MANAGEMENT OF TRAFFIC
AND PHYSICAL DISTRIBUTION

Management of
TRAFFIC
and
PHYSICAL DISTRIBUTION

By CHARLES A. TAFF, Ph.D.

Professor of Transportation and
Head, Department of Business Administration
College of Business and Public Administration
University of Maryland

3rd Edition · 1964

RICHARD D. IRWIN, Inc.

HOMEWOOD, ILLINOIS

Third Edition of *Traffic Management*
First Printing, January, 1964

Library of Congress Catalog Card No. 64–14783

PRINTED IN THE UNITED STATES OF AMERICA

PREFACE

EFFECTIVE traffic management continues to be an indispensable element in the successful and efficient operation of a business enterprise. It is a field of management which constitutes a major factor of service and cost and, as such, warrants particular attention. Additionally, it must be considered in its relationship to the areas of warehousing, inventory control, material handling, and packaging. Recognition by management of the importance of viewing the system as a whole has led to a broadened approach to traffic management in recent years and, in some companies, to the institution of physical distribution management. Traffic managers must be prepared to assume increasing responsibilities and to integrate the traffic and distribution needs of their company with production and marketing requirements.

The third edition has been oriented to the total approach, with emphasis upon alternates or trade-offs. This text has always treated the interrelationship of traffic management, warehousing, material handling, and packaging. Chapters dealing with these areas have been included since publication of the first edition, and the desirability of co-ordinating these functions has been stressed. This subject matter has been expanded, and a chapter added on inventory management. Managerial transportation responsibilities and the functions of traffic management, however, continue to receive major treatment. They are the nucleus of activities involved in the physical distribution of goods, and regardless of organizational structure are of paramount importance. Such topics as selection of media, rate negotiation, equipment management, private transportation, exporting and importing, transportation factors of plant location, and others included in the second edition have been revised and updated.

Data processing and analytical methods, including operations research, linear programming, systems analysis, and use of the probability theory, are thoroughly covered. Cases have also been added in this edition to encourage the development of reasoned judgment.

At the end of each chapter are discussion questions and problems which should stimulate interest in the subject matter. The American Society of Traffic and Transportation examination questions covering traffic management, which have been given twice yearly to those wishing to qualify as members of that society, have been brought up to date and are included in the Appendix. They should be very helpful to those people who are preparing for future examinations, and they should serve as class discussion questions.

The book is planned for college courses in traffic or physical distribution management or for use by those already active in the field. Each chapter is autonomous and may be presented in a different sequence if the instructor so desires. For courses in physical distribution, it may be advisable to move the chapters dealing with inventory management, material handling and packaging, warehousing, and locational factors forward to follow the chapter on management and analytical methods.

Suggestions from professors who have used earlier editions as a text have been helpful in the revision. The author also wishes to thank the many organizations and regulatory agencies that have generously supplied information. For invaluable aid in the preparation of the manuscript, the author is indebted to his wife, Glatha M. Taff.

CHARLES A. TAFF

College Park, Maryland
October, 1963

TABLE OF CONTENTS

PAGE

LIST OF TABLES xii

LIST OF FIGURES xiii

CHAPTER   PAGE

1. CONCEPTUAL FRAMEWORK 1

DEVELOPMENT OF TRAFFIC MANAGEMENT: Definition of Traffic Management. Noncompany Traffic Organizations. PHYSICAL DISTRIBUTION CONCEPT: Definition of Physical Distribution. COSTS OF TRANSPORTATION AND PHYSICAL DISTRIBUTION. MANAGEMENT OF PHYSICAL DISTRIBUTION. FUNCTIONS OF TRAFFIC AND PHYSICAL DISTRIBUTION MANAGEMENT: Routing. Rate Determination. Consolidation of Shipments. Rate Negotiations. Rate Litigation. Warehousing. Material Handling. Operation of Company-Owned and Leased Transportation Equipment. Locational Factors. Inventory Management. Diversion and Reconsignment. Handling of Claims. Application of Correct Classification. Sidetrack Agreements. Records and Statistical Data. Packaging. Transportability. Negotiation of Weight Agreements. Demurrage and Detention. Documentation. Maintenance of Adequate Tariff Files. Expediting and Tracing Shipments. Processing Transportation Bills for Payment. Directing Research. Arranging Transit Privileges. Auditing Freight Bills. Arranging for Movements of Household Goods. Loading. Handling of Export and Import Shipments. Arranging for Adequate Insurance Coverage. PROFESSIONALIZATION.

2. DEPARTMENTAL ORGANIZATION 28

TYPES OF MANAGEMENT ORGANIZATION: Line Organization. Line and Staff Organization. Functional Organization. Use of Committees in Line and Staff Organizations. TYPES OF TRAFFIC DEPARTMENT ORGANIZATIONS. TYPES OF OPERATIONS: Decentralized Operation. Centralized Operation. Combination Traffic Department. TRANSITION TO PHYSICAL DISTRIBUTION MANAGEMENT.

3. MANAGEMENT AND ANALYTICAL METHODS 44

MANAGEMENT POLICIES: Implementation of Policies. CO-OPERATIVE RELATIONSHIPS WITH OTHER DEPARTMENTS OR DIVISIONS. STAFFING. BUDGETING. REPORTS. ANALYTICAL METHODS: Research. Computers. Operations Research. Systems Analysis. Linear Programming. Probability Theory.

viii TABLE OF CONTENTS

CHAPTER   PAGE

4. THE TRANSPORTATION SYSTEM AND SERVICES 59

RAIL: LCL Services. Classification of Rail Carriers. Rail Freight Tons
and Revenues. MOTOR: Classification of Motor Carriers. Common Carriers. Contract Carriers. Exempt Motor Carriers. Private Motor Carriers.
Local Cartage. Package Service. WATER: Classification of Water Car-
riers. Domestic Water Transportation. Foreign Water Transportation
by American-Flag Vessels. Charters. AIR: Trunk-Line Carriers. Local
Service Carriers. Certificated Cargo-Only Carriers. Supplemental Car-
riers. Air Taxi Operators and Helicopters. Charters. Deferred Air
Freight. Air Express. International Air Carriers. PIPE LINES: Types of
Petroleum Pipe Lines. Crude-Oil Gathering Lines. Crude-Oil Trunk
Lines. Product Lines. Commingling of Shipments. Common Carrier
Status. Minimum Tender Requirements. Natural-Gas Pipe Lines. REA
EXPRESS. COMBINATION SERVICE: Trailer on Flatcar or "Piggy Back."
Trailership or "Fishy Back." Trainship. Motor-Air Service. FREIGHT
FORWARDERS: Surface Freight Forwarders. Air Freight Forwarders. PAR-
CEL POST: Surface Parcel Post. Air Parcel Post. BROKERS. COMPANY-
OWNED OR COMPANY-LEASED EQUIPMENT. SERVICE ASPECTS AND SHIPMENT
REQUIREMENTS.

5. DOCUMENTATION 93

COMMERCIAL BILLS OF LADING: Rail and Motor. Water. Air. Pipe Lines.
Express. Freight Forwarders. GOVERNMENT BILLS OF LADING: Preparation
of Government Bills of Lading. Accountability for Government Bills of
Lading. Conversion of Commercial Bills of Lading. OTHER DOCUMENTS:
Waybill. Arrival Notice. Delivery Receipt. Freight Bill. PROCEDURAL
SIMPLIFICATION. TERMS OF SALE.

6. CLASSIFICATION 118

RAIL: Consolidated Freight Classification. Uniform Freight Classification.
MOTOR: National Motor Freight Classification. New England Classifica-
tion. WATER. AIR. FREIGHT FORWARDERS. REA EXPRESS. CLASSIFICATION
COMMITTEE PROCEDURE: Rail. Motor. COMPANY CLASSIFICATIONS. EXCEP-
TIONS TO THE CLASSIFICATION.

7. CLASSIFICATION RULES 155

RAIL. MOTOR.

8. RATES 177

KINDS OF RATES. RAIL AND MOTOR COMMON CARRIERS: Line-Haul Rates.
Class Rates. Commodity Rates. Exceptions to the Classification. Freight—
All Kinds, or All Commodity Rates. Volume Rates. Local Rate. Joint
Rate. Proportional Rate. Through Rate. Differential Rate. Arbitraries.
Trailer-on-Flatcar Rates. Floating-In Rate. Cutback Rate. Standard
Rate. Minimum Rates. Any-Quantity Rates. Incentive Rates. Agreed
Charges. Export and Import Rates. Combination Rate. Aggregate of
Intermediates. Section 22 Rates. Reshipping Rate. Cube Rate. "Omni-
bus" Rule. Surcharge. Accessorial or Ancillary Charges. Released Value
Ratings. Actual Value Ratings. Allowances. Rate Structures. Factors

Affecting Rate Levels. MOTOR CONTRACT CARRIERS. WATER CARRIERS: Class Rates. Commodity Rates. Local Rates. Arbitraries. Minimum Rates. Heavy-Lift and Extra- or Long-Length Rates. General Cargo Rates. Charter Rates. Optional Cargo Rates. Ad Valorem Rates. Refrigerated Cargo Rates. Deck Cargo Rates. Dangerous Cargo Rates. Parcel Rates. Open Rates. Quantity Offered as a Shipment. AIR CARGO CARRIERS: Common Carriers. Contract Carriers. PIPE-LINE CARRIERS. FREIGHT FORWARDERS. REA EXPRESS. AIR EXPRESS. PARCEL POST. TRAFFIC DEPARTMENT RATE FORMS.

9. TARIFFS AND RATE FORMULATION 223

TARIFFS: Types of Tariffs. How to Look up a Rate. Priority of Rates. Exceptions to Priority Table. Conflict between Rates. Pertinent Principles of ICC Tariff Interpretation. Unofficial Tariffs. Traffic Manager's Tariff File. RATE BUREAUS AND CONFERENCES: ICC Supervision of Interstate Rates. TARIFF SIMPLIFICATION: Motor. AUDITING FREIGHT BILLS: Internal Audit Procedure. Outside Audits.

10. ROUTING AND CONSOLIDATION 259

ROUTING: Reciprocity. Rail. Determination of Rail Routing. Open Routing via Rail. Motor. Water. Air. Freight Forwarders. CLEARANCES. EMBARGOES AND QUARANTINES. INDUSTRIAL TRAFFIC MANAGEMENT ROUTING POLICY: Use of Premium Transportation. CONSOLIDATING SHIPMENTS: Shippers' Associations. Pool Cars. Definition of Pool Car. Industrial Use of Pool Cars.

11. CARRIERS' SPECIAL SERVICES 286

DIVERSION AND RECONSIGNMENT. STOPPING OF CARS IN TRANSIT TO COMPLETE LOADING. TRAP- AND FERRY-CAR SERVICE. PROTECTIVE SERVICES. ELEVATION. STORAGE. TRACING AND EXPEDITING: Tracing. Expediting.

12. TRANSIT PRIVILEGES 306

RAIL: Rules Governing Transit Privileges. Application Rules. Policing Rules. Types of Transit Privileges. Unit and Split Billing. MOTOR. TRAFFIC MANAGERS AND TRANSIT PRIVILEGES.

13. CARRIERS' TERMINAL SERVICES 322

TYPES OF TERMINAL SERVICES: Switching. Types of Switching Services. Switching Charges. Chicago Switching District. Pickup and Delivery. Weighing and Reweighing. Weight Agreements. Estimated Weights. Loading and Unloading. Transfer and Drayage. Lighterage and Floatage. WEIGHING AND INSPECTION BUREAUS: Activities of a Typical Rail Weighing and Inspection Bureau. Activities of Motor Weighing and Inspection Bureaus.

14. EQUIPMENT UTILIZATION 339

CAR SERVICE. PRIVATE CARS. DEMURRAGE AND DETENTION: Demurrage. Detention.

CHAPTER   PAGE

15. CLAIMS PROCEDURE AND PREVENTION 358

CLAIMS PROCEDURE: Causes of Claims. Loss and Damage Claims. Overcharge and Reparation Claims. Undercharge Claims. Rail Regulations
Governing Inspection of Freight. Motor Carrier Regulations Governing Inspection of Freight. Measure of Claims. Traffic Manager's Procedure and Prevention. CLAIM PREVENTION: Rail. Motor. INSURANCE.

16. REGULATION AND REGULATORY PROCEDURE 388

FEDERAL REGULATION OF DOMESTIC SURFACE CARRIERS: Development of the
Interstate Commerce Act. Composition of Interstate Commerce Com-
mission. Divisions of the Commission. Employee Boards. Functions of
the Commission. Procedure before the Commission. FEDERAL REGULATION
OF AIR TRANSPORTATION: Development of the Federal Aviation Act. Fed-
eral Aviation Agency. Composition of the Civil Aeronautics Board.
Functions of the Civil Aeronautics Board. Procedure before the Civil
Aeronautics Board. FEDERAL REGULATION OF AMERICAN-FLAG OCEAN CAR-
RIERS: Development of Merchant Marine Act. Maritime Administration.
Composition of Federal Maritime Commission. Functions of the Federal
Maritime Commission. Procedure before Federal Maritime Commission.
RE-EXAMINATION OF REGULATION. EMERGENCY FEDERAL TRANSPORTATION
AGENCY. STATE REGULATION.

17. MANAGEMENT OF PRIVATE INTERCITY TRANSPORTATION 422

MOTOR: Advantages. Feasibility of Conversion to Private Carriage. Equipment Purchase or Lease. Equipment Selection and Maintenance. Driver
Selection, Training and Supervision. Scheduling. Safety. WATER.

18. EXPORTING AND IMPORTING 438

TERMS OF SALE. EXPORTING: Direct Export Selling. Types of Direct Ex-
porting. Traffic Responsibilities. Packaging and Packing for Export.
Use of Containers. Causes of Preventable Losses. Marking. Documen-
tation. Indirect Exporting. Types of Indirect Exporting. IMPORTING:
Direct Importing. Customs Entries. Indirect Importing. Foreign Chan-
nels of Supply. Customhouse Brokers. Forwarding from Port. OCEAN
FREIGHT RATES: Space Weight Rates. Conference Rates. Additional
Charges. OCEAN FREIGHT FORWARDERS. FOREIGN-TRADE ZONES. MARINE IN-
SURANCE: Rights and Liabilities of Ocean Carriers. Types of Losses. Kinds
of Insurance Coverage. Surveying of Losses. INTERNATIONAL AIR SHIP-
MENTS.

19. PERSONAL EFFECTS AND PASSENGER TRANSPORTATION 475

Order for Service or Estimate Sheet. Rates and Charges. Released Value
Rates. Accessorial Services. General Rules and Regulations. Claims.
Movement of Office Equipment. PASSENGER TRANSPORTATION: Travel
Agents. Rail Reservations. Private Air and Charter. Air Line Reserva-
tions. Bus Transportation. Automobiles—Company-Owned, Leased, or
Rent-a-Car.

CHAPTER   PAGE

20. INVENTORY MANAGEMENT 492

Managing Inventory. Interdependence Aspects. Manufacturers' and Retailers' Inventories. Cost of Possession. Lead Time. Conditions of Certainty and Uncertainty. Inventory Standards. Economic Order Quantity.
Order Processing.

21. MATERIAL HANDLING AND PACKAGING 505

OBJECTIVES OF MATERIAL HANDLING. EQUIPMENT SELECTION AT SHIPPING
AND RECEIVING DOCKS. LOADING AND UNLOADING TO PREVENT DAMAGE.
CONTAINERIZATION. INDUSTRIAL PACKAGING.

22. WAREHOUSING 523

TYPES OF WAREHOUSING: Stock Location. Types of Public Warehouses.
THE UNIFORM WAREHOUSE RECEIPTS ACT: Negotiable and Nonnegotiable
Warehouse Receipts. LICENSING OF WAREHOUSES. WAREHOUSE SERVICES:
"Spot Stocks." Handling of Pool-Car Shipments. Distribution-Center
Public Warehousing and Storage in Transit. RATES AND CHARGES. CO-
OPERATION BETWEEN TRAFFIC MANAGERS AND PUBLIC WAREHOUSEMEN.

23. LOCATIONAL FACTORS 546

PRINCIPAL FACTORS. DECENTRALIZATION OF INDUSTRY. DEPARTMENTAL ROLE
IN PLANT LOCATION. EVALUATION OF FACTORS. ESTABLISHING THE CENTER
OF DISTRIBUTION.

APPENDIX A. TARIFF CONSTRUCTION 561

APPENDIX B. THE AMERICAN SOCIETY OF TRAFFIC AND TRANSPORTATION
             QUESTIONS ON TRAFFIC AND TRANSPORTATION MANAGEMENT
             FOR THE YEARS 1959–63 579

SELECTED BIBLIOGRAPHY 599

INDEX 605

LIST OF TABLES

TABLE   PAGE

2–1. Seven Major Stages of Company Growth 29

6–1. Relationships of the Various Ratings within the Official, Southern, and Western Territories 123

6–2. Comparison of Less-Carload Ratings 130

8–1. Scale of First-Class Rates (Class 100) Prescribed for Territory Covered by Docket No. 28300 179

8–2. Comparison of Export and Domestic Rates (In Cents)........... 190

8–3. Released Value Rating 199

10–1. Relative Advantages of Different Methods of Making Small Shipments 272

10–2. Tabulation of Shipments of Three Hundred Pounds and Less..... 274

11–1. Rail Diversion and Reconsignment Charges 291

11–2. Tracing and Expediting Data 302

14–1. Computation of Free Time, Chargeable Days, and Amount of Demurrage Charges Accruing per Car under the Straight Plan and the Average-Agreement Plan 354

16–1. Steps in Progress of Rate Proceedings 402

17–1. Per-Mile Cost of Operating a Tractor-Semitrailer 425

18–1. General Cargo Liner Carryings and Sailings on North Atlantic Route 462

23–1. Location of Weighted Center of Distribution: Recorded Data and Calculations 556

LIST OF FIGURES

FIGURE   PAGE

2–1. An Example of a Centralized Traffic Department 35

2–2. Organizational Chart of a Traffic and Distribution Service Department 39

4–1. Intercity Ton-Miles, Public and Private, by Kinds of Transportation, 1939–1962 61

4–2. Comparative Average Capacity of Tank Car, Tank Truck, and Tank Barge 71

5–1. Analysis of Railroad Bill-of-Lading Terms 96–97

5–2. Rail Uniform Straight Bill of Lading, Long Form............... 98

5–3. Motor Straight Bill of Lading 99

5–4. Specimen Bill of Lading Showing Listing of Articles Regularly Shipped by a Company 103

5–5. Specimen Air Bill 106

5–6. Specimen Government Bill of Lading 109

5–7. Specimen Motor Carrier Freight Bill 114

6–1. Sample Page from Early Tariff Showing Classification of Articles 119

6–2. Map of Rail Freight Classification Territories 120

6–3. Application of Letters, Numbers, or Reference Marks Appearing in Rating Columns, Consolidated Freight Classification No. 23.. 125

6–4. Sample Page from Consolidated Freight Classification No. 23.... 126

6–5. Explanation of Abbreviations and Reference Marks Contained in Uniform Freight Classification No. 6 131

6–6. Sample Listing from Uniform Freight Classification No. 6........ 132

6–7. Comparison of Articles Contained in Both Consolidated Freight Classification No. 23 and Uniform Freight Classification No. 6.. 133

6–8. Explanation of Abbreviations and Reference Marks Used in National Motor Freight Classification No. A–7 136

6–9. Sample Page from National Motor Freight Classification No. A–7 137

6–10. Form Used in Application for Change in Classification before Rail Classification Committees 141

6–11. A Sample Joint Docket Announcement as Used by Rail Classification Committees 143

6–12. A Proposal for a Change in Classification and Its Entry in the Classification 144

6–13. A Sample National Classification Board Docket Announcement.. 145

6–14. Application for Change in National Motor Freight Classification. 146

6–15. An Example of a Disposition Notice by the National Classification Board 148

6–16. Examples of Freight Classification Guides 150

6–17. An Example of Exceptions to the Classification Rules.......... 151

6–18. Sample of Motor Exceptions to the Classification Entry........ 153

6–19. Sample of a Motor Exception to the Classification Rules........ 153

7–1. Minimum Carload Weights, Rule 34 169

8–1. Example of a Title Page of a Commodity Rate Tariff........... 183

xiv LIST OF FIGURES

FIGURE   PAGE

8-2.   Application of Cube Rule 197
8-3.   Map of REA Express Blocks 217
8-4.   An Example of an Interoffice Letter Giving Rate Information.... 218
8-5.   An Example of an Inbound Rate Card 219
8-6.   An Example of an Outbound Rate Card 219
8-7.   Example of Freight Rate Schedule 220
9-1.   Major Railroad Rate Territories 234-35
9-2.   Organization of a Railroad Rate Conference, Associations, and
       Committees in the Eastern Territory 238-39
9-3.   Major Intraterritorial Motor Rate Territories 240-41
9-4.   Example of a Shipper's Proposal to a Rate Bureau.............. 242
9-5.   Recommendation of Standing Rate Committee of a Rate Bureau
       in Regard to a Shipper's Proposal 243
9-6.   Example of Notice of Approval of Action of Standing Committee
       of a Rate Bureau in Regard to a Shipper's Proposal........... 244
9-7.   Steps in Rate-Making Procedure When a Proposed Rate Is Pro-
       tested 247
9-8.   Example of a Rate and Route Sheet 254
11-1. A Copy of a Diversion and Reconsignment Order.............. 292
11-2. Schedule of Charges and Conditions for Stop-Off Privilege....... 295
11-3. An Example of a Tracing Order 303
12-1. An Example of a Transit Privilege 308
12-2. A Sample Motor Carrier Tariff 318-19
14-1. Example of a Car Supply Questionnaire Sent Out by Shippers Ad-
       visory Boards 341
14-2. An Example of a Daily Report of Cars 341
14-3. Sample of Record Maintained for Leased Cars 346
14-4. Sample of Disposition Instructions Furnished Carrier on Private
       Cars 347
14-5. An Inbound Car Record Form 348
15-1. Standard Form for Presentation of Known Loss or Damage for All
       Rail Transportation 366
15-2. Shipper's Form for Concealed Loss or Damage for Motor Carriers 367
15-3. Consignee's Form for Concealed Loss or Damage for Motor Car-
       riers 368
15-4. An Order of the Interstate Commerce Commission Awarding
       Reparations 371-72
15-5. Example of a Rail Overcharge Claim 374
15-6. An Example of an Indemnity Bond 375
15-7. An Example of a Stipulation Form 376
15-8. An Example of a Claims Documents Transmittal Sheet of an In-
       dustrial Traffic Department 382
15-9. An Example of a Claims Tracer Form as Used by an Industrial
       Traffic Department 383
16-1. An Organization Chart of the Interstate Commerce Commission. 392-93

FIGURE   PAGE

16–2. Interstate Commerce Commission Form Used in Presenting Formal
      Complaint 396–98
16–3. Form Used to Answer Complaint before Interstate Commerce
      Commission 399
16–4. Petition for Intervention Form in Complaint before the Interstate
      Commerce Commission 400
16–5. An Organization Chart of the Federal Aviation Agency......... 404
16–6. Organization Chart of the Civil Aeronautics Board.............. 405
16–7. The Usual Steps in Economic Proceedings before the Civil Aero-
      nautics Board 407
16–8. An Organization Chart of the Maritime Administration......... 409
16–9. An Organization Chart of the Federal Maritime Commission..... 411
16–10. An Organization Chart of the Office of Emergency Transporta-
      tion 417
17–1. Summary Sheet for Proposed Truck Transportation Project...... 424
17–2. A Portion of a Road Test to Be Given to Driver Applicants...... 431
18–1. An Example of a Booking Request Form Used in Exporting...... 447
18–2. A Copy of a Shipper's Export Declaration 449
18–3. A Copy of an Ocean Bill of Lading 450
18–4. Method of Operation of Foreign Trade Zone 466
19–1. Traffic Department Form for Notifying Mover 478
19–2. An Example of an Operating Expense Report of Company Auto-
      mobiles 489
20–1. Business and Federal Government Inventories for 1961.......... 492
21–1. Typical Handling Equipment 509
21–2. Cargo Containers in Gondola Container Cars—Capacity 6 Large or
      Medium or 12 Small Cargo Containers 512
21–3. Cargo Container with Skid Runners 513
22–1. Example of Manner in Which Public Warehouses Blend Fluctuat-
      ing Requirements into Reasonably Constant Volume 526
22–2. An Example of Nonnegotiable Warehouse Receipt 532
22–3. An Example of a Negotiable Warehouse Receipt 533
22–4. Standard Terms and Conditions on Back of Warehouse Receipt.534–35
22–5. Sample of Storage in Transit, with the Public Warehouse Acting
      As the Food Manufacturer's Agent 538
22–6. Portions of a Typical Warehouse Schedule 539–40
23–1. Map Showing Area (Shaded) Served from Chicago within Which
      Class 1 or 100 Rates Are Lower than from New York, New Or-
      leans, and San Francisco 548
23–2. Range of Value of the Five Most Important Factors in Specific
      Plant Location Survey 551
23–3. Map Showing Area to Be Economically Served on Cost-Compari-
      son Basis from Four Points 554
23–4. Map Showing Area to Be Economically Served if One of Four
      Points on Previous Map (Fig. 23–3) Is Relocated 555
23–5. Location of Weighted Center of Distribution 557

FIGURE   PAGE

A–1. A Title Page of a Rail Tariff 564
A–2. An Example of the Alphabetically-by-Name Method, Using Head-
      line, Sideline Points. The Rate Bases Are Used to Secure the
      Rate 569
A–3. Example of a Sideline Method of Publishing Rates.............. 570
A–4. Example of Distance-Scale Method of Publishing Rates Governed
      by a Distance Table Tariff 571
A–5. An Example of Commodity Alphabetical Method of Publishing
      Rates 572
A–6. Number of Supplements Permitted to Tariff 574
A–7. Requirements Regarding Volume of Tariff Supplemental Matter.. 574
A–8. Exceptions Allowed to Requirements Regarding Tariff Supple-
      mental Material 575

Chapter

1

CONCEPTUAL FRAMEWORK

Ever-changing business conditions present challenges to management. It must meet domestic and foreign competition, it must render consumer satisfaction, and it must operate efficiently enough to secure profits adequate to sustain the business enterprise and provide the basis for its growth. Management is responding, in great part, by reassessing the performance of each component of the business organization and analyzing its relationship to the whole. As an important component which involves substantial costs and has significant effects upon customer service, the management of traffic and transportation is receiving close attention. The advantages of integrating this area with inventory control, warehousing, material handling, packaging, and related functions are being recognized. In some companies, this has resulted in a realignment of responsibilities under a physical distribution department, whereas in other companies the structural organization is unchanged but co-ordination of traffic management and these areas is being increased.

DEVELOPMENT OF TRAFFIC MANAGEMENT

The ability to link supply of products, manpower, and natural resources with the many sources of demand has created a national economy unsurpassed anywhere in the world. Efficient transportation has provided the integrating factor responsible for the interdependence existing among the various constituent elements of our economy. Specialization of manufacturing industries and agriculture encouraged the production of tremendous quantities of goods which had to be transported from points of production to many areas of consumption. This accentuated the need for skillful management of transportation responsibilities.

Many of the functions were performed in earlier years by individuals who did not have the title of traffic manager. However, industrial traffic managers bearing such a title were found in the latter part of the nine-

1

teenth century at the headquarters or main offices of certain large industrial concerns. It is possible that the title "traffic manager" was borrowed from the railroads, since a number of lines in the 1870's and 1880's had a traffic manager or general traffic manager. Since the first traffic managers in industry came from the railroads to manage the traffic of industrial organizations, it is likely that this is the origin of the job title.

Two facts stand out in the early development of the traffic manager: (1) He existed where there were large-volume movements of freight and the transportation cost was an important factor in the total cost of the goods; and (2) in the industries where the transit privileges were first granted by railroads, the traffic manager appeared to supervise the fulfillment of the record-keeping requirements in regard to these privileges.

In the period before government regulation of transportation, the industrial traffic managers were chosen primarily because of their connections. Their main job was to secure for the manufacturer the most advantageous terms and largest rebates. This period of favoritism in rates and service was one in which the traffic manager was influential at the executive level of his company due to his bargaining ability. With the advent of federal regulation in 1887, which prohibited rebates and other forms of discrimination, the stature of the industrial traffic manager declined for the next twenty years.

The growth in the role of traffic management came with the advent of newer modes of transportation, motor and air; the revival of inland water transportation; and the continued growth of pipe line transportation. These factors gave business organizations much greater flexibility in the handling of their shipments. Not only were competitive rate aspects injected as a result of these alternative means, but there was service competition as well. The emphasis which business management has placed on distribution phases in recent years has been a contributing factor also, as well as the increasing availability of books and other publications devoted to the subject of traffic management, thus broadening the scope of understanding of this field. Organizations, such as traffic clubs, have also increased the appreciation of the importance of traffic management.

Over the years, the responsibilities of traffic managers have broadened from mere competence in rate analysis to the management of movement of material. This has been an evolutionary development since, in general, management inertia regarding the functions that could be efficiently performed through traffic management and the preoccupation of traffic managers with rate analysis were deterrents to the growth of management status. In the past two decades, however, management has recognized and accepted the fact that there is a wide spectrum of interrelated functions of traffic management that must be efficiently performed; and traffic managers have assumed management responsibilities over the broad area now encompassed by traffic management.

Definition of Traffic Management

Traffic management for business, both industrial and commercial,[1] and government organizations is responsible for the planning, direction, selection, purchase, and use by the company or organization of all aspects of transportation or transportation service, with the objective of serving the organization—business or government—in the most efficient manner possible. The people who perform this function are now referred to as "industrial" traffic managers, although at one time the term "commercial" was also applied to them. There are many variations in titles, such as "general traffic manager," "traffic manager," "director of traffic," "vice president of traffic," to name but a few.[2]

Efficient traffic management embraces many elements, one of which is economy. Thus, traffic management involves management of the myriad aspects of the purchase of transportation and transportation service by shippers or consignees, or by individuals or organizations on their behalf, which will include the use of facilities and equipment at a price or rate consistent with the services rendered in order to effect the efficient movement of persons and property from one point to another.

In this purchase of intraplant and interplant transportation, or transportation from or to all points as needed by the organization, many alternatives are available to the traffic manager; but the following are basic:

1. He may procure the transportation service directly from for-hire carriers, such as common or contract carriers, or indirect service, such as that of freight forwarders and parcel post.
2. He may purchase equipment in which the transportation service can be provided by his company.
3. He may lease equipment to accomplish the same purpose.
4. He may combine any or all of these alternatives.

However, it should be noted that the method of accomplishing these alternatives differs.

Noncompany Traffic Organizations

In some smaller business organizations the traffic management functions are handled by an outside organization, such as a traffic counselor, traffic consultant, or traffic service bureau. These persons or organiza-

---

[1] Examples of commercial establishments are wholesalers, jobbers, retail stores, and similar organizations.

[2] Since late 1949, *Traffic World*, the national traffic and transportation weekly news magazine, has published from time to time a feature article, "TraffiCareers," which contains a brief sketch of a prominent industrial traffic manager. These articles provide excellent descriptions of the comprehensive responsibilities of various traffic managers from a cross section of industry.

tions engage in full-time work by serving as the traffic department for a number of small companies. They endeavor to accomplish most of the same functions that an industrial traffic department performs. The extent of their activities, however, is usually outlined in the contract with the company they serve. Work may be performed on a short-term basis or over a long period of time and on a retainer or fee basis.

Two of the most common services available are the transportation rate card system and the auditing of paid freight bills. The rate card system consists of rates for specific commodities to desired destinations with information on file cards concerning the minimum weight, route, and any further information required for making a shipment.

The extent of these bureaus in particular areas can be ascertained by consulting a telephone directory.

Traffic management activities have also been undertaken for groups of business organizations by their trade associations. Such organizations do not actually ship or receive commodities, but their individual members do. They may provide such services as supplying freight rates to members, analyzing rate proposals affecting the association or its members, preparing testimony for presentation before regulatory agencies and others, publishing information bulletins on service, and preparing classification and freight rate guides.

A transportation and traffic division of chambers of commerce is quite common. This type of traffic activity, in which the organization is not a shipper or receiver, has often been referred to as "commercial traffic management." It is more appropriate, however, to refer to this work as "traffic activities." Some of the services rendered include routing traffic; quoting rates; reviewing legislation and informing members concerned; preparing location analyses for use in attracting new industries; and participating in transportation litigation. These services are either provided without charge or on a fee basis.

There is also widespread reference to what is called "carrier traffic management." The sales and rate organization of carriers is usually termed the "traffic department"; or, in some instances, it is a part of the carrier traffic department, and the management of this segment of a carrier's operation has been termed "carrier traffic management." Some carrier organizations have divided their traffic department and created a sales department. The carrier's traffic department, under these circumstances, performs such functions as the formulation of proposals for rates, publication and distribution of tariffs, presentation of testimony on rates before regulatory bodies, and classification of freight. The traffic department also plans the scheduling of service in conjunction with the operations department. Thus, it can be seen that the carrier's traffic department is engaged in activities which are complementary to those of the user of the service—the industrial traffic manager.

PHYSICAL DISTRIBUTION CONCEPT

During the early phases of our industrial growth, the emphasis was upon problems of production. This concern with productive problems dominated management activities for many years. The development of scientific management in the latter part of the last century and its successful application to production problems during the present century resulted in revolutionary improvements in productive techniques. The report of a committee on waste in industry recommended further refinements of productive activities and stimulated additional efforts in improving techniques and reducing production costs.[3]

In the evolutionary development of management science, three general divisions were recognized by organizations engaged in manufacture: production, finance, and sales. With the successful growth of these firms and the complexity of problems accompanying it, there were changes in management. During the present century, an awareness has developed concerning the distributive aspects of management. In the past, the manufacturer who produced most efficiently prospered, but technical advances in productive phases have resulted in the standardization of many fabricating processes. The competitive ability of individual firms, in the future, may depend proportionately more on the efficiency of their distribution.

Economists have frequently differentiated between production and distribution. Production, in the economic sense, is the addition of physical or form utilities to goods. This would involve the creation of useful materials or physical extraction of materials, with the necessary processing and fabrication to bring them eventually to a finished state. Distribution is the addition of time, place, and ownership utilities to goods. It is defined as including the transportation of goods from the point of original or intermediate production to the place of sale or further fabrication; the storage of goods until they are needed; the merchandising, display, and advertising of goods; and their actual sale or transfer into the possession of the ultimate buyer.[4]

The problems of distribution costs were brought into focus with the establishment of the Domestic Commerce Division in the Department of Commerce in 1924. The U.S. Chamber of Commerce also held domestic distribution conferences at about this time. These organized activities sparked an interest in this theretofore neglected field.

The term "distribution," used in its broadest sense, then, refers to the completed process from the time the finished product is ready for ship-

---

[3] Committee on Elimination of Waste in Industry of the Federated American Engineering Societies, *Waste in Industry* (Washington, D.C., 1921).
[4] Paul W. Stewart and J. Frederic Dewhurst, *Does Distribution Cost Too Much?* (New York: Twentieth Century Fund, Inc., 1939), p. 6.

ment until its delivery to the ultimate consumer. In this sense, distribution includes a number of fields of specialized management, such as sales, advertising, financing, traffic management, and warehousing. All of these costs constitute the total cost of distribution; and the majority of them are either directly or indirectly of vital concern to the traffic manager, although not his responsibility.

"Physical distribution" is a more restrictive term and appears to have emerged from the early writings in the marketing field. Over forty years ago references were made in a basic textbook in marketing to the function of physical supply which embraced transportation and storage; and the field of marketing was defined as consisting of "those efforts which affect transfers in the ownership of goods and care of their physical distributions."[5] Although references were made in subsequent marketing textbooks to physical supply, transportation as a separate area of specialization and study was well established, and very little of this subject was included in subsequent marketing textbooks.

In 1930, a survey of the relation of industrial traffic management to business made by the Department of Commerce refers to "physical distribution" and "transportation" as being synonymous.[6] This study alludes to the physical phases of distribution as including such functions as packaging, material handling, receiving, storing, transporting, and shipping.

It was not until after World War II, however, that the area of "distribution" appeared in organizational structures. At that time, a small number of business firms primarily in the food industry created the position of "distribution manager" which embraced traffic, warehousing, packaging, and material handling. On the other hand, there were and are far more traffic managers whose responsibilities encompass those of the distribution manager but who do not have that title. The physical distribution concept was not organizationally identified until the late 1950's and then by only a comparatively few large firms. Although still in an evolutionary stage of development, there is an increasing amount of interest in it. A re-evaluation of the organizational structure and the functional assignments of responsibility for traffic, warehousing, packaging, material handling, inventory control, and, in some cases, order processing is taking place.

Several factors have caused this general re-evaluation. One is the cost-profit squeeze confronting a great number of business organizations. A diminishing margin of profit is causing heightened concern for tighter cost control. A thorough probing of all components of cost has often revealed that some have been more rigorously controlled than others

---

[5] Fred E. Clark, *Principles of Marketing* (New York: The Macmillan Co., 1922), p. 1.

[6] Wayne E. Butterbaugh, Department of Commerce, *Industrial Traffic Management* (Washington, D.C.: U.S. Government Printing Office, 1930), p. 1.

and that the relative magnitude of production versus distribution costs is unbalanced. In the latter areas, management has not been as effective in its application of cost standards or controls.

Distribution costs are more complex than those of production. While the "let's reduce costs here" approach of production may also be applied to distribution, there are weaknesses in this method which may become apparent if the many components of distribution are not viewed as a system. The reduction of cost in one component can have a substantial effect upon others. For example, inventories may be cut, reducing capital investment and certain other costs, but if this is done without regard to other aspects of the distributive process, it may result in inadequate service to customers and dealers and thereby jeopardize future sales. Another factor that has focused attention on the physical distribution aspects has been the introduction of a wide range of automatic data-processing equipment. This can be programmed in such a manner as to give management more complete data in a much shorter period of time. In addition to enhancing advance planning, data processing can enable management to examine various cost alternatives.

An additional factor has been the systems approach to management which is being increasingly employed by business firms. In seeking to maximize profits, all components of the business enterprise and their inter-actions upon one another are analyzed. Various "trade off" possibilities are considered, such as reducing warehouse space by using faster premium transportation, and the total cost approach applied to the multiple choices available.

Definition of Physical Distribution

The public discourse among businessmen and educators on the physical distribution concept has been growing. Numerous articles, new periodi-cals, and other publications have appeared since 1958.[7] In addition, semi-nars and conferences dealing with the subject have been sponsored by such organizations as the American Management Association, the Ameri-can Society of Traffic and Transportation, and others. Among the many subjects covered is that of the definition of the term. One definition widely used in these discussions is that physical distribution is the moving of finished products from the end of a production line to customers.[8]

Others have defined it to embrace raw materials and finished products.[9] The first definition would not include the traffic function in many com-panies inasmuch as the traffic manager is usually responsible for both in-

---

[7] See E. J. Kelley and William Lazer (eds.), *Managerial Marketing: Perspectives and Viewpoints* (Homewood, Ill.: Richard D. Irwin, Inc., 1958), p. 359; and Edward W. Smykay, Donald J. Bowersox, and Frank H. Mossman, *Physical Distribution Management* (New York: The Macmillan Co., 1961).

[8] American Management Association, Inc., *Management of the Physical-Distribution Function* (New York: American Management Association, 1960), pp. 7, 14.

[9] Smykay *et al., op. cit.,* p. 1.

bound and outbound transportation. Since transportation is considered an integral part of the physical distribution function, this definition is rather limited.

One scholar has suggested that title follows function; therefore, the real issue is not so much a problem of semantics as it is an organizational problem.[10] The point is made that regardless of which higher executive traffic management is assigned to, it must also report to and work with other major executives. The creation of a physical distribution department does not eliminate this necessity. For example, the traffic manager will be expected to continue his contact with the manufacturing department and the sales department on inbound material. This expert feels that it is more important to establish a physical distribution department for the purpose of utilizing data-processing equipment in the alternative choice situations relating to the warehousing and transportation of finished products.

In the ferment of ideas and re-evaluation of the functional areas of management, the term "materials management" has been applied. This has been defined as including those ". . . activities involved in the acquisition and use of all materials employed in the production of the finished product. These activities may include production and inventory control, purchasing, traffic, materials handling, and receiving."[11] As defined, this would restrict materials management to incoming materials. On the other hand, another definition of materials management ". . . would embrace all activities concerned with materials except those directly concerned with designing or manufacturing the product or maintaining the facilities, equipment, and tooling."[12] This definition would include most of the activities of a company's purchasing, production control, shipping, traffic, receiving, and stores departments. The impetus for this definition appears to stem from purchasing agents or departments.

Another term that has been applied is "rhochrematics." The derivation of the word is from the Greek "rhoe" meaning a flow, as a river or stream, and "chrema" meaning products, materials, or things, and the abstract ending "ics" for any of the sciences.[13] This is defined as a scientific approach to the management of material flows and appears to be a very broad definition.

Some business firms have given consideration to the application of the logistics principles used in military operations to their company's organi-

---

[10] E. G. Plowman, Vice President–Traffic, U.S. Steel, *Traffic World*, October 8, 1960, p. 32.

[11] Vincent dePaul Goubean, *Materials Management—A Realistic Appraisal* (New York: American Management Association, Report No. 35, 1959).

[12] Dean S. Ammer, *Materials Management* (Homewood, Ill.: Richard D. Irwin, Inc., 1962), p. 12.

[13] Stanley H. Brewer, *Rhochrematics, A Scientific Approach to the Management of Material Flows* (Seattle, Wash.: Bureau of Business Research, University of Washington, 1960), p. 3.

zation. This gives rise to the application of the term "business logistics" which, when patterned after military logistics, embraces many areas. Military logistics encompass the functional fields of military operations; materiel requirements; production planning and scheduling; acquisition, inventory management, storage, maintenance, distribution and disposal of materiel, supplies, tools, and equipment; transportation, telecommunications, petroleum, and other logistical services; supply cataloging, standardization, and quality control; commercial and industrial activities and facilities including industrial equipment; and vulnerability of resources to attack damage.[14] Obviously, there are some functions of military logistics that do not have application to the business field. Furthermore, the profit motivation of a business firm is dominant, whereas there is none in a military organization. A primary problem in adapting military logistics to business management is to determine what functions can be logically grouped in organizational structure. From the businessman's point of view, the optimum balance of resources should enable him to place a competitive product or service in the consumers' hands and yet receive an adequate profit reward.

"Business logistics" has also been defined as a type of management activity that develops and uses procedures and techniques, especially of a mathematical nature, for planning and handling and transportation of inbound supplies and outbound finished products required by, or produced by, an enterprise.[15] It should be pointed out that "physical distribution" could be defined in the same way and that techniques and procedures of a statistical or mathematical nature can be, and are, used in many different types of management endeavor.

This definition of business logistics, however, is further indication of the search for an appropriate title for the position which is responsible for a number of functions, including transportation, warehousing, inventory management, industrial packaging, and material handling. "Business logistics," as here defined, is a more narrow definition than the business logistics definition that was discussed earlier.

It should not be implied from this discussion that a group of functions are being brought together, only one of which has previously been "managed." All have been managed in one way or another. The advantage the discourse about these terms does offer is that greater attention is being focused on the total cost concept than ever before. Some companies have concluded, after study, that there is no need for organizational restructuring or change in name to "physical distribution" since the institution of the systems approach to traffic management in their companies has accomplished essentially the same objectives.

A workable definition of physical distribution that will be used in this book is that it is the management of movement, inventory control, pro-

---

[14] Department of Defense Instruction No. 5000.8, dated June 15, 1961.
[15] E. G. Plowman, *Traffic World*, April 6, 1963.

tection, and storage of raw materials and processed or finished goods to and from the production line. This would embrace transportation, material handling, industrial packaging, warehousing, inventory control, and the communications network necessary for effective management.

The physical distribution concept is seldom accepted without a great deal of thorough preparation, development of facts concerning what can be accomplished, and selling the idea to top management. The need to convince the departments that are affected by a change in organizational structure is also paramount because reluctance to co-operate fully will jeopardize the success of the change.

COSTS OF TRANSPORTATION AND PHYSICAL DISTRIBUTION

There is a tendency on the part of management to attach a considerable degree of importance to the aggregate cost of any particular element of business enterprise. As a matter of fact, a part of the function of cost accounting is such identification. When there is a regrouping of functions, however, it is often difficult to secure the precise cost figures for each of the regrouped functions immediately. This certainly has been true in the case of the systems approach to traffic management or the physical distribution concept. It is usually but a matter of time, though, until these costs can be allocated and identified with the appropriate function. Transportation cost figures are readily available but certain of the other cost elements can only be estimated.

Wide cost variations exist in transportation costs among companies in the same industry as well as between industries. Surveys show that inbound freight costs expressed as a percentage of goods purchased varied from 3 to 23 per cent in the pulp, paper, and products companies, and from 2 to 312 per cent in stone, clay, and glass products. Expenditures for outbound freight, expressed as a percentage of sales, ranged from 1 to 30 per cent in food and kindred products, and from less than 1 to 50 per cent in stone, clay, and glass products.

Total expenditures for transportation for the year 1951, published in the first edition of this book, represented about 18 per cent of gross national product. By 1961, this was an amount equal to about 20 per cent of GNP, or more than $100 billion annually. Of this, freight was estimated to account for $44 billion, and passenger $53 billion. These figures do not reflect the cost of government expenditures unrecovered from users, estimated to be $2.5 billion; the cost of transmission of gas by pipe line, and the cost of transmission of electrical energy.

Our expenditures for highway movements for that year were $26.6 billion, rail $8.3 billion, water $2.7 billion, oil pipe line $1.0 billion, air $382 million, freight forwarders $428 million, and other shippers costs, such as loading and unloading freight cars, and the operation of traffic departments, $1.3 billion.[16] Freight transportation costs run a little less than 10 per cent of GNP.

Ascertaining the other elements of cost in physical distribution is much more difficult because they are not readily identifiable. The cost of carrying inventory is often computed as a proportion of average value of inventory, and a figure of 25 per cent has been used. This would include cost of storage, depreciation, interest, transportation, handling and distribution, obsolescence, insurance, and taxes. If transportation and handling and distribution costs are eliminated in order to avoid double counting between transportation and inventory carrying costs, the figure would be approximately 22 per cent.[17] The total of average value of inventories for 1960, as given by the Department of Commerce, amounted to more than $123 billion, so inventory carrying costs for that year was an estimated $27 billion or 5.4 per cent of GNP.[18]

The sum of transportation and inventory carrying costs is approximately 15 per cent of GNP. The production component is estimated to constitute 45 per cent of GNP, and promotion components, including sales, advertising, and merchandising, amount to 40 per cent. Physical distribution activities constitute the third largest cost component.

Cost figures for packaging are relatively minor when compared to transportation and inventory carrying costs and are usually included in the production and promotion components. They amount to about 3 per cent of GNP.

Transportation is the most important of the cost elements in physical distribution. Although the exact amount of transportation purchased by or arranged for the traffic manager cannot be precisely stated, he plays a significant role in all phases of transportation activity.

MANAGEMENT OF PHYSICAL DISTRIBUTION

A major organizational problem is the selection of a director for physical distribution. If an analysis is made of each of the components of physical distribution, it will be found that the area of traffic management has embraced a broader spectrum of managerial responsibilities than any of the other components. In larger firms, it has often encompassed most, if not all, of the physical distribution components. Where it has not encompassed all of them, traffic personnel have worked co-operatively with packaging, warehousing, material handling, inventory management, and data processing, in facilitating manufacturing, sales, and customer service.

---

[16] Transportation Association of America.

[17] J. L. Heskett, "Macroeconomic Cost of Physical Distribution," presented at annual meeting of American Transportation Research Forum, Pittsburgh, Pennsylvania, 1962.

[18] *Ibid.*

In any regrouping of functions in which one of the managers of the existing areas is chosen to head physical distribution, it must be recognized that one of the prerequisites will be the ability to weld these management areas into a strong supporting element with minimum friction. On the basis of present responsibilities and qualifications, the traffic manager is in an excellent position to assume management of the components of physical distribution.

Some of the management titles used in physical distribution include "vice president of distribution," "director of distribution," "distribution manager," "director of traffic and distribution services," "product distribution supervisor," "manager of material control and distribution," "production planning and distribution manager."

FUNCTIONS OF TRAFFIC AND PHYSICAL DISTRIBUTION MANAGEMENT

In management literature, there is no uniformity in the treatment of the functions or the phases of mangement. In some instances in each of the fields of specialized management, reference is made to the production function, the finance function, the personnel function, the traffic function, and so on, the idea being that there is only one function in each of these fields. In other instances, reference is made to production functions, finance functions, personnel functions, traffic functions, and the like, the principle in these instances being that there are a number of functions in each of the fields instead of a single function.

Where a single field, such as production, personnel, or traffic, is covered as a single subject, it is customary to explain the various functions in the particular field. In traffic management, these functions have been classified in a number of different ways. One such classification named administration, cost, service, physical handling, and transportation functions.[19] Another classification is one which has been divided into routine or service, constructive, and co-operative functions.[20] The routine functions are those related to the management of the routine or day-to-day transportation requirements of the company. Constructive functions seek to discover and develop new and improved methods of transportation. Co-operative functions are those performed in co-operation with the heads of other departments of the same company, with other traffic managers, or with representatives of the carriers to improve the transportation service. A similar classification recognizes four functions: protective, inherent or service, supervisory, and co-operative functions.[21]

---

[19] Wayne E. Butterbaugh, Department of Commerce, *Industrial Traffic Management* (Washington, D.C.: U.S. Government Printing Office, 1930).

[20] G. Lloyd Wilson, *Industrial Traffic Management* (Washington, D.C.: Traffic Service Corp., 1949).

[21] Leslie A. Bryan, *Traffic Management in Industry* (New York: Dryden Press, 1953).

An additional classification could divide the functions between those which are internal, which would include those functions performed wholly within the department or company, and the external functions, which would embrace those functions in which the traffic department deals with outside organizations, such as regulatory bodies, rate conferences, shippers' advisory boards, and others. Further, one might say that certain functions are operating functions and others are policy functions. This type of classification may be based on the type of organizational make-up that occurs in a large organization.

The purpose of any classification of functions is to place various functions in particular categories in order that there may be a better understanding of the activities of the traffic department. Whatever the division of day-to-day functions or activities and those which can be termed "long-range functions," there cannot be a complete divorcement of one group of functions from another. Even the matters that are handled routinely still have their effect upon planning functions.

The functions performed by traffic departments differ widely, depending upon a number of factors, such as the nature of the industry or business, volume of tonnage handled, number of shipments moved, value of goods shipped, distance goods are transported, possible economies which may be effected, and value of traffic management in the operation and control of a business. The major transportation functions or responsibilities of the traffic department are those concerned with freight movements. The passenger transportation functions may include the operation of company-owned or leased automobiles and company-owned aircraft or buses, as well as handling details incident to the purchase of passenger transportation from commercial carriers.

The functions of a department of physical distribution are broad. They generally include inventory management, warehousing, industrial packaging, material handling, and traffic management. As has been pointed out, some traffic departments in very large companies either have had charge of many of these broad functions of physical distribution or have worked co-operatively with other departments in the handling of these functions; and where there is a physical distribution department, traffic management functions are handled by a traffic section in such a department. For these reasons, there will be no attempt to separate the functions of traffic management and physical distribution because there will be overlapping of the functions in corporate organizations. All of the functions normally a part of traffic and physical distribution, however, are covered.

Because of comparatively limited experience with physical distribution management, there has been little discussion about classification of its functions. Some of the classifications applied in traffic management have equal application to physical distribution. There does seem, however, to be a somewhat stronger emphasis on planning and programming, customer orientation, and the use of analytical method-ologies.

Routing

Routing is an important responsibility of the traffic manager or the traffic section of a physical distribution department. It involves the choice of mode of transportation and the selection of carrier or carriers within that mode. Most shipments, both inbound and outbound, on which his company pays the transportation costs are routed by the traffic manager.

In order to perform this service, the traffic manager must have a thorough knowledge of the services offered by the various carriers. He must determine the route over which the shipment will be shipped, and have a knowledge of the places and times at which shipments are picked up and delivered by the different carriers. Whether or not a more expensive means of transport should be used in order to reduce inventory or ware-housing costs is another important determination that must be made in routing.

Through experience, many traffic managers have established standard routings for shipments between specific points. This is used in connection with frequent shipments having the same origin and destination points. Except for unusual circumstances, the standard routing will be used in connection with these shipments. Some traffic managers have files which can be referred to by their staff when it is necessary to provide routing between certain specified points. These routings must be carefully watched to assure that good service is maintained and that improvements are made when it is possible to do so. If these things are done, standard routings can be of value as timesavers.

Carriers sometimes impose an embargo on shipments to or within a specified area. This cuts the flow of goods, and the traffic manager will have to route goods via circuitous routes unless he is able to secure a permit to move the freight through the area affected by the embargo.

Rate Determination

Traditionally, the most important single function of traffic management has been that of securing the correct rate. Although carriers will supply rates to a shipper, there are many intricacies and complexities in the rate structure. Since there are many different types of rates by different modes of transportation, the traffic department or section may be able to find a rate more advantageous to its company than that quoted by a particular carrier. This does not infer that the carrier does not quote the correct rate, because there may be more than one rate which could be applied.

The rate function is broad. The traffic manager must consider not only individual modes of transportation but also common carriers and contract carriers within a mode. With contract carriers, the traffic department or section may negotiate rates with individual carriers on a contract basis.

Traffic personnel are interested in line-haul charges, as well as accessorial charges, and may find it necessary to seek adjustment in rates and charges due to changes in industrial or transportation conditions.

Consolidation of Shipments

In ascertaining the most advantageous rate, the traffic department or section should investigate the consolidation of shipments. It may be possible to consolidate shipments of less-carload lots into carload lots and ship them to distribution points, where they may be reshipped to destination. The savings between the less-carload rate on the individual shipments and the carload rate are substantial. Just as consolidation is used on outgoing shipments, so can it be employed on incoming shipments through consolidation of small lots at central points, where they may be reshipped in carload lots.

Rate Negotiations

Rate negotiation is an exacting and difficult job, but its results can be rewarding. Such work involves the initiation of requests to carriers, classification committees, or rate bureaus for adjustments in ratings and rates. Such requests are accompanied by the justification for the proposal, which will be submitted in accordance with procedures outlined by rate bureaus. It is far less time-consuming to prepare an adequate presentation at the outset in rate adjustment procedure; for, if it should be necessary to carry it into rate litigation before a regulatory body, the greater part of the work will have been done. Rate negotiation requires a thorough analysis of all aspects of a proposal.

This is a phase of work in which a traffic department or section should be on the alert for new ideas. One traffic manager used an idea to negotiate a rate which was most favorable to his company. His company made dog food, one of the principal ingredients of which was horse meat. Horses are ordinarily shipped in small numbers and require special handling, and so they normally take a fairly high freight rate. However, horses for slaughter can be loaded to car capacity and handled just like slaughter cattle; so it seemed to this traffic manager that they should take the same rate.

Exploring the subject, he found that, in certain rate territories, horses for slaughter actually did go at the fat-cattle rate. He made a thorough study of relevant Interstate Commerce Commission decisions and carefully prepared and presented his case to the proper authorities in his territory. As a result, his company's large shipments of horses travel at an 18 per cent lower cost.

Rate Litigation

Appearances before regulatory bodies by the traffic department or section are important in assuring that the best interests of a company are served. It sometimes becomes necessary to file complaints against carriers with federal or state regulatory bodies, or to intervene in investigations which have been instituted before these agencies. When industries affected by rate proposals submit all relevant data concerning the effect such proposals will have upon their company, the regulatory agency is better able to arrive at just conclusions.

Statistical data concerning rates and routes, exhibits, and presentation of evidence relating to the effects of the matter at issue should be prepared by the traffic department or section. Other departments of the company may present the facts concerning the matter as it affects their particular department, such as sales, purchasing, or production. The traffic manager is usually called upon as a witness, and he may be helped by legal counsel.

Warehousing

Warehousing is an important responsibility of physical distribution management, particularly where a manufacturer is engaged in producing consumer items. The optimal location in regard to minimal transportation costs, customer services, level of inventories, and company warehouses versus public warehouses are some of the matters that must be determined. In some large companies that do not have a physical distribution department, warehouses are operated by the traffic department, or arrangements will be made with public warehouses for the handling of the company's products. If public warehouses are used, the procedures to be followed by the warehouseman in the handling of the company's products may be formulated by the traffic department. This guidance may be in the form of a manual or similar document.

Strategic location of warehouses can give the customer better service and can also result in a reduction in transportation costs by moving carload, truckload, or bargeload quantities into the warehouses.

Material Handling

The development of material-handling techniques in recent years has been little short of phenomenal. The improved handling of material is not confined to production but applies to all phases of physical movement. The traffic department, because of knowledge of and familiarity with the physical movement of goods, has encouraged the use of material-handling equipment. Not only can proper equipment speed the operations in shipping and receiving, but it can make efficient use of storage space and reduce the cost of handling. The use of material-handling equipment, such as palletization with fork-truck operation, can also reduce loss and damage, since individual packages are subjected to less handling because they can be combined into larger units.

The benefits of material handling are not solely confined to the producer but may be beneficial to the consignee as well. In co-operation with the sales department, the traffic department can arrange for the movement of goods on pallets, on skids, or in other unitized lots, so that the consignee has less handling at destination.

When a company has a physical distribution department, one of the important responsibilities of that department is material handling, excluding the production line. In companies which do not have a physical distribution department, material handling is not generally a responsibility of the traffic department, but many of the activities of the traffic department involve material handling. The traffic manager, therefore, must be informed regarding developments in this field because he may act in an advisory capacity in this respect.

Operation of Company-Owned and Leased Transportation Equipment

The operation of company-owned transportation equipment, including intraplant equipment, is an important responsibility of many traffic departments or sections. Company-owned equipment may be operated because it is of special design and to insure an adequate supply of transportation equipment to meet the minimum shipping requirements of the organization.

One of the duties in the operation of company equipment is to suggest improvements in design. The traffic department or section has charge of scheduling the use of such equipment, scheduling the routes, and supervising the cost of operation.

Leasing or chartering of transportation equipment has become more common in recent years, and the arrangements for such leases are generally handled by the traffic department or section. An evaluation must be made of the relative merits of owning or leasing equipment.

Locational Factors

With the continuing growth of the individual units of economic activity, there is greater expansion, and new plant locations must be carefully chosen. Further, the trend toward decentralization of industry, which has been significant in the postwar period, has placed increased emphasis upon the site location that best meets the needs of the company.

An analysis of physical distribution aspects in plant location will include the market area, existing transportation facilities and rates, and warehousing. The importance of these factors in choosing a new plant site will vary, depending in part upon the nature of the industry. In some cases, the transportation elements are paramount, as in industries where the transit privilege is especially important. Where this is the case, the traffic department or section will establish the transportation advantage of one location over another or select several possible sites. The transportation factor will then be considered in relation to other location factors. In most instances, plant location results from a thorough analysis of all factors.

Inventory Management

Business firms recognize that too high an inventory level causes high carrying costs and potential obsolescence. Conversely, too low an inventory can result in high restocking and production costs, as well as the risk of lost sales and customer good will. Clearly, the control of inventories is extremely important in the successful functioning of many business firms. The level of inventories is related to such factors as the movement and storage of materials. The amount of material in the pipeline, that is, in storage, in transit, and in processing can be substantially altered through co-ordinated management by production, physical distribution, and sales. Capital costs in inventory, transportation and storage costs, and costs of inventory obsolescence are traded off in order to control total costs and maintain minimal inventory levels consistent with production needs.

Diversion and Reconsignment

It is sometimes necessary to change the routing of a shipment or its final destination after the shipment has been turned over to a carrier, the consignee remaining the same. This is called "diversion." Where the consignee is changed and perhaps the destination, this act is termed "reconsignment." Diversion and reconsignment are terms which are often used interchangeably, however.

When it is necessary to make changes of this sort, the traffic manager contacts the carrier which has the shipments and requests that the necessary changes in routing or delivery be made. This usually must be accomplished before the shipment has reached its original destination, or the lading will need to be reshipped on a new bill of lading if it has reached its original destination.

Handling of Claims

The procedure for detecting loss and damage and satisfactorily handling the claim with the carrier is a responsibility of the traffic manager. The claims for loss, damage, or delay must be prepared on standard forms and filed within a specified number of months in order to protect the claimant's rights should the claims be declined. Procedure should be established so as to expedite the handling of such claims.

Although the collection of claims is important, a claim-prevention activity is also part of the claim function. To effect such claim prevention, periodic analysis must be made of claim records in order to determine the causes. By determining such causes, remedial steps can be taken to minimize the causative factors and thereby improve the service rendered to the customer.

Another aspect of handling claims is that involving overcharges and undercharges of carriers' freight bills. Through the auditing of freight bills, errors may be found regarding the rates assessed, the weights used, and the total charges. Where overcharges are detected in freight bills, claims are filed against the carriers. Where the carrier collected less than the correct transportation charge, arrangements must be made to pay the amounts due.

Claims made by the shipper that the rates legally published in the carrier's tariffs are not lawful under the regulatory statutes are called "reparation requests." They constitute a very important phase of traffic responsibilities.

Application of Correct Classification

A most important responsibility of a traffic manager is to have a thorough knowledge of the product which his company produces. This will enable him to perform an essential function of the traffic department or section—namely, securing the proper classification for the goods. Classification mistakes can be costly, since improper classification can mean higher rates. This happened to a hardware supplier who shipped brass-covered steel rods to retailers who cut them to desired lengths. The shipments were assessed as curtain rods, whereas they should have been rated at the much lower level of iron or steel brass-coated rods. It may also happen that a trade name of a product may not be sufficiently explanatory for transportation purposes, since the classification of goods is based on transportation characteristics, both physical and economic. Goods may be sold and invoiced by a widely advertised brand name. However, the transportation documents used in connection with the shipment may bear the transportation classification description. It is necessary to convert these trade names into transportation descriptions in order that such transportation descriptions will appear on all of the shipping papers to assure the placement of the goods into the correct classification. This may be done by the preparation of a pamphlet which contains this information.

Sidetrack Agreements

The agreement entered into between a railroad and a shipper who has industrial tracks is necessary because the carrier does not have an obligation to render service throughout the industrial plant. Such agreements cover such important matters as the cost of construction of industrial track, its maintenance, liability, use by the two parties, and termination of the contract.

The traffic manager negotiates agreements of this nature. In larger organizations, such agreements may be checked by the legal counsel before final approval is given.

Records and Statistical Data

One of the tools of effective management is the maintenance and intelligent use of records and statistical data. There are many ways in which such material can be used which are beneficial to the company and which can help the traffic manager in his division of traffic among the carriers. Such material is useful in the presentation of matters before classification and rate groups, as well as other shippers' or carriers' committees, and regulatory bodies. Such records assist, also, in the handling of reciprocity matters between the company and carriers which are purchasers of the company's products.

The bill of lading or freight bill contains much useful information which, if tabulated, can be helpful in effecting greater consolidation of shipments and will indicate the density of shipments moving between specified points. One traffic department tabulates 100,000 freight bills each year and secures valuable information from this source.

The conversion of records to computers offers opportunities to analyze the data as to their usefulness for research application as well as enabling management to get a rapid feedback of facts which can be helpful in the development of business strategy.

Packaging

Packaging is one of the functions of physical distribution. Since packaging cost is an element of the total cost of the goods to the consumer, it is necessary that the latest techniques of packaging be known. Much research has been undertaken on the subject of packaging by container manufacturers, carriers, trade associations, and government agencies. In cosmetic and toiletry companies, the largest portion of the manufactured cost of the product is that of the packaging component.

The physical distribution department has to work with the sales department and manufacturing department in order to develop and use the proper packaging to accommodate the product and get it in the hands of the customer without damage.

In preparing goods for shipment, the traffic department or section must share its technical knowledge about this field with other departments. Certain packaging specifications and containers may be required by the rules contained in freight classifications or tariffs. Departments not familiar with transportation aspects must be apprised of the error of packing articles of different classifications together, with the result that the rate of the goods with the highest classification may determine the rate which applies on the entire package. An example which illustrates the importance of the systems approach is that of a company which produced an entire cabinet that was assembled by the purchaser. It had been shipping the cabinets in carload lots to four warehouses which supplied dealers throughout the United States. The rate was the same whether the cabinets were sent to the warehouses assembled or unassembled, since the components, when packed together, were considered to be a complete article. The traffic manager analyzed the rate structure and found that a saving of about 40 per cent could be achieved by sending the components of the cabinet separately, the shelving in one shipment and the bolts and nuts in another. The saving was made possible because the rates for components were lower than the rates for the complete article. In order to ship this way, however, the packaging of the parts had to be done at the warehouses rather than at the plant, where assembly line operations made packaging cheaper. The higher cost of packaging was $40,000 annually, while the saving in the transportation bill was $320,000, or a net saving of $280,000.

Transportability

A challenge which often confronts the traffic manager when large or unusual items are being procured or produced relates to the transportability of the item. Transportability is the capability of moving an item by highway, rail, water, or air carriers, or by self-propulsion. It is, therefore, extremely important that priority consideration be given to this in research, design, engineering, development, and modification programs. The development and complexity of military weapon systems accentuates the necessity for injecting the factor of transportability in design requirements and engineering programs in order to facilitate timely and efficient delivery.

Negotiation of Weight Agreements

The arrangements for agreements with inspection and weighing bureaus regarding rail and motor shipments of the same weight are a function of the traffic manager. Under such agreements, shipments are accepted for transportation under "agreed weights," thus eliminating the necessity of weighing individual shipments. These bureaus have the right to make necessary inspections and to make adjustments, where necessary. Such agreements represent savings in time to the shipper, and money to the carrier, through the elimination of individual weighing.

Demurrage and Detention

To assure that cars, trucks, barges, and pipe lines are released during the period of free time allowed by the carrier is another function of the traffic manager. Holding demurrage and detention charges to a minimum benefits the traffic department or section and releases transportation equipment for greater utilization. Average demurrage agreements may be established on inbound and outbound cars, so that credits earned through release of cars or other transportation equipment within the first twenty-four hours of free time may be used to offset debits accrued on equipment held beyond the free time.

Documentation

Correct documentation, including preparation of bills of lading and other shipping papers, is important to the smooth functioning of a traffic department. There must be close attention to the possibilities of errors in filling out the various documents. The traffic manager must be familiar with the different kinds of bills of lading and the purposes which can be served by each, as well as the conditions agreed to by the carrier, as shown on the bill of lading.

Maintenance of Adequate Tariff Files

This responsibility of a traffic manager has a direct bearing upon the effectiveness of the traffic program he directs. The staff of a traffic department cannot work efficiently without necessary tariffs. The application of the proper rate cannot be determined unless there are sufficient tariffs available to assure that the best possible rate, or combination of rates, can be ascertained.

Expediting and Tracing Shipments

The urgency of movement of some shipments makes it necessary for arrangements to be made to get the shipment to destination in the shortest possible time. This involves arrangements with the carrier's operating or traffic division in advance to advise them of the urgency of the shipment and to facilitate its movement, particularly at junction points. In arrangements of this type, the carrier's personnel notifies the traffic department periodically of the progress of the shipment. Expediting is more successful when arrangements are made prior to the time the shipment is given to the carrier; but even after it has been given to the carrier, expediting can be employed successfully.

Tracing involves the initiation of a procedure for finding shipments that have become lost in transit or delayed. Tracing forms are usually used on which each of the carriers via which the shipment was routed is requested to report on the shipment while it was being transported by the carrier.

Processing Transportation Bills for Payment

The traffic manager must provide a uniform system for processing transportation bills for payment. On collect transportation bills, for example, he will insure that they will be paid upon receipt of the shipment, unless credit arrangements have been made with the carrier. Regulatory bodies prescribe the maximum allowable credit periods for transportation bills, excluding Saturdays, Sundays, and legal holidays.

Directing Research

Research in traffic management and physical distribution is an important function which should be performed in order to insure that efficient operations are being conducted. Much of the research at the present time deals with rate matters, whereas there are many additional areas in which research should be performed, such as packaging, unit size, warehousing, material handling, inventory control, site selection, and others.

Research may be performed by departmental personnel, or it may be done under contract for specific projects.

Arranging Transit Privileges

One of the special services which carriers provide is the transit privilege. The granting of this privilege by the carrier permits the movement of a commodity from origin to final destination with a stop at an intermediate point where the commodity is unloaded, stored, processed, reloaded, and reforwarded. In effect, two separate transportation movements are involved, but the carrier will assess the through rate from origin to final destination. This very important privilege enables an industry to process commodities, such as grain, at an intermediate point.

The traffic manager must arrange for the establishment of such a privilege, and there are many technical aspects to it.

Auditing Freight Bills

Freight bills are usually audited by the traffic department after the freight charges have been paid. Many errors are found in such bills because of mistakes in applying the wrong rate or weight, as well as simple arithmetical mistakes. Some companies pre-audit their freight bills before payment and, in this manner, detect errors which can be rectified by carriers prior to the presentation of the next bill for a similar movement. Pre-auditing can lessen the necessity of filing claims for overcharges.

Auditing conducted by the traffic department is usually supplemented by sending the freight bills to an outside organization which specializes in this work and operates on a commission basis.

Arranging for Movements of Household Goods

It has become increasingly common for employees who are transferred or new employees to have the expenses incurred in the moving of their household goods paid by the employing company. Therefore, traffic managers have been given the responsibility of arranging for the transportation of household goods when they are moved at company expense. Although such arrangements are relatively simple, the traffic manager must pay particular attention to such shipments. Because employees are often not familiar with transportation matters, the traffic department may be particularly helpful to them.

Loading

In the loading of transportation equipment, there are standard practices and procedures which will facilitate the safe arrival of goods. Carriers have incorporated years of experience in loading-rules pamphlets which deal with the subject of how to load properly and to brace and stow the goods to be shipped. This function may be performed in collaboration with other departments; but the traffic department, as the user of transportation service, will receive and make available the latest information dealing with this subject.

Handling of Export and Import Shipments

The handling of traffic matters involving export or import shipments is generally a traffic responsibility, either directly or indirectly. Reservation of space, documentation, and insurance are some of the details the traffic department must handle. Where brokers and other intermediaries are used, co-ordination must be maintained with them. Arrangements must be made also for customs entries, of which there are many different types.

The terms of sale are very important in international trade and will determine the extent of the arrangements which the traffic department will need to make. In addition to the numerous alternatives for shipping domestically, there are choices of ports and carriers in international trade.

Arranging for Adequate Insurance Coverage

Where the company owns and operates transportation equipment, it is necessary that adequate protection be provided for the risks that exist in the use of company-owned equipment. Protection may be provided by the establishment of a self-insurance fund of the company, or arrangements may be made with insurance companies. There are many different types of insurance policies, so that the coverage desired can be tailor-made for the organization.

In addition to the insurance on transportation equipment, it may be desirable to provide insurance protection for shipments involving water transportation where the rates do not include marine insurance. Also, where there is a limited liability of the carrier, as in the case of released value, provisions may be made to carry insurance to protect against the hazards to which the goods may be exposed, since the maximum limit of the carrier's liability is inadequate.

PROFESSIONALIZATION

The American Society of Traffic and Transportation, formed in 1946, is a professional organization for traffic and transportation patterned, to some extent, on the professional societies or institutes of accounting, life underwriting, medicine, and law. There is no organization solely for physical distribution, and many persons in this field are members of the American Society. The objectives of this organization are to establish standards of knowledge, technical training, experience, conduct, and ethics, and to encourage the attainment of high standards of education and technical training requisite to proper performance of the various functions of transportation. The establishment of this organization was the culmination of many meetings and discussions extending over a thirty-year period on the subject of professionalization of traffic management.

Some of the requisites essential in the establishment of a profession are (1) that an adequate body of technical data exist, (2) that the technical data can be arranged and organized, (3) that a set of standards be met requiring mental training and effort, (4) that a code of ethics govern the conduct of members in their work, (5) that a spirit of public service exist, and (6) that the persons desiring to join the profession possess special competence and work for further advancement of the profession.

The standards for professionalization can be set by statutory enactment, by establishment of a specified curriculum in colleges or universities, or by a society composed of those already in the field to set standards. It is the latter procedure which the American Society has followed. There are four examinations, given semiannually, which cover the fields of (1) transportation economics; (2) the principles of traffic and transportation management including physical distribution; (3) general business, including principles of economics, marketing, political science, and finance; and (4) interstate commerce law and regulation. In addition, an original paper of from three to five thousand words on a special aspect of traffic management, transportation, or physical distribution is required. Persons who have passed the examination given by the Interstate Commerce Commission for Practitioners or who submit proof of membership in the bar of the Interstate Commerce Commission are exempted from the Society's examination in interstate commerce law and regulation. To be eligible for the examinations, the applicant must be at least twenty-one years of age and of good moral character, and must submit credentials to the Society of his educational background and business experience.

Upon passing the four examinations and having an original paper accepted, the successful candidate who becomes a member is granted a certificate by the American Society of Traffic and Transportation. By 1964, 640 persons had been certified, while 3,000 were in the process of taking the examinations.

Another class of membership is composed of founder members, who are persons of distinguished attainment in the field of transportation and traffic, and over forty years of age. These members are nominated by the Executive Committee and elected by the Board of Directors of the Society. There were more than 1,300 founder members by 1964.

In 1957, a new class of members was added by amendment to the constitution. This class is designated as "contributors" and includes corporations or firms, as well as individuals. The class of contributors was established in order to increase the financial strength of the Society and to broaden its scope.

Annual meetings of the Society are held; and in 1951, there was inaugurated a two-day national conference and seminar with an excellent program, which has been held biennially since that time. A number of state chapters of the Society have been established.

The ultimate goal of the future traffic manager is that of a professional status. The examinations of the American Society of Traffic and Transportation are designed to test competence; and through this means and by adherence to high ethical standards, professionalization will be accomplished.

Two other organizations are keenly interested in greater education and technical training in the transportation field: Delta Nu Alpha fraternity and the Associated Traffic Clubs of America.

Delta Nu Alpha is a fraternity of men who are interested in advancing their usefulness and satisfaction in their chosen field of work—transportation—by obtaining the benefits of education and technical training and by helping others to obtain these benefits. Its purpose is the promotion, in every possible manner, of the widening and deepening of the education of its members, both in technical traffic and in general business and economics. It encourages its members to take the examinations of the American Society of Traffic and Transportation.

The Associated Traffic Clubs of America has as its objectives the development of better relationships between shippers and carriers, and the stimulating and developing of interest in educational matters among member traffic clubs. Its educational program and the educational aids it publishes and distributes are focused on these objectives. The Associated Traffic Clubs of America Foundation has the mission of bringing forcefully to the attention of top management the importance of competent traffic management by skilled traffic executives.[22]

There is growing recognition of the need for formal education in traffic and physical distribution management. Young people entering the field at the present time are quite likely to be graduates of a college or university in which they have had some course work in business subjects including transportation. This is in contrast to a number of years ago and is, in part, a reflection of a general trend in all areas of business. Where the systems approach to traffic management has been applied, it has emphasized the need for a sufficiently broad background in order to understand fully the interrelated functions of business enterprise as well

---

[22] The National Defense Transportation Association seeks to bring to the attention of the public the necessity for transportation preparedness through meetings, conferences, and publications, as well as other objectives.

The Propellor Club of the United States seeks to foster a strong U.S. Merchant Marine through meetings and conferences of its membership.

as technical competence in traffic management. The application of the physical distribution concept requires a similar educational background. Like so many other phases of specialized management, the field of traffic management has developed competent technicians, but to carry out successfully the increased responsibilities of this field today, much more than technical proficiency is required.

DISCUSSION QUESTIONS AND PROBLEMS

1. Looking ahead ten years, what will be the relative position of physical distribution, business logistics, and the systems approach to traffic management in the twenty largest corporations? In small business firms? Why?
2. What suggestions do you have to secure more accurate figures on the aggregate cost of traffic and physical distribution in our economy?
3. What are the implications of the cost of transportation relative to our gross national product?
4. Set forth in an outline the ways in which traffic managers directly and indirectly affect transportation expenditures.
5. What basic alternatives are available to the traffic or physical distribution manager in securing transportation? Does this place any greater responsibility upon him than was true forty years ago?
6. In what ways has the development of the newer modes of transportation provided both an opportunity and a challenge to management?
7. "To be able to save 10 per cent of the yearly transportation or physical distribution bill is considered a good performance." Critically analyze this statement.
8. How does the day-to-day handling of traffic functions affect planning functions?
9. Since interest in distribution developed much later than that in production, would you consider this an advantage or disadvantage? Why?
10. "The competitive ability of individual firms, in the future, may depend proportionately more on the efficiency of their distribution." What is the role of traffic or physical distribution management in this situation?
11. Place the functions of traffic management into two categories based on direct and indirect responsibilities. How would this differ for two large corporations, one a coal producer and the other a producer of staple groceries?
12. What are the requisites for a profession? Has traffic management attained professional status? What evidence is there concerning a movement in that direction?

Chapter

2

DEPARTMENTAL
ORGANIZATION

THE proper organizational framework within which to accomplish efficient management is of prime importance. Since the Industrial Revolution, the successful planning of management organization in itself has been responsible for growth impetus. Some major organization principles are as follows:

1. Definite and clear-cut responsibilities should be assigned to each executive.

2. Responsibility should always be coupled with corresponding authority.

3. No change should be made in the scope or responsibilities of a position without a definite understanding to that effect on the part of all persons concerned.

4. No executive or employee, occupying a single position in the organization, should be subject to definite orders from more than one source. (This should not interfere with functional direction exercised by staff specialist departments, such as accounting, personnel, purchasing.)

5. Orders should never be given to subordinates over the head of a responsible executive.

6. Criticisms of subordinates should, whenever possible, be made privately; and in no case should a subordinate be criticized in the presence of executives or employees of equal or lower rank.

7. No dispute or difference between executives or employees as to authority or responsibilities should be considered too trivial for prompt and careful adjudication.

8. Promotions, wage changes, and disciplinary action should always be approved by the executive immediately superior to the one directly responsible.

9. No executive or employee should ever be required, or expected, to be at the same time an assistant to, and critic of, another.

10. Any executive whose work is subject to regular inspection should, whenever practicable, be given the assistance and facilities necessary to enable him to maintain an independent check of the quality of his work.[1]

---

[1] American Management Association's "Ten Commandments of Good Organization."

The simple problems of the owner-manager in meeting the demands of the market have been supplanted by multiple problems of increasing complexity. Many managements or managers are not owners, and they must consider the stockholders' interests in their decisions. With the growth in the size of companies, organizational problems, as well as others, arise. Major organizational problems which occur in the development of a one-man business to a large company have been identified in the seven major stages of company growth shown in Table 2–1. It is not to be inferred that in each stage of growth there is but a single problem of organization, but rather that the problem listed in each stage is the primary problem.

TABLE 2–1

SEVEN MAJOR STAGES OF COMPANY GROWTH

Stage of Growth	Size* (No. of Employees)	Organizational Problem and Its Possible Consequences
I	3–7 Any size	Formulation of objectives: *Division of work*
II	10	Delegation of responsibility: *The accommodation of personalities*
III	50–100	Delegation of more management functions: *Span of control*
IV	50–300	Reducing the executive's burden: *The staff assistant*
V	100–400	Establishing a new function (functionalization): *The staff specialist*
VI	100–500	Co-ordination of management functions: *Group decision making*
VII	Over 500	Determining the degree of delegation: *Decentralization*

* The figures in this column indicate very broadly the size of the company when the particular organization problem may arise for the first time. The rise of the organizational problem is not necessarily tied to the size indicated.
SOURCE: Ernest Dale, *Planning and Developing the Company Organization Structure* (New York: American Management Association, 1952), p. 22.

Traffic and physical distribution functions are important in all stages of growth of a business organization; but the degree to which they are accomplished may be dependent upon whether there is a departmental organization, how it fits into the business organization, and how efficiently it can perform its functions. Larger business organizations, with their specialization in the various management fields, usually assign the responsibilities of traffic management to a traffic manager or director of physical distribution, who is quite likely to have the staff with which to perform all the necessary functions. In smaller organizations, only a part of functions may be performed, owing to the lack of personnel and a lack of understanding of functions. This is true in so-called "small" business firms.[2]

Although organizational structure is necessary, the most important factor in the success or failure of a business is the quality of management.

TYPES OF MANAGEMENT ORGANIZATION

The organization of business firms may be of several types: the line organization, line and staff organization, functional organization, and the use of committees. When responsibility is delegated in any type of organizational make-up, care must be taken to assure that the necessary authority is also delegated, so that the responsibilities can be discharged effectively. A common failing of management is the assignment of responsibility without the necessary authority.

Line Organization

The line organization, which is widely found in smaller companies, has a line of authority from the owner directly down to employees. It is usually referred to as a "military" type of organization, and the orders in this type of organization travel according to the line of authority. The line organization infers that the owner or general manager is in constant touch with all phases of the business operation. One man is entirely responsible, so there is a clear-cut division of authority and responsibility.

Line and Staff Organization

As business organizations increase in size, certain disadvantages of a strictly line organization becomes apparent. This may lead to a combination of what is termed the "line and staff" organization. In such an organization, the line executive maintains undivided responsibility and authority to command, but a staff of managerial experts is created to provide ideas and technical information to the line executive in an advisory capacity. Thus, staff specialization can be accomplished throughout an entire organization. The staff specialists do not issue orders. However, the information which they possess may be transmitted to a line executive who

---

[2] The Small Business Administration, a government agency, has classified any manufacturing concern as "small" if it employs 250 or less employees, including affiliates; as "large" if it employs more than 1,000 persons. This definition applies for loans and purposes other than government procurement. Between these limits, a manufacturing firm may be classified as either "small" or "large," depending on its industry and in accordance with the Small Business Administration employment-size standards. For government procurement purposes, a business enterprise with less than 500 employees was classified as "small." However, a business enterprise with less than 500 employees cannot be considered "small" if it is dominant in its field of operation. On the other hand, a relatively small business enterprise primarily engaged in an industry characterized by a large number of employees may be certified as a "small" business, even though it has more than 500 employees.

possesses the authority and who may establish such information as an order for dissemination throughout the organization.

Functional Organization

Another type of business organization is the one in which the staff members are given broader responsibility in so far as the functions of the departments which they head are concerned. Instead of functioning in an advisory capacity, as was true in the line and staff organization, these staff members have authority to command within their own departments. Under this form of organization, expert advice is available, and there is a free flow of work of a technical nature between the various staff departments.

Use of Committees in Line and Staff Organizations

Larger companies have often found that the line and staff organization can be modified advantageously through the formation of committees which assist in meeting certain management requirements. Standing committees may be established at different levels of authority, such as an executive committee for top management, and at a lower level a research and development committee or an operating committee. The latter, for example, excludes any planning and deals solely with day-to-day operations of a plant. Such standing committees tend to become an accepted part of an organizational structure. Occasionally, a temporary committee is established to deal with special projects or problems. Ordinarily, the committee makes a recommendation which is then given to the executive responsible for making the decision.

TYPES OF TRAFFIC DEPARTMENT ORGANIZATIONS

There are a number of different types of traffic organization arrangements in which the traffic department, if there is one, or the traffic functions are a subdivision of an operating or service department. Traffic activities are also often co-ordinate with other departments such as purchasing, marketing, and production. Many small companies have no separate traffic organization, and the traffic functions are handled by personnel from other departments as part of their regular assignments. These functions may be supplemented by securing help from outside organizations, such as traffic consultants or counselors. Under such arrangements, it is customary to have a very limited number of traffic functions performed.

Another type of organization is one in which an individual is assigned the title of traffic manager but has no staff of his own. The personnel from other departments may have a certain portion of their time assigned to assist him in the traffic functions.

A traffic department which performs only certain specified traffic functions, such as documentation and rate and claims matters, is another type of traffic department organization. Additional functions which are normally considered to be traffic functions are performed by other departments. In a division such as this, the traffic department may be looked to for management improvements for all traffic management functions, even though the traffic department is not responsible for and does not perform certain of them.

A complete traffic department which performs all of the functions of traffic management but in which the head of the department reports to one of the operating or service departments is another kind of traffic department organization. Many of the traffic department heads in this type of organizational make-up are called "directors of traffic."

The most highly developed traffic department and the one which performs all of the functions of traffic management is that in which the traffic department is a separate entity within the company, headed by a vice president of traffic, who is at a comparable level with the other departmental executives. In a setup of this kind, the head of traffic is an active and direct participant in the policy-making activities of the company.

Larger companies which provide part of their own transportation service by operating owned or leased equipment have divided their departmental traffic organizations into two broad divisions. The *traffic management division* under this arrangement is generally concerned with the control or management of those activities incident to the procurement and use of commercial transportation; the other division may be referred to as *transportation management* and exercises control or management of those activities incident to the operation of physical transportation facilities owned or controlled by the company. This would include over-the-road operation of a fleet of trucks, as well as intraplant transportation and local pickup and delivery.

Where a line and staff organization is established, which is often true in large companies, the General Traffic Department is found as part of the staff organization. The plant traffic managers are directly under the general managers of the respective plants. In this type of management organization, the greatest effectiveness can be secured through the maintenance of a genuine spirit of co-operation between the General Traffic Department at staff level and the general managers who have line authority over the plant traffic managers. A procedure should be followed whereby the general plant manager is informed whenever a member of the General Traffic Department staff visits his plant, and he should be told of the purpose of the visit. After consultation with the plant traffic manager, a memorandum of the items which were covered and any suggested changes should be given to the general manager and the plant traffic manager. If it is a matter of great enough interest, a copy should be sent to higher authorities.

The extent to which the importance of traffic management has been recognized in a particular industrial organization is reflected in the management level at which the traffic manager operates. The size of the corporation and the volume of traffic are by no means controlling factors in the recognition and the place which traffic management is given in top-management councils. If this were true, one would find far more vice presidents of traffic in industrial organizational setups. Two of the first five largest industrial firms in the United States, with large volumes of traffic and substantial traffic expenditures, have a traffic manager and a director of traffic, respectively, reporting to a vice president, who is at the executive level, while they are not.

A comparison of the activities of the general traffic departments of a number of large industrial organizations shows a performance of similar activities; yet, some traffic managers are vice presidents of traffic and thus have a direct voice in the formulation of company policy, while other traffic managers have no direct voice in company decisions. They may make recommendations through channels to their superiors; but the effectiveness of this type of communication—having to pass, as it does, through several hands—will be less than that of a personal presentation by a traffic management official at the co-ordinate level of other top officials. In recent years, the physical distribution concept has been established in some larger companies. Where this has occurred, the traffic functions are the nucleus of a physical distribution department.

TYPES OF OPERATIONS

When a company has a number of plants, the organization of the traffic department may be geared to either a centralized or a decentralized type of operation, or a combination of the two types.

Decentralized Operation

The trend in company organization in the postwar period has been toward decentralization. This affects all departments of a company which decides to decentralize. Many traffic managers are reluctant to have decentralization of the traffic functions because they feel that a centralized department strengthens their ability to negotiate with carriers and also enables them to assemble and present more effectively their suggestions and reports to top management.

Top management, in deciding to decentralize, however, will balance the advantages and disadvantages; and if the decision is made, it must be assumed that what can be accomplished for the company as a whole outweighs the advantages of centralized control of one or more departments.

A very large manufacturing concern gave as one of the principal reasons for its decentralization into 118 operating departments, each with profit responsibilities and operating authority in a given business area, that it would make the corporation more directly competitive in serving specific customer requirements. Headquarters service divisions serve these operating divisions in an advisory capacity in accounting and traffic.

In a decentralized type of traffic operation, each of the plants operates independently. However, the traffic department at headquarters supplies technical information, where necessary. Policy guidance may be given by the headquarters traffic office, and the traffic units at the plants operate within the framework of these general policies. In this manner, it is possible to establish a decentralized traffic operation and retain some degree of control.

In some instances, decentralization of traffic management is complete, in that the headquarters traffic office has no direct or indirect control over the traffic functions or operations of the plant traffic departments.

Generally, the most advantageous type of decentralized traffic operation is the one in which there is some functional traffic control over the plant traffic departments by the headquarters traffic office. It is possible, under a decentralized traffic operation in which the headquarters maintains functional control, to have many traffic matters of a local nature handled efficiently by personnel who are familiar with local situations. Many of the functions of traffic management which are essential but of a repetitive nature can be performed at the local level, which gives the headquarters traffic personnel the opportunity to concentrate on those matters which will provide greater efficiency and economy of traffic aspects for the company.

Instead of supplying information directly to the plants, the traffic department may employ traffic representatives who are assigned to districts or specific plants. These representatives are liaison personnel between the headquarters traffic office and the plants. The traffic representatives may be furnished the information which they pass on to the plants; and, should the need arise, they may serve as advisers.

In 1956, the Secretary of the Army was designated as single manager for traffic management within the continental United States on those aspects of traffic service which are common throughout the military establishment. As a result, the Secretary of the Army organized the Military Traffic Management Agency which, in 1962, became the Defense Traffic Management Service under the Defense Supply Agency of the Department of Defense.

The principles governing this organization are (1) flexibility to enable immediate transition from peace to war operation; (2) assignment of responsibilities to support logistic requirements in order to assure uninterrupted service even though DTMA headquarters or a regional office was put out of action; and (3) centralization of direction and control and decentralization of traffic operations and services, as far as practicable, to installations of the military departments and to Agency regional offices.

This Agency is the largest domestic shipper, with freight expenditures of $464 million involving 24 million tons of freight and passenger expenditures of $126 million. The regional offices have facilitated very substantial decentralization of operations, yet are responsive to direction and control from headquarters.

Centralized Operation

Where a centralized type of traffic operation is established, the major traffic activities are handled at the headquarters traffic office. It is only necessary, under such an arrangement, to issue instructions to the receiving and shipping personnel at the plants. The shipping and receiving de-

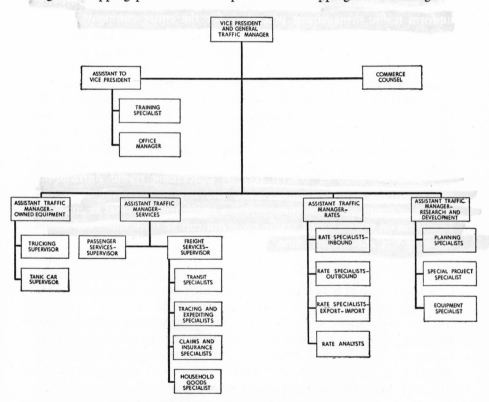

FIG. 2–1. An example of a centralized traffic department.

partments at the plants, under such a setup, are generally not under the traffic department, nor are they referred to as plant traffic personnel. The shipping information may be transmitted to the shipping and receiving activities at the plants, or such instructions may be given to the sales or purchasing departments, which in turn will handle the matters with the plants.

In this type of operation, centralized route and rate control may be established in which all outbound shipments from the plants exceeding a specified weight, such as 2,000 pounds, are required to be released from the plants through application to the headquarters traffic department for routing, at which time the rate for such a shipment will be affixed as well.

Much tighter control can be maintained over routing and traffic distribution in centralized traffic operations which may be of importance in rate negotiation with carriers to accomplish the best possible transportation cost for the company. Centralized control also permits the employment of highly skilled technicians to perform specialized duties. In this type of control, there is a focal point for the organization on all matters dealing with traffic management—rates, claims, routing, and a myriad of other responsibilities—and the centralized traffic department can provide uniform traffic management procedure for the entire company. Under this type of control, a single tariff file at the headquarters traffic department is all that is required. Figure 2-1 (p. 35) is an example of a centralized traffic department.

In many of the larger companies, there has been an organizational setup in which certain traffic functions are performed independently at the plants, subject to the prescription of policy by the headquarters traffic office. The latter office may find it necessary to direct certain phases of traffic plant operations through appropriate department liaison in order to accomplish company objectives.

The maintenance of central records concerning traffic distribution, claims, intraplant transportation costs, and cost of operating company-owned or company-leased transportation equipment provides essential information on which future traffic programs can be formulated and action taken at the appropriate time.

Combination Traffic Department

Some companies have a combination of both centralized and decentralized traffic operations. Certain divisions or plants control their own routing, rate negotiations, and other traffic activities, whereas other divisions or plants in the same parent company are controlled by headquarters. Often, this arrangement is transitional and occurs as a result of a merger when a new company or division traffic department is not disturbed until it is fully integrated into the parent organization.

TRANSITION TO PHYSICAL DISTRIBUTION MANAGEMENT

In some companies, the traffic department has for some years embraced all or a large number of the elements of physical distribution. Those most commonly encompassed in such departments are warehousing, plant location, material handling, and packaging. Although physical distribution has had its primary impetus in the larger companies, the traffic department has remained unchanged in a number of large companies and has under its purview many of the physical distribution components.

Over a decade ago, several large companies in the food industry recast their traffic management functions into a physical distribution department. At the time, there was only a limited amount of general interest in this action, the prevailing feeling among industrial traffic managers being that this development was largely the result of the emphasis that such consumer-oriented firms placed on the marketing aspects. Interest in physical distribution, though, has increased considerably in the last five years, although companies manufacturing consumer items have continued to show a more active interest than others. A number of factors have contributed to the increase in physical distribution departments which were discussed in the first chapter. These include the cost-profit squeeze which has necessitated improved cost control, the refinement of data processing, and the development of the total-cost approach.

An organizational opportunity exists between sales and manufacturing for pulling together the physical distribution functions into a department which can render staff assistance to all other departments. The assemblage of these functions should be analytically approached, component by component, and clear guidelines established for the operation of such a department. The heart of this department is the traffic and transportation component, since it affects so many of the aspects of physical distribution. Its role in trade-offs—for example, the balancing of transportation costs against warehousing, packaging, material handling, and inventory costs and its pre-eminence as the largest cost segment in physical distribution—require utmost co-ordination of this component with others. In addition to transportation, additional functions in the newly established departments include inventory control, warehousing, material handling (excluding the production line), packaging, and, in some instances, order processing. One of the most frequently cited advantages to the establishment of physical distribution departments is the ability to determine the total cost of these components, to weigh their total effect, and to achieve a better balance and improved service to customers. It is clear that before such a department is set up, sales, manufacturing, and other departments should be convinced of the value of the organizational change so their co-operation will be assured. Additionally, it is important that there be sufficient authority to carry out the responsibilities, a free flow of communications, and a clear delineation of the areas of control.

Some critical problems of overlapping control must be dealt with in formulating the proper organizational structure. For example, in the case of warehousing, responsibility may be divided between traffic and production, purchasing, or sales. Inventory control is usually under production, yet where field warehousing or distribution centers are necessary the control of such inventories may be a responsibility of sales and production. One approach to deal with the overlapping areas of control which may result in a better understanding of what the physical distribution relationships should be is to compile a list of the problems that have occurred in the past, and then study various organizational structures to see if there are logical relationships between the problems and the structures.

The close co-ordination of the physical distribution components of inventory, transportation, warehousing, packaging, and material handling which is required if there is to be an efficient system and a proper balancing of costs may be accomplished in some companies through an organizational change to a physical distribution department or through liaison between the traffic department and other components. In whatever organizational form, a systems approach which includes an analysis of the interrelationships between specific components and the entire physical distribution pattern is essential. A part of this analysis should be better identification of the cost components which would facilitate improved organizational structure. In the larger companies, the feeling may be that authority can be more logically assigned through a physical distribution department; although an organizational structure that places production, purchasing, finance, sales, and traffic on a co-ordinate level, with liaison and top executive decisions on interrelated factors could have the same results.

A large company grossing $340 million annually with 15 plants producing over 300 products and employing about 10,000 people has, over a period of years, formulated organizational changes as they were judged to be desirable. Prior to 1957, a customer service department was responsible for field and internal sales management liaison as well as for bringing together the various products produced at many different locations, for order processing, order assignment, and on-time deliveries. It was not responsible for the cost of distribution but was held accountable for all service implications in making delivery to the customer. The traffic department had complete responsibility for transportation, public warehousing, and all costs beyond the shipping point. The production service department was responsible for co-ordinating the physical distribution functions at the plant involving shipping, receiving, stores, and internal handling.

Among the problems was the fact that the traffic department had day-to-day cost responsibility but not customer service responsibility which caused conflicts between these two departments. The production service manager was responsible for plant shipping efficiency. However, the customer service manager was the one who assigned orders and demanded performance. The lack of effective control of the distribution costs as well as lack of full responsibility for customer service led to the

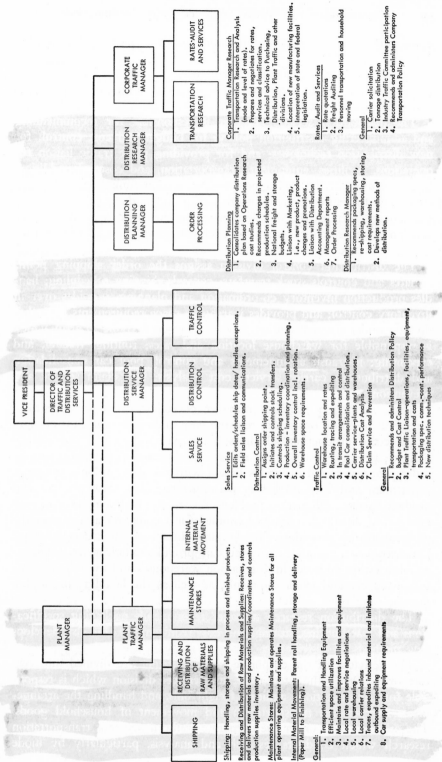

FIG. 2-2. Organizational chart of a traffic and distribution service department.

development of an organization embracing the physical distribution concept.

Under the new organizational structure, the director of traffic and distribution services at corporate headquarters has a number of managers under him, as shown in Figure 2–2.

The distribution service manager is responsible for recommending and administering distribution policy; for budget and cost control; for new distribution techniques; and for providing plant traffic liaison for operations, facilities, equipment, transportation, and costs. In addition, he is a member of the packaging and specification committee which was established to insure proper protection of products during transportation and storage. Under the distribution service manager is a sales service division which edits orders and schedules shipping dates, as well as providing field sales liaison communications.

The distribution control division assigns the order shipping point; initiates and controls stock transfers; controls shipping scheduling; handles production inventory co-ordination and planning; provides over-all inventory control; and provides warehouse space requirements. Another division under the distribution service manager is traffic control which is responsible for warehouse location and rates; routing, tracing, and expediting; in-transit arrangements and control; pool car consolidation and distribution; carrier service; cost analysis; and claim service and prevention.

The distribution planning manager consolidates company distribution plans based on operations research cost studies; recommends changes in projected production schedules; plans national freight and storage budgets; prepares management reports on distribution planning; handles order processing; and maintains liaison with the distribution accounting department and with marketing personnel regarding new product and product changes. Numerous problems related to the development of new methods of distribution are programmed for a computer as a part of the problem-solving procedure. By keeping abreast of these developments, the distribution planning manager can provide sufficient lead time to establish estimated needs in distribution warehouses and the requirements for mixed car and truck shipments, as well as the handling of display material, and other matters.

The distribution research manager recommends packaging specifications and warehousing, storing, and cost requirements. He also develops new methods of distribution.

The activities of the corporate traffic manager are divided into two categories. One is the rates, audit, and services division which is responsible for rate quotations, auditing freight bills, and handling the arrangements for personal transportation and movement of household goods. The other division under the corporate traffic manager is transportation research which conducts research and analysis, particularly by mode of transportation and level of rates. This division provides technical advice to other departments, such as purchasing, distribution, plant traffic, and others, a part of which involves the preparation and negotiation for rate adjustments, classification changes, and service changes. Another responsibility is the location of new manufacturing facilities and the interpretation of state and federal legislation affecting transportation. The corporate traffic manager recommends and co-ordinates transportation policy. He is also responsible for the distribution of tonnage and serves on industry transportation committees.

The plant traffic manager has responsibility for local rate and service negotiations; local warehousing; transportation and material-handling equipment; adequate supply and equipment requirements; tracing and expediting of inbound material and initiation of outbound expediting. Under the plant traffic manager is a shipping section responsible for handling, storage, and shipping of in-process and finished products. A receiving and distribution of raw materials and supplies division receives, stores, and delivers raw materials and production supplies; and co-ordinates and controls production supplies inventory. The maintenance stores division maintains and operates maintenance stores for all plant operating equipment and supplies. The internal material movement section is responsible for storage and handling of materials within the company.

CASE

The Quality Sales Company is a manufacturer of food products that has over sixty plants in the United States. It has nationwide distribution and uses its own and public warehouses. Its management has been alert to changes in merchandising and distribution methods and has made organizational changes over a period of years which it has felt would improve the efficiency of the organization.

The General Traffic Department in this organization originally reported to the Vice President of Manufacturing and Engineering. During this period, the major activities of the department concerned the refinement of plant traffic problems.

Later, the General Traffic Department was placed under the Vice President of Sales, during which period the traffic activities were primarily correlated with sales. Another step in the development was the organizational change that brought the General Traffic Department, as well as other service departments, under the Executive Vice President of the corporation. Still another change in organization made the Executive Vice President the chief operating officer, whose staff consisted of a corporate vice president to whom reported all service officers, such as Vice President—Controller; Vice President—General Counsel; Vice President—Manufacturing and Engineering; Treasurer; Vice President—Purchasing; Vice President—Traffic; Director of Research; Director of Public Relations; Director of Personnel Relations. A group of operating vice presidents also reported to the chief operating officer.

In the different stages of development of this General Traffic Department, the emphasis in traffic activities was concentrated in each instance in the respective area of the executive officer under whom the General Traffic Department was currently lodged, until finally it attained full stature and assumed the broad responsibilities of traffic management.

The responsibilities of the General Traffic Department of this large company are:

1. To develop, with the co-operation of the line organization and other staff departments, the corporate transportation and warehousing policies.

2. Upon request, or upon its own initiative, to furnish assistance, advice, and counsel to the line and staff organization in connection with transportation, location, and warehousing activities.

3. Upon request, or upon its own initiative, to keep the chief operating officer informed on important matters in the area of transportation and warehousing, as related to compliance with corporate policies, efficiency, effectiveness, and adequacy of traffic representation both in plants and in headquarters, as well as the need for revised or new objectives, policies, plans, methods, procedures, and techniques.

The general Traffic Department is divided into departmental sections:

1. Administrative.
2. Freight rates and classification.
3. Warehousing and pool-car distributors.
4. Claims.
5. Service, including passenger department operation of company airplanes and the like.

The administrative section, in addition to providing internal departmental administration, furnishes assistance, advice, and consultation on a broad basis to line and staff organizations on all phases of transportation and warehousing activities. In addition, this section works with the general traffic manager on the development and availability of special-type transportation equipment or facilities to move raw materials or finished products and participates in new plant location studies and plant relocation surveys.

1. Prepare an organization chart for this company embracing the physical distribution concept. On one page, describe for top management the reasons that such an organizational change would constitute an improvement.

DISCUSSION QUESTIONS AND PROBLEMS

1. In what way has the organization for management been responsible for the growth of business organizations?
2. Briefly define the different types of management organization. What are the basic differences between them?
3. "If the creation of a Physical Distribution Department simply adds one more management layer to the organization, why do it?" Carefully analyze.
4. If you were the traffic or physical distribution manager of a very large corporation, which produced at ten points and distributed nationally, would you recommend a centralized or a decentralized traffic operation? Justify your recommendation.
5. Consult the literature on management organization, and ascertain what the trend has been since 1946. In general, has it been toward decentralization? What challenge, if any, does this create in traffic department organization?
6. In a decentralized operation, what method of liaison with plant traffic personnel would you suggest as being the most effective?

7. What differences are there between industrial traffic organization and government traffic organization?

8. What factors would cause the use of a combination of centralized and decentralized traffic organization? Do you feel such an approach would work satisfactorily on a permanent basis? Why, or why not?

9. How would you differentiate between the traffic management division and the transportation management division of a department traffic or physical distribution organization?

10. In organizing a traffic department or section for a large corporation, would you set it up by function or by mode of transportation used? Explain your answer.

11. What deterrents are there to a transition to physical distribution management?

Chapter

3

MANAGEMENT AND ANALYTICAL METHODS

BUSINESS environment is constantly changing, and inertia cannot be tolerated. Traffic managers must be alert to the opportunities offered by additional transportation facilities, by greater specialization of equipment and service, by the availability of private transportation, and by competitive elements. If traffic is a part of a physical distribution department, transportation costs and services will also have to be considered as they relate to the total cost of physical distribution. It may be advantageous under certain circumstances to spend more on transportation in order to effect a reduction in total cost.

Within the organizational framework of a department, regardless of the type, the task of administering must be efficiently performed. Like the administration of other departments, the direction of the traffic or physical distribution department requires attention to detail; but consideration of the broad objectives of the company must be paramount. There should be willingness to try new methods and techniques. The sponsoring of research will provide innovations and improvements, as will the establishment of a training program. The feasibility of data processing as a management aid should be carefully considered. The goal of traffic and physical distribution management should be the best possible customer service at minimum total distribution costs in order to maximize profits.

MANAGEMENT POLICIES

There are two phases of policy matters that should be considered in a traffic or physical distribution department. If at the executive level, such a department can contribute substantially to the formulation of business policies for the company. This can be accomplished in conjunction with other company executives at the comparable policy level. It is in the formulation of policies, which in effect is the establishment of broad principles to serve as guides in the administration of business enterprise, that each of the specialized management areas in the business organization can facilitate the accomplishment of company objectives.

In the past, the traffic manager has frequently not participated in the formulation of company policies. With the increasing effectiveness of traffic managers in controlling transportation costs and the general management acceptance of the total cost approach to physical distribution, however, there is evidence of greater participation of traffic managers in policy formulation. Where a physical distribution department has been established, the director or manager of the department will unquestionably be at the policy level in order that the physical distribution functions can be analyzed and co-ordinated with production and sales.

The other phase of policy making deals with departmental policies. These policies should be recorded and made available to all personnel governed by them. Some departmental heads are reluctant to record policies because they feel that such a record might be used adversely by outsiders. While this possibility does exist, the advantages accruing to a stated policy program outweigh this disadvantage.

Too often, the assumption is made that the establishment of policies is a matter only for large concerns. This is not the case. Purposes and principles expressed in policies can serve as valuable guides in the building of efficient departments and should not be overlooked by business organizations that expect to grow.

In smaller business organizations, there is no line between policy making and policy execution. The policy formulators are the policy executors in this type of organization. As companies grow and greater specialization of activities is developed, a division appears between policy making and operations. Although there will always be some overlapping between these functions, the practice of disseminating stated policies promotes among personnel a better understanding of the principles to be followed in the traffic or physical distribution program. Policies should not be formulated without due consideration being given to their administration, for standards and operating procedures must be established within the framework of the policies. There also must be methods employed to insure that policies are being carried out wholeheartedly in a spirit of genuine co-operation.

The issuance of traffic or physical distribution management policies is particularly important where there is multiplant operation. Such policies, if properly administered, will insure adherence to established standards and will result in a greater degree of uniformity.

Guiding principles in the establishment of traffic or physical distribution policies which should be helpful in their formulation are as follows:

1. The statement of any policy should be definite, positive, clear, and understandable to everyone in the organization.

2. Policies should be translatable into practices, terms, and peculiarities of every department or division of the enterprise.

3. Policies, regardless of how fundamental, should not be inflexible; they should, however, possess a high degree of permanency.

4. Stability of policies is essential, and constantly changing policies are fatal to business success.

5. There should be as many policies as necessary to cover conditions that can be anticipated but not too many policies to become confusing or meaningless.

6. Policies should be predicated on fact and sound judgment, and should not constitute merely personal reflections.

7. Policies should not prescribe detailed procedure except in rare instances.

8. Policies should recognize economic principles, be in conformity with federal and other laws, and be compatible with the public interest.[1]

In the formulation of policies, the over-all goal of the department should be clearly stated, i.e., maximum service at minimum cost consistent with the profit objective. Essentially, such areas as warehousing, packaging, inventory, material handling, and transportation must be treated as subfunctions of the physical distribution function. Such subjects as the use of "premium" transportation and private or for-hire carriage, reciprocity, demurrage, and support of applications of common and contract carriers for operating rights and extensions may be included.

Implementation of Policies

The manner in which departmental policies will be implemented will vary in different companies. Traffic and physical distribution policies may be issued as a numbered series, called "Traffic and Physical Distribution Memoranda" or bearing a similar title. Such memoranda are often supplemented in functional areas by "General Traffic Letters" or "General Warehouse Letters" and others. Another method used is to issue a manual. In a physical distribution department, a manual might be issued in each of the general areas. The completeness of such manuals will depend upon the thoroughness with which policies and procedures are covered. Where the manuals contain both policies and procedures, it is customary for the policies to be found in the forward part. Instructions and procedures will occupy the bulk of the manual. Such manuals may furnish the instructions and procedures for each job function. This gives reasonable assurance that the functions will be understood and that performance will continue uninterrupted by changes in personnel. Since, under this arrangement, personnel assigned to many jobs do not have to make decisions, it is possible to employ personnel which will not be so costly to the company.

A typical traffic manual might contain the following material:

1. Traffic policies.
2. Preparation of goods to be shipped.

[1] L. P. Alford and J. R. Bangs (eds.), *Production Handbook* (New York: Ronald Press Co., 1948), p. 1383.

3. Marking of packages.
4. Ordering of transportation equipment.
5. Loading, bracing, and stowing of shipments.
6. Preparation of shipping documents.
7. Distribution of shipping documents.
8. Unloading of shipments.
9. Payment of freight charges.
10. Claims procedure.
11. Special regulations governing certain items, such as dangerous articles.

The use of traffic manuals has been somewhat limited thus far, but it is felt that the benefits which may be derived from their use merit their consideration. Those who have drawn up such a manual have sometimes found that its preparation results in a more satisfactory co-ordination and correlation of functions than was previously the case. Such manuals also serve to promote better understanding between departments.

Because of constantly changing factors, manuals must be supplemented *Supplements* from time to time in order to keep the latest information and procedures in the hands of the users. A loose-leaf manual in which pages can be inserted as they are issued provides a simple manner in which to keep the manual up to date.

CO-OPERATIVE RELATIONSHIPS WITH OTHER DEPARTMENTS OR DIVISIONS

One of the most important factors in the successful operation of a traffic department has been the ability to work closely and constructively with other departments. The emphasis has had to be upon the service that can be performed by efficient management of traffic. Some examples of the assistance given to individual departments follow:

Executive Division. Advise on plant location, advise on siding and other carrier agreements, arrange for transportation of executives, and participate in production planning.

Accounting Department. Audit freight bills or arrange for outside audit; furnish proof of delivery to credit division; file claims for overcharge, loss and damage, or reparations; and work out credit arrangements with carriers.

Sales Department. Furnish rate memoranda to salesmen, determine most desirable unit of sales on the basis of rates, furnish rate information to aid in extension of market areas, furnish information on competitors' rates and rate requests, furnish rates and other information for prospective customers, show most advantageous sales areas from traffic standpoint, assist customers in transportation problems, furnish information on warehouse location and related problems, operate or advise on operation of distribution warehouses, furnish data on impending rate and classification changes, and furnish automobile cost data for determination of salesmen's mileage allowances.

Purchasing Department. Show most advantageous purchasing areas from traffic standpoint, furnish information on most economical size of purchase, work with purchasing to consolidate less-carload shipments, assist in preparation of contracts in which terms affect traffic, and furnish information on impending rate and classification changes.

Manufacturing Department. Prescribe or advise on operation of shipping and receiving departments, maintain a steady flow of inbound and outbound traffic, and advise on product design.

Legal Department. Prepare rate case evidence, prepare loss and damage claim evidence, appear before rate committees and regulatory bodies, and advise on preparation of contracts for transportation equipment.

Personnel Department. Facilitate passenger movement of employees, and handle transportation of household effects for employees.

Advertising Department. Advise on descriptive matter on packages, and in advertising literature, with respect to classification probabilities; and place adequate advertising on company-operated transportation equipment.[2]

If a company adopts the physical distribution concept, the approach is broadened beyond that of conventional traffic management to that of systems analysis, involving a total cost approach. A balancing of cost factors is secured by analyzing all the components of physical distribution, and the best solution applied. Close co-ordination between all departments is mandatory if systems analysis is to be effective. Obviously, adjustments will have to be made in working relationships, especially in those areas where there are new organizational relationships.

A physical distribution department has to work closely with sales and can be of great help to the sales department in a number of ways. Improved order processing can result from co-ordination between these departments. Sales secures the order and knows the wishes of the customer regarding delivery. Extent of warehousing service and time in transit are important elements in the order cycle and are known by the physical distribution department. The selection of the best location for distribution warehouse centers to give maximum service at reasonable cost is also a factor of common interest to sales and physical distribution. Co-ordination in the establishment of the most desirable minimum sales quantity in terms of transport cost and susceptibility to damage en route is advantageous. Such matters as the feasibility of improving customer relations by operating a company-owned transportation system involves the sales department as deeply as the physical distribution department. The latter should also be a participant in the sales planning process in order to have advance knowledge of sales and advertising campaigns which might impose an unusual demand on the distribution system.

The physical distribution department has to plan and schedule movements to and from production. These varying demands require the utmost co-operation to insure a free product flow in accordance with scheduled production.

The work with the purchasing department involves the establishment of the least cost locations of raw materials, and the necessary arrangements to see that the material flows to the company as required. This may necessitate the establishment of points at which a number of raw

---

[2] Paul B. Blomgren and Joseph R. Hartley, *Getting the Most from Traffic Management*, prepared for Indiana State Chamber of Commerce, Indianapolis, May, 1954.

materials can be consolidated for movement in an orderly fashion into the plant. Production, purchasing, and physical distribution must co-ordinate their efforts to assure that there is sufficient material on hand to meet scheduled production runs for prescribed periods, plus adequate stocks to assure continuity of production. This requires a careful balancing of components so that inventory does not become excessive in terms of either physical demands on storage or financial demands on capital.

STAFFING

The success of a traffic or physical distribution department, in the final analysis, rests in the employment of qualified personnel. Personnel requirements will vary, depending upon the functions to be performed. There are some functions that require technical proficiency, such as rates, statistical analysis, and inventory control, which may be acquired through both training and experience. The specialists are likely to be found at headquarters and usually possess more formal training, whereas plant personnel may have general abilities and be capable of performing varied functions not requiring highly technical or specialized knowledge.

The person who assumes executive departmental responsibility must recognize the relationships of the various departments of the company, and the broad responsibilities he must discharge. The trend has been to broaden responsibilities of traffic managers and, with growing recognition of physical distribution, the need for individuals with managerial ability and breadth of knowledge is further accentuated. Job descriptions for such individuals usually run two to three pages.

In other positions, it is desirable to combine managerial ability with specialized knowledge which can be applied to their limited area of responsibility. While this does not mean compartmentization, emphasis should be placed upon the good performance of their tasks. They should also be systems-analysis oriented at low echelons in order that they can understand why such an approach will achieve company objectives. Some companies have hired a person with operations research or systems analysis experience who can assist in working out different concepts of traffic and physical distribution. Since these are newer approaches to problem solving, there is often a lack of education or experience in these methods and yet their advantages have proved to be of substantial value.

Traffic or physical distribution departments usually encourage their employees to participate in training courses. There are a variety of these, some of which are outside the company organization and are provided by colleges, universities, and vocational schools in day and evening classes or in correspondence courses, or classes sponsored by an organization such as a traffic club. Organization for training within the industry may be formal, in that regular classes are held; or informal, in the nature of an on-the-job training program.

It is important in establishing training programs to recognize the different levels of training that may be needed. Management should be alert to the development and application of new concepts which are often a part of management development programs offered by universities.

BUDGETING

A budget is used in business management as a device to plan and control the activities of the organization in order that the firm's objectives may be accomplished. Much of the emphasis in budgeting is on control, and it is possible to compare the results with the planned operations contained in the budget. If there is wide deviation between these two, action can be taken to control it. Thus, budgeting contains a measure of both planning and control.

Where the traffic or physical distribution department is a separate department at a co-ordinate level with other departments, a departmental budget will be submitted to the executive or committee in charge of budgeting. Where the traffic activity is under a physical distribution department, its expenses will be a part of the budget of that department.

In the preparation of a traffic or physical distribution department budget, the different elements of cost for which the department is responsible are computed and related to the sales budget. In a physical distribution department, those components would include transportation, warehousing, material handling, packaging, and also administrative expense. These components might be further subdivided into private transportation expense, common carrier, private warehousing, public warehousing, and others. Cost figures for the preceding three years in each of the categories are assembled. A rate of increase or decrease for each of the years is then computed, and a moving average arrived at for the three-year period. A tentative budget total for each category is computed using the rate of increase or decrease for the three-year period. This dollar figure is then reconciled with the ratio to net sales figure, and an actual budget figure for the following year obtained by averaging the two dollar totals. The dollar amounts for each expense category are totaled, and the budget figure for the department obtained.

REPORTS

A report may be the means by which to communicate effectively the accomplishments of a traffic or physical distribution department to top management and other departments. The type, form, content, and length of reports vary from company to company. In some companies, the form and length of the report are prescribed for all departments, so that the format is standardized. In other companies, the form may be adapted to the particular needs of the department. Some reports are in narrative form, others in statistical form; and still others are combinations of these. In formulating a report, it should be emphasized that there must be a fact or an idea, or a series of facts or ideas, that are worth reporting.

To aid in the evaluation of the report by the recipient, it should contain a basis of comparison or contrast or method of measurement. Further, it must be in understandable language; and, when possible, its form and timing should be adapted to the personality of the principal recipient.

Reports may serve any one of many purposes, or several: (1) to sell a new idea; (2) to reflect the financial facts of a given situation; (3) to compare the alternatives of proposed action; (4) to analyze a management problem; (5) or to estimate a future financial picture or technical or economic development and its effect on the company.

Monthly, quarterly, semiannual, and annual reports may be made, depending upon the size of the company and the scope of traffic or physical distribution activities. A topical outline of a monthly traffic department report would include such subjects as new rate proposals and their status, new transportation arrangements, personnel strength, demurrage and detention, claims handled, rate changes, consolidation of shipments, utilization of transportation equipment—owned and/or leased—and additional miscellaneous or general items as required. Much the same topics would be contained in other regular reports.

The traffic manager will secure data which may be used for departmental purposes and as the bases for some reports to management, such as the amount of carloads and truckloads, the amount of inbound and outbound tonnage, distribution of traffic among different modes of transportation, and rate adjustments. The information of the traffic department can be combined with that from other departments to establish averages or ratios which management finds useful, such as the percentage of transportation or traffic costs to total sales, or the amount of freight costs expended per unit to transport into a given sales territory. In addition to the foregoing, the physical distribution department would make reports on such subjects as the feasibility of higher cost transportation to reduce inventory, the use of distribution center warehouses, the physical distribution support aspects of marketing in new territories, or a study of new plant location.

A report should be an effective means of communication. A mass of figures which are not interpreted or not presented in an organized, meaningful manner may be of little value. A system of graphic reporting which accompanies the textual material may be used to make the report more interesting.

ANALYTICAL METHODS

Research

A very great expansion of research and development has taken place in the last decade. The dollar outlay, in 1962, for R&D totaled $16.5 billion, which was eight times the level of fifteen years earlier. The commitments of both business and government for R&D work continue to increase because of its proved value. In the case of business organizations, these expenditures have led to product discovery, technological innovations, and improved systems.

The role of research in traffic and physical distribution must be expanded, as has been done in other management areas. While research is being conducted in traffic and physical distribution by some firms, particularly in connection with rate cases and location problems, there are many areas in which little or no research is conducted.

The transportation industry, as a whole, spends only an estimated 0.7 per cent of its total budget on R&D as compared to a national industry average of 4.2 per cent.

There are two broad types of research activity. One is termed "basic" or "pure" research and is concerned with basic scientific investigations undertaken in order to discover or develop new fundamental facts, theories, natural laws, or relationships. The results of such research will usually have no immediate application in industry. The other type is called "applied" research and is the application of basic scientific knowledge to specific problems. Applied research is the type used in traffic and physical distribution.

A separate research and development section is the type of research organization needed to carry out many research undertakings which are not being adequately performed at the present time. A program of this kind must be under the direction of an individual with imagination. There must be full support on the part of top management, and it should be clear that it is established on a long-term basis. If research is undertaken with the sole expectation of short-run advantages, the results may prove disappointing.

A research and development section will cut across all aspects of the traffic or physical distribution department such as packaging, material handling, level of inventories, and warehousing. It will study, analyze, and develop plans, policies, and programs or procedures which are assigned to it, as well as undertaking on its own research which is considered appropriate. Some of the research methods which have been used for many years are time and motion study, marketing research, statistical quality control, and economic analysis. Scientific research methods are characterized by freedom from bias, judgment based on facts, objectivity, rationalism and reasoning, selectivity, and probabilities rather than certainties.

In the postwar period, there has been increasing use by industry of the management consulting firm. This type of firm may be hired to make a thorough survey of a company, analyze the performance of the various management functions, and recommend the proper organization and adequate staffing to insure efficient performance.

Historic — Past analyzed & interpreted
Deductive — logical concl. from generalization
Inductive — gen. corel. from controlled observations.
Analytic — discover true nature of interrelationships.

One of the reasons that these organizations are called upon is to secure a fresh look from a group of outsiders. The reasoning is that they have been doing similar work and can bring to the investigation the benefits of varied experiences secured in working with other companies. Often, the management consulting firm relies heavily upon the suggestions of company personnel, so that its recommendations include ideas that may have been previously advanced by company personnel and not accepted by company management until offered by this type of outside organization. One of the advantages that the management consulting approach offers is that the business organization may put recommended changes into effect *Research* much earlier than would have been the case had there been no investiga- *Process* tion or study made.

The steps in the research process are as follows: (1) formulation of *Formulate* the problem, (2) determination of sources of information, (3) preparation *Determine* of the data collection forms, (4) designation of the sample, (5) collection *Prepare* of the information, (6) tabulation and analysis of the data, and (7) *Designation* preparation of the research report. *Collect*
Tabulate
A scientific study meets certain standards. The procedure used must *Prepare* be objective and involve accurate measurements. Basic scientific methods that are accepted and recognized must be employed in the study. The person who conducts the research must possess a scientific mind—that is, he must be unbiased, constantly searching for new facts, and requiring logical solutions.

A number of basic methods are used in scientific research, which are sometimes modified in their particular fields. The historical method is one in which past events are analyzed and interpreted. These facts are then used as the basis of understanding existing problems and future events. In the inductive method, general conclusions are drawn from controlled individual observations. It is necessary that there be sufficient data to make it possible to generalize. This method is often referred to as the method of reasoning from the specific to the general. The deductive method is to arrive at logical conclusions drawn from generalizations. It is obvious that inductive and deductive methods are used together. The facts are gathered and generalizations developed by using induction. From these generalizations, the logical conclusions can be drawn, which is deduction. The analytical method is to attempt to discover the true nature or interrelationships of an intellectual problem or a substance that does not superficially reveal them. This method divides a complex whole into components that can be more easily observed and understood.

Computers

In the post-Korean War period, automatic handling of information has received increased attention, and systems of data processing have been installed to effect more efficient management of various functions.. During this period, electronic data processing (sometimes referred to as "integrated data processing" or "automatic data processing") has been used successfully in the solution of many problems, both in industry and in government. The first electronic data-processing computers were of the so-called "giant" type, which could be supported only by large organizations handling great workloads. Recently, manufacturers have produced equipment which falls into the category of "small" and "medium," and is characterized by reduced size, cost, speed, and capacity.

There is a general purpose computer which can do all types of arithmetical computations, store data, compare items, and prepare reports, as well as perform other functions. This type is regarded as one that is completely integrated and can perform the functions of data processing, such as receiving and converting information, storing and sorting data, collating, computing, transmitting, and making data into a usable form—namely, a readable output.

The special purpose computer is limited as to type of computations it can make and as to the functions it can perform.

Programming is a very important procedure in data processing. It is the means for translating a routine procedure into coded instructions which cause the machine to go through its automatic operations. The caliber of the programming will determine how well the objectives of the problem specifications are accomplished and how effectively machine time is utilized. The conversion to the data-processing system usually requires several months because of the necessity to train personnel properly in its use and then to get the procedures worked out satisfactorily.

There are several areas of traffic management, particularly in large industrial organizations, in which the use of computers appears feasible. One large firm with a centralized traffic organization which prepares rate and route sheets for shipments of all commodities to and from all destinations has much traffic of a repetitive nature and has found computers to be of great assistance. This traffic department maintains approximately 140,000 rate and route cards. During the numerous rate changes of the past few years, it has averaged 20 changes per year. This has necessitated changes on rate and route cards of from 25 to as many as 100,000 changes by hand, depending upon the nature of the rate change. Using the manual system, a typist could type 100 sheets a day. On general rate increases, it took as long as three months to get all of the rate and route cards changed, so that during this time, many shipments which used the old rate and route sheets were not moved at the correct rates.

By establishing a rate and route form which accommodates all the data shown on the old sheets plus space for additional information, it is possible to put this information into the machine and make a so-called "master" card which contains coded information as to the commodity, origin, destination, and the preferred route (although more than one route is often contained on the card). The minimum weight, rate, and break-point weight are also given. The break-point weight is the point at which a shipment may be shipped cheaper as a higher weight (the next minimum weight) at the next lower rate. In the event of a general rate increase, the increase is fed into the machine and added to the master cards. From these cards, new rate and route sheets can be run off in a matter of hours, instead of days or months as under the manual system.

This company receives approximately 350,000 freight bills per year. Using a computer, a card is punched containing the basic information on the freight bill that the carrier has submitted, including origin, destination, weight, and rates. These cards are fed into the machine and compared with the master cards. When the cards match, nothing need be done; but the machine rejects the freight bill cards which do not match the master cards. This operation is, in effect, a precheck or pre-audit before the bills are paid.

Another area of application for computers is that used by one company to simulate six months of sales and restocking under a new control and physical distribution system. The simulation showed that the new system could improve service to customers and cut the dollar value of inventories in half. Through use of the computer, ways were also found in which the system could be modified to improve inventory handling through certain periods of peak demand.

Firms are making increasing use of computers to simulate the probable consequences of business actions. Computer simulation is designed to reduce the risks of irrevocable decisions by testing complicated theories on computers. A mathematical model is set up for a particular proposal, such as building new plants or installing new inventory systems. Creating a mathematical model forces management to take an analytical approach to management problems and to consider all aspects of a problem.

Computers also speed up clerical processes, which improves service to other departments of a company and allows faster transmittal of information to plants. There may be some economies effected in the use of computers as well.

Data-processing systems may be purchased or leased, or may be leased with an option to purchase, depending upon the manufacturer involved. Repair parts and maintenance service are usually included under leasing arrangements. In traffic management control, there is transitional equipment available between the conventional tabulating equipment and the more elaborate data-processing systems which may be advantageously used. There is no necessity to move immediately to computers unless there is justification for it.

Data processing is inherently accurate if the right data are fed into it. A new factor in its use is that it proceeds to maximum benefits rather than randomly searching for them. Results are secured within time limits, enabling management to take advantage of the information for decision making.

Operations Research

Operations research was developed during and after World War II. It is research into the relationships and functions of an organized activity. Using scientific methods applied to business problems, its purpose is to provide executive departments with a quantitative basis for decisions regarding operations under their control, in order to use the resources on hand for optimum results.

Operations research uses a variety of specialists operating as a team, including economists, statisticians, sociologists, mathematicians, and cultural anthropologists. The prediction and comparison of the values, effectiveness, and costs of a set of proposed alternative courses of action are developed analytically. The approach is likely to be symbolic, and rather full use is made of mathematical models as a working device. Historical analysis of past actions or operational experiments is used to evolve the values of the basic actions, and conclusions are often shown as a range of alternate possibilities rather than as a single right answer.

Operations research differs in approach from customary business research in that the operations research team will generally attempt to study the relationship of the activity under consideration to all other pertinent elements of the business, and a definitive answer is not necessarily sought.

Systems Analysis

Systems analysis is a method used to study any particular aspect or segment of a system, yet it requires an understanding of the entire system. Ordinarily, the business or industrial system consists of such factors as manpower, materials, machines, consumers, competitors, management, and government. These factors are variously subgrouped, and their control and interrelationships must be studied in a systematical and analytical manner in order to assure maximum accomplishment of a company's over-all objectives. The techniques of operations research are particularly applicable in systems analysis. Ordinarily, as many of the factors as possible are reduced to quantitative terms. It is recognized, however, that the human element as it affects the system must also be analyzed.

The basic elements of a system consist of input, component, and output. The input acts as a signal which activates the system. The component will accept the input signal and perform a single or series of functions as directed. The output is the measurable risks in terms of costs or other specified corporate goals.

As applied to traffic and physical distribution, systems analysis is particularly useful in the total cost approach. Traffic and physical distribution objectives are established within the framework of existing constraints—managerial or physical—which limit the scope of the study. This emphasizes the interaction of various components of physical distribution. Models, either mathematical or nonmathematical, may be constructed as a result of postulating alternative types of systems. A model or models can then be tested, either in simulation or actual operation. This makes it possible to ascertain the capability and costs of alternative system components. The analysis may indicate that the relationship of commitments of manpower and capital to develop components should be substantially altered.

Linear Programming

Linear programming is another phase of research and involves the use of advanced mathematics. It is a means for determining the best course of action to follow under limiting or restricting conditions in situations where a large number of solutions are possible. The formulation of a proper statement of the problem to be solved is the phase of linear programming which is the most difficult, inasmuch as this involves putting numbers on factors, some of which are not usually quantified, and stating the problem in such a manner that a mathematical solution is possible. Linear programming may utilize manual or machine methods.

"Linear" refers to straight-line mathematical relationships. The mathematical equations used are expressed in the first power so that variables in the equation develop in direct proportion to each other—in other words, the influence of each element must be directly proportional to the quantity of the element involved in the problem. Each of the number of alternative methods is expressed in equation form and yields a particular input-output ratio. By comparing the ratios, the best procedure may be selected.

Probability Theory

The idea of probability is sometimes referred to as the "laws of chance." The factor of chance works in such a way that in certain cases a series of events, if free of man-made interference, will produce results that conform to a predictable pattern. The probability theory is applicable to those events that can be repeated many times under nearly the same conditions. This theory has been used in the physical and biological sciences and is being increasingly applied in the business field. Most decision making occurs in the face of uncertainty, and the use of probability concepts and statistical inference have been found to be helpful. The theory of probability deduces properties of a physical process from mathematical models while statistical inference is used to determine the properties of the model from actual observed data.

In many business situations, a great many variable factors have a bearing on whether the goal can be achieved. Through the use of the probability theory, efforts can be made to determine if certain methods would be successful in achieving the goal. The product of the analysis would be to indicate the relative degree of certainty with which the desired goal might be expected.

DISCUSSION QUESTIONS AND PROBLEMS

1. Describe briefly the co-operative relationship between the traffic or physical distribution department and other departments or divisions.
2. What information does the traffic department need and secure from other departments in order to manage traffic effectively?
3. Explain in detail the purposes and types of traffic or physical distribution department reports. Prepare the format of such a report.
4. "Too often, the assumption is made that the establishment of policies is a matter only for large concerns." Briefly comment on this statement.
5. In your opinion, what method is the most feasible one to implement traffic and physical distribution management policies?
6. The traffic manager asks you to prepare a traffic manual for use by his department or section. Prepare a detailed outline of the material you would cover, and state what sources would be helpful in compiling the information.
7. "Upgrading the personnel that are already a part of a traffic department does not mean that their efficiency increases." Do you agree with this statement? What are other alternatives?
8. What are some of the factors which should be considered in setting up a traffic management training program?
9. How is a traffic or physical distribution department budget different from a sales department budget? Are transportation expenses usually budgeted?
10. List the principles which would be helpful in establishing traffic management policies.
11. What type of research is used in traffic and physical distribution management? In your judgment, how should such research be conducted?
12. What is the role of the management consulting firm in research?
13. Outline how you would analyze the feasibility of an electronic data-processing system for a traffic and physical distribution department in a large corporation.
14. In what ways does the physical distribution function offer a challenge to management?
15. What are some specific examples of the application of probability theory and linear programming to traffic and physical distribution problems?

Chapter

4

THE TRANSPORTATION
SYSTEM AND SERVICES

In the development of our early modes of transportation, geographical factors were of primary importance for, in many instances, barriers such as rivers, lakes, and mountains served as deterrents to the economic development of certain areas. Although our early modes of transportation, water and rail, were limited by the facilities used to fixed waterways and roadbeds, the more recent development of motor and air transportation has injected a much greater degree of flexibility into our transportation system and has lessened the impact which physical geography heretofore had upon transportation.

Our transportation network is without parallel in the world today, and the service available is unprecedented. The traffic manager[1] has at his command a wide selection of service from which to choose, which represents both a challenge and a responsibility. To use transportation service as effectively as possible in the traffic activities of his company is a challenge to the traffic manager, for it requires a thorough knowledge of the type of service offered by each mode of transportation, the rates, routes, time in transit, and many other factors; and to use transportation service in such a manner as to strengthen our transportation system is a responsibility which the traffic manager should acknowledge.

In 1963, the American transportation system included the basic facilities of 29,000 miles of inland waterways; 3,418,314 miles of streets and highways; 135,000 miles of airways; 200,000 miles of petroleum pipe lines; and 220,000 miles of railroads. Included in our system are 103 larger railroads and 505 smaller lines, which own 1,550,000 freight cars, 25,500 passenger cars, and 28,500 locomotives; 81,630 airplanes, of which 1,620 (340 pure jets) are operated by 50 scheduled airlines in domestic service;

---

[1] Regardless of organizational structure—whether a traffic department or a physical distribution department—the transportation and traffic components will be handled by a traffic manager or director.

over 65,000 local, state, and interstate trucking companies with 12,730,-000 trucks of all kinds; 1,340 companies engaged in intercity bus service and using about 10 per cent of the 270,000 buses; over 70,000,000 passenger cars; more than 1,700 operators on inland waterways; 21,021 towboats, tugs, barges, and carfloats on the nation's rivers, canals, and harbors; a large fleet of ore and coal carriers on the Great Lakes; 9,352 craft on the Mississippi and Gulf intracoastal waterways; and pumping stations and other facilities for 200,000 miles of petroleum pipe lines.

The many services offered by transportation agencies range from highly specialized operations, such as those of pipe lines, to general commodity operations, such as those of railroads and motor carriers. This wide variety of transportation services provided by a transportation network totaling 4,002,314 miles has been developed and is offered by carriers which are private enterprise firms.

These transportation companies are comprised of different types of carriers. The for-hire carriers include those called "common carriers" and those called "contract carriers." Some common carriers haul general commodities, whereas others are specialized carriers limited to a single commodity class or a small number of commodities. As common carriers, they assume full responsibility for the safe delivery of shipments, unless limited by bill-of-lading or tariff provisions, and transport them in equipment under their direct control and responsibility to the public. Contract carriers, which are used under individual and special contracts, can be made virtually a part of the company's organization; or the contract can spell out any provisions that are mutually agreeable and in conformance with existing laws. There are services, such as the freight forwarders, which assume full responsibility for safe delivery but which do not physically transport the goods in equipment under their direct control. Other indirect methods are air and rail express and parcel post. The services of for-hire carriers or the indirect carriers are sometimes supplemented by the use of private carriage, in which case the transportation service is performed by a company for its own use in company-owned and/or leased equipment.

An illustration of the extensive use made of intercity transportation relates the for-hire and private intercity transportation to the population of the United States. The annual ton-miles[2] per person, approximately 8,000, is an increase of more than 90 per cent since 1939.

---

[2] The statistical units used to measure intercity volume of traffic are ton-miles and passenger-miles. Ton-miles are used in measuring freight transportation. One ton carried 10 miles would represent 10 ton-miles. Passenger-miles are used in passenger transportation, and one passenger transported 5 miles is 5 passenger-miles. It should be noted that the average distances vary among the modes of transportation. Airline distances, for example, are approximately 17 per cent shorter than rail distances, which factor should be recognized in comparing air ton-miles or passenger-miles with rail ton-miles or passenger-miles. Conversely, the distances in inland water transportation average greater than the average distances in rail transportation.

INTERCITY TON-MILES, PUBLIC AND PRIVATE,
BY KINDS OF TRANSPORTATION, 1939-1962

BILLION TON-MILES

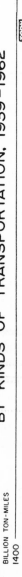

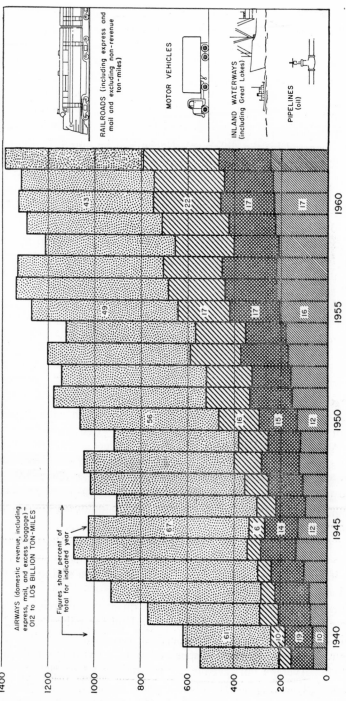

AIRWAYS (domestic revenue, including express, mail, and excess baggage)—
.012 to 1.05 BILLION TON-MILES

Figures show percent of total for indicated year

RAILROADS (including express and mail and excluding non-revenue ton-miles)

MOTOR VEHICLES

INLAND WATERWAYS (including Great Lakes)

PIPELINES (oil)

Source 1939-1959, I.C.C., Bureau of Transport Economics and Statistics, Intercity Ton-Miles, 1939-1959, Statement No. 6103; 1960, Annual Report of the Interstate Commerce Commission; 1961, staff estimates.

FIG 4-1. Intercity ton-miles, public and private, by kinds of transportation, 1939-1962.

The wide disparity in the utilization of transport facilities results in broad differentials in line density. In rail transport, for example, less than 10 per cent of total main line rail mileage, or 23,000 miles, carries 50 per cent of total freight ton-miles of traffic whereas 67,000 miles, or 30 per cent, account for only 2 per cent of rail freight ton-miles. Analysis of other modes would also show great differences in line density.

The revenue ton-miles transported by each mode of transport are shown in Figure 4–1. Significant shifts in the percentages of total ton-miles transported by the different agencies can be noted. In the postwar period, the railroads' share of the percentage total has declined from 66 per cent in 1946 to 43 per cent in 1962. Ton-miles transported by rail also decreased from 602 billions to 600 billions in that period although total ton-miles transported by all modes increased from 903 billions to 1 trillion, 395 billions.

It is expected that the ton-mile market will continue to expand. A projection to 1970, based on past linear relationships, 1939–59, between freight ton-miles and gross national product, would result in 2 trillion ton-miles in 1970. Such a projection does not reflect major technological innovations or wide swings in the business cycle. Approximately 67 per cent of total intercity ton-miles is moved by common carriers, which is a reduction from 1939 when it was 75 per cent.

RAIL

One of the types of rail service that carriers offer is based on the quantity which is to be moved as a single shipment. In rail transportation line-haul service, carload (CL) and less carload (LCL) are the two basic types. Although the definitions of carload and less carload may be found in tariffs, a satisfactory definition of carload is that it is a quantity of freight which can be loaded in or on a freight car and is entitled to a particular rate because the weight of the freight equals or exceeds that which is specified in the carrier's tariff for the application of that rate.

Railroads have interchange of traffic without transfer of lading, which permits the shipment to go from origin to destination in the same car. Seventy-five per cent of rail tons carried is interchange traffic. Interchange facilitates the movement of goods through a saving in time and the reduction of handlings.

Railroads are capable of carrying large quantities of freight over long distances very economically. The average haul for railroads in 1962 was 452 miles but average train speed between terminals was only 19.9 miles per hour. This is an increase in speed of slightly less than 4 miles an hour since 1946. Average rail revenue per ton-mile is 1.4 cents.

Rail freight service is performed by local or way freight trains through freight or expedited service. Most of the freight runs are not scheduled. A surcharge for expedited service, above the normal line-haul rate, has been established for guaranteed delivery at destination in a specified number of hours. Bulk freight moved in specialized equipment may be dedicated to a particular type of move, such as coal, and such operations are referred to as "integrated trains."

Goods may be tendered to carriers in a variety of ways, such as loose, in bulk, and in packages, as well as many others. In order to ship freight in its different forms, specialized equipment has had to be provided, in many instances by rail carriers. Open and closed cars are also provided, since many items are of a size that does not permit loading in closed cars. The different types of rail cars which are available are found in a quarterly publication, the *Railway Equipment Register.* This publication is filed with the Interstate Commerce Commission and has the status of a tariff.

Boxcar distribution is governed largely by the condition and suitability of the equipment, since all closed cars are not suitable for the loading of all commodities. There are four generally recognized classes of closed cars: Class A for flour, sugar, and similar articles; Class B for grain; Class C for merchandise traffic; and Class D for articles such as hides, sewer pipe, brick, and similar commodities, known as "rough loaders." According to length, there are two classes of closed cars: (1) cars 40 feet, 7 inches (which are considered "standard" cars) or less in length; and (2) cars 41 feet to 50 feet, 6 inches in length. For yard classification, they are generally referred to as (1) 40-foot cars and (2) over 40-foot cars.

Eighty-six per cent of the boxcars in service are 40-foot cars, and 32 per cent of these cars have a capacity of 3,700 to 3,800 cubic feet. Approximately 9 per cent of the boxcars are 50 feet in length, with capacities from 4,100 to 6,000 cubic feet. The trend is toward larger cars. There are an increasing number in use which are designed to minimize damage and to facilitate loading and unloading by material-handling equipment. The average tons per carload in a recent representative year were 43 tons. The average tons for products of mines were 59; animals and products, 14.75 tons per carload; and manufactured and miscellaneous, 32 tons.

LCL Services

LCL services which the railroads provide may be offered in a number of different ways. Many local way stations have *substituted freight service* in which the railroads have substituted trucks to handle LCL shipments and move them to and from larger terminals and break-bulk or concentration points.

Peddler cars, also, have been used to move LCL shipments to different consignees en route. The freight rate is paid to a specified final destination, but the lading is partly distributed at various intermediate points en route. The service performed by these cars is different from the way-car service or LCL shipments, in that the former shipments are delivered directly to consignees.

The use of *package cars* is another of the LCL services. They are loaded by the railroad with a number of LCL shipments in scheduled service, daily in some cases and several times weekly in others, in fast or expedited trains. Such cars are billed by the originating railroad to a carrier's local freight agent at the scheduled destination, at which point the contents of the car are unloaded. A portion of the contents may be held in the freight station for delivery to consignees, and the remainder may be transferred to another car for further movement. The transportation and traffic divisions of chambers of commerce frequently publish bulletins on the package-car service available in their respective cities. A bulletin of this kind contains tabulations of the on-time performance of such cars, as well as the service which is available.

A *pool car* is one in which a shipper consolidates all his LCL consignments at one destination to one consignee, who acts as an agent for the shipper in delivering the shipments. Where there are a number of combined LCL shipments for consignees at different destinations, the car will be billed as a carload to the shipper's agent at a central point; the agent will rebill and forward the individual shipments to their final destination.

Classification of Rail Carriers

Railroads are classified by the Interstate Commerce Commission for accounting and statistical purposes into two classes: Class I carriers are those railroads with gross operating revenues in excess of $3 million per year, and Class II are those with gross operating revenues of less than $3 million per year. This classification has been effective since January 1, 1956.

Class I railroads operate approximately 96 per cent of all railway mileage, employ 93 per cent of railway workers, and perform approximately 99 per cent of railway service as measured by passenger-miles and ton-miles. Currently, there are 103 Class I railroads, an additional 42 Class I switching and terminal companies, and 463 Class II railroads.

Although not classified by the Commission, there are so-called "short-line" railroads which have come to be regarded as railroads less than 100 miles in length. They play an important role in originating and terminating traffic for larger railroad systems.

Rail Freight Tons and Revenues

Class I railroads handle primarily carload traffic. There has been a steady decline of LCL car loadings since 1946, and it amounted to less than 3 per cent of gross freight revenue in 1963.

The Interstate Commerce Commission uses the following commodity groups for use in tabulating statistics: products of agriculture, animals and products, products of mines, products of forests, manufactures and miscellaneous, and less-carload traffic. The products of mines represented 51.6 per cent of the total tons originated in 1962 but produced only 23 per cent of the total revenue. On the other hand, the manufactures and miscellaneous group, which represented only 27.9 per cent of the tonnage originated, produced 48.4 per cent of the revenue.

MOTOR

The highway facilities used in motor transportation are public facilities and embrace a highway system of over 3 million miles of improved roads. They are owned by the states or political subdivisions thereof, except for a relatively small mileage of toll roads and federally owned roads in national parks and reservations.

The equipment used in motor transportation has been tailored to the job to be performed, with the result that there is a great diversity of equipment. Straight trucks may be equipped with many different types of bodies, such as platform, stake, dump, and van, as well as others. There are low-bed, tank, pole, and van full trailers, and semitrailers which are designed and used for general as well as specific purposes. The cubical capacity of van trailers varies, depending upon the length of the vehicle, which is influenced by size restrictions imposed by the states. A 40-foot van is being increasingly used. On some turnpikes, two 40-foot vans are operated in tandem. There are also heavy-duty off-highway trucks which may be used in special types of operations.

Whereas railroads derived less than 3 per cent of their revenue from less-carload service in 1963, motor carriers of general freight subject to Commission regulation secured 61 per cent of their revenue and 43 per cent of their tonnage from shipments which are defined as "less-truck-load" shipments, that is, shipments of less than 10,000 pounds each.

The average haul of Class I intercity common carriers has averaged about 260 miles since 1955; and, in 1962, it was 267 miles. The average haul for Class I motor contract carriers was 147 miles. The average revenue per ton-mile for common carriers is a little over 6 cents and for contract carriers 5.5 cents. *16% Trucks*

Classification of Motor Carriers

There are a number of different ways of classifying motor carriers that will assist in an understanding of the services offered by them. One of these is the accounting classification established by the Interstate Commerce Commission. Class I carriers are those whose gross revenues exceed $1 million per year; Class II are those whose gross revenues are from $200,-000 to $1 million per year; and Class III are those whose revenues are less than $200,000 per year. This classification has been effective since 1957.

Another classification is that which resulted from a national investigation by the Interstate Commerce Commission in 1937.[3] The latter

---

[3] *Classification of Motor Carriers of Property*, 2 MCC 703 (1937).

classifies motor carriers as common, contract, private, or exempt carriers, and brokers.[Service may be regular route, scheduled or nonscheduled, which means it is performed over designated routes; or it may be irregular route, radial or nonradial service.]Radial service is from a fixed base point or points to points or places located within a radial area, such as 75 miles from a base point.

There is a greater diversity of types of service available through the various kinds of carriers in the field of motor transportation than in any of the other modes of transportation. The fact that motor transportation can furnish store-door to store-door transportation without transfer of lading offers a very distinct advantage to many shippers.

Common Carriers

Part II of the Interstate Commerce Act, which subjects motor carriers to regulation, defines a common carrier by motor vehicle as any person which holds itself out to the general public to engage in the transportation of property by motor vehicle over regular or irregular routes in interstate or foreign commerce.[4] The common carrier serves anyone desiring service without discrimination among customers as to service or rates. The shipper is given a uniform bill of lading, or receipt, for each shipment, and the carrier has full responsibility for safe delivery of shipments unless it specifically limits its liability. The operating authority of a common carrier is a certificate of public convenience and necessity issued by the Commission and may be regular or irregular route. In motor transportation, there are many carriers which are specialized and transport but a very limited number of commodities, yet hold themselves out to the general public and are common carriers. Some of the specialized carriers are tank-truck operators, automobile haulers, and household goods carriers.

The general commodity common carriers are not all of the same type in the sense that the operations of some of them are those of distribution service to small towns and communities, while others have key-point operations in which service is rendered only between key-points such as two cities. Some motor common carriers operate over regular routes, whereas others operate over irregular routes. On June 1, 1963, 15,332 motor common carriers of property held certificates from the Interstate Commerce Commission.[5]

In motor transportation, the basic services are truckload (TL) and less truckload (LTL). The truckload may be equal to or more than the minimum specified for the application of a truckload rate, and it is understood to be the quantity a carrier can transport in a single vehicle. It may also be defined as a shipment which will fill the capacity of a trailer, and

---

[4] Section 203 (a) 14.
[5] Section of Certificates and Permits, Bureau of Operating Rights.

there are similar definitions. Motor carriers also make use of a volume minimum. The volume minimum may exceed the carrying capacity of the largest vehicle, and a shipment tendered under the volume minimum may be transported in two or more vehicles. The volume minimum was established in order to be competitive with the railroads, the latter originally having equipment of considerably greater cubical capacity.

Less truckload may be defined as a shipment which weighs less than the minimum weight prescribed by the carrier for the application of the truckload rate. There are also less-than-volume shipments in motor transportation, which are usually considered to be those shipments of less than an amount specified by the carrier, such as 5,000 or 7,000 pounds.

Contract Carriers

The term "contract carrier by motor vehicle" was first defined in the Motor Carrier Act of 1935 and was redefined by Congress[6] in 1957 to mean:

> . . . any person which engages in transportation by motor vehicle of passengers or property in interstate or foreign commerce, for compensation under continuing contracts with one person or a limited number of persons either (a) for the furnishing of transportation services through the assignment of motor vehicles for a continuing period of time to the exclusive use of each person served or (b) for the furnishing of transportation services designed to meet the distinct need of each individual customer.

The motor contract carrier subject to regulation by the Commission is issued a permit. Under the new definition, there are two types of contract carriers. The first of these is that of a contract carrier with a fleet of vehicles used exclusively by a single shipper, such as a chain store firm or a shipper of automobiles or any other large shipper with sufficient traffic to provide a profitable operation for the carrier without utilization of the vehicles for the transportation of goods for any other shipper. For example, a contract carrier serving a chain store firm may perform a distribution service from warehouses to retail stores. The second type of contract carrier is that which provides a transportation service for a group of affiliated companies and, in so doing, meets a distinct need for each shipper in the group, an example of which would be the co-ordination of the combined traffic of the group. Other contract carriers use the same equipment to serve several unrelated nonaffiliated customers; if the service for each customer meets a distinct need, the combined operation would appear to be of the second type. Contract carriers do not hold themselves out to render service to everyone nor do they issue a uniform bill of lading or receipt. They operate under long-term individual contracts, usually for six months or more, with one shipper or with a limited number of shippers.

---

[6] Public Law 85–163.

At common law, contract carriage is recognized as a form of private carriage. There were on June 1, 1963, 2,383 contract carriers which had been issued permits and were subject to regulation by the Commission.[7]

Exempt Motor Carriers

Another type of for-hire motor carrier operation is the exempt carrier operation. The carriers in this category move certain commodities for compensation, but they are specifically exempt from the Commission's economic regulation.[8]

The current exemptions include property carriers using motor vehicles controlled and operated by farmers engaged in the transportation of agricultural commodities or farm supplies; vehicles controlled and operated by co-operative associations as defined in the Agricultural Marketing Act; vehicles used in carrying livestock, fish, or agricultural commodities; vehicles used exclusively in the distribution of newspapers; vehicles used in the transportation of property incidental to transportation by aircraft; vehicles used in transportation of property wholly within a municipality or zone adjacent to or commercially a part of such a municipality; vehicles used in casual, occasional, or reciprocal transportation of property by motor vehicles as a regular business; and vehicles used in transportation within terminal areas by railroads, water carriers, or freight forwarders subject to the act in transferring, collection, or delivery service.

Court rulings through the years had the effect of broadening the agricultural exemption. The Transportation Act of 1958, however, amended the definition of the agricultural commodities exemption by adopting a ruling of the Commission's Bureau of Motor Carriers, which specifically lists the exempt and nonexempt items, thereby limiting the exemption.

The major activity of the exempt carriers is that of moving agricultural commodities, livestock, and fish. No exact figure is known as to the number of such exempt carriers; but the Commission has estimated that there are about 48,000, operating 225,000 vehicles.

Private Motor Carriers

The fourth type of carrier is the private carrier of property which is defined as a person not included in the common and contract carrier definitions in the Interstate Commerce Act and which transports in interstate or foreign commerce by motor vehicle property of which such person is the owner, lessee, or bailee when such transportation is for the purpose of sale, lease, rent, or bailment, or in furtherance of any commercial enterprise.[9] The Transportation Act of 1958 contained an amendment which provides that no person engaged in any business enterprise other than transportation shall transport property by motor vehicle in

[7] Section of Certificates and Permits, Bureau of Operating Rights.
[8] Sections 203 (b) and 202 (c).
[9] Section 203 (a) 17.

interstate or foreign commerce for business purposes unless such transportation is within the scope and in furtherance of a primary business enterprise, other than transportation, of such person.

It is relatively easy to engage in private carriage because equipment can be leased or purchased. If leased, there is no investment in equipment; and if purchased, the investment required for equipment is relatively small. There were an estimated 92,000 private carriers in 1963.

Local Cartage

In local cartage service, both common and contract carriers operate. Local cartage operations which deal with interstate commerce usually involve pool-car or pool-truck handling and distribution, and collection and delivery service of less-truckload and less-carload freight. In addition, there are many services largely local in nature, such as riggers specializing in mobile units which can make heavy lifts from office buildings or plants, general cartage services, armored car service, and retail delivery service.

Package Service

For many years, intercity bus operators have offered package freight service, transporting a wide variety of articles. Most carriers place a limit on the size of the package. The largest intercity bus operator has found that 80 per cent of the packages shipped weigh less than 30 pounds, and the average distance transported is 150 miles. Representative commodities carried include automobile and farm implement parts, medicines, and drugs.

The package express service offered in connection with the intercity bus carriers is generally available on a prepaid, collect, or C.O.D. basis. Service is usually provided from and to points on the lines of the transporting carrier. There are several carriers that have very extensive operating rights; and the service on these lines may be, in effect, coast to coast.

Small trailers, called "pup" semitrailers, are being used by some bus lines for hauling express and other matter behind buses.

Several companies have specialized in providing small package service, usually less than 50-pound shipments. This service is performed under contract with retail department stores. Another service that may be available is the delivering of small packages from manufacturers, wholesalers, and distributors to their customers within a several-state area. One company handles more than 140 million packages a year.

WATER

The provisions of the Interstate Commerce Act governing the issuance of operating authorities to domestic water carriers subject to Part III of the act are substantially the same as those for motor carriers. The definition of a contract carrier under Part III is somewhat broader than for a motor contract carrier under Part II. It provides that one who furnishes a vessel to a person other than a carrier subject to the act for use in transporting his own property is a contract carrier. Water carriers are also entitled to extend their services over uncompleted portions of waterway projects authorized by Congress, over the completed portion of which they already operate, as soon as such uncompleted portions are open for navigation.

Classification of Water Carriers

The Interstate Commerce Commission has classified the common and contract carriers to which it has issued certificates and permits. The certificates and permits which have been issued limit the carrier to transportation by (1) self-propelled vessels, (2) sailing vessels, (3) nonself-propelled vessels with the use of separate towing vessels (barge-line services), (4) towing vessels, or (5) vessels furnished to persons other than carriers for use by such persons in the transportation of their own property (restricted to contract carriers by statutory definition).[10]

For statistical purposes, domestic water carriers are classified into Classes A, B, and C. Class A carriers are those water carriers with annual gross revenue exceeding $500,000; Class B, from $100,000 to $500,000; and Class C, less than $100,000.

The primary exemptions from regulation by the Commission apply to (1) the transportation of commodities in bulk, when the cargo space of the vessel used is not being utilized for the transportation of more than three such commodities; and (2) the transportation of liquid cargo in bulk in vessels designed exclusively for such use. The Commission has held that nonbulk commodities cannot be included in a tow of bulk commodities without subjecting the entire cargo to regulation, regardless of the manner in which responsibility under the bills of lading might be divided among two or more carriers.

Water transportation is usually classified into the broad categories of (1) domestic and (2) foreign.

Domestic Water Transportation

In domestic water transportation, there are the categories of coastwise, intercoastal, Great Lakes, and inland water transportation.

Coastwise is considered to be movement by water from and to points on the Atlantic Coast, Gulf Coast, or Pacific Coast. The Interstate Commerce Commission has stated that such transportation as that from Houston to Texas City, Texas, by way of the Houston Ship Canal, is in coastwise commerce, which term, as judicially defined, includes movement over

---

[10] Interstate Commerce Commission *56th Annual Report* (Washington, D.C.: U.S. Government Printing Office, 1942), p. 141.

navigable inland waterways as well as by deep-sea vessels between domestic ports.[11]

Intercoastal water transportation embraces those movements between Atlantic and/or Gulf ports and Pacific Coast ports via the Panama Canal. The Intercoastal Shipping Act in 1933 stated that a common carrier by water in intercoastal commerce for the purposes of the act shall include every common and contract carrier by water engaged in transportation for hire of passengers or property between one state of the United States and any other state by way of the Panama Canal.

Great Lakes shipping between Great Lakes ports in the United States constitutes another phase of domestic shipping. The ships used in all three of these types of service can be of the type physically comparable to those used in foreign ocean shipping. Bulk carriers transport iron ore from the head of Lake Superior to Lake Erie ports at a cost of about 2 mills per ton-mile.

Inland water transportation uses the navigable rivers and canals, including the intracoastal waterways, for movement of commodities. Sometimes, Great Lakes shipping is included under inland water transportation.

Domestic water transportation is protected, in the sense that only ships of American registry can engage in such activity. This protection is the result of the principle of cabotage, which is the limitation of domestic traffic to vessels documented under the flag of that country.

The majority of tonnage moved by water in domestic transportation is in bulk. This is particularly true of the inland waterways, and the cost per ton-mile averages less than for any of the other modes of transportation, averaging slightly more than 3 mills per ton-mile. The minimum bulk shipments accepted range from 500 to 1,000 tons and in 1961 dry bulk comprised 60 per cent of the tonnage and 32 per cent of the revenue. The average capacity of three pieces of equipment used for hauling the same product is shown in Figure 4–2. Through the use of integrated

TANK CAR

8,500 gallons

TANK BARGE

TANK TRUCK

840,000 gallons

5,200 gallons

SOURCE: American Waterways Operators, Inc.

FIG. 4–2. Comparative average capacity of tank car, tank truck, and tank barge.

tows, eight or more barges can be moved with a 14,000- to 20,000-ton cargo, equal to four trains of 100 cars each. Such tows measure 1,170 feet in length, which is longer than the *Queen Elizabeth* or the *USS United*

---

[11] *Hanlon-Buchanan, Inc.* v *Burlington R. I. R. Co.,* 258 ICC 519, 522 (1944).

States at their water lines. On the lower Mississippi River, where there are no locks, the tows run up to 30 barges and as much as 30,000 tons.

Foreign Water Transportation by American-Flag Vessels

American ships engaged in foreign water transportation do so in a number of different types of service. Some act as common, some as contract, and others as industrial carriers. In addition, a carrier may offer a combination of these services.

The Shipping Act of 1916 defined a common carrier by water in foreign commerce as one which is a common carrier engaged in the transportation by water of passengers or property between the United States or any of its districts, territories, or possessions and a foreign country, whether in the import or export trade. Ferryboats running on regular routes and ships operated as ocean tramps are not considered to be common carriers.

Steamship companies often operate their ships in both common carriage and contract carriage. Furthermore, by loading the holds of the ship with cargo from a number of shippers under a uniform ocean bill of lading and loading the remaining holds with cargo from a particular shipper under a special contract or charter party, it is possible for the same ship between an origin and a destination to offer both common and contract carriage. Contract carriage, under these circumstances, is actually space chartering.

In ocean shipping, reference is frequently made to industrial carriers. An industrial carrier is sometimes understood to mean a for-hire carrier controlled by a business enterprise primarily engaged in some other form of industry, such as manufacturing, mining, or commercial activities, as contrasted to transportation. A carrier, such as an oil company, may transport its own product in ships it owns. If it has unused cargo space, it may also make such space available to shippers. Although the industrial carrier is basically not for hire, there are occasions when it will serve as a for-hire carrier.

Two of the services widely available in foreign ocean shipping are (1) liner service and (2) tramp service. Liner services are usually defined as those that operate on regular routes at regular intervals, which would mean a scheduled operation. The Maritime Commission, has defined a tramp vessel as one that operates on irregular or unscheduled sailings from one port of loading to one port of discharge, lifting one dry cargo commodity, usually of low value, without mark or count, and from one shipper to one consignee.

Liner services of American-flag vessels have been established between those ports with sufficient tonnage to justify a liner operation. Operations of this kind depend upon many shippers to secure adequate loading. A route between ports in a United States coastal area or areas to foreign markets is termed an "essential trade route" if it has been determined by the Maritime Administration under the provisions of the Merchant Marine Act of 1936 to be essential for the promotion, development, expansion, and maintenance of the foreign commerce of the United States. The majority of American-flag liner service is rendered over 35 essential trade routes.

Although usually hauling a single cargo, tramp ships sometimes carry as many as three commodities on any one voyage for not more than three shippers. Tramp vessels which seek to carry in shipload quantities are particularly adapted to the handling of seasonal or peak demands. Coal and grain and other cargoes of relatively low value per pound, when available in shipload quantities, are the types of commodities particularly adapted for tramp shipment.

Tramp service supplements liner operations. The vessels tend to be somewhat slower and without some of the conveniences, such as refrigeration, that may be found in liner vessels. It should not be inferred, however, that all tramp vessels are inferior to liner-type facilities, for there are occasions when a steamship line will charter a ship from a tramp operator, and there are other times when tramp operators charter vessels from liner operations. Ordinarily, tramp operations are of a contract carriage type. If there are sufficient bulk commodities available between two ports, it is possible for tramp operators to engage in operations comparable to those of a specialized common carrier.

The three basic types of vessels used in foreign operations are (1) passenger, (2) dry cargo, and (3) tanker. Any ship which carries over twelve passengers is classified as a "passenger" or "passenger-cargo" ship. Where a considerable portion of a ship's space and revenue is devoted to cargo, it is called a "combination" or "passenger-cargo" vessel. Ships of this type may carry over a hundred passengers.

Dry-cargo ships are those which carry general cargo and not more than twelve, if any, passengers. Dry-cargo vessels carry a wide variety of items, some boxed or crated, some in bags or bundles.

Tanker vessels are designed primarily to carry crude oil and oil in various stages of refinement. They also carry other liquid cargo, such as molasses and vegetable oil.

In addition to the three basic types of vessels which comprise the major part of the American Merchant Marine Fleet, there are a number of miscellaneous types of vessels, such as special-type bulk carriers which carry cargo of ore and grain, or sulphur, and refrigerated ships.

Charters

Vessels may be chartered where there is sufficient tonnage to justify it, or for other reasons. The two types of charters used are (1) time charters and (2) voyage charters. Under the provisions of a time charter, the shipper hires a specific vessel for a fixed period of time, such as 120 days. The voyage charter, on the other hand, is one in which the vessel is chartered for a single voyage between specified ports of call. Voyage and time charters are usually established on a per diem basis, which is stipulated in the charter.

Bare boat or demise charter is one in which there is the lease of a vessel, often referred to as a "dead ship" because it is leased without stores and crew. The burden of operation and maintenance is upon the lessee in this type of arrangement. The duration of such charters is usually one or more years. The United States government made extensive use of this type of charter during World Wars I and II, and it has continued this procedure in the last few years. This procedure is not common between shippers and carriers where time and voyage charters are widely used.

AIR

Until 1944, air transportation of property was essentially air express. One of the reasons for the delay in the development of an air cargo service was the restrictive nature of the agreement between the Railway Express Agency (now REA Express) and the air lines. One of its provisions stated that the air lines could not establish rates less than twice the first-class rail express rate without the consent of the Railway Express Agency. Another provision stated that the air lines could not accept express shipments from any party other than the Railway Express Agency. These provisions were removed as a result of Civil Aeronautics Board action in 1943.[12]

The real growth of air cargo has occurred in the period since 1946. There has been a revolution in the technology of air transportation in terms of speed and size during this period. With jet transports, air freight service is twice as fast as the fastest service available by air less than a decade ago. With speeds of 550 to over 600 miles an hour, service by air is so much faster than by other modes that no comparison would do it justice. Unfortunately, ground handling of air shipments diminishes the total elapsed store-door to store-door time.

Air freight is a service with the weight and size of individual shipments limited only by the ability of the aircraft available for transportation. Four-engine cargo aircraft can normally accommodate pieces as large as 60 × 80 × 90 inches and carry a maximum of 40,000 pounds. Two-engine cargo aircraft can normally carry pieces as large as 53 × 57 × 60 inches and carry a maximum of 6,000 pounds. Smaller aircraft can accommodate pieces as large as 20 × 24 × 44 inches.

Advance arrangements are generally required for individual pieces weighing in excess of 200 pounds, of unusual size or shape, or pieces with a floor-bearing weight in excess of 100 pounds per square foot which may have to be provided with suitable skids or bases by the shipper.

There have been some occasions in which provisions have been incor-

---

[12] *Railway Express Agreements*, 4 CAB 157 (1943).

porated in an air carrier's certificate which have permitted it to substitute truck service for air service to specific points. When a service of this type is inaugurated, the rates are usually the same as the air rates, even though the service is provided by truck.

There are several different types of domestic direct air carriers which offer air cargo service. These are (1) trunk line, (2) local service, (3) certificated cargo only, (4) supplemental, and (5) air taxi and helicopters.

Most air carriers operate on specifically designated routes but certificated cargo only, supplemental, and air taxi operators may operate over irregular routes.

Trunk-Line Carriers

The Civil Aeronautics Board has defined a trunk-line carrier as an air carrier authorized by certificate of public convenience and necessity to provide regularly scheduled service of an express, long-haul character. Currently eleven carriers are engaged in trunk-line operations. These carriers render combination service which includes the carrying of passengers, mail, and property. Some are regional in scope, whereas others have extensive authority. Four carriers operate transcontinentally.

Local Service Carriers

Local service carriers operate routes of lesser traffic density and between less populous urban communities than the trunk-line carriers. A principal characteristic of their service is the provision of relatively short-haul transportation. In the number of route-miles operated, some local service carriers exceed some of the trunk-line carriers.

Since the enactment of the Civil Aeronautics Act of 1938, a total of 23 local service carriers has been certificated by the Civil Aeronautics Board, 13 of which are in operation at the present time. These carriers offer a combination service.

Certificated Cargo-Only Carriers

In 1947, a number of cargo-only carriers filed applications for certificates of public convenience and necessity. That same year, the Civil Aeronautics Board established, under an exemption, a group of operators defined as "noncertificated cargo carriers." This group could engage as common carriers in the transportation of property only, pending action on their certificate applications in the *Air Freight Case*.[13]

In the finding in this case, the Civil Aeronautics Board issued certificates of public convenience and necessity, authorizing scheduled transportation of property-only carriers over two transcontinental routes, as well as certain other routes. These carriers are certificated air cargo-only carriers.

[13] *Air Freight Case*, 10 CAB 572 (1949).

In addition to these certificated cargo-only carriers which were certificated in the *Air Freight Case*, scheduled air cargo service by an all-cargo operator was certificated to operate between the United States and Latin America. A large irregular carrier was certificated to render this service.[14] Two additional carriers were certificated for domestic operations. There are presently five all-cargo lines which operate between designated areas in the United States and, in one case, to the Caribbean and, in another instance, to Europe. These carriers are authorized to carry mail on a nonsubsidy basis. The all-cargo carriers tend to concentrate their schedules between 9:00 P.M. and 3:00 A.M.

By the end of 1963, the cargo-only carriers handled 46 per cent of domestic air freight, and their average revenue per ton-mile was slightly more than 18 cents.

Supplemental Carriers

Fourteen supplemental carriers operate under interim authority until the Civil Aeronautics Board acts upon their applications for permanent certificates. These carriers have been granted unlimited interstate charters of persons and property, plus military planeload contract flights with certain back-haul civil charter rights. Some may also, for a two-year period beginning in 1962, carry individually ticketed passengers or individually waybilled cargo, the amount depending upon the carrier's past participation in these operations. In addition, carriers have overseas or foreign charter authorization, subject to certain conditions.

An association of supplemental air carriers provides a central point where information is available on the transport aircraft and their location at all times. This enables the shipper to charter an aircraft of the size he desires to transport cargo for a single trip or a series of trips.

Air Taxi Operators and Helicopters

It is estimated that there are over 2,000 so-called "air taxi" operators. These are operators of small aircraft, usually of less than 12,500 pounds gross take-off weight and generally possessing five passenger seats or less. Such operations make possible an extension of emergency freight shipments, should the need arise.

At the present time, there are three helicopter or rotary wing aircraft, certificated to operate in Los Angeles, Chicago, and New York. Companies of this type hold themselves out to carry property and passengers.

Charters

Opportunities exist for the shipper with sufficient volume to charter aircraft from certificated air carriers. The charter rate on file with the Civil Aeronautics Board is usually at a specific amount per plane-mile. It is

---

[14] *Latin American Air Freight Case*, 16 CAB 107 (1952).

possible, under such a charter arrangement, for a shipper to ascertain what the charge per 100 pounds is and compare it with other air cargo services, as well as with other modes of transportation.

The Board's *Economic Regulations* defines a charter flight as ". . . transportation performed by an air carrier holding a certificate of public convenience and necessity where the entire capacity of one or more aircraft has been engaged for the movement of persons and their baggage or for the movement of property, on a time, mileage, or trip basis."

Deferred Air Freight

In 1956, the Civil Aeronautics Board authorized the establishment of deferred air freight service. This service, which was designed to generate a new type of air cargo, is conducted on a "space-available" basis and utilizes otherwise wasted cargo capacity on combination and all-cargo planes. The authorization for making shipments under the delayed air freight system has been prescribed by the Board, so that there is a two-day minimum time lag between regular air freight delivery and the delivery of deferred air freight. Each package must be marked "deferred air freight." Some of the service is on a store-door to store-door basis.

Air Express

Air express is handled by the Air Express Division of REA Express, Inc., formerly the Railway Express Agency, and it is forwarded on the passenger planes of all scheduled certificated air lines of the United States. Air express shipments are flown direct between more than 1,800 cities having scheduled air carrier service and are moved to 21,000 off airline communities by plane, train, and truck routing. Air express service is available to shippers in all cities located on airline and rail routes.

There is pickup and delivery service without additional charge in all cities and principal towns within the regular REA Express vehicle limits. Air express will be delivered on the customer's demand, regardless of the time of day.

Shipments can be accommodated that range up to 100 pounds per square foot in the cargo compartment of aircraft. By special arrangement with the air lines, through the express agency, shipments of greater density can be carried. When unusually large or heavy shipments, up to 6,000 pounds, are to be shipped by air express, it is often possible for the express agency to arrange for a cargo plane.

Under the Federal Aviation Act, the Civil Aeronautics Board's economic regulatory jurisdiction extends both to those companies actually operating aircraft and to companies indirectly engaging in air transportation by holding out their services to the general public as carriers of property which they move on the aircraft of the direct air carriers. Indirect carriers, such as air express and air freight forwarders, cannot engage in air transportation under the act without first securing authorization from the Board. The Board, however, has exempted REA from having to obtain a certificate.

International Air Carriers

In international air transportation, there are now 18 certificated American-flag carriers. Some of these are predominantly domestic air carriers; and the majority are combination carriers, carrying passengers, mail, and property. Several of these carriers engage in overseas air transportation, that is, transportation between a place in continental United States and a place in one of its territories, or between a place in one territory and a place in another territory. Although these movements in international air transportation can be made rapidly in jet transports, the rates have remained so high that only a limited volume of shipments move in international service.

PIPE LINES

In pipe-line transportation, there is a relatively small number of shippers, and the facilities are operated more like plant facilities than like conventional common carriers found in other fields of transportation. The pipe line is a specialized carrier, in the sense that it transports a commodity in one direction. While it is possible to reverse the direction of flow in a line, this requires the resetting of pumping stations to conform to the new design. There are also instances where pipe lines have been changed from crude service to product service, and from product lines to crude lines, but this is not often done. For a specific operating period, then, a pipe line transports a commodity in but one direction.

The commodities moved by pipe line are moved by the direct application of power, pushing or impelling. In some of the larger crude pipe lines, the crude moves through the pipes at a speed of around $3\frac{1}{2}$ miles an hour.

Pipe-line transportation differs from other modes of transportation in a number of ways. Transportation by pipe line requires no packing or packaging. Further, there is no empty equipment which has to be deadheaded back to the origin. A relatively high power efficiency is achieved in pipe-line transportation because there is no dunnage dead weight to be moved or any vehicle or equipment which is moved. Pipe lines are the most automated of our transportation facilities. Microwave communication systems are being increasingly utilized.

There must be a continuous volume of sizable proportions for a pipe line to be constructed. Substantial risk is involved in such construction, since it requires a large financial outlay, which is one of the reasons why the ownership of these lines is in the hands of the larger oil companies. In pipe-line transportation, there must be continuous production at one end, with continuous processing at the other, if the existence of the pipe line is to be justified.

Types of Petroleum Pipe Lines

An extensive pipe-line transportation system has been developed in the United States. Although pipe-line mileage has been built primarily for the transportation of petroleum and petroleum products, there are other commodities which are being or have been moved by pipe line. A 10-inch pipe line to move pulverized coal mixed with water, which is called "coal slurry," has been constructed in Ohio; and a 6-inch pipe line has been constructed to carry gilsonite ore from which gasoline is extracted. The ore is carried in a slurry from mine to processing plant.

There are three types of pipe lines usually referred to in oil pipe-line transportation. These are (1) crude-oil gathering lines, (2) crude-oil trunk lines, and (3) product lines.[15] For statistical purposes, the Interstate Commerce Commission classifies as large pipe lines those which have a gross annual revenue over $500,000, of which there are 77. The average revenue per ton-mile since 1946 for crude and product pipe lines has been a little over 4 mills.

Crude-Oil Gathering Lines

Crude-oil pipe lines that are used to bring petroleum from the wells or tank batteries to tank farms, concentrating and storage points, and trunk pipe-line pumping stations, or to rail, motor, or water loading racks are referred to as "gathering lines." Gathering lines gather the oil from the various lease tanks which have received the production from the wells on the lease through lead lines from a pumping well or flow lines from a flowing well. The gathering lines are sometimes referred to as "feeder lines."

Gathering lines usually are of smaller pipe diameter and have less capacity than trunk lines. Gathering lines average four to five inches in diameter, although some are larger. Because they tap the oil-producing field, which output may diminish over a period of time, such gathering lines are often on the surface of the ground and may be moved from time to time. As a matter of fact, each year certain gathering lines are taken up, and new systems or extensions to the existing systems are made.

Crude-Oil Trunk Lines

Crude-oil trunk lines are pipe-line systems used for transporting crude oil from producing areas to refining centers or to water terminals. Crude oil trunk lines are of larger diameter than gathering lines. They vary in diameter from 6 to 30 inches, with the greatest concentration in the

---

[15] Petroleum Administration for Defense, *Transportation of Oil* (Washington, D.C.: U.S. Government Printing Office, 1951), p. 22.

12- to 14-inch sizes. Many of the new crude-oil trunk lines which have been constructed in the last 10 years to connect new fields or to increase the capacity of existing pipe-line systems have been 16 inches and over.

There are numerous factors which influence the size of the pipe to be used. One of these is the future, as well as the initial, required capacity. New lines are generally sized to provide an initial movement of two thirds or less of the ultimate anticipated demand. Under comparable operating conditions, a 20-inch line has a capacity 30 times that of a 6-inch and more than 5 times that of a 12-inch line.

Product Lines

Refined-oil pipe lines which carry gasoline, kerosene, and light fuel oil were developed in the 1920's. The first reported mileage of refined-oil pipe lines was in 1928, when 250 miles were reported in operation.[16] The diameter of refined-oil pipe lines tends to be smaller than the crude-oil trunk lines, although there is a products line 36 inches in diameter.

During the period 1949–58, the capacity of products lines rose by 232 per cent and crude lines by 51 per cent. Carriers deduct up to 1 per cent of the quantities received of refined products at origin points to cover losses due to shrinkage and evaporation incident to transportation and about ¼ of 1 per cent for crude products.

The development of the petroleum pipe lines is unique in our transportation system, in the sense that the ownership of the facilities used for transporting the petroleum products and the ownership of the product being transported are frequently the same. The economies of larger-diameter pipe lines have resulted in an increasing number of joint undertakings by two or more oil companies which form a new corporation to construct and operate the pipe line, or a multiple-ownership arrangement between pipe-line companies, with the company having the largest interest operating it. A substantial portion of pipe lines is owned or controlled by the major oil companies. The large companies are integrated and engage in production, transportation, refining, and marketing of their petroleum products. The few pipe lines built by interests not affiliated with oil production or refining have been product lines.

The traffic moved by gathering lines includes crude oil not only for the oil companies that own the pipe lines but also for independent producers. The proportion of traffic for independent producers which is moved in gathering lines is somewhat greater than is the case with the crude-oil trunk lines or the refined-product lines.

Commingling of Shipments

Commingling of products—or, as it is sometimes termed in the pipe-line industry, "contamination"—may or may not be permitted, according to

---

[16] Department of Commerce, Transportation Division, *Petroleum Transportation,* January–March, 1949, p. 26.

the individual pipe-line policy. Some crude trunk-line companies will effect delivery only of crude oil comparable to that it is already moving. If this is not done, it is necessary to separate the shipments, since the shipper of sweet crude does not desire to have his product mixed with sour crude. Pipe lines sometimes have as many as 70 different kinds of crude oil flowing through the system, one batch behind the other. There usually is no separating device used between grades, with the result that there is some mixture of each grade into the other at the interface, the volume of the mixture being from 50 to 2,000 barrels. The different grades are identified by gravity or other characteristic, so that the interface mixture is held to a minimum. For products, the interface is usually cut in the center or either end, depending on the two products. As an example, when one grade of aviation gasoline follows another, a center cut will not contaminate either grade; however, if premium motor gasoline is being displaced by a low grade, the cut is made on the first indication of a change in gravity.

Common Carrier Status

The Hepburn Act, an amendment to the Act to Regulate Commerce (now the Interstate Commerce Act), was enacted in 1906 to regulate interstate pipe lines which were common carriers. Some five years later, the Commission studied the status of oil pipe lines as common carriers and, after investigation, held that interstate pipe lines had the obligations of common carriers, even though they were built over their own private right of way and transported only their own oil.[17]

There have been several regulatory and court actions, extending over a number of years, concerning the common carrier status of petroleum pipe lines.[18] The most recent Supreme Court case is one in which the Court supported the Commission's order to file annual and special reports and to maintain a uniform system of accounts under Section 20 of the act; but the Court held that Congress did not intend Section 6, which requires the filing of tariffs, to apply to private lines whose services were unused, unsought, and unneeded by independent producers.[19]

There are several arrangements whereby oil is transported for the account of companies other than the one which owns the pipe line. One of these is the transporting of oil under exchange agreement with other petroleum companies in which a company will take a certain quantity of oil at one point and deliver a like quantity elsewhere, thereby avoiding duplication of pipe lines.

---

[17] *In the Matter of Pipe Lines*, 24 ICC 1 (1912).

[18] *The Pipe Line Cases*, 234 U.S. 548 (1914); *Valvoline Oil Co. v. United States*, 308 U.S. 141 (1939); *Champlin Refining Co. v. United States*, 329 U.S. 29 (1946).

[19] *United States v. Champlin Refining Co.*, 314 U.S. 290 (1951).

Minimum Tender Requirements

The crude-oil trunk lines and the refined-oil pipe lines usually establish a minimum quantity which will be tendered as a single run. This has given rise to a minimum tender requirement. During the Temporary National Economic Committee hearings in 1939 and 1940, such requirements varied from zero to 100,000 barrels. Quite a number of these minimum tender requirements exceeded 50,000 barrels. The Interstate Commerce Commission found tenders in excess of 10,000 barrels for a particular crude-oil pipe line to be unreasonable; and later, it applied this ruling to others.[20] A 25,000-barrel minimum tender was approved for refined-oil pipe lines in 1941.[21]

What constitutes a tender varies among the pipe lines. Some companies view tenders as accounting records against which the daily receipts and deliveries are charged; others view the accepted tender as a contract; and some use the tender as a method to permit the scheduling of traffic through the line.[22] The minimum tender is not to be construed as the amount that has to be delivered at one time by the shipper, inasmuch as the shipper may deliver a specified amount daily against the tender until the amount specified in the minimum tender has been delivered.

Natural-Gas Pipe Lines

Interstate natural-gas pipe lines are subject to regulation by the Federal Power Commission. The transmission of natural gas in pipe lines is the only practical means available for transporting natural gas in large quantities whereas petroleum can be carried by other means of transportation. The natural-gas pipe-line facilities are not as closely tied to the oil companies as is the case with petroleum pipe lines. Natural-gas pipe line mileage is about twice that of oil pipe lines.

REA EXPRESS   Railway Express Agency

The REA Express is an organization formed by the railroads to perform express service. This service for small shipments is more complete than less-carload freight service, in that pickup and delivery within a designated urban area are performed by the express company throughout the United States. REA will also accept for shipment articles that railroads will not accept, such as valuable papers and currency. Express service has usually been rendered in conjunction with passenger train service and, therefore, has been an expedited service as compared with ordinary rail freight. With the abandonment of many passenger trains,

---

[20] *Brundred Brothers v. Prairie Pipe Line Co.*, 68 ICC 458 (1922); *Reduced Pipe Lines Rates and Gathering Charges*, 243 ICC 115 (1940).

[21] *Petroleum Rail Shippers' Ass'n. v. Alton & Southern R. R.*, 243 ICC 589 (1941).

[22] George S. Wolbert, Jr., *American Pipe Lines* (Norman, Okla.: University of Oklahoma Press, 1952), p. 25.

some use has been made of freight trains, and, in addition, they are operating highway vehicles over-the-road. About 90 per cent of all shipments are still moved by rail. Service is also provided to many foreign countries. Air or surface transportation is used on such shipments outside the United States.

REA Express offers both LCL and CL service. The latter is used particularly in the movement of certain perishables, although a wide range of commodities is carried. Fast service, coupled with the convenience of pickup and delivery of small shipments, has led to extensive use of express service. The average revenue per ton-mile of REA averages about twice that of regulated motor common carriers, or 12 cents per ton-mile.

COMBINATION SERVICE

Trailer on Flatcar or "Piggy Back"

There have been numerous efforts over the years to facilitate the movement of goods through elimination, where possible, of the transfer of lading. This has led to the development of the trailer-on-flatcar idea, whereby a loaded trailer is moved to a rail terminal, where it is placed on a flatcar. Upon its arrival at destination, it is moved from the rail terminal to the unloading point. This practice started in the 1920's, when LCL freight was loaded into the railroads' own trailers, placed on flatcars, and transported between two cities. At the destination city, the trailer would be moved to a point to be unloaded.

During the early 1950's, the railroads instituted an increasing amount of piggy back service, and several variations developed which became identified by number. Currently, these are:

Plan I. Railroad movement of trailers or containers of common motor carriers, with the shipment moving on one bill of lading and billing being done by the trucker. Traffic moves under rates in regular motor carrier tariffs. Currently, there are 43 railroads offering this plan.

Plan II. Railroad performs its own door-to-door service, moving its own trailers or containers on flat cars under tariffs usually similar to those of truckers. 63 railroads are offering this plan at the present time.

Plan III. Ramp-to-ramp rates based on a flat charge, regardless of the contents of trailers or containers, usually owned or leased by freight forwarders or shippers. No pickup or delivery is performed by the railroad. 55 railroads are now participating in this plan.

Plan IV. Shipper or forwarder furnishes a trailer or container-loaded flat car, either owned or leased. The railroad makes a flat charge for loaded or empty-car movement, furnishing only power and rails. 38 railroads are offering this plan at the present time.

Plan V. Traffic moves generally under joint railroad-truck or other combination of co-ordinated service rates. Either mode may solicit traffic for through movement. Currently, there are 33 railroads offering this plan.

The Commission, in 1962, instituted a comprehensive investigation of piggy back in *Ex Parte* 230. In August, 1963, the examiners' report proposed 23 rules to govern and promote co-ordinated TOFC operations.

Greater use is being made of containers in trailer-on-flatcar service which is known as "COFC" service. These are closed, cargo-type body equipment without running gear into which a number of packages or a quantity of freight can be stowed. They may be physically transferred among rail, motor, water, and air carriers and could become a common denominator in the movement of goods.

There has been considerable interest in trailer-on-flatcar service, and it has continued to grow. The number of railroad and privately owned flatcars equipped to carry trailers or containers was approximately 15,000 at the beginning of 1963, or 3 per cent of total railway equipment. TOFC car loadings were 2.5 per cent of total car loadings in 1963. The most common type of TOFC service is in trailer loads, although some railroads accept less-trailer loads.

Trailership or "Fishy Back"

A similar type of service—in which trailers are rolled on ships and carried to destination, where they are rolled off—has been instituted. This is sometimes referred to as "trailership" or "fishy back" service. In recent years, coastwise service has been established, in which a demountable container is moved by truck trailer to shipside and the 40-foot van is lifted off its chassis and put on the deck of the ship. The special trailer bodies carry both truckload and less-truckload shipments. On truckload shipments, they are sealed at the shipper's loading platform and remain locked until delivery to the consignee. This service is from interior points to seaboard, thence by water to the seaboard point, and final delivery to destination, which may be an interior point. A trailership with self-contained loading cranes is also in use.

The Interstate Commerce Commission has authorized a coastwise carrier to engage in regulated transportation of commodities in truck trailers or containers on decks of vessels used in the nonregulated transportation of bulk petroleum without subjecting the petroleum to regulation between Atlantic and Gulf ports.

One of the reasons for the interest and development of the roll-on, roll-off type of ship is the fact that, excluding bulk cargo and ammunition, one fourth of the military support cargo is wheeled or tracked and can be more quickly loaded or unloaded in a ship designed for this type of operation.

The use of trailers or containers provides increased flexibility and greatly accentuates physical co-ordination. In addition, studies indicate that the use of such equipment can cut stevedoring costs to about one tenth, total cargo handling costs to about one third, and port time to about one fifth of that required in the loading of conventional ships.

Trainship

The first trainship operation was established in 1892 on Lake Michigan, when the first train ferry began operations. The use of boxcars placed on ships has been utilized in several operations, the most extensive of which is a company which operates between New York, Savannah, Georgia, New Orleans, and Texas City, Texas, with ocean-going vessels more than 400 feet long. They are designed to transport, by water, freight brought to or moved from ports by railroads without transferring the freight from the rail cars. The vessels used in this service have four decks, and each deck has four sets of railroad tracks on which can be placed some 100 loaded freight cars. In addition, there is tank space for approximately 4,000 tons of liquid cargo and containers are also carried. Operations are between fixed termini on regular schedules. Special loading facilities exist at each of the ports for the handling of the loaded boxcars. These facilities consist of a combination elevator and crane. The elevator shaft is erected on the dock, and the stationary arms of the crane extend from the frame of the elevator shaft over the hold of the vessel. The floor of the elevator is a movable platform on which is a single track.

The establishment of through routes with railroads to ports to or from which trainships operate results in extensive service between certain territories. Routings may be rail-ship or rail-ship-rail. Since the port points served generate considerable traffic, shippers located at these ports may, for service or for rate reasons, use trainship. The difference in the freight charge for shipments routed via trainship depends upon the length of the rail haul at origin or destination, or both. Beyond a certain distance from ports, there is no rate advantage to shipping via trainship.

Motor-Air Service

Most of the domestic airlines and the largest intercity bus carrier inaugurated, in early 1957, a joint air-bus package express service to about 6,000 communities not served directly by air freight service. Shippers can use bus service to ship items to the nearest airport city, from which packages are flown to any part of the country and then delivered by the bus carrier or an air carrier.

The service includes prepaid, collect, or C.O.D. shipments. Package size is limited to a maximum of 24 × 24 × 45 inches, with a limit of 100 pounds per package.

Truck-air freight service has also been established to provide a co-ordinated service to a large number of communities. The combination of air and truck service available at many points gives a greater flexibility to the shipper in moving his traffic, particularly shipments requiring rapid transit. In one truck-air agreement, a single bill of lading is used.

FREIGHT FORWARDERS

Freight forwarders are divided into two types: (1) surface freight forwarders which utilize surface common carriers for line-haul movements and (2) air freight forwarders which utilize certificated air carriers.

Surface Freight Forwarders

A freight forwarder is defined in the Interstate Commerce Act as any person other than a carrier subject to Parts I, II, or III of the Interstate Commerce Act which holds itself out to the general public as a common carrier to transport or provide transportation of property for compensation in interstate commerce and which (1) assembles and consolidates, or provides for assembling and consolidating, shipments of such property and performs, or provides for the performance of, break-bulk and distributing operations with respect to such consolidated shipments; (2) assumes responsibility for the transportation of such property from point of receipt to point of destination; and (3) utilizes in whole or in part the transportation services of carriers subject to Parts I, II, or III of the Interstate Commerce Act. The operating authority of such freight forwarders is a permit issued by the Interstate Commerce Commission, which also classifies them for statistical purposes as Class A freight forwarders if they gross $100,000 or more per year and Class B if they gross less than $100,000.

Although subjected to regulation since 1942, the role of the surface freight forwarders was often viewed as that of a shipper in their relation to the carriers they used. In 1950, Congress amended the Interstate Commerce Act and clarified this point by establishing freight forwarders as common carriers.[23] Surface freight forwarders are unique in that they have the obligations and rights of common carriers, yet own and operate no rights of way or line-haul equipment. They rely on rail, motor, and water carriers for the line-haul movement of freight.

Freight forwarders developed in the surface transportation field largely because of their ability to consolidate numerous less-carload shipments into a carload and thereby effect satisfactory service to shippers. Acting as a middleman, a freight forwarder operates on the spread between less-carload and carload rates. This spread varies with the different commodities. If, for example, there is a spread of 25 per cent between the less-carload rate and the carload rate, a freight forwarder can pick up the small shipments, consolidate them into carload lots, and consign them to various distributing or break-bulk points, at which points the forwarder unloads and delivers the individual shipments to the original consignees. The longer the carload or truckload haul between its stations, the shorter the haul beyond, and the greater the volume moving over its platforms, the better service it can render.

---

[23] Public Law 881, 81st Congress, 2d session, December 2, 1950.

The LCL shipper who uses freight forwarder service finds that the consolidation of his freight into carload freight results in faster service than the ordinary LCL freight receives. The reason for the reduced transit time is that the shipment moves over more direct routes and by-passes transfers, as well as avoiding terminal delays. Another aspect of freight forwarder operation is that since the freight forwarder does not physically transport the commodities between terminals, this operation may effect a co-ordination of service by using rail, motor, and water carriers.

In 1959, the Commission ruled that freight forwarders are not restricted to the handling only of small shipments and permitted freight forwarders to establish rates on volume shipments subject to minimum weights of from 10,000 to 30,000 pounds. Accordingly, freight forwarders are making trailerload shipments under Plan III, piggy-back. Essentially, this service is competitive with motor carrier service.

The average haul for 1962 per ton of freight forwarder traffic by Class I railroads was 1,129 miles. Surface freight forwarders spend approximately 67 per cent of total transportation purchased for rail transportation; 16 per cent for motor transportation; and 16 per cent for pickup, delivery, and transfer service. Average weight per shipment is about 308 pounds.

Although some freight forwarders have the authority to serve all points and places in the United States, others have a more limited territorial scope of operations. The greatest relative service advantage in freight forwarder operations exists when shipments move between on-line points, and this is the service area in which freight forwarders have concentrated their efforts. However, they render service to off-line points, usually by means of using services of motor carriers from the on-line or break-bulk points to the off-line point, which may be 50 or 150 miles' distance.

There are exempt freight forwarders which can operate on a for-hire basis if they (1) perform service on behalf of a co-operative association as defined in the Agricultural Marketing Act; or (2) where shipments are made of ordinary livestock, fish (including shellfish), agricultural commodities (not including manufactured products thereof), or used household goods. Another general exemption is that of shippers' nonprofit associations, which will be described later.

Air Freight Forwarders

Until 1948, the Railway Express Agency (now REA Express), through its Air Express Division, was the only company authorized to engage in air transportation as an indirect air carrier. After extensive investigation of indirect air services in the transportation of property in 1948, the Civil Aeronautics Board relieved those indirect air carriers which sought to operate as air freight forwarders from the requirement of securing certificates of public convenience and necessity. The Board permitted air freight forwarders to operate in domestic air transportation on a temporary five-year basis.[24]

In 1949, air freight forwarders were permitted to engage in overseas and foreign air transportation along the same lines as domestic air freight forwarders.[25] Thus, in air freight forwarding, firms specialize in domestic air freight forwarding, while others specialize in international air freight forwarding. In 1963, there were 75 air freight forwarders operating in domestic and foreign commerce.

PARCEL POST

Surface Parcel Post

Parcel post is a service available in the movement of small packaged articles which do not exceed certain prescribed weights and sizes. Packages shipped via parcel post receive about the same type of service as those shipped via REA Express.

Mail service is divided into domestic and foreign. It consists of mail matter deposited in the mails for delivery from one place to another and is divided into four classes. First-class mail consists of written matter sealed against inspection, postal cards, and private mailing cards. Second-class mail consists of newspapers and periodicals. Third-class mail is merchandise, printed matter, and other mailable matter, not exceeding 8 ounces in weight and not classified as first- or second-class mail matter. Fourth-class mail (parcel post) consists of merchandise, printed matter, and other mailable matter exceeding 8 ounces in weight and not included in the first and second classes.

From 1931 until January 1, 1952, the size and weight limits of parcel post, prescribed by the Postmaster General, were a maximum of 70 pounds in weight and a maximum of 100 inches in length and girth combined. By Public Law 199, Eighty-Second Congress, the weight limit on parcels mailed at first-class post offices for delivery to other first-class post offices was reduced to 40 pounds for local, first, and second zones; and it was reduced to 20 pounds for deliveries to points in the third through eighth zones. The size of parcels was limited to 72 inches in length and girth combined. Parcels mailed at or addressed for delivery to any second-, third-, or fourth-class post office remained subject to the former limits of 70 pounds and 100 inches in length and girth combined. Certain other exceptions to the smaller weight and size limits, such as agriculture products, were set forth in Public Law 199.

Complete information on parcel post regulations is contained in the *United States Official Postal Guide*, and it should be consulted to keep

---

[24] *Air Freight Forwarder Case*, 9 CAB 473 (1948).
[25] *Air Freight Forwarder Case (International)*, 11 CAB 182 (1949).

abreast of changes. There is no limit on the amount of parcel post that can be shipped to any one consignee on the same day. Generally speaking, on lightweight package shipments, parcel post charges are lower than those applicable via other services.

Air Parcel Post

The current domestic air parcel post service was inaugurated in 1948. This service is available on all packages exceeding 8 ounces in weight but not weighing more than 70 pounds. Packages over 100 inches in length and girth combined will not be accepted. This service is for fourth-class matter subject to special air parcel post rates established for eight postal zones.

Parcels on which postage is prepaid at the prescribed rates are entitled to the most expeditious handling, transportation (by surface or air), and delivery practicable, but not special delivery. For maximum speed, the special delivery service should be utilized for all matter sent by air. This is especially important if the mail is to reach the office of address on a week end or holiday.

A company which provides home delivery of retail store packages in 15 major metropolitan areas provides fast air parcel delivery of commercial shipments for manufacturers and wholesalers between certain points. This company also provides transcontinental delivery service of parcel-post-type packages which average less than 10 pounds by utilizing its ground delivery service with air service.

Both surface and air parcel post service are available to various foreign countries, and the *United States Official Postal Guide* should be consulted if use of these services is contemplated.

BROKERS

The operation of a broker is not one in which the broker physically performs a transportation service. The Interstate Commerce Act defines a broker as any person not included in the term "motor carrier" and not a bona fide employee or agent of such carrier which, as principal or agent, sells or offers for sale any transportation subject to Part II of the act, or negotiates for or holds itself out by solicitation, advertisement, or otherwise as one which sells, provides, furnishes, contracts, or arranges for such transportation. The Interstate Commerce Commission grants brokers a license.

In water transportation, there are ship brokers who perform the service of arranging for such transportation by bringing together the shipowner and the person who desires to use the ship.

A transportation broker neither assumes responsibility for the safe delivery of goods nor performs the transportation.

COMPANY-OWNED OR COMPANY-LEASED EQUIPMENT

Private interplant transportation, or transportation from and to the points where needed by a company, is one of the alternatives available to the traffic manager. In consideration of this type of transportation, the traffic manager will need to know many factors. All of the costs should be assembled. Comparative figures should be obtained on the cost of purchasing equipment or of leasing it from transportation lessor companies or from individual owner-operators who may lease on a trip lease (one-way) or long-term lease. Leasing or chartering of transportation equipment has become more common in recent years, and the arrangements for such leases are generally handled by the traffic department or section.

Company operation of equipment is found in motor, water, and air transportation and is treated in more detail in subsequent chapters. The use of leased or owned rail equipment is found in rail transportation, although the physical movement of this equipment is by the rail carriers.

In intraplant operation, the question of owned or leased transportation equipment arises, since there are many organizations with extensive intraplant operations. The necessary equipment may include rail, motor, and water. Special design considerations in securing the exact equipment needed are quite common, and there is co-operation with other departments on this matter.

Industrial railroads are usually plant facilities only. In some instances, they may be sufficiently extensive that service is extended to the public in addition to what the company hauls for its own needs. In cases of this kind, the Interstate Commerce Commission has usually held such an operation to be common carriage and subject to its regulation. Whereas railroads which are industrial plant facilities may receive a switching allowance, the common carrier type of intraplant operation would receive a division of the joint rates with other rail carriers. On several occasions, the Commission has investigated industrial railroads and tap lines, the latter term applying to industrial railroads which serve sawmills of lumber and timber companies.

Motor and water equipment can be especially designed for intraplant work, and extensive use can be made of the conventional equipment. The traffic manager must purchase and/or lease the right type of equipment to perform properly the assigned job.

SERVICE ASPECTS AND SHIPMENT REQUIREMENTS

In the systems approach to traffic or physical distribution management, total cost is related to customer satisfaction in the choice of transportation media. In examining the services available in the different modes of transportation and the carriers within each mode, a traffic department or section must consider these factors in selecting a carrier. A number of other considerations are: time the goods are in transit, perishability of goods, need for special handling, one-carrier versus multiple-carrier service, dependability, adequacy of schedules, and packaging. The choice of carrier will be influenced by the needs of the particular shipment.

In addition to the basic transportation service between terminal points, many accessorial or additional services have been established to facilitate movement. These include such services as protection from freezing or from heat, diversion to a different destination en route, exclusive use of the vehicle or car, inside delivery, and many others. Some transportation services include pick up and delivery as a part of the service whereas others provide merely terminal-to-terminal service.

CASE

The wide variety of transportation services enhances the position of shippers and consignees in their procurement of transportation service. The obligations of carriers vary among the different types, and service and rate differences also exist. A shipper may choose from among rail, motor, water, and air carriers, from specialized or general commodity carriers, and from common, contract, exempt, and forwarder operations.

Federal regulatory statutes define contract carriage in motor and water transportation, and although not defined in the Federal Aviation Act, there are contract carriers rendering service in this field. The most extensive use, however, is made of motor contract carriage. About 2,500 of these carriers are operating interstate at the present time and are widely scattered throughout the United States. These carriers are regulated by the Interstate Commerce Commission.

Over the years, motor contract carriers have had average ton-mile revenues of about ¾ of a cent less than motor common carriers, which indicates that, in general, their rates are lower. Contrary to what might be expected, though, these carriers have not shown the rate of growth that has occurred in motor common and private carriage. In 1939, they accounted for 24 per cent of the intercity ton-miles transported by regulated motor carriers but this declined to 6.8 per cent by 1961. During this same period, total ton-miles transported by regulated for-hire motor carriers increased more than 400 per cent, so while ton-miles transported by contract carriers have shown a slight absolute increase they have had a decided relative decrease.

Motor contract carriers enter into long-term contracts and may discriminate among shippers. Contractual terms are those agreed upon by the shipper and the carrier. Therefore, a company may contract to have its products transported by a contract carrier and know quite exactly what its transportation costs will be. Many contract carriers can furnish specialized equipment to meet a company's specific needs. Since most contract carriers pick and choose among shippers, they usually serve only a limited number. The shipper can make them virtually a part of his organization since he prescribes in the contract the tonnage to be moved and the schedules which must be met.

1. In view of the foregoing, how do you account for the limited growth rate of motor contract carriers?

DISCUSSION QUESTIONS AND PROBLEMS

1. How does the transportation service available present the traffic manager with both a challenge and a responsibility?

2. What types of rail service are available? What is pool-car service? How does rail equipment influence service?

3. Briefly describe the many different types of motor carriers. Is the flexibility they possess advantageous to the traffic manager? To the public?

4. Outline the difference between the services available in domestic water transportation as compared to foreign.

5. Enumerate the different types of ships' charters and some typical provisions found in such agreements. As a traffic manager, what would be your procedure in chartering a vessel?

6. What are the different types of air service available? How do the maximum size and weight of shipments of air carriers compare with motor carriers? Rail carriers? Water carriers?

7. Do the different kinds of pipe lines give rise to different types of transportation service? If commingling of shipments is not permitted in pipe-line transportation, is this a disadvantage to the shipper?

8. In your opinion, what are the advantages and disadvantages in the greater development of combination service, such as trailer-on-flatcar service, to the carrier? Shipper? Public?

9. Is there any indication of a growing use of company-owned or company-leased equipment by traffic managers in your geographical area? What situations might prompt such a tendency?

10. Prepare an outline for each of the modes of transportation, comparing the different classifications.

11. How does our transportation potential for defense purposes compare at the present time with that of 1945? Consult some of the trade journal articles in 1945 for information about that period.

Chapter

5

DOCUMENTATION

THE shipping document which is of paramount importance to the traffic manager is the bill of lading. He must be familiar with its various forms and the functions which it performs. A number of other shipping documents which the traffic manager should know are also explained.

COMMERCIAL BILLS OF LADING

The forms of the so-called "commercial" bill of lading will be described first. An explanation of the United States government bill of lading will follow.

Rail and Motor

Railroads originally had bills of lading that differed considerably between the carriers, and there was question as to the authority of the Interstate Commerce Commission to prescribe the form of the bill of lading for railroads. The Transportation Act of 1920 authorized the Commission to prescribe the rail bill of lading, which it did in 1922. This prescribed uniform bill of lading for railroads has remained basically the same since that time.

In the case of motor carriers, the Interstate Commerce Commission has not prescribed a uniform bill of lading. The Motor Carrier Act of 1935 (Section 219) required motor common carriers to issue a receipt or bill of lading for any property received for transportation. Later, in 1946, the Commission ordered that certain information be contained on the motor common carrier's bill of lading or receipt, such as the names of consignor and consignee, the points of origin and destination, and other information similar to that found in the railroad bill of lading. However, since the Commission has not prescribed a uniform bill of lading, the result has been a diversity of motor carriers' bills of lading. Some motor carriers follow the rail bill of lading, others use the bill of lading form contained in the National Motor Freight Classifications, and there are other forms as well.

Until 1906, the liability of the common carrier was determined by common law and the statutes of the different states. It had been customary for a railroad, prior to this time, to incorporate in its bill of lading a provision that it would not be liable for any loss or damage which had not occurred on its own line. The shipper, under such circumstances, was greatly inconvenienced in trying to determine on which of the several lines on a through-route movement the loss or damage had actually occurred.

The Carmack Amendment to the Act to Regulate Commerce changed this by requiring that a common carrier which received property for transportation from a point in one state to a point in another state be required to issue a receipt or bill of lading covering the shipment and be liable to the bill of lading holder for any loss, damage, or injury caused by the carrier or any common carrier to which the freight might be delivered and over whose line the freight might pass.[1] The effect of this amendment was to make the initial carrier liable for loss, damage, or injury to goods. It further provided that no contract, receipt, rule, or regulation should exempt a common carrier from the liability imposed by the amendment. It did not prohibit, however, limitations as to the amount of liability. Subsequent amendments were made in 1915 and 1916; and in 1916, the Federal Bills of Lading Act was passed. The latter act provided that a bill of lading which states that the goods are consigned to a specified person is a *straight bill of lading*, which is a nonnegotiable bill of lading. It cannot be bought, sold, or traded; and it is one in which it is stated that goods are consigned or destined to a specific consignee, which may be the consignee or another party. Where goods are consigned or destined to the order of a person, the bill of lading is an *order bill of lading*, which is negotiable— that is, it can be bought and sold, or conveyed by endorsement.

The negotiable aspects of the order bills of lading were enlarged by the Federal Bills of Lading Act. This act sought to limit carriers in their attempts to shift responsibility to the shipper by proving the kind and quality of goods covered by a bill of lading. Where goods are loaded by the shipper, the act provided that the carrier could insert the phrase: "Shipper's weight, load, and count" or a similar phrase; and the carrier was not responsible for damage caused by improper loading, nonreceipt, or misdescription of the goods on the bill of lading. If the goods were loaded by the carrier, its agent was to count the packages of freight or, if bulk freight, to determine the kind and quantity of goods which were shipped. The carrier was then liable for the number of packages contained on the bill of lading or for the kind and quantity of bulk freight described on the bill of lading.

---

[1] Carmack Amendment, June 29, 1906.

The bill of lading used by rail and motor regulated common carriers serves the following purposes:

1. It serves as a receipt for goods subject to the classifications and tariffs which were in effect on the date that the bill of lading was issued. It certifies that the property described on the bill of lading was in apparent good order except as noted; and that the property was marked, consigned, and destined as shown on the bill of lading. The bill of lading should be signed by both the shipper and an agent for the carrier, but a carrier cannot avoid its liability because it does not issue a receipt or a bill of lading.

2. It serves as a contract of carriage. A bill of lading, in serving as a contract of carriage, identifies the contracting parties and prescribes the terms and conditions of the agreement. This aspect of the bill of lading is often referred to as the "heart" of the bill of lading because the terms and conditions of the contract are set forth on the reverse side of the bill of lading. There, the limitations of the carrier's common-law liability are stipulated, as well as obligations of the carrier. The terms and conditions of the contract of carriage provide that the carrier is not liable for loss, damage, or delay due to acts of God, the public enemy, the authority of law, acts of defaults of the shipper or owner, or natural shrinkage. Another provision is that the carrier's liability is that of a warehouseman, which is deemed to be less than that of carrier liability, in cases where loss, damage, or delay has occurred after the expiration of free time and appropriate notice has been given to the shipper. There are numerous other important terms and conditions on the reverse side of the bill of lading which affect the contract of carriage. A thorough analysis of all of these provisions should be made.[2] (See Figure 5-1, pp. 96–97.)

3. It serves as documentary evidence of title. It is necessary, however, to qualify this statement. Although this is true of a negotiable bill of lading, in the case of the straight bill of lading, the person who has possession of this type of bill of lading *may* have title to the goods. That, however, depends upon the facts in the individual case. Such matters as the terms of sale have influence in establishing title to the goods covered by the straight bill of lading.

The railroad bills of lading are:

Uniform straight bill of lading (regular form).
Uniform straight bill of lading (alternative form).
Uniform order bill of lading (regular form).
Uniform order bill of lading (alternative form).
Straight bill of lading (short form).
Uniform through export bill of lading (straight form).
Uniform through export bill of lading (order form).
Uniform livestock contract.

The alternative form of the uniform straight bill of lading and the alternative form of the uniform order bill of lading are combination bill-of-lading and waybill forms which are authorized for optional alternative use with the respective regular form of bill of lading. The straight bill of

[2] A detailed analysis of bill-of-lading terms and conditions can be found in John M. Miller's *Law of Freight Loss and Damage Claim* (2nd ed.; Dubuque, Iowa: Wm. C. Brown & Co., 1961), pp. 31–51.

CARRIAGE

LIABILITY

LOSS OR DAMAGE. The carrier shall be liable as at common law for loss or damage to property accepted for transportation, until the expiration of the "free time" specified in tariff.

AS WAREHOUSEMAN. The carrier shall be liable only as warehouseman for loss, damage or delay caused by fire occurring after (a) expiration of "free time", (b) notice of arrival at destination has been daily sent or given, (c) placement of the property for delivery at destination, (d) tender of delivery of the property to party entitled to receive it.

COTTON COMPRESSION. The carrier has the privilege of compressing, at carrier's expense and risk, cotton or cotton linters, for greater convenience in handling; but the carrier shall not be liable for deviation or unavoidable delays resulting from the procuring of such compression.

GRAIN IN BULK. Grain in bulk consigned to a point where there is a railroad, public or licensed elevator, when delivered there, may (unless otherwise specifically provided in this bill of lading, and then if not promptly unloaded) be placed with other grain of same kind and grade; prompt notice thereof being given to the shipper. If so delivered, the shipment shall be subject to lien for elevator charges and all other charges hereunder.

CARRIAGE

ROUTE. The carrier may transport the property by any route and by any other carrier, in case of physical necessity.

REASONABLE DISPATCH. The carrier is not bound to transport the property (a) by any particular train, (b) in time for any particular market, (c) otherwise than with reasonable dispatch.

SHIPPERS' RISK. Property left to be shipped from a station where there is no regularly appointed railroad freight agent, shall be so left entirely at owner's risk until loaded into car; or except in case of negligence of carrier, if left in freight car, then it shall be so left at owner's risk until freight car is attached to locomotive or train.

CONSIGNEES' RISK. Property left by the carrier to be received at a station where there is no regularly appointed freight agent, shall be so left entirely at risk of owner after being unloaded from car; or except in case of the negligence of carrier, if left in freight car, then after the freight car has been detached from locomotive or train.

NON-LIABILITY

LOSS OR DAMAGE. The carrier shall not be liable for loss, damage or delay caused by (a) act of God, (b) authority of law, (c) public enemy, (d) act or default of shipper or owner, (e) natural shrinkage, (f) quarantine, nor, except in case of carrier's negligence, from loss, damage or delay resulting from (a) riots, (b) strikes, (c) country damage to cotton, (d) defect or vice in the property.

QUARANTINE. In case of quarantine, the carrier (a) may discharge the property 1—as required by regulations, at risk and expense of owner, 2—for carrier's dispatch at nearest available point, (b) may return property to shipping point (earning freight charges both ways) at owner's expense, (c) may fumigate or disinfect the property at owner's risk and expense, (d) shall be held harmless by the shipper, from any expenses or damages resulting from entry of the property into quarantine area.

EXTRAORDINARY VALUE. The carrier will not carry nor be liable in any way for documents, specie or any articles of extraordinary value not specifically rated in tariff, unless special agreement to do so and stipulated value of the articles are indorsed on this bill of lading.

EXPLOSIVES. If explosives or other dangerous property should be shipped without previous full written disclosure to the carrier, of the nature of shipment, the shipper, whether principal or agent, shall be liable for and shall indemnify the carrier against all loss or damage caused by such property, which may be warehoused at owner's expense or destroyed without compensation.

COOPERAGE. Except where due to the negligence of the carrier, necessary cooperage and baling of the property shall be at the expense of the owner.

SUITS. Suits can be instituted only within two years and one day from day when written notice is given by carrier to claimant that carrier has disallowed the claim or any part thereof. Where suit is not instituted within the stated time, the carrier shall not be liable.

INSURANCE. The carrier, when liable for loss or damage, shall have benefit of any insurance effected on the policy and provided the carrier shall not avoid the policy and provided the carrier shall reimburse claimant for premium paid thereon.

VALUATION. In all cases not prohibited by law, where a value, lower than actual value of the property (a) has been represented in writing by the shipper, or (b) has been agreed upon in writing as the released value as determined by classification or tariff, such lower value plus freight charges if paid, shall be the maximum amount recoverable for loss or damage, whether or not occurring from negligence.

CLAIMS. Claims must be in writing and may be filed with (a) receiving carrier, (b) delivering carrier, (c) carrier issuing this bill of lading, (d) carrier on whose line the loss, damage, injury or delay had occurred.

DELAY IN ACCEPTANCE. When property at destination is not removed by party entitled to receive it, within the "free time," the carrier may (a) hold the property subject to tariff charges for warehousing or storing, (b) remove the property at the owner's cost, to public or licensed warehouse at place of delivery or other available place, where it will be held without the carrier's liability, subject to lien for freight and other lawful charges, including reasonable cost of storage.

DELIVERY BY CARRIER. The carrier shall deliver the property to the owner upon payment of freight and other lawful charges made in connection with the shipment, except if otherwise lawfully authorized to relinquish possession of property.

PAYMENT OF CHARGES. The carrier has the right to require prepayment of the charges or guarantee of payment. (For details as to liability for payment, see Section 7.)

WRONG CLASSIFICATION. If upon inspection it is ascertained that the articles shipped are not as described in this bill of lading, the freight charges must be paid on the articles actually shipped.

PROPERTY NOT ACCEPTED. When shipment of non-perishable property is not received or is refused by consignee within 15 days after notice of arrival has been sent or given, the carrier may (A) sell the property at public auction to highest bidder, at place designated by carrier after (1) mailing or giving to the shipper a notice that shipment has been refused or is unclaimed and will be subject to sale if disposition be not arranged, (2) publishing after 30 days from date of above notice to shipper, a notice once a week for two consecutive weeks in a newspaper having general circulation at place of sale or nearest place where such newspaper is published; the notice to contain (a) description of the shipment, (b) name of consignee or party to be notified if sent "order notify," (c) time and place of the sale; (B) sell the property under such circumstances and in such manner authorized by law, if unable to sell as above.

When shipment of perishable property is refused or not received promptly by consignee, in order to prevent deterioration or further deterioration, the carrier may dispose of the property to best advantage by public or private sale, after giving notice to consignor or owner, if time permits, that shipment has not been accepted, and requesting disposition thereof.

SALE BY CARRIER. When shipment has been sold by the carrier as provided herein, proceeds shall be applied in payment of the following (1) freight charges, (2) demurrage, (3) storage charges, (4) lawful expenses in connection with the sale, (5) cost of any necessary care or maintenance of property. Any balance remaining shall be paid to the owner of the property sold.

FIG. 5–1. Analysis of railroad bill-of-lading terms.

SOURCE: *Distribution Age*, December, 1945

(Uniform Domestic Straight Bill of Lading, adopted by Carriers in Official, Southern, Western and Illinois Classification territories, March 15, 1922, as amended August 1, 1930, and June 15, 1941.)

UNIFORM STRAIGHT BILL OF LADING 1st SHEET

(Prescribed by the Interstate Commerce Commission)

ORIGINAL --- NOT NEGOTIABLE

Shipper's No._____

Agent's No._____

WESTERN MARYLAND RAILWAY COMPANY

RECEIVED, subject to the classifications and tariffs in effect on the date of the issue of this Bill of Lading,

at_____, 195___

from_____

the property described below, in apparent good order, except as noted (contents and condition of contents of packages unknown), marked, consigned, and destined as indicated below, which said company (the word company being understood throughout this contract as meaning any person or corporation in possession of the property under the contract) agrees to carry to its usual place of delivery at said destination, if on its own road or its own water line, otherwise to deliver to another carrier on the route to said destination. It is mutually agreed, as to each carrier of all or any of said property over all or any portion of said route to destination, and as to each party at any time interested in all or any of said property, that every service to be performed hereunder shall be subject to all the conditions not prohibited by law, whether printed or written, herein contained, including the conditions on back hereof, which are hereby agreed to by the shipper and accepted for himself and his assigns.

(Mail or street address of consignee—For purposes of notification only)

Consigned to_____

Destination_____ State of_____ County of_____

Route_____

Delivering Carrier_____ Car Initial_____ Car No._____

No. Packages	DESCRIPTION OF ARTICLES, SPECIAL MARKS AND EXCEPTIONS	*WEIGHT (Subject to Correction)	CLASS OR RATE	CHECK COLUMN	
					Subject to Section 7 of conditions, if this shipment is to be delivered to the consignee without recourse on the consignor, the consignor shall sign the following statement:
					The carrier shall not make delivery of this shipment without payment of freight and all other lawful charges.
					(Signature of Consignor)
					If charges are to be prepaid, write or stamp here, "To be Prepaid."
				*	Received $_____ to apply in prepayment of the charges on the property described hereon.
					Agent or Cashier
					Per _____ (The signature here acknowledges only the amount prepaid.)

*If the shipment moves between two ports by a carrier by water, the law requires that the bill of lading shall state whether it is "carrier's or shipper's weight."

NOTE—Where the rate is dependent on value, shippers are required to state specifically in writing the agreed or declared value of the property.

The agreed or declared value of the property is hereby specifically stated by the shipper to be not exceeding

_____per_____

Charges Advanced:

$_____

_____Shipper.   _____Agent

Per_____   Per_____

Permanent post-office address of Shipper_____

1

FIG. 5–2.   Rail uniform straight bill of lading, long form.

lading (short form) is a modification of the uniform straight bill of lading (regular form). It does not include the contract terms and conditions on the reverse side; in their stead, reference is made to the contract terms and conditions set forth in the classification governing the transportation of the shipment.

Section 41 of the Bill of Lading Act provides that any person who, knowingly or with intent to defraud, falsely makes, alters, forges, counter-

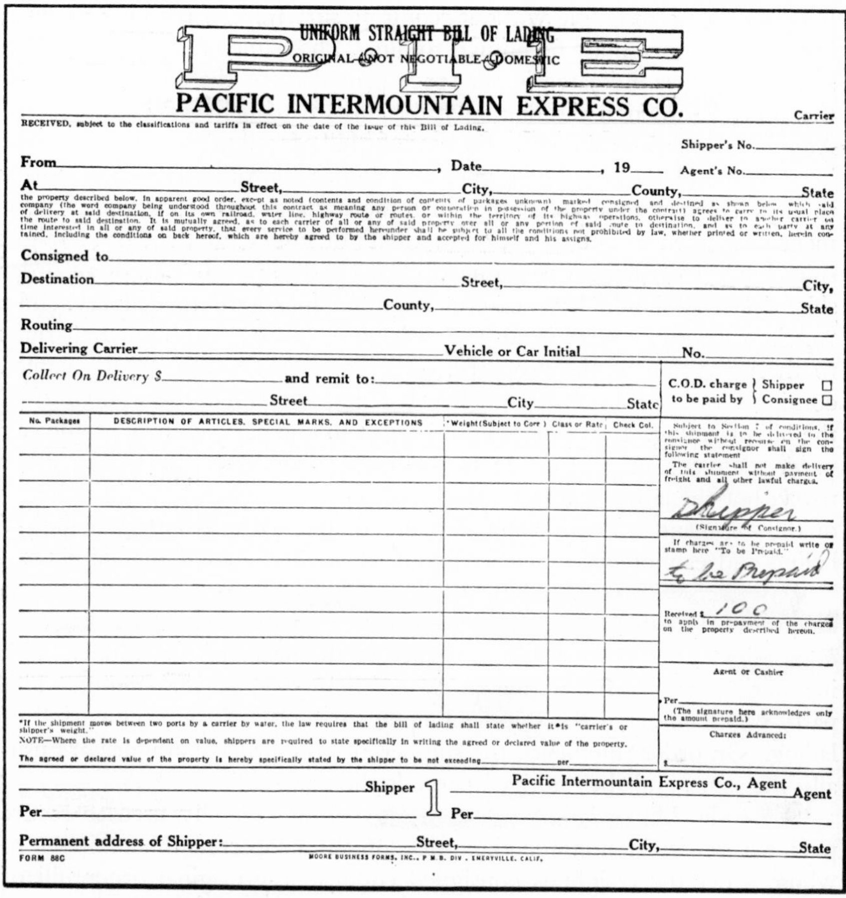

FIG. 5–3.   Motor straight bill of lading.

feits, prints, or photographs any bill of lading shall be guilty of a misdemeanor. Upon conviction, such person shall be subject to a fine of not exceeding $5,000 or five years' imprisonment, or both. A person who aids in any of the foregoing acts, or knowingly permits such a false bill of lading to be processed, is equally guilty and subject to the same penalties. Section 10 of the Interstate Commerce Act provides severe penalties for false billing by carriers or false representation by shippers.

A *straight bill of lading* is not negotiable. It states that goods are consigned or destined to a specific consignee, which may be the shipper or another party. Straight bills of lading may also be issued which designate a party other than the consignee to be advised or notified of the arrival of the freight, or in whose care the shipment may be delivered. The rail uniform straight bill of lading is shown in Figure 5–2, and one for motor is shown in Figure 5–3.

The carrier's agent at destination may make delivery of freight covered by straight bills of lading without requiring surrender of the bill of lading, but the consignee must be known to him. The name of the party shown as the consignee indicated in the space provided for the consignee and at the address shown is the one lawfully entitled to delivery of the goods. Any other notations shown in the straight bill of lading are merely for the information of the billed consignee and do not constitute lawful authority to make delivery to anyone other than the actual billed consignee. A shipment consigned to one party, or to advise or notify another, is a straight shipment for the named consignee; but it has also possibilities of an order shipment and should have careful attention in regard to delivery. The "advise-or-notify" party is not the consignee, and so has no inherent right to the possession of the property. Delivery is made only to the named consignee or upon his written delivery order, which may be written upon the bill of lading. If shipment is consigned to one party in care of another party, delivery may be made to the named consignee, or to the other party; but the latter "care-of" party has only the right to accept delivery of the shipment at the point of delivery designated in the straight bill of lading and cannot order a reconsignment or diversion of the shipment.

An *order bill of lading* is used when the shipper desires to retain title or control of shipment until the payment of invoice charges has been accomplished. The shipment is consigned to the order of the shipper, with instructions to notify another party of the arrival of the freight. This party can then claim the shipment upon surrender of the original bill of lading. On order shipments, the shipper and the order consignee are usually the same, and the "notify" party is the vendee.

The order bill of lading is negotiable and is generally used to secure payment at destination for the value of the property. The shipper to whose order the freight is consigned endorses the original order bill of lading and usually takes it to a bank with a sight draft attached thereto. The bill of lading and the sight draft are then forwarded by the bank to a bank at destination. The party on whom the sight draft is drawn obtains possession of the bill of lading by payment to the bank for the amount of the sight draft. The funds are transferred back to the origin bank, where they are credited to the shipper; and the title to the goods passes to the buyer when he obtains the bill of lading.

The holder in due course of an order bill of lading properly endorsed, upon the surrender thereof, is the only one entitled to receive the shipment or to direct delivery, diversion, or reconsignment. Delivery of order-billed property is usually not made until the original order bill of lading, properly endorsed, is surrendered.

If an order bill of lading is not available, however, the property covered by the bill of lading may be delivered in advance of surrender of the bill of lading to a party who states to the carrier, in writing, (1) that he is the owner or is lawfully entitled to the possession of the property; (2) that the bill of lading has been lost, delayed, destroyed, or otherwise is not immediately available at a bank; and (3) that he presents to the carrier, as a substitute for the bill of lading, a security in the form of (*a*) currency, certified check, or bank cashier's check in an amount equal to 125 per cent of the invoice or value of the property; or (*b*) at carrier's option a specified bond of indemnity with surety in an amount equal to twice such invoice or value; or (*c*) at carrier's option, a blanket bond of indemnity with surety; or (*d*) at carrier's option, an open-end bond of indemnity with corporate surety.

A specific bond of indemnity is one given to protect delivery of a particular shipment. A blanket bond of indemnity is one that can be used many times, until canceled as provided therein or at the option of the carrier. An open-end bond is one which may be used repeatedly until canceled. It applies separately, without limit, to each shipment in an amount equal to twice the invoice or value thereof.

Through export bills of lading are used only on shipments for export which move through coast ports and only when such shipments do not leave the possession of the rail carriers until delivered to the water carrier at the designated port. An export bill of lading, which may be issued in either straight or order form, is a combination of a domestic bill of lading and an ocean bill of lading, and it names the terms and conditions which are applicable to ·both means of transportation. The issuance of export bills of lading is usually delegated to general agents or division freight agents of railroads or other designated representatives of the freight traffic department. However, local freight agents may also be delegated such authority. The use of the export bill of lading eliminates the necessity for shippers' representatives or brokers to act for the shipper at the port, since it provides for the transfer of the shipment direct to the steamship and a continuous carriage to the foreign destination.

Before a shipment is offered for transportation to a port for export, it is customary for the shipper to apply to the traffic department of the railroad serving the port for a shipping permit, which will be issued only when evidence is submitted that arrangements for ocean space for transportation by vessel have been made. This permit is then sent to the freight agent at point of origin and authorizes him to accept the shipment for transportation, usually within certain stated dates.

Shipments for export through coastal ports may also move on domestic bills of lading if the shipper wishes to make his own arrangements for ocean transportation; or they may move on domestic bills of lading, to be exchanged for an export bill of lading before the arrival of the shipment at the port.

In shipping livestock, the usual railroad bills of lading are supplanted by a special document known as the *uniform livestock contract*, which must be executed for each shipment of livestock. The contract is prepared in duplicate. Both copies must be signed by shipper and agent, and signatures must be witnessed in the space provided therein. The face of the livestock contract requires the shipper to declare whether his shipment consists of "ordinary livestock" or "other than ordinary livestock." The latter includes cattle, swine, sheep, goats, horses, and mules which are chiefly valuable for breeding, racing, show purposes, or other special uses. This difference is necessitated by the Cummins Amendment to the Interstate Commerce Act, under which the Interstate Commerce Commission has ruled that the rates on ordinary livestock may not be made dependent upon value. The rates on other than ordinary livestock, however, may be dependent upon value. The uniform livestock contract, therefore, contains spaces for the shipper's declared value of such livestock. If the shipment consists of ordinary livestock, no value needs to be stated; but for other than ordinary livestock, the shipper must declare the kind and value of each animal. If a shipment consists of both ordinary and other than ordinary livestock, both declarations must be executed; but values are required to be declared and entered on livestock contracts only for animals "other than ordinary livestock."

Tariffs naming rates on livestock usually provide that an attendant may accompany such shipments. They also name the conditions under which carriers will provide for free transportation of such persons. An attendant assumes all risk of injury to his person while in charge of livestock during its carriage and delivery. Therefore, there is provided on the uniform livestock contract a separate contract with the person or persons in charge of the livestock. The latter contract is not executed with the shipper but with the man or men in charge, who are required to sign the separate contract, and their signatures must be witnessed.

Carriers generally furnish bills of lading for shippers; but where the latter have a substantial number of standard items shipped, it has become the practice of such traffic departments to have printed on the face of the bill of lading the articles being regularly shipped, as well as the name and address of the consignor. This lessens the possibility of error and speeds the paper work in the preparation of the bill of lading. A specimen of such a bill of lading is given in Figure 5–4. There is always sufficient space left when standard items are listed on the bill of lading for the addition of articles for a particular shipment.

When carriers furnish bills of lading, they furnish the long form, which is the form that provides the usual terms and conditions on the back of the bill of lading. Shippers, in providing the bill-of-lading form, can use a short form which has been in existence since 1949 for rail and motor carriers. On the face of the short-form bill of lading, there is a statement that the terms and conditions of the uniform domestic straight bill of lading contained in the governing classifications or tariffs are applicable to the shipments made on the short form. This eliminates the necessity for carrying the terms and conditions on the reverse side of the bill of lading, although they remain applicable. The Commission has held that a shipper is bound by the terms of a shipping receipt, although those terms may

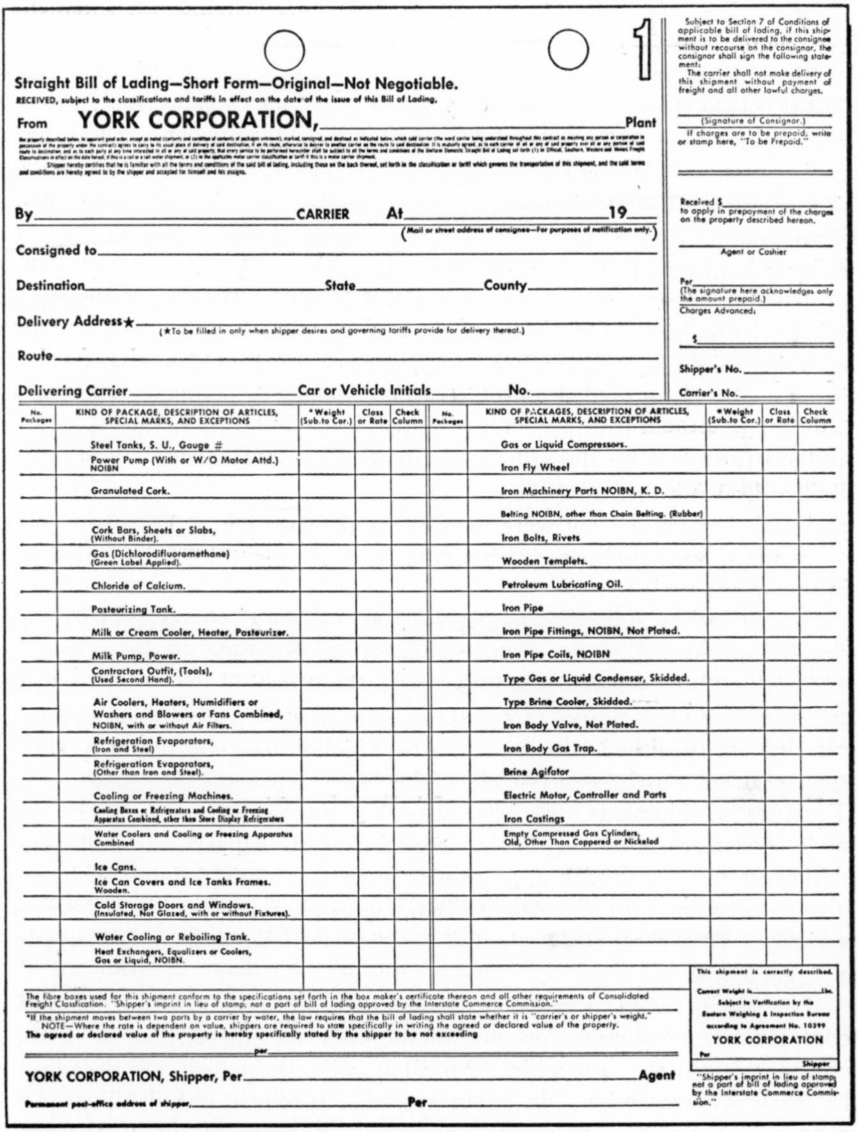

1

Straight Bill of Lading—Short Form—Original—Not Negotiable.

RECEIVED, subject to the classifications and tariffs in effect on the date of the issue of this Bill of Lading,

From **YORK CORPORATION,** ______ Plant

By ______ CARRIER At ______ 19__

(Mail or street address of consignee—For purposes of notification only.)

Consigned to ______

Destination ______ State ______ County ______

Delivery Address★ ______

(★To be filled in only when shipper desires and governing tariffs provide for delivery thereat.)

Route ______

Delivering Carrier ______ Car or Vehicle Initials ______ No. ______

Subject to Section 7 of Conditions of applicable bill of lading, if this shipment is to be delivered to the consignee without recourse on the consignor, the consignor shall sign the following statement:

The carrier shall not make delivery of this shipment without payment of freight and all other lawful charges.

(Signature of Consignor.)

If charges are to be prepaid, write or stamp here, "To be Prepaid."

Received $ ______ to apply in prepayment of the charges on the property described hereon.

Agent or Cashier

Per ______ (The signature here acknowledges only the amount prepaid.)

Charges Advanced:

$ ______

Shipper's No. ______

Carrier's No. ______

No. Packages	KIND OF PACKAGE, DESCRIPTION OF ARTICLES, SPECIAL MARKS, AND EXCEPTIONS	*Weight (Sub. to Cor.)	Class or Rate	Check Column	No. Packages	KIND OF PACKAGES, DESCRIPTION OF ARTICLES, SPECIAL MARKS, AND EXCEPTIONS	*Weight (Sub. to Cor.)	Class or Rate	Check Column
	Steel Tanks, S. U., Gauge #					Gas or Liquid Compressors.			
	Power Pump (With or W/O Motor Attd.) NOIBN					Iron Fly Wheel			
	Granulated Cork.					Iron Machinery Parts NOIBN, K. D.			
						Belting NOIBN, other than Chain Belting. (Rubber)			
	Cork Bars, Sheets or Slabs, (Without Binder).					Iron Bolts, Rivets			
	Gas (Dichlorodifluoromethane) (Green Label Applied).					Wooden Templets.			
	Chloride of Calcium.					Petroleum Lubricating Oil.			
	Pasteurizing Tank.					Iron Pipe			
	Milk or Cream Cooler, Heater, Pasteurizer.					Iron Pipe Fittings, NOIBN, Not Plated.			
	Milk Pump, Power.					Iron Pipe Coils, NOIBN			
	Contractors Outfit, (Tools), (Used Second Hand).					Type Gas or Liquid Condenser, Skidded.			
	Air Coolers, Heaters, Humidifiers or Washers and Blowers or Fans Combined, NOIBN, with or without Air Filters.					Type Brine Cooler, Skidded.			
						Iron Body Valve, Not Plated.			
	Refrigeration Evaporators, (Iron and Steel)					Iron Body Gas Trap.			
	Refrigeration Evaporators, (Other than Iron and Steel).					Brine Agitator			
	Cooling or Freezing Machines.					Electric Motor, Controller and Parts			
	Cooling Boxes or Refrigerators and Cooling or Freezing Apparatus Combined, other than Store Display Refrigerators					Iron Castings			
	Water Coolers and Cooling or Freezing Apparatus Combined					Empty Compressed Gas Cylinders, Old, Other Than Coppered or Nickeled			
	Ice Cans.								
	Ice Can Covers and Ice Tanks Frames. Wooden.								
	Cold Storage Doors and Windows. (Insulated, Not Glazed, with or without Fixtures).								
	Water Cooling or Reboiling Tank.								
	Heat Exchangers, Equalizers or Coolers, Gas or Liquid, NOIBN.								

The fibre boxes used for this shipment conform to the specifications set forth in the box maker's certificate thereon and all other requirements of Consolidated Freight Classification. "Shipper's imprint in lieu of stamp; not a part of bill of lading approved by the Interstate Commerce Commission."

*If the shipment moves between two ports by a carrier by water, the law requires that the bill of lading shall state whether it is "carrier's or shipper's weight."

NOTE—Where the rate is dependent on value, shippers are required to state specifically in writing the agreed or declared value of the property.

The agreed or declared value of the property is hereby specifically stated by the shipper to be not exceeding

______ per ______

This shipment is correctly described. Correct Weight is ______ Lbs. Subject to Verification by the Eastern Weighing & Inspection Bureau according to Agreement No. 10399

YORK CORPORATION

Per ______ Shipper

YORK CORPORATION, Shipper, Per ______ **Agent**

"Shipper's imprint in lieu of stamp not a part of bill of lading approved by the Interstate Commerce Commission."

Permanent post-office address of shipper, ______ Per ______

FIG. 5–4. Specimen bill of lading showing listing of articles regularly shipped by a company.

differ from oral arrangements made between the shipper and the carrier. Failure to examine the shipping receipt has been stated by the Commission as being the same as signing a contract without reading it.[3]

The duty of issuing bills of lading is not imposed upon the shipper, since the law requires that the carrier shall issue a receipt or bill of lading.

[3] *Eliasberg Bros., Inc.* v. *Railway Express Agency, Inc.*, 300 ICC 789 (1957) and 302 ICC 305 (1957).

That the form is prepared by the shipper does not change the fact that the carrier has issued it when the agent of the carrier affixes his signature.

There is an important exception to the extensive use of bills of lading, and that is in the movement of coal. Coal is moved from mines to a scale station, at which point its weight is entered on *mine cards* used by the coal operator. The mine card, which is subject to all the conditions of the uniform bill of lading, shows a car number, the capacity, the date, the consignor and consignee, the destination, and the route. When the rail car is moved to the scale station, the mine card is taken up by the coal billing agent, and a revenue waybill is made. The scale station is where the weight is obtained and the rate applied. The only time a bill of lading might be used is when an accident occurs in which a car of coal is lost and a claim is filed, in which case a request is usually made that a bill of lading be furnished. These mine cards are made of heavy paper and are furnished by the railroad to the shipper. The Baltimore & Ohio Railroad, which first used these mine cards, used red ones; and because of their color and size, they were soon referred to as "jokers."

In addition to their use in the movement of coal, mine cards are used in moving quarried stone.

One of the distinctions often drawn between the common and contract carriers is that the *common carrier* of general commodities issues a *uniform bill of lading* in rail transportation and one which is, to some extent, *uniform* in motor transportation. Thus, almost all shippers using common carriage are furnished with a document which is basically uniform. *Contract carriers*, on the other hand, make *individual* and *special contracts.* Technically, shipments are made by both common and contract carriage under contract. However, in the case of contract carriers, the individual shipments may be under a continuing contract, with different shippers given different contracts; while common carriers have a bill of lading which serves as a contract, which is basically uniform and applies to only a single shipment.

The receipts used in contract carriage depend upon individual shipper contracts. Some shippers provide in the contract entered into with the contract carrier that a specific form, such as the short-form bill of lading, be used; whereas others designate a special receipt. The liability of a contract carrier depends upon contractual arrangements with the shipper. The carrier may contract under any terms except for total exemption from liability because of carrier negligence. The majority of contracts, however, provide for full liability on the part of the contract carrier.

The *preparation* of bills of lading is important. The preparation of rail and motor bills of lading is similar, so it will be sufficient to describe some of the aspects of the preparation of a rail bill of lading.

Bill-of-lading forms are printed in triplicate, consisting of an original, a shipping order, and a memorandum. The original and the memorandum copy must be given to the shipper, and the shipping order is retained by the carrier's agent. The original bill of lading and shipping order should be signed by the shipper and must be signed by the carrier's agent or by his authorized representative.

The bill of lading is not signed, issued, or delivered to consignor until all property named therein has been delivered into the possession of the issuing carrier with the shipping order. The bill of lading is dated as of that day.

The carrier's agent must show on bills of lading the words "Shippers' weight, load, and count" when freight receipted for is not actually checked or weighed by the carrier's agent.

Section 7 of the uniform bill of lading provides that the consignor shall be liable for the freight and all other lawful charges, except when he stipulates by signature, in the section provided for that purpose on the face of the bill of lading, that the carrier shall not make delivery of the shipment without payment of freight and all other lawful charges. This is commonly known as the "no-recourse" or "without-recourse" section of the bill of lading. When the "no-recourse" section is signed, notation to that effect is shown on the waybill by the carrier's agent. The agent of the destination carrier does not make delivery of the shipment without requiring payment of freight and all other charges by the consignee.

When a shipment is contracted for fully prepaid and the shipper is a credit patron of the rail carrier, there is written or stamped in the space provided on the uniform bill of lading: "To be prepaid." When only a portion of the charges are to be prepaid, the amount of such charges collected is indicated on the bill of lading in the space provided, and the carrier agent's receipt for the money appears separate and distinct from the bill-of-lading signature. Thus, the bill of lading will show a specified amount of "Prepaid to apply," and the agent of the destination carrier collects all additional charges from the consignee.

If the "no-recourse" clause is signed on either partially or fully prepaid shipments, the agent at destination collects from the consignee any charges over the amount of prepaid charges shown on the waybill.

Similar rules relative to credit apply to forwarded shipments on which shippers desire to prepay the freight charges.

The description of property shown on a bill of lading is usually the only means that a carrier has of knowing the kind of material being transported and on which to assess charges. There are some instances of deliberate misdescriptions, known as "false billing," in order to secure lower charges. Under Section 10 of the act, severe penalties may be imposed upon conviction of either shipper or carrier employees.

Some shippers make notations on the bill of lading, such as "Handle with care—slightest damage makes useless." It is well to point out that the carrier's liability for loss and damage on interstate shipments is found in Section 20(11) of Part I of the Interstate Commerce Act and the bill-of-lading terms and conditions. The terms and conditions of a bill of lading cannot be changed or varied by a notation such as this, since it would lead to discrimination among the carrier's customers. There may be some psychological value, however, in the use of such a notation.

Water

Domestic water common carriers issue bills of lading similar on their faces to those issued by railroads. They issue both straight and order bills of lading. However, they do not assume any liability for loss or damage which might occur on connecting lines where there is a through movement. There is a substantial difference between the terms and conditions on the water carrier's bill of lading as compared with rail and motor, in that the water carrier's terms and conditions limit considerably the liability of the carrier.

Air

Although the Civil Aeronautics Board has not prescribed a uniform bill of lading for air carriers, several sections of the Federal Aviation Act can be interpreted as giving it such authority. Thus far, there is no uniform-

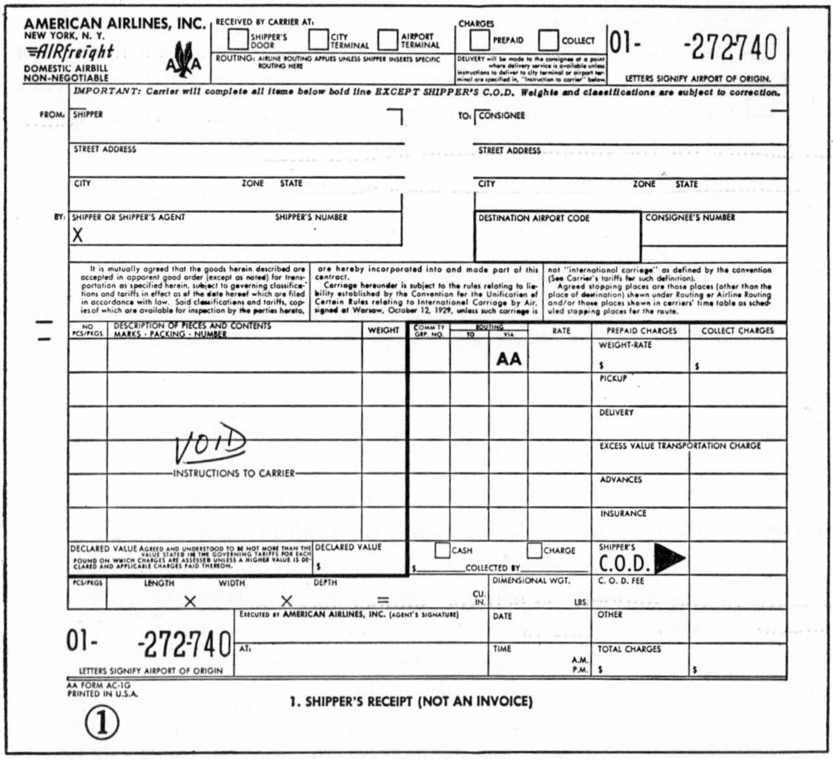

AMERICAN AIRLINES, INC.
NEW YORK, N. Y.
AIRfreight
DOMESTIC AIRBILL
NON-NEGOTIABLE

RECEIVED BY CARRIER AT: SHIPPER'S DOOR / CITY TERMINAL / AIRPORT TERMINAL

ROUTING: AIRLINE ROUTING APPLIES UNLESS SHIPPER INSERTS SPECIFIC ROUTING HERE

CHARGES: PREPAID / COLLECT

DELIVERY will be made to the consignee at a point where delivery service is available unless instructions to deliver to city terminal or airport terminal are specified in, "Instruction to carrier" below.

01- -272740

LETTERS SIGNIFY AIRPORT OF ORIGIN.

IMPORTANT: Carrier will complete all items below bold line EXCEPT SHIPPER'S C.O.D. Weights and classifications are subject to correction.

FROM: SHIPPER — STREET ADDRESS — CITY — ZONE — STATE

BY: SHIPPER OR SHIPPER'S AGENT — SHIPPER'S NUMBER

X

TO: CONSIGNEE — STREET ADDRESS — CITY — ZONE — STATE

DESTINATION AIRPORT CODE — CONSIGNEE'S NUMBER

It is mutually agreed that the goods herein described are accepted in apparent good order (except as noted) for transportation as specified herein, subject to governing classifications and tariffs in effect as of the date hereof which are filed in accordance with law. Said classifications and tariffs, copies of which are available for inspection by the parties hereto, are hereby incorporated into and made part of this contract.

Carriage hereunder is subject to the rules relating to liability established by the Convention for the Unification of Certain Rules relating to International Carriage by Air, signed at Warsaw, October 12, 1929, unless such carriage is not "international carriage" as defined by the convention (See Carrier's tariffs for such definition).

Agreed stopping places are those places (other than the place of destination) shown under Routing or Airline Routing and/or those places shown in carriers' time table as scheduled stopping places for the route.

NO PCS/PKGS.	DESCRIPTION OF PIECES AND CONTENTS MARKS - PACKING - NUMBER	WEIGHT	COMM'TY GRP. NO.	ROUTING TO	ROUTING VIA	RATE	PREPAID CHARGES	COLLECT CHARGES
					AA		WEIGHT-RATE $	$
							PICKUP	
							DELIVERY	
	VOID						EXCESS VALUE TRANSPORTATION CHARGE	
	INSTRUCTIONS TO CARRIER						ADVANCES	
							INSURANCE	

DECLARED VALUE AGREED AND UNDERSTOOD TO BE NOT MORE THAN THE VALUE STATED IN THE GOVERNING TARIFFS FOR EACH POUND ON WHICH CHARGES ARE ASSESSED UNLESS A HIGHER VALUE IS DECLARED AND APPLICABLE CHARGES PAID THEREON. — DECLARED VALUE $

CASH / CHARGE — $ ______ COLLECTED BY ______ — SHIPPER'S C.O.D.

PCS/PKGS — LENGTH × WIDTH × DEPTH = CU. IN. — DIMENSIONAL WGT. LBS. — C. O. D. FEE

EXECUTED BY AMERICAN AIRLINES, INC. (AGENT'S SIGNATURE) — DATE — OTHER

AT: — TIME A.M. P.M. — TOTAL CHARGES $ $

01- -272740

LETTERS SIGNIFY AIRPORT OF ORIGIN

AA FORM AC-1G
PRINTED IN U.S.A.

1. SHIPPER'S RECEIPT (NOT AN INVOICE)

①

FIG. 5–5. Specimen air bill.

ity in the air bill of lading, or "air bill," as it is termed. The air carriers which participate in the *Official Airfreight Tariff* use a uniform air bill, an example of which is shown in Figure 5–5. Their tariff provides that the shipper must prepare and present a nonnegotiable air bill with each shipment tendered for transportation subject to that tariff and tariffs governed thereby. If the shipper fails to present such an air bill to the carrier at the time of tendering the shipment, the carrier may accept the shipment if it is accompanied by a nonnegotiable shipping document or memorandum. No air bill or other shipping document or memorandum issued or accepted by a carrier is negotiable, regardless of the wording of such document or memorandum. Each shipment, regardless of the form of shipping document or memorandum accepted by the carrier, is subject to the carrier's tariffs in effect on the date the shipment is accepted by the carrier.

Prepaid shipments of newspapers will be accepted for local transportation without an air bill, provided advance arrangements have been made.

Unlike surface transportation where the bill of lading is prepared by the carrier, air carriers require the shipper to prepare and present the air bill to the air carrier at the time of shipment. Futhermore, the air bill has no contract terms or conditions but provides that the terms and conditions of all carrier tariffs in effect on the date of shipment are a part of the air bill. The presumption is that the shipper is familiar with the filed tariffs that govern the contract of carriage. In this field, when a shipment moves over the lines of two or more air carriers, the originating carrier assumes no liability for the shipment beyond its own lines.

Although all air carriers do not use a uniform air bill, they do issue the equivalent to a bill of lading. This is also true of air freight forwarders.

On air express shipments an air service uniform express receipt is issued. This receipt is similar to the REA Express receipt and is nonnegotiable. The air service uniform express receipt is issued in collect form for shipments sent air express collect and a prepaid form for prepaid shipments.

Pipe Lines

No prescribed bill-of-lading form for pipe lines has been required by the Interstate Commerce Commission. Pipe-line companies use a "tender of shipment," which is nonnegotiable. The tender is completed by the shipper in the minimum amount called for by the applicable tariff. It is submitted to the pipe-line company, which signs the tender and returns a copy to the shipper. When the shipper has a tank ready to run, the pipe-line company sends out a gauger, who makes out a run ticket on which is recorded information including oil level measurement, gravity, and temperature. At the end of each month, the shipper is sent a monthly statement of the runs and deliveries, and the current status of the tender is shown. The shipper does not have to deliver the amount of the tender at one time but delivers his daily shipping requirements, which are credited against the tender until the total amount of the tender has been delivered. A new tender is usually sent to the shipper when the current tender has been completed.

Express

The Interstate Commerce Commission has prescribed a uniform express receipt similar to the bill of lading used by railroads. Two forms of uniform express receipts are used, the collect form and the prepaid form, both of which are nonnegotiable. The terms and conditions are printed on the express receipt and should be carefully examined by users of express service.

Freight Forwarders

Surface freight forwarders are required by the Interstate Commerce Act to issue to their customers bills of lading which cover the individual-package shipments from time of receipt until delivery to the ultimate consignee. When the freight is consolidated into carloads for rail shipment, the railroad gives the freight forwarder its bill of lading, in which the forwarder is both the consignor and consignee. When the services of a common carrier by motor vehicle subject to Part II of the Interstate Commerce Act are utilized by a freight forwarder for receiving property from a consignor in service subject to this part of the act, such carrier may, with the consent of the freight forwarder, execute the bill of lading or shipping receipt for the freight forwarder. When the services of a common carrier by motor vehicle subject to Part II of the act are utilized by a freight forwarder for the delivery of property to the consignee named in the freight forwarder's bill of lading, shipping receipt, or freight bill, the property may, with the consent of the freight forwarder, be delivered on the freight bill, and receipted for on the delivery receipt, of the freight forwarder.[4]

GOVERNMENT BILLS OF LADING

One problem in moving government freight is that of shipping documents and their administrative handling. The number of government bills of lading rose to a peak of about 12 million during World War II. In peacetime, the number amounts to approximately 6 million a year. To identify and keep track of freight requires a system showing for whom it is destined, the location to which it is to be delivered, what it is, its size and weight, and when it was shipped, as well as other information. All this information has to be recorded on shipping documents which can be given to various parties concerned, so that they can plan the loading and unloading, transportation, segregation, and eventual use. The shipping

---

[4] Interstate Commerce Act, Part IV, Section 413.

| Standard Form No. 1103
5 GAO 3000
1103-106-01 | U. S. GOVERNMENT BILL OF LADING
ORIGINAL | B- 1282658
B/L NO. |

TRANSPORTATION COMPANY
TENDERED TO➤   **UNION PACIFIC RAILROAD CO.**

TRAFFIC CONTROL NO. MI 5724

STOP   THIS CAR OR TRUCK AT

IMPORTANT
Regulations permit this original bill of lading to be surrendered to the initial carrier or sent immediately to the consignee. The shipping agency will furnish specific instructions with respect thereto.

CAR-TRUCK LGTH., FT., INS.†		MARKED CAPACITY†		DATE FURNISHED†	DATE B/L ISSUED
ORDERED	FURNISHED	ORDERED	FURNISHED		
40'10"	40'10"	40'10"	40'10"		28 Sept 61

†FURNISH THIS INFORMATION IN CASE OF CARLOAD OR TRUCKLOAD SHIPMENTS ONLY.

FOR
CAR INITIALS AND NO.   UP 59315   KIND   FLAT

TRUCK NO.

IF EXTRA SERVICES ARE ORDERED SEE
ADMINISTRATIVE DIRECTIONS NO. 2 ON REVERSE

FROM

RECEIVED BY THE TRANSPORTATION COMPANY NAMED ABOVE, SUBJECT TO CONDITIONS NAMED ON THE REVERSE HEREOF. THE PROPERTY HEREINAFTER DESCRIBED, IN APPARENT GOOD ORDER AND CONDITION (CONTENTS AND VALUE UNKNOWN), TO BE FORWARDED TO DESTINATION BY THE SAID COMPANY AND CONNECTING LINES, THERE TO BE DELIVERED IN LIKE GOOD ORDER AND CONDITION TO SAID CONSIGNEE.

(SHIPPING POINT)➤   Warner, Utah
FULL NAME OF SHIPPER   John Manning Corporation

CONSIGNEE (NAME AND MAILING ADDRESS)
**Transportation Officer
Ft. Lewis, Washington**

MARKS

M/F: 127th Engr Co.

DESTINATION
Ft. Lewis, Washington

VIA (ROUTE SHIPMENT ONLY WHEN SOME SUBSTANTIAL INTEREST OF THE GOVERNMENT IS SERVED THEREBY)
UP

CHARGES TO BE BILLED TO (DEPARTMENT OR ESTABLISHMENT, BUREAU OR SERVICE AND LOCATION)
FINANCE CENTER, TDIV
U.S. ARMY
INDIANAPOLIS 49, INDIANA

SEAL NOS JMC 2097584

FOR CARRIER'S USE ONLY
WAYBILL NO.   FREIGHT BILL NO.

APPROPRIATION CHARGEABLE
2122010 01-2663 Q1521 S99-843

APPLIED BY Shipper

CONTRACTORS WILL RETURN UNUSED OR CANCELED BILLS OF LADING TO GOVERNMENT OFFICE FROM WHICH RECEIVED.

PACKAGES		DESCRIPTION OF ARTICLES (USE CARRIERS' CLASSIFICATION OR TARIFF DESCRIPTION IF POSSIBLE, OTHERWISE A CLEAR NONTECHNICAL DESCRIPTION)	NUMBERS ON PACKAGES	WEIGHTS*	FOR USE OF DESTINATION CARRIER ONLY			
NO	KIND				CLASS	RATE	DOLLARS	CENTS
1	EA	Tractors, NOI	V-5N	18,996	45	257	488	20
1	EA	Freight Trailer, NOI, Exceeding 44 Inches	V-50	14,750	50	286	421	85
1	EA	Scarifiers	V-5P	13,040	45	257	340	27
				46,786			1,250	32

SAMPLE

TARIFF OR SPECIAL RATE AUTHORITIES (CL-TL OR VOL ONLY)
PSCFB 1016

IF THIS SHIPMENT FULLY LOADS THE CAR OR TRUCK USED, CHECK ☐ YES

CARRIER FURNISHED   ☐ PICK UP–   ☐ TRAP CAR–
SERVICE AT ORIGIN   INITIALS OF SHIPPER'S AGENT _ _ _ _ _ _ _ _ _ _

NAME OF TRANSPORTATION
COMPANY➤ Union Pacific Railroad Co.

DATE OF RECEIPT OF SHIPMENT

INITIAL CARRIER'S AGENT. BY SIGNATURE BELOW, CERTIFIES HE RECEIVED THE ORIGINAL BILL OF LADING.
☐ YES (INDICATE BY CHECK)

SIGNATURE OF AGENT   PER
Leonard Mills

CERTIFICATE OF ISSUING OFFICER
I CERTIFY THAT THIS SHIPMENT IS MADE PURSUANT TO THE TERMS OF CONTRACT OR PURCHASE ORDER NO. Mov Order #1 Hqs, 6th USA, PSF DATED _ _ _ _ _
OR OTHER AUTHORITY FOR SHIPMENT F.O.B. POINT NAMED IN CONTRACT _ _ _ _ Calif.
ISSUING OFFICE Post Transp Office, Toole, Utah _ _ _ _ _ _

SIGNATURE OF ISSUING OFFICER Joseph Brooks, Procurement
DATE 28 Sept 61 TITLE Officer _ _ _ _ _ _ _ _ _ _ _

CONSIGNEE'S CERTIFICATE OF DELIVERY — CONSIGNEE MUST NOT PAY ANY CHARGES ON THIS SHIPMENT
I CERTIFY THAT I HAVE THIS DAY 10/28/61 _ _ RECEIVED FROM Union Pacific RR Co. _ _ _ _ _ AT Ft. Lewis, Wash. _ _
(DATE OF DELIVERY)   (NAME OF TRANSPORTATION COMPANY)   (ACTUAL POINT OF DELIVERY)

THE PROPERTY DESCRIBED IN THIS BILL OF LADING IN APPARENT GOOD ORDER AND CONDITION, EXCEPT AS NOTED ON REVERSE HEREOF.   CARRIER FURNISHED ☑ DELIVERY– ☐ TRAP CAR–
SERVICE AT DESTINATION.

Forty six thousand nine hundred eighty-six _ _POUNDS*   William Ryan, Colonel, TC _ _ _ _ _ _ _ _
(GROSS WEIGHT IN BOTH WORDS AND FIGURES)   (SIGNATURE OF CONSIGNEE OR AUTHORIZED AGENT)
*SHOW ALSO CUBIC MEASUREMENTS FOR SHIPMENTS VIA AIR, TRUCK OR WATER CARRIER, IN CASES WHERE REQUIRED.

FIG. 5–6. Specimen government bill of lading.

document, or invoice and receipt, and the bill of lading are two of the instruments that serve, among other purposes, as aids in solving the problem of the administrative handling of freight.

Transportation of property belonging to the government or to others, charges for which are to be paid by the government directly to commercial carriers by rail, highway, water, and air, are processed through the use of government bills of lading.

The government bill of lading was designed to meet the requirements of the administrative agencies of the government, the general accounting office which audits them, and the carriers. It has been designed from the standpoint of operations, as well as accounting, and for this reason differs from the uniform straight bill of lading which commercial shippers use. The government bill of lading provides for:

1. The name and title of the issuing officer.
2. The name of the issuing office.
3. The name of the government agency against which the charges are to be billed.
4. The appropriation chargeable.
5. The size of the car ordered and furnished.
6. The government bill-of-lading number and the departmental symbol.
7. The authority for the shipment.
8. A showing as to the actual delivery.
9. The extent of any loss or damage.

The government bill of lading serves as a receipt for goods, a shipping order, notice of loss or damage, a contract of carriage, a carrier's waybill, a delivery receipt, a description tally, and a freight bill to the government. Figure 5–6 is a specimen government bill of lading.

Some government shipments are originally documented with a commercial bill of lading and are later converted to a government bill of lading. Procedures exist for this conversion, and it is standard practice throughout the government to use the government bill of lading always. However, in certain emergency situations where it is impractical to secure the government bill, the commercial bill is used. In certain types of purchasing—particularly commodities such as coal, fresh produce, and lumber that move directly from countryside mines, points, or mills—the use of commercial bills of lading has been authorized for later conversion into the government bill of lading.

Preparation of Government Bills of Lading

The regulations and procedure to be used in connection with the accomplishment of freight and express transportation documents are specifically prescribed. It is the full responsibility of the issuing officer, shipper, or official authorizing the shipment to see that the correct forms are promptly and properly accomplished and immediately forwarded as required; and it is the full responsibility of the consignee to see that the carrier receives without delay the accomplished documents necessary to support its billing.

The forms comprising a set of bills of lading are made simultaneously by the use of carbon paper or by some other method. When carbon impressions of handwriting are to be taken, indelible pencil is preferable to pen and ink, and ordinary lead pencil should not be used. When a number of sets of bills of lading bearing identical information are to be prepared, duplicating machines are often used to advantage. Since subsequent records are made photographically in most cases, care should be exercised that bills of lading, including copies, are sufficiently legible for microfilming purposes. When loose or "cut" forms are used, one legible memorandum copy should be stamped "Property received" and another "Property shipped," since those words are not printed on memorandum copies furnished by the Government Printing Office in loose form.

The correct symbol and serial number appearing on the original bill of lading should be transcribed on the shipping order, the freight waybill (original freight waybill), carrier's copy, and all memorandum copies at the time the bill of lading is issued.

Each part in each carbon-interleaved set bears the serial number of the bill of lading. If any authorized memorandum copies are added to the carbon-interleaved set, the correct symbol and serial number should be added to such extra memorandum copies.

Whenever the serial number of a bill of lading is shown, in correspondence or otherwise, the symbol must also be shown. The symbol is part of the bill-of-lading number.

Normally, a separate bill of lading should be issued for each carload or truckload. Whenever a completed article is shipped in several cars, however, with each car containing portions that are useless without all the other components, the several bills of lading issued in connection therewith should be cross-referenced to each other.

The accomplishment of a bill of lading is the execution thereon of an acknowledgement that the service called for has been performed by the carrier, and a bill of lading so accomplished becomes the evidence upon which payment for the service will be made. The original copy must be forwarded by the shipper to the consignee for execution and surrender to the carrier upon delivery of the shipment. In order to ascertain whether the carrier has fulfilled all its legal and other obligations, every bill of lading is carefully compared with a strictly accurate tally of the shipment as delivered by the carrier.

Accountability for Government Bills of Lading

Government bills of lading are carefully safeguarded. Appropriate accountability records are maintained by the government services for the purpose of controlling the stock of printed bills of lading on hand and for fixing accountability upon employees responsible for their issuance and use. To facilitate such control, the bill-of-lading form, when printed, is serially numbered in the two places provided on the form, and such numerals are immediately preceded by symbol letters, which are approved by the Comptroller General. Such symbol letters must always be included in any reference to a government bill-of-lading number.

Conversion of Commercial Bills of Lading

When a shipment covered by a collect commercial bill of lading or collect commercial express receipt is received, and the transportation thereof is properly payable to the carrier from government appropriated funds, the consignee converts such commercial document into a government bill of lading without delay.

A serially numbered government bill of lading is prepared. All information required in the regular preparation of a government bill of lading is shown, but that clearly shown on the commercial document may be omitted. The government bill of lading is marked: "Converted from commercial shipping document attached," and the commercial document is securely attached. The government bill of lading is accomplished in accordance with regular procedure and turned over to the last line-haul carrier. Memorandum copies of the converted bill of lading are sent to the office of the government service concerned. Several commercial documents of one type, covering shipments from one point of origin to one consignor, via the same route, and received in one day, may be converted to one government bill of lading.

OTHER DOCUMENTS

Waybill

The waybill is a carrier document used to facilitate the movement of freight. In rail transportation, it is prepared by the freight agent of the originating line and contains the origin station, destination, routing, car initials and number, consignor and consignee, description of articles, weight, rate, freight charges, and any additional specific instructions, such as notations regarding delay, damage to contents or equipment, and similar information. The waybill is, in reality, a historical record of the movement of a shipment.

The form of the waybill varies, depending upon whether it is a local waybill—that is, one used for the movement from origin station to destination station on the same line—or an interline waybill for interline movement. A different form of waybill is usually issued to cover shipments moved pursuant to a transit privilege. The waybill usually accompanies the freight car and is made up from the shipping order, which is a duplicate of the bill of lading.

In motor transportation, some carriers make use of waybills as routing documents.

Arrival Notice

An arrival notice is sent to the consignee after preparation by the freight agent at destination, and carriers differ as to the form used. The notice contains the basic information in the waybill, as well as the name of the freight station at which delivery of the goods can be taken and the free time allowed before demurrage or detention or storage charges are imposed.

Notification by telephone is common, but the arrival notice is still forwarded, as it is the basis on which demurrage or detention action is established.

Delivery Receipt

A delivery receipt is prepared by the carrier's agent at destination and contains information similar to that found in the freight bill. In rail transportation, the delivery receipt is used where less-carload shipments are delivered at the freight station or where they are delivered by the delivery service. It is also used where carload shipments are placed on public team tracks, and, therefore, the carrier makes delivery at this point.

Carriers of all modes of transportation make use of some form of delivery receipt in order to insure an adequate record for delivery, as well as any possible future claim.

Freight Bill

The freight bill contains information similar to that on the bill of lading and shows the total freight charges to be collected. The freight bill is prepared by the agent at destination when charges are collect and by the origin carrier agent when freight charges are prepaid. When the freight charge is paid, the agent receipts the freight bill. Where freight charges are prepaid, the freight bill is sent or given to the consignor; and on a collect shipment, the original freight bill is presented to the consignee for payment. Payment must be made before the shipment is delivered, except that upon the request of any financially responsible shipper, credit is allowed and charges collected as promptly as possible, but within a period of 96 hours for carload shipments and a period of 120 hours for LCL shipments by rail.

On the reverse side of the rail freight bill are eight rules to be followed in its preparation by the carrier. The rail freight bills have been standardized, and the one in use has been recommended by the Commission.

Motor carrier freight bills differ as to format, but the essential information contained in the bill is much the same for all carriers. An example of a motor freight bill is shown in Figure 5–7. Motor carriers are required to bill shippers within 7 days after delivery of the freight, and the shipper is to pay within 7 days after the receipt of the bill.

In the case of rail and air express and surface freight forwarders, the credit period is 7 days. In domestic water transportation, the time allowed is 48 hours and, under certain conditions, 96 hours. The Civil Aeronautics Board, in 1962, began requiring air carriers to publish billing and payment practices in their tariffs. Carrier management may establish any practice in regard to billing and payment that is just, reasonable, and not unjustly

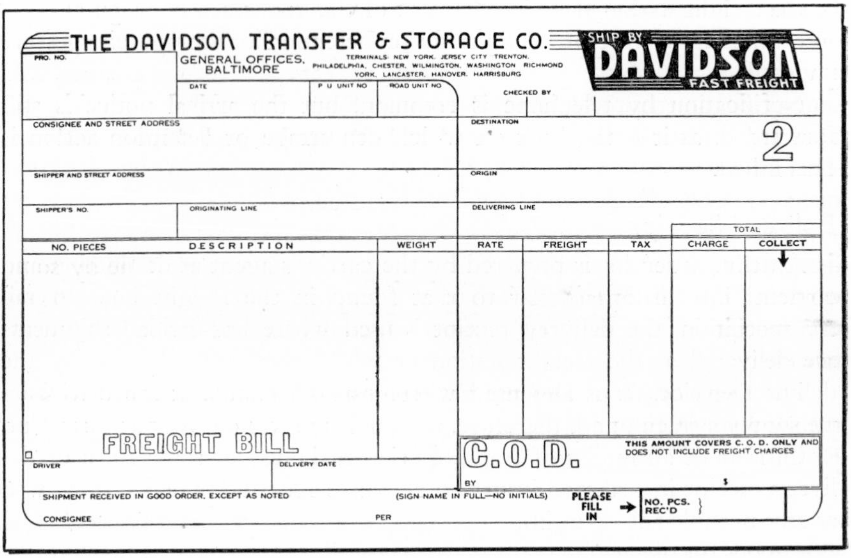

THE DAVIDSON TRANSFER & STORAGE CO.

SHIP BY DAVIDSON FAST FREIGHT

PRO. NO.

GENERAL OFFICES, BALTIMORE

TERMINALS: NEW YORK, JERSEY CITY, TRENTON, PHILADELPHIA, CHESTER, WILMINGTON, WASHINGTON, RICHMOND, YORK, LANCASTER, HANOVER, HARRISBURG

DATE | P U UNIT NO | ROAD UNIT NO | CHECKED BY

CONSIGNEE AND STREET ADDRESS | DESTINATION | 2

SHIPPER AND STREET ADDRESS | ORIGIN

SHIPPER'S NO. | ORIGINATING LINE | DELIVERING LINE

NO. PIECES	DESCRIPTION	WEIGHT	RATE	FREIGHT	TAX	TOTAL CHARGE	TOTAL COLLECT

FREIGHT BILL

C.O.D. THIS AMOUNT COVERS C. O. D. ONLY AND DOES NOT INCLUDE FREIGHT CHARGES

BY $

DRIVER | DELIVERY DATE

SHIPMENT RECEIVED IN GOOD ORDER, EXCEPT AS NOTED (SIGN NAME IN FULL—NO INITIALS)

CONSIGNEE PER

PLEASE FILL IN → NO. PCS. REC'D

FIG. 5–7. Specimen motor carrier freight bill.

discriminatory or preferential. The Board has approved an agreement of major air carriers that provides that charges are payable in cash at the time prepaid shipments are accepted or collect shipments are delivered. Credit may be extended, however, for a period of 10 days after the day of billing if arrangements for such credit have been made in advance.

In processing freight bills for payment, a traffic department approves the freight rate and classification; and it is the responsibility of the accounting department to pay the bill. The credit periods begin with the first 12:00 o'clock midnight following the delivery of the freight in those cases in which the freight bill is presented prior to or at the time of delivery of the freight; or with the first 12:00 o'clock midnight following the presentation or time of mailing of the bills in those cases in which the freight bill is presented subsequent to the time freight is delivered.

PROCEDURAL SIMPLIFICATION

A growing realization of the administrative burden and cost of handling documents has resulted in greater efforts to effect simplification and a reduction in costs. In general, documentation is the same for a 300-pound shipment as for a carload or truckload. Obviously, this disproportionate cost of small shipments is a factor of importance to carriers, shippers, and the public. The need to simplify documentation, particularly of small shipments, is highly desirable.

Where computers are available, documentation for all shipments could be adapted for computer use, which would allow for procedural simplification. This would likely involve a change in the size and design of such documents as the bill of lading and the freight bill. This could result in the acceleration of the processing of documents and permit a larger volume of documents to be handled per man-hour. It could also provide the basis for statistical data to be used in both carrier and shipper analyses. This information flow could be keyed to warehouse and inventory documents, as well, which would enhance its value.

Even without data processing, it is possible for documents to be redesigned in order to simplify their preparation as has been done by some carriers. The bill of lading, freight bill, waybill, arrival notice, and delivery receipt in the required number of copies can be made out simultaneously.

The Department of Defense has established a system designed to strip the supply system of extraneous paper work. It is called Military Standard Requisition and Issue Procedure, or MILSTRIP, and substitutes a standard system for over a dozen systems that had existed previously. The new system is customer-oriented so the Supply Transportation team will provide goods for the man who needs them— at the time he says he needs them. A priority chart is established so that the man in the field knows what his priority position is—for example, combat rates top priority whereas a reserve force has lower priority. MILSTRIP, based on priorities, has sought to speed up shipments in order to meet deadline requirements. In general, carriers have been required to shorten the period of time within which transportation is accomplished in order to adapt to the new requirements. All aspects of the requisitioning procedure, including documents, have been cut to the minimum so that this part of the procedure is streamlined.

The other part of the system is Military Standard Transportation Movement and procedure, or MILSTAMP. This involves the use of a single universal transportation document regardless of the mode of transportation and applicable on a worldwide basis. It can be used for shipment planning and advance notice as well as accumulation of data for management decisions and a check on the validity of transit times.

TERMS OF SALE

Shipments are usually made in contemplation of sale and/or as the result of a sale. A sale involves the transfer of title to goods, which is of concern to the buyer and seller and perhaps to other parties, such as carriers and insurers. The importance of terms of sale has led to many court actions, and it is now well established that risk follows title.[5] However, there are many misunderstandings between buyers and sellers concerning when title passes, who bears the risk at a particular time, and who is to pay freight charges.

[5] For a comprehensive discussion of this subject, see Thomas G. Bugan, *When Does Title Pass* (2d ed.; Dubuque, Iowa: Wm. C. Brown & Co., 1951).

Regulated common carriers are bailees in their relationship to shippers —i.e., they do not have title to goods but do have possession of the goods and do possess liability for shipments.

There are many terms of sale, such as F.O.B. (free on board) point of origin, F.O.B. factory, F.O.B. mill, F.O.B. buyer's cars, or F.O.B. destination. The freight charges may be absorbed or allowed, depending on the terms of sale. Traffic managers have often found that the transportation aspects of the terms of sale are not fully comprehended by other departments in the business organization, and it is necessary that they be understood in order that later difficulties be avoided.

CASE

The movement of household goods of military and civilian personnel of the Department of Defense is a large and complex undertaking. During the period July 1, 1961 to July 1, 1962, 658,200 tons of household goods were shipped at a cost of $114 million. 98,000 tons of this amount were moved in through bill of lading service to and from the continental United States, Alaska, Hawaii, and foreign countries. For many years, voluntary rate tenders were filed with installation transportation officers in the United States and overseas. These were accumulated at each installation in bulky tender files. With over 1,200 separate shipping installations and 1,600 carriers rendering service, there were many problems that arose involving uniform application of procedures, rotation of traffic among carriers, and the filing of rate proposals under Section 22.

On July 1, 1961, the Defense Traffic Management headquarters assumed the responsibility for reviewing, accepting, and distributing household goods rate tenders, and for the maintenance of a public file at its headquarters. The workload that resulted from this centralization of houshould goods rate tenders was far greater than expected and, in the following ten months, 41,039 tenders were received for review and acceptance. The heavy workload caused new procedures to be instituted, one of which was that reductions below and increases above the competitive rate would not become effective for 30 days after receipt by the Defense Traffic Management Service; changes to meet competitive rates would be accepted upon completion of a technical examination and approval by DTMS; and reductions below the competitive rate would be limited to one per month between any two points for each carrier. Such reductions were required to be delivered to DTMS during the first five working days of each month.

The new procedure was found to be inadequate to meet and solve the filing of rates problem and on February 14, 1962, DTMS established a moratorium on rate tender increases and decreases until June 1, 1962. The competitive or "me too" rate tenders were not included in the moratorium.

After June 1, 1962, any increases or decreases carried a 60-day delay in effectiveness. The acceptance dates for increases or decreases were set at the first five working days of each quarter, thus allowing a maximum of four changes in rate patterns per year. The manpower requirements were very heavy and necessitated the borrowing of an additional 17 rate analysts from other headquarters rate analysis work. Even with overtime, these rate analysts were unable to process a sufficient number of rate quotations to eliminate the backlog.

The large work volume caused consideration to be given to the use of a computer, and a program was developed of computer analysis of through government bill of lading household goods rate tenders. An IBM 1410 computer system was available for use, and the program was designed for use in this system. The rate tenders supplied by the carriers were in the form of cards which provided rate information. The computer edits, sorts, analyzes, and provides a print-out of all rates, listing the lowest rate first and then proceeding in ascending order to the highest. Rate print-outs are forwarded to installation transportation officers and to the Government Accounting Office (which audits government rates). The program has dramatically cut processing time and relieved 10 rate analysts of this work. The installation transportation officer now works from a single computer print-out in determining each carrier's costs.

1. What advantages, other than savings, would there be in a program of this kind to headquarters?

2. To installation transportation officers?

3. Can you visualize the application of similar methods in an industrial firm?

DISCUSSION QUESTIONS AND PROBLEMS

1. Secure a copy of the rail uniform straight bill of lading, and compare it with the motor common carrier straight bill of lading. What differences, if any, can you find?

2. Name the different types of railroad bills of lading. Carefully explain the difference between the order bill and the straight bill.

3. Assume that a shipper signs the "no-recourse clause," which is Section 7 of the rail bill of lading. What effect would this have upon the collection of freight charges?

4. If the shipper decides not to accept the terms and conditions of the rail straight bill of lading, will this affect the carrier's liability? The applicable rate? Is there a classification rule which applies to this?

5. Under what conditions may a shipment moving by rail or motor common carrier on an order bill of lading be lawfully delivered without the surrender of the original bill of lading?

6. What are the basic differences between the government bill of lading and the commercial bill of lading? Would the traffic manager for an aircraft plant producing planes under government contract ever use a government bill of lading?

7. The bill of lading of common carriers serves, in part, as a contract of carriage, and contract carriers also operate under a contract of carriage with the shipper. What basic differences, if any, are there between the two contracts?

8. Secure a copy of a bill of lading used by a well-known steamship line engaged in foreign shipping, and compare its terms and conditions with the rail domestic straight bill of lading.

9. What relationship, if any, exists between the terms and conditions of the bill of lading and the shipper insuring his shipment?

10. Outline the difference between the waybill and the freight bill.

11. Explain what is meant when it is said that "regulated common carriers are bailees in their relationship to shippers."

12. What action can the carrier take if it finds that the commodities shipped are not those described on the bill of lading?

Chapter

6

CLASSIFICATION

RAIL

Prior to the development of rail transportation, the classification of commodities for transportation purposes into a small number of classes or groups was practiced by river- and canalboat operators abroad. Later, a similar pattern was followed by such operators in the United States. The charges which were established by wagoners also made use, in many instances, of the classification technique. With the development of railroads, there was the adoption of this method of classifying traffic. Over 100 years ago, one of the railroads had in its tariff an "enumeration and classification of articles," which provided for 90 items in Class 1, 82 in Class 2, and 82 in Class 3.[1] Figure 6–1 is a sample page from this tariff.

In the establishment of charges to ship goods, each railroad originally grouped goods into a limited number of categories for the use of its own lines. This so-called "classification" meant that, through the establishment of such a procedure, a railroad could place the many items which were offered it for shipment into a relatively small number of categories, which greatly simplified its rate quotations. One of the first classifications of goods used by a railroad established two classes: (1) heavy goods and (2) light goods. The charges for the light goods were assessed in terms of the space occupied, while the tendency was to establish the charge for heavy goods on the basis of weight.

Later, refinements were made in classifications, and new groups were added. As time passed, this reclassifying continued to be based on the transportation characteristics of the goods offered for shipment. Since each individual railroad had its own classification, there were a large number of classifications within a given area, as well as differences concerning the method of classification.

[1] New York & Erie Railroad Freight Tariff, adopted April 20, 1852.

ENUMERATION AND CLASSIFICATION OF ARTICLES.

All articles not enumerated will be charged first class rates.

This character † refers to articles carried at estimated weights.

This character * refers to articles in the Third Class which are carried at Fourth Class Rate, in specified quantities.

First Class.

Apples, green.

Baskets, double weight, Batting, cotton, Blinds, Berries, Bonnets, Books, Boots and Shoes, Bread, Brushes and Brooms, Buffalo Robes, Bacon, loose, Beeswax, Beans and Peas, green, Bottles, empty, Boxes and Barrels, empty.

†Cabinetware, boxed, at owner's risk, Codfish, in bundles, Candies, in boxes, Cards Cotton and Wool, † Chairs, boxed, Cotton waste, in sacks or bales, Copper and Brass vessels, Carpetings, Cigars, Cigar Boxes in cases, † Carriages, well boxed, at owner's risk, Clocks and Weights, Cradles and Baskets, double weight, Cork, Covers and Sieves, Cocoa Nuts, † Cattle and Calves, Caps, Cassia, Cultivators, Camphene, at owner's risk of leakage.

Dry Goods, boxes and bales, Drugs, in boxes, Demijohns, empty, double weight, Deer Skins, loose in bundles.

Feathers and Furs, owner's risk, Furniture, old, loose, 1500 lbs. cart load at owner's risk, Fruit, green, at owner's risk, Figs, Flax, in bales, covered, Fish, fresh, at owner's risk, † Furniture, new well boxed, Fowls, in coops, one and a half weight.

Game at owner's risk, Garden Seeds, Glassware at owner's risk of breakage, Grapes, Glass, window, over 12 x 20, owner's risk.

Hair and Moss, upholster's, in sacks, Hats and Caps, Harnesses and Saddles, Hams, loose, † Hogs and Pigs, Hollow ware, Honey, † Horses and Mules.

Indigo, Ink, in boxes, at owner's risk of breakage.

Lemons and Oranges, packed, Looking Glasses, owner's risk of breakage, Leather, loose, going West, † Live Stocks of all kinds.

Machinery, well boxed, at owner's risk, Marble, wrought, at owner's risk of breakage, Mats and Rugs, Measures and Tubs, in nests, Medicines, owner's risk, Musical Instruments, Moss, in sacks, Muskets, and other firearms, Melons and Cucumbers at owner's risk.

Nuts, in bags.

Oysters, in kegs or cans.

Paper Hangings, in bundles, Palm Leaf, in bales, Paper and Stationery, Peaches, in baskets, prepaid, at owner's risk, Piano fortes, 1,200 lbs., owner's risk, † Pigs, Peltries, Ploughs, Pumps, Pineapples, at owner's risk, Porter and Ale, in glass, Plaster Paris Casts, owner's risk, Poultry, at owner's risk, Powder, not taken under any circumstances.

Quinces, at owner's risk.

Rattan.

Saddlery, Scale and Scale Beams, † Sleighs, well boxed, Shingles, loose, † Sheep and Lambs, Soap, fancy, Soda Water, Spirits of Turpentine, at owner's risk of leakage, Stove Pipe, Stove Furniture, at owner's risk, Stoves, mounted, at owner's risk, Straw Goods, Stove Plates, at owner's risk, Starch, Sweet Potatoes, Spices, ground.

Tinware, Trunks, Trees and Shrubbery, at owner's risk, Toys, boxed, Tea, Twine.

Umbrellas, boxed.

Veneering, Varnish, Veal and Lamb, dressed, at owner's risk, Venison, at owner's risk.

Waggons, children's, double weight, Waste, in sacks or bales, Wine, in boxes or baskets, Whips, boxed, Wadding, Wicking, Waggons and Carts, common, in pieces, Wheelbarrows, Whalebone, Wooden ware, Wool, in sacks, going West, Willowware, double weight.

Yarn.

Second Class.

Alcohol, in bbls., Ale and Beer, in casks,

Axes, Axletrees, iron, not car axles

Bacon and Hams, in casks, going West, Bags and Bagging, in bales, Bells, Brimstone, Beef, fresh, at owner's risk, † Beef, salted, in bbls., going West, Blankets, in bales, Burlaps, Binder's Boards, Broom Corn, pressed in bales, Boilers for engines, Brandy, Gin and Rum, in wood, Bulk Meat, Butter, Beans, in bags or bbls.

Cannon, Canvas, Candles, Cranberries, Carts and Waggons, common in pieces, closely packed in lots of five or more, Chair and Turned Stuff, Clover Seed, Coffee, Copper, plate, sheet and bolt, Copper, pig, wire, rods and nails, Crockery, boxes and bbls., Currants in bbls. or casks.

Deer Skins, closely packed in bales, Domestic Shirtings, and Sheetings, in bales, Dried Apples and Peaches, Dried Fruits, Domestic Woollen Goods, going East on manufacturer's account. Drugs and Dyewoods, in bbls. or bags.

Eggs, at owner's risk, Earthen and Stoneware.

Fish, pickled, dried, salted or smoked, Flax or Grass Seed, Forks, Hay and manure.

Glass, window, under 12 x 20, owner's risk, Glue and Gum, Groceries, not enumerated in other classes, Grass Seed, Gunny Bags.

Hair, Saddler's and Plasterer's, Hardware, Hops, Hemp, in bales or bags, at owner's risk, Hoofs and Horns, Herrings, in boxes or kegs, Hides, dry, less than 100, Hoes, Hay and Straw, pressed in bales.

Iron Sales, Iron, hoop, band and sheet.

Lead, in pipe, bars, pig and sheet, Leather, in rolls or boxes, Liquors, in casks or bbls., at owner's risk of leakage

Moss, in bales, Mahogany and other Foreign Wood of value, Marble, unwrought, in slabs, at owner's risk.

Nuts, in bbls., Nail Rods.

Oakum, Oil Cloth, Oils, at owner's risk of leakage, Oysters and Clams, in shell, at owner's risk, prepaid.

Paints and Dye Stuffs, Paper, Printer's, Paper Hangings, in boxes, Pasteboard, Pickles and Cucumbers, in casks, Pork and Mutton, fresh, at owner's risk, † Pork, salted, in bls. going West, Peas, in bags or bbls.

Rope, Rags, at owner's risk of fire and wet, Rice, Raisins.

Straw Paper, Scales and Scale Beams, boxed, Scythes and Snaths, Shot, in bags, Saleratus, Soap, common, in boxes, Sheep Skins, in bales, Spelter and Zinc, in pigs, Stoves and Stove Plates, by the car load, on manufacturer's account, at owner's risk, Shovels and Spades, Stove Plates, boxed.

Tobacco, in bales, Tow, pressed, Type, Tobacco, manufactured, going West.

Water, mineral, Wood, in shape, Wool, pressed in bales, Wines, in casks or bbls., at owner's risk of leakage, Whiskey; going West, at owner's risk of leakage.

Third Class.

Acids, Pyroligenous, in casks, * Anchors, Anvils, * Ashes, dry, house and leached, * Ashes, Pot and Pearl, Axes, going East on manufacturer's account.

* Bacon, in casks, * Bleaching Powders, in casks or bbls., * Bacon, in casks or boxes, going East, † * Beef, salted in bbls., going East, * Bark, Tanners, Bones, * Bran or Feed, in bags or bls., * Brick or Building Stone, to Pier only, * Burr Blocks, * Barilla.

† Charcoal, to Pier only, Cheese, in boxes or casks, at owner's risk of weather, Cider, * Clay, Marl and Sand, to Pier only, * Coal, Mineral, to Pier only, Codfish, in hhds. and boxes, Crockery, crates and hhds., Copper, Ore, * Cotton, in bales, * Cement, in bbls, * Chain Cables, Copper in boxes, * Chalk, * Car Wheel and Car Axles.

Dye Wood in sticks, Domestic Cotton Goods, on manufacturer's account going East.

* Earths and Manures, to Pier only.

† * Fire Wood, Posts and Rails, * Flour or Meal, in bags, † Flour and Meal, in bbls.

† * Grain of all kinds, in bags, *Grain of all kinds, in bbls., * Gypsum, Guano, Grindstones.

Hemp, Manilla, in bales, Hemp Yarn, in reals, * Heading and Staves, Hides and Skins, green, Hides, dry, in bales, Hog's Hair, in bales, * Hoops, and Hoop Poles, owner to load and unload.

* Iron, bloom, bar, scrap, pig, boiler, and railroad, * Iron Castings, plain and heavy, not machinery, * Iron Ore.

* Junk, Joiner's Work.

* Lard and Lard Oil, in bbls. and kegs, * Lath, actual weight, * Lead, in pigs or bars, going East, Leather, undressed, in boxes or rolls, going East, * Lime, in bbls. or casks, * Lime, in bulk, Locomotive Engines.

* Millstones, Molasses, * Marble and Stone, unwrought, in blocks, Mahogany, in log.

* Nails, Spikes and Bolts.

Oars, at owner's risk, to Pier only, owner to load and unload, * Oil Cake, m casks.

* Plaster, † * Pork and Beef, salted in bbls., going East, † * Potatoes and similar roots in bags or bbls., * Pitch.

Railroad Cars, * Rosin, Rigging.

* Salt, Saltpetre, * Soda Ash, * Shingles, in bunches, actual weight, Starch, in bbls., on manufacturer's account, Sugar, hhds., bls. and boxes, Shot, in kegs, * Steel, in boxes, bundles or bars, Steel Springs, going East on manufacturer's account, Sumac, † * Stone, unwrought.

* Tallow, in bbls., * Tar, Tin, * Tobacco, in hhds. or boxes, unmanufactured, Tobacco manufactured, going East.

Vinegar.

* Whiting, * Whiskey, going East, Wire.

* Zinc, in casks.

Fourth Class.

Anchors, 10 tons, Ashes, leached, 10 tons, Ashes, Pot and Pearl, 10 tons.

Bacon and Hams, in casks, 10 tons, † Beef and Pork, salted, in barrels, 10 tons, Burr Blocks, 10 tons, Barilla, 10 tons, Bleaching Salts, 10 tons, Bark, ground, in bags or casks, Bark, Tanner's, 10 tons, Brick and Building Stone, to Pier only, owner's to load and unload, 10 tons.

Chain Cables, 10 tons, Chalk, 10 tons, Coal, Mineral, 10 tons, to Pier only, Cement, 10 tons, Clay, 10 tons, Car Wheels and Axles, 10 tons, Cotton, in bales, 10 tons.

Earth and Manure, 10 tons, to Pier only.

† Flour, 100 bbls., Flour, in bags, 10 tons, Fish, salted, in bbls., 25 bbls., † Firewood, 10 tons, to Pier only, Feed, in bags, 10 tons, Feed, in bbls., 100 bbls.

† Grain, in bags, 10 tons, Grain, in bbls., 100 bbls., Gypsum, 10 tons, to Pier only, Guano, 10 tons, Grindstones, 10 tons.

Heading and Staves, 10 tons, Hoops and Hoop Poles, 10 tons.

Iron, bar, pig, scrap, bloom, bolt, shapes, boiler and railroad, 10 tons, Iron Ore, 10 tons, Iron Castings, heavy, not liable to damage, 10 tons.

Junk, 10 tons.

Lime, in casks, 10 tons, Lime, in bulk, to Pier only, owner to load and unload, 10 tons, † Lumber under 25 feet long, to Pier or Newburg, 10 tons, Lath, 10 tons, Lead, pig and bar, 10 tons, Lard and Lard Oil, in bbls., 10 tons.

Marble, unwrought, in blocks, 10 tons.

Nails, 10 tons.

Oil Cake, in casks, 10 tons.

† Potatoes, in bbls., 100 bbls., Pitch, 25 bbls., Plaster, 10 tons, owner to load and unload, Posts and Rails, 10 tons, owner to load and unload.

Rosin, 25 bbls

Spikes, common, ship and railroad, 10 tons, * Stone, unwrought, 10 tons, Steel, in boxes, 10 tons, Sand, 10 tons, to Pier only, † Salt, in bbls. or bags, 10 tons, Soda Ash, 10 tons, Shingles, 10 tons, Shooks, 10 tons.

Tallow, in casks, 10 tons, Timber under 25 feet long, 10 tons, Tobacco, unmanufactured, 10 tons, Tar, 25 bbls.

Whiskey, 10 tons, Whiting, 10 tons.

Zinc, 10 tons.

SOURCE: New York & Erie Railroad Co.

FIG. 6–1. Sample page from early tariff showing classification of articles.

It was not uncommon for one railroad to have a number of classifications. In many cases, there were two or more classifications which were effective on a single railroad, one governing local traffic and a second for through traffic. In addition, traffic going to or coming from a particular section of the country was often covered by an additional classification.

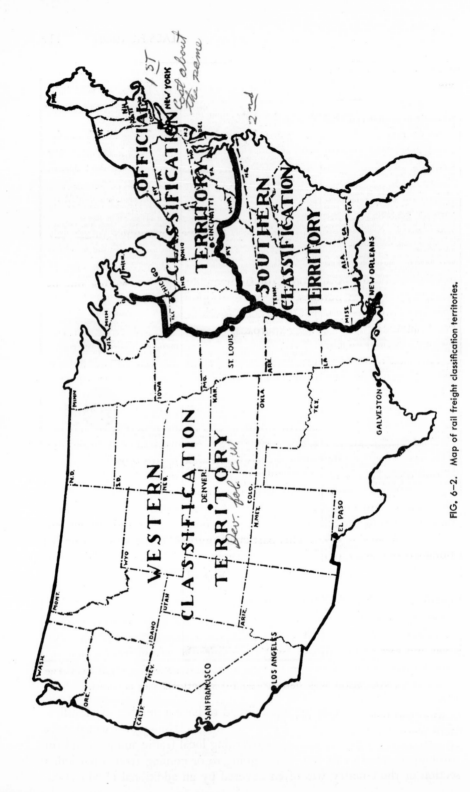

FIG. 6-2. Map of rail freight classification territories.

In the West, one railroad had 7 different freight classifications of its own: one governing eastbound traffic, one for westbound traffic, one for overhead traffic, and several others. In one of the geographical rate territory areas, it is estimated that at one time, there were 138 classifications.

So long as traffic did not move beyond the line of the initial carrier, the diversity of classification did not cause hardship. With the development of interline arrangements, however, the lack of uniformity caused considerable confusion. The origin carrier, in handling a particular type of freight, might feel that it was perfectly acceptable to receive freight in bundles and have a provision in its classification to that effect. On the other hand, a connecting line handling the same commodity might have had a somewhat different experience and so publish in its classification a provision that the articles had to be packed in boxes. Therefore, the articles would not be accepted for shipment by the connecting line because they were in bundles. Since the numerous classifications and the differences in these individual classifications made difficult the smooth interchange of traffic between railroads, it became apparent to both shippers and carriers that there was need for uniformity of classifications.

This lack of uniform classification of freight was one of the eighteen separate causes for complaint against the railroads by the Cullom Committee, which resulted in the passage of the Act to Regulate Commerce. In the Interstate Commerce Commission's *1st Annual Report*, the Commission referred to the lack of uniform classification and regretted that the same classification was not adopted by the rail carriers in all sections of the country. The statement was also contained in this report that classification is the foundation of all rate making.

A number of meetings were held in order to consider uniformity of classification. By 1890, a classification was agreed upon by a committee of traffic officials of the railroads and recommended for adoption by all railroads on January 1, 1891. This particular uniform classification proposal contained 16 classes, 10 of which were applicable to less-carload lots. This proposal of a uniform classification was not accepted, however.

Consolidated Freight Classification

In 1887, there had been established the Official Classification of 1887 in the Official Territory.[2] Two years later, the railroads south of the Ohio River and east of the Mississippi River adopted a classification which became known as the "Southern Classification." During the same year, the Western Classification was being used by practically all of the railroads operating from Chicago and St. Louis to the West, although a joint classification had been used by certain railroads in that area since 1883. Thus, there were developed three primary classifications, which took the place of the numerous and diverse individual classifications. Each of the three

---

[2] Figure 6–2 (p. 120) shows a map of the rail classification territories.

classifications had its own set of rules, descriptions of articles, and ratings,[3] and in some cases, they still were not uniform. In 1919, these three classifications were first published in a single volume, which was called the "Consolidated Freight Classification." The original volume was No. 1, and each subsequent issue has been consecutively numbered. The current volume is No. 23.

After the publication of the first Consolidated Freight Classification, the descriptions of articles, rules and regulations, and packing requirements became uniform throughout the three territories, although certain ratings were not the same in all territories. Over a period of time, Class 1, Class 2, and Class 3 were made uniform in all of the territories; but below that, there was no uniformity.

Until 1962 specific ratings applicable only to the Illinois and Southern Classification areas were included in the Consolidated Freight Classification. Currently, these are now contained in separate publications. The Illinois Freight Classification developed because, for transportation purposes, the territory embraced in the Illinois Territory was regarded as partly within Official Territory and partly within Western Territory, and to meet the need for fulfilling the requirements of an Illinois statute. The Illinois Classification area includes the state of Illinois, as well as border points in Wisconsin, Indiana, Iowa, Kentucky, and Missouri. It was originally published to apply on traffic within the state of Illinois and then was later filed with the Interstate Commerce Commission to apply on interstate traffic whose origin or destination was Illinois and adjacent territories. It was placed in the Consolidated Classification in 1933.

The Illinois Classification has the same ratings as those in Official Territory, except in those instances where Illinois shippers were in competition with shippers in Western Territory, in which case the Western Classification rating was adopted. This classification primarily governs (1) Illinois intrastate traffic and (2) the class rates between Illinois and points in the Indiana portion of the Chicago switching district.

One of the basic purposes of classification is to simplify rates. Commodities with like or similar transportation characteristics are grouped together into broad classes. Thus, 1,000 items might be divided into 10 groupings, based on their transportation characteristics. To each of the 10 groups, there would be affixed a rating. Class 1 constitutes 100 per cent, and the other classes bear a definite percentage relationship to Class 1. Instead of having 1,000 commodities, these commodities are placed in 10 groups with 10 rates which are applicable to the 10 classes. These groups are specified by either numbers or alphabetical letters. In the Official Territory, there are 6 numbered classes, plus Rule 26. In the Southern Territory, there are 12 numbered classes; and in the Western, there

---

[3] A rating is a number or a letter affixed to the classes. Class 1, for example, in the Consolidated Freight Classification is a rating; Class 2 is 85 per cent of Class 1 and is a rating.

are 5 numbered and 5 lettered classes. The relationships of the various ratings within the various classifications are indicated in Table 6–1.

TABLE 6–1

RELATIONSHIPS OF THE VARIOUS RATINGS WITHIN THE OFFICIAL, SOUTHERN, AND WESTERN TERRITORIES

Percentage of Class 1	Official	Southern	Western
100	1	1	1
85	2	2	2
70	3	3	3
55	R26	4	4
50	4	..	..
45	....	5	A
40	....	6	..
37½	....	..	5
35	5	7	..
32½	....	..	B
30	....	8	C
27½	6	..	..
25	....	9	..
22½	....	10	D
20	....	11	..
17½	....	12	E

SOURCE: ICC, Dockets No. 13494, No. 13535, No. 15879, and No. 17000.

The classification does not fix in dollars and cents the rates to be charged for moving the article but merely states the class or rating of each commodity. In order to ascertain the charge for moving the commodity between two points, reference must be made to a publication containing rates. The rate tariff will contain the rates which apply. The rating, then, in the classification merely indicates the class of the good, which is then used in conjunction with the rate tariff, where the rate will be found. Although the rating and the rate are interdependent, it should be emphasized that the rating and the rate are not the same.

Commodities are grouped into classes, those commodities in each class paying the same freight rate per 100 pounds. Frequently, a commodity is in several classes, depending upon whether carload or less-carload lots are involved and upon the method of packaging. One class is called "Class 1" or "Class 100," and each other class has been fixed as a percentage or multiple of Class 1. Thus, the freight classifications consist of lists containing descriptions of every commodity moving by freight and the class or classes to which it is assigned—that is, its classification rating or ratings.

In the publication of a tariff which contains class rates, one does not find the names of the various articles which may be shipped. The articles have, of course, been listed in the classification or the exceptions to the classification which shows the class or rating to which each article belongs. It will be recalled that in one class, there may be hundreds of different articles which take the same class or rating; and there is no need to reproduce all of these articles in the tariff, because the purpose of the classification has been to group them into classes and thereby simplify the quotation of rates.

There are ratings above Class 1 which run as high as four times Class 1, or 400 per cent of Class 1, and these are called "multiples" of Class 1. There are also ratings ranging down to 13 per cent of Class 1. The Consolidated Freight Classification is organized in the following order:

1. Cancellations.
2. Table of contents.
3. List of commissions with which this tariff is filed.
4. Names of chairmen and members of the Official and Western Classification Committees.
5. Participating rail carriers.
6. Participating water carriers.
7. Participating motor carriers.
8. Participating freight forwarders.
9. Index to rules.
10. Index to articles.
11. Rules.
12. Bill-of-lading forms.
13. Application of ratings.
14. Service orders.
15. Classification of articles (LCL, CL, minimum weights).
16. Authorized packages or shipping containers.
17. Explanation of abbreviations and reference marks.

In the use of the "Index to Articles" in the classification, where nouns are not sufficiently distinctive, articles are also indexed under their adjectives. All of the items, relating to different kinds of the same commodity are grouped together. For example, all items of tar are grouped under the general head of "tar" with the descriptive word following:

tar:
    candle
    coal
    hardwood
    pine

It is recognized that it is not practical to describe every article in a classification, so that the letters "NOIBN"—which mean "Not otherwise indexed by name"—are used in numerous instances where ratings for articles are not more specifically described in the classification. For example, there are a number of musical instruments specifically described, such as accordians and drums; but there is also the term "musical instruments, NOIBN," which includes other musical instruments not individually and specifically classified by name and description. This substantially broadens the description to include similar articles not specifically described. It is estimated that 5 million items in the military supply systems

TERRITORIAL RATINGS

The ratings shown in the columns opposite the separate descriptions of articles on pages 198 through 492 of classification as amended are to be used in connection with class rate tariffs which specify that class rates therein are governed by the Official or Western Classification, as the case may be.

APPLICATION OF LETTERS, NUMBERS OR REFERENCE MARKS APPEARING IN RATING COLUMNS.

Where two ratings or reference marks in lieu of ratings are shown in the rating columns, the first (reading from left to right) is for Official Classification and the second is for Western Classification.

Where only one rating or reference mark in lieu of rating is shown in the rating columns, it is for Official and Western Classifications.

1...............means First Class	1¾............... " One and three-fourths times 1st Class
2............... " Second Class	
3............... " Third Class	D1............... " Double 1st Class
R26............ " Rule 26 Class	2½t1............. " Two and one-half times 1st Class
4............... " Fourth Class	3t1............. " Three times 1st Class
5............... " Fifth Class	3½t1............. " Three and one-half times 1st Class
6............... " Sixth Class	4t1............. " Four times 1st Class
δ Denotes subject to rates and regulations of individual carriers.	A............... " Class A
	B............... " Class B
1¼...............means One and one-fourth times 1st Class.	C............... " Class C
	D............... " Class D
1½............... " One and one-half times 1st Class	E............... " Class E

Numbers higher than 12 (except R26 and rates in cents per car per mile on railway cars) provided for in the Classification, as amended, mean percentages of first class, except where columns in class rate tariffs are headed by such numbers, the column headed by number corresponding with the number in the Classification must be used.

SERVICE ORDERS

This Classification including supplements thereto is subject to:
Service Order Tariff No. 1-D, Agent Western Trunk Line Committee I. C. C. No. A-3949, C. T. C. No. A-1065, supplements thereto or successive issues thereof.

FIG. 6–3. Application of letters, numbers, or reference marks appearing in rating columns, Consolidated Freight Classification No. 23.

can be classified with 4,000 numbered descriptions. Figure 6–3 shows the application of letters, numbers, or reference marks appearing in the rating columns in Consolidated Freight Classification No. 23. Figure 6–4 is a sample page from the same publication.

Item	ARTICLES	Less Carload Ratings	Carload Minimum (Pounds)	Carload Ratings
11130	Blackboards (chalkboards), without stands, cloth or paper, in boxes....................	2	24,000R	R26-4
11140	Blackboards (chalkboards), without stands, metal, pulpboard or wooden, see Note 1, Item 11121, in boxes or crates, or in Packages 751 or 1013............................	3	30,000	5
11150	**BLACKS, DRY, NOT ACTIVATED, NOT DYES NOR DYESTUFFS:**			
11160	Blacks (carbon gas or oil blacks), compressed, electrostatically separated, filtered or granulated, density not less than 17 lbs. per cubic foot:			
	In barrels, boxes, double paper bags, see Rule 40, Section 10 (b), in steel cans, 5 gallons capacity or;more, or in Package 449..	2	40,000	5
	In Package 481, see Note, Item 11161..	....	60,000	5
11161	Note.—On shipments returned to point of manufacture, carload minimum weight will be 40,000 pounds.			
11170	Blacks (carbon gas or oil blacks), lamp black or vegetable black, nolbn, in double paper bags, see Rule 40, Section 10 (b) or in barrels or boxes, or in Packages 449 or 804; also CL, in cloth bags or Package 47..	1	20,000R	4
11180	Blacks, dry mineral earth or peat char, other than dry earth paint:			
	In double bags or in 4 ply paper bags...	3	30,000	5
	In barrels or boxes; also CL, in double wall paper bags............................	4	30,000	5
11190	Blacks, dry, nolbn, in barrels or boxes, or in double bags.............................	1	20,000R	4
11200	Bone, hydrocarbonated, in bags, barrels or boxes.....................................	3	36,000	5-A
11210	Bone, nojbn, drop or frankfort, in barrels, boxes or double paper bags...............	3	30,000	5
11220	Fertilizer blacks, in bags or barrels..	4	36,000	6
11230	Lamp black, filtered or electrostatically separated, compressed to a density of not less than 17 lbs. per cubic foot, in double-wall paper bags, or in barrels, boxes, or Package 900	2	40,000	5
11240	Bladders, nolbn, dried, in barrels or boxes...	2	30,000	37½-5
11250	Bladders, nolbn, pickled or salted, in barrels or boxes, in containers in crates, or in kits or pails..	3	30,000	37½-5
11260	Blasting machines, nolbn..	1	20,000R	3
11270	Bleach, laundry, nolbn, dry, in bags, barrels or boxes................................	R26-4	36,000	5
11280	Bleach assistant compounds, nolbn, dry, in double bags or in 5-ply multiple-wall paper bags, or in barrels..	R26-4	40,000	5
11290	Blocks, butchers', including butchers' cutting or chopping tables, or butchers' cutting or chopping table tops:			
	With legs exceeding 3 inches in length attached:			
	Wrapped in burlap..,	2	36,000	5-B
	LCL, in boxes or crates; CL, loose or in packages.................................	3	36,000	5-B
	With legs not exceeding 3 inches in length attached, in packages..................	3	36,000	5-B
	Without legs or bases or with legs or bases detached, LCL, in crates or wrapped, or with sides protected by paper wrapping; CL, loose or in packages.......................	R26-4	36,000	5-B
11300	Blocks, counter display, wooden, in the white, hollow, in packages; also CL, loose........	3	20,000R	R26-4
11310	Blocks, counter display, wooden, finished, covered or not covered with cloth or felt, LCL, in boxes or crates; CL, loose or in packages..	2	20,000R	R26-4
11320	Blocks, die, leatherboard or pulpboard, in crates or with surfaces protected by wooden cleats..	3	30,000	45-A
11350	Blood, dried, not human blood nor blood plasma, LCL, in bags or barrels; CL, in bulk or in packages...	3-4	40,000	6-E
11355	Blood, liquid, human, frozen or chilled, in refrigerated containers, see Note, Item 11356...	D1	10,000R	1
11356	Note.—Containers must be so constructed and sufficiently supplied with refrigerant to maintain a temperature of -12° Centigrade for a 24 hour period for frozen blood or blood plasma; or blood or blood plasma must be chilled to at least 35° Fahrenheit and containers must be supplied with refrigerant sufficient to maintain a temperature of 35° Fahrenheit for a period of seventy-two hours.			
11360	Blood, liquid, not human blood nor blood plasma:			
	In kits, or in metal cans in crates...	3	30,000	37½-5
	In barrels, or in metal cans in barrels or boxes....................................	3-4	30,000	37½-5
11365	Blood plasma:			
	Dehydrated, in boxes..	1	10,000R	2
	Liquid, frozen or chilled, in refrigerated containers, see Note, Item 11356............	4tl	10,000R	1
	Liquid, having value only for salvage, in glass bottles in boxes....................	2	15,000R	3
11370	Bluing, laundry, dry, in barrels or boxes...	2	30,000	4
11380	Bluing, laundry, liquid, in barrels or boxes..	3	30,000	5
11390	Bluing, laundry, combined with soap, washing compound or water softening compound, dry, in barrels or boxes...	4	36,000	5
11395	Boards, blocks or panels, honeycomb cellular construction, expanded, other than paper, faced or not faced, in packages...	D1	10,000R	2
11400	Boards, cutting, nolbn, in boxes or crates, or in Package 805.........................	2	30,000	4
11410	Boards or frames, building bulletin or directory, in boxes or crates..................	1	20,000R	3
11420	Boards or racks, bobbin or cone carrying, iron, or iron and wood combined, LCL, in boxes, crates, or in metal strapped bundles; CL, loose or in packages.......................	2	30,000	4
11430	Boards or racks, bobbin or cone carrying, wooden, loose or in packages................	1	16,000R	3
11440	BOATS, see Note 1, Item 11441, or PARTS NAMED:			
11441	Note 1.—Boats operated by electricity must have connecting wires between battery and motor disconnected.			
11450	Barges, flat top, open deck, steel, with or without wooden decks, loose or in packages ...	....	24,000R	40-A
11460	Barges, nolbn, SU, loose or in packages...	D1	10,000R	2
11470	Binnacles or binnacle hoods, in barrels, boxes or crates..............................	2	24,000R	R26-4

FIG. 6–4. Sample page from Consolidated Freight Classification No. 23.

In some instances, an article may be assigned two or more ratings, depending upon specified packing requirements. Less frequently, two or more carload minimum weights are specified for the same article.

A number of principles or elements that influence the classification of commodities are the following:

1. Weight per cubic foot as packed for shipment.
2. Value per pound as packed per shipment.
3. Liability to loss, damage, waste, or theft in transit.
4. Likelihood of injury to other freight to which it may come in contact.
5. Risks due to hazards of carriage.
6. Kind of container or package as bearing upon the matter of liability or risk.
7. Expense of, and care in, handling.
8. Ratings on analogous articles.
9. Fair relation of ratings as between all articles.
10. Competition between articles of different description but largely used for similar purposes.
11. Commercial conditions and units of sales.
12. Trade conditions.
13. Value of service.
14. Volume of movement for the entire country.
15. Adaptability to movement in carloads.
16. Carload minimum weights which are fair to carriers and shippers.

There are some 50 rules in the classification, the number fluctuating from time to time due to cancellations or additions to the rules. These govern the manner and form in which carriers will receive commodities, as well as the way in which they shall be packed and prepared for shipment. Some of these rules have been formulated with the co-operation of shippers, and they give protection to the shippers as well as to the carriers. They are important, and the principles contained therein should be mastered by the user of the classification. This is desirable, for the user can look up ratings for individual commodities without referring each time to about 50 rules. These rules are discussed in the chapter which follows.

Uniform Freight Classification

In 1939, the Interstate Commerce Commission instituted an investigation concerning the uniformity of classification.[4] One phase of this investigation, Docket No. 28310, involved the Consolidated Freight Classification and considered the lawfulness of descriptions of articles and carload minimum weights and ratings. It embraced the entire United States. Docket No. 28300 was an investigation of the lawfulness of interstate class rates established by ratings in the four rail classifications and the resulting charges between all points in the United States, except the Mountain-Pacific Territory and transcontinental class rates. The Commission has issued a number of findings in this extensive investigation.

The Uniform Freight Classification was in process of development for a period of more than six years, and there were over forty public hearings. The recognized classification principles were followed where exceptions ratings[5] were not a factor to be considered. However, the existence of

---

[4] ICC, Dockets No. 28300 and No. 28310.
[5] Exceptions ratings, which are exceptions to classifications, are discussed later in this chapter.

exceptions ratings was often a controlling factor on some important commodity groups, such as fresh fruits and vegetables, grain, grain products, salt, sugar, meats, and packing house products, as well as others. The carload class ratings were established sufficiently high so as not to interfere with the commodity rate adjustments on which the traffic moves. If the uniform carload ratings on some of these commodities were one class lower, it would have resulted in the class rates being lower than the commodity rates[6] in some instances but not in others. Except in very few instances, class rates do not apply on any of the commodities listed above. Thus, it does not make much difference what the uniform carload ratings are, so long as they do not interfere with the rate structure on which the traffic moves.

Where commodities moved primarily within a territory, the prevailing level of rates influenced the determination of uniform ratings. The level of rates in the South had much to do with the establishment of the uniform ratings on items which principally move in or from the South, such as naval stores and creosote oil. The prevailing level of rates to and within the Western Territory on items which move primarily within that area, such as agricultural implements and oil-well equipment, influenced the determination of the uniform ratings.

Because of the difficulties in classification ratings in violation of Section 3 of the Interstate Commerce Act, the Commission, in 1945, ordered that a uniform classification be prepared, with 30 numbered classes, ranging from Class 400 to Class 13. Each of these classes would represent a percentage of Class 100, or what was formerly Class 1. The order of the Commission prescribed that the uniform classification, when combined with a class rate scale based on mileage, should provide a basis for classification that is reasonable and just, nondiscriminatory and nonprejudicial.

After considerable litigation, the rail carriers filed with the Interstate Commerce Commission Uniform Freight Classification No. 1, which became effective on May 30, 1952. Dockets No. 28300 and No. 28310 were heard on the same record, and the establishment of the interstate class rates under Docket No. 28300 will be subsequently described in the chapter on rates. The Uniform Freight Classification was intended for nationwide application. However, the investigation of class rates in the companion Docket No. 28300 did not cover class rates in Mountain-Pacific Territory, or to or from that territory, so that the Consolidated Freight Classification continued to be used in the Mountain-Pacific Territory and on transcontinental traffic to and from that territory.

The Commission—as a result of the investigation in Docket No. 30416, *Class Rates, Mountain-Pacific Territory*, and Docket No. 30660, *Class*

---

[6] Commodity rates are generally lower than class rates and have more limited application. They are explained fully in the chapter on rates.

Rates, Transcontinental Rail 1950, which became effective in 1956—prescribed a class rate basis which was subject to the Uniform Freight Classification, so that it now has nationwide application. The Commission permitted certain truck competitive rates to remain in effect in the Mountain-Pacific Territory, with the result that within this territory, the Consolidated Freight Classification continues to be used. It is also used in connection with rates to and from Canada, certain freight forwarder tariffs, and on export-import traffic when the carriers have not converted such tariffs to the Docket No. 28300 class rate scale. The effect, then, is that the Consolidated Freight Classification has limited application.

In determination of the less-carload ratings, special attention was given to the principle that there should be an appropriate spread between carload and less-carload ratings. In many instances, the existence of an exceptions rating throughout the territories on carloads, with no exceptions rating on less carload, and vice versa, resulted in a spread either too little or too great. In so far as possible, such situations have been corrected in the Uniform Freight Classification.

The spread between less-carload and carload ratings has usually varied by one class or more, dependent upon the individual article shipped. Two items chosen from the Uniform Freight Classification indicate the differences:

Item	ARTICLES	Less Carload Ratings	Carload Minimum (Pounds)	Carload Ratings
13350	Bones, human, noibn, prepaid in barrels or boxes.	200	20,000R	100
	ALUMINUM:			
5550	Extrusions, noibn, loose (LCL, only if weighing each 25 pounds or over) or in packages..................	85	30,000	50

It is interesting to note how the Uniform Freight Classification compares with the Consolidated Freight Classification on less-carload and carload ratings. The average of all less-carload ratings in Consolidated Freight Classification No. 19, effective February 28, 1950, to October 14, 1951, was 87.07. The average of all less-carload ratings in Uniform Freight Classification No. 1 was 89.96, or practically the same. The average carload rating in Consolidated Freight Classification No. 19 is 50.40, as compared to average carload rating in the Uniform Freight Classification of 49.31. Table 6–2 (p. 130) shows the figures in detail.

Many people, upon their first introduction to transportation classifications, have felt that it was somewhat unusual that under the provisions of the Consolidated Freight Classification, the high-class freight started with

TABLE 6–2

COMPARISON OF LESS-CARLOAD RATINGS

	Less Carload	Carload
Consolidated Freight Classification No. 19:*		
Official	87.42	49.66
Southern	86.19	50.56
Western	87.59	51.05
All three	87.07	50.40
Uniform Freight Classification No. 1	89.96	49.31

* While Consolidated Freight Classification No. 23 is in effect, the average ratings of Consolidated Freight Classification No. 19 used in this table would result in no noticeable difference in the average ratings than if Classification No. 23 had been used.

Class 1, which is 100 per cent, and then the numbers went on up, such as Class 2, which is 85 per cent of Class 1, Class 3, Class 4, etc., while each of these classes constituted a lower rating than the preceding class, which meant that the transportation charge per unit was less for each succeeding higher number. The Uniform Freight Classification contains a change in this system, in that as the numbers decrease, the rating decreases also. Thus, the highest number, Class 400, will indicate the highest rating, whereas Class 85 is 85 per cent of Class 100.

The rail Uniform Freight Classification contains the 30 classes prescribed by the Interstate Commerce Commission. These are as follows: Classes 400, 300, 250, 200, 175, 150, 125, 100, 92.5, 85, 77.5, 70, 65, 60, 55, 50, 45, 40, 37.5, 35, 32.5, 30, 27.5, 25, 22.5, 20, 17.5, 16, 14.5, and 13. In addition, the Commission has authorized the use of Class 110, so there are a total of 31 classes which have been used since May 30, 1952, when Uniform Freight Classification No. 1 became effective. There is but a single rating for application on an article; whereas in the Consolidated Freight Classification, there are one or two ratings, depending upon territorial application. The arrangement of the contents of the Uniform Freight Classification is similar to that of the Consolidated Freight Classification.

The ratings shown in the columns opposite the separate descriptions of articles of the Uniform Freight Classification, and as amended, are used in connection with class rate tariffs which specify that class rates therein are governed by the Uniform Freight Classification. Number 13 and higher, except rates in cents per car-mile on railway cars, provided for in the Uniform Freight Classification, and as amended, mean the ratings assigned to the articles described and refer to columns in class rate tariffs headed by the same numbers.

Figure 6–5 is an explanation of the abbreviations and reference marks contained in Uniform Freight Classification No. 6. A sample listing from this classification is shown in Figure 6–6.

A comparison of articles as contained in both Consolidated Freight Classification No. 23 and Uniform Freight Classification No. 6, shown in Figure 6–7, indicates the simplicity of the latter.

EXPLANATION OF ABBREVIATIONS AND REFERENCE MARKS

AQ..............means any quantity.
CL..............means carload.
COD...........means collect on delivery.
DBA...........means doing business as.
KD.............means knocked down.
Lbs.............means pounds.
LCL............means less than carload.
Min. wt.........means minimum weight.

noibn ....means not otherwise indexed by name, except as to articles listed in the index prefixed with reference mark (*), and not rated more specifically in this Classification as amended, see Note.

RS or L.........means and other articles classified or rated the same or lower.

SU..............means set up.

R—Against carload minimum denotes subject to Rule 34.
    "   rating denotes reduction in rating.
    "   description denotes reduction by reason of change in description.
    "   carload minimum weight denotes reduction in carload minimum weight.
    "   rate or charge denotes reduction in rate or charge.
    "   rating denotes increase in rating.
    "   description denotes increase by reason of change in description.
    "   carload minimum weight denotes increase in carload minimum weight.
    "   rate or charge denotes increase in rate or charge.
★ Denotes new rule, or portion thereof, new item or new package.
    "   changes in wording which result in neither increases nor reductions in charges.
⊕CL rating is not applicable to Illinois intrastate traffic.
☐(with number (or letter, or number and letter) enclosed) Reissued from supplement bearing the number (or letter, or number and letter) enclosed within the square. See Rule 55.

#Rating will not apply on traffic moving between or destined to points in the following states:
Connecticut............All points.
Delaware...............All points.
District of Columbia....All points.
Indiana.................Rating not applicable on traffic moving between or destined to points in Indiana, except rating will apply on traffic moving between or destined to points in Indiana on C&EI, CMStP&P, Southern, L&N, IC and AW&W.
Kentucky...............Rating not applicable on Kentucky intrastate traffic nor on traffic moving between or destined to points in Kentucky on C&O, M&NF or N&W. Rating will apply on all other traffic moving between or destined to points in Kentucky.
Maine..................All points.
Maryland...............All points.
Massachusetts..........All points.
Michigan...............Rating will not apply on traffic moving between or destined to points on lower peninsula. Rating will apply on traffic moving between or destined to all other points in Michigan.
New Hampshire.........All points.
New Jersey.............All points.
New York..............All points.
North Carolina........Rating applies on all traffic moving between or destined to points in North Carolina, except rating will not apply on traffic moving between or destined to points in North Carolina on Abingdon Branch of N&W Ry. (Hurricane Branch to West Jefferson, inclusive).
Ohio...................All points.
Pennsylvania...........All points.
Rhode Island...........All points.
Tennessee..............Rating applies on all traffic moving between or destined to points in Tennessee, except rating will not apply from or to Bristol, Tenn. via N&W Ry.
Vermont................All points.
Virginia................Rating will not apply on traffic moving between or destined to points in Virginia, except rating will apply on traffic moving between or destined to points in Virginia on A&D Ry., ACL RR., D&W Ry., L&N RR., Interstate RR., SAL Ry., Southern Ry. and N&W Ry., stations Clarkton, Va. to Denniston, Va., inclusive, and Starkey, Va. to Ridgeway, Va., inclusive.
West Virginia...........All points.
Such traffic will be subject to rates and regulations of individual carriers.

Note.—Pending the amendment of tariffs governed hereby, the abbreviation "noibn" (not otherwise indexed by name) appearing in such tariffs will be read as meaning that the description of which it is a part applies on articles included in the same "noibn" description in the Uniform Classification, subject to any qualification shown in connection with the present description.

FIG. 6–5. Explanation of abbreviations and reference marks contained in Uniform Freight Classification No. 6.

Item	ARTICLES	Less Carload Ratings	Carload Minimum (Pounds)	Carload Ratings
	ADVERTISING MATTER—Concluded:			
2630	Displays, brick or tile facing or tile mounted on panels, prepaid, in boxes or crates............	70	24,000R	55
2640	Displays, consisting of empty bottles or cans in pyramids of six, prepaid, in boxes...........	92½	24,000R	55
2650	Displays, dummy articles, such as imitation bacon, butter squares, hams or sausage, prepaid, in boxes or crates..	100	20,000R	70
2660	Displays, figures or images, rubber, other than hollow outdoor, prepaid, in boxes or crates....	100	20,000R	70
2670	Displays, itinerant, consisting of portable material used in furnishing and equipping display windows for temporary merchandise displays, but not including the merchandise displayed or advertised, prepaid, in boxes..	110	20,000R	70
2680	Displays, store or window, paper or paperboard, prepaid:			
	Not flat nor folded flat, in packages.......................................	150	24,000R	55
	Flat or folded flat, in packages...	77½	24,000R	55
2690	Fans, advertising, paper or pulpboard, with pulpboard or wooden handles, in boxes..........	85	24,000R	55
2705	Agate, in the rough, in bags, barrels or boxes..	85	24,000R	55
2710	**AGRICULTURAL IMPLEMENTS, HAND, OR PARTS NAMED:**			
2720	Agricultural implement parts, hand, noibn:			
2730	Iron or steel, in packages...	85	24,000R	45
2740	Wooden:			
	Finished, in packages...	100	24,000R	45
	In the white, in packages; also CL, loose................................	60	36,000	30
2750	Cleaning, grading or separating machines (fanning mills), grain or seed:			
	SU, or partially taken apart:			
	Loose or on skids..	200	12,000R	70
	LCL, ends, tops and sides protected by crating, drums detached and in boxes or crates; CL, in packages..	150	12,000R	70
	LCL, in boxes or crates, or ends, tops and sides protected by crating, drums, dust hoods or wind chutes, fan boxes and sieves removed and secured within main frame; CL, in packages	100	12,000R	70
	Completely KD, in boxes or crates..	85	24,000R	45
2760	Cultivators, not wheeled, in packages..	77½	24,000R	45
2770	Cultivators, wheeled:			
	SU, loose...	200	24,000R	45
	SU, in boxes or crates...	150	24,000R	45
	KD, in packages..	77½	24,000R	45
2780	Cutters, feed:			
	SU, loose or in packages..	100	24,000R	45
	KD, in packages..	70	24,000R	45
2790	Cutters, seed potato, in packages..	85	24,000R	45
2800	Cutters, weed, in packages..	85	24,000R	45
2810	Distributors, fertilizer, wheeled:			
	SU, loose..:..	200	24,000R	45
	SU, in boxes or crates...	150	24,000R	45
	KD, in packages..	77½	24,000R	45
2820	Drills or seeders, wheeled:			
	SU, loose...	200	24,000R	45
	SU, in boxes or crates...	150	24,000R	45
	KD, in packages..	77½	24,000R	45
2830	Fingers, grain cradle, in bundles or in boxes or crates	85	24,000R	45
2840	Forks, metal tined, in packages..	77½	24,000R	45
2850	Forks, wooden tined, in packages..	85	24,000R	45
2860	Grain cradle bodies (cradles without scythes or snaths):			
	In bundles..	150	24,000R	45
	In boxes or crates...	85	24,000R	45
2870	Grain cradles:			
	SU, knives wrapped with burlap or straw rope, in bundles...................	300	24,000R	45
	KD, in bundles..	150	24,000R	45
	KD, in boxes or crates...	100	24,000R	45
2880	Heads, fork, hoe, manure hook, potato hook or rake:			
	In bundles..	77½	24,000R	45
	In barrels, boxes or crates...	60	24,000R	45
2890	Hoes, not wheeled, in packages..	77½	24,000R	45
2900	Hoes, wheeled:			
	SU, loose...	200	24,000R	45
	SU, in boxes or crates...	150	24,000R	45
	KD, in packages..	77½	24,000R	45
2910	Hooks, grass, in packages...	85	24,000R	45
2920	Hooks, manure or potato, in packages..	77½	24,000R	45
2930	Knives, cane, corn or hay, in packages...	85	24,000R	45
2940	Mulchers, wheeled:			
	SU, loose...	200	24,000R	45
	SU, in boxes or crates...	150	24,000R	45
	KD, in packages..	77½	24,000R	45
2950	Pea hullers:			
	Loose or on skids...	150	12,000R	70
	LCL, in boxes or crates; CL, in packages..................................	100	12,000R	70
2960	Peanut pickers (threshers):			
	Loose or on skids...	100	24,000R	45
	In boxes or crates...	85	24,000R	45

FIG. 6–6.   Sample listing from Uniform Freight Classification No. 6.

CONSOLIDATED FREIGHT CLASSIFICATION NUMBER 23

Item	ARTICLES	Less Carload Ratings	Carload Minimum (Pounds)	Carload Ratings
86280	Shoddy, silk:			
	In bags or boxes, or in bales not machine pressed or compressed to less than 12½ lbs. per cubic foot....	1	10,000R	2
	In bales compressed to 12½ lbs. or more per cubic foot....	2	30,000	R26-4-4
86290	Shoe horns, iron or steel, in boxes....	3	30,000	45-5-A
86300	Shoe horns, other than iron or steel, in boxes....	1	20,000R	3
86310	Shoe polishers, noibn, in barrels or boxes....	1	20,000R	3
86320	Shoe scraper and brush combined, in barrels or boxes....	2	24,000R	R26-4-4
86330	Shoe shining outfits, each outfit in separate carton, in boxes....	2	24,000R	R26-4-4
86340	Shutters, engine radiator, steel, automatic, in boxes or crates....	1	24,000R	3
86350	Shutters, engine radiator, steel, other than automatic, in boxes or crates....	2	30,000	4
86360	Sign fixtures, roller car route, metal, KD, in boxes....	2	24,000R	R26-1-4
86370	Signals, road traffic, light flashing:			
	SU or with head detached and packed in cabinet, in boxes or crates; also CL, loose, braced in car....	1	24,000R	3-4-4
	KD, loose or in packages....	2	30,000	4-5-A
86380	Signals or signs, road traffic or vehicle, reflector, in boxes or crates....	2	24,000R	R26-4-4
86390	Signs, cast iron, in boxes or crates....	3	30,000	4

UNIFORM FREIGHT CLASSIFICATION NUMBER 6

86280	Shoddy, silk:			
	In bags or boxes, or in bales not machine pressed or compressed to less than 12½ lbs. per cubic foot....	125	10,000R	85
	In bales compressed to 12½ lbs. or more per cubic foot....	85	30,000	55
86290	Shoe horns, iron or steel, in boxes....	70	30,000	45
86300	Shoe horns, other than iron or steel, in boxes....	100	20,000R	70
86310	Shoe polishers, noibn, in barrels or boxes....	100	24,000R	70
86320	Shoe scraper and brush combined, in barrels or boxes....	85	24,000R	55
86330	Shoe shining outfits, each outfit in separate carton, in boxes....	85	24,000R	55
86340	Shutters, engine radiator, steel, automatic, in boxes or crates....	100	24,000R	70
86350	Shutters, engine radiator, steel, other than automatic, in boxes or crates....	85	30,000	55
86360	Sign fixtures, roller car route, metal, KD, in boxes....	92½	30,000	55
86370	Signals, road traffic, light flashing:			
	SU or with head detached and packed in cabinet, in boxes or crates; also CL, loose, braced in car	100	24,000R	55
	KD, loose or in packages	85	30,000	45
86380	Signals or signs, road traffic or vehicle, reflector, in boxes or crates....	85	24,000R	55
86390	Signs, cast iron, in boxes or crates....	70	30,000	45

FIG. 6–7. Comparison of articles contained in both Consolidated Freight Classification No. 23 and Uniform Freight Classification No. 6.

Uniform Freight Classification No. 1 contained more than 23,000 ratings. There were some 10,270 LCL ratings, 52 any-quantity ratings, 120 mixed-carload ratings, and 12,938 carload ratings, with approximately 8,000 commodity descriptions.

Since the two rail classifications embrace all territories and there are certain exceptions to the classification, what is the correct classification or exception applicable for a given shipment? The title page of the tariff publishing the rate will refer to the classification and/or exceptions tariff which governs. This is a requirement of the Interstate Commerce Commission, and a tariff is not governed by a classification or exception unless this is indicated.

In addition to rail carriers which participate in the Consolidated and Uniform Freight Classifications, there are water and motor carriers, as well as freight forwarders, which are participants.

MOTOR

Upon the passage of the Motor Carrier Act in 1935, motor carriers subject to the act had to comply with one of the provisions which specified that motor carriers were to publish, post, and file classifications and tariffs.

In establishing classification ratings, the characteristics of the commodities which must be considered are generally as follows:

1. Shipping weight per cubic foot.
2. Liability to damage.
3. Liability to damage other commodities with which it is transported.
4. Perishability.
5. Liability to spontaneous combustion or explosion.
6. Susceptibility to theft.
7. Value per pound in comparison with other articles.
8. Ease or difficulty in loading or unloading.
9. Stowability.
10. Excessive weight.
11. Excessive length.
12. Care or attention necessary in loading and transporting.
13. Trade conditions.
14. Value of service.
15. Competition with other commodities transported.[1]

National Motor Freight Classification

There were a number of motor freight classifications filed with the Commission responsive to the act, but the one with the most general application and most widely used is the National Motor Freight Classification. The original issue of the National Motor Freight Classification, which became effective on April 1, 1936, consisted of two publications, the National Motor Freight Classification LTL–1, which contained less-truckload rates, and National Motor Freight Classification VR–1, which contained volume ratings. These two volumes were combined into one tariff in the next and succeeding reissues up to the present time.

An analysis of the original National Motor Freight Classification indicates that the motor carriers virtually adopted the railroads' Consolidated Freight Classification. The articles contained in the railroads' classification which ordinarily would not be expected to move by motor carrier were excluded from the National Motor Freight Classification. However, the great bulk of the articles contained carried the same ratings, the same minimum weights, and similar descriptions. Two primary reasons prompted such a complete adoption of the railroads' classification: (1) to be competitive with railroads and (2) to meet the requirements which the Motor Carrier Act imposed in regard to filing a classification by a specified date. The original form, then, of the National Motor Freight Classification and the Consolidated Freight Classification were very similar.

When the railroads established the Uniform Freight Classification, the motor carriers created their second classification which was similar to the second rail classification. For more than eight years, there were two

---

[1] *Motor Carrier Rates in New England,* 47 MCC 657, 660–1 (1948).

National Motor Freight Classifications similar to the two rail classifications. On December 31, 1961, the National Motor Freight Classification which was competitive with the rail Consolidated Freight Classification was canceled so that NMFC series A now has general application. The classes in the National Motor Freight Classification are as follows: 500, 400, 350, 300, 250, 200, 175, 150, 125, 110, 100, 92.5, 85, 77.5, 70, 65, 60, 55, 50, 45, 40, 37.5, 35—a total of 23 in all.

The contents of National Motor Freight Classification No. A–7 are as follows:

> Title page.
> List of commissions with which this classification is filed.
> Table of contents.
> Plan of contents.
> Cancellation notice.
> Participating interstate carriers.
> Participating carriers (under Federal Maritime Commission jurisdiction).
> Participating intrastate carriers.
> Index to articles.
> Index to rules.
> Rules and regulations.
> Bills of lading.
> Classification of articles.
> Specifications for numbered packages.
> List of provisions subject to expiration dates.
> Explanation of abbreviations and reference marks.

The classification uses numbers for ratings which are found under two headings of "LTL" and "TL." Originally, the "Volume" designation was used in order to be competitive with the rail classification, inasmuch as the minimum weights in the rail classification in some instances were so high that two trucks were required to move the commodities; and if it were designated as a truckload rating, then it might be limited to just the truckload. With the development of increased size of vans, the heading was changed to "TL." The truckload minimum weight factor is in the middle column. Motor carriers have used "NOI," which means commodities not more specifically described, rather than the "NOIBN" used by railroads.

The National Motor Freight Classification, since it was patterned after the rail classification, was basically a competitive classification, although many of the classification factors that normally would have been considered in the classification of articles were ignored. Thus, over 90 per cent of the entries in the National Motor Freight Classification were identical with those of the rail classification. The motor carriers soon found that many light and bulky articles would have to carry higher ratings than those contained in the National Motor Freight Classification, or a rule would have to be provided in the motor carriers' exceptions tariffs to assure adequate revenue on these commodities. Since the pub-

LIST OF PROVISIONS SUBJECT TO EXPIRATION DATES

The following provisions of this Classification are currently published subjected to reference marks (explained below) which provide a date with which the application of such provisions will expire, unless sooner cancelled, changed or extended:

Rule No.	Reference mark used therewith	Rule No.	Reference mark used therewith	Item No.	Reference mark used therewith	Item No.	Reference mark used therewith
Rule 110, Sec. 2 (b)	(A3)	Rule 260, Note 7	(B1)	46382 58776	(A2)	85680 85682	(B3)
Rule 260, Note 6	(A3)	Rule 290, Note 2	(A2)	67402 72006	(A2)	155253 155256	(B2)

EXPLANATION OF ABBREVIATIONS AND REFERENCE MARKS

Abbreviation	EXPLANATION
AQ	Any quantity.
Avdp.	Avoirdupois.
B&SG	Browne & Sharpe gauge.
BWG	Birmingham wire gauge.
COD	Collect on delivery.
Cont.	Continued.
cu. ft.	Cubic foot.
d/b/a	Doing business as.
E	East.
etc.	Et cetera (and other things, or the rest; and so forth).
F	Fahrenheit.
ft.	Foot.
I. C. C.	Interstate Commerce Commission.
i. e.	that is.
incl.	Inclusive.
in.	Inch.
KD	Knocked down.
lbs.	Pounds.
LTL	Less than truckload.
min. wt.	Minimum weight.
NMFC	National Motor Freight Classification.
NOI	Not more specifically described herein.
oz.	Ounces.
RSorL	Rated the same or lower.
r. p. m.	Revolutions per minute.
S	South.
(S)	Applies only as "South" rating (see Rule 70).
Sec.	Section.
sq.	Square.
sq. ft.	Square foot.
sq. in.	Square inch.
SU	Set up.
TL	Truckload.
t/d/b/a	Trading and doing business as.
U. S.	United States.
U.S.S.G.	United States standard gauge.
W	West.
wt.	Weight.
Vol.	Volume.
vs.	versus.

Reference Mark	EXPLANATION
↓	Indicates reduction.
↑	Indicates increase.
↕	Indicates change in wording which results in neither increases nor reductions.
*	Indicates new item.
o	degree.
♦	"East" classes (ratings) in this Classification are applicable on Wisconsin intrastate traffic and only insofar as they apply on less than truckload traffic for account of carriers parties hereto who have filed tariffs with the Public Service Commission of Wisconsin.
Ø	Applicable only on traffic having origin, destination and entire transportation in the following territory, viz.: Points in Illinois, Louisiana (west of Mississippi River only), upper peninsula of Michigan, Minnesota, Wisconsin, and all points west of the Mississippi River. All other traffic is subject to rates and regulations of individual carriers.
%	Indicates per cent.
v	Indicates mixed volume or mixed truckload entry.
@	Except as noted.
Ⓦ	Indicates water carrier.
Ⓡ	Indicates railroad.
Ⓕ	Indicates freight forwarder.
(MW)	Minimum weight factor, see Rule 115.
(A2)	Expires with December 21, 1963, unless sooner cancelled, changed or extended.
(A3)	Expires with April 1, 1964, unless sooner cancelled, changed or extended.
(B1)	Expires with July 1, 1964, unless sooner cancelled, changed or extended.
(B2)	Expires with September 30, 1964, unless sooner cancelled, changed or extended.
(B3)	Expires with January 31, 1965, unless sooner cancelled, changed or extended.

—finis—

FIG. 6–8. Explanation of abbreviations and reference marks used in National Motor Freight Classification No. A–7.

lication of the original National Motor Freight Classification, both of these courses of action have been followed.

An example of a light and bulky article is hassocks. Originally, hassocks were filled, and they weighed between 10 and 14 pounds per cubic foot; but now, many hassocks are manufactured hollow and provide storage space, thus weighing from 3 to 8 pounds per cubic foot. This is

Item	ARTICLES	CLASSES (Ratings) LTL	TL	Min. Wt. Factor (See Rule 115)
70090	Flavoring Compounds, lard or lard substitute, in bags, barrels, boxes pails or tubs.....	85	45	30.2
70110	Flax noils, in machine pressed bales.........	77½	40	36.2
70130	Flax Seed (Linseed), ground, in bags, barrels or boxes................	70	37½	36.2
70150	Flax Shives, LTL, in bags; TL, loose or in packages............	70	35	30.2
70170	Flax Straw, not threshed, in bales or bundles.........	85	35	24.2
70180	Flax Straw, Threshed, in bales.........	65	35	24.2
70200	Flax Straw or Hemp Stalks, partially decorticated:			
Sub 1	In bales compressed to less than 18 lbs. per cubic foot.......	70	50	20.2
Sub 2	In bales compressed to 18 lbs. per cubic foot or over...............	65	45	30.2
70220	Flintstone linings or Silica linings (Silex Linings), LTL, in boxes or crates; TL, loose or in packages....	50	35	50.2
70240	Flintstone, Silica or Quartzite pebbles, LTL, in bags, barrels or boxes; TL, loose or in packages........	50	35	50.2
70260	Floats, net, seine or lifeline:			
Sub 1	Aluminum, in bags or boxes...........	125	85	12.2
Sub 2	Cork, in bags or boxes........	300	300	AQ
Sub 3	Plastic, other than cellular or expanded plastic, in bags or boxes......	150	100	10.2
Sub 4	Wooden, in bags or boxes........	85	55	20.2
70270	Floats or Toys, water sports, cellular or expanded plastic or foam rubber, combined or not combined with other materials, see Note, item 70272, in packages.........	300	300	AQ
70272	Note—Applies on articles used by children or adults for play, instruction or safety.			
70300	Floats, stainless steel, chromium plated, steel, or monel metal, NOI, in boxes........	100	70	15.2
70340	Flocks, Cotton:			
Sub 1	In bales not machine pressed or in bags having a density of less than 20 lbs. per cu. ft..	100	70	16.2
Sub 2	In machine pressed bales, or in bags having a density of 20 lbs. or more per cu. ft......	55	35	36.2
70360	Flocks, rayon or synthetic fibre, NOI, in bags, bales or boxes having a density of:			
Sub 1	12 lbs. or less per cu. ft........	100	85	12.2
Sub 2	Over 12 lbs. per cu. ft..............	70	50	20.2
70380	Flocks, Hair or Wool:			
Sub 1	In bags, boxes or bales not compressed........	100	70	12.2
Sub 2	In compressed bales........	85	50	24.2
70500	**FLOOR COVERINGS OR RELATED ARTICLES:**			
70540	Carpet lining, felted paper pulp, in bales or boxes..............	100	70	20.2
70560	Carpet-lining, grass, in packages......	77½	45	24.2
70580	Carpet lining, paper, including felt paper, in packages:			
Sub 1	Indented........	65	35	30.2
Sub 2	Plain........	55	35	40.2
70600	Carpet or Rug Cushions, Cushioning, Lining, Pads or Padding, NOI, other than foam, cellular, expanded or sponge plastic or rubber, LTL, in packages; also TL, loose..	100	55	20.2
70640	Carpet or rug cushions, cushioning or lining, cotton, jute and glass fibres combined, with or without binder, in cartons or in wrapped bales or wrapped rolls........	300	85	10.2
70650	Carpet or Rug Cushions, Cushioning or Lining, or Floor Surfacing Underlayment, consisting of felt paper not less than .030 inch thick combined with foam rubber or cellular or expanded plastic not exceeding ¼ inch thick, in boxes or wrapped rolls....	85	55	20.2
70660	Carpet or Rug Cushions, Cushioning or Lining, sponge rubber, in wrapped rolls....	77½	45	30.2
70680	Carpets, Carpeting, Carpet Remnants or Rugs, soft surface (pile) fabric, power machine tufted or power loom woven, in cloth covered bales or rolls, in boxes or in Package 413.........	100	70	18.1
70700	Carpets, Carpeting, Mats, Matting or Rugs, floor, other than carpet or rug cushions, cushioning, lining, pads or padding:			
70720	Animal hair, wool, jute fibre, hemp fibre or rayon fibre, separate or combined, felted, not woven nor tufted, with burlap base, with or without coating or binder of latex or plastic, in packages....	85	55	24.2
70730	Cloth combined with foam rubber not exceeding ⅜ inch thick, in wrapped bales or rolls or in boxes......	100	70	18.1
70750	Fabric, woven paper, combined with cellular or expanded plastic or rubber not exceeding ⅜ inch thick, in packages........	85	55	24.2
70780	Grass, Straw, Twisted Paper Fibre, Reed, or Fibre NOI other than cotton, wool, silk or synthetic fibre; other than with pile surface, in packages.................	85	45	24.1
70800	Iron, steel or wire, in packages...........	77½	45	30.2
70823	Mats, fibreboard wallboard, in boxes.........	77½	45	30.2
70825	Mats, floor, made from old rubber tires and wire combined, in packages...........	65	35	30.2
70829	Mats, wood (not parquet flooring), in packages........	77½	45	30.2
70830	Mats or Matting, Cocoa or Coir Fibre or Yarn, woven, with or without pile surface, in packages........	85	55	24.2
70833	Mats or Matting, other than cloth, NOI, other than foam, cellular or expanded plastic or foam rubber, in packages........	100	70	18.2
70840	Metal combined with fibre, leather, rubber other than foam rubber or wood, NOI, LTL, in packages; also TL, loose........	77½	45	30.2
70910	Wood (parquet flooring), in packages.........	70	35	30.2
70912	Note—TL provisions also apply in mixed TL with not to exceed 10% of the weight on which the charges are assessed of floor tile cement, linoleum cement, floor wax, paper or paper felt carpet lining, steel linoleum rollers, caulking compounds, NOI, lacquer or varnish.			

For explanation of abbreviations and reference marks, see last page of this tariff.

FIG. 6–9. Sample page from National Motor Freight Classification No. A–7.

an example of a commodity which has changed over the years and is clearly in the light and bulky category today. Therefore, motor carriers which have sought to carry the modern hassocks at the ratings prevailing in the past have found that the trailer space is filled but they have very little weight and only limited revenue.

As was the case with railroads, the Commission has sought to achieve uniformity in motor classification and issued, in Docket MC–C–150, an order placing motor carriers on notice to effect uniformity of the National Motor Freight Classification. Unlike Dockets No. 28300 and No. 28310, the Commission did not issue a final order in the motor classification Docket No. MC–C–150.

The motor carriers revised the National Motor Freight Classification along the lines of Uniform Freight Classification No. 1 of the railroads. During 1963, there were over 5,000 motor carrier participants in the classification, and it is used in all of the rate territories except New England.

A tabulation of the ratings in National Motor Freight Classification No. A–6, including supplements, shows there are 11,518 LTL ratings and 14,817 truckload or volume ratings. The ratings in the classification range from 500 to 35. Over 50 per cent of the LTL ratings are Class 70 through Class 100; the lowest is Class 50, and the highest Class 300. More than 50 per cent of the truckload ratings are Class 35 through Class 55; the lowest is Class 35, and the highest Class 350.

Figure 6–8 shows an explanation of abbreviations and reference marks used in National Motor Freight Classification No. A–6; and Figure 6–9 is a page from that classification. The classification contains approximately 10,000 commodity descriptions. The National Motor Freight Classification is competitive with the Uniform Freight Classification. The following example, taken from National Motor Freight Classification No. A–6 and Uniform Freight Classification No. 6, indicates that the same description and the same ratings are used in both.

NATIONAL MOTOR FREIGHT CLASSIFICATION A-6

Item	ARTICLES	CLASSES (Ratings)		Min. Wt. Factor (See Rule 115)
		LTL	TL	
21480	Barber Poles, Revolving, metal and glass combined, in boxes or crates..................	100	55	20.2
21400	Barber Poles, other than Revolving, in boxes or crates...................................	85	55	20.2

UNIFORM FREIGHT CLASSIFICATION 6

Item	ARTICLES	Less Carload Ratings	Carload Minimum (Pounds)	Carload Ratings
9930	Barber poles, revolving, metal and glass combined, in boxes or crates........................	100	20,000R	55
9940	Barber poles, other than revolving, in boxes or crates..	85	20,000R	55

New England Classification

Although there are a number of individual classifications other than the National Motor Freight Classification, the establishment of the New England classification should be explained. The National Motor Freight Classification was originally used in the New England area, but many carriers felt that certain local conditions warranted the establishment of a classification emphasizing the element of shipping density.[8]

For shipments within New England, the Coordinated Motor Freight Classification is used. The rating determined by density is used as a base; and if there are commodities with unfavorable transportation characteristics, such as fragility or susceptibility to theft, the rating assigned will be one or two classes higher than the shipping densities would otherwise warrant. Certain traffic which is competitive with railroads and yet is desirable motor carrier traffic is assigned lower ratings than would be the case were shipping density of the article entirely relied upon to establish the rating. Ratings do not differentiate between less-truckload and volume shipments but apply for any weight unit. One of the objectives of the Coordinated Motor Freight Classification is to permit motor carriers to earn about the same revenue per truckload.

The classes established were numbered from 1 to 5. The most important factor in classification consideration, that of density, is shown in the tabulation below:[9]

Rating	Shipping Weight per Cubic Foot (Pounds)
Class 1	3 to 5
Class 2	5 to 10
Class 3	10 to 15
Class 4	15 to 20
Class 5	20 and over

There are also two multiples of Class 1 in the current issue of this classification applicable on those articles having a density of less than 3 pounds per cubit foot. These are: $1\frac{1}{2}$ times 1; and $2\frac{1}{2}$ times 1. No definite line is drawn between these two, but when density is this low, a classification committee decides each item on its own merits.

WATER

There are a number of water carriers engaging in domestic water transportation which participate in both the Consolidated and Uniform Freight classifications, as well as the motor carrier classification. Some steamship companies engaging in foreign transportation also have classifications.

AIR

Although at one time, air carriers made use of a freight classification, they abandoned this system and, at the present time, have not re-established it.

[8] *Motor Carrier Rates in New England*, 47 MCC 657, 661 (1948).
[9] *Ibid.*

FREIGHT FORWARDERS

Surface freight forwarders participate in the rail and motor classifications and do not have classifications, as such, of their own.

REA EXPRESS

REA Express has the *Official Express Classification* in which goods are classified into three general classes, as well as several special classes. First class includes all goods not otherwise classified or rated. Second class includes articles of food and drink, except alcoholic liquor, and the rates are generally 75 per cent of first class. Third class covers certain printed material, such as circulars and books. To handle shipments of valuable articles, such as securities and checks, there is a money classification.

The *Official Express Classification* is somewhat simpler than other carrier classifications. It contains rules which describe the application of rates and ratings as well as rules governing packaging, refrigeration, labeling, shipping or perishables, and similar matters.

CLASSIFICATION COMMITTEE PROCEDURE

Rail

The first rail classification committees were composed of representatives of the railroads which operate in the major geographical rate territories. There were, however, differing rules of procedure for the committees; and until 1914, the Official Classification Committee met twice a year to consider proposed changes. At that time, the Western Classification Committee adopted a different method. It established a committee that was not identified with any particular railroad. This Committee was given authority to handle classification matters, and it was to be in session constantly. The advantages of more expeditious handling and a greater degree of impartiality on the part of these committee members resulted in substantial improvement, which was adopted ultimately by other classification committees.

During World War I, the Consolidated Classification Committee, composed of the three classification committees—Official, Southern, and Western—was created by the Director General of the United States at the time the railroads were under government operation. Since that time, the chairmen of the three major classification committees have comprised the Consolidated Classification Committee which at present publishes both the Consolidated and the Uniform Freight classifications. The rail classification committees have a membership of from two to five members.

As is explained in the next chapter, one of the rules of classification permits articles to be classified by analogy. For example, a shipper may find some article already in the classification similar to the item he wishes to ship and ship it under that classification. He will then submit his proposal for classification to a classification board in order to insure that it is properly classified. In some instances, proposals are made to apply only in the Consolidated Freight Classification; but in other cases, proposals are made before that Committee and the Uniform Classification Committee as well. An application for change in classification before the Uniform Classification Committee is shown in Figure 6–10.

APPLICATIONS MUST BE MADE IN TRIPLICATE.
CATALOGUES, EXHIBITS, PICTURES OR CUTS, IF ANY, MUST ALSO BE FILED IN TRIPLICATE.

UNIFORM CLASSIFICATION COMMITTEE

OFFICIAL CLASSIFICATION COMMITTEE
No. One Park Ave. At 33rd St., New York 16, N.Y.

SOUTHERN CLASSIFICATION COMMITTEE
No. 101 Marietta Street, Atlanta 3, Ga.

WESTERN CLASSIFICATION COMMITTEE
Room 202 Union Station, Chicago 4, Ill.

APPLICATION FOR CHANGE IN CLASSIFICATION

The Classification Committees' Dockets close January 31, March 31, May 31, July 31, September 30 and November 30. In order to permit of proper investigation and publicity, applications for Classification changes should be filed with the Committees at least two weeks prior to the closing date if they are to appear on the following docket. If received later, it may be necessary to hold for subsequent docket.

Date_____

ARTICLE:—

NAME OF:_____

FULL DESCRIPTION OF:_____

SEND THREE CUTS OR PHOTOGRAPHS OF THE ARTICLE OR CATALOGUES, WHEN PRACTICABLE TO DO SO.

MADE OF:_____

USES:_____

HOW PACKED OR PREPARED FOR SHIPMENT (State whether in bags, barrels, boxes, bundles, crates or other packages or in pieces or in bulk)	DIMENSIONS OF PACKAGE OR PIECES, IN INCHES			WEIGHT AS PACKED FOR SHIPMENT		VALUE Per Lb. As Packed For Shipment
	LENGTH	WIDTH	HEIGHT	Weight Per Pkg. or Piece, Lbs.	Weight Per Cubic Ft. (See Foot Note), Lbs.	
WHEN SHIPPED L. C. L.						
WHEN SHIPPED C. L.						
IF KNOCKED DOWN, TO WHAT EXTENT						
IF NESTED, TO WHAT EXTENT						

	RATINGS					
PRESENT	UNIFORM CLASSIFICATION		CONSOLIDATED CLASSIFICATION			
			OFFICIAL		WESTERN	
Item No. Description	LCL	CL	LCL	CL	LCL	CL
MIN.C.L.WEIGHT						
PROPOSED						
Description						
MIN.C.L.WEIGHT						

(PLEASE SUPPLY INFORMATION REQUESTED ON OTHER SIDE)

FIG. 6–10. Form used in application for change in classification before rail classification committees.

Actual Weight That Can Be Loaded in Standard Cars 40 Ft. 6 In. in Length, 9 Ft. 2 In. Wide and 10 Ft. High (Inside Measurement). _____

Is the Article Shipped in Straight Carloads?_____If so, how many cars per annum, and territory in which moved?

_____

If shipped in Mixed Carloads with other articles, mention the other articles:_____

_____

Where Produced:_____

REASON WHY CHANGE OR ADDITION IS REQUESTED SHOULD BE FULLY STATED:

_____

_____

_____

_____

_____

_____

_____

_____

_____

_____

_____

_____

_____

_____

_____

_____

_____

_____

_____

_____

_____

_____

Applicant is requested to answer the following questions:

(a) Have you objection to your name being quoted as proponent in answer to inquiries that may be made as to who originated the proposition?_____

(b) Will you appear in person or by representative at public hearings?_____.

If so, where: Atlanta_____; Chicago_____; or New York_____?

Have you objection to this information being given to others upon inquiry?_____

Applicant's Address _____   _____ Applicant's Signature

NOTICE

Note—To ascertain the "weight per cubic foot" multiply together the three extreme dimensions of the article as packed for shipment, and where the result is in cubic inches, divide by 1728 to reduce to cubic feet, then divide the weight by the number of cubic feet thus ascertained.

FIG. 6–10—*Continued*

Each of the classification committees has a form to be filled out for changes in classification. This supplies the classification committee with the information necessary to assist it in properly classifying the goods. Periodically, a docket is issued, showing the proposed changes and indicating the time and place of the meetings. Publicity is given to these notices in the *Traffic Bulletin*. A joint docket announcement is shown in Figure 6–11.

Uniform Classification—Official Classification — Illinois Classification—Southern Classification —Western Classification

JOINT DOCKET 216

HEARINGS OF THE UNIFORM, OFFICIAL, ILLINOIS, SOUTHERN AND WESTERN CLASSIFICATION COMMITTEES

MAY, 1963

For consideration of proposals for changes in rules, descriptions, ratings and minimum weights as set forth herein

AT

Office 1015—101 Marietta St., Atlanta 3, Ga., beginning May 2, 1963
Room 324, Union Station, Chicago 6, Ill., beginning May 7, 1963
One Park Ave. at 33rd St., New York 16, N. Y., beginning May 14, 1963

Hearings by Appointment - See Page 2

For Atlanta hearings apply to A. H. Carson, Member, Southern Classification Committee, 101 Marietta St., Atlanta 3, Ga., for assignment.

For New York hearings apply to L. W. North, Chairman, Official Classification Committee, One Park Ave. at 33rd. St., New York 16, N. Y., for assignment.

For Chicago hearings apply to J. P. Hackler, Chairman, Western Classification Committee, Room 202, Union Station, Chicago 6, Ill., for assignment.

Written presentations at hearings are preferred and shippers are requested to furnish four complete copies of statements and exhibits.

In some instances, applicants of the subjects herein have proposed changes in Uniform Freight Classification 6 as well as Consolidated Freight Classification 23. Those applications have been docketed as requested. In other instances applicants proposed changes in one of the Classifications only. However, the Classification Committees will give consideration to appropriate changes in like items of both the Uniform and Consolidated Freight Classifications and interested parties should therefore express their views, if any.

The Changes proposed herein in Consolidated Freight Classification 23 do not include proposed changes in Southern Classification 65. No further amendments will be made in Southern Classification 65.

Proposed changes in Classification provisions as shown in this docket, whether initiated by shippers or carriers, after public hearing, may be deviated or varied from as warranted after consideration of the information and facts submitted.

Official Classification Committee	Southern Classification Committee	Western Classification Committee
J. D. SHERSON,	ELMER B. HULL	H. H. JOHNSON,
	ALVA H. CARSON,	
GEO. KATSAFOUROS	JAMES E. CAMP,	W. W. KNOBELOCH,
L. W. NORTH, Chairman,	R. E. BOYLE, Jr., Chairman,	J. P. HACKLER, Chairman.
	Illinois Classification Committee	
	H. R. JOHNSON, Chairman,	

CHICAGO 6, ILL., APRIL 13, 1963

(2900)   (Edw. Keogh Ptg. Co., Chicago—50783)   Printed in U. S. A.

FIG. 6–11. A sample joint docket announcement as used by rail classification committees.

Following public hearings, the classification board will vote on each proposal and will issue a recommendation advice to all members of the railroads' Traffic Executive Association. Unless objections are expressed within fifteen days from the date of the docket advice, the recommendations are deemed to have been concurred in. If not concurred in, they often are redocketed. If there is concurrence, all interested parties are notified, and the proposal is issued as a supplement to the classification. When the classification is reissued, these changes are contained in the new issue. A proposal and its entry, as recommended, in the classification are shown in Figure 6–12.

SUBJECT NO.	ITEM (Orig. issue except as noted)	ARTICLES	Less Carload Ratings	Carload Minimum (Pounds)	Carload Ratings
107	36320 UFC No.1	PRESENT Parachutes,noibn,in bales or boxes.	200	12,000R	100
		Ⓢ PROPOSED Amend Item 36320,UFC No.1 to read: Parachutes,noibn,in bales or boxes or in metal containers	100	18,000R 36,000	70 50

Ⓢ Proposed by shippers.

SOURCE: Joint Docket No. 156, May, 1953, p. 4

SUPPLEMENT No. 28 TO CONSOLIDATED FREIGHT CLASSIFICATION NUMBER 20

Item	Cancels Item (Original issue, except as noted)	ARTICLES	Less Carload Ratings	Carload Minimum (Pounds)	Carload Ratings
36320-A	36320	Parachutes, noibn, in bales or boxes ♦or in metal containers...............	1♦	♦18,000R	♦3

UNIFORM FREIGHT CLASSIFICATION NUMBER 2

Item	ARTICLES	Less Carload Ratings	Carload Minimum (Pounds)	Carload Ratings
36320	Parachutes, noibn, in bales or boxes ♦or in metal containers.............................	♦150	♦18,000R	♦70

FIG. 6–12. A proposal for a change in classification and its entry in the classification.

If the classification committees vote that a proposal fails of adoption, it may be appealed to the Traffic Executive Association—Eastern, Western, or Southern—which is composed of railroad traffic personnel.

Motor

Unlike rail classification, there is but one classification board for National Motor Freight classification. It is composed of not less than three or more than five full-time employees. The procedure employed is somewhat similar to the rail classification committee procedure. Proposed changes are docketed and publicized in *Transport Topics* and the *Traffic*

NATIONAL CLASSIFICATION BOARD

1616 P St., N. W.,
Washington 6, D. C.

DOCKET No. 108

MARCH-APRIL, 1963

For consideration of proposals for change in National Motor Freight Classification rules, descriptions, ratings, packing and minimum weights. As set forth herein hearings will be held on individual subjects only by appointment in the cities specified below:

Pick-Congress Hotel, 520 South Michigan Avenue, Chicago, Illinois, beginning March 19, 1963.
1307 Peachtree Street, N. E., Atlanta, Georgia, beginning March 25, 1963.
1616 P Street, N. W., Washington 6, D. C., beginning March 26, 1963.
Belmont Plaza Hotel, 49th Street and Lexington Avenue, N. Y., N. Y., beginning April 2, 1963.
Sir Francis Drake Hotel, San Francisco, California, beginning April 9, 1963.

Request for Hearing appointments should be made to the Secretary promptly for allotment of time for presentation of facts in support of or in rebuttal to proposals. Three complete copies of written arguments and exhibits should be furnished.

Proposed changes in this docket will be decided after public hearings, upon consideration of available facts. Effort is made to avoid publication of proposals which are obviously without merit or impossible of adoption. Publication of proposals on this docket does not imply endorsement of the National Classification Board.

The Classification Board is authorized to deviate from proposed changes and will accord consideration to all factors involved, including descriptions, ratings, rules, minimum weights and packing requirements.

Explanation of letters: (C) means change proposed by carrier; (S) means change proposed by manufacturer or shipper; and (B) means change proposed by National Classification Board.

NATIONAL CLASSIFICATION BOARD

N. F. Behme, Jr., Chairman
H. C. Willson, Member
J. E. Bordeaux, Member
E. H. Huffman, Member

F. T. Grice, Secretary

ISSUED MARCH 8, 1963

FIG. 6–13. A sample National Classification Board docket announcement.

Bulletin. A National Classification Board docket announcement is shown in Figure 6–13.

The functions of the National Classification Board are to consider proposals for changes in or additions to the classification with respect to commodity descriptions, packing requirements, minimum weights, and general rules and regulations. It must hold public hearings regarding all such changes and thereafter instruct the publishing agent as to resultant changes. All proposals must be submitted in writing to the Board; and any such proposals may be filed by any person, firm, or corporation. Forms for that purpose are provided by the Board; an example is shown in Figure 6–14. All proposals are subject to examination before being docketed.

National Classification Board

1616 P STREET, N.W. WASHINGTON 6, D.C. DUPONT 7-3200

APPLICATION FOR CHANGE IN
NATIONAL MOTOR FREIGHT CLASSIFICATION

__________ 19____

SUBMIT TWO COPIES OF APPLICATION TOGETHER WITH SUPPORTING EXHIBITS OR STATEMENTS. BE SURE TO ANSWER EACH QUESTION PRECISELY AND FULLY, FURNISHING ADDITIONAL INFORMATION ON SEPARATE SHEET IF NECESSARY.

Give full description of Article and Composition. State whether crude, rough, or finished. __________

1. Trade Nomenclature __________ 2. Is commodity fragile? Yes ☐ No ☐

3. Does commodity require refrigeration ____, Heat ____, Special Handling ____? 4. Is commodity flammable? Yes ☐ No ☐

Explosive? Yes ☐ No ☐ Liquid? Yes ☐ No ☐, Paste? Yes ☐ No ☐ Dry? Yes ☐ No ☐?

5. Is commodity SU ____: + KD ____: Flat ____: Other than flat ____: • Nested ____: ● Nested Solid ____: Not Nested ____

Wheeled ____: Not Wheeled ____: Wheels attached ____: Compressed ____: Not compressed ____:

+ KNOCKED DOWN ARTICLES: Ratings on articles provided for KD apply only when the article is taken apart, folded or telescoped in such manner as to reduce the bulk of the articles at least 33-1/3% from its normal cubage when set-up, assembled or expanded.

• NESTED: Three or more different sizes of the article enclosed each smaller within the next larger, or three or more of the articles placed one within the other so that each upper article will not project above the next lower article more than one-third of its height.

● NESTED SOLID: Three or more of the articles placed one within or upon the other so that the outer side surfaces of the one above will be in contact with the inner side surfaces of the one below and so that each upper article will not project above the next lower more than one-quarter inch.

6. Can the commodity be tiered for shipment? __________

7. Materials from which commodity is made (Show proportions by weight and bulk if possible). __________

8. Supporting DATA: Photos ____ Blueprints ____ Catalogs ____ Samples ____ Advertising ____

9. Area of movement within: East ____; South ____; West ____; All Territories ____.

10. What is predominant movement: LTL or TL? ____ Average weight of shipments: LTL ____ lbs.; TL ____ lbs. Tonnage for given period (Mos.) ____ (LTL) ____ (TL) ____.

11. Claim experience for a given period. (Show in dollars and cents if possible). __________

12. Name and address of shippers or manufacturers (Must be furnished when proponent is other than the shipper or manufacturer) __________

13. STATE FULLY WHY CHANGE OR ADDITION IS NECESSARY OR DESIRABLE. (If, as justification, applicant refers to ratings of other articles in the classification, complete information as to weight, value, packing, loadibility and other pertinent factors of such comparable items should be given. Use separate sheet if additional space is needed.)

FIG. 6–14. Application for change in National Motor Freight Classification.

PRESENT CLASSIFICATION: (Give reference to item number or explanation of how the commodity is now being rated.)	LTL	TL	MIN. WT. FACTOR
PROPOSED CLASSIFICATION: (Show description exactly as you propose it to be established in the Classification.)			

KIND OF PACKAGE (Bag, Box, Etc.)	OUTSIDE DIMENSIONS OF PACKAGE OR PIECES			WEIGHT AS PACKED FOR SHIPMENT (POUNDS)		WHOLESALE VALUE AS PACKED FOR SHIPMENT	
	Length	Width	Height	Pkge. or Piece	Per Cu. Ft.	Pkge. or Piece	Per Lb.

If package is of curved or irregular shape use extreme outside measurements.

To ascertain the "weight per cubic foot" multiply together the three dimensions of the article as packed for shipment and where the results is in cubic inches, divide by 1728 to reduce to cubic feet, then divide the weight by the number of cubic feet thus ascertained. To obtain the cubic feet of space occupied by a barrel, pail, etc., square the greatest diameter and multiply by the height.

APPLICANT IS REQUESTED TO ANSWER THE FOLLOWING QUESTION :

(1) Do you object to your name being quoted as proponent in answer to inquiries that may be made as to who originated the proposal? ______

Proponent's Name ______

Street Address ______

City ______

Signature ______

Title ______

FIG. 6–14—*Continued*

NOTICE OF DISPOSITION, ISSUED PURSUANT TO RULES OF PROCEDURE

National Classification Board

of the motor carrier industry

N. F. Behme, Jr., Chairman
H. C. Willson
J. E. Bordeaux
E. H. Huffman

1616 P STREET, N.W.
WASHINGTON 6, D. C.

February 28, 1963   Disposition Bulletin

There are set forth below the dispositions of various subjects listed on the dockets of the National Classification Board.

Recommended changes or additions will be published in the National Motor Freight Classification at the earliest practicable date. Any party interested in ascertaining the reasons for the National Classification Board's recommendations on any given subject(s) may receive them upon written request to the Chairman of the National Classification Board.

Docket 105, Subject 34 (B): Cloth or Fabric combined with foam rubber - It is proposed to amend the Classification to establish provisions for cloth or fabric combined with cellular, expanded or foam plastic not exceeding 3/8 inch thick at Class 150 AQ.

(870)   DISPOSITION: Approve as modified. Amend the Classification as shown below.

	LTL	TL	MWF
CLOTH, DRY GOODS OR FABRICS:			
49230 Cloth or Fabric other than rugs or carpeting, combined with foam rubber not exceeding 3/8 inch thick, NOI, in wrapped bales or rolls, or in boxes, see Note, item @	85	85	AQ
(New) Cloth or Fabric other than rugs or carpeting, combined with cellular, expanded or foam plastic not exceeding 3/8 inch thick, NOI, in wrapped bales or rolls, or in boxes, see Note, item @	125	125	AQ
(New) Note--When thickness of cellular, expanded or foam plastic or rubber exceeds 3/8 inch, rate per items157350, 157400 or 157440.			

Docket 106, Subject 17 (C): Pens or Pencils, ball point - It is proposed to add an item to the Classification for these articles reading as follows:

	LTL	TL	MWF
STATIONERY:			
(New) Pens or pencils, ball point, or parts thereof, wood or plastic combined with metal, actual value not exceeding 5¢ each, in boxes, see Note, item _____	85	55	24.2
(New) Note--Shipper must certify on shipping order and bill of lading the actual value of the property as follows: "Actual value of each pen or pencil or part thereof is hereby stated by the shipper to be not in excess of 5¢ each."			

DISPOSITION: Disapprove. Rate per item 179180 as "Stationery, NOI."

NATIONAL CLASSIFICATION BOARD

cc: F. G. Freund - Issuing Officer
All Parties of Record

FIG. 6–15. An example of a disposition notice by the National Classification Board.

Simple matters of clarification to correct an obvious error are permitted to be made without docketing. The Board usually holds five public hearings each year and not less than three at convenient places, usually Washington, New York, Chicago, and Atlanta, and occasionally some western point.

Following public hearings, a minimum of three Board members are designated by the secretary to vote on each proposal and then issue a disposition notice, within a reasonable time, copies of which are sent to all interested parties (Figure 6–15). Two methods of appeal are provided. Any 15 carriers participating in the classification may appeal from the decision of the Board within 30 days, provided they submit their reasons in writing for the appeal; or any 8 members of the National Classification Committee, which is composed of 100 representatives of various types of motor common carriers, may appeal a subject. On the other hand, if the proponent is dissatisfied, he may appeal to the Committee, basing his appeal upon pertinent grounds. If the Board reports a proposal as having failed of adoption, the proponent may appeal the decision to the Committee within 30 days, setting forth the grounds for the appeal. The full Committee must hear all appeals.

In the case of an appeal, the appellant is given an opportunity to appear before the National Classification Committee and present his case, perhaps submitting a written statement in support of his position. If no appeals are received, the publishing agent proceeds with the necessary publication. There has been a relatively small number of appeals.

The rules also provide that the Board may, in its discretion and for good cause shown, reopen or reconsider any docket subject upon which a disposition notice has been issued, provided that it is done within six months following the date of the initial notice and, further, that reconsideration cannot be given if publication has been made in the classification. After reconsideration, a revised disposition notice is issued—subject, of course, to all of the rules applicable to the initial disposition notice. The Board is not authorized to reopen any docket subject previously appealed and acted upon by the National Classification Committee. Additionally, the Board, upon request, provides interpretations of matters contained in the classification. These are opinions, not rulings, and number about 400 a year.

The National Motor Freight Traffic Association, Inc., is the publishing agent for the classification. It consists of motor common carriers, and its duties are to investigate, analyze, and disseminate information on classifications and tariffs. The National Classification Committee is an autonomous committee of NMFTA.

COMPANY CLASSIFICATIONS

The traffic departments of many companies have issued what is often referred to as a "company classification" for use by their personnel. Because the description placed on the bill of lading will influence the freight rate, it is necessary that the correct transportation description or classification be applied. Many commodities are sold by brand name and are invoiced to the customer. However, goods are classified for transportation purposes based on their *transportation* characteristics. Therefore, the bill of lading must contain the transportation description, or the shipper will pay higher charges for his shipments than would otherwise be necessary.

These freight classification guides can be easily prepared in loose-leaf form or some other simple arrangement. Probably the most voluminous such guide is that which the military departments have, which converts their standard stock catalog items into transportation classification items.

Some examples of conversion of invoiced products into transportation descriptions are shown in Figure 6–16.

Aphid and Mite Spray
  Agricultural Insecticides, N.O.I.B.N., Liquid

Product	Transportation Description
Bran Flakes	Flaked Bran Cereals

FREIGHT CLASSIFICATION GUIDE

APPLICATION OF UNIFORM FREIGHT CLASSIFICATION AND NATIONAL MOTOR FREIGHT CLASSIFICATION TO ENGINEER CORPS ITEMS

1. This compilation provides translation of Army-Air Force stock-list nomenclature into freight classification descriptions for billing purposes, and is primarily for the use of transportation personnel.

3. When the freight classification description shown in the freight nomenclature column of this guide contains the term "NOIBN" or is otherwise different from the Army-Air Force stock-list nomenclature, the latter will be shown on the bill of lading in parentheses beside or immediately below the freight classification description. See paragraph 21o(2), TM 55–550. The classification descriptions in the Uniform Freight Classification No. 1, and the National Motor Freight Classification No. A–1 will be used when the classifications referred to herein are not applicable to particular shipments.

Stock No.	Army-Air Force nomenclature (par. 3)	Freight nomenclature (par. 3)	See U. F. C. No. 1 or reissue item No.	See N. M. F. C. No. A–1 or reissue item No.
51–7200.500.200____ through 51–7200.500.300____	Polish, metal, liquid_____	Polishing compounds, noibn_____	6870	14700
40–6938.160–000____	Polishing machine, floor, electric_____	Machine, noibn (specify SU or KD)_____	31890	67570
40–6940.110–550____ through 40–6948.112–230____	Polishing and scrubbing machine, floor, electric.	Machine, noibn (specify SU or KD)_____	31890	67570

FIG. 6–16. Examples of freight classification guides.

EXCEPTIONS TO THE CLASSIFICATION

An exception is a specific rating, rule, regulation, or provision supplemental to or differing from the corresponding provision carried in the freight classification to which it is an exception. There must, however, be some published authority for thus deviating from the published classification, and this authority is obtained by incorporating the exception either in the tariff carrying the rate applying or in a separately published schedule known as "Exceptions to the Classification" or "Classification Exceptions."

The exceptions tariffs take precedence over the provisions of the classification. The general rules which are provided in the classification have often been modified (an example is shown in Figure 6–17) to meet industrial, commercial, and transportation conditions which existed in the

Freight Tariff No. 90-K.

SECTION 1
EXCEPTIONS TO OFFICIAL CLASSIFICATION RULES.

Item No.	RULES	TERRITORIAL APPLICATION (See Pages 42 to 50.)

310	**EXCEPTION TO RULE 5.**
	
	HIDES, SKINS, WOOL, HAIR, BRISTLES, GLUESTOCK, BONES, HOOFS, HORNS, PREVIOUSLY USED BAGS AND BAGGING, SEEDS FOR PLANTING, BIRD OR POULTRY FEEDINGS, OR MANUFACTURE (Import), less carloads:
	    Unless forwarded in tight cases or unbroken casks acceptable to the Inspector in charge, Bureau of Animal Industry, United States Department of Agriculture, at the Port of Entry, when bearing evidence of being freight "restricted" by the Bureau of Animal Industry, will be charged on the basis of the carload rate and carload minimum weight.
	    The stamps to be used by the Bureau of Animal Industry in connection with "restricted" freight will read as follows:
	      CARS NOT TO GO FORWARD UNTIL SEALED BY AN INSPECTOR OF THE UNITED STATES BUREAU OF ANIMAL INDUSTRY.
	      RESTRICTED IMPORT ANIMAL PRODUCT, CLEAN AND DISINFECT CARS, TRUCKS AND LIGHTERS.
	    (R. A. 25407.)
		From
		Baltimore (Note 3)___Md.
		Camden_____N. J.
		Chester_____Pa.
		Communipaw_____N. J.
		Delaware River Pier_Del.
		Eddystone_____Pa.
		Marcus Hook_____Pa.
		Newport News_____Va.
		New York (Note 4).N. Y.
		Norfolk_____Va.
		Philadelphia (Note 5)_Pa.
		South Amboy_____N. J.
		Wilmington_____Del.
		To
		A,B,C,D,E,F,G,H

320	**EXCEPTION TO RULE 5.**
	Meats in Refrigerator Cars.
	
	    Rule 26 rating will apply on shipments of Meats, cured, N. O. I. B. N. in Official Classification dried, dry-salted, pickled or smoked, loose, when loaded in refrigerator cars in quantities of 12,000 pounds or more, and shipped from one station, in one car, in one day, by one shipper, for delivery to one consignee at one destination. When ice is placed in cars for the protection of shipment the cost of same must be paid by the shipper.
	    (R. A. 68925, 86719.)
		From A To A,B,C,D,E,
		From B To A
		From D To A.D

FIG. 6–17.   An example of exceptions to the classification rules.

various classification territories by publishing rules contained in the Exceptions to the Classification. The special conditions and circumstances that led to the establishment of the Exceptions to the Classification were usually within one classification territory but not in others. Therefore, the modified rules found in the Exceptions to the Classification are generally published in issues such as Exceptions to the Official, Southern, or Western Classification, respectively.

There are a number of reasons why rail exceptions to the classification have been published. Among these are the following:

1. To meet motor carrier and other competition.
2. Because of convenience and expedition in publication.
3. To accomplish a more restricted application of particular rates.
4. To remove or reduce the amount of difference between class rates and between less-carload and carload rates.
5. To provide a quicker and less burdensome method of complying with Section 4 of the Interstate Commerce Act.[10]

A number of exceptions to the classifications are stated as percentages of Class 1, and they usually result in rates lower than would apply through use of the classification ratings. It should be pointed out also that in addition to the classification rules and to the Exceptions to the Classification, there are other exceptions specifically published in rate tariffs. These specific exceptions, since they are a part of the rate tariff, will take precedence over the classification rules and their exceptions.

---

[10] *Class Rate Investigation,* 262 ICC 447, 477 (1939).

An exception to the classification may have broad application throughout an entire rate-making area, or it may be limited to certain carriers or to but one carrier. The ratings established by exceptions are to be used in connection with class rates. The purpose of the exception is to remove articles from the classification and establish rates different from the normal class rates. An examination of the commodity descriptions found in exceptions will show that they are often broader than is the case in the classification.

Exceptions to the classifications have developed over a long period of years to the point where the volume of carload traffic which moved by rail under exceptions exceeds that which moved under class rates. The size of the volumes in which they were published almost equaled the classification itself. In effect, the classification exceptions established an additional classification which took precedence over the basic classification.

Although, technically, exceptions ratings were not at issue in Dockets No. 28300 and 28310, the Commission, in its Third Supplemental Report in that proceeding,[11] admonished the carriers to straighten out the tariffs involved in the exceptions class rates because their complexity was such as to verge on incomprehensibility. The Commission stated further in this report:

> We correct a misapprehension growing out of use of the term "exceptions" to the classification or classification ratings. The commodities so "excepted" are just as truly classified as the remaining articles which do take class ratings and to which class rates are applied. Setting apart the "excepted" commodities, and "excepting" them from the classification simply substitutes another classification rating for the general normal rating. The new "exception" rating, by whatever term called, is a classification rating, and is subject to all the requirements of the act.

It has been stated that 90 per cent of all the work, research, testimony, debate, argument, and compromise in the Dockets No. 28300 and No. 28310 proceedings had to do with exceptions ratings; and had no thought been given to exceptions ratings, an acceptable uniform classification could have been compiled in six weeks.[12]

As in the case of rail exceptions to the classification, motor carriers have found it desirable to publish such exceptions. The exceptions which are published may apply to ratings as well as to rules, descriptions, weights, and other items. In Figure 6–18, the volume rating for bottle caps is Class 35. However, in one rate territory, as shown in the example, exceptions are published to the National Motor Freight Classification on bottle caps; and the truckload rating, as shown in the second line under the "Caps and

---

[11] 281 ICC 213, 286 (1951).
[12] R. W. Boyle, Jr., "What Do I.C.C. 28300 and 28310 Rate Charges Mean to Shippers and Carriers in the Southeast?" Paper presented before the First Annual Southeastern Transportation Clinic, University of Georgia, Atlanta Division, December 10, 1952.

FREIGHT TARIFF No. 10-M

Item No.	ARTICLES	A. Q.	L. T. L.	T. L.
	SECTION 1			
	EXCEPTIONS TO NATIONAL MOTOR FREIGHT CLASSIFICATION			
	(See Rules 3 and 4)			
			RATINGS	
1540	**Caps and Covers Group:**			
	Can Ends, steel or tin, flat or nested, in packages. .			32½
	Caps, Covers or Tops, bottle, can or jar, metal with or without cork or paper lining, in packages			32½
	Caps, bottle, with medicine dropper inserts.		85	50
	Caps, composition, with or without cork, foil or paper lining (other than display) for bottles, glasses or jars, in packages ..			35
	Caps, jar, metal or glass combined, in packages...			32½
	Exception C of Rule 4 will **not** apply. (File P-A5397)			

Item	ARTICLES	RATINGS LTL	@Vol.	@ Vol.Min. Wt.-Lbs.
19350	Bottle caps, steel or tin, crimped edge, lined with cork or paperboard, without attachments, in barrels or boxes_____	55	35	30,000

FIG. 6–18. Sample of motor exceptions to the classification entry.

Covers" group, is a rating of 32½. Therefore, this particular kind of bottle cap moves under the exceptions rating, which is lower than would be the case were no exceptions published on it.

Competitive reasons appear to be one of the important causes for such publication of exceptions. If there is publication of a rail exception to the classification on an article which is competitive with motor carriers, this may result in a motor exception to the classification on the article. Figure 6–19 is a sample of a motor exception to the classification rules.

FREIGHT TARIFF No. 10-I

SECTION 1
EXCEPTIONS TO NATIONAL MOTOR FREIGIT CLASSIFICATION
(For General Rules See Section 2)

RULES AND REGULATIONS

RULE

MINIMUM CHARGE FOR INDIVIDUAL CARRIERS
(Exceptions to Rule 12 of N.M.F.C.)
(For Application of Rules 10A to 10Z, see Rule 10 of Tariff, or as amended)

Rule 13:

Loading and Unloading
(Exception to Rule 21 of N.M.F.C.)

The provisions of Rule 21 of the National Motor Freight Classification will not apply. Apply provisions of Rule 21 herein.
(File P-2690)

FIG. 6–19. Sample of a motor exception to the classification rules.

DISCUSSION QUESTIONS AND PROBLEMS

1. Trace the development of freight classification from 1850 to 1920, pointing out significant changes which have taken place during that period of time.
2. What are the basic purposes of classifications? Have these purposes become of greater or lesser importance over the years?

3. List the principles which influence the classification of commodities. Is any single factor dominant?

4. Prepare a map of the United States showing the area in which the Consolidated Freight Classification and the Uniform Freight Classification apply.

5. Carefully explain the development of the Uniform Freight Classification.

6. How can you determine which rail classification applies?

7. Place in tabular form the classes contained in the Consolidated and Uniform Freight Classification and the two motor carrier counterparts. What conclusions can be drawn from such a presentation?

8. Carefully examine Figures 6–4, 6–6, and 6–9. Explain fully five items chosen at random from each of the figures.

9. Assume that your company manufactures an article not presently in the rail classifications and, as traffic manager, you have reason to feel it should be entered. What steps would you follow to accomplish it?

10. Would you follow the same procedure if you wanted to reclassify an item?

11. What is the classification procedure before the National Classification Board? If your proposal fails of adoption, what, if any, appeal do you have?

12. How would you determine whether your company needed a company classification? How would you prepare such a classification?

13. Why have rail exceptions to the classification been published? Do exceptions ratings always supersede classification ratings?

14. Do you agree that the establishment of exceptions creates another classification?

15. If no thought had been given to exceptions ratings, an acceptable uniform classification could have been compiled in six weeks. Just what does this statement mean?

Chapter

7

CLASSIFICATION RULES

In order to apply the ratings contained in the classifications, it is necessary to know and understand the rules, for in this manner, the classification user can look up ratings for individual commodities without referring each time to all the rules. The majority of the classification rules includes the phrase "unless otherwise provided" because these rules have general coverage. Rules published to apply in specific instances may be at variance with the general rules; and in such cases, the use of this phrase in connection with the general rule permits the specific rule to apply.

RAIL

All freight rate tariffs are made subject to one or more of the classifications by name and number, such as the Official, Southern, Western, Illinois, or Uniform Freight Classification. All class rate tariffs are subject to both the rules and the ratings of the governing classification, while commodity tariffs are subject only to the rules and/or the description of articles of the governing classification, to the extent specifically provided in such commodity tariffs. Tariffs may specify that they are subject also to certain exceptions in the governing classification. The application and interpretation of the Consolidated and Uniform Freight Classification rules are discussed to provide a better understanding of this aspect of classification.

Shipments are ordinarily transported under one of the several types of uniform bills of lading prescribed for use in connection with interstate commerce by the Interstate Commerce Commission, and these are indicated in *Rule 1*. The contract terms of the bill of lading include provisions which limit the liability of the carrier in possession of any of the property covered in the bill of lading.

If the shipper chooses, however, not to release the carrier from its greater common-law liability, and a clause to that effect is printed, written, or stamped upon the uniform domestic bill of lading or uniform export bill of lading, as the case may be, the carrier is permitted, because of increased liability, to increase the through rate 10 per cent. This is subject to a minimum increase of 1 cent per 100 pounds over the rate applying under the uniform domestic bill of lading or uniform export bill of lading.

Rule 2 provides that the description of articles in the shipping orders and bills of lading must conform to the classification or tariff description. It further provides that when different ratings are provided for an article according to the type of packing or package, the shipping conditions must be shown. On LCL traffic, the shipping orders and bills of lading must specify the number of articles, packages, or pieces.

According to Section 2 of this rule, the carriers reserve the right to inspect the shipment, when necessary, to determine the lawful rating. When a shipment is found to be incorrectly described, freight charges must be collected according to the proper description. The railroads have delegated the supervision of weights and the inspection of shipments to the various weighing and inspection bureaus which they have established in each of the classification territories. Therefore, the facts concerning misdescription are usually determined by these bureaus.

Another provision is that if the description shown in the Bureau of Explosives tariff differs from the description contained in the classification, the exceptions, or a commodity tariff, the description shown in the Bureau of Explosives tariff must be shown first on shipping orders and bills of lading, with the classification description immediately following in parentheses.

By the terms of *Rule 3*, the carriers will not accept for shipment property of extraordinary value, such as bank bills, coins or currency, drafts, deeds, jewelry, valuable papers, postage stamps, letters, precious stones, etc., for they are usually handled by Railway Express. The first paragraph of this rule reads: "Unless otherwise provided in this Classification. . . . " An example of an exception to this rule is in Item 36015 of the classification, which provides for the transportation of envelopes or wrappers, government stamped, when shipped for the account of the United States government on government bills of lading in cars protected by government locks or seals.

Carriers are not obligated to receive freight which is liable to damage other freight or equipment under *Rule 4*. In the event that such article or articles are accepted, they are subject to delay for suitable equipment. The kind of freight covered by this rule would be materials giving off an offensive odor or materials susceptible to leakage, such as tar and molasses shipped in barrels which might under certain weather conditions allow the contents to seep through the barrels, covering the car floor or other materials loaded into the car.

The provisions of *Rule 5* are established for computing charges on shipments not complying with the classification requirements and miscellaneous rules. It provides that articles not properly packed may be refused for transportation. This rule broadens the application of certain specific shipping terms and imposes penalties on articles found in transportation shipped in unauthorized containers or forms of shipment. The first three sections provide that when packing specifications are not provided in the classification, articles will be accepted for transportation in any form of shipment, other than in trunks; when the term "in packages" is provided in connection with the separate descriptions of articles, such articles will be accepted for transportation in any container or in any shipping form other than "in bulk," "loose," or "on skids"; rates shown for freight in barrels will also apply on such freight in hogsheads, pipes, puncheons, tierces, casks, drums, or kegs; and ratings on glass inner containers will also apply on the same articles in earthenware.

Section 4 shows how to determine the ratings when articles do not comply with the rules in Sections 1 through 3, and it is often called the "penalty rule." It provides a basis for rates on articles found in transportation shipped in unauthorized containers or forms of shipment. A penalty of 20 per cent on LCL or AQ (any quantity) lots and 10 per cent on CL is assessed when articles are shipped in packages specified but which fail to conform to the rules for construction, material, packing, closing, or other regulations provided in Rules 40 and 41. The same penalty is assessed in several different cases for failure to ship in proper containers, such as shipments in crates, pails, or tubs, when the requirements are in barrels or boxes; or to ship articles "loose" when requirements are in packages. Penalties as high as 50 per cent are assessed under this rule, although in some cases, no penalty whatsoever is assessed, such as in a case where shipment is offered "in barrels" and requirements provide for "boxes."

When exception-sheet ratings or commodity rates are, by general reference to the classification, made subject to the packing specifications of that issue, the provisions of paragraphs A and B of Section 4 also govern in connection with such exception-sheet ratings or commodity rates.

However, when exception-sheet ratings or commodity rates have attached to them their own packing specifications, Section 4 of this rule cannot be applied to broaden such packing specifications. When an article is forwarded, therefore, in a container or shipping form provided for in the classification but not provided for in connection with exception-sheet ratings or commodity rates, classification ratings must be applied.

The marking of freight is covered in Rule 6, which provides that all less-carload traffic or any-quantity shipments must be marked, showing consignee and destination or place of delivery. However, freight to be transported at carload rates or ratings is not affected or covered by this rule. Order-notify shipments must be appropriately marked, and fragile articles must be properly marked. If the requirements as to proper identification have not been complied with, the freight will not be accepted for transportation.

An exception to this rule is that when shipment fully occupies the visible capacity of a car, or weighs 6,000 pounds or more, it need not be marked.

The provisions of *Rule 7* govern the execution of bills of lading. Bills of lading must not show more than one shipper, one consignee, and one destination, except that they may show the name of a party at the same destination to be notified of the arrival of the shipment. On straight bills of lading, the shipper may request carriers not to make delivery without written order or other required document. In the event of the loss of such order or document, the shipper may hold the carriers responsible for the loss. In such cases, the carriers may deliver the goods upon receipt of cash or certified check in an amount equal to 125 per cent of the cost of the goods, or they may accept bond in an amount which is double the cost of the goods.

An order-notify bill of lading is used by a shipper to guarantee payment of the goods by the consignee. Through the medium of an order-notify bill of lading, a carrier may not make delivery to the consignee until the shipper collects the cost of the goods. The consignee, upon payment, receives the order-notify bill of lading, properly endorsed, indicating that the invoice charges have been paid, and presents it to the freight agent for possession of the shipment. Should the agent deliver the goods to consignee without proper endorsement, the carrier is liable.

In cases where the original order-notify bill of lading has been lost or delayed, the consignee may secure possession of the goods upon receipt of a certified check or cash in an amount equal to 125 per cent of the invoice or value of the property, or upon receipt of a bond acceptable to the carrier in an amount which is twice the amount of the invoice or value of the property.

On both straight and order-notify bills of lading, the name of another party at a different destination may be shown when the consignee or party to notify is located at a river landing or other point inaccessible to the carrier's deliveries; or when the consignee is located at a prepay station, or on a rural free delivery route, or in the interior; or when the destination station and the consignee's post office address are differently named but adjacent to one another. In such cases, both addresses may be shown.

No charges of any description will be advanced to shippers, owners, consignees, or agents thereof, nor to their draymen or warehousemen, under the provisions of *Rule 8*. However, in practice, the effect of this rule has been lessened by the carriers which, for competitive or other reasons, have published a number of exceptions to this rule in various tariffs. Generally, these tariffs provide that inbound freight charges or other specific charges, such as customs and brokerage fees on imports and bonded freight, which accrue prior to delivery of the shipment to a railroad for movement over its lines, will be advanced to shippers.

Rule 9 provides that prepayment or guarantee of charges may be required by the agent at the point of origin or diversion point if, in his judgment, the agent at destination would not, at a forced sale of the goods, realize the total amount of charges due for transportation. It will be found that many articles described in the classification require that the charges be prepaid. These may be forwarded collect, provided that the shipper guarantees payment of the freight charges and the general freight department approves such guarantee. Examples of articles covered by this rule are Christmas trees, printed matter, and sales tickets.

The objective of *Rule 10* is to afford shippers the benefit of the lowest available freight charges for transportation of several different articles when shipped in a mixed carload.

Section 1 states that when several different articles for which straight carload ratings or rates are provided are shipped on the same bill of lading, the charges will be determined by applying the rate applicable to the highest-rated article in the mixed carload, subject to the highest carload minimum weight provided for any article in the shipment. For example, an article rated fourth class, carload minimum 21,000 pounds, and another article rated seventh class, carload minimum 30,000 pounds, are shipped in a mixed carload. Freight charges will be based on the actual weight of the mixture at the fourth-class rate, subject to a minimum weight of 30,000 pounds.

Section 2 provides that when the total charge on the entire shipment is made lower by considering the articles as if they were divided into two or more separate carloads, the shipment will be charged accordingly. If, however, the minimum weights vary according to the size of the car, they will be those applicable for cars not in excess of 40 feet, 7 inches long.

Section 3 provides that when the aggregate charge upon the entire shipment is less on the basis of carload rate and minimum weight of one or more of the articles, and on the basis of actual weight at less-carload rate for the other article or articles, the shipment will be charged for accordingly. Carload package requirements will apply on the LCL portion not subject to the penalties provided in Rule 5.

Section 4 declares that if a lower charge results under the application of Sections 1, 2, or 3 of this rule than under the provisions of a specific carload mixture, such lower charge will apply. For example, the classification will provide for specific carload mixtures, as will some of the tariffs. If any of the provisions of Sections 1, 2, or 3 produces lower charges, the lower charges will apply.

Carriers have published a number of exceptions to Rule 10, which contain more liberal mixed-carload provisions. This has become known as "streamlined Rule 10," which is used in the Official and Southern rate territories, and "modified Rule 10," which has had limited application in the Western Territory.

The streamlined rule provides that when a number of different articles, for which the same or different ratings or rates are provided when in straight carloads, are shipped at one time by one consignor to one consignee and destination in a mixed carload, they will be charged at the actual or authorized estimated weight and at the straight carload class or commodity rate (not mixed-carload rate) applicable on each article in the carload. The carload minimum is the highest provided for any article in the mixture, and any deficit in the minimum weight is charged for at the highest carload rating or rate applicable to any article in the carload. As in the case of general Rule 10 in the classification, the articles in the carload, for rate-making purposes, are separated into two or more carloads and rated accordingly if lower charges will result. Also, the less-carload rates apply on articles treated as such in the mixture.

Streamlined Rule 10 and modified Rule 10 read substantially the same, except that under the latter rule, "all-freight" rates cannot be used on the weight of freight in the mixed carload which would take the all-freight rate if shipped in straight carloads. Under the streamlined rule, straight carload rates and/or the all-freight rates can be used in rating a mixed carload. However, a somewhat greater uniformity in the application of the exception rules to Rule 10 of the Consolidated and Uniform Freight Classification may be expected as the result of recent Commission action.[1] Modified Rule 10 became effective on mixed-carload shipments moving within the Mountain-Pacific Territory as well as between that territory and the Western and Southwestern territories. Streamlined Rule 10 has been placed in effect on traffic moving east from the Mountain-Pacific Territory to the Official and Southwestern territories, although, westbound between these points, modified Rule 10 applies.

An example of how the exceptions to Rule 10 apply is as follows: It is assumed that a 40-foot, 7-inch car, containing a mixture of the following commodities, was tendered and that the weights and rates were as follows:

	Actual Weight	Min. CL Weight	Rate CL
Peas, cow, dried, in bags	24,000	36,000	$0.40 per cwt.
Pepper pods, dried, in barrels	12,000	20,000 R	1.00 per cwt.

Under Section 1 of Rule 10, the charges would be computed as follows:

	Charges
36,000 lbs. at $1.00 per cwt.	$360.00

Under Section 2 of Rule 10, the charges would be computed as follows:

Peas, cow, dried, in bags	36,000 lbs. at $0.40 per cwt.	$144.00
Pepper pods, dried, in barrels	20,000 lbs. at 1.00 per cwt.	200.00
	Total charges	$344.00

[1] ICC, Docket No. 3094, 291 ICC 427 (1954).

Under Section 1 of streamlined Rule 10, the charges would be computed as follows:

Peas, cow, dried, in bags............ 24,000 lbs. at $0.40 per cwt. $ 96.00
Pepper pods, dried, in barrels........ 12,000 lbs. at 1.00 per cwt. 120.00

Total charges $216.00

Under Section 2 of streamlined Rule 10, the total charges would be $344.00.

Since the highest carload minimum weight is 36,000 pounds, there would be no deficit (the difference between the total actual weight of the entire shipment and the highest minimum weight applicable to any one of the articles contained therein); and Section 1 of streamlined Rule 10 would result in the cheapest basis.

Unless otherwise provided in the classification, *Rule 11* provides that charges shall be computed upon gross weights, except that when estimated weights are authorized, such estimated weights shall be used. There are two types of estimated weights. The first type is that provided in the tariffs; the second type is the agreement weights, which are established through weight agreements under the supervision of the various weighing bureaus, to be described later. Temporary blocking or similar bracing or dunnage, when used, shall be charged for as provided in Rule 30.

Rule 12 contains the provisions for assessing freight charges on less-carload traffic, as well as providing the method of obtaining charges on carload traffic when the contents of the car are in one package.

Section 1 provides that a single LCL shipment of one class will be charged for at actual or authorized estimated weight and at the rating applicable. Section 2 provides that single LCL shipments containing more than one commodity, subject to different ratings when each class is in a separate package, will be charged at actual or authorized estimated weight and at the rating applicable to each class, subject to the exception provided in Rule 20, which covers parts or pieces constituting a complete article.

Section 3 states that the charge for a package containing freight of more than one class will be rated at the highest-classed article in the package. This applies also to carload shipments in one package, the minimum weight for which will be the highest carload minimum weight provided for any article in the package. In such cases, all articles need not be specified on the shipping order or bill of lading.

In Section 4 is provided the stipulation that when the less-carload description for an article specifies an individual minimum weight per package or piece (this does not refer to the weight of an inner container or article enclosed in an outer container) and no provision is made for packages or pieces weighing less than the specified individual minimum, the total charge for a number of packages or pieces of a lesser weight shall be the same as would accrue on a like number of similar packages or pieces, each of the specified individual minimum weight. For example, the classification provides that each steel telephone switchboard distributing frame, KD (knocked down), LCL, must weigh 50 pounds loose or in a package. Since there is no provision made for lesser weights per package or loose, the charge would be based on 50 pounds for each article if the weight of each was less than 50 pounds.

Section 5 provides that when the LCL description for an article in bundles specifies an individual minimum weight per bundle and no provision is made for the article loose, a single loose article or piece weighing as much as or greater than the specified individual minimum weight per bundle will be charged for as a bundle.

Section 6 covers the charge to be made when an article is differently rated LCL according to different weights of shipping packages or loose pieces. It provides that the total charge for a number of packages or pieces of a lesser weight shall be no greater than the charge for a like number of similar packages or pieces, each of a greater weight.

Rule 13 provides the minimum charge for LCL as well as carload shipments and is subject to exceptions that may be stated in the individual items of the classification. If classified first class or lower, the minimum charge for a single LCL shipment on one bill of lading will be arrived at on the basis of 100 pounds at the applicable rate; if classified higher than first class or Class 100, the minimum charge will be based on 100 pounds at the first-class rate. This means that if an article to be shipped weighs less than 100 pounds, it will be charged for at 100 pounds, except that if the article is classified higher than first class and weighs less than 100 pounds, the actual weight at the applicable rate will be used; but if 100 pounds at the first-class rate produces a higher charge, the higher charge will be used.

If the total weight of the single shipment is less than 100 pounds, the shipper will be charged for 100 pounds. However, if any one of the articles in the single shipment is rated higher than first class, the minimum charge will be based on 100 pounds at the first-class rate. For example, suppose that a package containing different articles, totaling 75 pounds, is offered for shipment on one bill of lading and one article is rated double first class, the balance being rated first class or lower. Under Rule 12, the charge must be made on the article taking the highest rating, that is, double first class at actual weight; but if 100 pounds at the first-class rate produces a higher charge, the higher charge is the charge which is assessed. In no case shall the charge on a single shipment be less than a stipulated amount which is contained in the rule.

On carload shipments, the minimum charge is stated in this rule; and in 1958, this was $34.86, subject to *Ex Parte* 206 increase. However, this charge does not apply on shipments of brick, cement, and certain other listed articles. On these commodities, charges would be determined on the basis of actual weight at the applicable rate. Nor does the minimum charge per car apply to switching charges. When two or more carload shipments are loaded in one car, the minimum charge is applicable to each carload shipment. When articles require more than one car due to the length of the articles, the minimum charge will be applied for each car used. However, this minimum would be applied to the entire shipment, regardless of the number of cars used when the article is subject to Rule 24 or another "part lot" or "overflow" rule.

Rule 14 defines a carload shipment. It provides that in order to be considered a carload and entitled to carload rating, a shipment must be made by one shipper to one consignee; freight must all be shipped from one station and (except as provided in Rule 24) must be loaded in one car. The shipper must make out one bill of lading to cover the entire lot, such bill of lading containing all the freight to one station, except as provided in the tariffs, and loading must be done by the shipper and unloading by the consignee. The minimum carload weight provided in the tariff or classification is the lowest weight on which the carload rating or rate will apply.

Another section of this rule allows split deliveries, which are deliveries to more than one party at the destination station, provided the service is authorized by tariff provisions. A further exception to this rule has been made to authorize stop-offs to complete loading or to partially unload. This section also provides an exception to the requirement that the shipper and the consignee shall load and unload carload shipments, provided that tariffs in individual cases authorize such loading or unloading by the carrier. If the shipper does not fully load a car but tenders it as a carload shipment and other freight is not put in the car, that shipment will be charged for as a carload.

Rule 15 provides that the charge for a less-carload shipment must not exceed the charge for a carload of the same freight at the carload rate subject to the carload minimum weight. However, since the carload rate does not usually include loading or unloading of a carload shipment by the carrier, and less-carload freight generally is loaded by the carrier, this rule contains a further provision. If a shipment tendered as less-carload freight and loaded by the carrier, or transported and unloaded by the carrier, is found to be subject to the carload rate, and the carrier's tariffs do not provide that the cost of loading or unloading is included in the carload rate, a charge will be made for such loading and a like charge for unloading, such charge, stated in cents per 100 pounds, to be based on the actual weight of the shipment.

A further provision of this rule is that the charge for a car fully loaded must not exceed the charge for the same lot of freight if taken as a less-carload shipment.

The provisions of *Rule 16* state that when both carload and less-carload ratings are provided for the same articles, the term "LCL" covers shipments in quantities less than the minimum weight provided for carloads, subject to Rule 15. A single shipment of LCL freight is defined as a lot received from one shipper on one shipping order or bill of lading at one station at one time for one consignee and one destination. It provides that two or more single shipments shall not be combined and waybilled as one shipment but must be carried as separate shipments and at not less than the established minimum charge for each shipment.

Rule 17

In the event that a carrier should receive for transportation an article that is not included in the classification, the rating for an analogous article is authorized under *Rule 17*. In such cases, the freight agent reports the facts to the carrier's traffic department in order that the rating may be verified and the necessary classification provided for future movements.

An example of the application of this rule is provided by an attempt to determine the ratings on television masts. Television masts were not named specifically in the original classification publications, nor were they covered by a description under the term "NOIBN." They were, therefore, by analogy, first made subject to ratings in an item covering "Masts, radio broadcasting, tubular steel, in sections, loose or in packages." Later, in accordance with the intended temporary use of this rule, the two classifications were amended by the addition of television masts, specifically described and rated. Item 67690 now reads: "Masts, aerial or antenna, radio or television, tubular metal, KD, telescoped or in sections, loose or in packages."

Rule 18

When not specifically classified, articles which have been combined or attached to each other will be charged at the rating for the highest-classed article of the combination; on shipments subject to carload ratings, the minimum weight will be the highest minimum weight provided for such highest rate or rating under the conditions of *Rule 18*. The classifications do have descriptions of many combination articles, such as radio receiving sets equipped with record players.

Rule 19

Ratings on KD articles apply only when an article is taken apart in such a manner as to reduce materially the space occupied. This generally means a reduction of one third or more in space. This matter is covered in *Rule 19*. — ⅓ space

Under *Rule 20*, all the parts of a complete article included in a shipment, whether or not the parts are assembled, are to be charged at the rate applying to the complete article, regardless of the higher or lower charges applying to the parts if shipped separately. For example, a carload shipment of automobiles, if shipped with bumpers detached but included in the car, would be charged for as a carload of automobiles. If, however, the number of bumpers included in the shipment exceeded the number of bumpers needed to complete the automobiles, the shipment would be considered as a mixed carload of automobiles and bumpers, and it would be subject to the mixed-carload provisions of Rule 10.

Rule 21 provides that the term "nested" means three or more different sizes of the articles are enclosed, each smaller one within the next larger, or that three or more of the articles are placed one within the other so that each upper article does not project above the next lower article more than one third of its height. The term "nested solid" means three or more of the articles must be placed one within or upon the other so that the outer side surfaces of the one above will be in contact with the inner side surfaces of the one below and each upper article will not project above the next lower article more than one-quarter inch. An example of the application of this rule is found in the uniform classification, which provides three separate less-carload ratings for tin lamp shades. When "not nested," the rating is 125; when "nested," the rating is 100; and when "nested solid," the rating is 92½.

The classification contains many articles described as "in the rough," "in the white," or "finished." This is covered in Rule 22, and an example is item 1105 of the Uniform Freight Classification. The term "in the rough" means wooden articles which are no further manufactured than sawed, planed, or bent. "In the white" refers to wooden articles further finished than "in the rough"; and the articles may include one coat of priming, but this does not apply when articles have been painted or varnished. "Finished" means wooden articles after they have been further manufactured than "in the white." To each of these categories, separate ratings are assigned.

Rule 23 provides that freight cannot be loaded in bunkers (ice-storage space) of refrigerator cars.

Unless otherwise provided in classifications or in tariffs, the provisions of Rule 24 apply only in connection with carload freight, the authorized minimum weight for which is 30,000 pounds or more. This rule is applicable when a consignment consists of sufficient freight to fill one or more cars but on which there is an overflow not sufficient to fill another car. The consignment must be made from one station, by one shipper in one day, on one bill of lading to one consignee and one destination. Each car, except the car carrying the excess, must be loaded as heavily as loading conditions permit; and each car must be charged at actual or authorized estimated weight, subject to the minimum carload weight at the applicable carload rate. The car carrying the excess will be charged for at actual or authorized estimated weight at carload rate, if loaded in a closed car, and at actual or authorized estimated weight at carload rate, subject to a minimum charge of 4,000 pounds at Class 100 or first-class rate, if loaded in an open car.

This rule will not apply when specific items in the classifications or tariffs provide otherwise; or on bulk freight, livestock, and traffic requiring special equipment, such as refrigerator cars and tank cars; or on freight for which the authorized minimum weight is less than 30,000 pounds; or on freight subject to Rules 34 and 29.

Unless the contrary appears, Rule 25 provides that the word "iron," wherever used in the classifications, includes also steel, and vice versa. Except as otherwise provided, where reference is made to the gauge of metal, it means U.S. Standard Gauge. This gauge is used in measuring the thickness of sheet iron or steel in connection with shipping barrels or drums.

There is currently no *Rule 26.*

According to *Rule 27,* owners are required to load and unload freight carried at carload rating or rates, unless the tariff of the carrier at origin or destination, or stop-off point, provides for loading or unloading by the carrier. The same provision applies with respect to heavy or bulky freight carried at the less-carload rate which cannot be handled by the regular station employees, or where facilities are not sufficient for handling. Other sections outline the requirements regarding the loading of closed and open cars to assure safe transportation and protection of equipment.

Unless the contrary appears, *Rule 28* provides that the word "rubber," wherever used in the classifications, includes artificial, guayule, natural, neoprene, or synthetic rubber.

Rule 29 contains the provisions for transporting long or bulky articles which it is not possible to transport in one car or to load through the side door of a boxcar. If a shipment of an article requires (because of its length) two or more open cars, charges will be assessed as follows, subject to actual or authorized estimated weight if greater:

If subject to Rule 34, the minimum weight for the longest car shall be used, to which will be added either 24,000 pounds for each additional car or the minimum weight prescribed for such car, whichever is lower. Further, if the article is of such length as could have been loaded on cars of the length ordered, the minimum weight for such cars will apply.

If not subject to Rule 34, the minimum weight for one car shall be used, plus 24,000 pounds for each additional car. No more than four cars shall constitute a series. If more than four cars are used, the additional car or cars shall be considered a new series.

There are several provisions of the rule which deal with specific measurements. When an LCL shipment, or a shipment for which no carload rating is provided, requires more than one car because of the length, shipments shall be charged for on the actual weight at the authorized rating or rate, but not less than 7,500 pounds at first-class rate for each car used.

A further provision of Rule 29 is that a shipment containing articles of dimensions other than those specified in the following paragraph (the dimensions of which do not permit loading through center side doorway, 6 feet wide by 9 feet, 4 inches high, without use of end door or window, in a closed car not more than 40 feet, 7 inches in length by 9 feet, 2 inches wide and 10 feet high) shall be charged at actual weight and authorized rating for the entire shipment, subject to a minimum charge of 4,000 pounds, at the Class 1 or Class 100 rate.

Unless a lower rate is otherwise provided, on a shipment which contains an article exceeding 24 feet, but not exceeding 40 feet, 7 inches in length and not exceeding 15 inches in diameter or other dimension, the entire shipment shall be charged at actual weight and authorized rating, subject to a minimum charge of 1,000 pounds at the Class 1 rate. For purposes of application of this rule, an article exceeding 40 feet, 7 inches in length actually loaded by the shipper on the car floor in an area not exceeding 40 feet, 7 inches in length or $8\frac{1}{2}$ feet in width will be deemed not to exceed 40 feet, 7 inches in length.

This rule is employed in connection with shipments of poles, cranes, and articles of unusual length that require more than one car. In so far as shipments of poles are concerned, tariffs publishing the through rates, in many instances, will set forth rules pertaining to shipments requiring more than one car which supersede the rules of the classifications.

Temporary blocking, flooring or lining, standards, strips, stakes, or similar bracing or supports not constituting a part of a car, also bulkheads, partitions, temporary doors or door protection, usually referred to as "dunnage," when required to protect or make carload freight secure for shipment, must be furnished by the shipper, as provided by *Rule 30*. No allowance is made for dunnage used in connection with bulk freight in closed cars; but an allowance of actual weight, not in excess of 2,000 pounds, will be made for dunnage used in closed cars or in or on flat or open cars in connection with other freight, provided that in no case shall less than the established minimum weight be charged.

When two or more carload shipments are loaded in one car, an allowance of actual weight, not in excess of 2,000 pounds, for dunnage used in closed cars will be made on such cars; and for the purpose of specifying the weight of the dunnage, it may be divided equally between the two or more carload shipments. In order to obtain the allowance for dunnage used in or on closed or open cars, the shipper must specify the weight of the dunnage on the shipping order and bill of lading. Transportation charges for dunnage, when they are made, shall be at the rate applicable on the freight which it accompanies. The term "dunnage" does not include hay, excelsior, sawdust, shavings, shredded paper, straw, packing cushions or pads, or similar packing material. When this type of material is used, the weight of such material is to be included in the gross weight of the shipment.

Rule 31 states that carload ratings do not include the expense of refrigeration. The charges for this service, when furnished, will be found in appropriate tariffs. The rule further provides that carriers are not obligated to furnish heated cars, or to maintain heat in cars, for the protection of the consignment, except upon conditions which the carriers' tariffs provide. On less-carload or any-quantity ratings, substantially the same conditions are applicable as on carload shipments.

Rule 32 covers the use of ice or preservative for the protection of freight. Unless otherwise provided in the classifications, a shipper may choose to place ice or other preservative in the bunkers or in the body of the car; and no charge will be made for its transportation, unless removed by consignee, in which case freight charges will be assessed on actual weight of the ice or other preservative in the car at destination at the carload rate applicable on the freight it accompanies. Ice or other preservatives placed in the same package with freight will be charged for at the rate applicable to the article shipped.

Currently, there is no *Rule 33* in the classifications.

Generally speaking, *Rule 34* is applicable to light and bulky freight, and to articles on which the carload minimum is 30,000 pounds or less. Practically all articles in the Consolidated and Uniform Freight classifications on which the carload minima are less than 30,000 pounds are specifically made subject to the rule, although there are a few exceptions. Many articles in the classifications with minima of 30,000 pounds are made subject to the rule, such as broomcorn, tobacco, and wool. However, in the commodity rate tariffs, many articles with minima less than 30,000 pounds are not made subject to the rule. Many commodity rate tariffs provide for two and sometimes three different carload minimum weights, depending upon the lengths of the cars used; and they are referred to as "alternative minima." Such commodity rate items are not subject to Rule 34. The objective of this rule, as well as similar rules in rate tariffs providing for varying minimum weights which increase with the size of the car used and are subject to alternative rate provisions, is to foster complete utilization of the loading capacities of the larger cars.

Under the present scale, closed cars 40 feet, 7 inches or less in length are used as 100 per cent and take the basic minimum weight. Cars over 40 feet, 7 inches and not over 50 feet, 6 inches in length are subject to a minimum weight 140 per cent of the basic minimum. Cars over 50 feet, 6 inches long are subject to a minimum weight 200 per cent of the basic minimum. Thus, for an increase of approximately 10 feet in maximum length, there is an increase of 40 per cent, or 4 per cent per foot, in minimum weight. In 1949, 91.5 per cent of the boxcars were less than 40 feet, 7 inches in length and were subject only to basic minimum weights, and 8.5 per cent were subject to the scale of graduated minimum weights where the commodity shipped in these cars was subject to Rule 34.

By using this rule, instead of repeating it in all of their tariffs, the carriers may provide, for example, that the carload rate on wooden boxes from A to B is 20 cents per 100 pounds, minimum weight 20,000 pounds subject to Rule 34 of the classifications. This would mean that if a car 40 feet, 7 inches or less in length was ordered by the shipper and furnished by the carrier, the total charges would be 0.20 × 20,000 or $40. If, on the other hand, the shipper should order a 50-foot, 6-inch car, and a car was furnished, Rule 34 of the classifications with the graduated minimum would require assessment of charges based upon a minimum weight of 28,000 pounds, whether shipper loaded that amount or not; in this situation, charges would be 0.20 × 28,000, or $56.

Rule 34 provides a basis for ascertaining the minimum weight when cars are furnished at variance with the shipper's orders. On closed cars,

Section 3. (a) Table showing minimum CL weights applicable on articles made subject to Rule 34, in closed cars, see Note 2.

Length of Closed Car	When Minimum CL Weight provided in Classification, exceptions thereto or applicable tariff for articles shipped is:						
	10,000 lbs. Charge not less than	11,000 lbs. Charge not less than	12,000 lbs. Charge not less than	13,000 lbs. Charge not less than	14,000 lbs. Charge not less than	15,000 lbs. Charge not less than	16,000 lbs. Charge not less than
	lbs.	lbs.	lbs.	lbs.	lbs.	lbs.	lbs.
Cars over 40 ft. 7 in. and not over 50 ft. 6 in. long..............	14,000	15,400	16,800	18,200	19,600	21,000	22,400
Cars over 50 ft. 6 in. in length......................	20,000	22,000	24,000	26,000	28,000	30,000	32,000

Length of Closed Car	When Minimum CL Weight provided in Classification, exceptions thereto or applicable tariff for articles shipped is:								
	18,000 lbs. Charge not less than	20,000 lbs. Charge not less than	22,000 lbs. Charge not less than	24,000 lbs. Charge not less than	26,000 lbs. Charge not less than	28,000 lbs. Charge not less than	30,000 lbs. Charge not less than	35,000 lbs. Charge not less than	40,000 lbs. Charge not less than
	lbs.	lbs.	lbs.	lbs.	lbs.	lbs.	lbs.	lbs.	lbs.
Cars over 40 ft. 7 in. and not over 50 ft. 6 in. long	25,200	28,000	30,800	33,600	36,400	39,200	42,000	50,400	56,000
Cars over 50 ft. 6 in. in length..............	36,000	40,000	44,000	48,000	52,000	56,000	60,000	72,000	80,000

(b) Where CL minimum weight provided is not shown as a base weight in Section 3 (a) the articles are subject to Rule 34, the minimum CL weight for cars exceeding 40 feet 7 inches in length will be as follows (see Note 2):

	Example using 17,000 lbs. as base weight
Cars over 40 ft. 7 in. and not over 50 ft. 6 in. long, 140% of base weight..	23,800
Cars over 50 ft. 6 in. in length.................... 200% of base weight...................	34,000

Note 3.   When shipper orders a car of specified length within and including the minimum and maximum lengths for which the same minimum CL weight is provided in Section 3, the furnishing by carrier of a car of any length between and including such minimum and maximum lengths will be a fulfillment of shipper's order.

Section 8. (a) Table showing minimum CL weights applicable on articles made subject to Rule 34, in open cars, see Note 4.

Length of Open Car	When Minimum CL Weight provided in Classification, exceptions thereto or applicable tariff for articles shipped is:						
	10,000 lbs. Charge not less than	11,000 lbs. Charge not less than	12,000 lbs. Charge not less than	13,000 lbs. Charge not less than	14,000 lbs. Charge not less than	15,000 lbs. Charge not less than	16,000 lbs. Charge not less than
	lbs.	lbs.	lbs.	lbs.	lbs.	lbs.	lbs.
Over 41 ft. 6 in. and not over 42 ft. 6 in........................	12,260	13,420	14,640	15,860	17,080	18,300	19,520
Over 42 ft. 6 in. and not over 46 ft. 6 in........................	14,200	15,620	17,040	18,460	19,880	21,300	22,720
Over 46 ft. 6 in. and not over 50 ft. 6 in........................	16,200	17,820	19,440	21,060	22,680	24,300	25,920
Over 50 ft. 6 in. and not over 52 ft. 6 in........................	17,200	18,920	20,640	22,360	24,080	25,800	27,520
Over 52 ft. 6 inches in length..............................	20,000	22,000	24,000	26,000	28,000	30,000	32,000

Length of Open Car	When Minimum CL Weight provided in Classification, exceptions thereto or applicable tariff for articles shipped is:								
	18,000 lbs. Charge not less than	20,000 lbs. Charge not less than	22,000 lbs. Charge not less than	24,000 lbs. Charge not less than	26,000 lbs. Charge not less than	28,000 lbs. Charge not less than	30,000 lbs. Charge not less than	35,000 lbs. Charge not less than	40,000 lbs. Charge not less than
	lbs.	lbs.	lbs.	lbs.	lbs.	lbs.	lbs.	lbs.	lbs.
Over 41 ft. 6 in. and not over 42 ft. 6 in........	21,960	24,400	26,840	29,280	31,720	34,160	36,600	43,920	48,800
Over 42 ft. 6 in. and not over 46 ft. 6 in........	25,560	28,400	31,240	34,080	36,920	39,760	42,600	51,120	56,800
Over 46 ft. 6 in. and not over 50 ft. 6 in........	29,160	32,400	35,640	38,880	42,120	45,360	48,600	58,320	64,800
Over 50 ft. 6 in. and not over 52 ft. 6 in........	30,960	34,400	37,840	41,280	44,720	48,160	51,600	61,920	68,800
Over 52 ft. 6 inches in length.................	36,000	40,000	44,000	48,000	52,000	56,000	60,000	72,000	80,000

(b) Where CL minimum weight is not shown as a base weight in Section 8 (a) and the articles are subject to Rule 34, the minimum weight for cars exceeding 41 feet 6 inches in length will be as follows (see Note 4):

	Example using 44,000 lbs. as base weight
Cars over 41 ft. 6 in. and not over 42 ft. 6 in., 122% of base weight..................................	53,680
Cars over 42 ft. 6 in. and not over 46 ft. 6 in., 142% of base weight..................................	62,480
Cars over 46 ft. 6 in. and not over 50 ft. 6 in., 162% of base weight..................................	71,280
Cars over 50 ft. 6 in. and not over 52 ft. 6 in., 172% of base weight..................................	75,680
Cars over 52 ft. 6 inches in length, 200% of base weight..................................	88,000

SOURCE: Uniform Freight Classification No. 6 and Consolidated Freight Classification No. 23

FIG. 7–1.   Minimum carload weights, Rule 34.

when the carrier is unable to furnish a car of the length ordered by the shippers and furnishes one of greater length, the minimum weight is that fixed for the car ordered; except that when the loading capacity of the car is used, the minimum weight may be that fixed for the car furnished. The reason for this provision is that it is difficult to determine if the freight offered for shipment could or could not be loaded in a car of the length ordered because cars of identical length have varying space capacity due to differences in height or other dimensions.

On open cars, when the carrier is unable to furnish a car of the length ordered and furnishes a longer car, the rule provides that the shipper will be charged the minimum weight for the car furnished; except if the articles are of such length as could have been loaded on a car of the length ordered, the minimum weight will be that fixed for the car ordered. Open cars of identical length vary little in car floor area so it is possible to determine exactly if a car of the size ordered could accommodate the shipment.

It is one of the most important rules of the classifications and is used much more frequently than most of the other classification rules. It consists of ten sections: Sections 1 through 4 apply to closed cars only; Sections 5 through 8 apply to open cars only; and Sections 9 and 10 apply to both. Minimum carload weights applicable on articles subject to Rule 34, in open and closed cars, are shown in Figure 7–1.

The classifications and specific commodity tariffs provide ratings or rates on practically all articles capable of being shipped in tank cars, and *Rule 35* applies to tank-car freight. Included in these articles are most liquids, such as water, acids, chemicals, gasoline, oils; compressed and liquefied gases; molasses, asphalt, tars, and fats. Shipments moving in tank-car equipment require a different kind of handling and require special considerations not necessary in the transportation of solids. All gases and some liquids are subject to expansion and contraction under temperature changes. The Interstate Commerce Commission has regulations governing the transportation of explosives and other dangerous articles in freight, express, and baggage services, as well as specifications for containers in which these commodities are to be shipped, including tank cars. The carriers have granted power of attorney to an agent to publish these regulations in tariff form, and that tariff is applicable whenever a commodity referred to therein is shipped. Many of the articles shipped in tank cars, being inflammable, corrosive, or poisonous, are subject to those regulations. The computation of weights on articles in tank cars presents conditions different from those of other freight, especially those commodities subject to expansion; as they weigh less per gallon in higher temperatures because they expand, the same quantity, by weight, occupies more space.

These are some of the factors which have led to the establishment of this rule, which forms a basic set of regulations for tank-car freight and is applicable when individual items in the classifications and carriers' commodity tariffs refer to it.

Rule 36 authorizes the disposition of fractions in computing rates based on a multiple or a proportion of another rate, such as $1\frac{1}{2}$ times first-class or double first-class rate. If the fractions are less than $\frac{1}{2}$ cent, such fraction is omitted; if $\frac{1}{2}$ cent or more, the result is increased to the next whole figure. This rule authorizes the disposition of fractions only when computing rates as specified in the rule, and for no other purpose. Generally, tariffs requiring computations carry their own rule for disposing of fractions resulting from such computations. When fractions result from computations other than designated in this rule and no rule is provided for their disposition, the product of the computations should be used.

At the present time, there is no *Rule 37* in the classifications.

Rule 38 states that unless otherwise provided in the governing tariffs, if there is in effect a commodity rate on a given shipment, that rate and not the class rate must be applied, except that rates, either class or commodity, specifically designated as applicable only on import, export, coastwise, or intercoastal shipments, must be applied on such shipments to the exclusion of all other rates not so designated. When both commodity rates and class rates are published for application on import, export, coastwise, or intercoastal traffic, the commodity rate will take precedence over the class rate unless the tariffs naming such commodity rates designate otherwise.

Rule 39 covers explosives and dangerous articles other than explosives, which must be shipped in containers and handled and marked in accordance with the rules and regulations prescribed by the Interstate Commerce Commission and found in Agent H. A. Campbell's Explosives and Dangerous Articles Tariff.

Rule 40 sets forth in great detail the specifications for materials that must be used in—and the method of constructing—shipping containers, other than fiberboard. The purposes of the detailed specifications, gauges, and tests shown in this rule are primarily to insure the safe transportation of the articles shipped.

Rule 41 is quite lengthy, for it sets forth the specifications governing the materials and the manner of construction for fiberboard, pulpboard, or double-faced corrugated strawboard containers. It also provides a penalty for articles tendered for transportation in fiber boxes not fully complying with the requirements and specifications of this rule.

Rule 42 provides that it is permissible to forward reshipping documents, invoices, or operating instructions with the articles covered thereby at the rate applicable on such articles.

In connection with shipments other than livestock, live wild animals, or ostriches, where tariffs provide transportation of a male attendant in charge, *Rule 43* provides that such attendant must execute a contract—the substance of which is that he assumes all risks of accidents and releases the carrier from claim, unless such accident is due to the carrier's negligence.

Rule 44 specifies the method by which items in the classifications which have been supplemented are canceled and the new entries numbered.

Rule 45 provides that advertising matter other than stationery or gift articles, advertising signs that are not electric (other than figures or images), or store display racks or stands may be shipped with the goods advertised, at the same rate, either carload or LCL, provided the advertising matter does not exceed 10 per cent of the gross weight of the goods and packing. Any excess will be charged for at the rate applicable to such advertising matter. On carload shipments, where actual weight is less than minimum weight, the weight of the advertising matter may equal 10 per cent of the minimum weight.

One premium may be placed in each package, except that in carloads, premiums may be in bulk but cannot exceed one premium for each package of the commodity. In such cases, the freight charges will be the same as on the commodity accompanying the premiums.

Rule 46 states the explanation of the words "and" and "or" and the use of parentheses. "And" is used to couple the terms between which it appears; "or" provides for alteration or use of either or both of the terms between which it appears; and the name of the article or articles appearing within parentheses constitutes another description of the identical article or articles immediately preceding the parentheses.

The explanation of indentations is given as being used where any part of the description of an article is found set away from the left margin in a position subordinate to the text preceding it, in which case the description is to be read within its context, and particularly with the preceding heading or headings. The effect of its position upon the meaning of a description should be carefully observed.

The term "rate," as used in the classifications, means the specific figure published in freight tariffs, class or commodity, to be used in computing the charge on the property transported. The terms "rating" or "column" signify the letters or numerals employed in the classifications or in exceptions thereto to identify the "rate" published in freight tariffs, class, or commodity.

Rule 47 provides that shipments moving on less-carload or any-quantity rates or ratings originating at or destined to agency stations in the United States may be consigned C.O.D.; and it provides that the carrier at the shipping point will accept such shipments subject to the provisions shown, while the agent of the carrier at destination will undertake to collect the amount designated on the face of the bill of lading as the value of the goods, subject to collection fees published in this rule. Marking and other conditions of C.O.D. shipments are covered by this rule.

Rule 48 states that reference in the classifications to items, pages, rules, etc., includes reference to reissues of such items, pages, rules, etc. Reference to other publications includes reference to supplements thereto or successive issues thereof. A similar rule is contained in most freight tariffs.

For the purpose of determining the merits of shipping containers not specifically provided for in the classifications, shipments in such containers, for the purpose of experimentation, will be accepted for transportation as covered in *Rule 49*. A permit must be secured from classification committees before presenting the shipment for transportation; and the shipper must agree to accept the decision of the classification committees in case of loss or damage to the shipments, as to the amount of the claim for such loss or damage.

Empty shipping containers, not exceeding a total weight of twenty-five pounds, may be included in straight or mixed-carload shipments of commodities in such shipping containers, according to *Rule 50*, the rate or rating to be applied being the highest carload rate or rating applicable on any commodity in such shipping containers contained in the car. To the extent provided in this rule, this is an exception to the mixed-carload provisions of Rule 10.

At the present time, there is no *Rule 51* in the Consolidated or Uniform Freight classifications.

Rules 52 and *53* are found only in the Uniform Freight Classification and provide the method of computing weights on liquefied petroleum gas (Rule 52) and butadiene (Rule 53) when shipped in tank cars. Each rule includes a table which is composed of two columns. Column 1 lists, in ascending order, a specific gravity rating of the liquid material. Column 2 is divided into two subcolumns: the first applicable during April to October, both inclusive, and the second applicable during November to March, both inclusive. In each subcolumn are listed weights per gallon applicable to the commodity of the specific gravity rating shown opposite in column 1.

The *Rule 53* which appears in the Consolidated Freight Classification deals with Fourth Section departures. By its terms, carriers will correct any unauthorized departures from the Fourth Section of the Interstate Commerce Act caused by changes in the classification. Corrections can be made on one day's notice by proper publication in the carrier's rate tariffs, by reducing any higher rate or charge to the rate or charge applying for the longer haul, or by reducing any through rate or charge which is higher than the aggregate of intermediate rates or charges, to the amount of such lower aggregate. Application is made to the Commission for authority to make reparation to the lower basis. Reparation procedure is a method used to permit refund of any overcharge resulting from the application of any legal published rate which is unlawful, in that it does not conform to all of the requirements of the Interstate Commerce Act.

When an article is not rated the same in all classification territories and a change is made in the rating in one territory without a corresponding change being made in other territories, a Fourth Section departure may result, particularly at stations on or near the border line between classification territories. This is due to the application, generally, of the destination territory classification on traffic moving between points in different classification territories, and occurs when the classification rating to the destination is lower than that applying to intermediate border points.

Currently, there is no *Rule 54.*

The method of denoting reissued matter in supplements is described in *Rule 55.* It provides that matter brought forward without change from one supplement to another will be designated as reissued by a reference mark in the form of a square enclosing a number, the number being that of the supplement in which the reissued matter first appeared in its currently effective form.

Rule 60 applies when specifically designated, railroad-owned flat cars of substantial capacity are used and specifies a minimum charge of 15,000 pounds at the first class or Class 100 rate.

MOTOR

Originally there were not as many rules contained in the National Motor Freight Classification as there were in the rail classifications but now there are about the same number. The motor rules are numbered from 1 through 320, and there are currently 57 rules. This numbering allows for additional rules to be added in the future and inserted near those rules dealing with similar subjects. Many motor classification rules cover the same subjects and are much the same as the corresponding rail classification rules. To facilitate a comparison of the subject matter and the rules, the following tabulation has been made:

Subject	Rail Rule No.	Motor Rule No.
Acceptance and billing of shipments	1, 2, 7, 42, and 45	10, 170, 175
Conditions under which carriers may refuse shipments	3, 4, and 5	15, 20, 30, 50, 200 thru 320
Marking of freight	6, 24, and 39	55, 65
Application of ratings	14, 16, 17, 18, 19, 20, 21, 22, 25, 28, 31, 35, 42, 45, and 50	5, 23, 60, 95, 100, 105, 130, 140, 170, 175
Application of rates	1, 10, 14, 30, 36, 38, 42, 45, and 50	5, 10, 60, 90, 135, 145, 170, 175
Application of charges	1, 5, 8, 9, 11, 15, and 47	10, 30, 50, 130, 135, 140, 150, 155, 165, 200 thru 320
Application of minimum charges	12, 13, 24, and 29	110, 130, 140, 160
Minimum weights	10, 12, 14, 15, 24, 29, 34, and 35	23, 110, 115, 130, 140
Mixed-load shipments	10	110
Freight requiring the use of more than one transportation unit	24, 29, and 34	23
Loading and unloading of freight	15 and 27	160
Perishable traffic	31 and 32	23
Dangerous articles	39	55
Package and container specifications	40, 41, and 49	30, 50, 185, 200 thru 320
Dunnage	30	135
Miscellaneous rules	23, 43, 44, 46, 48, 52, 53, 55, and 56	

An important motor rule is *Rule 34* which deals with minimum weights and cubic capacities. Prior to Rule 34, volume minimum weights were taken primarily from the rail classification. The present rule contains two tables, A and B. These tables show minimum weights for the different minimum-weight factors, based on vehicle cubic capacities. For example, Table A is predicated on a vehicle with a capacity of 1,850 cubic feet and above, and Table B on one of less than 1,850 cubic feet.

A minimum weight factor follows the description of each commodity and the ratings in the classification. This represents the rail competitive minimum combined with the density of the article. For example, a minimum weight factor of 10.1 would indicate a rail competitive minimum of 10,000 pounds (the figure preceding the decimal point), and the number following the decimal point, in this illustration "1" is the key to the density of the article. The rate tariff will indicate which table should be used by carrying a provision to this effect.

The application of a particular table is a matter decided by the various motor carrier rate bureaus. It is assumed that the bureaus designate the particular table which reflects the cubic capacity of most of the vehicles operating in their territories. If the rate tariff does not indicate application of a particular table, Table B applies. Minimum-weight factors go as high as 60.2.

In using Rule 34, the table letter shown in the carrier's rate tariff and the minimum-weight factor shown in the classification are all that is necessary to secure the truckload minimum weight.

DISCUSSION QUESTIONS AND PROBLEMS

1. Would a classification rule ever apply to shipments which move on other than class rates?
2. Why should the classification rules be mastered?
3. What classification rule gives the carriers the right to inspect a shipment when it is necessary to determine the ratings?
4. List the different ways in which articles may be offered for shipment under the ratings shown in the rail and motor classifications.
5. Determine the applicable rating for malt tonics, medicinal, shipped in glass carboys, in barrels, or in boxes. Check this item in the rail classifications, and then consult Rule 5.
6. Under what conditions, as provided in what rail classification rule, may (a) LCL freight be accepted without marking, (b) railroads require prepayment or guarantee of freight charges?
7. Compute the charges, under Rule 10 of the rail classifications, of the following: A mixed carload which weighs 65,000 pounds and consists of 38,000 pounds of lard substitutes, in metal cans, in boxes, and 27,000 pounds of leaf lard, in packages. In straight carloads, the items are lard substitutes, Class 5, 40 cents per 100 pounds, minimum weight 30,000 pounds; and leaf lard, Class 3, 70 cents per 100 pounds, minimum weight 21,000 pounds.

8. You have a shipment of two dies, automobile body stamping, iron, which each weigh 800 pounds. Check this item in the rail classifications; then consult Rule 12, and determine how the charges would be assessed.

9. What is streamlined Rule 10? Modified Rule 10? Where are they found?

10. Under the rail classifications, what is the minimum charge for carloads? LCL? What is your authority?

11. Assume you ship 6,000 pounds of an article at an LCL rate of 80 cents per 100 pounds. The carload minimum for this commodity is 10,000 pounds, and the carload rate 60 cents per 100 pounds. You instruct the carrier to bill the car through to destination without loading other freight in it. The carrier complies with the request. Consult Rule 14 to ascertain whether this can be done, and determine the charges.

12. What is the primary advantage to the shipper of the contents of Rule 24 of the rail classifications?

13. Using rail Rule 34, compute the following: The shipper loads work benches, NOIBN, SU (set up), which weigh 17,500 pounds, in a 40-foot closed car. The classification carload minimum weight is 16,000 R. Assume that a rate of $2.00 per 100 pounds exists between two points. What are the applicable charges?

14. Assume that the carload minimum weight on a commodity is 27,000 pounds, subject to Rule 34 of the rail classifications. The shipment is loaded in a 51-foot closed car. Compute the minimum weight.

15. You tender a carload of soap to a railroad and indicate that the shipment includes gift articles which do not exceed 10 per cent of the gross weight of the soap. Is there any rail classification rule which permits or prohibits these articles from taking the soap rate?

16. What motor classification rule governs the marking of freight? How must shipments be marked for handling?

17. What rating is applied on a motor shipment of differently rated articles packed in one container? What motor classification rule applies?

18. May a motor carrier charge more for a less-truckload shipment than for a volume shipment of the same commodity? What motor classification rule governs?

19. Is there any difference between the motor and rail classification rule which applies to the shipment of advertising and premiums shipped with the articles advertised?

20. What is the purpose of motor classification Rule 34?

21. In comparing the rule provisions of motor and rail classifications, it will be noted that some rail rules are more comprehensive. Do you feel that motor carriers have benefited by less stringent requirements? Have shippers benefited?

Chapter

8

RATES

THE utilization of the transportation service of a carrier by a shipper involves payment to the carrier for this service. This payment is computed by the carrier at an established rate or price per unit, the most common price unit being 100 pounds, expressed in cents per 100 pounds. Other determinable units may be and are used, such as gallon, barrel, cord, or ton—net (2,000 pounds) or gross (2,240)—among others. For example, in the steel industry, the gross ton is used in computing iron ore rates. It is estimated that there are more than a hundred different types of freight rates. The more important and frequently used are described in this chapter.

All rates filed with a regulatory body are legal rates since they are filed in accordance with statutory requirements. A regulatory body does not, in most instances, pass on the lawfulness of a rate at the time it is filed. If shippers challenge the lawfulness of a rate, which they often do, it is then determined by the regulatory body.

KINDS OF RATES

The rate applicable for the service rendered by common carriers may be classified into two broad groups. These are (1) the line-haul rate, which, as the term implies, is generally the rate from the origin terminal to destination terminal; and (2) the accessorial or ancillary charges.

The completeness of the service in the line-haul rate depends upon the mode of transportation and the quantity offered in one shipment. In motor transportation, the line-haul rate is a store-door to store-door service. This may or may not be the case in rail transportation, depending upon whether the shipper and receiver have rail sidings. This includes the spotting of cars for loading or unloading of carload shipments at public team tracks[1] or on industrial trackage, if this is located within

---

[1] Industries which do not have rail sidetracks which permit direct service can utilize the public team tracks or delivery tracks which railroads provide at one or more central locations for shippers and receivers of carload shipments who do not have rail facilities.

specified limits. In water transportation, the line-haul rate is a pier-to-pier rate; while in air transportation, this rate is an airport-to-airport rate.

RAIL AND MOTOR COMMON CARRIERS

Line-Haul Rates

Line-haul rates may be subdivided into *class rates, commodity rates,* and *exceptions to the classification.*

Class Rates

Class rates are governed by a rating in a classification, so that ratings and class rates are interdependent. They are applicable on the various classes designated in the applicable classification. The classification of freight is important for a number of reasons: (1) it embraces many of our manufactured items, (2) certain of our other rates are tied to the class rate structure, and (3) a class rate is always available to ship articles to and from all points in the United States which have carrier service. Only a very small percentage of total rail traffic moves at class rates. In 1960, an estimated 5 per cent of total rail revenue was derived from these rates.

Class rates are in the form of a schedule which shows the price per 100 pounds for moving Class 1 or 100 freight every possible distance it may be moved. The cost of shipment for a given commodity is determined by ascertaining its classification rating, the Class 1 rate per 100 pounds for the haul involved, and the percentage of the Class 1 rate to which the classification rating in question is subject.

In an earlier chapter, the development of the railroads' Uniform Freight Classification in Docket No. 28310 was discussed. The investigation of class rates by the Interstate Commerce Commission, Docket No. 28300, was heard on the same record as Docket No. 28310; and since both classification and class rates were involved, the case is often referred to as the "Class Rate Case." In scope of territory, the number of commodities, and the amount of revenue involved, it was the most extensive and most important freight rate revision ever undertaken. Probably, it constitutes the greatest step toward tariff simplification ever taken up to this time. Its accomplishment involved changes, however slight, in all class rates in the territories involved.

The rail carriers filed with the Interstate Commerce Commission National Rate Basis Tariff No. 1 and 12 class rate tariffs which became effective on May 30, 1952, in conjunction with the new Uniform Freight Classification, which supplanted some 60 tariffs previously used.

It is possible, in connection with class rates, to establish the charge in terms of cents per 100 pounds for specific distances, and this is exactly what is done. This is referred to as a "rate scale"; and in Dockets No. 28300 and No. 28310, effective on May 30, 1952, the Interstate Commerce

TABLE 8–1

SCALE OF FIRST-CLASS RATES (CLASS 100) PRESCRIBED FOR TERRITORY COVERED BY DOCKET NO. 28300

Distance	Rate, cents per 100 pounds	Distance	Rate, cents per 100 pounds
5 miles	58	950 miles	335
10 miles	64	975 miles	340
15 miles	69	1,000 miles	345
20 miles	73	1,025 miles	350
25 miles	76	1,050 miles	355
30 miles	80	1,075 miles	360
35 miles	83	1,100 miles	365
40 miles	86	1,125 miles	370
45 miles	89	1,150 miles	375
50 miles	91	1,175 miles	380
55 miles	94	1,200 miles	385
60 miles	96	1,225 miles	390
65 miles	99	1,250 miles	395
70 miles	101	1,275 miles	400
75 miles	103	1,300 miles	405
80 miles	106	1,325 miles	410
85 miles	108	1,350 miles	415
90 miles	110	1,375 miles	420
95 miles	112	1,400 miles	425
100 miles	114	1,425 miles	430
110 miles	118	1,450 miles	435
120 miles	122	1,475 miles	440
130 miles	126	1,500 miles	445
140 miles	129	1,525 miles	450
150 miles	133	1,550 miles	455
160 miles	136	1,575 miles	460
170 miles	140	1,600 miles	465
180 miles	143	1,625 miles	470
190 miles	146	1,650 miles	475
200 miles	149	1,675 miles	480
210 miles	153	1,700 miles	485
220 miles	156	1,725 miles	490
230 miles	159	1,750 miles	495
240 miles	162	1,775 miles	500
260 miles	168	1,800 miles	505
280 miles	173	1,825 miles	510
300 miles	179	1,850 miles	515
320 miles	185	1,875 miles	520
340 miles	190	1,900 miles	525
360 miles	196	1,925 miles	530
380 miles	201	1,950 miles	535
400 miles	206	1,975 miles	540
420 miles	211	2,000 miles	545
440 miles	216	2,025 miles	550
460 miles	221	2,050 miles	555
480 miles	226	2,075 miles	560
500 miles	231	2,100 miles	565
520 miles	236	2,125 miles	570
540 miles	241	2,150 miles	575
560 miles	245	2,175 miles	580
580 miles	250	2,200 miles	585
600 miles	255	2,250 miles	595
620 miles	260	2,300 miles	605
640 miles	265	2,350 miles	615
660 miles	270	2,400 miles	625
680 miles	275	2,450 miles	635
700 miles	280	2,500 miles	645
720 miles	285	2,550 miles	655
740 miles	290	2,600 miles	665
760 miles	295	2,650 miles	675
780 miles	300	2,700 miles	685
800 miles	305	2,750 miles	695
825 miles	310	2,800 miles	705
850 miles	315	2,850 miles	715
875 miles	320	2,900 miles	725
900 miles	325	2,950 miles	735
925 miles	330	3,000 miles	745

SOURCE: *Class Rate Investigation, 1939*, 281 ICC 213, 328 (1951). Increase granted under *Ex Parte* 175 not included.

Commission prescribed a scale of Class 100 rates for application in all territories governed by Docket No. 28300. This is shown in Table 8–1.

In examining the Class 100 rates and the mileage shown in Table 8–1, it can be seen that to transport 100 miles a commodity that is classified Class 100 the rate is $1.14 per 100 pounds. This scale of Class 100 rates greatly simplifies the determination of all other class rates. A commodity which, because of certain factors, such as high value or susceptibility to theft, is Class 400 in the classification, would be transported at a rate of 400 per cent of $1.14 for 100 miles, or $4.56 for 100 miles. Likewise, a commodity which, because of classification factors, is classified less than Class 100, perhaps Class 50, would move 100 miles at 50 per cent of Class 100, or 50 per cent of $1.14, or $0.57 per 100 pounds for 100 miles.

The uniform class rate scale differs from most mileage scales in that the rate of progression is more constant. An examination of the class rate scale adjusted to include the general rate increases, *Ex Partes* 162, 166, and 168, shows that the rate of progression varies from 2 cents to 6 cents up to 100 miles for each mileage block of 5 miles. From 100 miles to 240 miles, the rate of progression varies from 3 to 4 cents up to 240 miles for 10-mile blocks. For distances over 240 miles up to and including 540 miles, the rate of progression is 5 or 6 cents for each 20 miles. From 580 to 800 miles, the scale increases 5 cents for each 20-mile block. From 800 to 2,200 miles, the rate of progression is 5 cents for each 25 miles of additional distance; and then, for the additional distance beyond 2,200 miles, the scale increases 10 cents for each 50 miles. The rate of progression for the greater distances is more constant. In general, then, the class rate scale is relatively high for short distances but progressively lower as the distance increases.

National Rate Basis Tariff No. 1 provides the rate basis applicable from or to all points in Docket No. 28300 territory. A rate-basis point is generally the principal tonnage point in a square of about 40 miles. Stations within the square are assigned as their rate basis the principal tonnage point. The rate-basis numbers, generally speaking, are the shortest workable mileages over which carload traffic can be handled without transfer of lading. In the case of short-line carriers, rate-basis numbers and rates will not correspond exactly with the scale shown in Table 8–1 (the so-called "Appendix 18 scale") because of the addition of arbitraries to the rates provided in that scale.[2]

The prescription of such a rate scale will tend to emphasize the advantage or disadvantage of location where shippers rely upon class rates to move their commodities. With a single class rate scale having general application, this results in a more or less frozen level of class rates. This focuses greater attention on the classification than has been the case in the past for, in effect, the classification of the article determines what the freight charges will be.

---

[2] E. A. Nightingale, "Uniform Freight Classification and Uniform Class Rates," *I.C.C. Practitioners' Journal*, Vol. XX (1952), p. 171.

The new uniform class rate scale is lower than any scale of rates which formerly was in effect in any territory, as well as being lower than any scale or system of class rates which had been in effect heretofore between the several rate territories, except within the Official Territory, where the Class 1 (Class 100) rates have been slightly increased in some instances and slightly reduced in others. It has been reported that the uniform class rate scale reduced the former class rate scales in the South about 16 per cent; interterritorially, between the South and the North, the rates have been reduced an average of about 13 per cent; between the South and the Western Trunk-Line Territory, they have been reduced an average of about 21 per cent; between the South and Southwest, a little over 26 per cent; and in all of the territory between the Rocky Mountains and the Mississippi River, the reduction averages more than 21 per cent.[3]

A survey of New England traffic managers resulted in the conclusion that, to the extent that New England industries market their products beyond the borders of the Official Territory, they have profited by the new class rate adjustment, for the long-haul interterritorial class rates prescribed by the Commission have, in general, resulted in reductions, some of which are quite substantial. For New England industries which market their products largely within the Official Territory, the class rates have been so increased, with relatively few exceptions, as frequently to prove a real handicap.[4] This would be true especially where shippers do not have volume shipments.

In a general revision of such scope and magnitude as Docket No. 28300 and Docket No. 28310, the effect was to reduce rates in some instances and increase them in others. With or without uniformity of classification, the Commission's order in No. 28300 changes the class rates between all points east of the Rocky Mountains. If ratings effective prior to May 30, 1952, had been maintained without change, the rates and charges would be greatly changed by application of the Docket No. 28300 class rate scale; but there would be nothing but reductions within and between all territories (except in Official, where slight increases and reductions occur), because the Docket No. 28300 class rate scale is lower in all instances than the basic class rate scales formerly applicable within and between all territories, as mentioned earlier, except in the Official Territory, where the change is slight.

In Docket No. 30416, *Class Rates, Mountain-Pacific Territory*, and Docket No. 20660, *Class Rates, Transcontinental Rail, 1950*, which became effective in 1956, the Interstate Commerce Commission took interim action in the areas involved by prescribing Western rail-proposed scales to

---

[3] R. W. Boyle, Jr., "What Do I.C.C. 28300 and 28310 Rate Charges Mean to Shipper and Carriers in the Southeast?" Paper presented before the First Annual Southeastern Transportation Clinic, University of Georgia, Atlanta Division, December 10, 1952.

[4] Statement of W. H. Day before 2nd Annual Transportation and Traffic Management Conference, Northeastern University, May, 1953.

be subject to the Uniform Freight Classification. It generally provided for reductions in the existing class rates within the Mountain-Pacific Territory but not as great as those in the Docket No. 28300 scale. As a result of this action, there were reductions in transcontinental class rates from 16 to 29 per cent on most traffic. The carriers were permitted to maintain rates established to meet truck competition and to maintain short- and branch-line arbitraries. The rate scale prescribed serves as a minimum, but provision is made for alteration when commodity or classification exceptions rates are higher.

Commodity Rates

Commodity rates ordinarily will take precedence over class rates or exceptions ratings. They are sometimes termed "special rates." A rate of this kind is applicable to specific commodities or constitutes a so-called "specific commodity rate"; or it may be established on groups of commodities which bear some relation to each other. Commodity rates are published on specific commodities directly rather than through the medium of the freight classification. It was estimated in 1960 that commodity rates accounted for 79 per cent of the revenue of railroads and about 90 per cent of the tonnage.

Two of the important factors in the establishment of commodity rates by carriers have been the quantity offered for shipment and the regularity of movement. Examples of commodity rates are those applicable on the movement of cement, coal, brick, sand, gravel and stone, iron and steel, and lumber and forest products, as well as others. From time to time, a sample of the rail carload shipments moving on commodity rates made on a representative day by the Interstate Commerce Commission shows that over 80 per cent of such shipments are made at commodity rates. The title page of a commodity rate tariff is shown in Figure 8–1.

There are three general types of commodity rates:

1. Those tied to class rates, usually expressed as a certain percentage of Class 1, and termed "column rates."
2. Those rates not tied to class rates but constructed on a systematic basis, such as a distance scale.
3. Those special point-to-point rates not built upon any systematic basis but adjusted to meet the needs of particular shippers, localities, or competitive conditions.

Exceptions to the Classification

The exceptions to the classification may establish rules, regulations, or ratings different from those published in the classification. This usually results in the application of a class rate used in conjunction with the exceptions to the classification, and the rate will be one lower than the class rate when used in conjunction with the classification. The exceptions to the classification may be lower classes or percentages of class rates. Rail-ø - Except matter under suspension in I. & S. Docket No. M-5582.

MIDDLE ATLANTIC CONFERENCE, Agent

FREIGHT TARIFF No. S-60D
(CANCELS FREIGHT TARIFF No. S-60C)

Local, Joint and Proportional Freight Tariff)

OF

TRUCKLOAD COMMODITY RATES
INCLUDING EXPORT, IMPORT, COASTWISE AND INTERCOASTAL RATES

ON

IRON and STEEL ARTICLES

APPLYING

FROM POINTS IN:	TO POINTS IN:
MARYLAND NEW JERSEY NEW YORK AND PENNSYLVANIA	DELAWARE DISTRICT OF COLUMBIA MARYLAND NEW JERSEY NEW YORK PENNSYLVANIA VIRGINIA WEST VIRGINIA

For reference to governing classification and other governing publications, see Rule 1, page 3.

ISSUED JANUARY 15, 1954 **EFFECTIVE FEBRUARY 18, 1954**

Issued by
W. A. SUESS
Chief of Tariff Bureau
2111 E Street, N. W. WASHINGTON 4, D. C.
MAIL ADDRESS: P. O. BOX 686

Address inquiries regarding rates published herein to individual carriers, parties hereto.

FIG. 8–1. Example of a title page of a commodity rate tariff.

roads secured approximately 13 per cent of their revenue in 1960 from traffic moving under exceptions to the classification. Since the exceptions are related to the classification, they were explained fully in the chapter on classification.

Freight—All Kinds, or All Commodity Rates

An additional category might be added to these subdivisions of line-haul rates, although it is not of the importance of the class rates, exceptions ratings, or commodity rates. This is the all-freight rate or all-commodity rate and is applied to a mixture of freight in a shipment. It is applied when the same rate is made on all commodities, regardless of their classification. Such a rate may be on carload, truckload, trainload, or shipload lots. A rate of this kind is somewhat similar to the mixed carload charges that would apply under Rule 10 of the rail freight classification or the Modified or Streamlined Rule 10 of the classification exceptions. However, under FAK or ACR rates, a single factor is given for a mixture of any type of freight based upon a designated minimum weight instead of computing charges upon several different formulas as is the case of the application of Rule 10, Streamlined or Modified Rule 10.

Freight forwarders are extensive users of these rates. All-commodity or all-freight tariffs generally provide a mixing rule whereby commodities having a lower carload rating than the all-commodity rates are charged at the lower carload rate.

Volume Rates

There have been several instances in which rail rates have been published to apply on weights in excess of a carload. *Trainload rates* on molasses and ore between particular points are two examples. A rate of this kind is usually the result of competition from other carriers, such as barge-line operators which establish rates in amounts greater than single carloads.

Generally, the trainload rate applies to a quantity of freight loaded in more than 20 cars. A *multiple car rate* is one based on weight requiring more than one car but usually less than 20. In both of these, the shipment must be billed from one consignor to one consignee, on one day, and on one bill of lading.

A multiple car rate applying to five cars with a minimum of 450 tons was put into effect in 1963. This involved the use of jumbo cars, which are larger than hopper cars. The rates applicable to grain were a 60 per cent reduction over those previously applicable. Subsequently, a rate applicable to a single car, minimum of 18,000 pounds, was permitted, which was made 120 per cent of the five-car rates approved earlier.

Railroads have established *annual volume rates* under which the rate is reduced providing a minimum yearly total of tonnage is delivered. An example is that of bituminous coal from West Virginia to New York where a 50-cent per ton reduction in the freight rate was made on coal in excess of 3 million tons delivered to the consignee in the New York Harbor area during a one-year period upon the condition that the total receipts of the consignee were not less than 5.5 million tons. In another instance, a ten-year contract has been entered into in which an electric utility furnishes two 126-car integral trains to be used in the transportation of coal. The contract calls for an average of 4 million tons a year at a rate of $1.30 a ton, compared with the former rate of $3.17.

Volume rates are also used in motor transportation and are so characterized because of the volume minimum weight connected with the application of the rate. The volume minimum applies when a shipper tenders the volume minimum weight of a commodity, as provided for in the tariff, for transportation at one time, even though it may exceed the carrying capacity of the vehicle available.

The commercial minima established by rail carriers, under the conditions of which the shipper either presented that quantity for shipment or paid for that quantity, have been followed by the motor carriers. Although motor carriers could not, in some instances, legally transport in one vehicle the commercial minima they have established in order to be competitive, due to size and weight limitations, they have established commercial minima which would be competitive with the rail carriers and have placed the shipment in two vehicles. For example, a motor carrier commodity rate has been authorized on a minimum of 100,000 pounds, which is the same as the rail minimum and rail rate.

Local Rate

A local rate is one which applies on a movement in which the transportation is completely over the lines of one carrier, without regard for the length of haul.

Joint Rate

A joint rate is a rate applying from a point on one line to a point on another line. Thus, a joint rate will apply on a movement involving two or more carriers. A shipment may pass over the lines of several railroads but be subject to a single joint rate which applies from origin to destination. A joint rate essentially contemplates a through shipment over a through route on a through bill of lading.

Proportional Rate

A proportional rate is a portion of an already existing rate which must be combined with another part of a rate to make a complete rate. This rate may be used if the origin point is one located beyond the point from which a rate is published to apply, if the destination point is a point beyond which such a rate applies, or if the origin and destination points are beyond the points from and to which such a rate applies.

An example of such a rate would be:

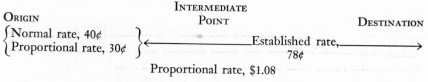

ORIGIN	INTERMEDIATE POINT	DESTINATION
{ Normal rate, 40¢ { Proportional rate, 30¢ }	← _____ Established rate, _____ → 78¢	

Proportional rate, $1.08

A proportional rate may be restricted to apply from or to certain points or territories. A tariff which names a proportional rate on cotton goods, for example, originating in North Carolina and naming points on the Ohio River, is made applicable only on traffic destined to points in the Western Trunk-Line Territory. In some cases, the tariff is not so restrictive, in that it merely states that the proportional rate is applicable on traffic coming from points beyond or destined to points beyond. The Commission has stated that a proportional rate is one which applies to part of a through transportation movement within the jurisdiction of the Interstate Commerce Act. A rate to a port for shipment beyond by water carrier not subject to the provisions of the act would not be a proportional rate.[5]

Through Rate

The term "through rate" is often confused with the term "joint rate." A through rate is the total rate from point of origin to destination and may be a local rate, a joint rate, or a combination rate made by adding together local, joint, or proportional rates. A through rate over a single line is often referred to as a "local through rate," and a through rate via two or more lines is referred to as a "joint through rate." A definition often looked upon as technically more nearly correct defines a through rate as a single rate from origin to destination published in but one tariff.

Differential Rate

A differential rate infers a deviation from some established standard. It can be looked upon as a rate established by adding fixed amounts to or subtracting them from certain basic rates regarded as standard. A differential rate is one which often applies over a route more circuitous than the standard direct route, or a route over which the service is decidedly inferior to the direct routes. The differential rates applying over such routes are frequently made by deducting specific amounts, called "differentials," from the rates applying via the direct routes with their faster service. Examples of these rates are the all-rail rates from New England Territory origins and Central Territory origins to Western Trunk-Line Committee Territory destinations via routes through Canada; and the rail-lake, lake-rail, rail-lake-rail rates between Western Trunk-Line Committee Territory and Central Territory Railroads, Trunk-Line Territory, and New England Territory.

Arbitraries

An arbitrary usually means a fixed amount to be added to the rate to the base point in order to arrive at charges to another destination or an amount added to the base rate for small shipments. For example in the first instance, a shipment is to move from Boston to a point 35 miles from Cincinnati. The rate to be applied is the base rate to Cincinnati, the base

[5] *Crescent Coal and Mining Co.* v. *C. & E. I. R. R.*, 24 ICC 155 (1912).

point, plus an arbitrary of a set amount per 100 pounds, such as $2\frac{1}{2}$ cents per 100 pounds.

Trailer-on-Flatcar Rates

The Commission, in 1954, after investigation of various legal questions concerning transportation of highway trailers on flatcars, found that transportation by a railroad of its own freight in its own trailers on flatcars is rail transportation under Part I of the act; and that terminal service by such trailers in addition to the rail haul is a movement within the partial exemption of Section 202(c)(1);[6] further, that railroads could handle the trailers of common carriers by motor vehicle on through route and joint rate or substituted service arrangements but could not handle the trailers of contract carriers, and that railroads could handle trailers of private carriers on an open-tariff basis.[7] In 1962 the Commission reversed itself and permitted motor contract carriers to participate in Plan I.

Railroad commodity rates applicable to trailer-on-flatcar service performed in rail equipment by the railroads apply to volume or trailerload minima and are generally higher than the commodity rates on regular freight-car service. Some tariffs also contain class rates. The required minimum volume is usually lower than the standardized carload minimum weights required in boxcar service.

Motor common carriers which have entered into arrangements with railroads for them to handle a portion of their movements have done so under substituted service, by which the railroads become parties to the motor carrier rates. Thus, joint motor-rail rates are established. Rates for rail movements of shipper trailers on shipper flatcars are based on a flat charge per car, whether loaded or empty.

An examination of trailer-on-flatcar tariffs of various carriers shows that one or more of the following services are available: diversion and reconsignment, pickup and delivery, loading and unloading, stop-offs and partial loading and unloading, split pickup and delivery, and inside pickup and delivery.

The Interstate Commerce Commission has ruled that a reasonable allowance may be made by the carrier when a shipper-owned trailer is used in trailer-on-flatcar service, although a proposed allowance of $18\frac{1}{2}$ cents per 100 pounds was not deemed to be reasonable.[8] The Commission suggested it would be more appropriate to pay such an allowance upon mileage.

Floating-In Rate

A floating-in rate is a line-haul rate usually associated with the movements of small lots of cotton from the gin in uncompressed bales for concentration and compression, and reshipment. This rate is designed to act

---

[6] Terminal zone exemption.
[7] *Movement of Highway Trailers by Rail*, 293 ICC 93 (1954).
[8] *Allowances for Use of Trailers*, 299 ICC 513 (1957).

as a lien on the goods; and if the terms under which it is published are not observed, the charges are revised to the basis of full local or joint rates.

Cutback Rate

A cutback rate is usually applied on traffic moving under the transit privilege. It is an arrangement whereby the carrier may refund to the shipper a portion of the local rate applied on freight that had been shipped into a transit point and then reshipped from transit point to destination via the same carrier.

Standard Rate

A standard rate is a line-haul rate usually referred to as a "standard all-rail rate." It is generally considered to be a rail rate applicable over a direct route between two territories. The standard all-rail rates are so referred to because there may be a rail-water rate in which the movement is partly by rail and partly by water.

Minimum Rates

In general, a minimum rate means that this is the lowest charge a carrier will assess for any given amount of freight between two points. Small shipments often move under minimum rates.

As a result of competitive situations among carriers of the same type or between different modes of transportation, the Interstate Commerce Commission sometimes prescribes minimum rates. The effect of such a prescription of rates is to bring about rate stabilization. After a period of time, the minimum rate order is canceled because the situation no longer requires it. At the time the rate order is issued, the minimum rates become the "going" rates.

Any-Quantity Rates

There is usually a difference between the rate applicable due to quantity offered as a single shipment. Thus, LCL and CL rates differ due to differing services rendered by the carrier and the difference in the amount tendered for shipment. In an any-quantity rate, the rate per 100 pounds is the same regardless of the quantity tendered.

Incentive Rates

Carriers publish rates on articles for which the minimum weight for a carload is 30,000 pounds. However, if the shipper tenders any amount above the minimum, the additional weight will be at a lower rate, such as 90 per cent. This "incentive" is to encourage better equipment utilization, as well as to meet competitive rates. Incentive rates are associated with weights that must be loaded in a single car and are sometimes referred to as "discount rates."

Another type of incentive rate is the alternative minimum weight

rate. Under this basis, a fixed charge per 100 pounds for a specified minimum weight per car is established but a higher minimum weight is also
specified which provides a lower rate if the larger quantity is shipped.
For example, under the alternating minimum, the shipper might pay
$1.00 per 100 pounds for the first 40,000-pound minimum carload and
80 cents per 100 pounds on an 80,000-pound minimum. The alternating
minimum would more likely be used by larger shippers than the discount
type of incentive rate.

Agreed Charges

In Canada and Great Britain, a rate-making system is used by railroads
whereby industries agree by contract to ship an agreed percentage of their
business by rail in consideration for a lower rate, which constitutes a
form of incentive rate. A large number of agreements call for 100 per
cent although it may be as low as 55 per cent. The agreed-charge contracts are open on equal terms to all carriers and to all shippers, regardless
of their individual volume of traffic, and the rates must be fully compensatory.

In Canada, notice of these contracts is published in the *Canada Gazette*.
They receive public hearing and approval before the Board of Transport
Commissioners, and the approved contracts are open to public inspection
at the stations.

The agreed-charge contracts were first authorized in Canada in 1938
and 545 had been negotiated by 1958. By 1963 an additional 1,032 had
been issued. In 1960, agreed charges accounted for 20 per cent of total
rail revenues.

U.S. railways operating in Canada may initiate agreed charges between
any two points on their lines in Canada and may also participate in agreed
charges as origin, intermediate, or terminal carriers when such agreed
charges have been made by Canadian railways.

A United States railroad, in late 1958, proposed a "guaranteed" rate
based on the agreed-charge principle. The railroad guarantees to the
shipper that no change would be made in its rate for a period of twelve
months, unless a minimum rate order of the Commission should require
the railroad to increase its rates. The railroad requires that at least 90
per cent of the shipper's tonnage would move via this railroad in the
twelve-month period. The rate would be 17 per cent lower than the
normal rate.

The Commission in this case[9] ruled that in the absence of a statutory
amendment, contract rates and agreed charges were deemed unlawful
per se. In 1962, this case was reopened for reconsideration. In another
case, the New York Central proposed lower contract rates on rug and
carpet shipments which would have been granted to shippers agreeing

---

[9] I. and S. No. 7151, *Guaranteed Rates—Sault Ste. Marie, Ont. to Chicago, Ill.* (1961).

to move 80 per cent of their shipments over that road but the Commission also found these rates to be unlawful per se.[10] A lower court affirmed these findings, but this has been appealed to the Supreme Court.

Export and Import Rates

Rates provided for the inland transportation of shipments to or from points outside the United States are called "export" or "import" rates. These rates, primarily used by railroads, are usually lower than the domestic rates for the same hauls. Based on rates applicable in 1958, the export rail rate on road-building machinery, including tractors, from Springfield, Illinois, to New York City—991 miles—was $15.80 per ton, while from Springfield to Chicago—185 miles—the rate was $15.20 per ton. In this illustration, the machinery was being transported an additional 806 miles for only 60 cents a ton more than the charge applying to

TABLE 8–2

COMPARISON OF EXPORT AND DOMESTIC RATES

(In Cents)

COMMODITY	FROM	TO BALTIMORE		TO SAN FRANCISCO		DIFFERENCE, EXPORT RATE UNDER DOMESTIC RATE TO:	
		Domestic Rate	Export Rate	Domestic Rate	Export Rate	Baltimore	San Francisco
Automobiles, passenger	Detroit, Mich.	A 118	A 45	A 450	A 193	A 73	A 257
Canned goods ..	Chicago, Ill.	A 47	A 47	A 88	A 73	A 0	A 15
Cigarettes	Durham, N.C.	A 61	A 61	A 170	A 115	A 0	A 55
Machinery and machines	Chicago, Ill.	A 62	A 62	A 178	A 88	A 0	A 90
Structural iron and steel	Chicago, Ill.	A 37	A 34	A 110	A 44	A 3	A 66
Wire rope	Springfield, Mass.	A 32	A 32	A 143	A 74	A 0	A 69
Airplane landing mats, aluminum	Blue Island, Ill.	A 85	A 85	A 275	A 165	A 0	A 110

A—tariff rates in effect on November 1, 1953.
SOURCE: *War Materials Reparations Cases*, Docket No. 29572, Examiner's Report, December, 1953.

Chicago. On the same kind of machinery, the export rail rate from St. Louis to New York—1,040 miles—was $15.60, whereas from St. Louis to Chicago—276 miles—the rate was $18.00. In this case, the rate was $2.20 a ton more for 764 fewer miles.

The purpose in establishing such rates has been to encourage the movement of shipments in foreign trade. An import rate is published to apply from a port on traffic which originates at a point in a foreign country or insular possession of the United States; or via coastwise movement by

---

[10] I. and S. 7250, *Contract Rates—Rugs and Carpeting From Amsterdam, New York* (1961).

water from another port in the United States; or via water through the Panama Canal from Pacific Coast ports. An export rate is published to apply to a port only on traffic when shipments are destined to a foreign country or an insular possession of the United States, or for coastwise movement by water to another port in the United States, or for movement by water through the Panama Canal to Pacific Coast ports. Table 8–2 shows the differences in rates in effect on certain commodities where the export rate is 50 per cent less than the domestic rate and in other instances where it is the same.

When export and import rates are designated as such, they take precedence over other rates between the same points via the same route, whether they are class or commodity rates. This means that if a commodity rate is published to and from a port but is not specifically shown as an export or import rate, it may not be used on an export or import shipment, even though it is lower than an export or import class rate published to or from the same port. The import or export rate on the same commodity may vary, depending upon the foreign origin or destination. Import rates, for example, from New Orleans, Louisiana, to Chicago will vary on the same commodity, depending on the foreign origin. Also, the rates from Chicago to southern ports are generally higher when destined to the Canal Zone, Cuba, and insular possessions of the United States than when destined to points in Europe and Africa.

This was the result of action taken by Southern carriers many years ago because of a competitive situation then existing. Prior to that time, traffic *from* Europe and Africa generally was routed via North Atlantic ports because the distance via ocean was shorter and shipping facilities and steamship movements were better than those via the Gulf ports. To overcome these handicaps, the Southern carriers lowered their inland rates on traffic from Europe and Africa as an inducement to shippers to use the Gulf route. This action was opposed by the Eastern lines and resulted finally in the "Todd-Knott Award," which represented a compromise. After that settlement, the Southern carriers were able to get the Interstate Commerce Commission to apply the same principles to export traffic *to* Europe and Africa.

The Commission has generally adhered to the policy of not prescribing export or import rates lower than corresponding domestic rates, unless a material difference in costs is shown[11] or the questioned rates are shown, by comparison with other export or import rates, to be unreasonable.[12] It has been repeatedly stated that there is nothing inherent in export or import traffic that entitles it to rates lower than those on domestic traffic,[13]

---

[11] *Imported Fertilizer Materials*, 161 ICC 649 (1930); and *Riverside Portland Cement Co. v. Director General*, 92 ICC 667 (1924).

[12] *Railroad Com. of Kansas v. Missouri P. Ry. Co.*, 22 ICC 24 (1911).

[13] *D. Nagase & Co. v. Director General*, 68 ICC 539 (1922); and *Pullman Standard Car Mfg. Co. v. Pennsylvania R. Co.*, 281 ICC 445 (1951).

but the establishment of such rates has been left to the carriers' managerial discretion, provided that they do not violate any provision of the act.

Export and import rates are usually published as "shipside rates." Thus, the rates apply not merely to or from the freight depot but to or from the side of a ship. Such rates include the cost of moving the articles between a car and the side of a ship, but they would not include the cost of loading or unloading a ship. In 1958, the railroads proposed and the Commission approved a charge of 6 cents per 100 pounds on water-borne traffic, since it was held that such traffic received more port terminal services than domestic traffic.

Combination Rate

A combination rate is a combination of two or more rates which are added together and apply from point of origin to point of destination. It may be a combination of class rates, local rates, and joint rates, or a combination of two or more of these or other rates. The combination rate must be a combination of factors in effect on the date the shipment was accepted for transportation at the point of origin. It may be used only in those instances where there are no published local or joint rates from the point of origin to destination, unless otherwise authorized by tariff application.

If a rate is published as a through rate, it is the legally applicable rate. This is the case even though such a rate may be higher than the aggregate of intermediate rates. This is in accordance with Rule 5–a of Tariff Circular No. 20. Under Rule 56 of Tariff Circular No. 20, however, carriers legally may not publish rates which are unreasonable; and the publication of a through rate in excess of the aggregate of intermediate rates is usually evidence in itself that the through rate is unreasonable. Under this rule, the carrier is obligated to protect the through rate; but the shipper may obtain reparations by presentation of the facts to the Interstate Commerce Commission. The Commission, in such an instance, probably would order the carrier to charge no more than the aggregate of intermediate rates.

Rule 56 is applicable to all rail rates, although carriers publish, in some tariffs, a rule known as *Alternative Application of Combination Rates*, which is sometimes referred to as a "wildcat" clause. This has the same effect as Rule 56, except that it eliminates the necessity for a shipper to file a complaint with the Commission when the aggregate of intermediate rates is lower than the through rate. When this rule is placed in a tariff, it makes the lower aggregate of intermediate rates the legal rate, and carriers are obligated to protect such a lower rate.

The difference between a combination rate which is applied because of the lack of a through rate and a combination rate protected because of the alternative combination rule is not always understood. In the case of the former, the shipment need not necessarily move through the base point, which is the point on which the combination is made, provided that certain conditions specified in Rule 55 (*c*) are met.

Rule 55 (*c*) states:

If in applying combination rates on a through shipment, the shipment moves from a point of origin or to a point of destination intermediate to a base point upon which the lowest combination makes, such combination must be applied, and it is not necessary to haul the shipment to such base point and back again through or to such intermediate point of origin or destination; provided that the rates used in such combination are applicable over the route the shipment would have moved had it been hauled to the base point and back again over the same route, and also that compliance with routing instructions will permit movement to the base point and back again over the same route.

In the case of a combination rate used under authority of the alternative combination rule published in the tariff, the above rule does not apply, for the reason that it is applicable only when a through rate is not published from origin to destination or, if published, is not applicable to the particular shipment. The alternative combination rule will definitely state whether a shipment must move through the base point or not. Many tariffs which contain the alternative combination rule stipulate that shipment must move through the base point if the lower combination is to apply. In other tariffs, this may be modified to allow movement through points other than the base point, with certain restrictions. In ICC, Docket No. 13535, which deals with tariffs applying between the Southwestern Territory, on the one hand, and the Southern and Official territories, on the other, the alternative combination rule provides that as long as the shipment moves over routes provided in the tariff containing the through rate, a combination rate may be made via any base point or over any railroad.

Section 4 of the Interstate Commerce Act makes it unlawful for rail carriers to publish rates higher for shorter distances than for longer distances when the move is over the same lines or routes in the same direction. These are often referred to as *Section 4* rates. Although rail carriers publish many commodity rates between points, which rates are generally lower than class rates, a violation of Section 4 of the act occurs when shipments move between points from and to which commodity rates are not published, and which points are intermediate to points from and to which commodity rates are published, at rates higher than those published from and to intermediate points.

The Commission has provided a method whereby the carriers may apply the next-more-distant-point rates on shipments which move between intermediate points. Rule 27 of Tariff Circular No. 20 permits rail carriers to publish in their tariffs a rule which authorized the establishment of the next-distant point applicable from or to the intermediate point when such shipments occur, but requiring the carriers to file with the Commission an application for authority to make refund to the shipper on any shipment based on the rate from or to the next-more-distant-point.

Many carriers have incorporated Rule 27 of Tariff Circular No. 20 in their tariffs. Under this rule, if a shipment moves from or to a point for which a specific rate is not published and the tariff publishes a specific rate from or to a more distant point via the same route, the carrier will protect and assess the rate from or to the more distant point. The use of this procedure eliminates the necessity of applying to the Commission for authority to make refunds.

The figure below illustrates the use of a simple intermediate rule:

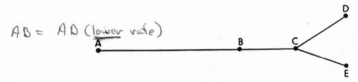

In this figure, a shipment moves from A to B. There is no commodity rate published between these two points. However, a commodity rate is published to the more distant point C. Under the intermediate clause, the rate from point A to point C will apply from A to B.

Where there are branch or diverging lines, there will be two or more next-beyond points. The rate to be applied in this instance is to the next-beyond point resulting in the lower charges. The following illustration indicates the application of this provision of the intermediate rule:

In the figure above, a shipment moves from point A to point B, and there is no commodity rate published. There is a commodity rate published, however, from A to D of 44 cents and A to E of 48 cents. Lines to D and E diverge at C, so that there are two next-beyond points. Under the terms of this provision, the lower rate of 44 cents will be applicable.

It sometimes happens that the intermediate point will be located between two points to which rates are named. In other words, a shipment will pass through a point to which a rate is named before arriving at the destination; and there will also be a rate published to a point beyond, as shown below:

For example, a commodity rate of 47 cents is published to C, and a commodity rate of 44 cents is published to D. There is no rate from point A to B. Although a lower rate is published to the next-beyond point, D, the destination is located between C and D; and since the rate to point C is higher, it must apply.

There are further provisions of the intermediate rule, but these examples are illustrative.

Some tariffs do not refer to Rule 27 but refer to Interstate Commerce

Commission Fourth Section Order No. 9800, which is similar in many respects to Rule 27 of Tariff Circular No. 20, except that Order No. 9800 applies only to commodity rates, whereas Rule 27 may apply, if it so states in the tariff, to class rates as well as commodity rates. Interstate Commerce Commission Fourth Section Order No. 9800 also has a provision that if the class rate on the article shipped from or to the intermediate point is higher than the class rate on the same article from or to the more distant point, the more distant point commodity rate cannot be applied as the legal rate; but shippers are required to file a petition with the Interstate Commerce Commission for authority to obtain reparations based on the next-more-distant point commodity rate plus the difference between the class rate from or to the intermediate point and the class rate from or to the more distant point. Under this rule, if the class rate from or to the intermediate point is the same as or lower than the class rate from or to the more distant point, the more distant point commodity rate is the legally applicable rate.

Aggregate of Intermediates

Aggregate of intermediates means the total of the separately established rates applying to different parts of the movement between a given origin and destination. There are instances where a published through rate exceeds the combination of separately established intermediate rates in effect between the same points. For example, assume that there is a through rate of 70 cents per 100 pounds in effect between points A and C, and that via the same route in the same direction, there exists a lower combination of rates, making 65 cents per 100 pounds, as shown in the following example:

```
A            (70 CENTS)            C    THROUGH RATE


A    (30¢)    B        (35¢)       C    COMBINATION RATE
```

Shippers moving freight between points A and C would soon note this difference and, under some of the aggregate of intermediate rules, would be required to pay only the lower combination rate of 65 cents. However, under certain other aggregate of intermediate rules, the shipper would have to pay the higher through rate of 70 cents; but he could notify the carrier of the difference, and the carrier would in turn apply to the Commission for authority to award reparation on the basis of the lower combination.

There are various aggregate of intermediate rules. The purpose of the aggregate rule, when published in a tariff, is to prevent violations of Section 4 of the Interstate Commerce Act, which makes it unlawful to charge any greater compensation as a through rate than the aggregate of the intermediates, subject to the provisions of the act. Another form of the aggregate of intermediate rule provides:

If the lowest combination of rates (joint, local or proportional) applicable on interstate traffic and contained in tariffs lawfully on file with the Interstate Commerce Commission via any route over which the through rate published in tariff as amended applies, produces a lower charge than the through rates published in this tariff, as amended, such lower combinations of rates will apply via the route over which such combination is made.

In a tariff which carries this particular rule, the combination rate in the foregoing example could be applied only via the route over which such combination is made, which would mean from *A* to *C* through point *B*, and only if such route is authorized in the tariff naming the through rate.

Section 22 Rates

Section 22 of the Interstate Commerce Act provides "that nothing in this part shall prevent the carriage, storage, or handling of property free or at reduced rates for the United States . . . or the transportation of persons for the United States Government free or at reduced rates. . . ." The provisions of Section 22 are permissive and permit carriers embraced by the Interstate Commerce Act to grant to the government free or reduced rates for the transportation of persons and property.

Public Law 85–246, passed in 1957, requires that Section 22 quotations be filed with the Commission and thereby be open for public inspection. This law also provides that carriers may collectively make Section 22 quotations, provided that they have filed a Section 5a[14] agreement which has been approved by the Commission, thereby making the carriers immune from antitrust prosecution. Between 15,000 and 30,000 Section 22 quotations are filed annually with the Commission.

Reshipping Rate

A reshipping rate is a line-haul rate. It is defined as one applicable to the outbound movement by rail of a shipment from a station into which it was previously consigned by rail.

Cube Rate

With the trend toward lower density on certain traffic due to improved manufacturing and packaging techniques or to other factors, motor carriers have found that the classification machinery has lagged in interrelating this trend into the class rate structure. Since classification is on a national scale, full recognition is not and cannot be given to variations from the normal or average in the densities of products moving locally. The result is that the carriers may transport freight which does not adequately meet the cost of its transportation. They have, therefore, adopted a measure of protection in the form of "cube rules." Cube rules are established in rate tariffs and apply on light and bulky articles. The rat-

---

[14] Section 5a is explained in the chapter which follows.

ings in the governing classification are subject to minimum weights per cubic foot. Thus, when the applicable class rating of a shipment of a minimum density, as shown in column 1 of Figure 8–2 of the cube rule,

MINIMUM DENSITY IN POUNDS PER CUBIC FOOT (1)	LESS–THAN–TRUCKLOAD RATINGS (2)
15	CLASS 55 OR LOWER
10	ABOVE CLASS 55 BUT NOT ABOVE CLASS 70
7	ABOVE CLASS 70 BUT NOT ABOVE CLASS 85
5	ABOVE CLASS 85 BUT NOT ABOVE CLASS 100
3	ABOVE CLASS 100 BUT NOT ABOVE CLASS 150
2	ABOVE CLASS 150 BUT NOT ABOVE CLASS 200
1	ABOVE CLASS 200 BUT NOT ABOVE CLASS 300
LESS THAN 1	ABOVE CLASS 300 BUT NOT ABOVE CLASS 500

FIG. 8–2. Application of cube rule.

is lower than the lesser of the ratings shown opposite it in column 2, the higher of the two ratings shall apply on the shipment, subject to certain other tariff stipulations.

"Omnibus" Rule

The "omnibus" rule is often referred to as the "catchall" rule, in that by its provisions, there can be included numerous special or accessorial charges which will apply in conjunction with a rate tariff without specific reference to such individual tariffs. The following is a typical "omnibus" rule:

In the absence of specific provisions in this tariff to the contrary, shipments transported under this tariff will be entitled to such allowances and privileges and subject to such charges, rules and regulations of originating carriers parties to this tariff, for property while in their possession and of any of the intermediate or delivering carriers, parties to this tariff, for property while in their possession as are provided in tariffs lawfully in effect and on file with the Interstate Commerce Commission as to interstate traffic, with Canadian Transport Commission and with State Commissions covering traffic subject to their jurisdiction, providing for terminal or transit privileges or services, including also

Car Rental	Elevation	Reconsignment	Transit
Car Service	Lighterage	Stop-off	Privileges
Cartage	Loading	Storage	Unloading
Demurrage	Private Car	Switching	Weighing
Diversion	Mileage	Transfer	

Surcharge

Due to increased cost of handling small shipments, carriers have established, in some instances, a surcharge per shipment on those weighing less than a specified amount, such as 5,000 pounds. The amount of the surcharge varies in the different rate territories. Some surcharges are on a sliding scale, i.e., the larger the shipment the lower the surcharge.

Accessorial or Ancillary Charges

The second broad category mentioned earlier was that of accessorial or ancillary charges. These are charges made for additional, special, or supplemental services, although some of these may be absorbed in the line-haul rate. The Interstate Commerce Commission has required in Rule 10 (*a*) of Tariff Circular No. 20 for rail carriers and Rule 11 (*a*) of Tariff Circular MF No. 3 for motor carriers that each carrier or its agent shall publish, post, and file in tariffs in a clear manner all of the rules, rates, and charges for demurrage, switching, car floatage, lighterage, wharfage, storage, transfer and drayage, weighing, trap-car or ferry-car service, which are referred to as "carrier terminal services"; and diversion, reconsignment, icing, refrigeration, heat, elevation, peddler-car service, feeding, grazing, and other transit services, absorptions, allowances, expedited service, stop-off charges to unload partially or load, which are usually referred to as "special services"; as well as other charges and rules which in any way increase or decrease the amount to be paid on any shipment. Inasmuch as there will be further explanation of these services in other chapters, no further description will be given at this time.

Released Value Ratings

Rail and motor common carriers and freight forwarders are responsible, under the Interstate Commerce Act, for the full value of merchandise which they carry. When freight is lost or damaged, shippers may file claims in order to recover the value of the goods lost or damaged. Such common carriers are often referred to as "insurers" of the goods they carry. With the majority of goods which move, the liability of these common carriers is not limited. However, the Commission, under the provisions of the Interstate Commerce Act, can permit carriers to establish rates on so-called "released value." The released value constitutes the maximum which the shipper can recover from a carrier in the case of loss or damage of a shipment, and it is a method whereby a carrier may limit its liability. Other reasons for establishing released value rates are because it is sometimes difficult to determine precisely the actual value of the article, susceptibility of the traffic to loss or damage may be comparatively high, and a wide range in the value of the commodity may make the amount of any claim difficult to estimate.

Where the carrier desires to limit its liability by means of establishing rates on the basis of released value, it must make application to the Commission for this authority. If the Commission approves, a released rates order will be issued. Common carriers by rail, motor, or freight forwarders, which are parties to the Consolidated Freight Classification No. 23 and Uniform Freight Classification No. 6, with supplements thereto or reissues thereof, have been authorized to establish released ratings on graphite; crucibles; ores; fur or fur-lined clothing; office records; clock watches; scrap leather; emigrant movables; motion-picture films; printed matter; household goods; rugs; silk; titanium metal; earthenware or stoneware with restaurant or hotel equipment; hides; pelts, or skins; paintings or pictures; chinaware, earthenware, porcelainware, or stoneware; drugs; medicines; toilet preparations; and essential oils.

Ratings on these classified items are dependent upon the value declared in writing by the shipper, or agreed upon in writing as the released value. The released rates orders contain a provision which stipulates that changes may be made in any rating, minimum weight, or packing specification; but the commodity description may not be broadened to embrace other articles, nor may any change be made in the released valuations upon which the ratings are dependent without specific authority from the Commission. Some of the released rates orders provide for a number of released values from which the shipper may choose. Table 8–3 is a sample

TABLE 8–3
Released Value Rating

	UFC No. 6 LCL CL
Clothing, fur or fur-lined, NOIBN, in boxes, or in salesmen's trunks, locked and sealed with metal seals:	
Released value not exceeding $1.50 per pound	100–12,000R–85
Released value exceeding $1.50 but not exceeding $5.00 per pound..........	250–12,000R–150
Released value exceeding $5.00 but not exceeding $7.50 per pound..........	300–12,000R–200
Released value exceeding $7.50 per pound, NOT TAKEN.	

Source: Uniform Freight Classification No. 6.

of a commodity which has a released value rating. The shipper, in this instance, has three options: (1) the described clothing may be shipped at a released value not exceeding $1.50 per pound; (2) it may be shipped at a released value exceeding $1.50 but not more than $5.00 per pound; or (3) it may be shipped at a released value exceeding $5.00 but not exceeding $7.50 per pound. As Table 8–3 indicates, the released value has a bearing on the rate which the carrier charges. In some instances, commodities which have a value beyond a specific amount are not accepted by the carrier.

Rail and motor carriers and freight forwarders engaged in moving general commodities have established released value ratings on a comparatively limited number of commodities. However, the specialized motor carrier group of household goods carriers, which carries the generic classification of household goods, has established released value rates on all such goods. There is, therefore, one segment of motor common carriers, most of whose movements are based on released value. Released value rates for household goods carriers and for Express are discussed in other sections.

Rail and motor common carriers of general commodities sought authority, in 1955, to establish rules limiting liability on articles in the freight classifications with respect to loss and damage in transit to $3.00 per pound, and in the case of motor carriers to $150 per package, whichever is greater. Rail carriers also sought a maximum of $200,000 per shipment and motor carriers $100,000 per shipment.[15]

The carriers also proposed to establish valuation charges of 10 cents for each $100 of value above the stated maxima. The objective of the proposal was to require shippers to give notice of the value of property tendered for transportation, so that proper protection in transit could be given it by the carriers, and to provide release against claims for loss of and damage to property of especially high value. The Interstate Commerce Commission held that it had no power to issue a "general" released rates order but, on appeal, a district court held that the Commission does inherently possess such power. The Commission reopened these cases for reconsideration and held that since the evidence in the proceeding was general in nature and did not conform to standards set in prior proceedings, the proposed rules were not shown to be just and reasonable either as to the affected traffic as a whole or as to any particular commodity.

An indication of the number of applications for authority by rail and motor common carriers and freight forwarders under Sections 20(11), 219, and 413 of the act to establish rates dependent upon declared or agreed values can be found in the *Annual Reports* of the Interstate Commerce Commission. The *76th Annual Report* states that there were 75 applications filed during a one-year period. At the close of the year, 40 of these applications had been granted.[16]

Actual Value Ratings

There have been a few actual value ratings published. This has been accomplished where the range of value is so wide that it has been difficult to establish one rating based on an average value. The shipper, in such actual value ratings, must designate the rating and certify the actual value of the article on the bill of lading or on the shipping order. The liabil-

---

[15] Ex Parte MC–49, *Released Rates Rules–National Motor Freight Classification* and Ex Parte No. 197, *Consolidated Freight Classification and Uniform Freight Classification,* 306 ICC 495 (1959) and 309 ICC 380 (1960).

[16] Interstate Commerce Commission, *76th Annual Report* (Washington, D.C.: U.S. Government Printing Office, 1962), p. 42.

ity of the carrier under actual value is quite different from that under released value.

Allowances

When shipper-owned equipment is used by regulated for-hire carriers, the shippers may be given an allowance covered by tariff provision. The allowance is usually in cents per loaded mile when the shipper's equipment is used in line-haul or over-the-road service. If the allowance is authorized for a service such as pickup and delivery, it will usually be in terms of cents per one hundred pounds.

Rate Structures

In the evolutionary development of the freight rate structures, the rates in various territories developed with a considerable degree of independence in the respective territories. In rail transportation, some of the smaller rate bureaus merged, creating larger geographical freight rate areas, which tended to lessen the differences in the freight rate structures. The population growth and industrial development of different territories also influenced the trend toward greater similarity. The interterritorial rate structure had never had the wide differences which had existed between intraterritorial rates.

The rate structures which have emerged were originally the product of a compromise between the carriers' traffic representatives, who were responsible for the establishment of rates, and the shippers, who were seeking advantageous rates. With the development of regulation and the ultimate granting of sufficient rate authority to the state and federal regulatory bodies, these bodies have become an additional factor in the establishment of the rate structure.

The regional rate structures which developed in rail transportation came about partly as a result of the fact that relatively few railroads extended beyond the boundaries of any one of the three major classification territories. The railroads within a given territory co-operated in the establishment of a rate structure for the territory, although there were several territorial subdivisions which had deviations in rate structures from the larger territory of which they were a part.

The class rate structures in four of the five major rail rate territories were the result of investigations made by the Interstate Commerce Commission, starting in the 1920's. Although there was no extensive investigation of the entire class rate structure in the Mountain-Pacific Territory at that time, there were scales of rates prescribed by the Commission in a number of cases in that territory.[17] These class rate investigations re-

---

[17] *Arizona Corporation Commission* v. *Arizona and Eastern Railway Co.*, 113 ICC 52 (1926); *Public Utilities Commission of Idaho* v. *Oregon Short Line Railroad*, 146 ICC 168 (1928); *Utah Shipper Traffic Ass'n.* v. *Atchison, Topeka and Santa Fe Railway*, 172 ICC 306 (1931); and others.

MANAGEMENT OF TRAFFIC AND PHYSICAL DISTRIBUTION

sulted in the establishment of a basic scale of Class 1 rates which had general application within the respective territories.[18]

These class rate scales were based on distance. However, they were modified by some degree of grouping of origins and destinations, by certain special adjustments, and by key-point rates which did not adhere exactly to the scale.[19] The class rate scales prescribed by the Commission in the various territories were different in each territory. This resulted in differences in the levels in Class 1 rates in the various rate territories.

The Commission, as a result of Docket No. 28300, *Class Rate Investigation, 1939,* prescribed a class rate scale in all of the major rail rate territories except the Mountain-Pacific Territory. In a subsequent investigation, the Commission made effective, in 1956, an interim class rate scale in the Mountain-Pacific Territory which was 20 per cent higher than the class rate scale prescribed in Docket No. 28300. Both of the scales are based on distance but are modified by the grouping of points.

In the construction of the line-haul freight rates, a number of different bases are used. These are mileage or distance blocks, group, zone, territorial block, or point to point or station to station. Some of these bases used in rate construction have become associated with particular types of rates, and combinations of the bases are often found as well. As noted earlier, blocks—or the use of a distance scale—have been associated with class rates. Railroads have established rates in which a large area is blanketed. For example, rates on certain commodities have been blanketed so that rates from a Pacific Coast producing territory to the Atlantic Coast area are no higher than the rates from the same Pacific territory to Denver, Colorado. Chicago is sometimes given the same transcontinental rate as Atlantic seaboard points, both eastbound and westbound. Eastbound rates on lumber and related products are blanketed so as to be no higher from West Coast producing points to the Atlantic seaboard than from the same points to Indiana. In the establishment of transcontinental rail freight rates from the Mountain-Pacific Territory, competitive market conditions are the main factor, and mileage is relatively unimportant, because this is an agricultural and raw-material-producing area which must find markets in the East. Transcontinental rates from the Mountain-Pacific Territory are relatively lower than from any other territory.

The majority of goods moving is intraterritorial in nature. In the development of the class rate structure, the interterritorial class rate structure was more complex than that of intraterritorial class rates. The usual procedure was to blend the different intraterritorial class rate levels to

---

[18] *Eastern Class Rate Investigations,* 164 ICC 314 (1930), and supplemental decisions; *Southern Class Rate Investigation,* 100 ICC 513 (1925), and supplemental decisions; *Western Trunk-Line Class Rates,* 164 ICC 1 (1930), and supplemental decisions; *Consolidated Southwestern Cases,* 123 ICC 203 (1927), and supplemental reports.
[19] Board of Investigation and Research, *Summary Report on Study of Interterritorial Freight Rates,* 78th Congress, 1st session, House Document No. 145 (Washington, D.C.: U.S. Government Printing Office, 1943), p. 4.

secure the interterritorial class rate. Since the intraterritorial class rate level differed in each of the rate territories, this blending of rates resulted in rates which were usually higher than would result from applying the scale of the lower-rated territory for the full distance, and lower than would result from applying the scale of the higher-rated territory for the full distance.

With the growth of motor and water competition, rail carriers made extensive use of the publication of exceptions to the classification, some of which had a limited territorial application, whereas others applied throughout a rate territory. The exceptions to the classification resulted in rates that were lower than the class rates used in conjunction with the classification. In effect, the exceptions to the classification established a new classification for those articles placed in the exceptions category. These exceptions ratings became an important part of the rate structure. Generally, exceptions ratings were accorded to those articles in which there was some volume of movement.

Because of the variety of bases on which commodity rates have been made, it is difficult to analyze this rate structure unless a group of commodities accorded such rates are studied in detail. On some commodities, there are differences in commodity rate levels within a major rate territory. It was found that on logs or pulpwood, and on sand, gravel, and crushed stone, there are many levels in the same territories, often with individual line scales maintained by different railroads.[20] On brick, cement, coke, fertilizer and fertilizer materials, lime and sand, and gravel and crushed stone, there are different levels in two or more of the subdivisions of the Official or Eastern Territory.[21]

When mileage is the basis for the formulation of the rate, the shortest mileage that the car can travel without transfer of lading is the mileage used. Because a number of railroads, several of which may have to cover greater distances to compete for the traffic than one which has a direct route, may be competing for the same traffic, the Commission has permitted the inclusion of an amount in calculating cost per mile plus a fair profit as a basis for freight rates. This is an allowance for circuity, which averages 14 per cent, according to the Bureau of Accounts, Cost Finding, and Valuation.[22]

Thus, 14 per cent is added to the line-haul portion of the rate for the short-line hauls, which the Bureau finds reasonably compensatory, to cover the extra mileage over the circuitous routes. This enables the carriers which have circuitous routes to compete with carriers with more

---

[20] Board of Investigation and Research, *Report on Interterritorial Freight Rates*, 78th Congress, 1st session, House Document No. 303 (Washington, D.C.: U.S. Government Printing Office, 1943), p. 148.

[21] *Ibid.*

[22] Senate Subcommittee on Interstate and Foreign Commerce, *Surface Transportation Ratemaking Bills* (Washington, D.C.: U.S. Government Printing Office, 1957), p. 243.

direct routes, but this is reflected in higher class rates. In prescribing the class rate scale in Docket No. 28300, an allowance of 12 per cent for circuitous hauls was included in the costs on which the uniform class rate scale was predicated.[23]

As might be expected, there is considerable diversity in the commodity rate structure. However, on a small number of commodities, the Commission has established uniform levels in two or more territories.[24] The territorial commodity rates are, in some instances, on the basis of a full combination of rates to and from border points. In other instances, they are combinations of proportionals, or of locals and proportionals. In still other cases, they may be tied to a distance scale.[25]

Interterritorial commodity rates may or may not be precisely related to the intraterritorial level of commodity rates. Some interterritorial commodity rates are based on the level of the higher-rated territory; whereas in other instances, they are on the level of the lower-rated territory. In still other cases, they may be a blend of the two levels. These are but a few of the variations. Commodity rates from points in one territory to points in another may be higher in one direction than in the opposite direction. The differing commodity rate levels, as well as the different bases, are to be expected on the majority of commodity rates. Many of these rates are on volume movement between specific points—in other words, a localized movement, to meet the needs of particular shippers. From the carrier's point of view, the commodity rates which have a limited application may reflect its transportation costs to a greater degree than is true of some of the other types of rates. However, there are commodity rates which have nationwide application.

Rail rates and the rail rate structure have served as the pattern for the development of rates and the rate structure of competitive modes of transportation. The rate structure of motor carriers is very similar to that of rail. There are more rate territories, however, in motor transportation; and the geographical areas are not so extensive. The rate structure of motor carriers is more fluid and contains more levels of rates due to the specialization of carrier operations.

In order to insure a competitive relationship, motor carriers, except household goods carriers, use rail distances on most class rates and commodity column rates instead of highway distances. For example, from Parkersburg, West Virginia, to Lexington, North Carolina, the rail rate-making mileage is 498 miles, and the actual highway mileage is 352, or a difference of 146 miles. Although it has been urged that highway mileages be used by motor carriers, this would require a great number of computations. The use by motor carriers of rail mileage results, in many instances,

---

[23] *Class Rates in the United States*, 294 ICC 662 (1955).
[24] *Op. cit.*, p. 149.
[25] Board of Investigation and Research, *Report on Interterritorial Freight Rates, op. cit.*, p. 219.

in higher rates when compared to private trucking, which uses the most direct route and is subject to costs reflecting actual distance.

In recent years, motor carriers have made many changes in their classifications, one of which is the reclassification of light and bulky commodities. This has resulted in different and generally higher ratings for class rates.

Another change is the use of *class rate stops* or *minimum rate stops*. Motor common carriers have not observed the same relationships as rail carriers throughout the class rate scale. On certain articles bearing lower classification ratings, higher class rates are fixed as minima. For example, one group of motor carriers established minimum class rates on less-truckload shipments based on Class 75 for distances up to 760 miles, and on truckloads Class 60. Therefore, even though an article is in less-truckload quantities and is Class 50, the class rate which will apply is the class rate applicable to Class 75. Individual motor carriers who do not want to handle traffic at the specific published rate will also publish a note or exception to this effect and thereby "flagout" the rate.

Another difference between motor and rail class rates is the addition by motor carriers in some rate territories of a freight charge, or "arbitrary," on all shipments under 6,000 pounds. In some cases, this is applicable to two weight categories, a higher arbitrary applying on shipments weighing less than 2,000 pounds and a lower one applying on shipments weighing between 2,000 and 5,999 pounds.

Another difference is that some motor carriers have retained the groupings; whereas the rail carriers, in establishing the Docket No. 28300 class rates, revised—and to some extent—expanded their groupings.

Factors Affecting Rate Levels

Differences in the levels of rates in the various rate territories can be attributed to a number of factors. Some of these are:

1. Density and distribution of population.
2. Geographical characteristics of the territories.
3. Types of industrial development.
4. Concentration of industrial development.
5. Concentration of sources of raw materials.
6. Location of primary and secondary markets.
7. Balance or imbalance of freight traffic within the territory.
8. Predominant type of traffic.
9. Seasonal movement of traffic.
10. Distances goods must be transported.
11. Distribution of the volume of traffic moving through the territory—i.e., overhead or bridge traffic, and the volume of traffic to or from or within the territory.
12. Nature of intercarrier competition—railroad, water, motor, air, or pipe-line transportation.
13. Availability of water, motor, and pipe-line competition.
14. Carrier policy in establishing rates to meet carrier competition.

15. Market competition within the territories.

16. Relative costs of performing transportation services in the rate territories.

17. Economic policy of the carriers or government in the development of industries or regions.

18. Policies of state and federal governments with respect to the regulation of transportation.[26]

Basically, there are two approaches to rate adjustments, either increases or decreases. These are the horizontal—or so-called "across-the-board"—increase and the vertical increase. In the horizontal increase, a proposal may be made to increase all rates and charges by a given percentage, such as 10 per cent. Since World War II, the railroads have generally used this method. This type of adjustment is frequently subject to "hold downs"—that is, the carriers, with Commission approval, may hold down the increase on certain commodities to a level below the general across-the-board increase. In the case of a particular 6 per cent horizontal increase, the Commission prescribed that rates on baled cotton, in carloads, would be subject to a maximum increase of 9 cents per 100 pounds. Another example is the rate on pears from California to Chicago which, in 1940, was $1.42 per 100 pounds. If the full percentage of all the increases since that time had been levied and there had been no hold-downs, the rate would have been $2.98 in 1958, instead of $2.13, the actual rate.

In an across-the-board increase, the railroads often find that it is not desirable for them to take the full increase authorized because of competition. As a result, the amount of increase applied by the railroads is often less than that authorized.

The vertical adjustment applies to a selected commodity or commodity group and does not cause the distortions that appear in an across-the-board adjustment. The tendency is to take the full amount authorized. During the past three years the ICC has admonished rail carriers to use vertical and not horizontal increases in order to remain competitive.

MOTOR CONTRACT CARRIERS

Motor contract carriers are required to publish in their schedules which are filed with the Interstate Commerce Commission the actual rates or charges for the services they perform. This change was made by Public Law 85–124, enacted on August 13, 1957. Previously, they had had to file only minimum rates and charges. The 1957 amendment contains an exception which states that any contract carrier serving a single customer may continue to file minimum rates if it has served the customer for at least a year unless the Commission, after a hearing, determines that the public interest requires the carrier to file actual rates.

Contract carriers may charge rates in accordance with the specialized

[26] G. Lloyd Wilson, "The Elements of Freight Rate Making," *Traffic World*, February 18, 1950, p. 64.

service they render and do not have to maintain the same rates, rules, and regulations for the same service for all shippers served.

WATER CARRIERS

The Interstate Commerce Commission has authorized water carriers operating in domestic transportation to establish rates in some instances lower than the rail rates for competitive traffic. The differential permitted has varied, depending upon the commodity, the length of haul, and the degree and nature of competition. When there is a combination service, such as rail-water, which is in competition to rail, the typical differential for the combination service is 8 per cent under the rail rate.[27]

Water transportation rates for freight are not as complex or as extensive as rail rates; but there are certain descriptive designations which follow, in a general way, the rail terminology. Many of them are described in the paragraphs which follow.

Class Rates

Class rates are those which apply in the groups or classes into which the various articles are divided. Due to the relatively small number of ports of origin and destination covered by a given service, a classification may be used which refers to the rate tariff or rate section giving the applicable rate, thus giving rise to class rates.

Commodity Rates

A commodity rate is a special rate on specific articles, usually removing the application of the class basis. Water rates are quoted predominantly on a commodity rather than a class basis.

Local Rates

Local rates are those which apply on freight carried from origin port to destination port by one water carrier.

Arbitraries

An arbitrary is a stipulated amount above a rate between two points and is used to make a through rate. It is sometimes called a "differential," although a differential may be made by either adding to or subtracting from a basic rate. The arbitrary is usually applied by adding a fixed amount covering transference and carriage to an inland point or a near-by port to the base port-to-port charge.

---

[27] Bureau of Transport Economics and Statistics, Interstate Commerce Commission, *Rail-Water Rate Adjustments* (Washington, D.C.: U.S. Government Printing Office, December, 1954).

Minimum Rates

Minimum rates are rates below which, by law or agreement, the rates of a carrier may not fall.

Heavy-Lift and Extra- or Long-Length Rates

Heavy-lift and extra- or long-length rates are those which, because the cargo weight or length exceeds the specified maximum, are added to the basic rate or quoted separately. These are sometimes referred to as "penalty charges."

General Cargo Rates

General cargo rates are those rates applicable in the absence of specific commodity rates or classification rates.

Charter Rates

Charter rates are those rates paid under the contract of affreightment for the use of an entire vessel.

Under the time charter, it is the obligation of the charterer to pay the owner a charter hire as well as all port charges, cargo-handling charges, fuel oil charges, and others pertaining to the cargo carried and the ports visited. In the time charter, the rate is usually quoted as a certain amount per dead-weight ton per month. This is sometimes modified so that the charge is a stated amount per month. There are two primary forms of the time charter. The one most widely used for all charters entered into in the United States is a form approved by the New York Produce Exchange. The other is the Baltine charter, issued by the Baltic and International Conference in Copenhagen, which is widely used abroad.

Under a voyage charter, the owner agrees to place the vessel at the disposal of the charterer to carry a certain cargo from one port to another. The owner may bear all of the expenses of the voyage, in which case the charter is said to be a gross-form charter; or the charterer may agree to load and/or discharge, so that these expenses are borne by him. The basis for the voyage charter rate is usually a weight ton, and the rate is quoted as a certain amount per weight ton. However, the rate is sometimes given on a space-unit basis.

Optional Cargo Rates

Optional cargo rates are those rates assessed in return for the privilege of declaring an option as to the port of call at which the cargo shall be discharged.

Ad Valorem Rates

Ad valorem rates are rates charged in cases where the value of the shipment is declared to be in excess of the bill-of-lading limits of liability.

These rates may be assessed on value alone or in addition to the regular charges assigned.

Refrigerated Cargo Rates

Refrigerated cargo rates are those rates assessed in addition to the usual charges for similar items because of the services involved in transporting the cargo under refrigeration.

Deck Cargo Rates

Deck cargo rates are those rates charged for the carriage of goods on the deck of the ship rather than in the holds. Such charges are usually somewhat less than under-the-deck stowage rates.

Dangerous Cargo Rates

Dangerous cargo rates are the rates assessed by special arrangement with the transporting company when transporting hazardous or dangerous cargo. Movements of this type are usually under Board of Underwriters' rules and special conditions in the bill of lading.

Parcel Rates

Parcel rates are those rates assessed by some carriers for the transportation of small parcels not forwarded upon a bill of lading. However, some lines may issue instead a bill of lading for small parcel shipments, collecting the minimum charges made for the service of issuing a bill of lading.

Open Rates

Open rates are rates upon which the carriers in a conference cannot agree. Consequently, each carrier is allowed to charge whatever rates it wishes to charge. If no conference agreements in any trade are in force, all rates are open rates.

Quantity Offered as a Shipment

The terms "carload" and "less carload" are misnomers when applied to water transportation, but it is the general practice of water carriers engaged in intercoastal transportation to maintain commodity rates on carload and less-carload bases. This is attributable to the fact that the competitive transcontinental rail rates are on such bases, and because rail movements at carload and less-carload rates frequently precede or follow the water transportation. However, the Commission has never held that water carriers are under any obligation to maintain carload rates. Moreover, the application of any-quantity rates has been approved in the absence of a showing that a public demand would not be adequately served unless carload rates were established.[28]

---

[28] *Kahn Mfg. Co.* v. *Boston & M. R.*, 276 ICC 556 (1949).

AIR CARGO CARRIERS

Common Carriers

The scheduled air lines operating after the passage of the Civil Aeronautics Act in 1938 did not publish air cargo rates as such. Rather, the rates for the carrying of such cargo as was tendered were published by the Railway Express Agency (now REA Express). The Railway Express Agency contracts with the air lines at that time provided for the air lines to carry air express furnished them by the Railway Express Agency. One of the provisions of the express agency's contract with the air lines, which was removed after Civil Aeronautics Board investigation in 1943, was the proviso in the contract limiting the air lines to accepting shipments only from the Railway Express Agency.[29]

The removal of this restriction, coupled with the emphasis on air transportation which had developed through the widespread use by the military services of air cargo transportation during World War II and the increased use of air express for emergency shipments needed for prosecution of the war, resulted in the filing of the first air freight rates contained in an air freight tariff by American Airlines. At the time of the filing of this tariff, air express rates averaged about 70 cents per ton-mile, whereas the rates in American's air freight tariff averaged about 44 cents per ton-mile on a door-to-door basis, with an allowance made if the shipper or receiver performed the pickup or delivery service.[30]

There were four classes established—A, B, C, and D—and the charge per ton-mile was 50 cents, 43 cents, 36.5 cents, and 30 cents, respectively. The ratings were subject to released valuations: Class A, $2.00 per pound; Class B, $1.65 per pound; Class C, $1.35 per pound; and Class D, $1.00 per pound. These rates were formulated on the basis that the cubic measurements did not exceed 400 cubic inches per pound. Where this was exceeded, the charge was assessed on the basis of one pound for each 400 cubic inches. The density factor, therefore, was important in rate determination.

American Airlines' initial tariffs classified commodities into different classes in a manner similar to those of rail and motor carriers. These classes established class rates and were based on mileage blocks. In addition, special commodity rates were established. A similar system was followed by other air lines, which started individual freight services approximately a year later. There were refinements, however, in the establishment of rates on an airport-to-airport basis, with pickup and delivery charges in a different section of the tariff.

The filing of subsequent tariffs led to further changes; and in 1946, one air line established a single cargo rate for all articles acceptable for air

---

[29] *Railway Express Agreements*, 4 CAB 157 (1943).

[30] Harold W. Torgerson, "History of Air Freight Tariffs," *Journal of Air Law and Commerce*, Winter, 1948.

transportation. Furthermore, five weight brackets were established, and the rate per ton-mile decreased as the weight within the brackets increased. The purpose of the graduated weight bracket was to encourage larger shipments and to serve as an incentive for freight forwarders to utilize air carriers.

There were fourteen tariffs filed between 1944 and 1946. However, the air lines canceled their individual issues and filed with the Board three consolidated tariffs, consisting of a Rules Tariff, a Pickup and Delivery Tariff, and a Freight Tariff, which were to become effective on August 1, 1947. The rates provided in the consolidated tariff averaged about 20 cents per ton-mile. All carriers which were participants in this tariff limited their liability to 50 cents per pound, with a provision for a higher declared value. Moreover, in this tariff, the density factor was computed as 300 cubic inches being equal to 1 pound. The largest noncertificated carrier which filed its tariffs in 1947 assessed charges at the rate of 6.5 pounds per cubic foot, or 1 pound equaling 266 cubic inches. At the present time, the air lines participating in the Official Airfreight Tariff use 250 cubic inches as equal to 1 pound, except in the case of flowers, in which the figure is 266 cubic inches equal to 1 pound. The former figure is identical to that used by the International Air Transport Association in international air transportation. Although the IATA figure used to be lower and that of our domestic carriers higher, the present figure represents a compromise. The importance of the density factor can be shown by the following illustration: When articles such as fashionable women's hats, which occupy 300 cubic inches but weight but one-half pound each, are shipped by a scheduled air carrier, the rate charged would be for two pounds.

The Civil Aeronautics Board established minimum rates in 1948 in order to limit competition that had developed between the trunkline carriers and all-cargo carriers. Various modifications were made in these rates during the following decade, and on October 1, 1961, the Board revoked all outstanding minimum rate orders on the basis that they were no longer desirable.

In 1956, the Board authorized special lower rates for air freight which would be delivered on schedules slower than those of regular air freight but faster than those of surface transportation. These are known as "deferred" air freight rates.[31] Shipments under the deferred air freight system are subject to release not prior to the third day after receipt when the movement is under 2,100 miles and not prior to the fourth day when the movement is 2,100 miles or more. Under certain conditions, carriers can offer a combination of deferred and regular service.

The following table shows the delivery schedule for shipments under the deferred rates:

---

[31] CAB Order Serial No. E–1705–9, April 13, 1956.

Shipments Received Prior to Midnight on:	*Shall Not Be Released Prior to 7:00 P.M. on:*	
	Under 2,100 Miles	*2,100 Miles or Over*
Monday	Thursday	Friday
Tuesday	Friday	Saturday
Wednesday	Saturday	Monday
Thursday	Monday	Tuesday
Friday	Wednesday	Wednesday
Saturday	Wednesday	Wednesday
Sunday	Wednesday	Thursday

The Official Airfreight tariffs published on behalf of the certificated air carriers consist of Rules Tariff; a General Rate Tariff, which contains general commodity rates; a Pickup and Delivery Tariff, which names rates for this service which are in addition to the airport-to-airport rates; and a specific Commodity Rate Tariff, which names rates on specific items. In addition, there are miscellaneous publications which include a Special Pickup and Delivery Tariff; a Restricted Articles Tariff; an Official Air Cargo Tariff; a Circular (federal and state laws and regulations governing the transportation of such items as live animals and drugs); an Official Air Cargo Station Directory (information as to types of aircraft operated, maximum shipment weights, and sizes); and All-Cargo Flight Schedules, as well as others. Most air cargo business is at the specific commodity rates.

Air lines provide local and joint airport-to-airport rates, as well as general commodity rates. Separate pickup and delivery charges are available. In addition, they have provided exceptions to general commodity rates, charges, and rules. Some air carriers have provided "premium" commodity rates, i.e., rates applicable to specific commodities which are higher than the general commodity rate. Such rates would be similar to class rates used by other modes of transportation.

Scheduled air carriers usually provide that unless a higher value is declared on the air bill, shipments are deemed to have a value of $50.00 for any shipment weighing 100 pounds or less and 50 cents per pound for each pound of any shipment weighing in excess of 100 pounds. Any value declared in excess of the amount will be subject to a charge of 10 cents per $100.00 declared value or fraction thereof. In the movement of flowers and nursery stock, shipments are deemed to have a value of $10.00 for any shipment weighing 100 pounds or less plus 10 cents per pound for any shipment weighing in excess of 100 pounds; a charge of $2.00 will be made for each $100.00 or fraction thereof of excess valuation.

There are articles of extraordinary value, such as negotiable securities and precious metals, that are accepted only at the actual value, which must be declared on the air bill at the time of receipt from the shipper.

Pickup and delivery service averages about 55 cents per 100 pounds with but few exceptions, and there is a minimum charge of $1.30 per shipment. Special rates apply for this service on week ends, on holidays, and for trips outside local limits.

Contract Carriers

Some of the certificated air cargo carriers, as well as supplemental air carriers, operate in contract carriage in the movement of air cargo, particularly for the military departments, on a plane-mile basis, depending on the type of aircraft used. The rate varies from approximately 57 cents per ton-mile for a 2-engine plane to approximately $1.31 for a 4-engine plane. Based on ton-miles transported, they vary from a low for a 2-engine plane of 11.7 cents per ton-mile to 13.9 cents for the 4-engine aircraft. In addition to these ton-mile costs, there are numerous costs—such as terminal and communications facilities, cargo-handling equipment, and others—which are borne not by the carrier but by the military departments. Approximately one third more would have to be added to the ton-mile costs to get the actual cost of the service. Some industrial concerns use air contract service.

PIPE-LINE CARRIERS

The rates charged by petroleum pipe lines for crude oil are based on a standard barrel of 42 standard gallons at 60 degrees Fahrenheit. The tariffs consist of two parts: (1) the tender rules and (2) the rates. Sometimes, they are published together; at other times, separately. The rules part of the tariffs regarding acceptance of the shipment varies from company to company.

Crude oil accepted for shipment must be marketable or merchantable, which means that it must be properly settled and contain less than a stated percentage of basic sediment and water. Another customary tariff requirement is the limitation concerning the temperature at which the oil may be accepted. To facilitate handling, some tariffs also establish limits on gravity and viscosity.

In product lines tariffs, the requirement is often established that the products will be accepted only when storage facilities for the particular commodity are available at the destination. Another common proviso is that products of the same quality and specifications are being handled at that time in the products line. Oil which is involved in litigation or oil against which there is any lien will not be accepted by a carrier.

Pipe lines usually maintain only sufficient tankage space to receive deliveries from the shipper; and at destination, the tariffs may provide for the pipe line to furnish sufficient tankage which can be used by the consignee during a specified period. If the consignee does not accept delivery in accordance with the time limits provided in the tariff, a demurrage charge, varying from one eighth to 1 cent per barrel per day of delay, is charged. There are special and terminal services for which additional charges exist. These include such items as storage, gathering services, and blending in transit, to name but a few.

Uncertainty regarding the amount of flow has often resulted in an initially high tariff rate to guard against unexpected depletion of a field. Both local and joint tariffs are issued in pipe-line transportation, and they are generally not of the volume found in motor or rail transportation.

FREIGHT FORWARDERS

The LCL rates of surface freight forwarders to shippers are generally the same as the LCL or LTL rates which the shipper would pay via rail or motor common carrier. However, there are some forwarder rates slightly below the rail or motor rates. This formerly was more prevalent than is the case today.

The Commission ruled in 1959 that freight forwarders are not restricted to the handling of small shipments only. It approved freight forwarder trailer-load volume commodity rates under Plan III piggyback, subject to minima ranging from 10,000 to 30,000 pounds, in which assembly and consolidation of shipments are performed. This ruling was upheld by the Supreme Court in 1962.[32]

"Freight—all kinds" or "all-commodity" rates established by rail, motor, and water carriers at a specific rate applicable to the entire shipment, even though it is mixed freight, are widely used by freight forwarders. Surface freight forwarders, like motor common carriers of general commodities, have established minimum class rate stops.

The rates of air freight forwarders generally are those which the air carriers charge. Since air carriers have a decreasing scale for larger-quantity shipments, the air freight forwarder, through consolidation, can operate on the same type of spread between charges for small shipments as compared to large shipments that the surface freight forwarder does.

In 1957, the Civil Aeronautics Board ruled that joint rates between air freight forwarders and direct air carriers were not authorized. However, it added that special reduced rates for air freight forwarders are not unlawful per se, and a regulation prohibiting the filing of such rates would be premature. This matter is in litigation in the courts.

REA EXPRESS

The types of rates used by the REA Express are similar to those of railroads. The *Official Express Classification* is used in conjunction with class rates, but there are also exceptions to the classification. This classification differs somewhat from others. Unlike other classifications, it lists only the commodities that are exceptions to the general rule and does not

---

[32] *Eastern Express, Inc.* v. *United States* (1962).

list those commodities that take the basic rate. Most types of merchandise take the first-class rate. Second-class rates, which apply on food and drink items, are 75 per cent of first-class rates. Other rates used are commodity rates; merchandise rates, which apply on the transportation of ordinary merchandise; money rates, applicable to items of unusual value; basing rates, which are those made by adding or subtracting arbitraries from other rates; and pound rates, which are basic rates multiplied by the number of pounds in a shipment and the product divided by 100. For example, the charge on a shipment weighing 75 pounds between points taking a rate of $3.65 for 100 pounds would be determined by multiplying $3.65 $\times$ 75 and dividing the product by 100, which equals $2.7375, or $2.74.

Both carload and less-carload rates are published, based on the amount offered for shipment. There are also rates for container service, which involves the use of special metal containers for carrying small packages. Accessorial charges—such as refrigeration, terminal, switching, and C.O.D. charges—are also established.

Quantity or "incentive" rates apply on wearing apparel when the charges are prepaid, and the total weight is 300 pounds or more rendered and receipted for at one time from one shipper to one address, and certain other stipulations. On shipments of 300 to 1,499 pounds, the applicable charge is 75 per cent of first class; 1,500 to 2,499, 70 per cent; and 2,500 pounds and over, 65 per cent.

Express rates on the declared value of the goods are based on an amount not exceeding $50 per 100 pounds, or 50 cents per pound. Extra charges for each $100 valuation are made if the shipper wants the additional valuation added.

The rate structure of REA Express is much simpler than the rail or motor carrier rate structure. The United States is divided into blocks constituting the area between the intersecting parallels of latitude and longitude. The blocks are numbered consecutively from west to east, starting in the northwest corner with number 101, the second tier with 201, and so on. There are 58 such blocks; and from north to south, there are 25 blocks, with block number 100 parallel to the latitude of the Puget Sound area and block number 2500 parallel to Key West. (See Figure 8–3.) Between each of the blocks, there is a rate scale. Each block is divided into 16 squares and lettered A to Q inclusive (omitting the letter J), so that the rate can be computed from subblock to subblock.

In 1961, a cube rate for small shipments was made effective which discarded the conventional weight-times-distance method of computing freight charges. It is based instead on the number of pieces comprising a shipment and total cubic volume. The shipment piece-count charge is determined from a one-page schedule, and the cubic line-haul charge is determined from a table based on a fixed charge of 7 cents per cubic foot per 100 miles. Basically, the cube rate means that the greater the density and the fewer the pieces the shipper can achieve per shipment the lower the charges. This is the case even though the total shipment weight may be the same or more than other shipments moving at higher charges if the latter are bulkier or involve handling a greater number of pieces. Recently REA has instituted "unitized" charges to apply on freight on pallets, skids, or in pallet containers.

AIR EXPRESS

The REA Express publishes the air express rates which apply on shipments from 1 to 40 pounds between particular points, although the basis for charges on shipments of more than 40 pounds is provided. Commodity rates have been published to apply on certain items. Due to minimum charges applicable on air freight, the rates on small shipments are generally lower via air express. Usually, the rate break between air express and air freight is between 25 and 35 pounds.

The liability of the express company is limited in air express shipments to not over $50 per 100 pounds, or 50 cents per pound. Additional coverage can be secured for each $100 of valuation declared.

PARCEL POST

A parcel post rate can be secured by writing to the origin-point post office or by obtaining in person a copy of the Official Parcel Post Zone Key for that particular point. This key will show the parcel post zone from the particular origin point to all post offices in the United States by reference to destination unit numbers. The *United States Official Postal Guide* shows unit numbers for all post offices in its list of post offices, by states. The *Guide* also contains parcel post charges by zones, of which there are eight. Special handling, which will expedite the movement to the office of destination, is available at a nominal charge. Parcel post can be insured or sent C.O.D.

Air parcel post rates are somewhat higher than parcel post rates. The zone rates for parcels carried by air are based on the eight postal zones applicable to fourth-class, parcel post mail. Parcels weighing less than 10 pounds and measuring more than 84 inches, but not more than 100 inches, in length and girth combined must take the 10-pound rate.

Air parcel post may be sent either as first-class mail or as fourth-class mail, depending on its contents. Air parcel post that is first class may be registered, while fourth-class air parcel post may be insured or sent C.O.D. Both classes may be sent special delivery. The sender must guarantee any return or forwarding postage necessary for registered, insured, or C.O.D. air parcel post.

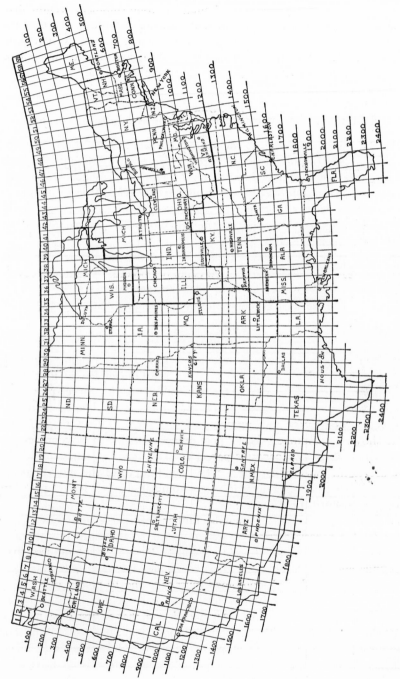

FIG. 8–3. Map of REA Express blocks.

TRAFFIC DEPARTMENT RATE FORMS

The industrial traffic department or section has numerous company forms which are used in conjunction with rate matters in its organization. While the forms used differ in number and structure in different companies, the ones described in the following paragraphs are representative of those in general use.

There are often requests from other departments of an organization for freight rates. An interoffice letter, such as Figure 8–4 below, may

FROM

To	Noted	Date	
			Advise
			Note
			File
			Handle
			See Me
			Return

Date Sent

Date Returned

KEMAR CORPORATION

INTER-OFFICE CORRESPONDENCE

To

Attention of

From

Date

Dictated by

SUBJECT FREIGHT RATES File

Per your request of we quote below the rates effective as of the date hereof. These rates are subject to change and therefore SHOULD NOT BE USED IN THE FUTURE UNLESS CONFIRMED BY THE GENERAL TRANSPORTATION DEPARTMENT.

Rates are shown in cents per 100 pounds unless otherwise noted

Commodity:

FROM	TO	Rate	Min. Wt.	Rate	Min. Wt.

FIG. 8–4. An example of an interoffice letter giving rate information.

INBOUND RATE CARD

Rates in cents per hundred pounds except as otherwise indicated

Material	Destination
Origin	Origin Carrier

Tariff Description and Package	Tariff Reference	* CL	* LCL	Min. Weight	TL	LTL	Date
Route							

* Subject to Ex Parte 175 Increases except as otherwise indicated

FIG. 8–5. An example of an inbound rate card.

be used to transmit this information. The frequent changes in rates which take place prompt the statement that rates quoted are those effective on a given date.

Some traffic departments have outbound and inbound rate cards (often called "rate and route" cards), on which pertinent rate information is contained. A typical inbound rate card, shown in Figure 8–5, contains information on the rates via different modes of transportation, as well as

TF-10176

DATE ISSUED	CANCELS SHEET DATED	CHECKED BY:
FROM	DESTINATION	
CONSIGNEE		
ROUTE		
	ROUTING INSTRUCTIONS ISSUED BY	

EXP. SCALE		P.P ZONE		ROUTE	RAIL AND OTHER LCL	VOL.	MINIMUM	ROUTE	TRUCK LTL	VOL.	MINIMUM
TOOTH BRUSHES, NOIBN											
COMBS, NOIBN											
SYNTHETIC RESIN ARTICLES, NOIBN											
STORE DISPLAY, STANDS, SET UP, O/T FLAT IN PKGS.											

FIG. 8–6. An example of an outbound rate card.

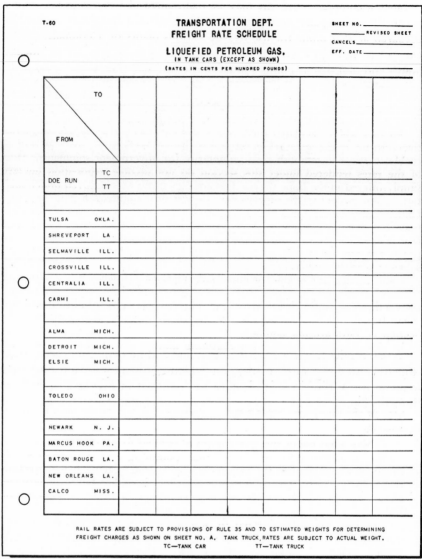

FIG. 8–7. Example of freight rate schedule.

tariff description and reference and package. An outbound rate card, on which the articles being shipped from the producing point are printed on the rate card, is shown in Figure 8–6. In this particular case, the card provides space for movement by any means.

The use of rate cards depends in part on the routing control exercised by the headquarters traffic department in larger organizations. If centralized control is established, the plant traffic departments have to secure a release from the headquarters traffic department before a shipment can be made.

Since a complete tariff file may be maintained at but one point, which is usually at company headquarters, there is often a freight rate schedule prepared at that point for use by the various plants of a company. This can be set up as in Figure 8–7, with origin points on the left or sideline points and destination points shown in the headline points.

CASE

An area where regulated for-hire carriers have been able to exercise initiative with minimal regulatory constraint is that of Section 22 rates. Section 22 enables carriers to establish rates voluntarily for government shipments. Most of the rates tendered under this section do not involve negotiation but are simply offered in the hope they will encourage traffic to be moved under such rates. Government traffic officials have consistently emphasized that these rate tenders are voluntary and find it hard to believe that carriers would file rates that were not compensatory. For example, in fiscal 1962 the Defense Traffic Management Service of the Department of Defense originated only 375 proposals for rate or classification adjustments, whereas there were 51,535 unsolicited tenders received from carriers.

Some carrier and shipper groups have repeatedly sought the abolition of Section 22 and have charged that these rates enable the government to ship commodities at rates lower than other shippers can move similar shipments. They feel this casts a burden on commercial shippers since, it is alleged, the Section 22 rates are not compensatory.

In 1956, Congress passed a law requiring that all new Section 22 rates had to be filed with the Interstate Commerce Commission unless they involved shipments affecting national security. Actually, such quotations had been available for public inspection long before the Interstate Commerce Act was so amended.

One of the arguments against the continuance of Section 22 rates is quoted as follows:

"There is no doubt the government is entitled to reasonable rates on its traffic, but it should be prohibited from sponsoring destructive competitive practices which weaken the nation's transportation system. It is regrettable that certain government departments and agencies either fail to understand, choose to ignore, or just do not believe in the National Transportation Policy.

"No one has ever objected or would ever object to the government obtaining Section 22 lower rates for the movement of military goods, troops, freight of extremely unusual character, or freight destined to or from any port in connection with any national emergency.

"Most objectors disapprove of the government putting its traffic up for bid regardless of the economic effects which the resulting rates will have upon carriers and industry. From an economic point of view, what do these bargain rates accomplish? In the short run, they may help balance each government agency's current budget. In the long run, it helps destroy the common carrier system which it should maintain, promotes cutthroat competition and inhibits modernization of equipment that requires some assurance of future traffic for adequate financing."

1. How would you go about determining if Section 22 rates cast a burden on other traffic?

2. Generally, the federal government does not make use of private carriage

in freight transportation. Would you feel that the government should be able to engage in private carriage if Section 22 rates are eliminated? Why or why not?

DISCUSSION QUESTIONS AND PROBLEMS

1. Explain fully for each mode of transportation the completeness of service covered by the line-haul rate.

2. Enumerate the reasons why class rates are important. How does classification simplify rates?

3. How does a class rate scale work? Does such a scale make a more rigid rate structure?

4. Make a chart which will show the uniform class rate scale progression. Why does it not increase in direct proportion to distance increases?

5. What are some of the adjustments in the class rate scales which have occurred as a result of the prescription of the uniform class rate scale?

6. List the different types of commodity rates. What are some of the reasons for their establishment?

7. Trainload or multiple-car rates have been authorized by regulatory bodies in but a few instances. Why? Is this beneficial to shippers? Carriers? The public?

8. Differentiate clearly between proportional and differential rates.

9. Carefully explain what is meant by incentive rates. Do you feel there is a justification for incentive rates?

10. What factors have influenced the establishment of export and import rates? Why are such rates as much as 50 per cent lower than the domestic rates?

11. Explain the difference between a combination rate which is applied because of the lack of a through rate and a combination rate protected because of the alternative combination rule.

12. Show, by diagram, some of the different applications of the intermediate rules.

13. What is a volume rate? Is it the same as a truckload rate?

14. Explain the meaning of released value ratings. What is the trend in the use of such released values by carriers? Do you feel that it is wise for shippers to encourage such ratings in order to get reduced rates?

15. What are the dominant factors in the development of our freight rate structure?

16. Of what significance to the traffic manager is the Commission waybill study, which shows that 91 per cent of the rail carload tonnage moves by commodity rates?

17. In water transportation, identify the following: heavy-lift rates, optional cargo rates, ad valorem rates, open rates, and parcel rates.

18. Trace the development of air cargo rates. Is density of any importance in air cargo movements?

19. What are the similarities and differences in the rates of railroads as compared to pipe lines? Freight forwarders? REA Express? Air Express? Parcel post?

20. Explain the purpose of a traffic department's rate and route card.

21. What are agreed charges? Are they similar to any other type of rate?

Chapter

9

TARIFFS AND RATE FORMULATION

TARIFFS

TARIFFS are of a wide variety, with each type quite different in material. An explanation of the contents of individual tariffs or interpretation thereof is a highly, complex subject. To add to the problem is the fact that during a one-year period, over 190,000 freight and passenger tariffs and supplements (about 700,000 pages) are received by the Interstate Commerce Commission for filing.

The Interstate Commerce Act provides that every common carrier subject to the act shall print and keep open to public inspection schedules showing all interstate rates and charges for transportation between different points on its own route, and between points on its own route and points on the route of any other carrier by railroad, pipe line, motor, or water when a through route and joint rate have been established.

If no joint rate over the through route has been established, the carriers are required to print, file, and keep open to public inspection the separately established rates and charges applied to the through transportation. These printed schedules are referred to as "tariffs"; in effect, they constitute a price list. These tariffs must plainly state the places between which property will be carried and contain the classification, if any, of freight in force. They must state separately all terminal charges, storage charges, icing charges, and all other charges which the Commission may require; all privileges or facilities granted or allowed; and any rules or regulations which in any way change, affect, or determine any part of the aggregate of such rates and charges or the value of the service rendered to the shipper or consignee. It becomes apparent that it requires thousands of tariffs in order to publish all the various types of rates, charges, rules, and regulations of the carriers. Tariffs vary from a single page to over a thousand pages in size.

Carriers are required to post or file, at each station at which freight service is available and at which an agent or attendant is employed, tariffs and supplements thereto which contain the rates applying from or to that point; they must also post or file tariffs publishing terminal or other charges applicable at that station which are issued by the carrier or by an agent for the carrier's account.

Under certain conditions, however, the Commission, by specific order, as a result of applications filed by the carriers showing good and sufficient justification therefor, has permitted the carriers to deviate from the above requirement, so that under present-day conditions, the only tariffs which it is necessary for an agent to have on file are those he must use in the normal conduct of business at his station. This relief from the necessity to comply fully with the requirement referred to is known as "posting relief."

Where advantage is taken of the posting relief so granted, notices must be posted at the stations involved, stating at what point a complete public file of all tariffs is maintained. Further, the carrier must, within ten days after receipt of request for the posting at a station of any tariff, post such tariff at that station.

The tariff has the force of a statute as long as it is effective and is recognized as such by both carriers and shippers. The Court has said that "the tariff, so long as it is of force is, in respect to the rates named to be treated as though it were a statute, binding as such upon railroad and shipper alike."[1]

Tariffs of carriers subject to the Interstate Commerce Act must be prepared and filed with the Interstate Commerce Commission in accordance with the provisions of the applicable tariff circular. Such a circular specifically, and in detail, outlines the form, size, and some of the phraseology to be used in tariffs. The present rules and requirements are the result of years of study and experience of the Commission and competent tariff men of the carriers and associations co-operating with the Commission. These rules have as their objective the statement of rates, rules, and regulations in freight tariffs in a simple manner, with a view to making it possible for any user of a tariff to determine readily the rates, rules, and regulations applicable to a given shipment. The Civil Aeronautics Board prescribes similar requirements for air carriers subject to its jurisdiction.

For uniformity in constructing tariffs, it is necessary to eliminate ambiguity and superfluous wording in order to have a more standardized publication. Therefore, tariffs of carriers subject to the Commission's jurisdiction must be constructed in the form and manner prescribed by the Interstate Commerce Commission's tariff circulars.

Types of Tariffs

Generally, rail freight tariffs are divided into the five following groups:

[1] *Pillsbury Flour Mills Co.* v. *G. N. Ry. Co.,* 25 Fed. (2d) 66 (1928).

1. *Class Rate Tariffs*. Those publications requiring use of a classification for ratings of various articles are class rate tariffs. These tariffs name class rates, carload, less-carload (less-truckload, volume, or truckload for motor carriers) on any articles named in the governing classifications referred to. Class rates, in the broad sense, include rates for ratings either in exceptions tariffs or in classifications.

2. *Commodity Rate Tariffs*. Those publications containing rates for articles grouped under generic headings, which for various reasons do not move under class rates and therefore receive special treatment, are commodity rate tariffs. These tariffs name rates applying on specific commodities or groups of commodities only. Commodity rates are specific as to the articles described or as to those which are grouped under a commodity title. Rates named in these tariffs cannot be applied on analogous articles. (See Rule 17 of the Consolidated and Uniform Freight classifications.)

3. *Class and Commodity Tariffs*. Those publications which contain class and commodity rates and rules governing alternate application in any instance where the articles could be rated under either section of the tariff are class and commodity tariffs.

4. *Mileage Tariffs*. Those publications which contain rates published on the basis of mileage or on the basis of minimum rates protected under circuitous operations are mileage tariffs. These tariffs are frequently used to specify minimum rates, particularly when the through service is via two or more carriers, one of which desires to assure itself of a minimum rate for the distance traveled over its route.

5. *Special Service Tariffs*. Those publications containing rates and charges to cover special services and privileges, accessory services, and services not included in line-haul movements are special service tariffs. These tariffs name charges for special services performed by transportation companies or authorized shippers, such as heating, refrigeration, local switching, diversion and reconsignment, stopping in transit, pickup and delivery, storage and/or processing in transit, collection of invoice values, and other special services as specified in the tariff.

Rates as contained in all the foregoing tariffs are published in some of the following kinds of tariffs:

Local Tariffs. These tariffs contain and name rates from and to, or between, stations on the line of a single carrier and are ordinarily published by the individual line.

Joint Tariffs. These tariffs contain and name rates from and to, or between, stations on the line of one carrier and stations on the line of another; or from, or between, stations on the lines of two or more carriers. Joint tariffs are issued by individual lines or by tariff-publishing agencies.

Agency and Individual Carrier Tariffs. It is most difficult to outline clearly a definite procedure to be followed in locating the tariff containing the rate in question, inasmuch as no established rule is observed in the publication of tariffs, i.e., whether issued by a tariff-publishing agent or by the individual lines. The majority of class rate tariffs are agency issues, however, and are published to apply from certain origin points to specified destinations, although some tariffs, commonly referred to as "between" tariffs, are applicable in both directions.

In a so-called "between" tariff, in order to keep the size of the publication to a minimum, some publishing agents have confined the headline points to the smallest territory covered by the tariff and used the base points for the larger territory as the sideline points. In those instances in which a tariff is published to apply from and to certain points, care must be taken to insure that, in looking up the rate, the origin and destination are not reversed, for in these tariffs, the same rate does not apply, in many cases, in both directions, due to the fact that the groupings which are used for the origin and destination may differ.

Individual carriers generally publish commodity rates which apply locally within one association territory, while tariff-publishing agents issue commodity tariffs which apply from the territory under the jurisdiction of the rate association of the issuing publishing agent to destinations in another rate territory. There are, of course, many exceptions to the above generalizations. Specific commodity tariffs are published by agents which apply within only one rate territory, and individual carriers publish commodity tariffs containing rates which apply interterritorially.

A survey of applicable tariffs discloses that rates which have been prescribed by the Interstate Commerce Commission are generally compiled and issued by tariff-publishing agents, whereas rates published in commodity tariffs by carriers are those based on proposals initiated by the individual carriers and are limited to destinations within the origin rate association territory.

Agency Tariffs. These tariffs are those publications naming local rates applicable for the account of one carrier, or joint rates applicable for the account of two or more carriers and for which carriers the publisher is acting as a tariff agent under powers of attorney issued individually by the carriers and filed with the Interstate Commerce Commission. Carriers participating in such agency tariffs cannot file with the Commission any other tariff or tariffs containing rates applicable on the same articles between the same points.

Joint Agency Tariffs. Tariffs quoting rates between two territories published jointly by agents acting for the railroads in each territory as, for example, Trunk-Line Territory Railroads Tariff Bureau No. 107–C, naming rates *between* Western Trunk-Line *and* Trunk-Line and New England territories, are joint agency tariffs.

There are no uniform systems among the various railroads or tariff-issuing agencies of designating the tariffs issued by each. In the majority of instances, however, serial numbers, together with letter prefixes or suffixes, are used. For example, a railroad or an agency issues a series of numbers, such as series 100 or series 200, for use in designating its different tariffs. Tariffs coming under the 100 series may often contain class rates; the 200 series, commodity rates; and the 300 series, class and commodity rates, and so on.

When it is necessary to cancel a tariff, and the new tariff is given the same series number as the one which it replaces, a letter prefix or suffix is also necessary to differentiate between the current and the canceled issues. Thus, if a tariff designated as Freight Tariff 500 is canceled, the one issued to take its place is designated as Freight Tariff 500–A or A–500, depending upon whether the prefix or suffix is used. When 500–A is canceled, its subsequent issue is 500–B.

The Interstate Commerce Commission does not require that a carrier use a number other than the ICC number.

How to Look up a Rate

The Interstate Commerce Commission requires that each carrier publish, post, and file a complete index of effective tariffs to which it is a party, either as an initial or as a delivering carrier. The publication of a tariff index simplifies the procedure for finding the applicable rate. The user of a tariff should become familiar not only with the tariffs but also with the tariff index, since the latter document is helpful in determining the tariff which should be used in looking up the rate.

Tariff indexes are arranged by sections. Section 1 contains all of the tariffs in which the carrier is the initial carrier, listed in the following order: specific commodity tariffs, general commodity tariffs, class and commodity tariffs, class tariffs, and miscellaneous issues. Section 2 contains a list of all tariffs in which the carrier is listed as the delivering carrier. Section 3 contains a numerical list of ICC numbers of the issuing carrier, as well as state numbers. It may also show its own individual tariff numbers, which are often added as Section 4. An additional section is sometimes added, showing the participating carriers in tariffs published by the issuing carrier.

There are a number of methods which can be used in looking up the applicable rate. There is disagreement, even among those who have spent many years in rate work, as to which is the best procedure. However, the following method is a representative one that can be used to determine the correct rate.

If the correct name of the commodity, the quantity to be shipped, and the origin and destination are known, the first step is to ascertain whether or not a specific commodity tariff is published which covers the commodity described, packing requirements, and the points of origin and destination. Since a specific commodity tariff is one which names rates on a certain commodity or on that particular commodity and its related articles, the rate which is named in such a tariff is the applicable rate, and the only one that may be used via the route or routes over which the commodity rate is applicable, even though a class rate or some combination of rates might be lower.

Tariffs which publish rates on a number of different commodities are known as "general commodities tariffs," whereas the "specific commodity tariff" names rates on a certain commodity. If there is no specific commodity tariff which is applicable, the second step is to determine whether a general commodity tariff is effective which would cover the commodity to be shipped, the packing requirements, and the points of origin and destination. If the rates are not found in any of the foregoing tariffs, the next step is to secure the ratings of the commodity from the classification or the exceptions to the classification in order to find the class rate which is applicable. The procedure is to go to the exceptions to the classification first, for if the rating can be found there for the commodity to be shipped, it must be used in lieu of the rating in the classification. In the event the exception to the classification is not applicable, recourse must be made to the classification. The classification should provide a rating on the article to be shipped.

After the rating in the classification for the article is found, the class rate in a tariff having the rate which is applicable to the rating must be ascertained. A general procedure for checking the rate, once the applicable tariff is found, is as follows: Read the title page of the tariff to determine if it is lawfully on file with the various commissions; the governing classification and exceptions; the effective date; the origin and destination territory; the commodity description; and whether the rates are local, joint, import-export, etc. Next, the table of contents should be scanned to locate the list of origin and destination points, the application of rates, the exceptions to the application of rates, the rules and regulations, rate sections, commodity descriptions, minimum weights, and routing instructions. Next, when checking the origin and destination stations, the rate basis, the station group, or the item number should be referred to by the person looking up the rate. The commodity description will also refer to various item numbers or section numbers of the tariff. A check of the rate-base station groups and item numbers will determine the rate which is applicable. Particular attention should be given to all reference marks, notes, rules and regulations, applications of rates, and references to other tariffs or publications which might affect the rate.

After securing the rate, the routing instructions must be checked to determine the route or routes over which the rate is applicable. The effective supplements to the tariffs, if any have been issued, must be carefully checked also, to determine whether or not anything in the supplements affects the rate which has been found in the original tariff. Finally, reference may also be made to the carrier's tariff index which most carriers publish.

Priority of Rates

The procedure for looking up a rate indicates that some rates take precedence over others. In order to give some idea of the priority of rates, a brief outline follows:

1. Through specific commodity rate:
   a) Between specified points.
   b) Between specified groups of points.
   c) Rates made by rule of intermediate application.
   d) To or from base points, and application extended under switching and absorption rules.
   e) Rate to or from base point extended by arbitrary or differential amount.
2. Through distance commodity rate.
3. Through specific class rate (subdivided [a] to [e], as in 1).
4. Through distance class rates.
5. Combination rate (i.e., rate made by addition of two or more rates over the same route; order of priority is considered in connection with each factor).
   a) Specifically authorized bases (each factor is considered as in 1–4, inclusive).
   b) Proportional specific commodity rates (each factor is considered [a] to [e], as in 1).
   c) Specific commodity rate (each factor is considered [a] to [e], as in 1).
   d) Distance commodity rates.
   e) Proportional class rates (each factor is considered [a] to [e], as in 1).
   f) Specific class rates (each factor is considered [a] to [e], as in 1).
   g) Distance class rates.

Exceptions to Priority Table

Export and import rates take precedence over domestic rates on export and import traffic, respectively.

Conflict between Rates

If there is a conflict between rates on a shipment, the following principles apply:

1. More specific rate takes precedence over less specific rate.
2. When two or more rates are established on same date in the same schedule, the lower rate takes precedence.
3. Through rates include all terminal charges at intermediate interchange points.

Pertinent Principles of ICC Tariff Interpretation

The regulatory bodies have had to interpret the application of the provisions of tariffs, so that there are numerous principles which are helpful in understanding tariffs. Some of the representative principles, with citations, are contained in the following paragraphs:

1. Although doubt as to the meaning of a tariff must be resolved in favor of the shipper and against the carrier which compiled it, the doubt must be a reasonable one.[2]
2. An exception attached to a general provision excepts from that provision only that portion to which the exception specifically refers.[3]

[2] 159 ICC 219 (1929).
[3] 148 ICC 273 (1928).

3. Where two descriptions and tariffs are equally appropriate, the shipper is entitled to have applied the one specifying the lower rates.[4]

4. When a commodity shipped is included in more than one commodity description in the same tariff, the rate on that description which is more specific is applicable. As between two unequal commodity rates, both adequately descriptive, the applicable rate is the one making the lower charge.[5]

5. When there are an overlapping classification description and conflicting ratings, the rating which most specifically and accurately describes the article must be applied. Where there is no clear choice, the lowest rating is applicable.[6]

6. Where a commodity shipped is embraced within two tariff descriptions, one general and one specific, the specific description and the rate in connection therewith must be applied.[7]

7. When two interpretations of a classification description are possible, the one which avoids conflict should prevail.[8]

8. A commodity rate must be applied strictly and not by analogy.[9]

9. Doubt as to the meaning of a tariff must be a reasonable one, and neither shippers nor carriers may be permitted to urge a strained or unnatural construction. In arriving at a proper determination of this question, a tariff must be considered in its entirety. If it may be said, after consideration of pertinent provisions and limitations, that a fair and reasonable construction expresses the intention of framers, such intention should control.[10]

Unofficial Tariffs

There are numerous publications which are often termed "unofficial" tariffs, in that they are not filed with a regulatory body and therefore do not have the effect of a statute, as is the case of tariffs which are so filed. However, they are useful publications and may be directories like the *Motor Carrier Directory*. Carriers sometimes issue memorandum tariffs as rate guides showing rates from a particular point or points. These are a convenience to shippers, and such tariffs have no legal status. There are also several rate guides, such as *Leonard's Guide*, which are compiled by organizations which sell such service. These publications vary widely as to content. Some publish all rates and charges from a city or state throughout the United States, whereas others may publish a rate guide which covers a very limited area.

Traffic Manager's Tariff File

It has been common practice for railroads to furnish tariffs to shippers without charge. Motor common carriers and air carriers have usually furnished individual issues gratis to shippers, but their agency publications are on a subscription basis in most instances. However, since the individual carrier members of the tariff bureau or conference which publishes the tariff are entitled to a specified number of copies, the carriers may distribute free copies to some shippers.

[4] 268 U.S. 542 (1925).
[5] 159 ICC 342 (1929).
[6] 195 ICC 757 (1933).
[7] 210 ICC 245 (1935).
[8] 238 ICC 25 (1940).
[9] 196 ICC 691 (1933).
[10] 121 ICC 275 (1926).

There are many satisfactory arrangements for filing tariffs. Filing on shelves, in file cabinets, or in special sectional drop-section files are some of the methods used. One widely used method is to file tariffs and supplements in four-pronged binders. When not in use, binders are placed upright in a file case which should be accessibly located to the tariff user. All binders in the file are numbered consecutively, so that they may be returned to their proper place when removed from file.

Tariffs issued by the various agencies are filed in these binders in separate sets, alphabetically according to issuing agency name; each set is in issuing agency number order, regardless of tariff application. Tariffs issued by the carriers are filed in like manner, except that it is advantageous to group specific commodity tariffs. Commodity tariffs so grouped are filed in issuing carrier number order. Usually, the rail issues, both individual and agency, are grouped together; the same is true with motor, while miscellaneous schedules are kept separately. Unofficial tariffs are also generally kept separately.

Abbreviations of issuing agencies, such as IFA (Illinois Freight Association), MAC (Middle Atlantic Conference), and commonly known abbreviations of issuing carriers are stenciled on the front of binders. Issuing agency numbers without suffix are also shown on the front of binders. When practicable, issuing carrier numbers without suffix are shown on binders containing carrier issues.

It is suggested that the fronts of binders containing agency tariffs be stenciled with abbreviations. Binders containing the National Motor Freight Classification, the Consolidated Freight Classification, the Uniform Freight Classification, the Open and Prepay Station List, and the Railway Equipment Register may be kept in a separate section of the file case. These binders should be stenciled with appropriate abbreviations.

Supplements are filed behind the original tariff in numerical order, or alphabetically when supplements are designated by alphabetical letters. Canceled supplements should be retained in the file.

There are numerous independent "watching" services which can be employed by a traffic department or section to supply a daily or weekly list of the publications filed with a regulatory body which will affect rates. This enables the traffic department to anticipate changes in rates and, where necessary, to participate in such proceedings. The *Traffic Bulletin*, which is published weekly by the Traffic Service Corporation, contains abstracts of all tariffs, supplements, and classifications filed with the Commission by common carriers, and it is widely used in keeping abreast of tariff changes.

Many carriers, in order to provide a through service to shippers, must enter into agreements with as many as five other carriers on a single shipment. They confer and establish agreements on the rates to be charged and the apportionment of the charge to the participating carriers. This means that they are often dealing with their competitors. There is no similar situation in any other industry, and it has necessitated specific legal arrangements in rate-making.

RATE BUREAUS AND CONFERENCES

Carriers originally published rates by issuing them in their own tariffs. Later, traffic committees, which were composed of carrier representatives from a geographical area, were established. The increasing volume of traffic by rail which moved between carriers was a factor in the development of these so-called "rate territories." Sometimes, carriers had depended upon agreements made between them to govern the rates on competitive traffic. This took the form of money or traffic pools. With the passage of the Act to Regulate Commerce in 1887, both money and traffic pools were prohibited, so that railroads which had made agreements through their traffic associations on competitive freight rates ended this procedure. However, traffic associations, which established the machinery through which rates could be formulated and, as a part of such procedure, had carriers enter into formal rate agreements, soon found this procedure questioned because the Attorney General of the United States secured injunctions, under the Sherman Antitrust Act of 1890, against two of these traffic associations. The Supreme Court handed down decisions in these two cases, stating that these formal rate agreements were illegal under the provisions of the Sherman Antitrust Act.[11]

Subsequent to these decisions, the Official Classification Committee of the railroads in the Official Territory, in 1899, prepared a new classification. Although the Interstate Commerce Commission was not charged with enforcing the Sherman Act, it nevertheless sent a statement of facts to the Attorney General, but he declined to act. The Attorney General differentiated between the findings in the earlier cases—the Trans-Missouri and the Joint Traffic Association cases—and this instance by finding that there was no showing of contract, combination, or conspiracy which was forbidden by the antitrust act. In this particular instance, it was pointed out that the carriers, in making the informal agreement, preserved the right of individual action to each carrier; that there was no penalty against a carrier which changed a rate fixed by the manager of the association; and there was nothing to show compulsion, combination, or arbitrary action suppressing competition.

The various rate bureaus and associations then adjusted their organizations and procedures along the lines of the opinion rendered by the Attorney General. These bureaus and committees functioned openly and were an accepted part of the rate-making procedure. However, the Department of Justice later brought suit against railroad associations for alleged violations of the antitrust laws. A similar suit was filed against certain motor carrier associations, with the result that the well-established procedure in rate formulation was questioned.

---

[11] *United States v. Trans-Missouri Freight Association*, 166 U.S. 290 (1897); *United States v. Joint Traffic Association*, 171 U.S. 505 (1898).

With the threat of modification of the conference method of rate making as a result of the litigation, carriers urged Congress to enact legislation which would permit the use of the conference method but, at the same time, relieve them of any possibility of violating the antitrust laws. The Congress, after extensive hearings, passed the Reed-Bulwinkle Act, which is incorporated as Section 5a of the Interstate Commerce Act. This section authorizes carriers, as defined in the section, to apply to the Commission for approval of any agreement between or among two or more such carriers relating to rate and other matters contained within the language of that section upon such terms and conditions as the Commission may prescribe. The parties to any agreement which is approved by the Commission and any other persons are relieved from the operation of the antitrust laws with respect to the making of the agreement and with respect to the carrying-out of the agreement in conformance with its provisions and prescribed terms and conditions. The Commission has prescribed rules and regulations governing the form, contents, filing of applications, maintenance and preservation of accounts and records, and filing annual reports, under Section 5a. They prescribe that there be public notice of the filing of each application, which will indicate how a hearing upon the application can be secured. Additional conditions are that the agreements must be in furtherance of the national transportation policy and that the agreements shall permit the individual members of a rate bureau the right to take independent action either before or after any determination made under the rate bureau procedure.

As matters now stand, the carriers subject to the jurisdiction of the Interstate Commerce Commission can formulate rates through rate bureaus, conferences, or associations without fear of antitrust proceedings, if such agreements are on file with and approved by the Commission. As of 1963, there had been sixty-five agreements approved—9 railroad, 7 water, 1 freight forwarder, and 48 motor.

An examination of Section 5a filings approved by the Commission shows similarities, particularly in those dealing with a single mode of transportation; but there are, even in these instances, some procedural differences. In other instances, the procedures and methods employed differ widely. The railroad rate agreements subject to Section 5a provide that a carrier or shipper can request a change in rates of the chairman of the rate bureau which has jurisdiction over the rate involved or of a carrier member of that bureau. The major railroad rate territories are shown in Figure 9–1 (pp. 234–235). The proposed change is then distributed to all members of the bureau, and it is placed on the public docket by publication in a national traffic publication at least 14 days prior to any action being taken. A shipper can request a public hearing; and if such a request is filed, it must be granted.

The proposal must be disposed of through a majority vote of the

CANADIAN FREIGHT ASSOCIATI
WESTERN LINES

NORTH PACIFIC
COAST
FREIGHT
BUREAU
TERRITORY

PACIFIC SOUTH COAST
FREIGHT BUREAU
TERRITORY

WESTERN TRAFFIC ASSOCIATION TERRITORY

WESTERN TRUNK LIN
COMMITTEE TERRITOR

SOUTHWESTERN FR
TERRITO

TRANSCONTINENTAL EASTERN BOUNDARY
OF WESTERN DEFINED TERRITORY
(Eastern boundary of North & South Pacific Coast Territories)

LEGEND

✿ ✿ ✿ ✿ ✿   EASTERN TERRITORY:

●━●━●━●   CENTRAL TERRITORY RAILROADS - FREIGHT TRAFFIC
          COMMITTEE TERRITORY.

▮▮▮▮▮▮▮▮   ILLINOIS FREIGHT BUREAU TERRITORY.

★ ★ ★ ★ ★   NEW ENGLAND RAILROADS - FREIGHT TRAFFIC
            COMMITTEE TERRITORY.

━◄━◄━◄━   TRUNK LINE TERRITORY RAILROADS - FREIGHT
          TRAFFIC COMMITTEE TERRITORY.

◄━◄━◄━◄   SOUTHERN FREIGHT ASSOCIATION TERRITORY:

, ·   WESTERN TRAFFIC ASSOCIATION TERRITORY:

━ ━ ━ ━ ━   NORTH PACIFIC COAST FREIGHT BUREAU TERRITORY.

● ● ● ●   PACIFIC SOUTH COAST FREIGHT BUREAU TERRITORY.

\\\\\\\\   SOUTHWESTERN FREIGHT BUREAU TERRITORY.

●●●●●●●   WESTERN TRUNK LINE COMMITTEE TERRITORY.

TRANSCONTINENTAL TERRITORY RATES APPLY FROM AND TO RATE GROUPS
   IN OTHER TERRITORIES.

SOURCE: SECTION 5A FILINGS OF ASSOCIATIONS

FIG. 9-1. Major railroad rate territories.

members attending the meeting at which the proposal is considered. The disposition of the docketed proposal is then published in a national traffic publication. If the action of the bureau is not acceptable to the shipper, he can request reconsideration by the same committee or request a review by the Traffic Executive Committee of that association. However, the provisions for review by the Traffic Executive Committee vary in the different rail rate territories. In the Western Traffic Association Territory, which is composed of nine rail rate-making bureaus in the area west of the Mississippi River, the shipper can appeal to the Traffic Executive Committee of the Western Traffic Association. Within 10 days after receiving notification of the disposition notice from the chairman of the Western Traffic Association's Executive Committee, the shipper can be granted a conference with the traffic executives of the interested member lines. Publication will be withheld for 30 days to give the shipper the opportunity to have this conference.

The larger bureaus, such as the Southwestern Freight Bureau, have a Standing Rate Committee composed of three or more members who are Bureau employees selected by the Bureau Executive Committee. The Standing Rate committees make the initial examinations and analysis of all proposals, conduct public hearings, and make recommendations to member lines on all proposals. The Standing Rate committees have no authority in the final determination of proposals.

If there is no objection within 14 days to the recommendation of the Standing Rate Committee, the recommendation is deemed to have the approval of the individual lines, and an effective date is set for publication of a change in a tariff.

In the Western Traffic Association Territory, where a rate proposal involves traffic moving through two territories, such as the Western Trunk-Line Committee and the Southwestern Freight Bureau, the proposal is docketed with the bureau in which the proposal originated.[12] If that bureau approves it, it is then submitted to the other bureau involved. Should the latter approve, the rates are published, if the Commission approves.

In the Eastern Territory, which embraces three rail rate territories, a rate proposal which would apply to a movement entirely within the Central Territory Railroads' area may be placed, upon request of a member carrier, on the docket of the General Traffic Committee—Eastern Railroads, and the determination will then be made by the latter committee.[13]

The organization of the railroad rate conference, associations, and committees in the Eastern Territory is shown in Figure 9–2 (pp. 238–39).

There is not the division of subterritories in the Southern Freight

---

[12] *Western Traffic Association—Agreement,* 276 ICC 183 (1949).
[13] *Eastern Railroads Agreements,* 277 ICC 279 (1950).

Association Territory that exists in the other primary rail rate associations. There is a Standing Rate Committee and a General Freight Committee. A recommendation of the General Freight Committee may be reviewed by the Executive Committee of the Southern Freight Association.[14]

Requirements of motor carrier rate agreements were reviewed by the Commission in the application which the Middle Atlantic Conference made. The procedure is basically the same for motor carriers as for rail carriers, but the Commission questioned the power of the Conference to request suspension of rates. It stated that if such procedure was used by the Conference and, in so doing, there was any violation of the Sherman Antitrust Act, this action would not fall within the exemption granted by Section 5a.

In the case of motor general commodity carriers, there are more rate territories than is true of rail. Figure 9–3 (pp. 240–41) shows the major intraterritorial motor rate territories.

The following associations also publish interterritorial rates: the Middle Atlantic Conference, Southern Motor Carriers Rate Conference, General-Central Eastern Conference, Central and Southern Motor Freight Tariff Association, Middlewest Motor Freight Bureau, Pacific Inland Tariff Bureau, Pacific Southwest Tariff Bureau, Rocky Mountain Motor Tariff Bureau, Interstate Freight Carriers Conference, and Southwestern Motor Freight Bureau.

The persons employed by motor rate bureaus and committees are not employees of the carriers but are employees of the bureaus, committees, or conferences. The general procedure is that a proposal can be docketed for a hearing with the Standing Rate Committee, usually composed of employees of the conference, bureau, or committee experienced in rate and related matters.

This Committee analyzes the proposal by comparing the proposed rates with other rates already in effect on the same or similar commodities applying from and to the same points or in the same general territory. The commodity descriptions are examined to assure that they clearly describe the articles being shipped. The rates of competing carriers are verified by a check of tariffs which have been filed. The Committee evaluates the information furnished it voluntarily by shippers and carriers, and compares all of the facts with those submitted by the proponent carrier.

The Committee will conduct an open hearing which carriers, shippers, and other interested parties may attend, with hearings docketed for a specific place and time. The normal procedure is for a public hearing which provides an opportunity for competing carriers to present their points of view. They may be supporting the proposal and would concur in it; or they may be opposing the proposal, but after hearing the presen-

---

[14] *Southern Freight Association–Agreement*, 283 ICC 245 (1951).

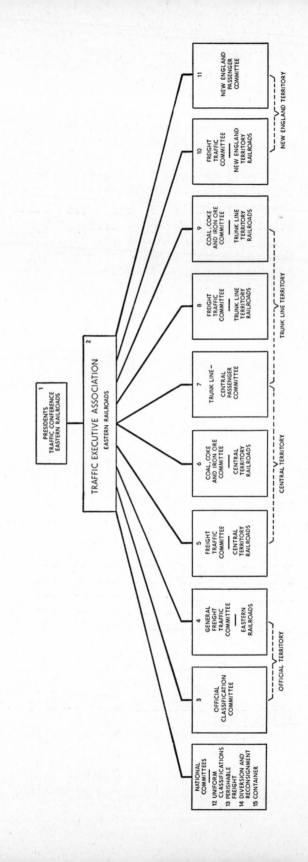

1. PRESIDENT'S TRAFFIC CONFERENCE -- EASTERN RAILROADS. The Conference may consider any traffic matter involving or affecting carriers in Eastern Territory, and will review any traffic matter which it is requested to review as provided in Article III, Section 12(b).

2. TRAFFIC EXECUTIVE ASSOCIATION--EASTERN RAILROADS. The Association may consider any traffic matter involving or affecting carriers in the Eastern Territory whether considered by any subordinate organization or not, and will, upon request, review recommendations of subordinate organizations (Committees Nos. 3-15).

3. OFFICIAL CLASSIFICATION COMMITTEE. Considers classification ratings subject to approval of Traffic Executive Association -- Eastern Railroads.

4. GENERAL FREIGHT TRAFFIC COMMITTEE -- EASTERN RAILROADS. Considers (i) all interterritorial freight proposals to it other than those relating to coal, coke (the direct product of coal), and iron ore, and (ii) all other freight proposals to it of traffic matters involving or affecting generally the carriers in Eastern Territory having membership in the Committee, other than proposals relating to coal, coke (the direct product of coal), and iron ore.

5. FREIGHT TRAFFIC COMMITTEE -- CENTRAL TERRITORY RAILROADS. Considers all proposals to it of traffic matters involving or affecting only the carriers in Central territory having membership in the Committee other than proposals relating to coal, coke (the direct product of coal), and iron ore.

6. COAL, COKE, AND IRON ORE COMMITTEE --CENTRAL TERRITORY RAILROADS. Considers all proposals involving traffic matters relating to coal, coke (the direct product of coal), and iron ore which, as provided in Appendix G to the Agreement, are to be presented to it.

7. TRUNK LINE - CENTRAL PASSENGER COMMITTEE. Considers all proposals to it of passenger traffic and related traffic matters involving or affecting the carriers in Trunk Line or Central territories having membership in the Committee.

8. FREIGHT TRAFFIC COMMITTEE -- TRUNK LINE TERRITORY RAILROADS. Considers all proposals to it of traffic matters involving or affecting only the carriers in Trunk Line territory having membership in the Committee, other than proposals relating to coal, coke (the direct product of coal), and iron ore.

9. COAL, COKE, AND IRON ORE COMMITTEE -- TRUNK LINE TERRITORY RAILROADS. Considers all proposals involving traffic matters relating to coal, coke (the direct product of coal), and iron ore, which, as provided in Appendix G of the Agreement, are to be presented to it.

10. FREIGHT TRAFFIC COMMITTEE -- NEW ENGLAND TERRITORY RAILROADS. Considers all proposals to it of traffic matters involving or affecting only the carriers in New England territory.

11. NEW ENGLAND PASSENGER COMMITTEE. Considers all proposals to it of passenger traffic and related traffic matters involving or affecting the carriers in New England territory having membership in the Committee.

12. UNIFORM CLASSIFICATION COMMITTEE. Formulates ratings for uniform classification as required by Interstate Commerce Commission in No. 28310. Class Rate Investigation, 1939, 262 I.C.C. 447.

13. NATIONAL PERISHABLE FREIGHT COMMITTEE. Considers proposals pertaining to the protection of perishable traffic.

14. NATIONAL DIVERSION AND RECONSIGNMENT COMMITTEE. Considers traffic matters pertaining to the diversion and reconsignment of traffic.

15. NATIONAL CONTAINER COMMITTEE. Considers proposals relating to containers.

NOTE A: Article II, Section 15 of the Agreement provides that any organization provided for in Article II, before which is properly pending a proposal of any traffic matter for interterritorial application, shall cooperate with any similar organization in other affected territory, either in joint meeting or through correspondence, in considering and determining such matter, and makes provision for an agreement among the carriers of the Eastern, Western, and Southern groups for the use by each group of its own procedures in such consideration of interterritorial traffic matters. See Agreement, Art. II, Sec. 15 and Appendix M thereto.

NOTE B: The Agreement makes provision in Article II, Section 19, for the maintenance of such assistants and research groups as in the judgment of the Chief Traffic Officers of the carriers involved are reasonably necessary to aid the members of any organization in its functions; also for the designation of any organization of sub-committees or special committees to investigate and report on any traffic matter before the organization.

SOURCE: Section 5a, Application No. 3 filed with ICC by Eastern Railroads, December 7, 1948, p. 127.

FIG. 9-2. Organization of a railroad rate conference, associations, and committees in the Eastern Territory.

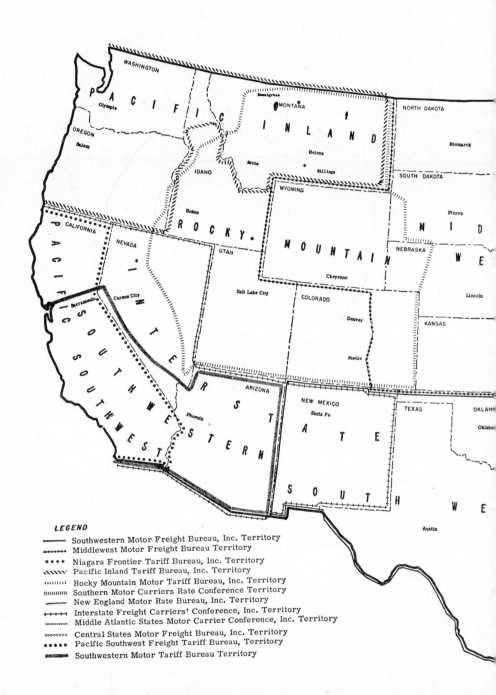

LEGEND

——————— Southwestern Motor Freight Bureau, Inc. Territory
••••••• Middlewest Motor Freight Bureau Territory
•••• Niagara Frontier Tariff Bureau, Inc. Territory
ᵥᵥᵥᵥ Pacific Inland Tariff Bureau, Inc. Territory
ıııııı Rocky Mountain Motor Tariff Bureau, Inc. Territory
ıııııııı Southern Motor Carriers Rate Conference Territory
——————— New England Motor Rate Bureau, Inc. Territory
+++++ Interstate Freight Carriers' Conference, Inc. Territory
•••••••• Middle Atlantic States Motor Carrier Conference, Inc. Territory
ₒₒₒₒₒₒₒₒ Central States Motor Freight Bureau, Inc. Territory
•••• Pacific Southwest Freight Tariff Bureau, Territory
▓▓▓▓▓ Southwestern Motor Tariff Bureau Territory

SOURCE: Section 5a Filings of Associations

FIG. 9–3.   Major intraterritorial motor rate territories.

tations at the hearing, they might decide to concur in it. Shippers who are affected by a docketed proposal have the opportunity to be heard, for the proposal may have important repercussions upon the marketing of their products, involving competitive relationships as well as other important factors.

An example of a shipper's proposal to a rail rate bureau and the reasons given which seek to justify the proposal are shown in Figure 9–4 below.

TRANS-CONTINENTAL FREIGHT BUREAU
CHICAGO 6, ILL.

APPLICATION NO. D-9704   March 3, 1953
(File 681-2)

TO MEMBERS:

THE PROPOSAL SET FORTH BELOW HAS BEEN PRESENTED FOR CONSIDERATION

Action on the proposal will not be restricted to its exact scope, but may include other points of origin and destination or other commodities or recommendations varying from, but directly or indirectly related to, the changes proposed.

W. H. DANA, Chairman

SHIPPERS' PROPOSAL

CANNED APPLE SAUCE, CL, EB: Request for rate of 100 cents to 105 cents per 100 lbs., not subject to Tariff X-175-series, min. C.L. wt. 60,000 lbs., from Sebastopol, Cal., to Denver, Colo. (Group J), Tariff 2-S.

PRESENT

See reasons.

REASONS

We are advised by *****, Sebastopol, that a request with the *** railroad for a reduction in the carload rate on canned apple sauce from Sebastopol to Denver, Colo., territory has been initiated.

I am advised that the present carload rate, including all ex parte increases is $1.47, minimum 40,000 lbs. and $1.36 minimum 60,000 lbs.

He also advises me that he considers a rate of $1.00 to $1.05 minimum carload 60,000 lbs. should be established covering this traffic. I understand that if consideration is given to the publication of such a rate, it would induce the shipment of approximately ** carloads by the *** annually to that territory. At present the majority of this commodity is being shipped by truck to Los Angeles and to Denver territory. The trade in Denver advise that they are very much interested in securing supplies of apple sauce from this source; however, because of the high rail rate they are unable to compete with eastern carriers on certain shipments and must resort to the use of trucks. Our people would much prefer to handle this business by rail and it is felt that the rate suggested herein would be fair compensation to carriers for handling the traffic.

The canning of apple sauce in California is a new industry and is worthy of your assistance in this department. There is no question but what if given this help, it will develop into something worth while for both canners and carriers.

FIG. 9–4. Example of a shipper's proposal to a rate bureau.

This proposal was distributed to the members of the rate bureau. The recommendation of the Standing Rate Committee on this proposal was that it be declined. This action and the reasons for it are indicated in Figure 9–5. However, the carrier members of the bureau can object to this action by a specific date, if they desire.

The report of the Standing Rate Committee in this case was approved by member carriers, and this notice of approval is shown in Figure 9–6.

TRANS-CONTINENTAL FREIGHT BUREAU
UNION STATION
CHICAGO 6

M.F. EDBROOKE, Chairman   July 2, 1953

STANDING RATE COMMITTEE
E.C. PIERRE, CHAIRMAN
C.J. HENNINGS
LEROY D. SMITH

TO FREIGHT TRAFFIC MANAGERS COMMITTEE -
TRANS-CONTINENTAL FREIGHT BUREAU

REPORT ON APPLICATION NO. D-9704
(File 681-2)

CANNED APPLE SAUCE, C.L., E.B.

Unless objections are received not later than July 17, 1953, following recommendation
of Standing Rate Committee will be considered as approved and announcement of approval issued.

RECOMMENDATION

That the application be declined.

REASONS

This application is for a rate equivalent to from 88 cents to 93 cents per 100 lbs.,
subject to Tariff X-175-series, on canned apple sauce, minimum carload weight 60,000
lbs., from California to Group J, to meet truck competition.

The present rate at 60,000 lbs. minimum is $1.24, subject to Tariff X-175-series,
which proponent contends is too high for rail movements (Item 3800-series of Tariff 2-S)

Request has also been received for reduction in rate from the North Coast to Group
J corresponding with any reduction made from California.

Another shipper supports the application but only if the reduced rate is made applicable on the entire canned goods list.

Eastern producers of canned apple sauce in Virginia and New York have registered
opposition unless they are given the benefit of a corresponding reduction in westbound
rates to Colorado.

The carriers now have under consideration on Application D-8924 and supplements
various shipper requests for reduction in the eastbound and westbound trans-continental
rates on canned goods. The subject is to be considered at the August meeting of the
Executive Committee, and if any readjustment of rates in these items should be made it
would apply on canned apple sauce.

The rates requested in the present application are lower than any of the rates between the Pacific Coast and Group J requested in Application D-8924 or any supplement
thereto, which likewise were predicated on truck competition, and the Standing Rate
Committee does not see how the present application could be approved without jeopar-
dizing the entire canned goods adjustment, with revenue losses which could not possibly
be offset by any added tonnage of canned apple sauce.

The Committee recommends that the application be declined.

M. F. EDBROOKE

Chairman.

FIG. 9–5. Recommendation of Standing Rate Committee of a rate bureau in regard to a
shipper's proposal.

Should the proposed action of the Standing Rate Committee as a result
of the docketing procedure not be acceptable, the procedures provide for
an Appeal Committee. Unlike the Standing Rate Committee, the Appeal
Committee is usually comprised of a majority of carrier representatives,
augmented by some of the Standing Rate Committee members. The principle back of carrier composition of the Appeal Committee is that since
carriers render the service, it is they who should determine the final ac-

TRANS-CONTINENTAL FREIGHT BUREAU
UNION STATION
CHICAGO 6

M.F. EDBROOKE, Chairman
STANDING RATE COMMITTEE
E.C. PIERRE, CHAIRMAN
C.J. HENNINGS
LEROY D. SMITH

July 20, 1953

Application D-9704

File 681-2

NOTICE OF APPROVAL

TO FREIGHT TRAFFIC MANAGERS COMMITTEE -
TRANS-CONTINENTAL FREIGHT BUREAU

CANNED APPLE SAUCE, C.L., E.B.

Standing Rate Committee's report of July 2, 1953, that

Application D-9704 be declined, stands approved.

M. F. EDBROOKE

Chairman

WS/bg

Copy to:
EXECUTIVE COMMITTEE--TRANS-CONTINENTAL FREIGHT
BUREAU. RATE ADVICE MAILING LIST.

FIG. 9–6. Example of notice of approval of action of Standing Committee of a rate bureau in regard to a shipper's proposal.

tion which is taken. Often, they have participated in the original action, but this procedure makes it the carriers' decision.

Emergency proposals will be received from any carrier member and acted upon by the Standing Rate Committee within fifteen days. The bureaus have emergency procedures which apply in the case of emergency proposals. Emergency proposals are defined as those which have for their purpose:

1. The meeting, or more nearly meeting, of a motor common carrier competitive rate, when the proponent carrier furnishes evidence that it is handling, or has recently handled, all or a substantial portion of the traffic.

2. The meeting, or more nearly meeting, of a reduction made by a competing carrier, other than motor common carriers, within the last forty-five days, when the proponent carrier furnishes evidence that it is handling, or has recently handled, all or a substantial portion of the traffic.

3. The establishment of rates to move traffic for the federal government.

4. The establishment of temporary rates for movement of supplies to relieve injury, damage, or suffering.

5. The establishment of rates on a level heretofore recognized as being proper for the removal of a plant, factory, or other establishment.

6. The meeting of any condition of an extraordinary nature which requires prompt relief and which, in the Committee's judgment, would justify an application to the Interstate Commerce Commission for authority to publish on less than statutory notice.

One of the large motor carrier rate bureaus, during the years 1950 through 1957, published a total of 43,120 reduced rates, or an average of 5,390 reduced rates per year. This was during an inflationary period, in which several general or horizontal freight increases became effective; yet, as a result of emergency and independent-action dockets, this very substantial number of reduced rates was instituted.

In air transportation, the tariffs are a great deal simpler than in rail and motor transportation due, in part, to the fact that there are fewer commodities and carriers and a limited number of joint rates. Rates are published for individual carriers by a tariff publishing agent, the Airline Tariff Publishers, Inc., although some air lines issue individual tariffs on particular traffic. The ATP is unlike surface rate bureaus in that the latter have rate committees which collectively consider tariff changes and publish disposition notices. So far air carriers do not possess any immunity from the antitrust statutes to permit them jointly to consider and agree on rates. However, the charter of ATP permits a carrier to advise other carriers of an intended tariff change and this is often done.

It should be understood that the ultimate decision on interstate rates rests with the Interstate Commerce Commission in the case of surface carriers subject to federal regulation; and the Civil Aeronautics Board in the case of air carriers subject to federal regulation.

ICC Supervision of Interstate Rates

There is some misunderstanding as to the amount of supervision which the Interstate Commerce Commission exercises over the initiation of rates filed with it. The system used by the Commission for reviewing and checking rates and tariff schedules before they become effective takes several forms. The first of these is that when tariffs are received, they are checked for compliance with the rules and regulations issued by the Interstate Commerce Commission which govern the form and content of tariffs. In July, 1956, a complete examination, for test purposes, of a random selection of 36 motor tariffs and schedules was made by the Commission. It was found that deficiencies existed in all of the filings. Some of the errors warranted rejection of the tariff, whereas others were of a nature which would have resulted in controversy between carriers and shippers. More than 123 provisions, rules, or rate items were found not to comply with the tariff circular rules. Only 9 irregularities would have been discovered if a mere cursory examination, as is customary because of lack of personnel, had been made of these tariffs by the Commission. If, in checking, the tariff examiner finds rates to be noticeably out of line, they are referred to the Commission's Suspension Board for consideration and possible recommendation of suspension; or the matter is taken up with the carriers which have filed the tariff, with a view to bringing about a voluntary adjustment.

Since the Interstate Commerce Act provides that a carrier may apply to the Commission for a reduction in the time required for a tariff to remain on file with the Commission before it becomes effective, carriers frequently request a so-called "short-notice" filing. The ordinary time that a tariff is on file with the Commission is 30 days; but if there is an adequate reason, it can be reduced to a minimum of 1 day, which enables carriers to meet emergencies. Many such applications are filed. Such short-notice filing, however, will involve the examination of the proposed rates to determine the propriety of granting the application before the tariff schedules become effective. As a brake on unwarranted rapid fluctuation in rates, the Commission's tariff rules require rates to remain in effect 30 days.

When protests are made against a proposed rate filed with the Commission, there is a rate review of the rate proposal. This review is made by the Commission's Bureau of Traffic, and a decision to suspend or not to suspend the proposed rate or rates will be made. Of the large number of rate changes proposed each year, the total number of suspensions by the Commission is relatively small. An outline of the rate-making procedure when a proposed rate is protested is shown in Figure 9-7.

Another phase of the review and checking of rates relates to the Commission's administration of Section 4 of the Interstate Commerce Act. Application for relief from that section (long-and-short-haul provision) calls for an examination of the proposed rates and a final decision by a division of the Commission.

The formal complaints filed by shippers or filed upon petitions of carriers or investigations initiated by the Commission on its own motion constitute another way in which, in effect, rates are reviewed. When decisions are reached in these investigations, the tariffs filed to put the results of the investigation in effect will show why they are filed. Generally, a "spot check" by the Commission will indicate their legality and

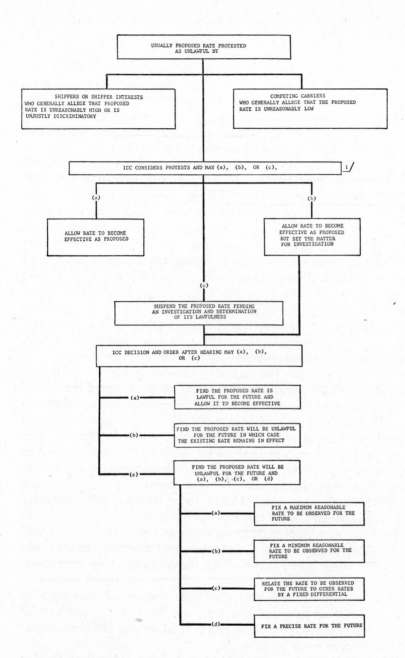

USUALLY PROPOSED RATE PROTESTED
AS UNLAWFUL BY

SHIPPERS OR SHIPPER INTERESTS
WHO GENERALLY ALLEGE THAT PROPOSED
RATE IS UNREASONABLY HIGH OR IS
UNJUSTLY DISCRIMINATORY

COMPETING CARRIERS
WHO GENERALLY ALLEGE THAT THE PROPOSED
RATE IS UNREASONABLY LOW

ICC CONSIDERS PROTESTS AND MAY (a), (b), OR (c),   1/

(a)

ALLOW RATE TO BECOME
EFFECTIVE AS PROPOSED

(b)

ALLOW RATE TO BECOME
EFFECTIVE AS PROPOSED
BUT SET THE MATTER
FOR INVESTIGATION

(c)

SUSPEND THE PROPOSED RATE PENDING
AN INVESTIGATION AND DETERMINATION
OF ITS LAWFULNESS

ICC DECISION AND ORDER AFTER HEARING MAY (a), (b),
OR (c)

(a) — FIND THE PROPOSED RATE IS
LAWFUL FOR THE FUTURE AND
ALLOW IT TO BECOME EFFECTIVE

(b) — FIND THE PROPOSED RATE WILL BE UNLAWFUL
FOR THE FUTURE IN WHICH CASE
THE EXISTING RATE REMAINS IN EFFECT

(c) — FIND THE PROPOSED RATE WILL BE
UNLAWFUL FOR THE FUTURE AND
(a), (b), (c), OR (d)

(a) — FIX A MAXIMUM REASONABLE
RATE TO BE OBSERVED FOR THE
FUTURE

(b) — FIX A MINIMUM REASONABLE
RATE TO BE OBSERVED FOR THE
FUTURE

(c) — RELATE THE RATE TO BE OBSERVED
FOR THE FUTURE TO OTHER RATES
BY A FIXED DIFFERENTIAL

(d) — FIX A PRECISE RATE FOR THE FUTURE

1/ ICC MAY ON ITS OWN MOTION AND WITHOUT ANSWER OR OTHER FORMAL PLEADING ENTER UPON A HEARING CONCERNING THE LAWFULNESS OF A PROPOSED RATE AND PENDING
SUCH HEARING AND DECISION SUSPEND THE OPERATION OF THIS RATE.

SOURCE: Office of the Undersecretary of Commerce for Transportation.

FIG. 9–7. Steps in rate-making procedure when a proposed rate is protested.

propriety. The latter review, in effect, constitutes a pre-audit of the tariff schedules before they are filed with the Commission.

Thus, there are both pre-audit and post-audit checks of the voluminous rates filed with the Commission. Each ". . . carrier is entitled to initiate rates and, in this connection, to adopt such policy of rate-making as to it seems best."[15] It has been stated that during a twelve-month period a number of years ago, 157,869 freight and passenger tariffs were received by the Commission for filing, of which 62,524 tariffs, or 39.6 per cent of the total, were pre-audited and reviewed from the standpoint of the lawfulness of the rates contained in the tariffs.[16]

The Commission considers a *fully compensatory rate* to be one that covers fully distributed costs and provides an average, or more than average, profit in addition. Fully distributed costs include the cost of moving the particular commodity from origin to destination plus a percentage factor to compensate for the return movement; a proportionate share of the overhead or administrative expenses including terminal expense; special charges; and a nominal percentage profit.

A rate which is said to be *reasonably compensatory* is somewhat different, in that it covers the out-of-pocket or line-haul costs for the movement of a particular commodity from origin to destination, with a percentage factor included to compensate for empty return movement. Therefore, the carrier must look to other commodities to make up the proportionate share of overhead expenses lost in such a movement.

In the past, the Commission has refused to adopt any precise formula, mathematical or otherwise, for use in determining the justness or reasonableness of a given rate on particular traffic without giving consideration to the particular facts involved in the movement of such traffic, as well as the prevailing level of rates maintained by other carriers for the same or similar transportation services. The test of reasonableness of a rate considered by the Commission to be the best is a comparison with other rates on like traffic in the same general territory or between points similarly situated. Rate comparisons of this type should be supported by a showing of similarity of transportation conditions and characteristics, as well as evidence that there is such a movement and that the rates are not merely "paper rates," and a showing that the compared rates are not depressed to meet competition.

In 1930, the majority of protests filed against proposed rates were by shippers and involved proposed rate increases. By 1960, 90 per cent of proposed rate adjustments involved rate reductions and less than 10 per cent of the protests were by shippers.

The Transportation Act of 1958 included an amendment to Section

---

[15] *United States* v. *Chicago, M. St. P. & Pac. R. Co.*, 294 U.S. 409, 506 (1935).

[16] Statement by Commissioner Alldredge in *Study on Monopoly Power*, House Subcommittee of the Committee on the Judiciary, 81st Congress, 2d session (Washington, D.C.: U.S. Government Printing Office, 1949), p. 775.

15a of the Interstate Commerce Act which provides that in a proceeding involving competition between carriers of different modes of transportation, the Commission, in determining whether a rate is lower than a minimum reasonable rate, "shall consider the facts and circumstances attending the movement of the traffic by the carrier or carriers to which the rate is applicable," and that "rates of a carrier shall not be held up to a particular level to protect the traffic of any other mode of transportation, giving due consideration to the objectives of the national transportation policy." This appeared to indicate that the factor of cost should be of greater importance and that there should be less emphasis upon the effect which the reduced rates might have on other competing modes of transportation.

Subsequent rulings of the Commission, however, have reflected little change in policy as a result of the amendment to Section 15a. The Commission denied reduced contract rates proposed by a rail carrier provided the shipper moved at least 80 per cent of its traffic within a one-year period. It was stated that protesting motor carriers indicated they would follow with similar rates, and the Commission felt that the end result would be destruction of the rate structure. These contract rates were held to be unjust and unreasonable.

On the other hand, where the competition was market rather than carrier competition, the Commission approved reduced rates which were conditioned upon shippers moving a minimum tonnage per year. In this case involving the movement of coal, it was stated that the reduced rates were necessary to meet market competition, which was residual fuel oil moving into the area from abroad.

Where intermodal rate competition exists, the Commission has sought to ascertain not only if the rate is compensatory but also if it is unlawful, even though compensatory, because it is destructive to competition. It is in the latter area that the Commission appears to be open to criticism. The charge is often made that the Commission is protecting the status quo regardless of the need to adjust to changes in marketing and transportation conditions. Where rates are compensatory, the Commission should not be so protective of all carriers and should allow rate innovations to become effective.

In another case, the Commission disapproved rail trailer-on-flatcar rates on a level with sea-land rates and sea-train on the grounds that these rates constituted a destructive competitive practice and fixed a differential of 6 per cent for TOFC over sea-land rates.[17] A federal court set aside this decision of the Commission requiring railroad piggyback rates to be 6 per cent higher than competing rates of water carriers in the coastwise trade.[18] The court felt that the prohibition of Section 15a(3) against "umbrella rates" was intended to be qualified only when

[17] I&S No. M–10415, *Commodities—Pan-Atlantic S.S. Corp.*, 313 ICC 23 (1960).
[18] No. 8679, *New York, New Haven & Hartford Railroad Co.*, v. *U.S.A. & I.C.C.* (1961).

factors other than the normal incidents of fair competition intervened such as a practice which would destroy a competing mode of transportation by setting rates so low as to be harmful to the proponent as well as its competitor. This ruling was appealed to the Supreme Court by the Commission.

The Supreme Court remanded the case to the Commission, stating that the Commission had erroneously applied the "broad policy" of the national transportation policy and failed to apply the "more particular-, ized mandates" of that policy and of Section 15a(3), which prohibits the holding up of rates of one mode of transportation to protect the traffic of another mode.[19]

Another court decision set aside a Commission ruling which had condemned rail rates as destructive even though the rates appeared to be compensatory and in most instances exceeded full costs.[20]

A rate may be found by the Commission to be unreasonably low if (1) the rate fails to cover the out-of-pocket costs of the carrier; or (2) the rate, although returning out-of-pocket costs, is below the rate level of a competing lower cost mode of transportation. Shippers and localities have asked the Commission to find rates unreasonably low on one or the other of these grounds when competing shippers or localities would receive an allegedly unwarranted advantage of lower rates.

Three provisions of the Interstate Commerce Act are designed to protect shippers from specific kinds of discrimination. Section 2 applies when different rates are charged for "a like and contemporaneous service" on "a like kind of traffic under substantially similar circumstances and conditions." A complaint of discrimination under Section 4 will be sustained when a greater charge is exacted for a shorter haul than for a longer haul over the same route in the same direction. Section 3(1) is designed to protect shippers from the more general kinds of rate discrimination. However, the protection in Section 3 is limited because the rule has been construed not to provide protection from undue rate prejudice against shippers and communities unless the same carrier or carriers effectively participate in the rate on both the prejudiced and preferred traffic.

TARIFF SIMPLIFICATION

The complexity of freight tariffs has long been a source of dissatisfaction to both shippers and carriers. Although the regulatory bodies have outlined in their tariff circulars general principles concerning the composition of tariffs, this has not been a specific prescription of a single pro-

---

[19] No. 108, *Interstate Commerce Commission* v. *New York, New Haven, Hartford Co., et al* (April, 1963).

[20] *Exceptions Ratings on Agricultural, Roadmaking, and Other Articles*, 315 ICC 9 (1961); 203 Fed. Supp. 629 (1962).

cedure. The result has been differing approaches by publishing agents. In rail transportation alone, freight tariffs are compiled by as many different tariff bureaus as there are operating railroads. In addition to this, numerous agency bureaus publish rates jointly for a number of carriers. The same general situation prevails in motor transportation, except that there are more than twice the number of joint agency bureaus.

When it is recognized that thousands of articles are shipped between thousands of stations or points, with differing quantities being offered in different containers and with hundreds of routes available, one can appreciate the complex nature of rates. In the period since World War II, there have been additional tariff complications because of the general rate increases.

As a result of the increasing complexities of tariffs, the railroads, after considerable consultation with a leading shipper organization (the National Industrial Traffic League), agreed that the railroads would establish and finance an organization to undertake tariff research. The Railroads' Tariff Research Group started operations on September 1, 1951, and was under the supervision of an administrative committee of railroad traffic executives. The research group submitted recommendations for improvement of the freight tariffs to the administrative committee. This group sent out questionnaires on particular phases of tariff simplification, the results of which gave them viewpoints of interested parties. A publication containing a number of tariff-making specifications and a Tariff Maker's Manual were issued. Numerous other suggestions were also made.

Some of the opportunities for accomplishing tariff simplification as reported by the Railroads' Tariff Research Group are:

1. Every common rule ought to have a common location in all tariffs through the controlled alignment of item numbers.
2. Every tariff provision having the same meaning or similar effect should appear under a single explanatory title in every tariff carrying the provision.
3. Every tariff provision of common meaning and intent should read exactly the same.
4. A single design or pattern for the arrangement of matter on title pages of tariffs should be uniformly used throughout the country.
5. A single set of principles for the construction of a table of contents should be observed.
6. A limited number of standard patterns for the arrangement of rate tables should be prescribed for nationwide use.

The Railroads' Tariff Research Group completed its work by January 1, 1958. The separate organization was terminated; and an organization of railroad employees, called the National Freight Tariff Committee, was formed, with the responsibility of tariff simplification in addition to its regular duties.

Simplification of the language used in tariff compilation is still badly needed. Users of a tariff should readily understand the intent and meaning of tariff provisions. The following is an actual example of a proposed tariff rule which appears to border on the incomprehensible:

> On shipments made under the provisions of items 140, 142, 143, 145, 160, 165, 175 and 180, and where there are published in tariffs of originating lines, parties to this tariff, provisions that when a carload shipment received at one of the origin points named in the above mentioned items is ordered by shipper to be stopped off at some other point on its line for completion of loading with freight which is not loaded in accordance with provisions in above mentioned items, the originating carrier may for operating convenience place a separate car or cars at stop-off point to be loaded with freight that would otherwise be loaded there into the car or cars containing the shipment ordered to be stopped and such shipment and the car or cars so loaded at stop-off point shall be treated as though such car or cars had been partially loaded at point of origin and actually stopped off at stop-off point for completion of loading, such provisions will apply in the application rates determined under the provisions of items 140, 142, 143, 145, 160, 165, 175 and 180.

Motor

Motor carriers also have instituted steps to accomplish simplification of tariffs. A Special Committee on Uniform Tariff Rules and Regulations of the National Motor Freight Traffic Association conducts research into tariff simplification. This Committee has continued the work of an earlier committee formed in 1951. A number of reports containing recommendations have been issued by the Committee for use by motor carrier tariff makers, as well as a Model Rules Tariff. A joint committee of the National Industrial Traffic League and the National Motor Freight Traffic Association was formed in 1958 to implement a program of tariff improvement and simplification.

AUDITING FREIGHT BILLS

The auditing of freight bills is an important part of traffic management. There are two types of auditing: (1) the internal or company audit and (2) the external or outside audit. Some traffic departments refer to this as "checking freight bills," since any audits are performed by the accounting department.

With so many opportunities for mistakes to be made at various stages in the preparation of documents used in transportation, one of the control devices which must be used to minimize company losses is the establishment of an internal audit. The traffic manager should decide the minimum amount below which bills are not checked. This can be determined by experience, or a very simple time study can be helpful in establishing the minimum. Common minima in use at the present time are $15, $25, and $40.

The number of freight bills received by many of our large corporations is tremendous. One corporation has 55,000 per month, or some 700,000 per year, and another has over a million freight bills per year. The recovery for overcharges may run as high as $1 million. When the complexity of tariffs and the large volume of supplemental tariff matter in the postwar period, due in part to the freight rate increases, are combined with the human element, there will inevitably be mistakes. Then, too, no carrier representative or company traffic employee can be sure at any time that the lowest legal rate has been quoted. The use of an outside audit, therefore, should not be regarded as a reflection upon the efficiency of the traffic department or section. The most competent traffic managers of some of the largest corporations consider this as a necessary supplement to their own audit.

The outside auditing firm is particularly valuable to the smaller industrial traffic departments. These departments cannot afford to spend $3,000 or $4,000 a year to maintain a complete tariff file. Such a department cannot justify the expense of the files in which to keep the tariffs and the filing clerk to maintain them, or the additional personnel to check thoroughly each freight bill. The result is that such departments may maintain a file of perhaps 25 per cent of the necessary tariffs, which are those used for the majority of their traffic. Under these circumstances, the value of the outside audit is substantial for, in effect, the work done with a portion of the freight bills has not been previously performed.

Internal Audit Procedure

The procedure for the internal audit may vary, depending in part upon whether or not there are centralized or decentralized systems of routing and rate control, or a combination of these. Traffic managers with centralized routing and rates will have cards or sheets that have been set up in order to furnish this information upon request from the various plants. Since these cards or sheets will show the legal tariff rates, as well as the carload or truckload minimum weight, the container, and the complete route that affords the cheapest means of transportation, the freight bills can be checked against these cards. Figure 9–8 is an example of a rate and route sheet. The rate cards or sheets will have to be made up to cover the date of the shipment in order to be used in this manner. If the rate card or sheet is not applicable on the date of the shipment, the tariffs will have to be consulted.

Although the freight rate is the rate of charge per unit assessed by the carrier for the transportation of freight, usually stated to apply in connection with units of weight such as per 100 pounds, the freight charge generally refers to the total charge assessed against a shipment, including charges for services incidental to the transportation. There are many possible errors that may arise in arriving at the total transportation charge.

The steps which might be taken in the internal auditing of freight bills follow:

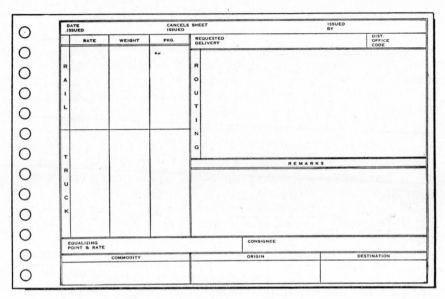

FIG. 9–8.   Example of a rate and route sheet.

1. In order to determine the correct commodity description, rating, package, and carload or truckload minimum weight, the freight classification should be checked.

2. In the use of the tariffs, be sure that the effective supplements are filed with the tariff available.

3. The agency or individual tariffs should be checked to determine whether or not a specific commodity rate is applicable. Are there any arbitrary rates to be added or subtracted from the rates?

4. If a specified commodity rate is not published, an additional check of the tariff should be made to see whether an intermediate application rate on the commodity would apply between the points involved.

5. If there is no specific commodity rate, the exceptions to the governing classification used in connection with the tariff or the exceptions in the tariffs themselves should be checked to see if any special rating applies.

6. Check to see whether combination rates, either commodity rates or class and commodity rates, might be applicable.

7. The alternate application should be checked in sectional tariffs since, in many such tariffs, the sections apply to class rates or commodity rates but permit the application of the lowest rating.

8. The class rate application should be checked also, for it may be found to be lower than the commodity rate and have application via a routing on which the commodity rate would not apply.

9. Tariffs which contain rates applying via joint hauls should be checked, for such rates may provide a lower rating than that provided in local tariffs.

10. Individual lines' tariffs may contain class rates and/or commodity rates not found in agency tariffs, so they should be checked.

11. Two or more carriers may serve the same points or general area but do not necessarily provide for the same rate, so that the individual tariffs should be consulted.

12. There must be verification of the weight, for the freight bill may show gross, tare, or net weight.

13. Another item to be checked is whether or not ICC service orders change or suspend any of the base rates.

14. Upon ascertaining the base rate, it must be determined whether the shipment is subject to all of the postwar ex parte increases. In this connection, the percentage of increase applicable and whether the commodity is subject to any maximum increases should be determined.

15. Whether or not the commodity is subject to any accessorial charges should be checked.

The information developed as a result of freight auditing shows that there are a number of factors that should be watched which may result in savings.

1. Where possible, less-carload shipments should be consolidated into carloads and less-truckloads into truckloads.

2. When it is possible, shipments should be held until sufficient weight is available to make a minimum carload or truckload, thus avoiding the payment of a penalty on the deficiency in weight.

3. Separate weights of different articles should be shown if this permits the application of respective rates.

4. The proper size and type of car should be ordered, so that penalties will not be paid on graduated minimum weights on articles subject to Rule 34 of the Consolidated or Uniform Freight classifications.

5. Two carriers should be used instead of three if through the use of the third carrier, the rate would be increased.

6. All goods should be properly billed.

7. When possible, Rule 24 of the Consolidated and Uniform Freight classifications should be used. Under this rule, the shipper is permitted to have the actual weight in the follow-lot car move at carload rates which have a minimum of 4,000 pounds or more. Certain conditions must be observed if this rule is used.

8. Transit privileges should be used wherever possible.

The assignment of freight audit tasks varies from company to company. One company may assign rate personnel to check freight bills in certain specified territories, such as Southern Freight Association, New England, Trunk-Line, Trans-Continental, and others. Because the territories may have their own rate peculiarities, the assignment by territory gives the individual assigned a familiarity with a particular territory.

Another method of assignment is to have rate personnel auditing the freight bills only for certain plants. The principle behind this method is to achieve continuity, as well as to insure a complete familiarity with the tariffs in a given territory or those used in connection with certain plants. This system can be and is arranged so rotation permits each individual to be able eventually to check the rates and handle the problems of any territory or plant.

Rate personnel sometimes are assigned to spend a minimum of one day per week in auditing freight bills. This is another method of conducting internal audits. Thus, each member of the traffic staff spends four days in rate quotation, checking rates, and similar matters; and the fifth day is spent in auditing freight bills in a specific territory or from certain plants. This procedure provides that the auditing is carried on each day by a part of the rate personnel, and the rest of the staff perform their usual functions.

Companies with numerous plants may establish a pre-audit procedure whereby a cursory examination of the freight bill is made prior to its payment by the plant. This may be done within the credit period which is permitted by the carrier, or it may occur after the freight bill is paid but prior to the forwarding of the freight bill to the central office for auditing. Such pre-audits may turn up many errors in extensions. The pre-audit may be quite limited, since the policy of the company may be to provide for a centralized freight audit and the maintenance of a complete tariff file only at headquarters.

The number of tariffs maintained in a tariff file may depend upon the commodities which the company distributes, as well as the geographical areas in which this is accomplished. A few tariff files contain almost 25,000 tariffs. Some of the tariffs in a complete tariff file are particularly valuable because the publishing agent's supply of certain tariffs is sometimes exhausted.

Outside Audits

Many traffic departments or sections, upon the completion of the internal audit, will send their freight bills to a traffic audit firm which specializes in this work. It is reported that 90 per cent of the largest industrial corporations use outside traffic audits. The firms which specialize in this work are called "traffic bureaus," "traffic associations," "traffic consultants," or similar names.[21] This type of traffic audit firm works on a contingency basis, which is covered in the contract drawn between the traffic audit firm and the industrial traffic department. It may provide that the traffic audit firm receive 60 per cent of the total collections made as a result of their work, or the firm may receive as much as 70 per cent or as low as 40 per cent. On claims loss or damage, the fee may be 20 per cent of the amount recovered. A clue as to the efficiency of the internal audit can be secured from the percentage for which the traffic audit firm is willing to undertake the audit. A company may grant 50 per cent initially, and the traffic audit firm may find that the internal audit is being done so

---

[21] Some organizations are termed "traffic bureaus" or "traffic counselors" whose primary business is that of serving as the traffic department for a number of small manufacturers which do not feel that they have a sufficient volume of freight to justify the employment of a traffic manager. In addition, one aspect of the services which these companies offer is that of auditing freight bills. This audit service may be offered to business firms other than those which are regular clients. The outside audit firms which bear titles of freight traffic associations or bureaus should not be confused with freight traffic rate bureaus which are carrier-supported agencies.

successfully that the firm is not justified in continuing on that contingency basis. Accordingly, the firm will raise the percentage to a higher figure. Some of the firms engaging in rate audit work have as many as 2,000 active clients.

The traffic audit firms are specialists which, in reality, supplement inside auditing. They look for certain details from which experience has shown there is likely to be some recovery made. For example, an obscure provision in a tariff that a competent rate man in the industrial traffic department may not be familiar with is a type of situation traffic audit firms have detected, and for which recoveries have been made. A commodity rate used by the traffic audit firm for the construction of a combination of rates lower than the assessed through rate is another example of the manner in which additional recovery can be made.

Some industrial traffic departments make a practice of sending the same bills to a second traffic audit firm after the completion of an outside audit of their freight bills. This firm will then attempt to find, and usually does find, additional errors which will be the basis for filing claims.

In the course of a day's work, a freight auditor of a traffic audit firm is reported to check between 500 and 1,500 freight bills.

DISCUSSION QUESTIONS AND PROBLEMS

1. "The tariff has the force of a statute as long as it is effective." What does this mean to shippers and carriers?
2. Describe the different groups of rail freight tariffs. In what manner does a mileage tariff differ from a class rate tariff?
3. Outline the general pattern found as to which tariffs are agency publications and which are individual publications.
4. The Interstate Commerce Commission does not require that a carrier shall use a number on the title page of the tariff other than the ICC number. Is that the procedure followed?
5. Consult the volumes of ICC orders and decisions, and compile a list of principles of tariff interpretation from them.
6. Consult the volumes of Civil Aeronautics Board decisions and orders, and ascertain what principles of tariff interpretation have been stated.
7. You are asked to set up a tariff file for a company organization which distributes breakfast cereals by motor and rail in the New England states. How would you proceed? Apply this problem to your own region, and indicate what tariffs you would need.
8. Trace the background of Section 5a of the Interstate Commerce Act.
9. Carefully explain the procedure for a rail rate proposal. What if it fails of adoption?
10. A rate approved by a rail or motor rate bureau or conference automatically becomes effective. Comment upon this statement.
11. What explanation can you give for the large number of motor carrier rate bureaus as compared to rail?
12. "There is some misunderstanding as to the amount of supervision which

the Interstate Commerce Commission exercises over the initiation of rates which are filed with it." Exactly what supervision does it exercise?

13. List the methods for accomplishing rail tariff simplification which have been stated by the Tariff Research Group of the railroads.

14. What tariff simplification activities have motor carriers participated in during the past several years?

15. Is there any advantage to an outside rate audit? Would you favor a company pre-audit?

16. Would an internal rate audit be of any greater value in a decentralized than in a centralized traffic department or section?

17. What are the different methods of assigning rate personnel to company rate audits?

18. List in sequence the steps to be followed in looking up a rate. After obtaining a working knowledge of tariffs, what steps might be consolidated?

19. Outline the priority of rates and any exceptions or conflicts that might exist.

Chapter

10

ROUTING AND
CONSOLIDATION

ROUTING

Routing is a responsibility of the traffic manager that is of considerable importance in carrying out his work efficiently. It is through the medium of routing that traffic can be and is divided among carriers. The routing function is first that of evaluation of the modes of transportation to determine which one will most satisfactorily meet the needs of the company. The nature of the shipment may preclude the use of certain modes of transportation, in which case the determination of the mode is simplified. After the choice of the mode of transportation is made, selection of the carrier or carriers within that mode is the next step. While the past record of service of the carriers available to render the service can narrow the number of carriers considerably, the routing alternatives available to a traffic manager today are more numerous than was true in the past, allowing him more latitude in his selection of carriers.

The traffic manager considers a number of factors in his routing of shipments: the rates via certain routes may differ; the availability of special services, such as diversion and reconsignment, must be taken into consideration, and the fact that transit privileges may be available only via a particular route; the facilities of one delivering carrier via one route may be superior to those of another delivering carrier via a different route; and items of extraordinary value as provided in the rail or motor classifications will not be accepted for shipment, limiting the choice of the transportation agency for moving such articles.

Rail car shortages have occurred with some frequency in recent years. This emphasizes the point that a traffic manager who has several rail carriers available but uses only one of them may find himself in a somewhat awkward position during a car-shortage period, due to the inability of his rail carrier to furnish all the cars that would be needed.

The matter of routing is the subject of company policy in a formal or informal manner in most industrial concerns in order to secure efficient traffic management. Routing can be made a traffic manager's tool of inestimable value to his company. The emergency shipment to keep a production line going is the most often cited example of the great importance of choosing a carrier to move the commodities to meet the emergency. Such occurrences are not infrequent in traffic management, but routing can also be used effectively in trade-offs. For example, routing can be accomplished to use the transportation pipeline instead of warehousing. This may be done through routing via a more circuitous route or by using a slower form of transportation which results in longer time in transit. Some traffic managers plan their routing so that a definite percentage of their company's inventory is continuously en route, thus reducing the amount of required warehouse facilities. For example, a lumber broker in the Pacific Northwest may start a car of lumber before he has a buyer for it and then try to sell it while it is in transit. The rail tariff permits him to route a shipment from Bellingham, Washington, to Buffalo, New York, southeast and then north, moving through Oregon, California, Arizona, New Mexico, Colorado, Kansas, Nebraska, Iowa, and Minnesota to Minneapolis; then to St. Louis, up to Chicago, and then to Buffalo, a total distance of 5,203 miles, at the same rate as the short-line route of 2,708 miles. The railroad is providing storage for the load until it is sold.[1] Similar practices are permitted in shipping fruits and vegetables from California to the East. Grain merchants, brokers, and millers also make extensive use of indirect routes.[2]

Reciprocity

Reciprocity is a subject on which there seems to be a great difference between the theory advocated and the actual practice. A careful reading of the many statements on reciprocity indicates the feeling that reciprocity is not a scientific manner in which to conduct business. Even though this principle appears sound, reciprocity is widely used.[3] In the late 1920's, reciprocity was carried so far as to involve a scheme by which groups of

[1] Senate Interstate and Foreign Commerce Committee, *Surface Transportation Ratemaking Bills.* 85th Congress, 1st session (Washington, D.C.: U.S. Government Printing Office, 1957), p. 247.

[2] *Ibid.*

[3] In 1963, the Justice Department filed a civil antitrust suit in which it sought to require General Motors to divest itself of its Electro-Motive Division, the principal manufacturer of diesel locomotives in the United States. Its complaint charged General Motors with unlawfully monopolizing the domestic market for new and rebuilt locomotives, alleging practices such as giving preference in routing freight traffic to railroads which bought locomotives from Electro-Motive; routing freight traffic so as to remove or reduce the volume shipped over railroads which purchased locomotives from their competitors; and increasing the volume of traffic routed over railroads which General Motors believed to be contemplating the purchase of locomotives.

railway supply companies, seeking to increase their share of the market, bought the right from large shippers to route their traffic. It is not uncommon, even today, for a carrier's representative to drop ceremoniously upon the traffic manager's desk copies of purchase orders of the carrier from the company from which he is soliciting business.

Some firms have established a company policy governing reciprocal dealings, so that the traffic manager will have to treat this subject within the framework of this policy. However, it is a matter that can and should be treated realistically. If a factual evaluation shows that, in the opinion of the traffic manager, the company is losing by following such a policy, this matter should be referred to the proper executive officer. If, as a result of reciprocity, a particular carrier is favored, it should be clearly understood that should there be any sacrifice in the efficiency of traffic management due to this factor, it should not be charged against the traffic manager.

Rail

The shipper's right to route carload traffic by rail is permitted under Part I of the Interstate Commerce Act. Section 15(8) provides:

> In all cases where at the time of delivery of property to any railroad corporation being a common carrier, for transportation subject to the provisions of this part to any point of destination, between which and the point of such delivery for shipment two or more through routes and through rates shall have been established as in this part provided to which through routes and through rates such carrier is a party, the person, firm, or corporation making such shipment, subject to such reasonable exceptions and regulations as the Interstate Commerce Commission shall from time to time prescribe, shall have the right to designate in writing by which of such through routes such property shall be transported to destination, and it shall thereupon be the duty of the initial carrier to route said property and issue a through bill of lading therefor as so directed, and to transport said property over its own line or lines and deliver the same to a connecting line or lines according to such through route . . . .

The right of the shipper to route freight in rail transportation gives him great latitude, since for many commodities between certain points, rail carriers have established many routes. The railroads established rates on the more circuitous routes which are competitive with the short-line mileage in many instances, and they actively seek traffic over these more circuitous routes. The Commission has permitted an unlimited amount of circuity on rail traffic moving at class rates and rates made at a fixed percentage of the class rates. In some cases, on special commodity rates, it has permitted as much as 70 per cent circuity when short-line distances are 150 miles or less, 50 per cent circuity for distances up to 1,000 miles, and 33⅓ per cent circuity for distances over 1,000 miles. This gives rise to a tremendous number of routes. The available and authorized routes on class rates between Dallas, Texas, and Detroit, Michigan, are reported to be 4,717,664.[4]

The rail carrier is obliged to follow the shipper's routing, except when conditions exist beyond its control. A further exception to this is that, through the issuance of service orders, the Interstate Commerce Commission can permit carriers to disregard the shipper's routing because of floods or other exigencies. No similar provision in Part II which applies to motor carriers, in Part III which applies to water carriers, and in Part IV which applies to freight forwarders requires the carrier to follow the shipper's routing. The result is that a great deal of controversy exists, particularly regarding motor carriers.

Determination of Rail Routing

The rate between an origin and destination point is not necessarily the same via all routes. In order to determine the route or routes to which a rate applies, reference must be made to the rate tariff. The tariffs may provide specific routes, or they may stipulate that the rates will apply via all routes made by use of the lines of the carriers which are parties to the tariff. However, a tariff can combine both of these plans, as well as provide exceptions that will broaden or restrict the application of the rates. Many rail tariffs have a provision which reads as follows: "The rates herein apply via all routes made by use of the lines of any of the carriers parties to this tariff, except as otherwise specifically provided on pages ...... in individual rate items, or in connection with individual rates."

Through this provision, rail carriers can indicate affirmative routes—that is, carriers and junction points via which shipments may be transported under the rates named—or negative routing—that is, routes or carriers via which rates do not apply. Rather than provide the affirmative routes in rate tariffs, they may be published in a separate publication, in which case reference must be made in the rate tariff to this publication. These are termed *routing guides.* Routing guides have been widely used, particularly for general application within a given rate territory, although they have been published also to apply between points in more than one rate territory. These are referred to as *local* and *joint routing guides.*

Another type of routing guide has been issued for use in connection with a commodity or a group of related commodities. The third type is the *gateway routing guide,* which provides routes to and from gateway points and is usually published by an agent for all carriers in a given

---

[4] House Committee on Interstate and Foreign Commerce, *Transportation Policy,* 84th Congress, 2d session (Washington, D.C.: U.S. Government Printing Office, 1956), p. 423. This computation was made by counting routes from Dallas to Memphis, Memphis to Louisville, Louisville to Detroit; from Dallas to St. Louis, St. Louis to Chicago, Chicago to Detroit, etc., then multiplying one against the other, and considering the different railroads and operating routes between each gateway.

territory. The gateway routing guides are published because it is not practical, in many instances, to publish through routing from points in one rate territory to points in another, due to the large number of routes that it would be necessary to include. Another practical reason is that the division of through interterritorial rates is over the contact point or the connection of one group of carriers with another, and the tariffs usually name the gateway through which traffic passes from one rate territory to another.

Another type of routing guide is that provided by individual carriers which will indicate the routing that applies as far as a particular rail line is concerned. Many of the rail routing guides are quite voluminous because of the many possible routes. One of the four rail trunk lines from New York to Chicago has 40 direct points of interchange with one of the other trunk lines and 42 with a third trunk line. In addition, there are indirect connections which can be made by use of intermediate lines through additional junctions. One of the trunk lines which does not serve St. Louis, Missouri, direct out of New York has more than 130 published routes between New York and St. Louis.

The *Official Guide of the Railways* is very helpful in routing freight, since it contains rail maps and junction points. However, it is an unofficial publication.

Routing instructions are usually published in the back of a tariff. In some instances, they are on the same page which carries the rate; in other cases, the tariff will refer to a routing guide. To determine the correct routing, the following procedure might be used:

1. Note the title page for the application of the tariff.
2. Secure the index number of the carriers at both origin and destination, which is found in Section 1.
3. Having secured the origin and destination index numbers, refer to the table in which the origin and destination numbers are listed; from this, the route reference number is determined.
4. The route to be used from origin to destination is secured by referring to the route reference number, which may be listed numerically in another section.

A number of situations in rail transportation arise due to failure to insert the rate or route on the bill of lading or the insertion of the rate but not the route. These so-called "rate and route conflicts" have led to a number of Commission decisions regarding the obligations of the carriers.

The first situation is where the shipper shows neither the rate nor the route on the bill of lading. The Commission requires that the origin carrier must forward the shipment via the least expensive available route. In the words of the Commission: "While it is the duty of the initial carrier to adhere to its established rates, it is also the duty of the initial carrier, in the absence of routing instructions to the contrary, to forward shipments, having due regard to the interests of the shipper, ordinarily by that reasonable and practicable route over which the lowest charge for that transportation applies."[5] This policy has been consistently followed by the Commission.

Another matter of concern to the Commission is when the shipper inserts the rate on the bill of lading but specifies no routing. The Commission has stated, in this regard, that the rate inserted in the bill of lading is equivalent to routing, provided the rate shown is the correct rate.[6]

Another situation is that in which the shipper indicates the routing on the bill of lading but does not show the rate. In this instance, the Commission has stated that it is the obligation of the carrier to follow the shipper's routing, in spite of the fact that a lower rate might apply via another route. In other words, the shipper is presumed to have a knowledge of the applicable rates, which would be reflected in his choice of routes.[7]

If the shipper shows both the rate and the route on the bill of lading and the rate shown is correct, the carrier must observe the routing, the Commission has ruled. Where both the rate and the route are inserted by the shipper but the rate did not apply over any route and the carrier moved the goods over another route on which the rate was higher than that placed on the bill of lading by the shipper, the Commission has held that since the rates inserted by the shipper were not applicable over any route and the rates charged were the lowest available over any route, there was no damage resulting from any misrouting.[8]

The Commission has issued a ruling, also, regarding circumstances in which the shipper places on the bill of lading the routing and the rate, as well as instructions to stop off for partial loading and unloading. However, the rate inserted by the shipper is not applicable via the stop-off point. The Commission has held ". . . that where the rate named in the bill of lading was not applicable over the designated route and no lower rate was in effect over any route and the shipment was forwarded over the route specified the charges are applicable on the basis of the lowest rate over that route and the shipment is not misrouted."[9]

The Commission held, in another instance, that where the shipper tenders a shipment to the rail carrier, the carrier, in accepting the tender, is not obligated to turn the shipment over at the point of tender to a competitor. The Commission has held that "the initial carrier is under no obligation to turn over to a competing carrier shipment delivered to it upon bill of lading containing routing instructions and a rate applicable only over other lines to which the consignor might have given the ship-

[5] *Hennepin Paper Co.* v. *Northern Pacific Ry. Co.*, 12 ICC 535, 537 (1907).

[6] *Plainfield Grain Co.* v. *Elgin, Joliet & Eastern*, 41 ICC 608 (1916); and *Everist* v. *C. M. St. P. Ry. Co.*, 92 ICC 473 (1924).

[7] *Western Sugar Refinery* v. *Southern Pacific Co.*, 101 ICC 114 (1925).

[8] *Williams & Sons* v. *Baltimore & Ohio R. R. Co.*, 153 ICC 54 (1929).

[9] *Crane & MacMahon, Inc.* v. *N. Y. C. & St. L. R. R.*, 168 ICC 319 (1930).

ment and that it is not chargeable with misrouting when the shipments are forwarded over the cheapest available route affording it a line haul."[10]

Sometimes, a shipment is given to the carrier, and it is only partially routed. Where the initial carrier bills it to a junction with its connection, without indicating the route beyond the connecting line, the second carrier should request the initial carrier for further routing instructions. If it does not do this, the Commission has held it to be responsible for any excess charge that results from its error in forwarding the shipment to its destination via other than the cheapest available route.[11] Again, if a shipper names in the bill of lading some, but not all, of the railroads that are to participate in the haul and some or none of the junctions, the shipper has partially routed the shipment. Under such circumstances, each carrier named must receive a line haul via the junctions shown, if any, or via junctions through which the lowest rate applies and add to the waybill whatever carriers or junctions are necessary to form a through route via which the lowest rate applies.

Open Routing via Rail

Carriers with published rates must protect such rates via any route over lines of carriers named in the tariff. This is termed "open routing." A tariff published with open routing must be in conformance with the Delmar case, in which the Supreme Court held that where there is a choice of two or more routes, a carrier cannot be required to move a shipment via a route which would result in a violation of the Interstate Commerce Act.[12] The Supreme Court stated that "the railway can transport the shipments over the shorter and customary route without violating Section 4, but if the tariff is constructed to require it to take them over the longer route, it must violate that Section and incur the resulting penalties. In this situation we think the tariff should be construed as applying only to the shorter route and not as giving the shipper the option between two routes at the through rate."[13]

A shipper who furnishes routing may insert the name of a railroad system, such as the Southern Railway System. Many of the railroad subsidiaries of a system maintain their separate identity and file their own tariffs so that, in routing, reference must be made to individual railroads and not just the system. Routes which are water-rail or rail-water-rail and are competitive with all-rail routes can be used by shippers; but the Commission has held that the shipper, when he delivers the shipment to the initial carrier, must specify such routing. Otherwise, it is understood that the shipment is to move all-rail.[14]

---

[10] *McLean Lumber Co. v. L. & N. R. R. Co.*, 22 ICC 349 (1912). See also *St. Louis Cooperage Co. v B. & O. R. R. Co.*, 161 ICC 259 (1930).

[11] *Duluth & Iron Range R. R. Co. v. C. St. P. M. & O. Co.*, 18 ICC 485 (1910).

[12] *Great Northern Ry. Co. v. Delmar Co.*, 283 U.S. 686 (1931).

[13] *Ibid.*

[14] *South Alabama Grocery Co. v. Central of Georgia Ry. Co.*, 129 ICC 327 (1927).

Some traffic departments, in routing rail shipments, do not show the junction points on the bill of lading. One of the reasons for this is that where the junction is shown on the bill of lading, the railroads have to move the cars through that junction. However, if there is a lower rate via some other junction and the carriers have complied with the shipper's request, the shipper cannot file a claim for overcharge. When the junction point is not shown, it is possible for the shipper to insist upon the lowest applicable rate. Where junctions are not shown, the initial carriers handle the cars via their working routes. As a general rule, this is the carrier's service route, and traffic may be expedited. Service routes are the shortest and fastest routes. The transit time on these routes, which may involve two or more railroads, may be, in some instances, 24 to 48 hours shorter than if one direct-line carrier had been used.

Another reason that junction points are not shown is that some traffic departments have a volume of traffic so large that if all the junctions were specified, it would entail a great deal of work. On the other hand, if a car is to be stopped off in transit for partial unloading, the junctions may be shown, to be certain that the through rate will be applied and the stop-off actually accomplished. The insertion of the junctions to insure the use of the through rate can make possible the avoidance of the payment of the combination of rates or a local rate from stop-off point to destination.

Motor

Part II covering motor carriers does not grant the shipper the right to route his freight, so that a great deal of controversy has risen concerning this subject. In some of the early cases, the Commission pointed out that there are no provisions in Part II which give the shipper the power to route his shipment.[15]

One of the administrative rules issued by the Commission's Bureau of Motor Carriers, stating the Bureau's view of the correct interpretation of Part II of the Interstate Commerce Act in the absence of authoritative decisions on the subject by the Commission, expressed the view that "if the initial carrier performed the transportation in a manner contrary to the shipper's instructions, the question as to whether it violated its contract and whether the shipper may recover damages therefor are for the Courts to decide."[16] However, this ruling is not followed, in view of modifications occasioned by subsequent cases decided by the Commission. In these more recent cases, the Commission has indicated that Section 216 (b) of the act requires that carriers must establish, observe, and enforce just and reasonable regulations and practices, and that one of these practices is routing. Thus, the general tenor of these cases is that motor carriers

[15] *Central Territory Motor Rates*, 8 MCC 233, 252 (1938); and *Hausman Steel* v. *Seaboard Freight*, 32 MCC 31, 34 (1952).
[16] Administrative Ruling No. 24, dated September 2, 1936.

should follow a shipper's routing instructions; and if unable to do this, the carrier should obtain rerouting instructions from the shipper. Failure to do this may make the carrier liable for misrouting and has been held to be an unreasonable practice.[17]

It is estimated that less than 1 per cent of the motor carrier bills of lading received from shippers carry routing instructions beyond the initial carrier. The initial carrier is thus left the responsibility of providing the routing beyond its line. If a shipper feels injured by misrouting when more than one route is available, the Commission has stated that regardless of the fact that the statute does not specifically authorize the shipper to route his shipments, the carrier has the obligation to route the shipment over the lines of connecting carriers that result in the lowest charge.

Where a motor common carrier refuses to accept a shipment because the bill of lading carries shipper's routing via designated motor carriers, the shipper has no satisfactory recourse.

The Commission has held that motor common carrier through routes may exist without the maintenance of joint rates, and the Commission has no authority to require the establishment of through motor common carrier routes, or any power to prevent the closing of such routes.[18]

Where the shipper desires to route in motor common carriage, it is helpful to make certain that the selected route is an open one via which the through route is applicable.

Some motor carrier tariffs provide the routing applicable for the movement of property, whereas other motor carriers have issued routing guides showing the routing to points they serve or serve in conjunction with other motor carriers in joint hauls. There are two widely used national routing guides, *Motor Carrier Directory* (American Trucking Associations, Inc.) and *National Highway and Airways Carriers and Routes.*

Water

Part III of the Interstate Commerce Act governing water carriers does not contain any provision which gives the shipper the right to route traffic. However, water carriers under Section 305 (*b*) of the Interstate Commerce Act have the duty to establish reasonable through routes with common carriers by railroad; and they may establish reasonable through routes with common carriers by motor vehicles. Where there is a joint rail- or motor-water movement, the bills of lading of the originating railroads and motor carriers usually provide that the bill-of-lading conditions of water carriers govern over the water carrier's portion of a joint through route. It has been widespread practice, however, when use is made of the

[17] *Great Atlantic & Pacific Tea Co.* v. *Ontario Frt. Lines,* 46 MCC 237 (1946); *Metzner Stove Repair Co.* v. *D. & R. Forwarding Co.,* 47 MCC 15 (1947); *Eastern Aircraft* v. *Fred Olson & Son,* 47 MCC 363 (1947).
[18] *Rocky Mountain Lines, Inc.—Elimination of Participation,* 31 MCC 320 (1941); *Rayons between Trunk Line and New England Territories,* 44 MCC 280 (1944).

intercoastal water route, that a separate bill of lading is issued to cover the intercoastal carrier's port-to-port shipment.

Air

In air transportation, the Federal Aviation Act contains no provision which gives shippers the right to route freight. However, there are a relatively small number of routes, as well as carriers, in air transportation as compared with motor and rail transportation. In air transportation, one-carrier service is relatively more extensive than in either motor or rail, so that the extensive routing found in some of the other modes of transportation is not necessary. Some air carriers which provide a joint freight service may limit the routing to that which they designate in a tariff. Any shipment which is tendered to air carriers unrouted will be routed by the carrier.

Freight Forwarders

Part IV of the Interstate Commerce Act, governing surface freight forwarders, does not give the shipper the right to route traffic. Freight forwarders utilize the common carrier facilities of the regulated surface carriers. The shipper tenders to the freight forwarder less-carload or less-truckload freight which the shipper could not route were he to turn it over to a rail carrier or a motor carrier; nor is he able to route it via a freight forwarder.

CLEARANCES

When shippers have unusually large and heavy objects, such as transformers, generators, or boilers, it may be necessary to ascertain in advance from the railroads whether or not clearances are sufficient to permit their being routed via the line. Clearance limitations are based on overhead obstructions, such as bridges and tunnels; on roadside structures, such as platforms, mail cranes, and track curvatures; on limit and length of cars; and on the weight-carrying capacity of bridges and trestles.

Data concerning railroad line clearances, maximum car dimensions, and weight limitations can be found in the publication *Railway Line Clearances*, which is not a "tariff" and is not "filed" with the Commission.

All states impose size and weight limitations upon motor carriers transporting property. For shipments of unusual size or shape which the shipper might wish to move via truck, he should rely upon a group of specialized carriers called "heavy haulers." Each state usually designates a person or office within the state government who has authority to issue special permits for movement of shipments by motor carrier of unusual size and weight which exceed the limits set by the state. The usual procedure is for the heavy hauler to secure the necessary permit.

EMBARGOES AND QUARANTINES

An embargo is the refusal by a carrier, for a limited period, to accept any commodity duly tendered for transportation to or from any area. Carriers sometimes find that, to prevent a complete breakdown of service at a particular point, it is necessary to impose an embargo. An embargo may be issued for various reasons, such as congestion at a terminal or an other-than-carrier labor difficulty. Such embargoes are filed with the Commission and/or the Civil Aeronautics Board, and abstracts of them appear in trade journals. Carriers usually notify traffic managers of embargoes, for they will influence routing.

Numerous articles shipped are subject to quarantine laws and regulations designed to prevent the spread of animal and plant diseases. Digests of quarantine laws, rules, and regulations affecting receipt, transportation, and delivery by common carriers of livestock, food products, nursery stock, and other articles are published in tariff form. However, the tariff does not contain the laws, regulations, and duties imposed upon shippers concerning disinfecting, inspection, packing, and the like.

Quarantines regulate or prohibit the transportation of certain articles; and those items shipped in violation of quarantines are subject to immediate confiscation or destruction at the option and expense of carriers, consignors or owners, consignees, or their agents.

INDUSTRIAL TRAFFIC MANAGEMENT ROUTING POLICY

The traffic department or section of a large industrial organization might have a routing policy similar to the following: In choosing transportation companies, consideration should be given to previous service rendered, service available, cost of service, material-handling facilities available at both shipping and receiving stations, financial stability of carrier, and carrier claim record. Such a routing policy would apply to so-called "normal" transportation, and a special authorization would be necessary to use premium transportation.

Information concerning distribution of traffic by a company among carriers is generally not made available to the general public. However, occasionally, such information is contained in a hearing before a regulatory body. One such example shows that during July, 1952, all outbound shipments from the Boeing Company plants were divided between the various types of transportation as follows: by rail, 22.69 per cent; by freight forwarders, 3.66 per cent; by motor carriers, 68.04 per cent; by air and rail express, 1.52 per cent; and by air freight, 4.09 per cent.[19]

Another example of routing policy which applies to the largest domestic shipper, the Department of Defense, is as follows:

---

[19] Docket No. 30994, January 27, 1954, p. 11.

General

In the employment of its own transportation resources and in the procurement of commercial transportation, the Department of Defense will be guided by and pursue policies which will not contravene the National Transportation Policy enacted by Congress in the Transportation Act of 1940 and the Declaration of Policy by Congress to the Civil Aeronautics Authority, as contained in Section II of the Civil Aeronautics Act of 1938. These policies are cited in the attached enclosure for the guidance of all in connection with any reference thereto in Department of Defense transportation and traffic management policies.

Policies

A. The economic resources of the Department of Defense inherent in its large procurement of commercial transportation will not be employed in such a manner as will adversely affect the economic well-being of the commercial transportation industry.
B. In view of the reliance of the military services during periods of mobilization or war on all modes of transportation, preferential consideration in the routine procurement of transportation will not be accorded one mode of transportation as against another.
C. Commercial transportation service will be employed for the movement of personnel or things when such service is available or readily obtainable and satisfactorily capable of meeting military requirements.
D. Administrative procedures will be frequently reexamined and perfected so as to employ on a routine basis each form of transportation in such a manner as to recognize its inherent advantages. Such review shall include, among other things, the following considerations:
    1. In the movement of personnel, the utilization of the productive time of men being transported, and
    2. In the movement of things, the conservation of stocks through reduction of pipeline and storage requirements and the better utilization of critical and controlled items.
E. Such requirements as are deemed necessary to assure safe and expeditious movement of personnel and things will be prescribed and clearly indicated to all agencies concerned.
F. Administrative procedures will not be promulgated, nor actions taken, which result in an assumption of statutory responsibilities vested in transportation regulatory agencies.[20]

The use of this routing policy has resulted in the distribution of traffic based on revenue for the year 1962 as follows: rail, 27.3 per cent; motor, 53.6 per cent; air, 10.3 per cent; forwarders, 4.8 per cent; pipe lines, 2.7 per cent; and water, 1.1 per cent.[21] This was domestic traffic moving on government bills of lading, and the total expenditure was $459 million.

The degree of control over routing may depend upon whether there is centralized or decentralized traffic control. If there is centralized control, the use of rate and route cards serves as a means of routing control, for the policy may be established that all inbound shipments of 2,000

---

[20] Department of Defense Directive No. 4500.9, dated January 6, 1956.
[21] Department of Defense, 1963.

pounds or more must be routed by headquarters traffic. On outbound traffic routed by the company, it may be the same or a different figure.

The Defense Traffic Management Service, which is responsible for traffic management for the Department of Defense in domestic transportation, operates in a similar manner. It has provided that installation transportation officers may select the mode of transportation and routes within the mode for air freight of less than 1,000 pounds; and the regional offices, 1,000 pounds and over. Another aspect of decentralization has been the issuance of standing route orders to installations which are valid until rescinded. Thus the installation officer has a number of routes and carriers from which he can select.

When more than one carrier serves a given shipping point a company may attempt to allocate traffic to each carrier during slack periods on a percentage of the traffic handled for the company by each carrier during peak or emergency periods, when all available carriers were working at their maximum capacity.

The principle involved in this routing policy is that the carriers that have served during the peak periods should be rewarded during the slack periods. This has the advantage of insuring that carriers will make more of an attempt to take care of the company's traffic during a peak period in order to get a higher percentage during a slack period. Postcard reports from consignees are used by some traffic managers as a basis for their carrier performance records.

In some instances, a railroad does not directly serve all buildings or facilities at a plant location. Under such circumstances, additional expenses may have to be incurred by the industrial traffic department to move commodities to or from the rail point at the plant to other points in the plant area. In contrast to this, a motor carrier can serve all plant facilities. In cases such as this, the rail carrier suffers a "disability." This disability is taken into consideration in routing by the industrial traffic manager, who is interested in the total cost of transportation.

Some companies make it a practice, when adding a new carrier to the routing list, to secure a report on the carrier, such as a Dun & Bradstreet Mercantile Report. This supplies information about the financial record of the company which is of importance in its ability to settle claims and is indicative of its reliability as a carrier.

Carrier salesmen have forms called "routing orders." They attempt to convince industrial traffic managers of the advantages of shipments via their company and ask traffic managers to accept routing orders which provide that henceforth all shipments will move via that particular carrier. Many large industrial traffic departments do not honor routing orders.

The chart shown in Table 10–1 has been compiled by an organization of retail stores which depends upon small-volume shipments in order to supply guidance for its members in routing shipments. For purposes of

TABLE 10–1

RELATIVE ADVANTAGES OF DIFFERENT METHODS OF
MAKING SMALL SHIPMENTS

Transportation Chart

Carrier	Relative Service	Relative Cost	Pickup	De-livery	Minimum Charge*	Features
Parcel post.	Good	Cheapest under 40 lbs.	No	Yes	None	Varying restrictions on size and weight. Must be prepaid.
Railway Express ..	Good	Economical from 50–60 lbs.	Yes	Yes	$2.07	No tracing of shipments.
Truck	Good	Low on over 65 lbs.	Yes	Yes	$3.00 to $5.00	Great variance on LTL by carriers.
Freight forwarder	Good	Low on over 65 lbs.	Yes	Yes	$2.65	May have surcharge to smaller communities.
LCL–rail ..	Slow	Economical	Usually	Yes	$3.09	Service better where through merchandise cars.
Air freight..	Fast	Expensive	Extra	Extra	$4.00	Does not service all towns.
Air fast freight ...	Fast	Expensive	Usually extra	Usually extra	$6.50 Up	Does not service all towns.
Premium air (parcel post express—emergency)	Fastest	Highest	Varies	Yes	High $3.50 to $9.00	Rates prohibitive except for small packages or emergencies.
Water	Slow	Cheap	No	No	$10	Limited in area served.
Garment carriers ..	Good	Expensive	Yes	Yes	$1.59 garment	Saves packaging costs.

* Minimum charges shown are approximations only and may vary by different carriers or different regions.

SOURCE: American Retail Federation.

illustration, a chart of this kind is very helpful, but it should be emphasized that the relationships between different methods of shipping and carriers' customary charges change. Therefore, these facts must be taken into consideration in using such a chart.

A few larger companies have mechanized their routing by use of electronic data-processing equipment. A listing is made of all points from which supplies are received, and a freight routing based on size, cost, and other factors is determined. This enables them to apply a routing to each purchase order and to furnish a nationwide traffic routing manual for other departments, such as purchasing, sales, and manufacturing.

Use of Premium Transportation

Because delivery dates must be met in order to insure satisfactory customer service, a traffic department may be called upon to move "urgent" shipments to meet a deadline. This necessitates the use of what is termed "premium transportation," i.e., transportation more costly than conventional rail, motor, or water freight service. Some traffic and physical distribution departments are also using premium transportation at certain times when the higher transport costs can be offset by lower inventory or warehouse costs. When total costs are lowered, such transportation is not actually "premium" transportation.

CONSOLIDATING SHIPMENTS

Surveys at various plants often reveal that sufficient attention is not given to consolidating shipments. For example, one plant on one day shipped 20 separate pieces of freight, totaling 21,221 pounds, to one common destination. Had these shipments been consolidated, a great saving in time, labor, and money would have resulted.

Shipments of LCL traffic are the ones on which consolidation efforts can be concentrated. LCL traffic and small shipments are defined for statistical purposes by the Commission as consisting of shipments of under 10,000 pounds. Shipments weighing 300 pounds or less constitute over 90 per cent of all small shipment traffic and have been a problem for both carriers and shippers in the inflationary period since World War II. It is estimated that small shipments cost over 2 billion dollars annually. The number of shipments under 10,000 pounds accounted for 81 per cent of the total number of Department of Defense shipments yet represented only 3.4 per cent of the total weight. Some shippers feel that a single agency should handle all small shipments rather than having them handled by a number of agencies.

A comparison of the number of small shipments, total weight, average weight per shipment, and average revenue per shipment via different modes of transportation is provided in Table 10–2.

The cost and other problems associated with small shipments provide an incentive for the traffic manager to accentuate consolidation. The Commission, in Docket No. 29556 and MC–C–543, has investigated rail and motor small shipments, respectively.

In some large industries, incoming shipments are cleared through a central receiving department. Documentation is prepared, or receipted, and recorded. The papers are forwarded to the purchasing office to

TABLE 10–2

TABULATION OF SHIPMENTS OF THREE HUNDRED POUNDS AND LESS

Agency	Number of Shipments (000)	Total Weight (000 Pounds)	Average Revenue per Shipment	Average Weight per Shipment (Pounds)
Railway Express Agency, Inc...	78,716	3,148,640	$3.21	40
(Air Express)	(4,297)	(109,873)	(7.14)	(26)
Class I railways*	27,168	3,694,896	2.60	136
Class I intercity motor common carriers of general commodities†	117,745	15,777,774	1.47	134
Class I, II, and III motor carriers of passengers	p 17,664	p 429,238	p 0.65	p 24
Freight forwarders (large)†	12,222	1,344,354	N.A.	110
Fourth-class mail	1,247,574	7,727,586	0.369	6.2
Air parcel post................	14,924	30,998	1.72	2.1
Total	1,516,013	32,153,486	.....	....

N.A.—Not available.

p—Preliminary data, subject to change on basis of final figures.

* Approximate estimate on basis of data from earlier year not corrected for possible changes.

† It is known that an indeterminate number of small shipments, not consolidated into truckloads, are carried by motor common carriers for freight forwarders. The extent of the resulting duplication cannot be stated.

SOURCE: Bureau of Transport Economics and Statistics, Interstate Commerce Commission, *Statistics of Small Shipments*, Statement No. 5325, Table 1, 1953, for the year 1951.

notify it that the purchases have been received in whole or in part; and on the basis of this notice, the purchasing office may approve the vendors' invoices to the cashier for payment.

Similarly, all outgoing shipments in an industry may clear through a central shipping department. After bills of lading are prepared, a daily shipping report is forwarded to the sales department and to the sales invoicing department. From these reports, the sales department is informed that its sales have gone forward, and the sales invoicing department knows that it may prepare sales invoices against the customer.

Unless purchase orders issued by a company dictate shipping dates, routing quantities, and frequency of movement, the traffic manager (or the buyer) has little control over incoming material, although the traffic department can assist the purchasing department in determining the most economical sources of supply from the standpoint of transportation costs. Naturally, if his company is paying the freight charges, more control of movement can be exercised by the consignee.

Conversely, the traffic manager at a shipping point has the most control of the manner of shipping. This is true particularly when his company is paying the transportation charges. He must concern himself with the most economical method of transportation consistent with giving service to the customer of his company. Methods which give the traffic manager a fair control over the shipment until it reaches its destination will be selected by him whenever practicable.

Traffic management does not function independently of production, and many industries have scheduling departments to co-ordinate activities. Articles requiring the use of the same machine, or machine attachment, are scheduled together in order to reduce the number of machine changes and labor cost thereof. Likewise, shipments of several articles produced in different departments, but destined to a common consignee, are scheduled for concurrent production, and shipping orders make cross reference to each other to avoid separate shipments being made.

Organization of a central shipping and receiving department is limited by existing facilities. Wherever practicable, it should be organized with several locations, each for specific purposes or for handling of commodities which by their very nature would require segregation, such as explosives, perishables, and vehicles. Full carloads and truckloads should not be physically handled through the central shipping and receiving department. By the same token, large or heavy shipments, even though less carload or less truckload, should not necessarily be physically handled through the central shipping and receiving department. However, shipping and receiving papers should clear through this department to the traffic department.

A local policy should be established to specify the heaviest weight which would be automatically delivered to the central shipping and receiving department. For less-carload and less-truckload shipments weighing in excess of this established weight, proper co-ordination should be established with the supply agencies and the central shipping office. In such a case, the shipment might be loaded directly into a car for subsequent switching to the central shipping and receiving department for completion of lading, or a partially loaded car might be switched from this department to the supply agency for completion. Similarly, if intended for shipment by motor carrier, the priority of loading into the truck would be determined by the chief shipper. In instances where no additional tonnage is immediately available for consolidation, it might be decided that the shipment will be delivered to the central shipping and receiving department for holding and subsequent shipping under the most advantageous circumstances.

It should not be inferred that the consolidation of shipments should be limited to shipments destined to a common consignee. On the contrary, consolidation can be accomplished with separate shipments for many consignees, which is one purpose in having all shipping papers cleared through a central shipping department.

Carrier tariffs provide for certain shipments to be stopped in transit for partial loading and unloading at certain designated locations at a slight additional charge. By proper consolidation of shipments at point of origin and proper billing and routing through tariff-designated break-bulk points, traffic managers can take advantage of this privilege and obtain the benefit of carload or truckload rates.

As previously mentioned, available facilities are a controlling factor unless, of course, new facilities will be constructed or old ones remodeled. The shipping room might be laid out in lanes or spaces alphabetically, according to actual destinations or directions, or perhaps by selected modes of carriage. The traffic manager can best determine the most practicable layout after a period of observation of the quantities and frequency of movement to various destinations. In addition, the appropriate layout may be determined through a recapitulation of previously issued bills of lading.

The receiving room should have spaces set aside and marked for each of the principal using agencies. A space should be set aside for parcel post, express, and air freight. Incoming and outgoing movements can be handled in the same space due to the usual simultaneous pickup and delivery for or by these agencies of carriage.

A small space enclosed by wire and equipped with padlock should be set aside to handle restricted material or astray freight while awaiting receipt of identity. Furthermore, damaged packages may be segregated and held in the enclosure to avoid further damage while awaiting carrier's inspection and placing of responsibility. Such a space may be useful for storing surplus car-seal supplies required to be kept in locked storage.

Space should also be allowed for the temporary deposit of pallets, four-wheel trucks, tow motors, lift trucks, and other material-handling equipment when not in use.

The floor should be at the level of the rail car door or truck platform, with ramps to permit free operations of tow vehicles between shipping and receiving departments, on the one hand, and other units of the company, on the other hand.

The rail siding should be on one side; and preferably, a highway for motor trucks should be on the other side. The highway or spotting space should be sufficiently clear of main driveways to permit full-length spotting. Offices could be at either end of the building. The shipping and receiving spaces should be adjoining to permit expansion and contraction of each as required. Outside platforms on the rail and truck sides of the building will permit convenient use of four-wheel trucks, palletizing, tallying, and other handling, including continuous work after the warehouse is closed for the night.

In operations, outgoing less-carload and less-truckload shipments sent to the central shipping department are deposited in appropriate locations. The shipping documents are referred to the traffic manager, who selects the mode of transportation. A daily planning chart or similar system to record approximately the tonnage by destination will be helpful and can be used. The documents should be formulated to show the information desired by the traffic manager and the company. Documents are retained in the shipping department until shipping is ordered by the appropriate authority.

By analysis of the planning chart or similar system, it may be determined which shipments may be consolidated, or held for consolidation, into carloads or truckloads for one common consignee. In addition, the traffic manager determines how many of the shipments are destined in one general direction or could be routed via one common intermediate freight station. For example, from a plant located at Kansas City, shipments to Miami, Jacksonville, Atlanta, Birmingham, Mobile, and Memphis would travel via Memphis, thence to beyond points. Accordingly, the traffic manager could order the loading of shipments to these points into one car marked for break-bulk at the Memphis freight station of the carrier. These shipments would be loaded in reverse order for quick handling at Memphis, where the Memphis, and perhaps Mobile, freight would be unloaded by the carrier and replaced with freight destined to Birmingham, Atlanta, and so on. The objective of consolidating less-carload and less-truckload shipments is to make them into carloads and truckloads wherever possible in order to take advantage of the lower carload or truckload rate.

Care must be exercised in loading consolidated cars or trucks and controlling the paper work. Shipments are sometimes loaded and not billed, or billed and not loaded. They are sometimes loaded into the wrong cars or trucks. Some plants use the "envelope on the car" system. Under this arrangement, the traffic manager selects those shipments which can be loaded in one car for carding to a break-bulk point. He should know where junction points and interchange points are located or where cars should be carded normally, and he has car cards made in advance. In the case of a car carded Memphis, he would arrange to have a Memphis car card nailed temporarily on the side of the car. In addition, he would give the car a number, perhaps 101. If he is loading two such cars for Memphis, with the second one started before the first one is completely loaded, he would give the second one the number 201. In other words, Memphis is designated by the number 1. Cars for Chicago might be numbers 102, 202, and so on; cars for Dallas might be 103, 203, and so on.

The car number (101, 102, etc.) given by the traffic manager is written on a large envelope which is nailed to the side of the car. The loading crews are instructed to load, either by name or break-bulk point or by envelope number; and as the freight enters the door of the railroad car, the shipping documents are tallied, signed, dated, and placed in the envelope. In this manner, all papers are kept together.

It may be found that several small packages are delivered to the central shipping department daily, and because of the weight only, these shipments are marked for parcel post or express. Destinations may be close enough that overnight service by truck could be expected, but shipment by rail or truck is subject to minimum charges. Further exploration may show that these shipments are regularly consigned to a few common points and that no necessity exists for an expedited service. Similarly, small packages may be received regularly by parcel post or express from another plant, the same one to which the traffic manager is making these small shipments regularly. Whenever practicable, small packages can be accumulated for one destination.

Generally, incoming bills of lading are received in advance of the freight. These are recorded in bill-of-lading ledgers and placed in suspense files. When the freight arrives, the carrier receives a temporary receipt on his freight bill and gives one copy to the receiving department. The receiving department must obtain a receipt from any supply service to whom the goods are delivered.

Saving in transportation time is an item not usually recorded for later references. Nevertheless, it has a value. Saving in transportation costs through consolidation, plus the several advantages of joint utilization of manpower, equipment, and space, can readily be shown in justification for consolidating shipments.

Shippers' Associations

Part IV of the Interstate Commerce Act, which regulates freight forwarders, states in Section 402 (c) (1) that the provisions of this part of the act do not apply to the operations of a shipper or a group or association of shippers in consolidating or distributing freight for themselves or for the members thereof on a nonprofit basis for the purpose of securing the benefits of carload, truckload, or volume rates. Under Section 402 (c) (2), these provisions likewise do not apply to the operations of a warehouseman or other shippers' agent in consolidating or distributing pool cars, whose services and responsibility to shippers in connection with such operations are confined to the terminal area in which such operations are performed.

Individual shippers who originate and have traffic destined to common points may form and have formed shippers' associations, particularly since the end of World War II. The basic reason for the formation of these organizations is to take advantage of the difference in rates between small shipments and large shipments. Such organizations consolidate small shipments which, when combined, become large shipments and are transported at the rate accorded large shipments. The establishment by motor carriers of a surcharge on small shipments also has been a factor in the formation of these associations, for consolidation into truckload or carload lot eliminates the surcharge and the lower carload rate or truckload rate may be secured. The membership of these associations is often limited to shippers who have high-rated commodities or to shippers who benefit from the association because there is sufficient spread between the carload or truckload and less-carload or less-truckload rate of their commodities to accomplish savings after deducting all costs.

The establishment of a shippers' nonprofit association usually results in the hiring of a very small staff by the association to handle the routing and clerical work, and the renting of a small office space. A central depot, which is usually platform space located on a railroad siding, is established to facilitate assembling and loading cars. The loading is generally done by hired assemblers using their own equipment. Each shipment which arrives at the platform is covered by the necessary bills of lading, which will list the items to be shipped, the general destination of the shipment, and the name and address of the consignee. The association's employees will make up a manifest covering the entire car which, with the bills of lading, is given to the carrier. At destination, the shippers' association may appoint an agent, such as a warehouseman or a local cartage company, to distribute the contents of the pool car to the consignees. Loss and damage claims are handled by the shippers' association. Members of the association will be charged the carload or truckload rate, plus the actual cost of assembly and distribution.

Consignors and consignees are usually divided into separate shippers' associations. Consignee shippers' associations usually ask their vendors to deliver shipments to the association's origin terminal; but if this is not done, the association will arrange for pickup and will charge the cost of it to the member.

The Interstate Commerce Commission undertook an investigation of one such association in 1947 and found that the freight charges received by the association, whether from its member or its nonmember consignors, were on the basis of the less-carload forwarder rate from origin to final destination, plus 3 per cent of the total charge, which was added in order to equalize the association's charge with that of the freight forwarder. The fact that nonmember consignors would sell goods to members on a delivered basis but pay the association the LCL freight rate raised the question in the Commission's investigation as to whether the difference between the less-carload rate received by the association from nonmember consignors and the carload rate that the association paid the railroads represented a profit; if so, the association was operating on a for-hire basis.[22]

The Commission found the operations of this association to be those of a freight forwarder. However, this decision was reversed by court action, and the reversal was upheld by the Supreme Court.[23] There is nothing in the language of the act or the legislative history to suggest that Congress intended the extent of the exemption to be determined by the type of shipment involved, whether F.O.B. origin or F.O.B. destina-

---

[22] *Pacific Coast Wholesalers' Association, Investigation of Status,* 264 ICC 134 (1945); 269 ICC 504 (1947).

[23] *Pacific Coast Wholesalers' Association* v. *United States,* 81 Fed. Supp. 991 (1949); *United States* v. *Pacific Coast Wholesalers' Association,* 338 U.S. 689 (1950).

tion or delivered price. The determining factor was felt to be the nature of the relationship between the members and the association or group.

One of the most debated aspects of the consignee shippers' associations has been the practice of some of them to bill freight charges to the prepaying consignor in the same manner as outlined above. The Commission has frowned upon a consignor shippers' association sending freight bills to consignees for payment and crediting the savings to the consignor.

In 1962, the Commission ruled that shipper associations do not qualify for exemption from economic regulation as freight forwarders if they are corporations as that term is commonly understood.[24] In a later case, the Commission stated that if a corporate charter of a shipper association relieves its members of liability or responsibility for corporate obligations, it is the type of organization not covered by the exemption.[25]

Although the high-rated, less-carload traffic lends itself to the operations of shippers' associations, savings may also be effected in lower-rated commodities. However, the savings will not be so great. In order to determine the feasibility of a shippers' nonprofit association, the commodities to be shipped can be listed, and the less-carload rate applicable thereto shown. The costs of pickup (which vary with classification, distance, and weight), the loading cost, the number of shipments, minima, and carload costs are totaled. The difference between the total of these costs and the less-carload rate will show whether or not such an association is worth consideration.

It is not known exactly how many shippers' nonprofit associations have been formed. There are at least one hundred of them, since there are approximately that number listed in the Commission's files. The Commission has investigated a number of them on the basis of complaints received, principally from freight forwarders. The most common complaint is that they are not acting as nonprofit associations.

The shippers' associations formed thus far have not been confined to a single group of commodities. Department store and mail-order merchandise are classes of traffic that have led to the formation of quite a number of these associations. However, there have been associations to consolidate pipe, iron, and steel in bargeload lots for movement on inland waterways. Hardware items are another kind of traffic which has been the basis for the formation of organizations of this kind.

There are no exact figures as to the volume handled by the shippers' associations, although some indication can be derived from the statistics of one located in Atlanta, Georgia, having about 275 members. It receives 15 to 20 cars a week from New York and Chicago, which amount to approximately $1\frac{1}{2}$ million pounds per month. Since this is only one of many

---

[24] *Atlanta Shippers Association, Inc., Atlanta, Georgia—Investigation of Operations,* May 14, 1962.

[25] *Carload Shippers Association, Inc.—Investigation of Operations,* June, 1962.

such associations, it is apparent that there is a substantial volume of tonnage being shipped by associations of this kind.

One shippers' association in Houston reports that the over-all charges of its association have averaged at least 10 per cent under rail less-carload and freight forwarder rates; and in many instances, the savings have been greater.[26] One member of this shippers' association reported that a boxed game that retails for $1.98 per game cost him on the average $11.40 per dozen F.O.B. New York. This company charged the retail variety stores $14.40 a dozen for this item, thus realizing a gross profit of $3.00 a dozen. The usual weight of the game per dozen was 25 pounds, and it cost $1.54 to ship it from New York via freight forwarder or $1.28 per dozen by water carrier. By handling it through the shippers' association, the item was brought to Houston at a cost of 84 cents a dozen, or a saving in freight charges of almost 50 per cent.

It appears that shippers' nonprofit associations may work together, and two of them could co-load or commingle shipments. Although not formally ruled upon by the Commission, there is serious question as to whether a freight forwarder and a shippers' nonprofit association could commingle shipments, because of the discriminatory aspects which might arise.

It is difficult to distinguish between the service a shipper receives from a shippers' nonprofit association and that provided by regulated freight forwarders. Annually, since 1951, the Commission has requested that Congress amend this statutory exemption. It wishes to have the exempt status granted only after a shippers' association has applied and proved its eligibility.

Pool Cars

Many warehousemen offer as one of their services that of pool-car service. Local cartage companies also offer pool-car service. Railroad tariffs do not provide for distribution or assembly of pool-car lots. The warehouseman or local cartage company is often termed a "consolidator" and will perform the pickup, sorting, consolidation, and loading; or at destination, it will perform the unloading and distribution at an agreed rate per 100 pounds. Fifty local cartage companies in Los Angeles indicated, in a hearing before the California Public Utilities Commission in 1953, that they were handling a combined total in excess of 2,000 pool cars per month.

The rate charged may be a flat charge, or it may vary, depending upon the classification of the freight. The carload or truckload rate is applied when a pool car or pool truck is used. An important factor in considering the use of the pool car is that the greater the distance, the larger the

---

[26] House Committee on Interstate and Foreign Commerce, *Transportation Policy*, p. 1109.

spread between less-carload or less-truckload rates and carload or truck-load rates.

Definition of Pool Car

A pool car constitutes a carload composed of several small lots which is shipped to one point to one consignee, the latter usually a distributing, agent, such as a warehouseman or local cartage company, which delivers the goods to the various consignees whose shipments are in the car. Large industrial shippers may make use of pool cars in a somewhat different manner. They often consolidate less-truckload and less-carload lots of material received from various shippers in one area at a specified point, and the pool car will then move to a company location in some other area.

Industrial Use of Pool Cars

In determining the feasibility of pool-car or pool-truck service, a primary factor to be considered is whether sufficient quantities of less-carload or less-truckload orders move regularly—that is, daily or every second day —to certain destination cities. If there is insufficient tonnage for specific cities, the tonnage destined for areas within a given range of key cities is considered. It may be found that it would cost little more to include the orders beyond the city, but over-all savings would still be large enough to justify the use of pool cars or pool trucks.

An example of the use that can be made of pool-car and pool-truck service is that which has been worked out by the Traffic Department of the Ford Motor Company. The Ford Company and most of the assembly plants were constructed on the assumption that the bulk of the material would be received by rail, the freight would move into the plant, and it would be unloaded onto the conveyor line. In this manner, no substantial inventory would have to be maintained.[27] At that time, however, the greatest portion of the material used in the construction of Ford cars was made by the Ford Company. There were relatively few outside suppliers, and most of them were in the Detroit area, so there was little problem in handling these shipments.

This situation has changed over the years, and particularly since World War II. At the present time, some 6,000 suppliers furnish material for the Ford plants. With suppliers more widely scattered and shipments more numerous and smaller in volume, there were many traffic problems. Not only was freight cost a factor; but also, there were many thousands of covering or protecting shipments moving by Railway Express or air freight in order to insure continued production, due to the lack of control over the less-truckload and less-carload shipments.[28]

---

[27] George H. Russel, "Operation Funnels," *American Cartagemen,* September, 1953, p. 16.

[28] *Ibid.,* p. 30.

Pool-car operation was inaugurated to improve this situation. In the Ford pool-car operation, a cartage company serves as the agent. It takes shipments coming from each of many suppliers and may sort them into as many as 15 or 16 separate freight cars. Since there are numerous suppliers funneling supplies into each of 7 different pool-car locations, the volume handled exceeds 500 million pounds per year. In 1950, some 15,000 pool cars were handled in this manner at a total savings to the company of about $4,360,000.[29]

The savings are not merely monetary, for there has been a reduction in transit time of shipments which has permitted less material in transit and therefore less cash tied up in inventory. It has reduced the congestion at shipping and receiving locations, and has resulted in a reduction in telephone and telegraph cost, as well as labor cost involved in expediting shipments. In the Ford pool-car operations, there are cars which contain an average of eighty individual suppliers' shipments which go on a single bill of lading with but one car to trace and a single receiving spot required for unloading.

Analysis was made, also, of the less-truckload quantities which moved between certain points, and it was found that much of this material could be consolidated into truckloads. The result was the establishment of pool-truck operations. The arrangements for handling this were similar to those of the pool-car service, in that a local cartage company was appointed agent to assemble and sort the individual shipments. Seven pool-truck locations have been organized. The inbound pool trucks often carry some service and assembly plant production parts which are carried to the Detroit pool-car location for redistribution to points beyond Detroit.[30]

CASE

The Bachelder Company is a major supplier of the automotive industry. It produces over 400 types and sizes of brakes, power steering equipment, carburetors, radios, fuel pumps, and other products. It has more than thirty plants throughout the United States, about half of which are within 100 miles of large metropolitan areas.

A troublesome problem at all of the plants is occasioned by the tremendous volume of inbound small shipments. The rates on these shipments run from 25 to 50 per cent higher than on carload or truckload. In addition to higher rates, many shipments fail to arrive on schedule which necessitates a substantial amount of tracing. Another aspect of the problem is congestion at the receiving platforms. Since there are deliveries made by many carriers, delays in unloading trucks may be as long as two hours. It was decided to analyze this problem at the Canton, Ohio, plant and try to find a solution which could be applied to other plants as well.

It was found that there was sufficient space at the Canton receiving area for enlargement of the dock, which would cost $20,000. While this would

---

[29] *Traffic World*, March 3, 1951, p. 35.
[30] *Ibid.*, p. 41.

relieve congestion, two additional employees would need to be hired at a combined annual cost of $11,500, including overtime.

An analysis of one month's shipments indicated a tonnage of 554,600 pounds of collect LTL shipments and 112,663 pounds of prepaid LTL shipments. Shipments of less than 10,000 were considered LTL shipments in the compilation of the statistics. It was found by examining the bills of lading that although these shipments came from many suppliers, they were generally routed through Cleveland. The possibility of having shippers forward shipments to a consolidator in Cleveland where they would be consolidated into truckloads appeared as a solution to the problem.

In addition to the foregoing tonnage, it was found that 141,000 pounds moved from Cleveland suppliers to Canton on an F.O.B. Canton basis. It was decided to see if the F.O.B. basis could be changed to Cleveland, with suppliers delivering to the consolidation center without cost and with a possible reduction in total price based on the freight charge from Cleveland to Canton. If this could be accomplished, this tonnage could be added to the other which would be consolidated and would add to the expected savings.

In order to ship in truckloads, it was considered necessary to hold for consolidation which initially would mean a 24-hour delay in shipments. Under these circumstances, a minimum of 24 hours would have to be added to the transit time, and the adjustment made in production scheduling and procurement. It was felt that within six months, the adjustment could be made so there would be a frequency of truckloads adequate to eliminate the 24-hour consolidation delays. An agent would be appointed to serve as a consolidator in Cleveland, and the suppliers would have to be notified to send their shipments to the consolidation point in care of the agent. The consolidation would be expected to effect a net savings of about 15 cents per 100 pounds.

1. What do you feel is the best solution?

2. Would there be any limitations on your recommendation when applied to all plants?

DISCUSSION QUESTIONS AND PROBLEMS

1. What are some of the factors considered in the routing of shipments?
2. If you were the traffic or physical distribution manager of a large rubber tire manufacturing plant with nationwide sales and were served by motor, rail, and water transportation, what would be a good routing policy for your company?
3. Select a particular type of manufacturing concern, and set forth what you feel would be a defensible and workable policy on reciprocity.
4. What are affirmative routes? Where may they be found?
5. Explain the different types of rail routing guides. Do motor carriers issue routing guides comparable to rail routing guides?
6. In rail routing, what happens when: (a) A shipper shows neither the rate nor the route on the bill of lading? (b) A shipper shows the routing on the bill of lading but does not show the rate?
7. All rail shipments should be routed by the traffic manager to show the junction points. Comment on the validity of this statement.
8. Why does not Part II of the Interstate Commerce Act grant the shipper the right to route his freight? What is the present ICC trend found in motor carrier cases on motor carrier routing?

9. What statutory provisions govern the routing of water and air shipments?

10. Formulate a routing policy on behalf of a large company in your area. How would you determine whether your policy was being followed?

11. Would the routing policy for a private business organization differ from that of a government agency? How?

12. What is the "small shipment" problem? Would consolidation be beneficial to shippers?

13. How does a central receiving department function? Discuss its advantages and disadvantages.

14. What are shippers' associations? Are they identical to freight forwarders?

15. A pool-car and pool-truck service may be advantageous under what conditions?

Chapter

11

CARRIERS' SPECIAL SERVICES

Carriers offer many special services that have been designed to accommodate shippers. These services, for which there is usually a charge, are provided for in carriers', tariffs; and some of those more frequently used are described in this chapter. There are many others, the titles of which are explanatory, such as exclusive use of vehicle or car, inside delivery, Saturday and Sunday collection and delivery, segregation of shipment, redelivery, and articles requiring special handling.

DIVERSION AND RECONSIGNMENT

The terms "diversion" and "reconsignment" are often used interchangeably, although, strictly speaking, a change in the destination of a shipment while en route is termed a "diversion," while the term "reconsignment" is generally applied to a change in the destination of a shipment after it has reached its originally billed destination.

A shipper, consignee, or owner may desire to change the name of the consignee, effect a change in the name of the consignor, make a change in the destination, or change the routing of a carload or truckload shipment after the bill of lading has been executed and the shipment has left the point of origin. There are certain commodities, such as perishables—including fruits and vegetables, dairy products, and others—which may start in the general direction of their market and, prior to their arrival at the particular market or after their arrival at the billed destination, can be diverted or reconsigned to a different market to accomplish a better balance of supply and demand. This particular service is a great benefit to shippers, as well as the general public, for it can accomplish a balance of supply in the market and can enable a shipper, consignee, or owner not only to effect a savings in transportation costs but also to realize a more satisfactory price in the sale of his commodity.

In other instances, the diversion and reconsignment privilege may be used because conditions or circumstances necessitate its use. The original customer or consignee might desire to cancel an order for commodities after they have been shipped, and the shipper may be able to sell the goods to another customer while the shipment is en route. The new buyer may be located at the same destination or at a different destination, and the diversion and reconsignment privilege makes possible such a change. A reconsignment often occurs, also, when the original customer resells the commodities to another party who is located at the original destination or another destination.

Diversion and reconsignment are frequently subject to the following conditions:

1. That shipment has not broken bulk, except such as incident to an inspection.

2. That there is no back haul on the shipment, except as provided for in the tariff.

3. That requests are made to the carrier within a reasonable time.

4. That an order for diversion or reconsignment not be accepted at a station or at a point of delivery against which an embargo is in force, although a shipment made under an authorized permit is not subject to this condition.

5. That on a straight bill-of-lading consignment, the original bill of lading be surrendered or other proof of ownership established.

On a shipment consigned to order, an order to divert or reconsign is not effective until the original bill of lading is surrendered for cancellation, endorsement of diversion or reconsignment, or exchange; or in its absence, the property may be diverted or reconsigned in advance of the surrender of the bill of lading only under specific provisions.

Shipments on straight bills of lading, showing consignment to one party with instructions therein or on which instructions are otherwise given to notify or advise another party and deliver only upon the surrender of a written order, or deliver only upon surrender of the original bill of lading, or consigned in any other manner which imposes upon the carrier the obligation not to make delivery or permit diversion except upon surrender of the original bill of lading or a written order, are treated as shipments billed to order unless the reconsignment or diversion order is given by, or the delivery is to, such originally billed consignee or his agent. The advise-or-notify party is not considered by most carriers to be the consignee.

6. That a request for diversion or reconsignment is made or confirmed in writing, and an order for diversion or reconsignment which specifies that the through rate is to be protected is not construed as obligating carriers to protect other than the lawful rate and charges. When an order for diversion or reconsignment requires protection of a rate and/or route which cannot be lawfully applied via the point at which diversion or reconsignment is made, prompt notice is given to the party requesting the diversion or reconsignment. Unless such an order contains the alternative of forwarding the car as originally billed, the car will be stopped for orders.

7. That, in most instances, all charges against the property, whether accrued or accruing under the rules of diversion or reconsignment, are paid or guaranteed to the satisfaction of the carrier before the car is diverted or reconsigned.

The diversion and reconsignment privilege must be provided for in a tariff of the carrier. The tariff provision enables the shipper to get the benefit of a through rate from the point of origin to the point of ultimate destination rather than having to pay the combination rates to and beyond the reconsignment point. In contrast to this, the Commission has stated that a consignee has the right to reship goods received by him without removal from the car upon payment of the freight charges to that point, the goods going forward under a new transportation contract. Whereas reconsignment is covered by special rules and conditions contained in the tariff, the through rate applies from the initial point to that of ultimate delivery, which is often less than the sum of the intermediate rates in and out of the point of original destination.[1] A reshipment does not preserve the continuity of the shipment from the point of origin to final destination.

In the case of perishable items, the carriers have tended to grant liberal diversion and reconsignment privileges. One railroad, which transports a substantial volume of perishable fruit, provides that no charge shall be made for the first three reconsignments, and a nominal charge will be made for the fourth and fifth reconsignment. Where such liberal diversion and reconsignment privileges are granted, the carrier's tariff usually provides that the number of diversions and reconsignments that occur on the lines of other carriers will be included in the total allowed. Even though the carrier's tariff states that five diversions and reconsignments are all that are permitted, the carrier's tariff can provide that a shipment can be reforwarded from the point where the reconsignment subsequent to the fifth diversion and reconsignment is effected. However, under these circumstances, the freight charges may be assessed on the basis of the full local or joint rate from the reforwarding point, plus other applicable charges which previously or subsequently accrue.

With the development of large food store chains, there has been more direct purchasing and consequent reduction in the diversion of rail cars. This is not true of sales made by brokers. It is estimated that at the present time, more than half of the rail traffic out of California and Florida is reconsigned at least once.

In contrast to the liberal diversion and reconsignment privilege granted on perishable commodities, nonperishable commodities generally, depending upon the tariff, are permitted but a single change in destination at the applicable through rate from the point of origin to final destination.

The Commission has felt that reconsignment charges should not be established at points via which there is no single through rate; and the shipper must pay the combination of local rates in and out of the point of reconsignment, the reasoning here being that the carrier, in performing the diversion or reconsignment service, does not incur any additional ex-

---

[1] *Detroit Traffic Association* v. *L. S. & M. S. Ry. Co. et al.*, 21 ICC 257 (1911).

pense over that which would have been incurred in the handling of two local shipments.[2]

Although there is a National Diversion and Reconsignment Committee which handles matters of a national nature regarding diversion and reconsignment privileges, there is not a national reconsignment and diversion tariff in effect. The general procedure has been for each carrier to publish its own diversion and reconsignment tariffs. Rules and regulations are suggested by the National Committee, and rules are generally the same on all railroads. The diversion and reconsignment tariffs of the carriers ordinarily will provide for back-haul or out-of-line charges, or out-of-route movement. However, there are instances where there is no charge made for out-of-route service. As an example, the Erie Railroad's main line does not reach Cleveland, Ohio, but a branch line runs from Leavittsburg, some thirty miles to Cleveland. The Erie, in order to be competitive with the New York Central and Pennsylvania railroads which serve Cleveland directly, provides in its tariff that carload shipments which originate at points in western states and move via the Erie from Chicago to Cleveland may be reconsigned at Cleveland to a point on or via the Erie Railroad east of Salamanca, New York, without charge for the additional out-of-route miles hauled from Leavittsburg to Cleveland and return.

The rail tariffs covering diversion and reconsignment usually provide that amounts less than a carload may be accorded these privileges. The usual requirement is that freight which is shipped at less-carload or any-quantity ratings, when forwarded in one car from one station on one day by one shipper on one bill of lading for delivery to one consignee at one station, will be diverted or reconsigned subject to the same rules and charges which are applicable on carload freight, provided the revenue paid thereon is not less than charged for the minimum quantity of 15,000 pounds or where car is loaded to its full visible capacity. Some rail tariffs carry a provision on this subject providing that less-carload shipments which are charged at less-carload rates when forwarded in the same car with carload shipments from one station on one day by one shipper on one bill of lading for delivery to one consignee at one destination will be diverted or reconsigned along with the carload shipment without additional charges, such cars to be subject to the same rules and charges as are applicable to the straight carload shipments.

The Commission has stated that reconsignment charges are to be determined as of the date of the origin of the shipment.[3]

The amount of the reconsignment charge varies, depending upon a number of factors, which are outlined as follows:

[2] *Chestnutt Lumber Co.* v. *Director General as Agent*, 89 ICC 236 (1924); and *Traffic Bureau Chamber of Commerce* v. *Southern Ry. et al.*, 115 ICC 625 (1926).

[3] *Carolina Portland Cement Co.* v. *Director General*, 83 ICC 383, 391 (1923).

Nature of Service and Charge	*Conditions under Which Applicable*
1. For diversion or reconsignment in transit* $13.00 per car.	If order placed to permit service being performed prior to arrival at billed destination or terminal yard.
2. For diversion or reconsignment to points within destination switching limits after arrival of car, but before place for unloading.	
No charge assessed.	If order received at destination direct from consignee or owner prior to arrival of car at destination.
Charge* $10.12 per car.	If order received within 24 hours after arrival.
Charge* $20.95 per car.	If order received subsequent to 24 hours after arrival.
3. For diversion or reconsignment to points outside of destination switching limits, after arrival of car, but before placed for unloading, charge* $20.95 per car.	After arrival of car at billed destination but before placement for unloading.
4. For diversion or reconsignment after car is placed for unloading and forwarded without being unloaded.	Apply combination of locals to and from the point of reshipment and not through rate.

* All charges in Official Territory and include increases through *Ex Parte* 223.

It will be noted that there are different charges where (1) a charge is made while the car is en route when diverted or reconsigned to points outside the switching limits on orders received before the arrival of a car; (2) diversion or reconsignment to points outside the switching limits after arrival but before placement (placement, as used in diversion and reconsignment rules, refers to the placement of cars on the consignee's private or assigned track or siding, and a freight car which is placed on a carrier's public delivery track is not considered as having been placed for unloading under the terms of the reconsigning tariff); and (3) diversion or reconsignment to points within the switching limits before placement.

Ordinarily, diversion or reconsignment to points outside the switching limits after placement is not permitted at the through rate; but there are numerous exceptions to this, particularly concerning commodities which move in tank cars. Where diversion or reconsignment is effected to points which are within the switching limits after placement, there usually is not a diversion or reconsignment charge; but the shipment will be subject to the rate or charge for local movement within the switching limits, in addition to the other charges which have accrued between the point of origin and the billed destination. These points represent the general rules, but there are exceptions. For example, where carload freight has been stopped short of the billed destination at the request of the shipper, consignee, or owner and held for orders, there are tariff provisions which apply; and the diversion or reconsignment charges vary, depending upon where the shipment is stopped.

Uniform diversion and reconsignment charges were authorized by the Interstate Commerce Commission in the *Reconsignment Case*, decided in 1919. This authorization and the *Ex Parte* increases are as shown in Table 11–1.

TABLE 11–1

RAIL DIVERSION AND RECONSIGNMENT CHARGES

	As Authorized	Increased under *Ex Parte* Authorizations (within Official Territory)*
1. For change in name of consignor with no further change in billing instructions	$1.00	$ 6.06
2. For diversion or reconsignment prior to arrival of car at billed destination.	2.00	10.12
3. For diversion or reconsignment at billed destination to a point outside of switching limits before placement for unloading	5.00	20.95
4. For diversion or reconsignment to points within switching limits before placement:		
a) Within 24 hours after arrival....	2.00	10.12
b) After expiration of 24 hours after arrival of car	5.00	20.95

* *Ex Parte* increases vary, depending upon the point where the D/R is accomplished. Includes increases through *Ex Parte* 223.

Generally speaking, it is the owner of a shipment who can divert or reconsign a shipment, although actually, anyone who is lawfully entitled to possession of a shipment may reconsign it. In a court case, it was ruled that where a carrier executes a reconsignment order which was given by a party who the carrier knows is not entitled to make the order and the carrier delivers the property to a party not entitled to receive it, the carrier is guilty of conversion and is liable to the lawful owner of the shipment.[4]

There is extensive use made of order bills of lading for those shipments in which there is anticipated use of diversion and reconsignment. Since an order bill of lading is negotiable and the holder is assumed to be the owner of the goods or entitled to their possession, there is little question, in so far as the carrier's agent is concerned, if the order bill-of-lading holder executes the order for diversion or reconsignment. The order bill must be surrendered to the carrier in order to execute the reconsignment,

---

[4] *Esterville Produce Co.* v. *Chicago Rock Island & Pacific R. R.*, 57 Fed. (2d) 50 (1932).

FILE NO.

DATE

CONFIRMING PHONE CALL TO

DATE OF CALL

CAR NO.

DIVERSION - RECONSIGNMENT ORDER

CONTENTS

CONSIGNED TO

WEIGHT

AT

ROUTED VIA

FOLD HERE   SHIPPED BY

FROM

DATE

OUR REQUEST   (CHECK THAT WHICH APPLIES)

( ) TRACE   ( ) EXPEDITE   ( ) RECONSIGN   ( ) DIVERT

TO

ADDRESS

VIA

CHARGE TO

PLEASE CONFIRM PROMPTLY WHEN THIS ORDER HAS BEEN ACCOMPLISHED AND STATE POINT OF INTERCEPTION.

FOR:

DIRECTOR OF TRANSPORTATION

CONTACT			PASSING			NOTIFIED			
CARRIER AND REPRESENTATIVE	TIME	DATE	POINT	TIME	TRAIN NO.	PERSON	DEPARTMENT	TIME	DATE

FIG. 11-1. A copy of a diversion and reconsignment order.

although the carrier's agent can, if he is satisfied that the person who makes the reconsignment order is lawfully entitled to request it and a bond is posted, make the reconsignment. If a straight bill of lading is used and the shipper anticipates diverting or reconsigning the goods while en route, the usual procedure is to consign them to himself. Inasmuch as both the shipper and the consignee are the same, it would be a simple matter to issue the order for diversion or reconsignment.

In some merchandising activities, the consignees in the straight bill of lading may be brokers or commission men; and it is possible for some confusion to arise as to whether the shipper or consignee, where a straight bill of lading is used, should make the reconsignment order. The carrier must take the necessary action to insure that the party that issues the reconsignment order is lawfully entitled to do so.

A copy of a traffic department diversion and reconsignment order is shown in Figure 11–1.

Where rail cars have been stopped, diverted, or reconsigned, the tariff provisions usually permit 24 hours of free time at the point where the diversion or reconsignment is accomplished. If the car is detained longer than 24 hours, demurrage charges are assessed in accordance with the demurrage tariff.

Motor carriers grant the reconsignment and diversion privilege in a manner similar to the railroads, although there is little uniformity in the motor rules. Each of the rate territories appears to have some differences in rules, but the principle of the reconsignment and diversion privilege is the same.

STOPPING OF CARS IN TRANSIT TO COMPLETE LOADING

Railroads instituted the practice of stopping cars in transit for partial loading or unloading of building materials and agricultural implements. Established during the early part of the present century, this privilege was inaugurated when the country was sparsely settled, and it has been continued since that time. Under this privilege, a manufacturer can sell goods to two or more customers, load the goods in one car, and bill to the final destination, with instructions to stop at the intermediate point or points where part of the goods will be unloaded, after which the car will continue on its way with the balance of the load to the ultimate destination. The stop-off privilege to complete loading makes possible the purchase of goods at two or more origin points. The material which is purchased at the first point is loaded, and the car is billed to final destination to stop at one or more intermediate points for loading the additional merchandise.

As this privilege was originally established, the stop-off point had to be directly intermediate on the route from the original point of shipment to the final destination, and the rate with the stop-off privilege had to be applicable via or through the point at which the car was stopped. After a few years' experience with the stop-off privilege, the railroads extended it to branch lines, in order that those railroads which had branch lines that reached points which were direct routes on other railroads could meet competition; in this case, it became customary for the railroads which had to reach these competitive points by branch lines not to make a charge for the out-of-line haul necessary to reach the stop-off point. The treatment of branch-line points as being located on the main line for stop-off purposes enabled the rail carriers to secure the long haul on traffic which they originated. On a shipment from Buffalo, New York to New York City on the Erie Railroad, a shipment can be billed for a stop-off at Newburgh, New York, which is located on a branch line of the Erie Railroad. The Erie waives the out-of-route haul between Greycourt, New York on the main line and Newburgh because Newburgh is located on the main line of a competing railroad, the New York Central.

The rules governing stop-off privileges will stipulate that the shippers at the point of origin must designate on the shipping order or the bill of lading (1) the stop-off privilege which is requested, whether it is to complete loading or to unload partially; (2) the point or points where the car is to be stopped; and (3) the name and address of the party which will load or unload at the stop-off point. The tariff rules governing stop-off provide that, where cars are stopped to unload partially, no freight may be loaded at stop-off points; and where cars are stopped to complete loading, no freight may be unloaded at the stop-off points.

The rate which is applicable is the carload rate which is in effect at the time the shipment is made from the origin point to destination, plus the stop-off charge; but there are certain exceptions to this, of which the following is an example: When the rate from the stop-off point to the final destination on cars stopped to complete loading is higher than the rate from the original point of shipment to such destination, the rate from the stop-off point to the final destination will govern the through movement from the original point of shipment to the final destination, plus stop-off charge of $25 per car per stop in the East. The transportation charges are based upon weight at the final destination of the shipments in cars stopped to finish loading and upon the initial weight of cars stopped to be unloaded partially, subject to minimum carload weights. For example, on a car from Akron, Ohio which is stopped off in transit at Youngstown, Ohio to complete loading and reforwarded to Jamestown, New York, the final destination, the charges are computed from the weight of the car after the loading is completed at Youngstown, Ohio, the stop-off point, at the rate applicable from Akron, which was the original point of shipment, to Jamestown, the final destination, subject to the carload minimum weight.

Some tariffs on stop-offs to complete loading and to unload partially provide that a carload shipment may be stopped at a transloading station, where the railroad, on request of the shipper, will transfer those portions of the shipment destined to stop-off points or the final destination and forward them in another car or cars. This transfer or stop-off is called "transloading" and may eliminate delays caused by handling cars to or from out-of-line stations and delays at stop-off stations. There is no charge assessed by the carrier for the transloading, charges being computed as if the original carload had made all the stop-offs for partial unloading.

The stop-off in transit is also granted by motor carriers, although it is an extra transportation service for which a motor carrier receives compensation. Figure 11–2, which is a portion of such a stop-off rule, shows the charge and indicates that the conditions of motor carriers are similar to those of rail.

Rule 28

Truckload shipments of freight may be stopped at point of origin or destination, or at points directly intermediate between origin and destination, for completion of loading or for partial unloading under the following conditions (Note D):

a) All freight charges must be paid in full at one time, by either the shipper or the consignee named in the bill of lading.

b) Only one bill of lading and one shipping order shall be issued for the entire shipment.

c) The bill of lading and shipping order shall show, in the space provided therefor, the name of only one consignee and one delivery address and only one shipper and one shipper's address.

d) The names of places or addresses (Note B) at which vehicles are to be stopped for completion of loading or partial unloading shall be shown either in the body of the bill of lading and shipping order or in a separate paper which shall be attached to and considered a part of the shipping documents.

e) Except as otherwise provided, only three stops whether for completion of loading or partial unloading or for both purposes, shall be permitted (Note A).

f) Except as provided in paragraph (*g*), the charge for each stop shall be at the rate of ¶12 cents per 100 pounds for the weight of the freight received or delivered thereat, subject to a minimum charge of ⊙ $7.06 per stop, in addition to the rate provided for in paragraph (*h*) (Note A).

Truckload shipments of freight may be stopped at point or origin or destination, or at points directly intermediate between origin and destination, for completion of loading or for partial unloading under the following conditions (Note D)—concluded:

g) On any traffic consigned to a pier or wharf to be stopped off for partial unloading or consigned to some other place to be stopped off at a pier or wharf for partial unloading, or on any traffic originating at a pier or wharf to be stopped-off for completion of loading or originating at any other place to be stopped off at a pier or wharf for completion of loading, the charge for each stop shall be at the rate of §19 cents per 100 pounds for the weight of the freight delivered or received thereat, subject to a minimum charge of ¶$17.66 per stop, in addition to the rate provided for in paragraph (*h*) (Note A).

h) Except as provided in paragraph (*i*), the rate from the original place of shipment to the place of final delivery will apply on the total weight of the shipment (the weight after completion of loading, if a stop for that purpose is made, or the weight before the first stop is made for partial unloading, if a stop for that purpose is made).

i) If the rate from any place where a stop is made for the completion of loading is higher than the rate from the original place of shipment, such higher rate will apply; or if the rate to any place where a stop is made for partial unloading is higher than the rate to the place of final delivery, such higher rate will apply.

j) Unless otherwise specifically indicated, the provisions of this rule will NOT apply to shipments of:

(1) Fresh and salted meats, except as provided in Note E.

(2) Any commodity moving under refrigeration, or any commodity indicated on bills of lading or package markings as perishable, except as otherwise provided in Notes C and E.

(3) Freight moving on C.O.D. basis.

(4) Freight consigned to order, or to order-notify, or otherwise so consigned as to require surrender of a bill of lading, written order or any other document in advance of delivery.

NOTE A: Three stops are permitted exclusive of the receipt of the original part of the shipment and the final delivery at destination. The word "stop" or "stops" as used herein, means stopping for the purpose of completing the loading or for partial unloading, not including the receipt of the original part of the shipment nor the final delivery at destination.

NOTE B: A party tendering or receiving freight at such places or addresses shall NOT be deemed a consignor or consignee.

NOTE C: Shipments of commodities in containers in which a refrigerant is placed by the shipper, or shipments of cheese, salad dressing, mayonnaise, sandwich spreads, oleomargarine, and yeast are NOT subject to the restrictions in paragraph (*j*), subparagraph (2).

NOTE D: On shipments moving from points in New York State in single-line hauls via Mushroom Transportation Co., Inc., or Shirks Motor Express Corp., Philadelphia, Pa., will be considered intermediate to Baltimore, Md., or Washington, D.C., in the application of this rule.

NOTE E: Shipments moving under refrigeration for local hauls via Chesapeake Motor Lines, Inc., Fowler & Williams, Inc., Greenleaf Motor Express (Note 1), Masten Trucking Co., Inc., Ontario Freight Lines Corp., Preston Trucking Company, Inc., Refrigerated Food Express, Inc., Rodgers Motor Lines, Inc., S&D Motor Lines, Inc., or Victor Lynn Lines, Inc., are NOT subject to the restriction in paragraph (*j*), sub-paragraphs (1) and (2). (Files R–513; P–2040, 2089, 2310, 3824, 3531, 3553; SR–727; P–4202; R–148; P–3829, 4448, 4449, 5732; M–779; P–6060; R–512).

SOURCE: Middle Atlantic Conference Freight Tariff 10–J, MF–ICC No. A–500

FIG. 11–2. Schedule of charges and conditions for stop-off privilege.

Under the stop-off privilege granted by carriers, it is possible to consolidate shipments to different customers in different cities. Perhaps a company in Pittsburgh receives a 12,500-pound order from a customer in Des Moines, Iowa, and an order of 17,500 pounds from a customer in Omaha, Nebraska. If shipped separately, the orders would move at the LCL or LTL rate; but using the stop-off privilege of unloading, they could be shipped as a carload or truckload from Pittsburgh to Omaha, with a stop-off in Des Moines. The shipper would pay the carload or truckload rate to Omaha, plus a modest stop-off charge.

An examination of rail tariffs will show that there are some commodities which are excluded from this stop-off privilege, such as freight in bulk, freight in tank cars, coke, and others. Cars which are stopped in transit to complete loading or to unload partially are subject to demurrage rules. Another common rule is that stop-offs to complete loading or to unload partially are not permitted on freight consigned to order, or order-notify, or otherwise so consigned as to require the surrender of the bill of lading. Where the stop-off privilege is involved, there is but a single bill of lading which is used from origin to destination.

Cars which are placed on connecting-line tracks at stop-off points are subject to connecting-line switching charges for both inbound and outbound switching movements, in addition to line-haul and stop-off charges. Some tariffs specifically provide for origin and destination territory, with the intermediate stations where the stop-offs will be permitted. The rules in some tariffs permit less-carload shipments, which are charged for at LCL rates, to be loaded by a shipper at the point of origin in the same car with a carload shipment billed to stop in transit to unload partially, if the less-carload shipment is consigned to the same party at the stop-off point as the carload portion, without additional stop-off charge. However, the weight of the less-carload shipment may not be used to make up the minimum weight of the carload shipment, and the unloading of the less-carload shipment must be accomplished by the party unloading the carload portion of the shipment at the stop-off point.

TRAP- AND FERRY-CAR SERVICE

"Trap car" or "ferry car" is a term used for a car placed at an industry or private sidetrack into which is loaded one or more less-carload shipments that may be switched to the freight station, or forwarded directly to the transfer point for rehandling or to destination; or cars containing one or more less-carload shipments switched from a freight station or directly on arrival at receiving yards to an industry which has a private sidetrack. Livestock, highly inflammable or combustible articles, powder, high explosives, and similar commodities cannot be handled in this manner.

Trap- or ferry-car service is furnished at stations named in the Official List of Open and Prepay Stations, where authorized by specific tariffs. No extra charge over regularly published less-carload rates is made on freight loaded in such cars, provided that such cars are loaded to specified minima or are loaded to full visible capacity. The following are examples of weight minima which might be used by a carrier:

1. Freight rated Class 250 or higher—2,500 pounds per car.
2. Freight rated Class 200—3,000 pounds per car.
3. Freight rated Class 150—4,500 pounds per car.
4. Freight rated Class 125—5,500 pounds per car.
5. Freight rated Class 100 or lower—6,000 pounds per car.
6. On mixed cars containing less than the minima required by items 1–5, the minimum weight will be based on the lowest-rated freight loaded in the

car, except that if there is sufficient weight of any one class of higher-rated freight to equal or exceed the minimum weight applicable thereto, as per items 1, 2, 3, or 4, this will govern.

7. On freight of light or bulky character, loaded to cubical or visible capacity of the car, or shipments too heavy to be handled at freight stations, including plate glass, boxed (in boxcars), iron or steel safes, loaded and blocked by shippers, and so forth, no minimum weight will be required.

8. When a trap or ferry car contains one or more single shipments of less than 100 pounds each, and charges on such single shipments are assessed on the basis of 100 pounds, the weight of each such single shipment will be computed at 100 pounds in arriving at the minimum weight of the trap or ferry car.

9. In case the actual weight of the shipment or shipments loaded in any trap or ferry car is not sufficient to entitle it to free switching, the shipper or consignee shall have the right to add to the actual weight of any shipment sufficient weight to bring the total weight up to the required minimum, with freight being charged on such final weight furnished. A proper notation showing how much the actual weight figures were increased must be made on the bill of lading and waybill covering outbound shipments.

The handling and movement of less-carload freight is facilitated by the use of trap or ferry cars, and this service is used quite extensively by large less-carload shippers. It is a service made available by the rail carriers to meet the needs of the shipping public.

Many of the larger industrial concerns had geared their freight handling to movement by railroads, and the trap- or ferry-car service could be made available and less-carload shipments handled very easily under this arrangement. In recent years, the dock facilities of the industrial concerns have been improved so that motor carriers can render service to and from plants without the congestion previously encountered. This factor has somewhat lessened the use of trap- and ferry-car service. Traffic managers of some of the larger plants have made arrangements with the railroads that serve them to load less-carload shipments in station order, thereby eliminating the necessity of sorting and handling at the local freight house; and these cars can be put right into the freight train.

PROTECTIVE SERVICES

There are numerous perishable articles, such as fresh fruits and vegetables, which require protection against heat or cold. It is necessary, under these circumstances, for the rail carriers to provide special equipment and service in order to maintain the proper temperature for the preservation of the perishable freight. Refrigerator cars or ventilator-type boxcars are two of the types of special equipment which are furnished for the handling of perishable freight, and there are a number of different types of heaters which are placed in cars to protect against cold. The protective services provided by railroads consist of icing, refrigeration, ventilating, or heater service. These special services are available only when provided for by a tariff; and each of the aforementioned services has a different rate or charge, which is dependent upon the type of service required for a particular commodity. Most of the protective services and charges are published by the National Perishable Freight Committee, and the current tariff is Perishable Protective Tariff No. 17 ICC No. 34.

It will be recalled that Rule 31 of Consolidated Freight Classification No. 23 and Uniform Freight Classification No. 6 indicates that carload ratings do not include the expense of refrigeration; nor do the ratings provided for freight in carloads obligate the carrier to furnish heated cars for freight requiring such protection, except under conditions which carriers' tariffs provide. Rule 32 of Consolidated Freight Classification No. 23 and Uniform Freight Classification No. 6 relates to ice or preservatives used for the protection of freight. The protective service charges are in addition to the line-haul transportation rates.

There are numerous rules in the tariff, and the shipper can select the type of service he desires, inasmuch as there are several classes of refrigeration. Standard refrigeration is protective service against heat by using ice, which is placed in the bunkers of a refrigeration car which has been furnished the shipper for loading, with re-icing en route whenever necessary. If the shipper desires a colder temperature, he may indicate the amount of salt to be added, and the carriers will supply this service in addition to the icing. The supplying of salt, however, is an extra service, and an additional charge is assessed. Where a mixed carload is shipped, the commodity on which the highest refrigeration charge applies governs the charge on the mixed carload.

Another rule covers top or body icing service, which permits shippers to put ice over the top of freight loaded in the car, in which case the shipper must specify on the bill of lading the quantity of ice to be used. The charges for this icing differ, depending upon the amount of ice used.

Another rule deals with precooling of citrus fruits which originate at western points. The precooling of a shipment is a means by which it is cooled after loading into the car. Where precooling is performed by the carrier, it usually is done by means of a mechanically operated fan which circulates air within the car. The shipper can provide precooling, and this is done in many instances. Pre-icing refers to icing the bunkers of an empty car before it is placed for loading and, technically, is not precooling. The charges for the carrier's precooling are provided from origin to destination, and the shipper has to specify on the bill of lading the kind of service desired.

One section of the Perishable Protective Tariff contains rules governing ventilation service. By manipulating the hatch covers of refrigeration cars and the doors and windows of ventilator-type boxcars, the amount of air which can go through the cars can be controlled. This makes possible some control over the temperature or moisture content inside the car. The rules provide that the shipper must show on the bill of lading the class of ventilation services desired.

Contained in the tariff to protect against cold, the Perishable Protective Tariff defines the so-called "heater" territory, which is generally the area of the north-central part of the United States extending to Cincinnati, Ohio, in the East and South, and to some of the more northern California points in the West. The carriers can protect against cold by operating heaters in the bunkers of refrigerator cars. Shippers can request this service, which is usually at a given charge per car per trip, although on some commodities between certain points, protective service against cold is compulsory.

The rules provide for shippers' protective service, shippers' specified service, and carriers' protective service. The latter is that in which the carriers are responsible for exercising good judgment in controlling the temperature in the car. In the shippers' protective service, the shipment is tendered to the carrier with the heaters furnished, installed, and initially fueled by the shipper, and the carrier then follows bill-of-lading instructions on proper heating. In the shippers' specified service, the carriers will furnish heaters at certain stations, and the shippers specify instructions for proper heating on the bill of lading. Another section of this tariff covers rules and charges for the furnishing of dry refrigerator cars, which are used for the transportation of evergreens, holly, bulbs, tubers, potatoes, and shelled peanuts which originate in the Southern Territory. The provision of these dry refrigeration cars will be at charges in dollars and cents per car furnished and is in addition to the line-haul rate.

Motor carriers provide protective services of a similar nature. Special equipment is available and the services are covered by tariff provisions.

ELEVATION

A special service which is offered by rail carriers in connection with the movement of grain is elevation. There are two types of elevation:

1. Transportation elevation, which consists of passing the grain through an elevator for the purpose of transferring it from car to car and ascertaining its weight. This type of elevation is an incident to the transportation of grain.

2. Commercial elevation, which involves various processes in the treatment of grain itself, such as cleaning, mixing, clipping, drying, and the like. This type of elevation is an incident to the merchandising of grain.[5]

The Interstate Commerce Act, Part I, provides that the term "transportation" includes " . . . all instrumentalities and facilities of shipment or carriage . . . and all services in connection with the receipt, delivery, elevation and transfer in transit, ventilation, refrigeration or icing, storage and handling of property transported." From the foregoing, it should be noted that elevation is a service required by the act. Transportation elevation is an obligation of the carriers, whereas commercial elevation is

[5] *In the Matter of Elevation Allowances at Points Located upon the Missouri, Mississippi, and Ohio Rivers and on the Great Lakes*, 24 ICC 197, 199 (1912).

not, although it is beneficial to the shipper, and carriers may furnish commercial elevation. Where commercial elevation is provided by a carrier, such service and the charges are contained in a tariff. The railroad does not have to own the elevator but may enter into a contract providing for transportation elevation. Where the carrier has transportation elevation provided for it by a shipper or an elevator operator, a reasonable allowance may be given by the carrier for such service.

STORAGE

Storage is a service in connection with transportation and is an actual part of transportation service only to the extent of normal and necessary holding of property during the movement and for the period normally required to make delivery. Demurrage charges are assessed for the detention of freight cars; and like these charges, carriers' storage charges are established to discourage consignees or owners of goods from permitting shipments to remain in the possession of the carrier unnecessarily, which will easily lead to congestion of freight. Demurrage is assessed on the basis of a specified amount per car-day, whereas storage applies strictly to the freight itself, with charges assessed on the basis of so much per 100 pounds per day for the time the freight remains on carriers' premises beyond the expiration of a specified free time.

Storage generally is thought of as only applying to less-carload shipments warehoused by carriers before transportation service has begun or after it has been completed; but under certain conditions, storage also applies to carload shipments. Whether or not the shipment subject to storage charges is carload or less-carload, the liability of the carrier is merely that of a warehouseman and not a common carrier. The daily storage is assessed on the basis of an upward sliding scale, dependent upon the time the freight remains on the carrier's premises. Under the bill-of-lading terms, the carrier can remove a shipment from its premises and place it in public storage, where it will be held without liability on the part of the carrier and subject to a lien for freight and other lawful charges, which could include a reasonable charge for storage.

Section 4 (a) of the Uniform Bill of Lading Contract Terms and Conditions provides that the consignee or owner of the freight agrees to remove goods promptly after their arrival at destination; and if he is unable to do so, he obligates himself for the payment of storage charges which will be assessed.

The storage of property by a common carrier may be voluntary storage, which is a type not contemplated by any conditions incorporated in the uniform bill of lading. Such services would result from the mutual consent of the parties and are performed on a for-hire basis. Involuntary storage is the storage by carriers of freight which is transported for hire and is a service necessarily incident to the transportation of such property.

There are two kinds of carload storage: (1) track storage, when the shipment remains in a rail car; and (2) warehouse or ground storage, when the shipment is unloaded and placed in or on the premises of the railroad. Track storage charges and rules differ at various terminals. Under certain conditions, track storage will be in addition to demurrage; while under certain other conditions, it will be in lieu of demurrage. Carriers also may provide ground storage free of charge, subject to the owner's risk. Certain shipments, such as export or import freight at the port of export or import and domestic shipments received from or intended for movement by ocean or lake vessels while at the port of transshipment, may not be subject to storage charges for warehousing while awaiting transportation service beyond the port. As there are no standard rules and charges for carload storage, current carriers' tariffs covering storage must be checked.

In addition to the types of storage discussed, there is both private and public warehousing, which includes storage and other service aspects.

The storage rules and charges which are published in Freight Tariff No. 4F, H. R. Hinsch, Agent, naming car demurrage rules and charges, and storage rules and charges, are uniform, but there are some exceptions. Other tariffs, both agency and individual issues, contain storage rules and charges that apply particularly in certain localities, and such tariffs should be consulted where applicable. The rules and charges in the Car Demurrage and Storage Tariff do not apply on freight stored in warehouses owned and operated by railroads as exclusively storage warehouses; export and import freight at the port of export or import; domestic freight received from or intended for delivery to ocean or lake vessels at the port of transshipment and freight subject to lighterage at seaboard points, when other rules and charges applicable thereto are provided in the tariffs of an individual railroad; carload lots of coal, coke, or ore; freight refused or unclaimed when and for the time held for the convenience of a railroad beyond legal requirements; and less-carload freight, until it is loaded into cars or after it is unloaded from cars at a nonagency station.

One of the rules of the storage tariff specifies the furnishing of notice. If a consignee or party entitled to receive freight is not given a notice of arrival or, in the case of a consignor, notice of the shipment being unclaimed or refused by the consignee or the party entitled to receive it, collection of storage charges ordinarily would be unlawful. This notice is to be given within 24 hours after the arrival of the shipment for billing at destination. Where refused or unclaimed freight is held by the carrier, the consignor has to be notified within 24 hours after refusal of less-carload shipments.

Notice within 24 hrs

TRACING AND EXPEDITING

Tracing

The traffic manager may need to trace shipments. Tracing is usually started when a shipment is delayed en route. Tracing bureaus are maintained by many carriers, whereas others have a particular department that

TABLE 11-2

Tracing and Expediting Data

Freight Forwarder	LCL	CL	Railway Express	LTL-TL	Air
Material.	Material.	Material.	Material.	Material.	Material.
No. of pcs.	No. of pcs.		No. of pcs.	No. of pcs.	No. of pcs.
Weight.	Weight.		Weight.	Weight.	Weight.
Fwdrs bill of lading reference.	Waybill No.		Waybill No.	Pro No.	Airbill No.
Date shipped.	Date shipped.	Date shipped.	Date shipped.	Date shipped.	Date shipped.
	Car No.	Car No.—Train No.	Car No.—Train No.	Truck No.	Flight No.
	Point car carded.	Classification pt.	Point car carded.	Interchange or freight point.	Transfer.
Route.	Route.	Route.		Route.	Route.
Consignor.	Consignor.	Consignor.	Consignor.	Consignor.	Consignor.
Consignee.	Consignee.	Consignee.	Consignee.	Consignee.	Consignee.
Origin.	Origin.	Origin.	Origin.	Origin.	Origin.
Destination.	Destination.	Destination.	Destination.	Destination.	Destination.
				Name of driver.	Airport.

ORDER FOR TRACING

To _____

   TRAFFIC DEPARTMENT

From _____

_____

ROOM	PHONE	DATE

DATE SHIPPED	WAYBILL NO. (IF LCL OR LTL)
SHIPMENT CONSISTING OF	
SHIPPED BY	FROM
CONSIGNED TO	AT
CAR INITIAL AND NO.	CARDED TO (IF LCL OR LTL)
COMPLETE ROUTING	
REMARKS	

(DO NOT WRITE BELOW HERE)

SHIPMENT DELIVERED	TIME	DATE
	PER	

FIG. 11–3.   An example of a tracing order.

handles this work. The traffic manager will have a tracing order which contains space for information that will be helpful in tracing the shipment, a copy of which is shown in Figure 11–3. The carrier is supplied the necessary information and traces the shipment, reporting results to the traffic manager. Less-carload shipments are handled similarly to carload, except that a "waybilling reference" must be first obtained from the originating carrier's "less-carload tracing clerk," and this information is used in the same way a car number is used for tracing.

For both tracing and expediting, the carrier must have certain basic information. In so far as it is possible, the following information should be forwarded to the carrier with the request for tracing or expediting: shipper, origin, consignee, destination, date shipped, commodity, release or route number, route, car initial and number, waybill number and bill-of-lading date and number. Table 11–2 lists information that will be helpful in tracing and expediting via the different transportation services. Some carriers are using computers in car tracing, which greatly facilitate this action.

Truckload shipments and less-truckload shipments are referred to the originating motor carrier's tracing bureau, which furnishes a "pro" (which is the abbreviation of "progressive") number corresponding to a waybill number and a trailer number. Additional information may be required. Sometimes, a connecting carrier will have its own billing reference, which supersedes the original "pro" in following the shipment from carrier to carrier.

Parcel post and express shipments generally cannot be traced, as no records are kept by the Post Office or the Express Company for this purpose. However, express shipments moving on high-value receipts may be traced, as the Express Company gets a receipt for each handling all the way from origin to consignee.

Air express, air freight, and air freight forwarder shipments may be traced by calling the originating air line's tracing bureau.

Expediting

The expediting of shipments is a service performed frequently by a traffic department or section. It may involve the expediting of shipments to other departments of the company in order to keep an assembly line moving, or it may involve shipments to customers which they are desirous of receiving in a hurry. The shipment to be expedited in a given situation may be one that is in transit, or it may not have left the origin point. These are facts that will have to be ascertained by the person attempting to expedite the shipment. In many firms, a particular individual is assigned to the job of expediting shipments, since knowledge of the different carriers' operations and the information needed by carriers to find and expedite a particular shipment are invaluable.

The arrangements for expediting differ somewhat according to the volume of the shipment and the mode of transportation concerned. When carload freight is to be expedited, the normal procedure would be to contact the agent's office or the car service or car record office of the carrier. Urgent matters may be handled by a call to the yardmaster's office of the carrier to assure that the car is forwarded on the first train that is available. If the car has been shipped and is in transit, the yardmaster may be able to arrange for a special switch for the car.

Less-carload freight is frequently transferred more than once in transit, which may result in delays. In expediting outbound less-carload freight, the local agent should be contacted to see if the freight can be loaded the same day that it has been picked up from the consignor. It is well to ask the local agent on inbound shipments to have the car in which the freight is contained unloaded promptly and arrange to have it placed on the first available truck. If this cannot be accomplished, arrangements should be made to have a company truck there to pick it up and deliver it.

Usually, a truckload of freight will proceed to its destination without being transferred while in transit. After securing the necessary information for truckloads of freight, the traffic expediter should inform the consignee of the scheduled arrival time, the driver's name, and the tractor and trailer number. There should be frequent checking by the expediter to make sure that the truck goes forward as promised.

Less-truckload shipments may be transferred while in transit, so it is important to know the transfer point or point of interchange so as to insure that the shipment continues on the first available load. If a shipment is to be expedited, care should be taken to insure that it is loaded in the rear if it is to be delivered first, or placed in the truck first if it is to be unloaded last. While these are matters considered by trucking companies in their loading, extra care in this regard may mean greater speed in delivery.

The procedure to be used for the other agencies of transportation may vary somewhat, but the basic information contained in Table 11–2 on expediting and tracing should be supplied, and the person or persons to contact with each carrier should be determined.

Extensive use is made of expediting by traffic departments which use private cars. This accounts in part for the high utilization of such cars.

Expediting is most successful when arrangements are started prior to the movement of the shipment. However, even when the shipment is en route, expediting can be effective and is usually handled by telephone or telegram. A card record of each case of expediting should be maintained, in order to show what action was taken, as well as to ascertain how effective it is.

DISCUSSION QUESTIONS AND PROBLEMS

1. To what tariff conditions are diversion and reconsignment privileges made subject by the carriers?
2. Why are nonperishable commodities, where authorized by the tariff, permitted but a single change in destination under the diversion and reconsignment privilege?
3. Ascertain from carrier agents in your area some examples of out-of-route service in connection with diversion and reconsignment privileges, and the competitive situations responsible.
4. Who can divert or reconsign a shipment? Are straight or order bills of lading generally used? Why?
5. What is the stop-off privilege? What are the typical conditions of the rail stop-off privilege?
6. Compare the provisions of rail and motor carriers regarding the stop-off privilege.
7. What is the purpose of trap- or ferry-car service? Is it of greater or lesser importance today as compared with twenty-five years ago? Why?
8. Are there special charges for protective services? Describe some of the different types of protective services.
9. Carefully explain what is meant by elevation. What is the obligation of the carrier in elevation?
10. What are the duties of a carrier in connection with storage? Name and explain the types of carload storage.
11. If you were traffic or physical distribution manager of an automobile assembly plant, how would you set up tracing and expediting?
12. Traffic managers make extensive use of expediting in the movement of their private cars. Why?

Chapter

12

TRANSIT PRIVILEGES

A MOST important special service, and one which possesses many technical aspects, is the transit privilege. Although it is basically a special service or arrangement which has been developed and offered by the railroads, there is an increasing number of transit privileges granted by motor carriers. The first recorded transit privilege, in 1870, covered the rebilling and reshipping of grain. The transit privilege applicable to grain is probably the one most extensively used at the present time. It enables many small communities with small flour mills to be placed on a parity, transportationwise, with larger mills located at some of the larger cities. Although the transit privilege is applicable to many commodities, a general guide as to the commodities on which transit has been granted or may be granted is that it generally applies to commodities that receive the same rating or rates, or approximately the same rating or rates, in the forms in which they are shipped to and from the transit point.

RAIL[1]

The establishment of transit privileges permits the movement of many different commodities from origin to final destination, with a stop at an intermediate point, where the commodities are unloaded, stored, processed, reloaded, and reforwarded. Actually, there are two separate transportation movements involved, but the transportation from origin to final destination is considered to be an interrupted through movement. Instead of applying the sum of local freight rates to and from the point at which the stop is made, the through rate from origin to final destination is charged, plus a separate nominal charge termed a "transit charge."

[1] A comprehensive study of rail transit privileges is contained in R. V. Hobbah, "Railroad Transit Privileges," Supplement to Vol. XVII, No. 3 (1944), of the *Journal of Business of the University of Chicago.*

Transit charges must be authorized by tariffs and generally apply to a given quantity, usually a carload of a commodity. In many instances, where the commodity reaches the transit point, at which point some manufacturing or commercial processing to that commodity is accomplished, the final destination may not be known to the shipper or the carrier. There are a number of reasons for the establishment of transit privileges: (1) industrial competition, (2) carrier competition, and (3) facilitation of a free movement of traffic.

The following illustration indicates the general nature of a transit privilege and the benefits which can be derived from it.[2] Transit is considered as it affects a carload of grain or grain products which is moved from Springfield, Illinois, to Chicago, at which point it is milled and the product reshipped to Philadelphia. In this illustration, the rate from Springfield to Chicago is 17½ cents per 100 pounds. From Chicago to Philadelphia, the local rate on grain is 48½ cents. In the absence of a transit privilege, the miller at Chicago would pay the sum of these two rates, or 66 cents. Railroads, however, have provided a through rate from Springfield to Philadelphia, via Chicago, which rate is 53½ cents. The establishment of the transit privilege at Chicago enables the Chicago miller to use this through rate, since at the time of the movement to the transit point, Chicago, the local freight rate is paid.

Upon reshipment from Chicago, the difference between the local rate paid into Chicago and the through rate from origin, Springfield, to final destination, Philadelphia, is paid. This difference is the transit balance rate; and in this illustration from Chicago to Philadelphia, it is 36 cents (53½ cents less 17½ cents), instead of the local rate of 48½ cents, which would have been applicable if the transit privilege had not been granted. The effect of such an arrangement is that a miller in Chicago is on an equal basis, from a transportation standpoint, with a miller in Springfield or Philadelphia. This enables him to penetrate the Philadelphia market area in competition with the Springfield or Philadelphia millers, assuming that each secures his grain products in the Springfield area. The Springfield grain producer has a market for his grain in Chicago as well as in Springfield and Philadelphia, and the purchaser of flour in Philadelphia can secure it not only from Springfield and Philadelphia but also from Chicago. Figure 12-1 (p. 308) shows how the transit privilege works in this case.

The competition between carriers, as well as between industries, is present in the consideration of transit privileges. For example, a city which is served directly on a main line by a railroad may be established as a transit point by one railroad. A second rail carrier may serve this same city, although not directly, since the city is located on a branch line which

---

[2] The rates quoted are those which were applicable in 1948. Subcommittee of Senate Interstate and Foreign Commerce Committee, *Study of Pricing Methods*, 80th Congress, 2d session (Washington, D.C.: U.S. Government Printing Office, 1948), p. 1010, Appendix, p. 3.

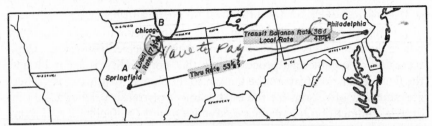

SOURCE: Subcommittee of Senate Interstate and Foreign Commerce Committee, *Study of Pricing Methods*, 80th Congress, 2d session (Washington, D.C.: U.S. Government Printing Office, 1948), Appendix, p. 3.

FIG. 12–1. An example of a transit privilege.

extends from the latter railroad's main line. In the latter case, a through rate would not apply via the branch-line point; yet, this railroad desires to participate in the traffic; it accomplishes this by establishing a provision in the transit tariff to the effect that rates are applicable via the main-line point closest to the branch-line point, and no charge will be made for the out-of-route or back haul. The following illustration is an example of such a situation. In this case, a shipment for transit at *B* and

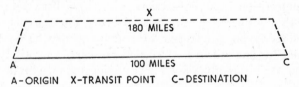

reshipment to *C* would go to *X*, then to *B*, back to *X*, then on to *C*. The back haul would be that from *B* to *X*. Some tariffs provide that in such cases, the through rate from *A* to *C* will be protected without extra charge, although other tariffs provide an extra charge that is generally based on a mileage scale.

　　In other instances, a transit privilege might be established on a branch line and a provision placed in the tariff that the branch-line point will be considered as a main-line point; and a reasonable out-of-route charge will be established for the branch-line service. A shipper on a branch line, therefore, might be in a better position competitively with a main-line-point shipper. The following diagram is an example of an out-of-line or out-of-route shipment which is accorded transit at a transit point that is not on a direct route or a route that would normally be used between origin and destination. A direct shipment from *A* to *C* would travel 100

```
                       X
    r-----------------------------------¬
   /             180 MILES               \
  /                                        \
 /                                          \
 L------------------------------------------- 
A                 100 MILES                   C

A-ORIGIN   X-TRANSIT POINT   C-DESTINATION
```

miles, while a shipment transited at *X* and reshipped to *C* would travel 180 miles, or a distance of 80 miles out of the usually traveled route. This 80 miles is the out-of-route portion of the haul. Some tariffs provide that no extra charge shall be made for this service, while other tariffs provide for charges similar to the back-haul scale of charges.

Another competitive aspect of the transit privilege relates to switching. If a transit operator's plant is served by one carrier but other carriers at that point have access to the plant by absorption of the inbound and outbound reciprocal switching charges of the railroad serving the plant, there is usually a rule in the transit or switching tariffs providing for such absorption of switching charges due to the competitive elements.

Rules Governing Transit Privileges

The transit privilege is granted by an individual railroad, and a party seeking the privilege is required to make written application to the railroad. Transit tariffs contain differing rules governing the application of transit privileges which can be divided into two general groups: application rules and policing rules.

Application Rules

Transit tariffs ordinarily have as one of the first application rules the description of the inbound commodity or commodities, which restricts the transit privilege to the commodity or commodities named. This rule, like all other application rules, may be worded differently in different tariffs, as the application rules are not uniform, although substantially the same.

Another rule is that concerned with the definition of the transit process permitted, which will specifically state the manner and extent of the process. The next rule is a description of the form or condition in which the inbound commodity or commodities may be reshipped after having been processed. The latter two rules are quite similar.

Another factor which is stressed covers the point or points where the transit applies. This may be a specific city or some other specified point. The territorial application of the transit tariff is contained in the next rule and covers the origin territory of the inbound commodity or commodities and the destination territory of the outbound commodity or commodities. This enables carriers, through concurrences, to participate in the movement of commodities which are accorded transit privileges in a rate territory other than the point of origin or point of destination.

The charge which is established for the transit privilege is indicated in the next rule. This charge is in addition to the through transportation rate. It is a nominal charge and is generally applicable, although there are some railroads which assess no transit charge. It usually is quoted in cents per 100 pounds, but sometimes it is established on a per-car basis. Some transit tariffs require that the transit charge be collected on the inbound shipment, whereas others specify that the charge applies on the outbound shipment.

The next rule establishes the time period which is allowed for the transit privilege. The time period most generally used is that of 12 months. On occasion, the shipper may not be able to ship the transit freight out within the maximum time period, in which case some rules provide an extension of an additional 12-month period, if there is justification. Where the extension is granted, it is usually subject to a penalty charge of so many cents per 100 pounds.

The rate which is applicable is contained in the next rule; and unless otherwise stated, the through rate applies from origin to destination. It is important, in this connection, to ascertain that the through rate is applicable via the transit point, for a transit privilege does not broaden the scope and application of a rate tariff unless there is incorporated in the transit tariff a specific provision whereby the through rate in the rate tariff can be used in connection with transit. The rate rule often applies a so-called "two-way" application. On some commodities, a higher rate would apply after processing than would apply on the commodity when it is a raw material. The rule in the transit tariff ordinarily will provide that the through rate to be applied is the higher of the two if a difference exists between the through rates on the commodity in its unprocessed and processed condition. Some transit tariffs provide a further refinement, which is referred to as the "three-way" rate rule. The following three rates are concerned in a situation of this kind: (1) through rate from point of origin to final destination, (2) rate from point of origin to transit point, and (3) rate from transit point to final destination. The highest of these rates will be applied on the transit movement. The most widely used of the rate rules is the application of the through rate from origin to destination. The through rate is the one which is in effect on the date the inbound shipment left the point of origin, and a transit tariff could not be applied unless it was in effect on the date the inbound shipment left the point of origin.

The miscellaneous rules or provisions are the last of the application rules. One of the miscellaneous rules of importance is that defining nontransit commodities or tonnage. A typical nontransit commodity rule provides that the term "nontransit commodities" named in the separate sections of the tariff means commodities which, because of tariff limitations, are not subject to transit rates, namely: (1) transit commodities upon which the time limit for the transit privilege has expired, (2) transit commodities originating at or purchased locally at the transit point, (3) transit commodities originating at points not subject to the transit rate via or from the transit point, and (4) transit commodities destined to points not subject to transit rates via or from the transit point.

A further provision concerning nontransit commodities can provide that when outbound shipments consist of a mixture (not physical) of transit commodities and nontransit commodities which are also named as transit commodities in the same car, the identity of transit and nontransit having been preserved, the transit carload rate applicable on the transit portion, according to the representative inbound transit freight bills surrendered, and the local carload rate from the transit point on the non-transit portion, respectively, will apply. The entire carload is subject to the highest carload minimum weight applying on any commodity in the car (actual weight, if in excess thereof). Any deficiency in weight will be added to the nontransit portion.

The foregoing rule permits transit and nontransit commodities to be shipped where there is no physical mixture in a mixed carload from the transit point. If a mixed carload of transit and nontransit tonnage is shipped, the transit tonnage involving a less-carload quantity secures the benefit of a through carload rate from origin to final destination; and the less-carload quantity of nontransit tonnage is paid for at the local carload rate from the transit point to final destination. On certain commodities which have been processed, the transit operation includes both transit and nontransit tonnage in an outbound carload shipment from the transit point; and the rule just described allows a lower rate than otherwise would be the case.

[handwritten margin note: Not physical mixed, both rates.]

Some transit tariffs have a further refinement of the mixture rule which provides for mixed shipments of transit, nontransit, and other commodities. When this rule is in the tariff, a mixture of transit, nontransit, and other commodities is permitted; and the latter group, which is in less-carload quantities, is charged at the local carload rate from the transit point to final destination provided, with some exceptions, that this weight is not used to make up the minimum weight applicable on the transit tariff or transit and nontransit commodities which comprise the majority of the mixed-carload shipment. There are other miscellaneous rules that may be found, but the ones which have been mentioned are representative of this particular kind of rule.

Policing Rules

The second group of rules found in transit tariffs is usually referred to as "policing" rules. The Commission has stated that "transit arrangements rest upon the fiction that the incoming and outgoing transportation services, while distinct, are applied to a continuous shipment from origin to destination. Movements to and from the transit point are parts of a through move upon which a through rate ultimately is collected. . . ."[3]

The stop which is made may be for as long a period as twelve months, so that it becomes necessary, with the granting of as liberal a privilege as the transit privilege, to insure adequate policing. The carriers therefore specify, in their transit tariffs, rules covering policing which permit inspection, establish the necessary record keeping, and other similar requirements. The Commission, in 1954, after a preliminary survey, indicated that rail transit policing "left something to be desired." The policing

---

[3] *Fredonia Linseed Oil Works Co.* v. *Atchison, T. & S. F. Ry. Co.,* 201 ICC 40 (1934).

rules are enforced by the weighing and inspection bureaus in the various railroad freight association territories.

Types of Transit Privileges

There are many transit privileges which have been granted, one of the most unusual of which the author has found is the stopping of beef to be blessed in transit as part of a religious ritual. Some of the primary privileges are described as follows:

1. The privilege of storage in transit permits the stopping, unloading into storage or warehouses (transit houses) for storage, and reforwarding only when in straight or mixed carloads. Storage-in-transit arrangements cover many different commodities, such as agricultural implements, alcohol, coffee, dairy products, frozen fish, foodstuffs (canned or preserved), fresh and frozen fruits, grain, sugar, wool, and the like.

2. Fabrication in transit is another type which permits the stopping and unloading at fabrication points of carload shipments of certain iron and steel articles for any of the following purposes:

Bending	Gagging	Shearing
Bolting	Painting	Straightening
Boring	Planing	Tapping
Burning	Punching	Threading
Countersinking	Reaming	Welding
Drilling	Riveting	Zinc coating
Flanging	Sawing	

Reshipping follows in carloads in an unfinished state, knocked down, to destination territories provided for in applicable tariffs.

The privilege of stopping inbound material for the purposes specified above is accorded on the following articles of iron and steel in carloads:

Angles	Columns	Rivets
Bars	Ells	Rods
Beams	Girders	Tees
Bolts	Masts	Trusses
Castings	Nuts	Washers
Channels	Plates	Zees

It should be noted that the fabricating processes do not permit the complete manufacture of a finished iron and steel commodity. Its purpose is to allow the conversion of specified iron and steel articles into semifinished materials for use in certain types of construction.

3. Transit on lumber and forest products is another of the types of transit. This is accorded to lumber and other forest products taking lumber rates or related to lumber rates as designated in a tariff publishing the rate, with certain woods excepted. Cooperage stock (consisting of staves, heading, hoops, and head liners), shingles, poles, lath, shavings, and sawdust, consisting of carloads, may be stopped in transit for the purpose of (a) dressing, drying, glueing, sorting, planing, preserving by treating,

resawing, or storing; (*b*) fabrication into box material, crate material, or box shooks, including wirebound box and crate material; also fabrication into plywood which in turn is fabricated into box material, crate material, or box shooks; (*c*) manufacturing into flooring blocks and squares, not polished, varnished, or waxed, not exceeding eighteen inches in length, consisting of two or more pieces of lumber or wood flooring, with or without paper backing, or reinforced with dowel pins or metal or wooden splines, but not inlaid; and (*d*) manufacturing into flooring.

4. Refining in transit, another of the kinds of transit, is permitted on oils and oil foods, such as cocoanut, corn, cottonseed, fish, linseed, palm, peanut, soybean, and the like, which may be stopped and subjected to one or more of the following: (*a*) refining, (*b*) solidifying (hydrogenating), except fish oils; (*c*) blending; (*d*) storing or packaging; (*e*) dehydrating (castor oil only); and (*f*) modifying (linseed oil only); and be reshipped to destination as provided by governing tariffs.

5. Miscellaneous transit privileges such as cutting, freezing, grading, and reconditioning butter; blending, grinding, and roasting coffee; grading, recandling, and shelling eggs; and blending and bottling wine.

6. The transit privilege on grain and grain products is extensively used and, in terms of the tonnage, is one of the most important transit privileges. One kind of grain cannot be substituted for another kind, but substitution has been permitted of one grade of wheat for another grade of wheat and one color of corn for another color of corn. Some of the numerous transit privileges on grain are outlined as follows:

a) Storage of grain. Grain may be stopped for unloading into elevators and warehouses (transit houses) for a number of different purposes, such as storage, treating, drying, cleaning, clipping, grading, mixing, or sacking, after which the grain or its equivalent is reshipped to destination.

b) Inspection of grain. Grain carloads screenings from grain, unground, meeting certain requirements as to content, are placed on hold tracks and notice of location sent to the consignee, or posted on bulletin boards where such is the practice, for the purpose of inspection and disposition. This inspection is the taking of a representative sample or samples and establishing the official grade of the contents of the car by competent and impartial authority independent of both vendor and vendee and only in accordance with national or state Board of Trade or Grain Exchange authorization or requirements.

A disposition order on a car held by a consignee after arrival means a specific order for each individual car, showing number and initials, given to the carrier in writing or to be confirmed in writing after inspection has been made, which authorizes (1) immediate tender of the car for unloading at the station where the inspection was made, or (2) the immediate reforwarding of the car to a connecting line or to another destination.

c) Milling in transit. Under this arrangement, grains such as corn, oats, rye, wheat, buckwheat, barley, and the like may be shipped and stopped for unloading into mills, elevators, and warehouses (transit houses) for any of a number of purposes, such as milling, malting, brewing, distilling, or otherwise converting into products, and reshipped in straight or mixed carloads to destination provided for in tariffs. Under the milling process, the whole grains are converted into various grain products and by-products.

d) Mixing in transit. Mixing arrangements permit the grinding, screening, storage, mixing, blending, repacking, shelling, or converting of grains into various kinds of feed, and reshipment in straight or mixed carloads to destinations provided for in tariffs.

A through-rate transit arrangement of the milling in transit of wheat is described to illustrate such a transit arrangement: The transit tariff will state that carload shipments of wheat originating at point *A* may be milled in transit at point *B*, and the product of the wheat may be shipped to point *C*. The tariff will state that the wheat must be billed from origin to the transit point at the flat rate (usually called the "local rate") and that the shipment of the flour from the transit point to destination will be charged the difference between what was paid on the inbound shipment and the rate on flour from origin *A* to destination *C*. It will be assumed that the transit tariff states, in effect, that an equal amount of tonnage may be shipped from the transit point as was received by rail at the transit point from point *A*.

Suppose the carload rate on wheat from *A* to *B* is 20 cents per 100 pounds, minimum weight 80,000 pounds. It will also be assumed that the carload rate on flour from *A* to *C* is 30 cents per 100 pounds, minimum weight 35,000 pounds. The shipment of wheat from *A* to *B* weighed 80,000 pounds; 10,000 pounds of wheat is wasted through the process of milling; and two shipments of flour, each weighing 35,000 pounds, were shipped from *B* to *C*. On the inbound shipment of wheat, the shipper would pay $160 per car, and the miller would have 80,000 pounds of wheat in his transit account. If he ships one car of flour weighing 35,000 pounds, he pays 10 cents per 100 pounds, the difference between what he paid in on 35,000 pounds of wheat (20 cents per 100 pounds) and the rate of flour from *A* to *C*.

What is left in the transit account after the above shipment of flour? There were 80,000 pounds shipped into the transit point, and 10,000 pounds were wasted in the manufacture of the flour. (Transit tariffs applicable to milling of wheat into flour usually have a cancellation of but 2 or 3 per cent for loss in milling, since bran and middlings go out as mill feed or grain products on the grain or grain products rates). The tariffs usually require that the amount of material wasted because of the manufacturing process be canceled from the amount of tonnage available for transit. Therefore, from the 80,000 pounds of wheat, 10,000 pounds of wastage is deducted, and the 35,000 pounds of flour are shipped. This leaves 35,000 pounds still in the transit account, against which 35,000 pounds of flour may be shipped. When the second car of flour is shipped, it will move out at the difference between what was paid in on wheat and the rate on flour from *A* to *C*.

The carrier's compensation was:

Inbound shipment $160
First outbound shipment 35
Second outbound shipment 35
$230

The carrier received the same revenue it would have received if two cars of flour had been shipped from *A* to *C* at the rate of flour and 10,000 pounds of wheat (the amount wasted) had been shipped from *A* to *B* at the carload rate, disregarding the minimum weight attached to the wheat rate, thus:

First car of flour from *A* to *C* (35,000 pounds @ 30¢)............ $105
Second car of flour from *A* to *C* 105
10,000 pounds of wheat from *A* to *B* @ 20¢ .... 20 — *lost.*
$230

The effect of the transit arrangement is to place the flour manufacturer at point *B* on a competitive basis with the flour manufacturer at point *A*. Both manufacturers pay 30 cents per 100 pounds to have their flour transported to point *C*.

What would be the situation if there were no transit arrangement in effect at point *B*? The shipment of wheat from *A* to *B* would be considered one shipment, and the two shipments of flour from *B* to *C* would be considered totally separate and apart from the wheat shipment. What difference would there be in the transportation cost? The rate on wheat from *A* to *B* was 20 cents per 100 pounds, and it will be assumed that the rate on flour from *B* to *C* is 20 cents per 100 pounds, minimum weight 35,000 pounds. In the absence of transit, the following would be the charges:

Wheat, *A* to *B*.. $160
Flour, *B* to *C*.. 70
Flour, *B* to *C*—second car 70
$300

The transit privilege then resulted in a saving of $70 on this one car of wheat.

The example cited is one of the most simple ones. A somewhat more complicated one will now be considered. In this case, there are three origin points, one transit point, and one destination. The transit privilege allowed will be galvanizing of iron and steel.

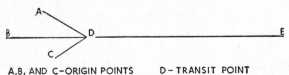

A,B, AND C—ORIGIN POINTS   D—TRANSIT POINT
E—DESTINATION

The minimum weight will be the same from all origins to the transit point and the destination, with a minimum weight of 50,000 pounds. The following rates will be used:

A to D	20 cents per 100 pounds
B to D	25 cents per 100 pounds
C to D	15 cents per 100 pounds
A to E	40 cents per 100 pounds
B to E	50 cents per 100 pounds
C to E	30 cents per 100 pounds
D to E	20 cents per 100 pounds

A minimum carload shipment of iron and steel articles moved from each origin to the transit point. This means that there are 150,000 pounds of iron and steel in the transit house. It will be assumed that the transit process, galvanizing, adds 2 per cent to the weight of the iron and steel, and that the transit tariff states that any weight added in transit shall be considered nontransit tonnage and shall be subject to the carload rate from the transit point to destination. The transit operator ships a carload shipment from D to E which weighs 51,000 pounds and surrenders the following billing:

A to D	10,000 pounds
B to D	5,000 pounds
C to D	35,000 pounds
	50,000 pounds

The differences between the rates paid into the transit point and the rates from origin to destination are:

A to E 40¢ minus A to D 20¢ = 20 cents
B to E 50¢ minus B to D 25¢ = 25 cents
C to E 30¢ minus C to D 15¢ = 15 cents

The outbound shipment from the transit point would be rated:

TRANSIT
10,000 lbs. @ 20¢ = $20.00
5,000 lbs. @ 25¢ = 12.50
35,000 lbs. @ 15¢ = 52.50

NONTRANSIT
1,000 lbs. @ 20¢ = 2.00

Unit and Split Billing

In this example, the carrier permits the use of tonnage from several origins to make up one outbound car from the transit point and permits the surrender of billing from several points. This is known as "split billing." In some cases, the carriers only permit surrender of billing from one origin to cover the outbound car, even though the outbound car may contain articles from several different origins. This is known as "unit billing." In some instances, the tariffs limit the number of split billings to an outbound car to a certain number, such as 3 or 5. In the last example, there were three splits. However, some transit tariffs are unlimited, and an outbound car from the transit point may be subject to inbound billing from 10 or 20 different origins. When tonnage from 20 different origins is surrendered for one outbound car, the billing of the shipment becomes quite complicated.

The examples just described dealt with what is known as "balance-out transit" or "balance-of-the-through-rate system." That is, the shipment moves from the transit point on the difference between the rate paid into the transit point and the rate from origin to destinations. Under this method of settlement, there is no money outstanding that is due either to the carrier or to the shipper.

Under the other method of settlement—the claim method—the shipment moves into the transit point at the applicable flat rate from origin, and the outbound shipment moves at the applicable rate from the transit point to destination, just as if no transit had been authorized. The shipper then files a claim with the carrier for a refund of charges. The following example will illustrate this method. It applies to the storage in transit of iron and steel:

A	B	C
A – ORIGIN	B – TRANSIT POINT	C – DESTINATION

A to B .... 20 cents
B to C .... 20 cents
A to C .... 30 cents

Shipment—50,000 lbs. to transit point
                 50,000 lbs. from transit point

Charges— To transit point.................... $100
                 From transit point................. 100
                                                                   $200

                 From origin to destination.......... 150   _claim_
                 Refund due to shipper under
                    claim method of settlement....... $ 50

When the claim method is used, the tariffs require the claim to be filed within a certain length of time, usually twelve months, from the date of the outbound shipment from the transit point. If the claim is not filed within the specified time, there is no adjustment of charges.

In order to be entitled to transit privileges, transit operators are required to make written application to a local agent at the transit point, division freight agent, or general freight agent and agree to abide by all the rules and regulations as published in applicable transit tariff. They must also keep records in the manner prescribed; make statements, when requested, as to tonnage and representative freight bills on hand; make affidavit, when required, as to the accuracy of such records and statements; and permit inspection thereof at any time by the proper inspection bureau representatives having jurisdiction.

There are many additional transit privileges, such as compression of cotton, concentration of such items as dairy products and packing house products, and the feeding of livestock, to name but a few.

Transit privileges have been granted in a limited number of cases by motor carriers. In the period since the end of World War II, an increasing number of transit privileges have been filed. Some of the different ex-

---

FREIGHT TARIFF S-64

RULES

RULE 1:   Commodities
     This tariff is applicable on Paper and Paper Products, in truckloads, as follows:
          Fibreboard, not corrugated or indented, in bundles, rolls or on skids.
          Pulpboard, not corrugated or indented, in bundles, rolls or on skids.
          Paper, Printing, other than newsprint or carbonized print, not printed nor im-
               printed, in boxes, bundles, rolls or on skids.
          Paper, Wrapping, in bundles, rolls or on skids.

RULE 2:   Origin, Destination and Route

     This tariff is applicable only on shipments originating at Covington, Va., destined to New York, N.Y., via Novick Transfer Co.

RULE 3:   Processing Defined

     (a) Shipments moving from Covington, Va., to New York, N.Y., under this tariff may be stopped in transit at Philadelphia, Pa., for cutting and trimming and subsequently, after being so processed, reshipped via Novick Transfer Co., to New York, N.Y.
     (b) Shippers or consignees desiring to use the transit privilege accorded by this tariff must make their own arrangements for processing at Philadelphia, Pa., and for reshipment therefrom to New York, N.Y.

RULE 4:   Application of Rates and Charges

     (a) Shipments hereunder will be subject to the applicable through rate on file with the Interstate Commerce Commission from point of origin to final place of delivery, plus a stopping in transit charge of 11¢ per 100 pounds.
     (b) Charges will be based on the gross weight of the shipment received at Covington, Va., with no allowance for loss of weight in processing at Philadelphia.

RULE 5:   Prepayment of Charges

     All charges, including the stop-off charge, must be prepaid at Covington, Va., based on the rate and charges provided for in Rule 4.

RULE 6:   Bill of Lading Notations

     (a) Bills of lading issued by the carrier at Covington, Va., should bear a notation substantially as follows:
          To be stopped in transit and delivered to

....,
          (name and address of person in Philadelphia to whom shipment is to be delivered)
          under the rules of MF-I.C.C. No. A-479, Middle Atlantic Conference, Agent.

     (b) Bills of lading or receipts covering outbound shipments of the processed paper from Philadelphia, Pa., to New York, shall show the gross weight (See Rule 4(b)) of the paper and shall bear a notation substantially as follows: (concluded on next page)
                                        -2-

FIG. 12–2. A sample motor carrier tariff.

FREIGHT TARIFF S-64

RULE 6: (Concluded)
    This shipment consists of paper originating at Covington, Va., and
processed at Philadelphia, Pa.
    The original shipment of unprocessed paper was received from Novick
Transfer Company at Philadelphia, Pa., on . . . . ,
covered by Freight Bill (or Pro) No. _____ , Dated _____ .
Shipment was made under the rules of MF-I.C.C. A-479, Middle Atlantic
Conference, Agent.

RULE 7:   Records

    (a) The consignee of the unprocessed paper and the shippers of the processed paper at
Philadelphia, Pa., must keep a record of all inbound shipments and all outbound shipments
of processed paper and such record must at all times be available for inspection by the
carrier or its agent.
    (b) The records should show the date of the receipt of the inbound paper and the gross
weight thereof, as well as the date of forwarding of the processed paper.
    (c) Outbound shipments of processed paper must be tendered to the carriers at Phila-
delphia, Pa., not more than 10 days after the delivery of the unprocessed paper at Philadelphia.
    (d) Against each inbound freight bill a truckload of processed paper weighing not more
than the inbound unprocessed paper must be tendered.
    (e) If such an outbound shipment is not made within the time limit of 10 days, the in-
bound freight bill will be cancelled for the purposes of this tariff and corrected freight bill
will be issued based on the rate applicable for local movement from Covington, Va., to
Philadelphia, without the "stop-off" privilege herein authorized. Any subsequent shipment
from Philadelphia to New York will be treated as a local shipment and assessed at full
tariff rates applicable on actual weight.
    (f) The carrier will keep complete records of the deliveries of unprocessed paper at
Philadelphia and the outbound shipments of processed paper shipped from Philadelphia, Pa.,
to New York, N.Y. The carrier's billing of all movements under this tariff shall bear
proper notations which shall clearly identify the shipments and indicate that they are moving under the processing-in-transit rules of this tariff.
    (g) As reshipment is made against each inbound freight bill such bill shall be cancelled
and proper notation made of the use thereof for the reshipment of the processed paper
from Philadelphia, Pa. No further shipment of processed paper may be made against the
same freight bill.

-3-

FIG. 12-2—Continued.

amples of transit privileges which have been granted by motor carriers
are the following:

1. A number of these tariffs grant storage in transit, and the rule provisions are similar to the rules of railroads in this connection. The most
common type of transit privilege in motor transportation appears to be
that of storage in transit. One general commodity motor carrier grants
storage in transit at a number of specified points on a wide range of commodities, including canned or preserved foodstuffs, fresh fruit, frozen
fresh fruit, fresh fruit juice, frozen fresh fruit juice, and others.

2. A number of individual carriers have granted the transit privilege on such things as cellulose acetate, storage on frozen food stuffs, and unfinished fabrics.

3. The agent for one carrier publishes a tariff on transit privileges applying on liquid chemicals for rehandling, further treatment, or storage. Under this privilege, the liquid chemicals are brought to a designated transit point in tank trucks in bulk. Some of the processing that is permitted is that of the addition of inhibitors and dye or coloring matter, as well as the denaturing of alcohol, after which the chemicals may be reshipped in packages.

4. One motor carrier transit tariff provides a dipping-in-transit privilege on shipments of tire fabrics.

5. Another motor carrier has granted processing in transit on paper and paper products. The transit tariff authorizes the cutting and trimming of the paper at a specified point.

6. The transit privilege granted by individual motor carriers on butter, cheese, eggs, and fresh meat permits storage, repacking, or rehandling. This particular privilege applying to dairy products makes it possible for butter, for example, to be moved in tubs to a transit point, where it is packaged and forwarded to ultimate destination.

As with rail carriers, there is usually a nominal transit charge, the most common figure being 10 cents per 100 pounds.

Figure 12–2 is a sample motor carrier transit tariff covering processing in transit. It will be noted, in this transit tariff, that many of the rules are similar to those found in rail transit tariffs; but there are not nearly as many, nor are they as voluminous as is the case with rail transit tariffs. Although some motor transit tariffs follow the rail transit tariffs in granting twelve months' time at the transit point, Rule 7 (c) of this motor transit tariff provides that outbound shipments of processed paper must be tendered to the carrier not more than 10 days after the delivery of the unprocessed paper at Philadelphia. The time limit, therefore, on this transit privilege is but 10 days.

TRAFFIC MANAGERS AND TRANSIT PRIVILEGES

The traffic manager has two primary responsibilities regarding transit privileges. The first of these is that of securing a transit privilege if it is advantageous to his company. This will require a familiarity with the nature of transit privileges and their relation to his company's products. A good source of information regarding transit privileges are the innumerable ICC cases concerning this subject. The second responsibility regarding transit privileges follows the securing of a transit privilege. The traffic manager, then, has to insure that the necessary records are kept in a manner which meets the requirements of the weighing and inspection bureaus.[4] In addition, special company records may be required.

[4] The functions of weighing and inspection bureaus are discussed in a later chapter.

The advantages offered by the transit privilege make it well worth consideration by the traffic manager.

DISCUSSION QUESTIONS AND PROBLEMS

1. What is the transit privilege? Is it the same as stopping in transit to load partially or unload?
2. List the benefits of the transit privilege to the shipper, the carrier, and the public.
3. Carefully explain how the out-of-line or out-of-route provisions work in connection with the transit privilege and what effect they have.
4. Outline the subjects which are generally covered under the application rules in transit tariffs.
5. What are some of the different approaches used in establishing a charge for the transit privilege?
6. Explain what is meant by the two-way and the three-way rate rules as contained in transit tariffs?
7. Of what significance is the transit tariff rule defining nontransit commodities? Can transit and nontransit commodities be mixed? What conditions are stipulated concerning mixtures?
8. Who polices the transit rules? Why are policing rules necessary?
9. List the different types of transit privileges. Which general group is the most extensively used? Why?
10. Fabricating in transit does not permit the complete manufacture of a finished iron and steel commodity. Why?
11. What is the difference between unit and split billing?
12. Give an example of each of the different methods of settlement of transit accounts.
13. List the different types of motor carrier transit privileges. Do you feel that such privileges will increase in the future?
14. Exactly how does the traffic manager proceed in attempting to secure a transit privilege?

Chapter

13

CARRIERS' TERMINAL SERVICES

TYPES OF TERMINAL SERVICES

THE terminal operations of carriers constitute the hub of transportation activities. The carriers provide certain services which are largely in connection with the terminal phase of their operations and are therefore referred to as "terminal services."

Switching

"Switching" is the term applied to movements of cars within the limits of a yard, terminal, or station, as distinguished from the movement between stations, which is called "road haul" or "line haul." Switching involves the movement of cars to or from the place of delivery or receipt following or preceding line-haul movements, as well as the movement of cars on which there is no line haul— that is, movement between two points within the limits of a yard, terminal, or station. Switching limits are prescribed in most cases by specifying in the switching tariff the limits at each station within which the published rates, rules, and regulations will apply.

At smaller stations, switching is done by local, way freight crews who bring freight to or take it from the station. The switching services needed at a particular station are performed while the train is stopped at that point to detach cars destined to, or to pick up cars originating at, that point. At larger stations and terminals, switching service is performed by so-called "switching crews" who work only at that particular station, terminal, or yard. Practically all stations are equipped with tracks accessible to highway vehicles, these tracks being commonly called "public team tracks," where carloads—and, in some cases, certain types or quantities of less carloads—are received or delivered, the shipper or consignee handling directly to or from the car.

Private sidings are spurs or sidings connected with the railroad's tracks. These are owned and maintained by industries on their own property and invariably are located adjacent to their warehouses, factories, or building, permitting the direct handling of freight to and from cars. These sidings are used exclusively for the handling of freight by the owning industry.

The railroad rates for line-haul traffic have always been recognized as including delivery or receipt of carload traffic on public tracks or private sidings of the origin or destination carrier. Therefore, switching carloads at origin or destination from either a public team track or a private siding is at no additional cost to shippers when performed by the line-haul carrier. However, a business firm with a private siding on one railroad may find it necessary for some reason to receive or forward freight over the line of some other rail carrier serving the same town or city. In such instances, the rates of the line-haul carrier include the obligation of effecting delivery or receipt only on its public team tracks, in which case it would be necessary to truck the freight between such public delivery tracks and the concern's place of business, despite the fact that it has a private siding right to its door.

In order to assist in effecting most economical operations and to foster the growth of industries having private sidings on their tracks, rail carriers generally establish moderate rates, usually stated in amounts per car, between points of interchange, with connecting carriers and private sidings at stations where they connect with other carriers. In addition to this, carriers reaching those stations in line-haul service ordinarily provide that they will absorb switching charges assessed by their connections in reaching a given industry, provided the line-haul revenue equals or exceeds a certain specified amount. This so-called "absorption" means that the line-haul carrier will pay to the switching line the amount of its switching charge. As a result, the industry obtains service to and from its private siding facilities at no cost above the line-haul rate to and from the city or town in which it is located.

Carriers generally will not absorb switching charges when the absorption results in a net transportation charge (exclusive of switching and other terminal charges) less than a certain minimum per car, which varies with different railroads. If the transportation charge does not permit absorption of the entire switching charge, the carrier will absorb only as much of the switching charge as will leave the minimum net transportation charge.

The switching rates between private sidings and junctions with connecting carriers are commonly referred to as "reciprocal switching" rates because there is a measure of reciprocity in their establishment, inasmuch as all carriers at a given point customarily publish the same rates between points of interchange and industries on their respective lines. Thus, through reciprocal switching rates established by the delivering carriers and their absorption by the line-haul carriers, industries have the privilege of selecting the line-haul carrier which best meets their transportation requirements, without depending for line-haul movement solely upon the carrier with whose rails their private siding connects. At the same time, all carriers reaching that point can serve all firms which possess private siding locations on an equal basis in so far as rates to the shipper are concerned. While it is expected that an industry will favor the railroad with which its private siding is directly connected, it does not have to do so from the standpoint of transportation cost.

In individual switching tariffs, the limits of the switching area may be set by the carriers and do not necessarily have to follow the municipal boundaries of the city. However, a switching district must possess reasonable limits which would reflect the industrial areas, transportation conditions, and commercial competition. In many of the agency switching tariffs, it has been general practice to define the switching limits as the corporate limits of the city. "Switching limits" and "switching district" are terms which are used interchangeably to define the area within which a carrier performs switching services subject to the rules, regulations, and charges published in applicable tariffs.

Many switching tariffs are individual publications, but there are a number of them which are published by an agent, and a consolidated switching tariff may be published at a particular point.

Types of Switching Services

The variety of switching services can be seen in the following classification:

1. Intraterminal movements—originating at one point and destined to another point on the same carrier's lines within the switching limits of one station or industrial switching district.
2. Interterminal movements—originating at one point and destined to another point on different carriers within the switching limits of one station or industrial switching district.
3. Intraplant movements—originating at one point and destined to another point within the trackage limits of the same plant or industry.
4. Interplant movements—originating at one plant or unit of a single industry destined to another plant or unit of the same industry on the same railroad.
5. Intermediate switching—movement of a car from the junction with one line-haul carrier to a junction point with a second line-haul carrier. This service permits the interchange of traffic between carriers whose rails do not connect at interchange points via which both rates are published.

Switching Charges

Switching rates to and from the point of interchange with connecting lines are published on a per-car basis, with few exceptions. It has proved impracticable to reflect the same refinement in them as in line-haul rates. For practical reasons, it is desirable that switching rates be somewhat on a postage-stamp basis, regardless of weight, comparative length of haul, and other factors.

Industrial switching is sometimes charged on a per-car basis, sometimes on a per-ton basis, and occasionally on a classification basis. When charging on a per-ton or classification basis, it is necessary, of course, to obtain weights. Where interterminal switching is involved—that is, switching between two points on different carriers within one switching area—the movements usually are subject to each carrier's separate switching rates to and from the point of interchange. However, there are several places where these interterminal movements are subject to through charges applicable from the point of loading to the point of unloading. In such cases, the covering tariff must be concurred in by the railroads participating in such joint rates or charges, and divisions of them between interested carriers must be arranged.

Switching and absorption tariffs are generally issued individually by each railroad, although at a few large centers, publication is in an agency tariff.

Usually, carriers do not make a charge for switching service when it is in connection with traffic which originates on private or assigned sidings at one point and is consigned to private or assigned sidings at another point when the same carrier originates and terminates the traffic as well as performing the line-haul transportation. Generally, the charges for switching services are made under the following circumstances: (1) where, at the point of origin, cars are loaded on private sidings of one carrier for movement from the shipping point to destination in line-haul service of another carrier; (2) where, at the point of destination, cars are to be unloaded on private sidings of a delivering carrier other than the carrier performing the line-haul service from the point of origin; (3) where cars move within a switching district in intraplant, interplant, intraterminal, and interterminal service. In some instances, the Interstate Commerce Commission has prescribed maximum amounts for switching charges or divisions which may be paid to tap lines by trunk-line railroads out of rates on interstate shipments of lumber and forest products from points on the tap lines.

Usually, a carrier does not open its public team tracks to reciprocal switching, and it will not ordinarily authorize the loading or unloading of freight on its public team tracks where it has not secured or will not secure a line-haul movement and the revenue from such shipment. The line-haul rates usually will include the switching services which are required in the placement of cars for loading or unloading on public team tracks or private sidings, or on spur or interchange tracks owned by an industry; but the holding-out to make the deliveries will be contained in the published tariffs. Some of the larger industrial companies have plants which cover a large area, and there are widely scattered buildings which are linked together by rail facilities. The rail carrier, in these instances, may place a car on interchange tracks which connect the main-line railroad tracks with those owned and operated by industrial companies. In this form of delivery, the cars may be handled from the interchange track to the point of unloading within the industrial plant by the engine and crews of the industrial plant facility railroad. However, the carrier also may hold itself out to make delivery at points within the industrial plant where the cars may be unloaded. Where this delivery service is performed by an industrial plant facility railroad, an allowance is paid to the industry, usually an amount per car or per ton, by the line-haul carrier, and this is referred to as a "terminal allowance."

The Commission, in 1955, broadened certain aspects of rail carrier switching at industrial plants. Under the Commission's rulings, rail carriers are required to provide switching service from the main line to industrial plant locations, usually to the first "spot" (first unloading point). Team track or interchange track delivery only is not sufficient.[1] Line-haul rates include delivery to the unloading spot, even though it is within the industrial plant area beyond the interchange delivery track, according to the Commission. Further, rail carriers may deliver on and remove from privately owned sidetracks or industrial tracks near and connecting with the carrier's tracks, cars of freight moving at carload rates, without any additional charge, provided there are no conditions which make it unsafe for the carrier's locomotives to operate over such tracks or that prevent the carrier from receiving or delivering the cars at its ordinary operating convenience in a continuous movement. If receipt or delivery of the cars cannot be accomplished in a continuous movement because of interruptions or any other condition caused by the shipper or consignee, the carrier can make delivery but must charge for the delay to the locomotive in accordance with a prescribed formula, or may place the car or cars on a hold track and return at a later time to complete the receipt or delivery, which latter movement is subject to a specific shipping charge.

"Continuous movement" is defined as a movement between the carrier's tracks and the loading or unloading locations, a hold track or tracks, or other place where cars are received or delivered without any delay or any suspension or break in time or in continuity of the movement, due to any circumstances or conditions for which the industry is directly responsible.

The definition of "ordinary operating convenience" means the time selected by the carrier when it is most advantageous to the carrier, in relation to its co-ordinated switching activities in a particular switching zone, when the terminal services are performed by switching locomotives, or at the time the train arrives at the plant site when the terminal services are performed by road-haul locomotives. Ordinarily, it contemplates only one switch a day.

In the case, *Carrier Switching at Industrial Plants in the East*, the Com-

---

[1] *Carrier Switching at Industrial Plants in the East*, 294 ICC 159 (1955); *Practices of Carriers Affecting Operating Revenues or Expenses*, Part II: *Terminal Services*, 294 ICC 705 (1955).

mission approved an amendment to a tariff describing more completely the scope of the terms in connection with operations, as follows:

The operations named below where performed by the carrier as necessary incidents to the placement and removal of cars moving at published carload rates, shall not be deemed (a) to break the "continuous movement," (b) to be in excess of the "ordinary operating convenience" of the carriers, (c) to be an "interruption, interference or any other condition caused by the shipper or consignee," nor (d) to be a "circumstance or condition for which the industry is directly responsible" as those terms are used in these rules:

1. The temporary holding of cars on tracks of the carrier or industry for instructions from the shipper or receiver.

2. The removal and replacement of cars, partially loaded or unloaded when incident to the placement or removal of other cars.

3. The service of securing the weight of freight, irrespective of the ownership of the scales used, where the weights obtained are used by the carrier for billing purposes.

4. Classifying, sorting and lining up cars on industry or carrier tracks.

5. Delay and interruption resulting from the operations of a common carrier by rail on industry tracks.

6. Operations performed in providing a service for which a separate charge is authorized pursuant to a published tariff.

The Commission permits an allowance for each loaded and empty car switched by the private industry in lieu of the service which the railroad is obligated to perform under the line-haul rates.

Chicago Switching District

Chicago is the largest railroad center in the United States. A brief description of the switching district there will indicate the importance of such an activity.

The Chicago switching district, which comprises an area of approximately 400 square miles, measuring some 40 miles in length from north to south and from 7 to 15 miles from east to west, is the largest switching district in the country. It is served by over 30 railroads which are parties to the Chicago Switching Tariff, 20 of which are line-haul carriers and 17 industrial or terminal lines. In the Chicago switching district, there are over 5,000 miles of track, with 160 yards, and more than 70 freight stations. In the case of freight houses and team tracks, they are restricted to the individual carrier's line-haul traffic, except for certain freight houses which are located in outlying sections of the switching district. The rate tariffs of carriers are made subject to the Chicago Switching Tariff by means of special reference, or by the "omnibus" rule.

Pickup and Delivery

In the Interstate Commerce Commission's *3rd Annual Report* in 1889, the Commission pointed out that 65 railroads provided free delivery of less-carload freight at certain stations. In the development of less-carload service, however, rail carriers did not universally provide a free pickup and delivery service until 1936. The development of competitive freight forwarders and motor carrier service in the early thirties caused numerous experimental pickup and delivery services by railroads to be instituted on this traffic, with local cartage companies performing this service under contracts as agents of the railroads.

If pickup and delivery service is performed by the carrier, the cost is generally included in the line-haul charge. However, tariff provisions have been published which provide that if the service is performed by trucks owned or hired by the shipper or consignee, the rail carrier will make an allowance per 100 pounds to the shipper or consignee. Pickup service is furnished by the carrier on request if there are tariff provisions which offer such service. Delivery service is furnished by the carrier if provided in the tariff and under any of the following conditions: (1) consignor noting or stamping on the bill of lading and shipping order a statement that delivery service is desired, together with the address of the consignee; (2) consignee filing with the carrier's agent at destination written instructions on the extent to which delivery service is desired; and (3) specific instructions of the consignee on specific shipments.

Ordinarily, the tariff provides that pickup or delivery service is confined to the corporate limits of cities and towns; but at points not having corporate limits, service is provided within a radius of one mile of the carrier's freight station. Except in those cases where shipments require the surrender of a bill of lading before delivery, with delivery service to be given to the shipment, no notice of arrival is sent, and only one tender of delivery will be made. If exceptions to the general boundaries exist they will be shown in the tariff, and the Open and Prepay Station List contains the stations throughout the United States at which such service is available.

The tariffs governing pickup and delivery service contain numerous rules. For example, articles are named on which the service is not available; and specifications are given concerning the loading or unloading of shipments which because of their weight, size, or character require additional labor beyond that ordinarily furnished on dray or truck. Free pickup and delivery service on less-carload freight is not available throughout the entire United States, for in August, 1953, the rail carriers in the Eastern Territory canceled their tariff covering this service. Certain other rail carriers have also discontinued this service.

Motor carriers, by offering store-door to store-door service, offer a complete service to shippers. This means that pickup and delivery, as well as the line haul, is performed by the motor carrier. It was the institution of this type of service that was largely responsible for the railroads' offering their free pickup and delivery.

In addition, in some motor rate territories, provision is made for a so-called "pickup and delivery" at locations beyond points at which pickup and delivery are considered to be part of the line-haul service. The general rule provides for pickup without charge from, and delivery to, a platform, doorway, or other location where the shipment can be placed adjacent to a point accessible to the vehicle of the carrier.

Inside pickup and delivery are provided for in a special rule in the tariff, and a specified charge is made in addition to line-haul rates. In one rate territory, however, a special rule affecting a group of carriers has been published which enables them to perform inside service to and from more than one floor, if elevators are available, without additional charge.

Motor carriers may offer what is termed "multiple pickups and deliveries." The Commission has restricted the number of stops to a total of 4 for pickups and 4 for deliveries but, in a later case, imposed no limitation on the number of stops. There has not been much uniformity in the past in the number of stops in transit allowed, the range being from 1 to 10, but some commodity rate items have been permitted an unlimited number. This service is generally authorized in connection with prepaid shipments.

There is strong shipper interest in this particular type of service, since it enables them to serve those unable to purchase in truckload quantities and also enables them to meet competition located closer to common markets.

Weighing and Reweighing

The ascertainment of the correct weight is of importance in transportation, for carriers generally state their rates in terms of a weight basis. Rates are usually quoted on a per-100 pounds or per-ton basis. However, since there are a number of different tons, it is well to point out that 2,000 pounds, or the net ton, may be the basis; it may be 2,204.6 pounds, or the metric ton; or 2,240 pounds, or the long ton, may be the basis. The long ton is used in the movement of certain commodities of the iron and steel industry.

There are different kinds of weights used by rail carriers. Carriers' tariffs, in some instances, publish a figure which has been determined as a standard weight on a specific measurement of commodity. For example, transportation charges on petroleum in tank cars in one section of the United States are to be computed on a weight of 6.6 pounds per gallon. Another type of weight is actual weight. Track scales are maintained by carriers at all of their larger terminals for the purpose of weighing carload shipments which are not covered by a tariff weight or a weight agreement. The track scale makes it possible for the entire freight car to be set on the scale; and after the gross weight has been taken, the marked tare or empty weight of the car, which is stenciled on the side, is deducted from the gross weight to arrive at the net weight of the contents. This is the weight the railroad uses for assessment of freight charges.

All initial weighing by carriers to ascertain the weight of a shipment for assessment of the proper transportation charge is performed without cost to shippers. One of the car service rules issued by the Association of American Railroads provides for light-weighing and weight-stenciling of all new freight cars, as well as for periodic relight-weighing and restenciling with tare weights of various types of cars. Over a period of time, freight cars lose weight due to wear of parts and weathering, with the result that the shipper may actually have 200 or 300 pounds transported free. Where the shipper sells his commodity on the basis of the railroad scale weight, it would be the receiver who would gain under such circumstances.

Before accepting delivery of a carload of freight, a consignee may request the delivering carrier to reweigh the loaded car if the consignee thinks that the billed weight is incorrect. The carrier will reweigh the loaded car; and if the new weight does not differ from the billed weight by more than a stated tolerance, the carrier reweighing the car will assess the consignee a moderate charge. Tolerance is the difference in the weight of lading due to variations in scales or weighing which may be permitted without correction of the billed weight. On brick, gravel, stone, and other specified articles, when loaded in open cars, the tolerance is $1\frac{1}{2}$ per cent of the weight of the lading. If the new weight differs from the billed weight by more than the stated tolerance—1 per cent on most commodities—billing will be corrected, transportation charges assessed on the new weight, and no charge made for the reweighing service. For example, one rail tariff provides a stated tolerance of 300 pounds on scrap.

The rules and charges covering reweighing are published in carriers' tariffs; and although there is no national publication that serves this purpose, the Association of American Railroads' Code of Weighing Rules provides uniformity where its recommendations are followed. The charges for reweighing are stated in dollars and cents per car. They vary in amount, depending on where the service is performed; whether railroad or private scales are used; whether it is before or after placement; whether it is at origin, en route, or destination; and if it is by the line-haul or switching carrier.

Motor carriers permit the use of estimated weights and have provisions governing weighing and reweighing in some tariffs, but the wide variation in such tariff provisions requires careful checking.

Weight Agreements

Where reasonably accurate weights can be secured without weighing each carload, the shipper, as well as the carrier, may benefit. There are economies to the railroad in reduced switching costs, and the loss of fewer car-days may be reflected to the shipper in greater availability of equipment. One way in which this matter can be facilitated is through the use of a weight agreement. Under a weight agreement, the carrier's agent will accept the shipper's weights, determined prior to the loading and inserted in the bills of lading. In return, the shipper agrees to keep his records accessible and in such form that a subsequent check of the weights of all such shipments can be made easily by representatives of the carrier's weighing bureau. If it is ascertained that undercharges exist, the shipper agrees, under the weight-agreement method, to pay promptly.[2]

The majority of rail carriers are members of weighing and inspection bureaus, although there are a small number of railroads which deal directly with a shipper when arranging for a weight agreement. One phase of these bureaus' operations has to do with weight agreements, and they represent railroads in matters concerning a weight agreement. Where there is a weight agreement, the shipper uses a rubber stamp which identifies the weighing and inspection bureau, or the shipper can have printed on the bills of lading he uses a facsimile of the weight-agreement stamp. Weight agreements usually apply to carload shipments, although they may be also executed for less-carload shipments by some of the weighing and inspection bureaus.

A typical weight agreement will cover such matters as the purpose of the agreement which is not having to weigh the shipper's particular commodities (which are covered in the weight agreement), the use of a certification stamp, the duration of the agreement, shipper's certification as to correctness of weights, maintenance of scales in good condition, shipper notification if weights of containers or commodities are changed, disposition and adjustment of errors by either party, maintenance of shipper's records, and application of regular tariff rates.

During World War II, national weight agreements were entered into between various weighing and inspection bureaus on behalf of their member railroad carriers and the military services. This provided for the acceptance of the government's tendered weights on carload or less-carload traffic shipped from all points in the United States on government bills of lading or on commercial bills of lading endorsed to be converted to government bills of lading, expediting such traffic and making it unnecessary for carriers to weigh shipments. A similar uniform national weight agreement has been entered into between the government and the railroads, which was effective in the middle of 1951.

The Western Weighing and Inspection Bureau, which operates in the territory generally west of the Indiana-Illinois state line and the Mississippi River, to but not including the Pacific Coast, states that it had 7,500 weight agreements in effect in 1963.[3] This Bureau also had 1,294 railroad-owned track scales and 790 industry-owned and -operated track scales which were under the supervision of that Bureau. In this area, an estimated 5 million cars were handled under weight agreements. The weighmasters who perform the weighing are employees of a railroad or an

---

[2] Odell v. *Michigan Central R. Co.*, 92 ICC 643 (1924).

[3] Information supplied by Mr. F. A. Piehl, Manager, Western Weighing and Inspection Bureau.

industry who have executed a weighmaster's oath and have read the section of the Interstate Commerce Act pertaining to false weighing or false reporting of weights.

Canned goods, which are packed twenty-four cans in a fiber box, represent uniform packages; and there are many instances where agreements are made to ship canned goods under weight agreements. A test weighing operation is conducted jointly by an industry and a weighing and inspection bureau representative, and an average weight is established. This weight is the one used in computing the total weight of the contents of the car. Another example of weight agreements is those entered into by concerns that use refrigerator car equipment exclusively, which often move under ice for which no freight charge is assessed. As a result of the agreement, both the shipper and the railroad have a net weight to use for computing freight charges. Weight agreements are filed with the Interstate Commerce Commission.

The traffic manager should investigate the possibilities of weight agreements and other matters involving weighing to facilitate the movement of goods for his company.

Estimated Weights

Estimated weights may be used under certain circumstances, but there must be a justifiable reason for their use. The purpose of the use of estimated weights is to avoid the delay, expense, and labor incident to the actual weighing of each shipment. The use of the estimated weight must be provided for in the tariff, and it must reflect the averages of actual weights.

Loading and Unloading

It is the obligation of the shipper or consignee to load and unload rail carload freight anywhere in the United States. The railroad itself loads or unloads anywhere in the United States, however, at the request of the shipper or consignee. A representative charge for the simple service of unloading in one territory was $2.86 per ton, or $4.09 per ton for a complete service, which includes such items as checking, coopering, sorting, stowing, and others.

Generally, loading and unloading of freight onto and off the carrier's vehicle are part of the motor carrier's customary service when this service can be performed by one man. There are numerous exceptions to this.

Transfer and Drayage

Frequently, rail carriers do not have common points of interchange, and they hire local drayage companies to transfer the goods between freight houses within the city. Also included is the movement of property between points within the same city or locality by use of local freight haulers not engaged in competitive intrastate or interstate transportation. In some instances, drayage firms are a subsidiary of a common carrier and have rates or charges on file with a governing regulatory body. With the development of motor carriers, the amount of transfer by means of local drayage companies between rail carriers not having common points of interchange has lessened and is not as important as it has been in the past.

Lighterage and Floatage

Within the limits of a harbor, freight is often handled in lighters, barges, scows, and floats in the loading and unloading of vessels as an incident to line-haul transportation. Such service is known as "lighterage service." The Port of New York is unique, in that the great bulk of water-borne traffic is lightered between the railroads and steamships docked at piers not served directly by rail. There is limited lighterage service at some of our other ports, such as Philadelphia, Baltimore, and Hampton Roads. The term "lighterage" has been extended through usage to include the movement of freight by use of lighters and other small craft between docks, terminals, and vessels located at points within short distances of each other. This concept of lighterage includes transfer, collection, and delivery of shipments, as well as short extensions of line operations.

Lighterage is generally performed within certain limits, but the terms "lighterage free" and "free lighterage limits" which are used have often been misunderstood. In New York, lighterage free is applicable to freight on which no charge is made over and above the New York, New York rate, as contrasted to freight on which an additional charge is made. Free lighterage limits apply to points such as the pier, vessel, or landing place within defined limits in the harbor where lighterage free freight may be received or delivered without a charge above the New York, New York rate as contrasted to points beyond the defined limits from and to which a charge is made for the towing service. The so-called "free lighterage service" is analogous to switching service when performed within the railroad switching district.

Shippers moving freight for export may have a carload which is consigned to customers in points in different foreign countries. Such a shipment through the Port of New York would normally require delivery at more than one steamship pier in the New York harbor. Tariff rules commonly provide for split deliveries even involving lighterage services, one such rule reading that a carload shipment of lighterage-free freight will be entitled to two free export lighterage deliveries or one free export lighterage delivery and one station delivery for export use of each carload assessed at the carload rate. In this particular rule, two free split deliveries and three additional split deliveries, the latter subject to a charge, are the maximum permitted for each carload.

The New York Lighterage and Terminal Tariff, an agency publication, contains numerous rules which are applicable to both domestic and import and export freight, and it contains a list of prohibited or restricted articles.

Barges, which are nonpropelled boats with roof and sides, are ordinarily used to lighter freight. Their capacity ranges from 3 to 6 carloads. Car floats are flat-bottomed, nonpropelled boats equipped with railroad tracks upon which the railroad cars are placed. There are both 2-track and 3-track car floats, which vary in capacity from 8 to 21 cars. The rail cars are moved on and off car floats over a float bridge by locomotive power, and the floats are moved in the harbor area in destination as well as transfer service.

WEIGHING AND INSPECTION BUREAUS

Weighing and inspection bureaus originally helped establish and police proper freight classification, descriptions, and weights of commodities, although their field of activity has broadened over the years. They do not operate under any law or regulation but have the sanction of the Interstate Commerce Commission. There are five rail weighing and inspection bureaus. These bureaus are not associated with one another and cover large geographical areas. Motor carrier weighing and inspection bureaus have been formed, and there are sixteen of them at the present time. At the time of their formation, some consideration was given to weighing and inspection bureaus on a national basis. However, they have been developed largely in connection with existing tariff bureaus and state motor carrier associations.

Traffic departments work co-operatively with weighing and inspection bureaus. Such bureaus are helpful in many phases of traffic work.

Activities of a Typical Rail Weighing and Inspection Bureau

The Western Weighing and Inspection Bureau is a typical weighing and inspection bureau. Some of its functions are described in order to give a better understanding of organizations of this kind. It was organized in 1887, with about 33 railroads participating in its services at that time. By 1963, 217 railroads, with over 120,000 miles of track in the territory covered by this Bureau,[4] were participants in this organization. The Bureau itself is comprised of a manager, a number of assistant and district managers, and an average of 1,200 employees.

Weighing supervision is one of the important functions of the Bureau; and a total of 2,084 track scales, railroad-owned and industry-owned and -operated, are under its supervision. These scales, used for weighing the cars, are built right in the tracks and are usually located at terminal points. Periodical checks of the various scales are made by the Bureau's fieldmen

---

[4] The Territory generally west of the Indiana-Illinois state line and the Mississippi River, to but not including the Pacific Coast states, as well as perishable freight inspection and demurrage supervision in the states of Washington and Oregon.

and local representatives, at which time they check to see that the weighing is performed by authorized parties and that the records are properly maintained; and if anything remiss is noted, they act to correct the matter.

Weight agreements, which have been described, are another of the aspects of weighing and inspection that are the responsibility of this Bureau. Some 7,500 such agreements have saved the railroads the cost of weighing, expedited movements, and eliminated disputes in regard to weight, thereby saving the expense that might be incurred in the investigation of overcharge claims.

The policing of transit privileges is performed by this Bureau. After an investigation by the Interstate Commerce Commission of certain practices followed in connection with the application of transit privileges, it was recommended by the Commission that a neutral agency should perform the function of policing these agreements. Weighing and inspection bureaus were delegated to supervise the transit privileges; and the Western Weighing and Inspection Bureau, during a typical year, supervised and handled the accounting on about 3 million cars which were accorded transit privileges. In the territory served by this Bureau, transit is granted on about 100 different commodities, and these privileges are granted to about 6,000 firms. In some cities the Bureau maintains validating offices, where transit papers must be presented for validation before the railroad accords the transit privilege. In other cities, the validation is handled by the railroad; and then, both the inbound freight bill and the outbound waybill are sent to the Bureau with the shipper's statement for accounting and verification. In addition, the Bureau's field and local representatives perform an audit of the transit operator's records to determine that the particular shipment which moved under transit privileges was entitled to the lower rates secured on the outbound shipment.

Although there is not as much misdescription of freight as was earlier the case, freight inspection is still an important function of the Bureau. One of the purposes of this inspection of freight is to determine that the proper description has been furnished by the shipper, so that the railroad may apply the proper rate. Freight inspectors are assigned to various freight houses throughout the territory to assist in the proper classification of freight offered for shipment. Considerable educational work is conducted by the Bureau in order to acquaint shippers with the correct manner of describing their freight.

Loss and damage inspection is another of the services performed by the Bureau. This represents an inspection of freight which has been transported and arrives at destination in damaged condition. The extent of the damage is determined, and its cause, and a report filed with the freight claim department of the Bureau to assist in the disposition of the claim when it is presented. In larger cities, a Bureau representative calls upon receivers for all the railroads which participate in the Bureau, which eliminates the necessity for each railroad to have inspectors perform this service, as is the case in cities where the Bureau does not perform this service.

Since 1933, the Western Weighing and Inspection Bureau has handled perishable freight inspection service at nearly all the principal cities throughout its territory, instead of having it done by outside contractors, as had been the case theretofore. When carload shipments of fruits and vegetables arrive, Bureau inspectors take the seal record, record the commodity temperature, and get a general description of the load. As the car is unloaded, the freight is inspected; a record is made of the damage, if any; and coopers repair crates or boxes where the damage is slight, thus assuring delivery of the freight in good condition and avoiding a claim. There are certain features of this service also that are performed for the freight claim department to expedite and facilitate the handling of claims.

Damage prevention is an important program supported by the Bureau. Many facts regarding causes of damage are developed by the inspection service, and the Bureau works with railroad organizations for claim or damage prevention. At border points, Bureau inspectors examine freight that comes in from Mexico to insure that the shipment is properly braced and loaded and that the packages are in condition for safe transportation. Of this type, also, is the inspection, at New Orleans and Chicago, of freight which is moving to and from steamships.

In connection with the movement of livestock, the Bureau performs a veterinary livestock inspection. Veterinarians, located at some of the principal markets, determine the cause of death in animals; and inspectors inspect the animals as they are unloaded, inspect the car to determine if it was properly prepared, and make reports in regard to dead or crippled animals to the freight claim agent.

The supervision of demurrage and storage is also performed by the Bureau. In order to have cars available for new shipments and not detained unduly, a charge is made for cars held beyond a certain time in loading or unloading. In each Bureau district, there is a demurrage supervisor who handles problems that arise through controversies between shippers, receivers, and the railroads.

Another service performed by contractors prior to 1934 and taken over by the Bureau at the request of the railroads is that of grain-door reclamation and coopering. This service involves the application of the grain door inside the regular storm door to prevent grain from leaking out en route. In many places, the cars are coopered with grain doors; and at the same time, these doors are reclaimed when cars are unloaded and returned to the railroad that brought them to the terminal. At one point in the Bureau's territory, during the wheat harvest months, as many as 1,000 cars per day are received. The job of reclaiming grain doors and seeing that they are returned to the loading point to be used again involves a great deal of work. Annually, the Bureau coopers more than 475,000 cars with wooden doors and 120,000 with paper-type doors (doors made of heavy Kraft paper or corrugated fiberboard with steel bands, which recently came into use and must be reclaimed for use again) and reclaimed about 7 million wooden doors for reuse.

The functions which have been described represent the more important of the many functions performed by this Bureau and others of its kind.

Activities of Motor Weighing and Inspection Bureaus

Some of the functions of the motor carrier weighing and inspection bureaus performed for motor carriers are identical to those of rail weighing and inspection bureaus performed for rail carriers. The policing of transit records and weight agreements constitute two very important rail functions not usually performed by motor carrier weighing and inspection bureaus, although the motor carrier weighing and inspection bureaus do assist shippers and motor carriers in arriving at an agreed weight. Shippers sometimes turn over freight to motor carriers with a rail certification stamp on the bill of lading, which is evidence of a weight agreement. The usual procedure in a situation of this kind is that the motor carrier accepts this shipment at the agreed weight between the shipper and the railroad, even though it moves by motor carrier, with no weight agreement in effect.

Some of the activities of motor carrier weighing and inspection bureaus are those of determining proper descriptions to be used on bills of lading; checking weights shown by shippers on bills of lading; recommending improved packing and shipping methods; determining causes of damage; inspecting damaged shipments; testing carriers' scales; recommending improved methods of freight handling, loading, and stowage for claim prevention; and assisting in disposition of over, short, and damaged freight. Weighing and inspection bureaus are supported by the carriers, although the functions they perform are beneficial to both shippers and carriers.

DISCUSSION QUESTIONS AND PROBLEMS

1. Why are the terminal operations of carriers often referred to as the "hub" of transportation activities?
2. What is reciprocal switching? What effect does it have upon competition between carriers?
3. Compare the switching limits of railroads with the commercial zones of motor carriers in your area, and report upon any differences.
4. Outline the different types of switching services, with an example of that type which you feel is most widely found.
5. What are the usual conditions under which charges are made for switching?
6. By whom are switching and absorption tariffs usually published? Why? What are some of the different methods of charging for industrial switching?

7. How would a traffic manager secure a terminal allowance? What is the carrier's obligation in switching cars to an industrial plant?

8. Do motor carriers generally grant an allowance to the shipper or consignor who picks up or delivers freight to the carrier's terminal? Why?

9. The establishment of a weight tolerance by carriers accomplishes what purpose? Are there any charges in connection with reweighing?

10. What are some of the factors that a traffic manager would consider concerning the use of a weight agreement?

11. Are estimated weights permissible? What is the advantage of using estimated weights?

12. Prepare a report on the similarities and differences between a rail switching tariff and a lighterage tariff.

13. Compare the functions of rail and motor weighing and inspection bureaus.

14. Trace the development of rail weighing and inspection bureaus, and indicate their present status.

Chapter

14

EQUIPMENT UTILIZATION

THE most effective utilization of carrier equipment is a joint responsibility of shippers and carriers. Improvident use of equipment can cause serious shortages of equipment, with attendant inconvenience and inability to deliver commodities when promised.

CAR SERVICE

Freight cars in active service are estimated to be in the hands of shippers and receivers approximately 50 per cent of the time. The responsibility for securing better utilization while in the hands of shippers and receivers rests largely with the regional Shippers Advisory boards, of which there are thirteen. These organizations work with the railroads and their association through education in those fields where co-operation is effective. Railroads have stated many times that more can be accomplished with shippers and receivers through co-operation than through inflexible rules and penalties, although the demurrage rules and other traffic provisions are used to encourage better use of cars. Some of the ways in which car shortages are accentuated are holding cars for prospective loading, demanding slow schedules and circuitous routes, delaying in transit for sale or reconsignment, and failing to unload dunnage and debris. There are also numerous carrier practices which contribute to the failure to secure greater use of equipment. It has been estimated that one day saved in the average rail car turnaround time would add 100,000 units to the supply of cars available.

Railroads, through the formulation of car service rules, have established principles governing the selection of a car to be furnished a shipper. In brief, these rules provide that once freight cars have been loaded off the rails of the owning railroad, every practicable effort should be made to find loading for them which will take them back to, toward, or via the owning road. Shippers can greatly assist in the carrying-out of this objective by placing advance car orders with the serving road showing routing and/or destination of the intended loadings and by requiring loading forces to select from the empty cars available at the platform for the day's loading as many cars as practicable which will, by the lading placed in them, be advanced toward the owner's rails.

The first approach to education of shippers and receivers toward the realization that in their hands rested a good part of the means toward securing better car supply and rail service was in the organization of the Shippers Advisory boards, starting in 1923. These bodies have a membership of over 22,000 shippers and receivers of carload freight. The purposes and functions of the Shippers Advisory boards are:

1. To form a common meeting ground between shippers, local railroads, and the carriers as a whole, as represented by the Association of American Railroads' Car Service Division, for better mutual understanding of local and general transportation requirements, to analyze transportation needs in each territory, and to assist in anticipating car requirements.

2. To study production, markets, distribution, and trade channels of the commodities local to each district, with a view toward effecting improvements in trade practices when related to transportation and promoting a more even distribution of commodities where practicable.

3. To promote car and operating efficiency in connection with maximum loading in the proper handling of cars by shippers and railroads.

4. To secure a proper understanding by the railroads of the transportation needs of shippers, so that their regulations may fit shippers' requirements; and, likewise, to secure understanding by the shippers and their co-operation in carrying out necessary rules governing car handling and car distribution.

5. To acquaint shippers and the railroads in each section of the country with the seasonal requirements in their section in order to promote cooperation in the handling of equipment between the different districts of the country.

6. To adjust informally car difficulties which may arise in each local territory between the carrier and the shipper.

7. To give the shipping public a direct voice in the activities of the Car Service Division on all matters of mutual concern.

The regional boards are voluntary organizations in which participation by traffic managers is to their advantage. There are no membership fees, dues, or salaries. Railroad representatives are encouraged to attend board meetings and participate in discussions on the floor at these meetings, although they are not accorded membership or voting power in the boards.

A quarterly carloading questionnaire is sent out, in order to ascertain the need for cars in the next quarter. Such forecasts have proved helpful in moving cars from surplus areas to forecasted deficit areas. The boards periodically send out a questionnaire, as shown in Figure 14–1, which is the basis for information which is passed through the Car Service Division of the AAR to the appropriate railroads.

The Interstate Commerce Commission exercises jurisdiction over car service matters. When substantial freight car shortages begin to occur, the Commission, after study of the situation, issues—under its emergency

Please check all items in which you are directly interested:

	EXCELLENT	GOOD	FAIR	POOR
(a) CAR SUPPLY				
(b) CONDITION OF CARS PLACED FOR LOADING				
(c) MAINTENANCE OF SCHEDULES (CARLOAD)				
" " " (LESS CARLOAD)				

(d) TRACING INFORMATION   SATISFACTORY _____ UNSATISFACTORY _____
(e) FREIGHT STATION SERVICE   SATISFACTORY _____ UNSATISFACTORY _____
(f) WHERE CARS ARE DELAYED 72 HOURS
    ACCOUNT BAD ORDER IN TRANSIT, DO
    YOU GET REPORTS   YES _____ NO _____

(On items checked "POOR" or "UNSATISFACTORY" please give complete details with advice as to your handling with carrier or carriers concerned to permit further attention.)

FIG. 14–1.   Example of a car supply questionnaire sent out by Shippers Advisory Boards.

powers—a car service order designed to minimize the shortage. For example, an emergency situation resulted in the issuance of a car service order, Service Order No. 910, "Railroad Operating Regulations for the Movement of Loaded Freight Cars," issued in March, 1956. This order was instituted after an investigation showed that slow schedules and circuitous routing were major factors contributing to an acute car shortage. Typical of these practices was the so-called "thirty-day" slow schedule from Pacific Coast states to Missouri River crossings. Such schedules, together with certain published out-of-line routes, served as an invitation to shippers to use freight cars for storage. The result was that many car-

NAME OF INDUSTRY_____
        DAILY REPORT OF CAR SITUATION AS OF 9 AM, _____19_____.
    (Report should be sent to each Department Head daily after assembled by Traffic Manager.)

Plant Track Capacity, Cars _____

Cars on our tracks, LOADS_____EMPTIES_____

Loads held out on
Constructive Placement _____

) When plant tracks are full carriers are permitted to put
) cars on "constructive placement" and hold them out on
) other railroad tracks, and begin demurrage same as if
) actually placed on our tracks. Department heads should
) study delayed cars shown below to assure themselves that
) material is not being received in greater quantities than
) needed.

CAR			DAY &		#	#	
INITIAL	NUMBER	CONTENTS	HOUR PLACED*	HOURS DELAY	LOAD LIMIT CAPY., Lbs.	WEIGHT OF SHIPMENT	REMARKS – WHEN HELD OVER 24 HOURS EXPLAIN WHY DELAYED

* Show date placed thus: 8/1 7AM(A) for actual placement.
                         8/1 7AM(C) for constructive placement.
Use these columns to check into opportunities for heavier loading, with consequent saving in number of cars needed.
  The Load Limit capacity of each car will be found stencilled thereon.
NOTE: This form intended for use by shippers and receivers for own compilation and information in co-operating with railroads in elimination of car delays. Additional supply of forms will be furnished without charge upon request to Car Service Division, Assn. of American Railroads, Transportation Bldg., Washington, D. C.

FIG. 14–2.   An example of a daily report of cars.

days were lost. The Commission sought to stop this abuse by issuing the service order.

Traffic managers should keep themselves well informed on the current car service orders, for the orders may require heavier loading, higher demurrage charges, and many other aspects of car service.

A daily report which shows the freight cars on hand is maintained by many traffic managers. The form can show the length of time each car has been held, the explanation for delay, and the car capacity utilized. One such form in use is shown in Figure 14–2.

In motor transportation, there have been several efforts to organize a shipper-carrier group along regional lines similar to that of the Shippers Advisory boards, but this appears to be in the developmental stage. The Middlewest Shipper–Motor Carrier Conference was formed in 1952 and has a membership composed of shippers and carriers in twelve states. Each participating carrier or shipper may elect only one member to the conference, and the membership is balanced between shippers and carriers. Some of the subjects which are discussed at the regular meetings are freight claims, congressional action on impending legislation of mutual interest, rate and commodity classification problems, tracing, and research on improving service for the shipper and eliminating loading delays for the carrier. Similar groups have been formed since that time in other areas.

PRIVATE CARS

A railroad car that is not owned directly by a railroad company but rather by a shipper, or a car-line company with which the shipper or the carriers arrange for its use, is referred to as a "private car." Privately owned cars were used as early as 1867, but it was not until about 1885 that a sufficient number of them were being utilized to make them a factor to be considered in the transportation problems of the country. The development of freight traffic proved that many commodities could be transported more advantageously in cars which were especially adapted to the character and peculiar qualities of particular articles than in ordinary cars furnished by the carriers. Therefore, some shippers undertook to provide their own cars for the transportation of their commodities. Although initiated in a small way with regard to a few articles, the use of private cars has been rapidly expanding. Private cars now in use are not owned by shippers alone but, in large numbers, by private car lines which furnish particular types of equipment to shippers.

Some industries have need for a constant and adequate supply of a special kind of car in order to conduct business on a large and economical basis. When a shipper furnishes his own car, or a car he has leased from a private car line, for transportation of articles requiring a special type of equipment, he relieves the carrier of a certain amount of its obligations as a common carrier. The shipper who is assured of the exclusive use of special-type equipment thereby enjoys an advantage. By owning or leasing their own cars, shippers are assured of suitable equipment, available when it is needed. Using a car only for a particular product enables the packer or refiner to eliminate delays which would result from the cleaning, conditioning, and transferring of cars by the carrier. Thus, it is more economical for certain shippers to own or lease special-type equipment.

The rates under which carriers transport traffic include the use of the equipment in which it is transported. Therefore, following the custom that prevailed between connecting carriers in respect to the use of each other's cars, the carriers became the hirers of shippers' cars and, as such, began paying for their use on the basis of a certain amount per mile on loaded, or loaded and empty, movement. This practice still prevails. Under the requirements of the Interstate Commerce Commission, such allowances are published in tariff form.

A separate tariff sets forth the rules governing the payment of mileage allowances, also the equalization of mileage on private cars used in the transportation of freight traffic. The rules of the tariff cover cars transported over the lines of the carriers which are parties to the tariff, including movement to and from shops for repairs or reconditioning. They do not, however, apply to movements of empty cars for which charges are assessed under tariff authority; or to empty movement of new or newly acquired cars from the point at which they are manufactured or acquired to the point at which they are first loaded, or to a point at which the owner's shop or track is located or any point where the owner has contractual arrangements for construction, repairs, or storage of his equipment; or to movements of cars leased to or operated by carnival, circus, or show outfits; or to movements of cars not properly listed in the Official Railway Equipment Register.

Mileage allowances for the use of privately owned cars are paid for, whether loaded or empty movements, only to the car owner and not to a lessee. The mileage is computed on the basis of actual distance contained in the freight mileage tables of the individual lines via the route of movement from the station of origin or the station at which received from the connecting line to the destination station or to the station at which delivered to the connecting line.

When a private car is both loaded and unloaded within a switching district, no mileage will be allowed, and the mileage between an industry or public track and freight station to the station of origin or destination will not be allowed.

There are provisions for the equalization of mileage covered in the tariff. Equalization anticipates an equal number of miles of loaded car movement to be matched with an equal number of miles of empty car movement over the rails of the same carrier. The tariff rules governing equalization of mileage on privately owned tank cars and privately owned freight cars other than tank cars differ; but in principle, they are the same.

In the equalization of mileage for tank cars, the rule provides that if the total empty mileage of cars of private ownership on June 30 of each year, or at the end of such yearly period as may have been agreed upon, is more than the total loaded mileage of such cars, this excess must be paid for by the private owner. This may be done either by an equivalent loaded mileage during the succeeding six months or at applicable mileage rates contained in applicable classification and tariffs, without minimum, plus an amount equal to the mileage allowance that has been paid by the railroads on the excess empty mileage cars not entirely unloaded. The remainder of the lading returned from destination to the point of origin at less-carload charges will not be considered as loaded cars in mileage equalization. The excess, if any, of loaded mileage over empty mileage of cars at the end of the accounting period is continued as a credit against the empty movement of such cars for the succeeding twelve months only.

On the equalization of mileage on privately owned cars other than tank cars, the rules provide that if the total empty mileage of any owner's cars exceeds the total loaded mileage, the excess must be paid for by the owner, either by an equivalent loaded mileage or at applicable mileage rates named in the Consolidated or Uniform Freight Classification, without minimum, plus mileage allowance that has been paid by the railroad to the owner on such excess empty mileage whenever the amount of excess mileage warrants such action.

Private cars of different classes cannot be combined in one equalization account, and separate accounts must be kept for each class of equipment. The mileage rate allowance which the carrier pays to the car owner varies, depending upon the type of equipment, from 6 mills per car-mile to 3 cents. The General American Transportation Corporation and the Union Tank Car Company furnish a majority of the private tank cars. Refrigerator cars are available from private car lines, and the railroads have established subsidiaries which provide refrigerator cars. Pacific Fruit Express, for example, is owned by the Southern Pacific Railroad and the Union Pacific Railroad. The Fruit Growers Express Company is another example of a company owned by a number of railroads, including the Baltimore and Ohio and the Pennsylvania, as well as others. Shippers often furnish their own equipment, and some of them have established subsidiary companies which own the equipment. The extent of the private car fleet and the diversity of interests can be found through an examination of the Railway Equipment Register. In 1962, there were 28 owners of 1,000 cars or more, and the total number of privately owned cars in that year was 321,507.

Traffic managers using private cars have been attempting to lower transport costs by heavier loading and use of specialized equipment. An additional factor in the new cars is that they have been designed for more efficient loading and unloading and minimization of damage to the freight. The advantages gained through the use of new cars are offset, in substantial measure, by the low mileage rate the shipper receives for furnishing the car. The latter is often noncompensatory for the new cars and should be formulated on a different basis—possibly on a sliding scale, with higher-than-average payments for higher capacity or specialized cars, and lower-than-average for older, low capacity, or general service cars. The possibility of establishing a differential payment basis with larger payments for loaded than for empty mileage might also be considered.

The nature of some commodities which are moved for the military departments has resulted in the purchase of specialized car equipment by the military establishment. There has been an increase in the ownership of such cars.

From the foregoing description, it can be seen that the use of private cars may come from the following sources: (1) Private-car companies; (2) car lines owned as subsidiaries of railroads; (3) cars owned by industrial shippers or their subsidiaries; and (4) cars owned by various agencies of the federal government, predominantly the military departments.

The Interstate Commerce Commission has held that a railroad has an obligation to furnish only those cars reasonably necessary for the transportation of commodities ordinarily offered for transportation. This was true even though the tariffs of the carriers provided rates which would require specialized equipment for the movement.[1] This ruling has been consistently followed. The Commission has held that the carriers have the exclusive right to furnish cars, and therefore a private-car owner did not have the right to have his cars used in transporting freight without consent of the carrier.[2]

Among the reasons for the use of private cars are (1) the commodities shipped require specialized equipment, (2) regular volume of shipments permits maximum equipment utilization, and (3) production requirements are dependent upon a constant supply of cars.

The manager of a private-car division has the responsibility of developing and recommending programs and policies which will assure efficient and economical operation of the cars. In order to accomplish this, he must develop and suggest specific operating and maintenance policies and programs, and recommend the purchase, lease, or retirement of rolling stock. His assistance in the lease of rolling stock will involve recommendations on the negotiation of long- and/or short-term leases. For leased cars, a record is maintained showing mileage loaded and empty, mileage allowance, rental paid, and other information, as shown in Figure 14–3. Estimated car requirements, receipts, and shipments at various shipping points must be analyzed in order to determine the most efficient distribution and routing of empty cars. The movement of cars for maximum car utilization and mileage earnings must be expedited. Car tracing and reconsign-

---

[1] *Pennsylvania Paraffin Works* v. *Pennsylvania Railroad Co.*, 34 ICC 179 (1915).
[2] *Use of Privately-Owned Refrigerator Cars*, 201 ICC 323 (1934).

FROM AND TO	RAILROADS	DATES	MILEAGE		MONTH MILEAGE ALLOWED	MILEAGE ADJUSTMENTS	REMARKS	RENTAL PAID	AMOUNT
			LOADED	EMPTY					

LESSOR ______ PERIOD ______ RENTAL ______ INITIAL ______ NO. ______

FIG. 14–3. Sample of record maintained for leased cars.

ment must be provided to assure adequate cars at shipping points. The traffic manager must maintain current records of loaded and empty car movements. A maintenance program may be required to assure minimum time out of service for rolling stock. This will reflect surpluses or shortages and assist in the most efficient use of the fleet.

Upon unloading private cars, disposition instructions must be furnished the carrier. This is usually done on a form similar to Figure 14–4.

Where private cars are owned, they may be leased to the consignee upon arrival if the carrier is notified prior to the movement, thereby avoiding demurrage charges which might otherwise accrue if there was delay in loading or unloading.

Efficient utilization of other carriers' equipment is also important. However, the free-time allowances of carriers other than rail carriers are usually not as liberal as in rail transportation, so that there tends to be somewhat better utilization of equipment.

The increasing use of private carriage by transportation shippers has caused many traffic managers who are responsible for private transportation to establish management controls over owned or leased trucks and barges, as well as other transportation equipment. These records, which are similar to those described for rail but modified to reflect the particular equipment involved, must be maintained and used if this aspect of traffic management is to be handled properly.

SHIPPING NOTICE — EMPTY CAR

DATE_____195____

AGENT_____RAILROAD

_____

DEAR SIR:

FORWARD EMPTY CAR PROMPTLY

	CAR		LAST CONTENTS
	INITIAL	NUMBER	

TO_____

_____

ROUTE_____

YOURS TRULY,

_____

_____   PER_____

_____

DATE SHIPPED LOADED_____

WHEN EMPTY PLEASE RELEASE PROMPTLY, AND:–

1. FILL IN TIME AND DATES		ARRIVED LOADED	PLACED	UNLOADED	RELEASED	REMOVED FROM SIDING
	TIME					
	DATE					

COMMENTS_____

_____

_____

RAILROAD AGENTS COPY

FIG. 14–4. Sample of disposition instructions furnished carrier on private cars.

DEMURRAGE AND DETENTION

Demurrage is basically a charge assessed by carriers in order to penalize shippers or consignees for the detention of freight cars held by shippers or consignees for loading or unloading or for furnishing of disposition orders when the cars are held beyond a specified period of time. The assessment of this charge is expected to discourage the holding of cars and to speed their return to transportation service. It also compensates the carriers for the shippers' use of cars for storage. "Detention" is the term used by motor carriers for this charge.

Management control of demurrage and detention requires careful planning, accurate and regular reports of performance, and proper education

CABAHA COMPANY
CAR REPORT
(SEND DAILY TO TRAFFIC DEPARTMENT)

NAME OF COMPANY_____PLANT_____DATE_____

CARS RECEIVED

CAR INITIAL AND No.	L OR E	COMMODITY	CONSIGNOR	ORIGIN	COMPLETE ROUTING

CARS SHIPPED

CAR INITIAL AND No.	L OR E	COMMODITY	CONSIGNEE	DESTINATION	COMPLETE ROUTING

CARS ON TRACK

CAR INITIAL AND NO.	DATE REC'D.	L OR E	B. O. OR O. K.	CAP.	CAR INITIAL AND NO	DATE REC'D	L OR E	B. O. OR O. K.	CAP.	CAR INITIAL AND NO.	DATE REC'D.	L OR E	B. O. OR O. K.	CAP.

FIG. 14–5. An inbound car record form.

of employees who are concerned with the functions of loading and unloading.

Some companies have maintained a perfect record of no demurrage charges. Others have not exercised sufficient management control over this phase of traffic management, with the result that demurrage and detention become expensive items. An example of an extreme situation that came to the attention of the Commission was that of a company which held 47 cars 165 days for billing, and 54 cars 107 days for unloading, totaling 101 cars for 272 days.

In establishing a program for reducing or eliminating demurrage and detention charges, the methods of loading, unloading, and storage must be carefully analyzed. There must be co-ordination of information from the purchasing, sales, and production departments, so that the loading and unloading personnel may have knowledge of shipping movements. There are occasions when the loading or unloading crew will have to be held over and paid overtime if the plant desires to avoid a demurrage charge on a particular car. When the overtime would exceed the demurrage charge, a car is ordinarily detained an additional day, at which time the car could be loaded or unloaded during a normal day's work.

A car record or vehicle record is an important means of effecting control of demurrage and detention. An inbound car record form is shown in Figure 14–5. Proper maintenance of a record of this type shows the demurrage situation at a glance. Demurrage status can also be shown in regular reports to top management and to other department heads. If there are a number of plants, the reports by plant can be used as one indication of traffic performance and can be compared as to the number of cars handled versus demurrage paid.

The traffic manager must work closely with carriers to assure that carrier equipment is lined up to facilitate loading and unloading. Prompt loading and unloading may depend, to some degree, on material-handling equipment, and it is important to have such equipment available when it is needed.

Demurrage

Demurrage was first applied in the maritime field and was the amount paid by the charterer of a vessel to the owner of the ship if the ship was detained in port beyond the time agreed upon. With the shortage of rail equipment during the Civil War, one railroad decided to collect demurrage at the rate of $5.00 per day after 24 hours' free time. However, few carriers attempted to impose demurrage because of the competition between the carriers, and those that did found it difficult to collect such charges. Although, as early as 1884, there were demurrage circulars issued by a few carriers which provided a $1.00 per day charge after 24 hours' free time, it was not until some 4 years later that the demurrage idea spread. With the opening of the transcontinental railroads and the increased development of commerce in this country, the demand for freight cars increased. One of the factors that limited the availability of cars was the practice of shippers to hold cars in terminals and at their own warehouses as long as it suited their convenience. Therefore, demurrage rules and regulations were established by demurrage bureaus or car service associations and were widespread by 1891.

The demurrage rules were published in car service publications, freight classifications, special circulars, and freight schedules. Under the organization of the car service associations, a railroad could be covered by a number of different demurrage bureaus, each operating under different rules and regulations. This lack of uniformity resulted in many inequities. Some commodities were not subject to demurrage, whereas others were; the free time permitted for loading and unloading differed in various parts of the country; and larger shippers were favored over the smaller ones.

A nationwide car shortage developed in 1906 and 1907, and some twenty-five states enacted car service laws. In 1908, the Interstate Commerce Commission established a committee to investigate demurrage. The report of this committee resulted in the appointment of another committee, headed by one of the Interstate Commerce commissioners, to prepare a set of uniform rules and regulations for demurrage. The Interstate Commerce Commission, in 1909, endorsed the rules that were prepared and recommended that they be made effective; and practically all the railroads published tariffs providing for uniform application of the code. Since 1919, the demurrage rules and charges have been published in a single agency tariff, called the "Car Demurrage Rules and Charges." Changes in the rules or charges as they are required are developed through committees of the Association of American Railroads, representing the carriers, and the National Industrial Traffic League, representing the shippers, meeting in joint session with representatives of the Interstate Commerce Commission.

The carrier's obligation as a common carrier of carload freight and the rate paid for transportation includes, in addition to the actual movement of the car from the point of origin to final destination, the tender of or placement of the car, plus a reasonable time for loading or unloading. The free time allowed for loading or unloading is a part of the service included in the freight rate. However, the carrier's common-law obligation and the transportation rate do not provide for car detention for any purposes other than those directly connected with loading or unloading. The basic transportation rate, then, will not include use of a car for storage or warehouse purposes, detention for testing or analysis of the contents, or arrangement of disposal of the shipment.

There are a number of reasons that occasion demurrage charges; some are foreseeable and can be prevented, and others may be caused by factors temporarily beyond the control of the shipper or consignee. Some of the reasons for delays beyond the free time in loading and unloading are lack of adequate and efficient industrial facilities for handling commodities, use of freight cars for storage purposes, congested private sidings and plant facilities, ordering too many cars or ordering cars too far in advance, lack of adequate car records, improper billing, delays in securing order bills of lading, and bunching of shipments by the shipper and consignee.

Although the Car Demurrage Rules and Charges Tariff governs the application of demurrage charges, there are several special tariffs to cover particular types of traffic. The uniform demurrage rules generally are not applicable on export freight awaiting ships at port, or on coal for transshipment at lake ports or tidewater. Another demurrage tariff contains rules and assessments of charges on coal and coal products at mines, washing plants, coke ovens, weighing stations, and the like. Another one covers coal, coke, crushed stone, and sand loaded in open-top equipment for transshipment by lake.

There are two types of demurrage charges under the Car Demurrage Rules and Charges Tariff. One method is the straight demurrage, whereby each car placed for loading or unloading is considered separately. The other is the average-agreement plan, which provides for a system of credits which may be used to cancel certain debits in arriving at a monthly total for assessment of demurrage charges.

The types of cars upon which demurrage applies are defined, as well as those cars exempted from demurrage. The cars of either railroad or private ownership which are held by consignors or consignees for loading, unloading, forwarding directions, or any other purpose are subject to certain rules. Where cars are held for loading a railroad company's own freight, they are subject to the rules, unless the loading is done by the railroad for which the freight is intended and on its own tracks. There are a number of cars exempt from the rules. These are cars under load with company material for the use of and consigned to the railroad holding the cars; cars loaded with livestock, although this rule does not include cars held for loading livestock for or by the shippers—a federal statute requires that livestock being transported cannot be held in cars for more than 28 consecutive hours (this can be extended to 36 hours upon written request of the owner or the party in charge of the shipment);[3] cars held by railroads containing refused or unclaimed freight which is to be sold by the railroads for charges; cars containing refused or unclaimed freight held beyond legal requirements at the convenience of the carrier; and private cars on private tracks, when the ownership of the track and the cars is the same. Under this last provision, it has been the custom of those traffic departments which use private cars to lease the car to the consignee. Thus, the consignee, if he has a private siding, can hold the car beyond the expiration of free time, since he is also the lessee and, as such, is the owner. Most traffic departments have special forms which have been provided for this purpose; and in this manner, demurrage charges can be minimized on private-car movements.

Forty-eight hours constitutes the free-time period and has been looked upon as a reasonable period for a shipper to load or unload. This free-

---

[3] Livestock Twenty-Eight Hour Act, 34 Stat. L. 607.

time period has been in effect since the establishment of the Car Demurrage Rules and Charges more than 30 years ago, and it has remained relatively unchanged during periods of car shortages such as the two World Wars. Despite the free time, about 17 per cent of cars in 1962 were held beyond the free time. A 24-hour free-time period applies on cars held for diversion, reconsignment, or reshipping or held in transit on orders of the consignee, consignor, or owner.

Saturdays, Sundays, and legal holidays, but not half-holidays, are not counted in computing time for demurrage purposes until after the car has been held for four working days or two days beyond the free time. These days are counted in computing time, however, where average agreements are in effect.

Where cars are held for loading or unloading on private tracks, the free time is computed from 7:00 A.M. of the day after actual or constructive placement and without notice of actual placement. Actual placement is that time at which the engine is cut loose from the car or cars. Constructive placement consists of actual placement or of holding the cars on orders of the consignor. In the event that latter situation exists, the agent has to send or give the consignor written notice of all cars he has been unable to place because of conditions of the other-than-public-delivery track, or because of other conditions attributable to the consignor. Cars held for loading on public delivery tracks will have the time computed from 7:00 A.M. of the day after placement. If the carrier fails to place the car within twenty-four hours after 7:00 A.M. of the day for which the car was ordered, the time will be computed from the first 7:00 A.M. after the day on which the carrier sends or gives notice of placement to the consignor. On inbound cars held for orders, surrender of the bill of lading, or payment of freight charges, the free time starts on the first 7:00 A.M. of the day after the notice of arrival is sent or given to the consignee or the party entitled to receive such notice.

When an industry performs its own switching for itself or for others, cars are considered to be delivered by the railroad when they are accepted by the industry on an interchange track, which is a track connection between a railroad and an industry. In this particular case, time is computed from the first 7:00 A.M. following actual or constructive placement of the car on the interchange track by the railroad and continues until the car is returned to the same or another interchange track.

When cars are ordered for loading on privately owned sidings by the consignor, the carrier assumes that siding space is available. If there is no space available, the carrier holds the car under constructive placement, and time is computed from the first 7:00 A.M. after such constructive placement.

Shippers sometimes make use of cars that have been unloaded on their sidings without the formality of placing an order for them. Such cars are referred to as "appropriated cars," and they are considered as having been ordered and actually placed at the time they are appropriated. If the cars are not loaded after the shipper has appropriated them, there is no free time authorized.

As indicated earlier, demurrage charges can be assessed for the detention of cars in two ways: (1) under the straight plan or (2) under the average-agreement plan, dependent upon the consignor's or consignee's desires. Demurrage charges are assessed at a certain amount per car per day or fraction of a day under the straight plan and are graduated upward the longer the cars are detained. Charges are increased during periods of car shortages. The average-agreement plan is a written agreement between a shipper and a carrier, whereby the demurrage charges are computed on the basis of the average time of detention of cars which are released during a calendar month. Under this plan, an allowance of one credit for each car released within the first 24 hours of free time is permitted, and there is the assessment of one debit for each of the first 4 days a car is held after the expiration of the free time. At the end of the month, the total number of credits is deducted from the total number of debits, and $4.00 is charged for each remaining debit. Where the credits exceed the debits, no charge is made, except for the detention of cars beyond the fourth debit day at the rate of $8.00. The excess credits from one month cannot be carried forward to the second month, nor do carriers make any payments for an excess of credits. There is no interchange of debits or credits permitted on inbound or outbound cars, which means that credits earned on inbound cars may not be used to offset debits accruing on outbound cars; nor may inbound debits be offset by outbound credits.

Where there is sufficient volume of car movements, traffic managers have found it advantageous to enter into an average agreement. Not only can savings in demurrage charges be effected, but the consignee or the consignor secures the maximum free time to load or unload each car and has the advantage of using unexpired free time on some cars to offset detention beyond the free time on other cars. The average agreement is beneficial to the carrier, in that it can place cars for loading or unloading without consideration as to the order of arrival, and thereby eliminate unnecessary switching.

Approximately 90 per cent of the cars subject to demurrage rules are covered by average agreements. Table 14–1 shows the charges under the straight plan and the average-agreement plan. Average annual demurrage collected during the decade 1952–62 amounted to a little more than $32 million.

There are a number of causes for cancellation or refunding of demurrage charges, the first of which is weather interference. If, during the free-time period, weather conditions are such as to render impossible the

TABLE 14–1

COMPUTATION OF FREE TIME, CHARGEABLE DAYS, AND AMOUNT OF
DEMURRAGE CHARGES ACCRUING PER CAR UNDER THE STRAIGHT
PLAN AND THE AVERAGE-AGREEMENT PLAN

PLACED AFTER 7 A.M. ON:	RELEASED AFTER 7 A.M. ONE WEEK LATER													STRAIGHT PLAN TOTAL DEMURRAGE	AVERAGE AGREEMENT TOTAL DEMURRAGE (USING CREDITS TO OFFSET UP TO 4 DEBITS PER CAR)
	Tuesday	Wednesday	Thursday	Friday	Saturday	Sunday	Monday	Tuesday	Wednesday	Thursday	Friday	Saturday	Sunday		
Monday ..	F	F	$4	$4	$4	$4	$8							24	8
Tuesday ..		F	F	$4	F	$4	$4	$4						16	0
Wednesday			F	F	X	X	$4	$4	$4					12	0
Thursday .				F	X	X	$4	$4	$4	$4				16	0
Friday					X	X	F	F	$4	$4	$4	$4		12	0
Saturday ..						X	F	F	$4	$4	$4	$4		16	0
Sunday ...							F	F	$4	$4	$4	$4	$8	24	8

F—Free time.
X—Excluded day.

loading or unloading of the cars without serious injury to the freight, an extension of the regular free period of 48 hours is granted until a total of 48 hours free from such interference shall have been allowed to secure the extra free time due to weather interference. A claim must be presented to the railroad within 30 days after the demurrage bill is presented. Where the lading of a car cannot be unloaded due to its being frozen or congealed, 48 hours' additional free time will be permitted, provided the consignee informs the carrier in writing within the first 24-hour period of this situation. Floods, earthquakes, hurricanes, or tornadoes, with their resultant aftermath, occasion detention which will be eliminated when the consignors or consignees cannot get to the cars to load or unload.

Another reason for the waiving of demurrage charges is that of bunching. This is a daily tender of cars by the carrier to the consignor or consignee in excess of the number which he has the ability to load or unload, resulting in an accumulation of cars. If a carrier makes irregular deliveries or has delays in filling orders for cars which result in accumulated numbers beyond the shipper's daily requirements, the shipper is allowed free time for loading on all cars that he normally would have had if they had been placed for loading as he ordered. A carrier's negligence, or such things as floods or earthquakes, may cause cars coming to the consignee via the same route from one point of origin to be bunched and tendered for delivery in excess of the requirements of the consignee. The consignee will be allowed the free time he normally would have had if the cars had not been bunched, but he must file a claim with the carrier in order to receive this allowance. This must be done within 30 days after the demurrage bill is presented. An illustration of bunching may be described as it applies to a shipper in New York who regularly ships 3 carloads a day to a consignee in Akron, Ohio. The consignee can unload 3 cars a day when they are placed for unloading. However, due to one of the aforementioned causes, the consignee receives no cars for 3 days, but on the fourth day the carrier places 3 cars and notifies the consignee of constructive placement of 9 cars due to delays in transit. The consignee could secure an adjusted free time on the 9 cars.

Another cause for waiving demurrage charges is that of delay or improper notice by the railroad. A notice of arrival which does not contain adequate information so that the consignee can identify the shipment will result in his requesting the carrier, within the free-time period, to supply him with the information omitted. The time which elapses between the receipt of the request for additional information by the carrier and the furnishing of the omitted information will not be charged against the consignee. When the detention results from an error directly chargeable to the carrier, there may be cancellation or waiver of demurrage charges. There is also a provision which applies to "run-around" cars, by which is meant the placement of recently arrived cars ahead of previous arrivals.

Additional free time is provided on cars containing import freight which are delayed by United States Customs or Department of Agriculture. The free time is not extended when the Department of Agriculture permits the filing and acceptance of a bond and the consignee or owner of the freight delays or fails to file such a bond. Thus, if delay is caused or contributed to by the consignee or owner, additional free time will not be allowed.

The last of the causes that may justify the suspension or waiving of demurrage charges is interference due to strikes. When cars are detained because of a strike of employees and the consignor or consignee is unable to load or unload cars, an adjustment from the regular demurrage charges may be secured. In order to secure cancellation or refund of demurrage charges assessed or collected, the consignor or consignee must present a claim in writing to the carrier within thirty days, stating the date and time such interference began and ceased. The period of time for which charges are assessed starts on the first 7:00 A.M. after the strike begins and runs until the first 7:00 A.M. after it ceases.

Where railroads deliver freight in harbor and terminal areas via lighters, barges, or car floats which are used to deliver freight to vessels carrying goods for export or to domestic customers, the rules, regulations, and charges for the use of this equipment will be found in separate tariffs. When this marine equipment reports at its destination, the shipper consignee or steamship agency which is directing the freight movement must provide a berth for the marine equipment. Two days' free time is permitted from the time the barge reports, and these free days are called "lay" days. Demurrage charges accrue, depending upon the marine equipment involved. In the New York harbor, an agreement can be entered into regarding boat demurrage. On goods moving in export, the free time is seven days; but this is modified, from time to time, by service orders. The apparent liberality in free-time allowance has been based largely on the fact that ships sometimes do not arrive as scheduled. There are also tidewater demurrage rules on cars containing anthracite or bituminous coal or coke for transshipment to vessels, and the individual tariffs covering these matters must be consulted.

Demurrage charges on barges on the inland waterways are applied on the basis of the length of the barge, and free-time allowance is based on the amount of cargo. For 300 or less tons, the free time allowed is three days, with a graduated scale upward to 701 to 900 tons and a free-time period of 8 days. The charges on barges of 175 feet or less in length on each of the first 3 days or fraction are $30 and, graduated upward to barges of over 200 feet in length, $60 for each of the first 3 days.

In ocean shipping, wharf demurrage is assessed when the cargo remains on the pier beyond a specified period of time. Ordinarily, the owner of the cargo is responsible for this, and the charge is made against him. It sometimes happens, however, that cargo is on the pier beyond the allotted free-time period due to the carrier's failure to make its schedule date. Under these circumstances, demurrage charges are made against the ship and not against the cargo.

Detention

Motor carriers have not established rules, regulations, and charges for detention of vehicles which are uniform, as has been the case with the railroads. In motor transportation, the reference will be usually found in the motor carrier tariffs and is referred to as a "detention charge." The purpose of this charge is identical with that of the rail demurrage charges —to secure prompt release of equipment. The free time for loading or unloading trucks varies from area to area; and upon the expiration of free time, many of the tariffs provide a charge based not on a given amount per day but a specified amount per hour. Even though such charges are published, many motor carriers do not collect them.

One of the major interterritorial motor rate bureaus publishes a detention tariff which provides, on truckload lots, 8 hours of permissible free time. For the first 24-hour period after the free time, the charge is $10; for the second 24-hour period, $15; and for the third 24-hour period, $25.[4] In another specific detention tariff, the free time permitted for delivery is on a graduated scale, based on the number of pounds, as follows:[5]

---

[4] Central and Southern Motor Freight Tariff Association, MF–ICC No. 118.
[5] Ohio Motor Freight Bureau, MF–ICC No. 629.

Weight (in Pounds)	Free Time (in Minutes)
2,000 or less	40
2,000–5,000	60
5,001–12,000	120
12,001–20,000	210
20,001–30,000	255
Over 30,001	360

The free time for pickup differs from that for delivery.

Where the loading or unloading of freight is delayed beyond the free time provided, a charge of $2.50 per vehicle for each 20 minutes or fraction thereof is provided in some motor tariffs.

The existence of considerably higher motor detention charges than rail demurrage charges has, no doubt, partly accounted for a higher degree of equipment utilization in motor transportation.

DISCUSSION QUESTIONS AND PROBLEMS

1. "The most effective utilization of carrier equipment is a joint responsibility of shippers and carriers." Why?
2. What are Shippers Advisory boards? What are the purposes and functions of the boards? List the benefits to a traffic manager in joining a Shippers Advisory Board.
3. Prepare a report, as traffic manager for a company, indicating whether it would be advisable to own or lease special-type equipment for moving a liquid chemical in large quantities to 5 customers located from 500 to 2,000 miles from the plant.
4. Explain the mileage allowance for private cars. Where will it be found?
5. How is equalization of mileage on private cars computed?
6. Secure a copy of the Railway Equipment Register, and determine how extensive a private-car fleet is now existent. What is the trend in the use of private cars?
7. What management controls should be exercised over privately owned or leased equipment?
8. One writer has stated that the investment in rail cars exceeds $1 billion; yet, the cars are actually moving but 15 per cent of the time. What is the relationship, if any, between this statement and demurrage?
9. The free time for loading and unloading boxcars is far more liberal than that granted by motor carriers. Are railroads too liberal? What suggestions do you have on this problem?
10. Summarize the rules governing demurrage.
11. Carefully explain demurrage charges under the straight plan and the average-agreement plan. How would you determine whether you should operate under an average-demurrage agreement?
12. Why is there basically a single tariff covering demurrage for railroads but not a single one for motor carrier detention charges?

Chapter

15

CLAIMS PROCEDURE
AND PREVENTION

CLAIMS PROCEDURE

A LL carriers strive to give service to shippers which will meet the ship-pers' needs and insure that the goods arrive in satisfactory condition. Although the loss of goods en route or the damage to goods can be ad-justed and payment made for the damages, the fact remains that the shipper and the consignee have made the shipment in response to a potential or actual order, and the failure of the goods to arrive causes inconvenience and perhaps monetary loss. Thus, even the satisfactory adjustment of loss and damage claims is a poor substitute for the arrival of a shipment in good condition.

Causes of Claims

The causes of loss of or damage to goods may not be entirely a carrier responsibility, for such factors as the method of packing have influence in the safe arrival of a shipment. This co-responsibility of shippers and carriers has led to a relationship between carriers and shippers unique in its spirit of co-operation. The Association of American Railroads has a Freight Claim Division that has three primary activities. The first involves the uniform, equitable, prompt, and lawful settlement of claims with claimants. The next activity is the proper interline distribution among the interested railroads of the amounts paid to claimants in settling their claims for loss, damage, or delay. The third area of primary interest is to ascertain the causes for loss of and damage to freight, in order that this information may be made available to interested organizations which can develop remedies to minimize recurrences. The American Trucking Asso-ciations, Inc., has a National Freight Claim Council which conducts similar programs.

To assist in the implementation of these programs, the railroads and motor carriers maintain codes of regulation, which are (1) Principles and Practices for the Investigation and Disposition of Freight Claims with claimants; (2) Freight Claim Rules for interline apportionment of amounts paid; (3) Prevention Practices and Recommendations, supplemental to item 4, which follows; and (4) Rules of Order, the constitution used to guide the Freight Claim Division of the AAR and the By-Laws of the National Freight Claim Council of the American Trucking Associations, Inc.

The railroads and motor carriers have territorial organizations, which are called "Freight Claim conferences," to aid in the handling of loss and damage claim problems on a regional and terminal basis. There are 10 of these rail organizations, 8 of which are in the United States and 2 in Canada. These groups co-operate with each other on interterritorial matters, as well as with the Freight Claim Division of the AAR on matters of general or nationwide concern. There are several regional motor carrier Freight Claim conferences, and more are in the process of being formed.

The railroads and the Fibre Box Association jointly conducted a transportation and packing survey on causes of claims which covered a three-year period and involved 3,440 carloads of products in fiberboard boxes from more than 1,000 different manufacturers. The three most prominent causes of damage found in this study were (1) rough handling of the car by the railroads, which accounted for 27 per cent of the damage; (2) poor arrangement of the load by the shipper, which caused 19 per cent of the damage; and (3) loose loading of the boxes in the car, which caused 16 per cent of the damage. The remaining 38 per cent was divided among 18 other minor causes.[1]

An arbitration procedure has been established for use whenever a difference of opinion between the railroads arises as to the proper application of any of the provisions of the codes. Through the years, rail carriers in different parts of the country did not have the same opinions as to carrier liability on claims of identical nature, nor did the claimants in different parts of the country have the same opinions as to carrier liability. The result of this was that claims which were similar often were not adjusted uniformly. To business organizations distributed over a wide area, these variations were particularly noticeable. Railroads were increasingly confronted with these divergencies and asked why such conditions existed. The general tendency was that the most liberal policy followed by a carrier with its claimants was the one advocated by shippers to be adopted generally in all territories. The existence of a situation such as this led to the development of the code of Principles and Practices for the Investigation and Disposition of Freight Claims, which was originally issued by the railroads in 1933. The principles and practices in this code are not arbitrary statements of carrier liability but do represent the

---

[1] *Traffic World*, March 28, 1953, p. 72.

consensus of opinion of the legal counsels of the railroads as to the meaning and intent of the various statutes, rulings of administrative bodies, and other decisions on the subject.[2]

The purposes of establishing this code were to secure uniformity by carriers and to give uniform treatment to claimants in disposing of claims of like nature, thereby maintaining harmonious relationships in freight claim matters among carriers and effecting more efficient handling of claims.

Although there have been many suggestions for including other types of claims than those currently contained in the code of Principles and Practices, the items that are included are those which have been sustained by a consensus of the railroads' legal counsel. The following outline of the sections contained in the code indicates that most of the contingencies regarding claim adjustments are included:

1. A preamble setting forth purposes and observance.
2. Claim-filing requirements.
3. Support of claims.
4. Measure of damage.
5. Destination inspections.
6. Claims for damage or deterioration from improper protective service of perishables.
7. Claims for damage by delay.
8. Claims for damage at intermediate points.
9. Claims based on unauthorized inspection.
10. Claims for lost packages from consolidated carloads of LCL.

The Bill of Lading Act fixes the responsibility for the loss or damage that might occur in transportation upon the railroad which issues the contract of carriage to the owner of the shipment, regardless whether such loss of shipment or damage occurred on its own line or with some other connecting railroad. The shipper is not concerned directly about the interline apportionment of claims among carriers, except that arrangements have been made to facilitate the apportionment in such a manner as to permit more efficient handling of claims.

There are definitions in the Freight Claim Rules of terminology used which assist in the more precise determination of responsibility. Such terms as "receiving carrier," "loading carrier," "unloading carrier," and "delivering carrier," are defined, to name but a few. The following definitions are of particular interest to shippers in the Freight Claim Rules: "Concealed loss or damage" is defined as freight which has been received at an initial point, carried and delivered without valid exception to receiving, checking, loading, unloading, or handling of freight at any point or between points, or during transportation, the loss or damage developing

---

[2] From an address, "Freight Loss and Damage Claims," given by Lewis Pilcher, Freight Claim Division, Association of American Railroads, at Transportation and Traffic Management Conference, Northeastern University, Boston, Massachusetts, May 21–22, 1952.

after delivery to consignee. "Unlocated loss and unlocated damage" is defined as loss or damage which is observed *before* delivery to consignee of freight received at initial or junction point and received under perfect record up to the destination point. The term "perfect record," just referred to, is considered to be one which a carrier has when investigation fails to locate any exception to receiving, checking, loading, sealing, waybilling, carding, and unloading of freight at any point, or between points, or during the transportation.

Although the initial carrier may be expected to investigate and settle claims under the provisions of the Bill of Lading Act, later legislation has provided that when a destination carrier delivers freight to a consignee in an incomplete or damaged condition, it is presumed at law that this resulted from an act of the destination railroad, which has to accept and adjust the claim with the claimant. However, the carrier has recourse against another carrier or carriers which participated in the transportation of the shipment.

The railroads try to control the many elements comprising their transportation service in order to minimize loss, damage, or delay to a shipment. There are nonrailroad responsibilities which may contribute to loss or damage and are not the result of handling but are caused by the inherent nature of the commodity or due to some cause that occurred before the freight was turned over to the railroads or after its delivery. Many of these nonrailroad responsibilities are areas in which the traffic manager, through proper attention, can co-operate with all interested parties in eliminating or minimizing the claims that might arise due to these factors. Among the nonrailroad responsibilities are the following:

1. Deterioration in transit due to the inherent nature of the goods transported. Examples of this are diseases of fruits, melons, and vegetables which have had their origin in the growing fields.

2. Manufacture of commodities in such a manner as to make them less liable to handling damage. Examples of this would be more sturdy construction of some of the more fragile articles, such as earthenware, glassware, and furniture.

3. Preparation of the article for transportation, which may include proper wrapping and boxing prior to its being placed in a shipping container.

4. Placement of the article within the shipping container, and sufficient inner packing to prevent damage through the contact of one article with another and to cushion shocks.

5. Securing the shipping container so as to assure that the contents will be maintained in good condition when shipped.

6. Proper and complete marking of the package. There are a surprising number of cities with identical names in the United States, which fact requires that the correct and complete marking be placed on the package. For example, there are more than twenty Springfield's in the United States. Of course, each individual package in a carload shipment does not have to be marked with consignee and consignor and other relevant information. In the case of a discrepancy between the bill of lading and the marks on the packages, the marks on the packages govern.[3]

---

[3] *Ibid.*

Shippers of carload freight are obligated to see that their articles for shipment are properly loaded, stowed, and secured prior to transportation. Consignees, in a similar manner, are obligated to unload carload shipments or handle freight at stop-off points or destination; and they must exercise a great deal of care in unloading in order to minimize loss or damage.

Motor carriers have benefited by the experience of the railroads in the establishment of their freight claim rules. The Principles and Practices for the Investigation and Disposition of Freight Claims for motor carriers consists of the following:

1. The purposes of the Principles and Practices.
2. Time limit for filing claims.
3. Documents required in support of claims.
4. Destination inspection.
5. Claims for deterioration.
6. Claims for damage by delay.
7. Claims for damage developed at intermediate point.
8. Measure of damages.
9. Two or more claims presented on same shipment.
10. Claims refiled.

Loss and Damage Claims

There are a number of different types of claims, one group of which is the loss and damage claim. The Commission does not have jurisdiction over the settlement of loss and damage claims, so that the shipper, if dissatisfied with claim adjustment, has recourse to the courts. This type of claim is a process in equity. As will be discussed later, the Commission does have jurisdiction over overcharge claims. A claimant may seek reparation through the courts for an overcharge claim but, in so doing, cannot seek further redress from the Commission.

Loss and damage claims entail the demand from a shipper for the payment of total or partial loss or damage to goods incurred in their transportation. This also will include claims which involve monetary losses due to the failure of rail carriers to transport the commodity with reasonable dispatch. Those articles in which there is a daily recorded market price, such as fruits and vegetables, livestock, and grain, are examples of shipments in which losses can be involved due to delay. For example, a carload of green beans originating in Florida and consigned to New York City might be due in New York for the market of the fourth day; but because of a defect, the car might be stopped and so not arrive until the fifth day. The market for green beans might have been $1.75 per basket on the due date and $1.50 on the date actually delivered, or a market decline of $0.25 per basket. Upon the proper presentation of the facts, the carrier would be liable for the loss sustained by the shipper. If the car has been delayed one or two days and the market remains the same during this time, there would be no market loss for which the carrier could be charged, assuming that there was no deterioration of the contents of the car because of the delay.

Carriers, in many instances, have established operating schedules for the handling of certain traffic. These operating schedules, over a period of time, have come to be accepted by the shipper and the carrier as constituting reasonable dispatch. Delays beyond these schedules are chargeable to the carrier if a loss results, unless the delay was occasioned by one of the excepted perils, such as an act of God. Other freight is often referred to as "dead freight," and some transportation delay ordinarily would not be justification for filing such a claim on this particular type of freight.

In cases involving delay, the carrier has been found to be liable only for damages which would, in the usual and ordinary course of things, result from its failure to perform. Such damages are called "general damages." All other damages are termed "special." For example, if the carrier is given notice of circumstances or certain conditions which may develop if there is delay in transit, and the delay occurs, the shipper can secure special damages, such as profits which would have been realized had there been no delay.

Freight which has become separated from the regular revenue freight bill is termed "astray freight" and is covered by an astray freight bill. "Over freight" is freight with or without marks (including articles in excess of quantity on billing) which is found at any point without a regular revenue or astray bill.

The filing of loss and damage claims with railroads is made to the freight claim agent, which is usually under the freight claim department. However, other types of claims are handled by the auditor of freight traffic, as will be explained later. A loss and damage claim, supported by the necessary documents required by the carrier, may be filed with the local freight agent of the carrier against which the claim is pending, or it may be mailed directly to the freight claim department of the carrier.

Section 2 (b) in the Bill of Lading Terms and Conditions states that claims must be "filed" with the carrier within nine months from the date of delivery of the shipment at destination. A claim is not considered filed until it is actually received by the carrier—that is, received either by the local freight agent or by the freight claim department. Where railroads pay for claims which involve loss, damage, or delay to freight, this payment does not include interest on such amounts, except where suits have been filed and the order of the court requires the payment of interest. Rail common carriers assume extraordinary liability as insurers of goods, subject to exceptions shown in Section 1 of the Bill of Lading Terms and Conditions. These exceptions are an act of God, the public enemy, the authority of law, the act or default of the shipper, and natural shrinkage or the inherent nature or vice of the goods. If there is a loss of goods while in the possession of a common carrier as bailee, which was caused by one of the perils just cited, the carrier might be liable if it could be shown that it failed to use reasonable care either to avoid the peril or to minimize the loss or damage after the goods were actually exposed to the peril. If the loss is occasioned by one of the aforementioned perils, it must be proved that the carrier's negligence was the proximate cause and not the remote cause of the loss.

The railroads' liability for loss or damage to freight is detailed by the contract terms and conditions of the uniform bill of lading. Whether or not such bill of lading is actually issued, most rate tariffs refer to the Consolidated Freight Classification or the Uniform Freight Classification which, in Rule I, contains the provision that unless otherwise provided in the classification, the acceptance and use are required of the uniform domestic straight or order bill of lading or the uniform export straight or order bill of lading. The exception to this is contained in the same rule, which permits the shipper to ship his goods under carrier liability at an increased freight rate of 10 per cent. In this case, the shipments are handled under common-law liability. Under common-law liability, shipments are transported subject to the five exceptions to liability which have already been mentioned; but carriers are not relieved from liability for loss or damage caused by (1) fire occurring after the expiration of forty-eight hours after notice of arrival is sent or given consignee and/or while the property is being held by the carrier as a warehouseman only (Sections 1 [b[and 4[a] of bill of lading); (2) riots or strikes (Section 1 [b] of bill of lading); (3) loss, damage, or delay to property stopped and held in transit upon request of the shipper, owner, or party entitled to make such request unless such loss, damage, or delay is caused by one or more of the five excepted causes (Section 1 [b] of bill of lading); (4) country damage to cotton (Section (1) [b] of bill of lading); and (5) property left exposed to theft or the elements at a nonagency station after unloading from a train (Section 4 [f] of bill of lading). Traffic managers rarely ship their goods under the rule provision providing for common-law liability.

Under the Uniform Bill of Lading Terms and Conditions, the rail carrier is liable sometimes as a warehouseman and not as a common carrier. Liability as a common carrier exists only for the period of free time allowed by the tariff for the removal of the goods after arrival at destination. After the expiration of free time, with the proper notice having been sent or given, the liability of the carrier is that of a warehouseman. The basic difference between liability as a common carrier and the common carrier as a warehouseman only is that the common carrier, as such, is liable as an insurer of the property with the five peril exceptions mentioned in the bill of lading, whereas the carrier as the warehouseman is liable only for losses resulting from negligence. As a warehouseman, the carrier must exercise ordinary care; whereas as a carrier, it must exercise extraordinary care.

The following example illustrates the differences in liability. A shipment of freight arrives at destination, and the usual arrival notice is sent to the consignee or party entitled to receive it. It is allowed to remain on hand in the warehouse of the carrier beyond the free time allowed by the tariff for the removal of such freight. After the expiration of free time, and before the removal of the freight by the consignee, the warehouse in which it is stored catches fire from some source other than lightning, through no negligence of the carrier; and the carrier, with the exercise of ordinary care, cannot prevent the destruction of the goods. In that event, the carrier is not liable for the loss, even though the fire was not caused by either of the excepted perils, because the goods were being held as a warehouseman only and a warehouseman's liability does not include losses by fire not caused by his negligence. Let us suppose that there was another identical shipment in the same warehouse on which the free time had not expired and which was being held by the carrier as a carrier. The second shipment was destroyed by the same fire as that which destroyed the first shipment and under the same circumstances. Since the fire resulted from a cause that did not exempt the carrier from liability as a common carrier, regardless of its efforts to preserve the goods, it would be liable for the loss. This exception would not apply to freight intended for "store-door delivery" and being held by the carrier for its own convenience.

Railroads analyze types of claims filed and group them into listed causes, together with the percentage that each group represents of the total freight claims. A typical example of this shows the following causes and the approximate percentages:

	Per Cent
For unlocated damage	48
Unlocated loss	16
Concealed loss and damage	12
Delays	6
Defective or unfit equipment	4
Train accidents	3
Improper handling in trains, yards, or stations	1
Error of employee	1
Temperature failures	1
Fire, marine, and catastrophes	1
Miscellaneous, aggregate	7

Individual carriers formulate prevention programs which emphasize their past experiences. The following is an outline of the various aspects which receive particular attention in one carrier's program:

1. Preparation of cars for loading.
2. Acceptance of shipments for transportation properly packed and marked.
3. Careful physical handling.
4. Proper stowing of freight.
5. Accurate and complete platform records.
6. Continuing education and instruction of station employees.
7. Proper handling of miscellaneous matters, such as claims correspondence, billing, handling of pickup and delivery, and other matters.

The loss and damage which is visible and which has been received with an exception made at the time of delivery is often referred to as "known loss or damage." The standard form for presentation of rail loss and damage (shown in Figure 15–1) is used, supported by the orig-

---

Standard Form for Presentation of Loss and Damage Claims

Approved by the Interstate Commerce Commission; Freight Claim Division, Association of American Railroads; National Industrial Traffic League, and the National Association of Railway Commissioners

(Claimant's Number) ‡

_____
(Name of person to whom claim is presented)

_____
(Address of claimant)

(Carrier's Number)

_____
(Name of carrier)

_____
(Date)

_____
(Address)

This claim for $_____ is made against the carrier named above by_____
(Amount of claim)   (Name of claimant)

for_____ in connection with the following described shipments:
(loss or damage)

Description of shipment _____

Name and address of consignor (shipper)_____

Shipped from_____, To_____
(City, town or station)   (City, town or station)

Final Destination_____ Routed via_____
(City, town or station)

Bill of Lading issued by_____Co.; Date of Bill of Lading_____

Paid Freight Bill (Pro) Number_____; Original Car Number and Initial_____

Name and address of consignee (Whom shipped to)_____

If shipment reconsigned enroute, state particulars: ____ _____

DETAILED STATEMENT SHOWING HOW AMOUNT CLAIMED IS DETERMINED.

(Number and description of articles, nature and extent of loss or damage, invoice price of articles, amount of claim, etc.)

	Total Amount Claimed

IN ADDITION TO THE INFORMATION GIVEN ABOVE, THE FOLLOWING DOCUMENTS ARE SUBMITTED IN SUPPORT OF THIS CLAIM.*

1. Original bill of lading, if not previously surrendered to carrier.
2. Original paid freight ("expense") bill.
3. Original invoice or certified copy.
4. Other particulars obtainable in proof of loss or damage claimed:

_____

REMARKS_____

The foregoing statement of facts is hereby certified to as correct.

_____
(Signature of claimant.)

‡ Claimant should assign to each claim a number, inserting same in the space provided at the upper right hand corner of this form. Reference should be made thereto in all correspondence pertaining to this claim.
*Claimant will please place check (x) before such of the documents mentioned as have been attached, and explain under "Remarks" the absence of any of the documents called for in connection with this claim. When for any reason it is impossible for claimant to produce original bill of lading, or paid freight bill, claimant should indemnify carrier or carriers against duplicate claim supported by original documents.

FIG. 15–1. Standard form for presentation of known loss or damage for all rail transportation.

STANDARD FORM FOR THE HANDLING OF CONCEALED LOSS
AND CONCEALED DAMAGE CLAIMS

SHIPPER'S FORM

INFORMATION REQUIRED FROM SHIPPER IN SUPPORT OF CLAIM FOR CONCEALED
LOSS OR CONCEALED DAMAGE

SHIPPER'S CLAIM NO..CONSIGNEE'S CLAIM NO...................................

POINT OF ORIGIN..DESTINATION..

DATE...NUMBER OF PACKAGES....................................

SHIPPER..CONSIGNEE..

COMMODITY...

INFORMATION REQUIRED	ANSWERS
1. When were the goods packed, if known?.................................	....
(a) Where were the goods packed?...	....
2. Were all the articles for which claim is made packed in container in good order?	....
(a) Was each article in (this package) (these packages) examined when packed or re-shipped, before delivery to the carrier?..............	....
(b) Does your record indicate whether or not the container was packed to its full capacity with the property shipped?........................	....
(c) If not packed full, what material occupied the remaining space?.........	....
3. Was the package protected against abstraction of or damage to contents by being strapped, sealed, corded, or otherwise specifically protected?....	....
(a) If so, how?..	....
4. On what date was shipment delivered to truckman?......................	....
(a) Was the shipment delivered truckman before or after 12 o'clock noon?.....	....
(b) Was the delivery made to the carrier by your own truck?..............	....
(c) If not, give name of trucking company...........................	....
(d) Give name of driver in either case, if known......................	....
(e) If not delivered by truck, state how delivered......................	....

I hereby certify the foregoing statement of facts to be true in every particular, to the best of my knowledge and belief

Dated at...   Signature...

Date..., 19....   ....
                                                                    in what capacity employed

FIG. 15–2. Shipper's form for concealed loss or damage for motor carriers.

inal bill of lading or bond of indemnity, the original freight bill or bond of
indemnity, and the original invoice or a certified copy. The concealed
loss or damage is that received with no loss or damage visible at the time
it is delivered, and the shipment is received without exception. The shipper's form and consignee's form used in handling concealed loss or damage for motor carriers are shown in Figures 15–2 and 15–3. Rail forms
are very similar. The carrier's agent, after notification by the shipper of
concealed damage, will make an inspection within 48 hours after delivery
of the freight. Claims for concealed damage must be filed within 15 days

**Standard Form for the Handling of Concealed Loss
and Concealed Damage Claims**

CONSIGNEE'S FORM

**Information Required From Consignee in Support of Claim for Concealed
Loss or Concealed Damage**

Shipper's Claim No. .... Consignee's Claim No. ....

Description of Shipment

Point of Origin .... Destination ....
Date Received .... Number of Packages ....
Shipper .... Consignee ....
Commodity ....

1. When (date and hour) was shipment received at your place of business? ....
....
2. Name of truck driver, if known ....
3. If not received by truck, state how received ....
4. On what date was loss or damage discovered? ....
5. On what date was carrier notified of loss or damage? ....
6. Kind of container? ....
7. How was package protected against abstraction of or damage to contents (strapped, sealed. or otherwise)? ....
....
8. Was container examined before opening? .... Or after opening? ....
9. If condition of container at time of such examination indicated cause of loss or damage, explain fully ....
....
10. If condition of contents or interior packing indicated loss or damage, explain fully ....
....
11. If property received did not fill container to capacity, what material occupied the remaining space? ....
12. What condition of container or contents indicated that loss or damage occurred while in possession of carriers? ....
....

I hereby certify the foregoing statement of facts to be true in every particular.

Dated at ....
                                                        (signature)
Date ....19.. ....
                                                        (In what capacity employed)

FIG. 15–3. Consignee's form for concealed loss or damage for motor carriers.

after date of delivery. The original bill of lading or bond of indemnity, the original destination freight bill or bond of indemnity, the original invoice or certified copy, the inspection report by the carrier's agent, and any other evidence which may be of aid in proving the claimed loss and damage should accompany a claim for concealed loss and damage.

Some claimants have misunderstood the 15-day rule and have pointed out that the law and the bill of lading are very specific in authorizing the filing of a claim within 9 months after delivery, or within 9 months after a reasonable time for delivery has elapsed. However, there is no conflict between the 15-day provision and the 9-month limitation for filing claims. Since carriers have the right to decline a claim where investigation indicates that it is not the carrier's liability, the 15-day provision simply provides a basis upon which a seasonably filed claim may be declined. Upon receipt of the written declination, the claimant has 2 years to bring suit against the carrier when it believes the claim is justified.

No statutory rule of liability exists for air cargo, and there are very few cases to provide guidance as to the law on this subject. In practice, air carriers limit their liability for loss and damage to that caused by their own negligence and only on their own lines. Moreover, they may limit this liability to a specified released value per shipment or per pound, which they have done by limiting it to 50 cents per pound.

Scheduled air carriers require that they be notified in writing within 30 days after delivery on known loss or damage and 15 days on concealed loss or damage. Claims must be filed within 270 days after delivery of the goods.

A deterrent to the establishment of through service and joint rates between different modes of transportation relates to liability. For example, where airlines and motor carriers have established through service and joint rates, the Commission has permitted such rates to be predicated on the air carrier's limited liability of 50 cents per pound. Shippers considering the use of joint air-truck movement should weigh the effects of this limitation of liability. This impediment to joint movements should be removed by legislative action, if necessary.

International air carriers will not assume liability in excess of the amount allowable under the Warsaw Convention ($7.48 per pound) unless shippers make a declaration of excess valuation. The latter provision carried in the bill of lading enables the shipper to increase the carrier's liability by paying an additional 40 cents per $100 of value. Recovery is permitted, however, only when the shipper proves negligence on the part of the carrier.

Overcharge and Reparation Claims

One group of overcharge claims arises because the carrier collects charges in excess of those based on the legally published rates. This kind of overcharge claim is most frequently presented. Overcharges of this kind are usually settled through presentation of the claim by the shipper to the carrier, although recourse can be made to the Interstate Commerce Commission by the shipper if the claim is declined by the carrier.

Another kind of overcharge claim is that which arises when the shipper feels that the rate charged, although legally applicable, is unreasonably or unjustly discriminatory or unduly preferential, i.e., is not lawful. The majority of this kind of overcharge claim alleges unreasonableness. The shipper may complain to the Commission which, if it finds the complaint to be valid, may award reparation in the case of rail and water transportation but not motor. Reparation is an award of damages, more in the form of a kind of retroactive rate adjustment than a claim.

There are a number of circumstances which give rise to such claims for reparation against railroads. For example, an industrial plant may be built at a point and shipments move from that point prior to the establishment of rates from such a point. Again, commodities have moved at class rates which should ordinarily move on commodity rates. Another example is the movement of commodities at commodity rates which are not on a proper basis. Also, it sometimes happens that rates are erroneously published or omitted in the issuing of supplements or in the reissue of a tariff. Sometimes, published rates are not protected by appropriate Fourth Section relief. Another instance is where published rates exceed the aggregate of intermediates via the route of movement and the tariff does not contain the aggregate of intermediates clause.

The Commission has held that it cannot award reparations on shipments which have moved under rates prescribed by it or approved as to maximum reasonableness.

Contrary to the general rule, the Commission has denied reparations when exceptions rates have exceeded uniform class rates provided by the Uniform Freight Classification and the Docket No. 28300 scales, basing its denial on the complex problems faced by the carriers in bringing their rate structure into alignment with uniform class rates prescribed in 1952.[4] The Commission allowed a five-year period as being the maximum for making such adjustments. In a subsequent case, the date set by the Commission was May 30, 1957. Notwithstanding these decisions, the carriers continued to maintain many commodity and exceptions ratings that produced charges higher than those resulting from application of the Uniform Freight Classification and class rates. In a 1957 case, the Commission prescribed rates for the future and granted reparation to the uniform class basis on all shipments made after May 30, 1957.[5] The railroads petitioned that the period of grace be extended to January 11, 1960, when all of the anomalous situations were eliminated by the publication of alternation rules providing for the application of class rates and Uniform Classification if they produced lower rates than commodity and exceptions rates. Fourteen cases were filed by the federal government, and these and others on file involve millions of dollars in reparation claims.

A special docket application is filed by the rail carrier with the Interstate Commerce Commission on interstate traffic where reparations are sought. In the application, it is necessary to give the commodity, number of shipments, aggregate weight, point of origin, destination, consignor, consignee, carrier issuing the bill of lading, dates and point at which bills

[4] *Page Belting Co.* v. *Boston & M. R.*, 291 ICC 21; 294 ICC 307 (1952).

[5] *Mannington Mills, Inc.* v. *Abilene & Southern Railway Co.*, 301 ICC 275 (1957) (1958).

of lading were issued, detailed information as to junction points via which shipments moved, aggregate freight charges actually collected, date charges were paid, by whom paid to carrier, date of delivery, rate and carload minimum weight legally applicable, rate sought to be applied, complete tariff authorities for both rates (ICC number, page of tariff, and

ORDER

INTERSTATE COMMERCE COMMISSION

No. 29974

ACME PEAT PRODUCTS, LTD., ET AL.
v.
AKRON, CANTON & YOUNGSTOWN RAILROAD COMPANY ET AL.

No. 30260

ALOUETTE PEAT PRODUCTS, LTD.
v.
ATCHISON, TOPEKA & SANTA FE RAILWAY COMPANY

IN THE MATTER OF AWARDING REPARATION BASED ON RULE-100 STATEMENTS FILED HEREIN

PRESENT: CHARLES D. MAHAFFIE, Commissioner, to whom the above-entitled matter has been assigned for action thereon.

It appearing, That on April 7, 1950, the Commission, by division 2, entered its report in the above-entitled proceeding, which report is hereby referred to and made a part hereof, and this proceeding now coming on for further consideration on the question of reparation, and the parties having filed agreed statements with respect to the shipments in question, showing among other things, the dates on which payment of the charges assailed was made; we find that complainants shown in the following table are entitled to awards of reparation from the defendants named below, insofar as the transportation over their lines took place in the United States, in the amounts set opposite their respective names, with interest:

Complainants	Defendants	Amounts
	Docket No. 29974	
Acme Peat Products, Ltd.	BCE-CP-SOO-CGW	$ 30.16
ditto	BCE-CP-SOO-CGW-SLSF	65.12
ditto	BCE-CP-SOO-CMSTP&P	65.12
ditto	BCE-CP-SOO-CMSTP&P-AT&SF	30.16
ditto	BCE-CP-SOO-CRI&P	66.40
ditto	BCE-CP-SOO-C&NW	32.80
ditto	BCE-CP-SOO-CMSTPM&O-MP	36.00
ditto	BCE-CP-SOO-GN	33.44
ditto	BCE-CP-SOO-GN-CB&Q	35.76
ditto	BCE-NP-SP	85.50
ditto	BCE-NP-SP-AT&SF	90.88
ditto	CN-GN-CB&Q	134.72
Alouette Peat Products, Ltd.	CP-NP	27.43
ditto	CP-NP-CB&Q-AT&SF	35.67
ditto	CP-NP-SP	1,862.54
ditto	CP-NP-SP-AT&SF	121.25
ditto	CP-NP-SP-AT&SF-M&ET	35.49
ditto	CP-NP-SP-NWP	29.96

FIG. 15–4.   An order of the Interstate Commerce Commission awarding reparations.

Docket No. 29974 - Sheet 12

Complainants	Defendants	Amounts
Alouette Peat Products, Ltd.	CP-NP-SP-NWP-P&SR	$ 25.88
ditto	CN-NP-SP-PE	118.41

It is therefore ordered, That the defendants, named in each of the groups shown in the above table, be, and they are hereby, authorized and directed to pay unto the complainants shown opposite said groups, on or before   February 19, 1954   , the amounts set opposite their respective names in said table, with interest thereon at the rate of 4 per-cent per annum, from the respective dates of payment of the charges assailed shown in the aforesaid agreed statements, as reparation on account of unreasonable rates charged and collected on numerous carload shipments of ground peat, shipped from points in British Columbia, Canada, to points in the United States, insofar as the transportation took place in the United States.

Dated at Washington, D.C., this   30th   day of December, 1953.

By the Commission, Commissioner Mahaffie.

GEORGE W. LAIRD,

Secretary.

(SEAL)

FIG. 15–4—Continued

effective date of tariff), and what the aggregate freight charges at the claimed rate would be.

It is necessary that a statement, known as a "Rule 100 Statement," accompany the special docket application. A Rule 100 Statement contains the following information for each shipment involved in the application: waybill date, waybill number, car initial and car number, origin, destination, route, commodity, weight, rate and freight charges paid, rate and freight charges at the claimed rate, and amount of reparation claimed. There is a space provided in the application for setting forth the facts in support of the request for authority to pay reparation. However, sometimes, the carrier will make the argument a part of the Rule 100 Statement. An order of the Commission awarding reparations is shown in Figure 15–4.

One phase of the reparation claims is the so-called "misroute claims." These claims can be adjusted without specific authority from the Interstate Commerce Commission or state regulatory commissions, since these bodies have granted the carrier blanket authority to adjust such claims. The claims involving misrouting are presented to the carrier on the standard form for presentation of overcharge claims; and the paid freight bill, as well as the original bill of lading, plus the bills covering the additional expense incurred as a result of the misrouting of the carrier, should be included. Claims which arise as a result of misrouting are due to the following causes:

1. Carrier's agent forwarding shipments to the improper destination.
2. Carrier's agent forwarding shipments covered by unrouted bills of lading over routes other than the route or routes via which the lowest rate applies.
3. Carrier's agent erroneously forwarding shipments over routes via which higher charges are applicable than applied via the route furnished by the shipper.

When overcharge claims arise because the carrier collects charges in excess of those based on the legally published tariff rate, and the shipper's claim has been declined and he has complained to the Commission, the Commission merely decides whether the rate complained of was the legal rate for the carrier to apply. There are many causes of this type of overcharge claim. For example, a carrier's rate clerk may use a class rate on a shipment instead of the commodity rate. Another example is where a carrier employee uses a class rate published from origin to destination when there is a commodity rate in effect from a more distant point applicable through the origin point to the destination, or beyond the destination point making the destination point intermediate, in which case a commodity rate would produce a lower charge. In billing shipments, another error which often occurs is the failure to consider Rule 15 of the Consolidated and Uniform Freight Classifications, which provides that the charge for a less-carload shipment must not exceed the charge for a minimum carload of the same freight at the carload rate. It also provides that the charge for a car fully loaded must not exceed the charge for the same lot of freight if taken as a less-carload shipment. The basis of many claims is occasioned by the application of combination rates versus through rates. If there is a published through rate from origin to destination, that rate is the legal rate via the routes specified in the tariff, unless the tariff contains a provision which authorizes the use of the aggregate of intermediates. Some of the aggregate of intermediate clauses in tariffs provide that where there is a lower combination via one route, such lower combination can be protected via all routes authorized in the tariff. However, others permit only the use of the lower combination rate via the route on which the combination is applicable.

There are many other errors which can be made by employees of the carrier that can result in overcharge claims, such as the use of rates on a gross-ton basis instead of a net-ton basis, billing to an erroneous destination, and billing shipment on a collect basis when charges have been prepaid at the origin point. Other causes of overcharge claims are failure to observe the correct amount of free dunnage, paying percentage increases in lieu of maximum increases, and paying interstate rates instead of intrastate rates.

Our concern in this chapter is primarily with overcharge claims which arise because the carrier collects charges in excess of those based on the legally published tariff rate. In filing claims, many traffic managers file

Standard Form for Presentation of Overcharge Claims

Approved by the Interstate Commerce Commission, December 2, 1913.
Accounting Division, Association of American Railroads and National Industrial Traffic League

(Name of person to whom claim is presented) (Address of Claimant) (CLAIMANT'S NUMBER)

(Name of Carrier) (Date) 194

(Address) CARRIER'S NUMBER

This claim for $______ (Amount of Claim) is made against the carrier named above by ______ (Name of Claimant)
for Overcharge in connection with the following described shipments:
Description of shipment ______
Name and address of consignor (shipper) ______
Shipped from ______ (City, town or station). To ______ (City, town or station)
Final Destination ______ (City, town or station) Routed via ______
Bill of Lading issued by ______ Co.; Date of Bill of Lading ______
Paid Freight Bill (Pro) Number ______; Original Car Number and Initial ______
Name and address of consignee (To whom shipped) ______
If shipment reconsigned enroute, state particulars: ______
Nature of Overcharge ______ (Weight, rate or classification, etc.)

DETAILED STATEMENT OF CLAIM

NOTE.—If claim covers more than one item taking different rates and classification, attach separate statement showing how overcharge is determined and insert totals in space below.

	NO. OF PKGS.	ARTICLES	WEIGHT	RATE	CHARGES	AMOUNT OF OVERCHARGE
Charges Paid:		Total				
Should have been:		Total				

Authority for rate or classification claimed ______
Give, so far as practicable, Tariff reference (I. C. C. or C. R. C. number, effective date and page or item).

IN ADDITION TO THE INFORMATION GIVEN ABOVE, THE FOLLOWING DOCUMENTS ARE SUBMITTED IN SUPPORT OF THIS CLAIM*

( ) 1. Original paid freight ("expense") bill.
( ) 2. Original invoice, or certified copy, when claim is based on weight or valuation, or when shipment has been improperly described.
( ) 3. Original bill of lading, if not previously surrendered to carrier, when shipment was prepaid, or when claim is based on misrouting or valuation.
( ) 4. Weight certificate or certified statement when claim is based on weight.
5. Other particulars obtainable in proof of Overcharge claimed;† ______

Remarks ______

The foregoing statement of facts is hereby certified to as correct.

(Signature of Claimant)

§ Claimant should assign to each claim a number, inserting same in the space provided at the upper right hand corner of this form. Reference should be made thereto in all correspondence pertaining to this claim.
* Claimant will please place check (x) before such of the documents mentioned as have been attached, and explain under "Remarks" the absence of any of the documents called for in connection with this claim. When for any reason it is impossible for claimant to produce original bill of lading, if required, or paid freight bill, claimant should indemnify carrier or carriers against duplicate claim supported by original documents.
† Claims for overcharge on shipments of lumber should also be supported by a statement of the number of feet, dimensions, kind of lumber, and length of time on sticks before being shipped.
Claims based on rates quoted in letters from traffic officials should be supported by the original or copies of such letters.
Claimants will please show correctly and distinctly their name and address, including street and number, Post Office box number or Rural Free Delivery (R. F. D.) number.
Claimants will please advise carrier promptly if overcharge is adjusted through any channel after presentation of claim.
(See quotation from Section 10 of the Act to Regulate Commerce, appearing on back of this form.)

FIG. 15–5. Example of a rail overcharge claim.

overcharge claims with the rail carrier collecting the freight revenue. In the case of prepaid shipments, this would mean the origin carrier; and on collect shipments, it means the destination carrier. Railroads, on the other hand, prefer that the origin carrier be the one with which claims are filed because interpretation of tariffs, rules, and regulations is usually recognized to be the prerogative of that carrier. Overcharge claims are usually handled by the railroad's auditor of freight traffic. Figure 15–5 is an example of a rail overcharge claim form.

THE ABC RAILROAD

Dated at _____.

_____19__

......................hereby represent and certify that the

original paid freight bill covering shipment...........from.........

......to.............Waybill No. ....dated at...........

........19 , has been lost, mislaid, or is otherwise not immediate-

ly available, and in consideration of refund of $ by.........

.....................account overcharge on said shipment...........

hereby agree to indemnify and save harmless.................... and

any other carrier participating in the transportation of the prop-

erty herein, from and against any and all loss, damage, or expense

whatsoever sustained or which may be sustained by any of the afore-

said carriers, or any claim or demand whatsoever heretofore made or

which may be made hereafter against any of the aforesaid carriers,

through the payment of the aforesaid refund without the presenta-

tion of the original paid freight bill herein by the undersigned.

Signed _____.

Witness:_____

FIG. 15–6. An example of an indemnity bond.

The documents which should accompany the overcharge claim are the bill of lading, original paid freight (expense) bill, and weight certificate or certified statement when the claim is based on weight; and claims for overcharges on lumber should also be supported by a statement of the number of feet, dimensions, and kind of lumber. The original paid freight bill is required in all cases; and in connection with certain claims, the original bill of lading is required to be submitted for overcharge. If the original documents cannot be submitted, a claimant must indemnify the carrier or carriers against a duplicate claim which might be supported by the original documents. This is done by filing an indemnity bond, a form of which is shown in Figure 15–6. The fact that the paid freight bill must be submitted with the overcharge claim does not mean that the claimant has to be the party which pays the freight charges, but he

```
————————————————————— Vs.—————————————————

        The Kurut  Railroad Company et al.
————————————————————————————————————————————

        THE UNDERSIGNED                                    the consignor

of _____loaded with_____

from_____  to _____

date_____  and _____

the consignee thereof, stipulate and agree that any adjustment made

in freight charges collected on this shipment to be in favor

of_____


————————————————————————19__
                                     ————————————————————————
                                     Signature of Consignor

                                     By_____

                                     Title_____


————————————————————————19__
                                     ————————————————————————
                                     Signature of Consignee

                                     By_____

                                     Title_____
```

FIG. 15–7. An example of a stipulation form.

must be a party to the transportation contract. If he has in his possession the paid freight bill, this entitles him to the refund. If the claimant is neither the consignor nor the consignee, a stipulation must accompany the claim papers. This document must be executed by the consignor and the consignee, stipulating that any refund due is payable to a third party. Figure 15–7 shows a stipulation form.

A section of the Interstate Commerce Act provides that actions at law shall be started or complaints filed with the Interstate Commerce Commission against a carrier within 2 years from the time of the cause of action, in claims for reparation. Overcharge claims must be started within a 3-year period by private shippers. The federal government is allowed a 3-year period, both for overcharge and for reparation claims.[6]

Interest is paid on overcharges not refunded within 30 days from the

------

[6] Public Law 85–762.

date of collection of the charges. Interest of 4 per cent is paid by rail carriers. It is felt that the carrier has the use of the money if the overcharge is not refunded within the 30-day period.

In the case of any claim which involves REA Express, it must be filed within 6 months after delivery of the shipment, and suit must be brought within 2 years and a day after the written declination of the claim.

Under Part II of the Interstate Commerce Act, the Commission does not have any jurisdiction and authority to order motor carriers to pay reparation. But the Commission ruled, in 1944, that when unlawful rates were charged, it was the duty of a motor carrier to refund any overcharges without an order by the Commission or a court order. Until 1959, it was possible for shippers to secure reparations for unlawful rates charged by motor carriers but in that year the Supreme Court held that a shipper of goods by certificated motor carrier could not challenge the reasonableness of a carrier's charges made in accordance with the tariff governing the shipment after the shipment had been made. The Court stated that Part II of the Interstate Commerce Act gave no right to reparation for past unreasonableness of rates, and that any common law right to such recovery was superceded by provisions of the Act.[7]

The Supreme Court, in 1962, held that where motor carriers misrouted shipments, shippers may recover reparation charges caused by such misrouting.[8] This decision held that "rate reasonableness" was not involved because the question was not one of rates but of routes. In 1963, the Commission issued guidelines to govern motor carrier misrouting which provide, among other things, that if the shippers and carriers are unable to agree on refunds the Commission will ascertain the amount of the claims.

The Commission does not have any authority for awarding reparations against freight forwarders for damages arising from violations under Part IV of the Act.

Undercharge Claims

Undercharge claims are those where the applicable charges have not been collected and there is a balance due the carrier or carriers under the tariffs legally on file with the Interstate Commerce Commission. If carriers are unable to collect the applicable charges, they must file suits in the courts to collect the charges. It should be noted that this is different from overcharge claims, where the shipper has recourse to the Commission. The statute of limitation for undercharge claims is the same as for overcharge claims, namely three years from the time the cause of action accrues.

---

[7] T.I.M.E., Inc. v. United States and Davidson Transfer and Storage Company, Inc. v. United States, 359 U.S. 464 (1959).

[8] Hewitt-Robins, Inc. v. Eastern Freightways, Inc., 371 U.S. 84 (1962).

Some of the common causes of bills for undercharges are based upon improper weights, errors in extension of the freight charges, use of rates not applicable to the article transported, failure to comply with restrictive tariff provisions, misdescription of goods, and failure on the part of the shipper to specify value when rates are published according to released valuations.

Carriers have definite procedures for the handling of undercharge claims, and every effort is made to avoid having to file a suit to secure outstanding charges. However, where necessary, such suits are instituted. Under Section 7 of the Uniform Bill of Lading Terms and Conditions, the shipper and receiver are actually liable for the payment of all freight charges, except in those instances where the consignee is not the beneficial owner and files the necessary nonbeneficial ownership notice naming the correct beneficial owner. The shipper can relieve himself from the payment of additional charges by executing the Section 7 clause on the face of the bill of lading. Where this clause, the nonrecourse clause, has been executed, the carrier has to look to the consignee for the payment of all charges, except as stated in the preceding sentence, where the consignee is not the beneficial owner of the property and proper notice has been filed. The Terms and Conditions of the Bill of Lading, Section 4 (c) state that "the proceeds of any sale shall be applied by the carrier to the payment of freight, demurrage, storage and any other lawful charges and the expense of notice, advertisement, sales and any other necessary expenses and of caring for and maintaining the property, if proper care requires special expenses, and should there be a balance it shall be paid to the owner of the property sold hereunder."

Where freight is refused or is unclaimed, it can be placed in public warehouses at the risk and expense of the owner of the goods; and unless he furnishes disposition, the goods will be sold to cover the transportation and storage charges. Where such refused or unclaimed shipments are sold by carriers for the charges owed on them and the proceeds of the sale are more than the charges due, the balance is paid to the owner. On the other hand, if the amount from the sale is not sufficient to cover the charges, the carrier has to collect the difference from the owner of the goods. There are some exceptions to the latter condition which will be found in tariffs. For example, an item in a tariff states that if the amount realized from the sale of refused or unclaimed fresh fruits and vegetables is less than the amount assessable against the shipment, the charge for the transportation and any accessorial and terminal services shall be the amount realized from the sale less the selling cost. However, if the goods at the sale are sold to the consignee or his representative, the transportation charges published in the tariff shall apply.

Rail Regulations Governing Inspection of Freight

The following rail regulations govern the inspection of freight before or after delivery to consignee and adjustment of claims for loss or damage thereon, and have been approved by the railroads and the National Industrial Traffic League:

Rule 1. When a package bears indication of having been pilfered while in possession of carrier, it shall be carefully weighed by the delivering agent before delivery and such weight endorsed on the freight bill and a joint inventory of contents of package by carrier and consignee shall be made before delivery or immediately upon receipt by consignee and claim for shortage so discovered shall be promptly adjusted.

Rule 2. Loss or damage discovered after delivery of shipment to consignee shall be reported by the consignee or consignor to agent of carrier immediately upon discovery, and in any event within fifteen days after receipt, and contents and container held for inspection by carrier, with a statement of facts or circumstances evidencing loss prior to delivery by carrier. Inspection by carrier shall be made when practicable, and in any event within forty-eight hours, and shall include examination of package and contents for evidence of abstraction of the missing goods, checking contents with invoice and weighing for comparison with shipping weight; also investigation of cartman's record of handling shipment. Report of inspection shall be made in duplicate on **A. A. R.** Standard Form No. FCD–16 and signed by carrier's agent and consignee, one copy thereof to be retained by consignee and attached to claim for loss if made. In case no inspection is made by carrier's agent, consignee's inspection shall be accepted as carrier's inspection. If investigation develops that the loss occurred with carriers, the 15 days' clause shall not be invoked. (NOTE: See Rule 7.)

Rule 3. Shortage from a package delivered consignee without exception when based only upon the consignee's failure to find the entire invoice quantity in package or when package remains in possession of consignee more than 15 days before the goods are unpacked and shortage discovered, shall not be regarded as a responsibility of the carrier unless investigation develops that loss occurred with carrier. When package remains in possession of cartman over night and not in a warehouse, carrier shall require proof that loss did not occur with cartman.

Rule 4. When a package bears evidence of damage while in possession of carrier, a joint examination of contents by carrier and consignee shall be made before delivery or immediately upon receipt by consignee and claim for damage so discovered shall be promptly adjusted upon its merits.

Rule 5. Damage to contents of package discovered after delivery of shipment to consignee shall be reported to agent of carrier immediately upon discovery or in any event within 15 days after receipt, with a statement of facts or circumstances evidencing damage prior to delivery by carrier, unless investigation develops that the damage occurred with carriers, then the 15-day clause shall not be invoked. Inspection shall be made by carriers when practicable, and in any event within 48 hours after notice. In case no inspection is made by carrier's agent, consignee's inspection shall be accepted as carrier's inspection. Report of inspection shall be made in duplicate on standard form and signed by carrier's agent and consignee, one copy thereof to be retained by consignee and attached to claim for damage if made. (NOTE: See Rule 7.)

Rule 6. Shortage or damage discovered by consignee at time of receiving freight in any quantity from car, warehouse or other premises of carrier shall be reported to agent of carrier before removal of entire shipment, in order that the cause and extent of loss or damage may, if possible, be definitely determined and proper record made thereof. Unloading of freight should not be retarded or discontinued awaiting inspection.

Rule 7. Notice of loss or damage may be given carrier's agent by telephone or in person, and in either event shall be confirmed by mail.

In case of loss or damage as provided for in Rules 2 and 5, and inspection is not made by carrier's representative, detail of findings of inspection by consignee shall be furnished carrier's agent immediately upon completion of inspection.

Rule 8. Failure of consignee to comply with the foregoing regulations shall be regarded as indicating complete delivery of freight by carrier in good order.

Rule 9. Where packages which indicate loss of or damage to contents are recoopered by the carriers, proper record of this exception shall be noted on the waybill and station records and shall be available to consignee.[9]

Motor Carrier Regulations Governing Inspection of Freight

The following motor carrier regulations govern the inspection of freight before or after delivery to consignee and adjustment of claims for loss or damage thereon:

Rule 1. The carrier delivering freight to consignee must require consignee to sign delivery receipt certifying that the freight was received in good order except as noted. Consignee must check freight and notate on delivery receipt any damage or shortage that is not of a concealed nature. Carriers should instruct drivers to refuse to permit consignees imprinting or writing on the delivery receipt any general exceptions not of a specific nature.

Rule 2. When a package bears indication of having been pilfered while in possession of carrier, it shall be carefully weighed by the delivering carrier before delivery and such weight endorsed on the freight bill and a joint inventory of contents of package by carrier and consignee shall be made before delivery or immediately upon receipt by consignee and claim for shortage so discovered shall be promptly adjusted.

Rule 3. Loss or damage discovered after delivery of shipment to consignee shall be reported by the consignee to the delivering carrier at his nearest terminal immediately upon discovery, and in any event, within fifteen days after receipt and contents and container held for inspection by carrier, with a statement of facts or circumstances evidencing loss or damage prior to delivery by carrier. Inspection by carrier shall be made when practicable and in any event within forty-eight (48) hours, and shall include examination of the goods, checking contents with invoice and weighing for comparison with shipping weight. In case no inspection is made by carrier, consignee's inspection shall be accepted as carrier's inspection. Report of inspection shall be made in duplicate on standard form and signed by carrier's agent and consignee, one copy thereof to be retained by consignee and attached to claim if made. If investigation develops that the loss or damage occurred with carriers, the fifteen-day clause shall not be invoked. (NOTE: See Rule 6.)

Rule 4. Shortage from a package delivered consignee without exception when based only upon the consignee's failure to find the entire invoice quantity in package or when package remains in possession of consignee more than fifteen days before the goods are unpacked and shortage discovered, shall not be regarded as a responsibility of the carrier unless investigation develops that loss occurred with carrier.

Rule 5. When a package bears evidence of damage while in possession of

---

[9] Freight Claim Division, Association of American Railroads, *Principles and Practices, Freight Claim Rules, Chicago,* 1957, pp. 101–2.

carrier, a joint examination of contents by carrier and consignee shall be made before delivery or immediately upon receipt by consignee, and claim for damage so discovered shall be promptly adjusted upon its merits.

Rule 6. Notice of loss or damage may be given carrier by telephone or in person, and in either event shall be confirmed by mail.

In case of loss or damage as provided for in Rule 3, and inspection is not made by carrier's representative, detail of findings of inspection by consignee shall be furnished carrier immediately upon completion of inspection.

Rule 7. Failure of consignee to comply with the foregoing regulations shall be regarded as indicating complete delivery of freight by carrier in good order.

Rule 8. Where packages which indicate loss of or damage to contents are recoopered by the carriers, proper record of this exception shall be noted on receiving carrier's records and shall be available to consignee.

Rule 9. Consignees shall retain container and damaged merchandise on shipments found to have damage until carrier has completed its investigation. If the carrier liability is undisputed, carrier shall promptly take possession of the salvage for disposal and its failure to do so promptly shall be regarded as abandoning the damaged goods to the consignee who shall dispose of it in such manner as will serve the best interest of the carrier if the goods have any value. If carrier fails to establish carrier liability within 30 days after claim is filed, consignee shall notify carrier in writing that the damaged goods are being held for its account and will be salvaged or destroyed, as the facts may warrant, after expiration of fifteen days from date of notice unless carrier arranges for their disposition. This rule will not apply where the value of the goods in undamaged condition exceeds $5.00, in which event, consignee shall retain container and damaged merchandise until carrier has completed processing of the claim.[10]

Measure of Claims

Rail and motor carriers and freight forwarders are subject to Section 20, paragraph 11, of Part I of the Interstate Commerce Act, which provides that common carriers shall be liable to the owner of the goods for the full actual loss, damage, or injury to property caused by the carrier. Carriers and shippers are in general agreement concerning this section of the act. However, there is no general agreement as to the meaning of some of the court decisions which have developed involving this section.

The courts, in the past, have generally based their decisions upon the rule that the destination value, regardless of the actual loss sustained by the owner of the goods, is the measure of the carrier's liability. The tendency, in more recent decisions, is to restrict the owner to his actual loss, as determined from evidence placed before the court, depending upon the terms of the contract of sale, the business methods of the plaintiff, and the circumstances under which the shipment was made.

Traffic Manager's Procedure and Prevention

Although there are standard forms for the presentation of loss and damage or overcharge claims, many of the traffic departments of indus-

[10] National Freight Claim Council, American Trucking Associations, Inc., *Principles, Practices, and Rules Covering Loss, Damage and Overcharge Claims*, Washington, D.C., 1962, pp. 44–45.

CLAIMS DOCUMENTS ⊙ TRANSMITTAL SHEET	THIS SPACE TO BE COMPLETED AND RETURNED TO ORIGINATOR WHEN CLAIM IS PAID OR OTHERWISE DISPOSED OF BY CARRIER.		
	MATHIESON CLAIM NUMBER	CARRIER'S CLAIM NUMBER	DATE PAID
	CARRIER	CREDIT PROCEEDS TO ACCOUNT NO.	
DO NOT WRITE IN SPACE AT RIGHT FOR USE OF TRANSPORTATION DEPT.-BALTIMORE	CHECK NUMBER	CHECK DATE	AMOUNT

	SHIPMENT IDENTIFICATION		
TO: Transportation Department - Baltimore	DATE SHIPPED	PURCHASE ORDER NO.	OTHER IDENTIFICATION
FROM: (PLANT)			

The attached papers are submitted to support claim to be filed against carrier for loss and/or damage to shipment. (Check those items that apply)

( ) Prepaid Inbound Shipment.
( ) Collect Inbound Shipment.
( ) Original Bill of Lading (or certified true and exact copy if original not obtainable).
( ) Original Freight Bill receipted by carrier's agent (memo copy not acceptable).
( ) Copy of Invoice (in duplicate) certified to be true and exact.
( ) Copy of Inspection Report, which Plant PA must obtain from carrier's agent or inspector.
( ) Salvage Receipt if same was issued to Plant PA by carrier's agent for goods salvaged.
( ) Itemized certificate of salvage expense where labor and/or materials were necessary to salvage damaged goods.
( ) Value of goods, if different from price shown on invoice (properly certified).

$ _____

R⊙RKS:

SIGNATURE OF ORIGINATOR	TITLE	DATE

⊙   DISTRIBUTION

TRANSPORTATION DEPT.-BALTIMORE - ORIGINAL & 2 COPIES
DIRECTOR OF PURCHASES - BALTIMORE - 1 COPY
ORIGINATOR - 1 COPY

FIG. 15–8. An example of a claims documents transmittal sheet of an industrial traffic department.

trial concerns have forms which have been designed either to accompany the standard forms or to be used as the basis for completing the standard form. The claims documents transmittal sheet of an industrial traffic department is shown in Figure 15–8. One of the reasons for a special company form is to accomplish uniformity, particularly where there are numerous widely scattered plants. Another reason is that it makes possible the maintenance of a record of the claims filed, thereby assuring a method for checking on the progress of claims adjustment periodically. In this connection, some traffic managers trace each pending claim every thirty days after it has been filed. A claims tracer form is shown in Figure 15–9. Such a systematic method has been found to encourage adjustment within a reasonable time.

The supporting papers which the carrier requires, as outlined in the preceding material, should be attached to the claim, and also any other relevant information that will help in its adjustment. Where the freight bill does not carry any notations of exceptions, the claim has to be sup-

TRACER - CLAIMS

Date_____

Carrier Claim No._____
Our Claim No._____
Loss and/or Damage Amt. $_____
Overcharge Amount $_____

Dear Sir:

Claim as numbered above was filed with your office under date of_____
As claim voucher has not been received, please advise present status and when we may expect adjustment.

FOLD HERE

Yours very truly,

FIG. 15–9. An example of a claims tracer form as used by an industrial traffic department.

ported with additional documentary evidence. Traffic managers have found that the maintenance of adequate and accurate receiving records constitutes one of the most effective methods of substantiating claims. Although, for loss and damage claims, the time limits for filing the claim apply to shipments which move all-rail or partly by rail and partly by motor carrier, the filing of the claim within the required time limit on the latter type of movement with the motor carrier does not always meet the requirements of the railroad bill of lading.

Traffic departments try to present loss and damage claims to carriers as soon as possible after receipt of the shipment. Often, there is a delay in the presentation of the claim due to inability to determine immediately the amount of damage; or the article may have to be repaired, which cannot be accomplished immediately. Under these or similar circumstances, since there is a time limit for filing a claim, the protracted delay may necessitate filing a preliminary claim. Such preliminary claim will give the carrier the same information required if a regular claim were filed, with the exception of the amount of the claim. The claim amount in the preliminary claim will be an arbitrary figure, which will be corrected as soon as the exact amount is determined.

Most traffic departments will establish a claim minimum, since the smaller claims may cost more to adjust than the amount of the claim received. A typical minimum for overcharge claims is $3.00, and for loss and damage claims, $10.00.

It is often necessary to adjust a loss and damage claim on the basis of a compromise. Traffic managers realize that there are cases of divided responsibility between the shippers and the carriers which may justify some adjustment. For example, the shipper's records concerning the shipment may not be sufficiently accurate; and claims based on shipments involving the shipper's weight, load, and count often involve some compromise. The carrier is not bound by the shipper's count; and it is necessary, therefore, that the shipper prove the actual quantity loaded and the actual amount delivered at destination. Since the carrier is liable for loss of any goods actually delivered to it and accepted by it, these claims involve adjusted settlements.

The action of traffic managers regarding the filing of claims where a shortage exists varies. Some feel that an immediate claim should be filed, to spur the efforts of the carrier to locate the shortage. Other traffic managers, however, feel that the individual carrier and the distance the shipment is transported are the two factors, taken together, which must be given consideration as to when to present a claim. The procedures of carriers regarding over, short, and damaged freight vary to such an extent that the most logical practice for a traffic manager to follow seems to be one based upon his past experience with the individual carrier.

The attitude of traffic managers regarding the acceptance of damaged shipments differs considerably. Some organizations make a practice of accepting all damaged shipments of their own products. There are two primary reasons for this action. One is to minimize the loss, since the business organization can have the necessary repairs made somewhat more simply than the carrier. Secondly, were the damaged freight to be abandoned and sold by the carrier, and hidden internal damage in the goods show up later, it would be harmful to the company, since the products bear the company name.

CLAIM PREVENTION

Rail

Much of the claim activity of the railroads is of a preventive nature. One method used to accomplish this is to maintain a continuous positive program by individual carriers to protect freight from loss or damage. Through the combination of efforts of individual railroads in the same geographical or terminal area, much preventive work can be accomplished. The National Freight Loss and Damage Prevention Committee, which is headed by a chairman who is also a full-time director of the Freight Loss and Damage Prevention Section of the Association of American Railroads, co-ordinates the activities of individual lines, as well as the territorial activities, into a general campaign.

The prevention work of the Association of American Railroads falls into these general categories:

1. Impressing all interested parties with the seriousness of the loss and damage problem.

2. Encouraging individual railroads to establish close liaison with each class of officers and employees engaged in the handling of freight or interested in rendering efficient service to the shipping public.

3. Co-ordinating the prevention work of departments which are engaged in loss and damage activities of individual carriers so as to sustain interest in problems local to each line and territory, as well as to foster a continuing interest in the loss and damage problem of the carriers as a whole.

4. Emphasizing the items of greatest importance, as reflected in the charges, to the causes and commodities, as shown in claim payment statistics.

5. Encouraging other organizations, such as the AAR Mechanical Division and the Freight Loading and Container Bureau, to develop improved methods for the loading of commodities in open-top and closed cars, respectively, in carload consignments in order to prevent damage or loss. The Container Bureau is encouraged to develop improved shipping containers which will do a better protective job at lower cost with lighter but stronger materials.[11]

Although the railroads have been engaged in freight claim organization work for many years, it was not until shortly after the turn of the present century that an organized loss- and damage-prevention effort was made in this country. The loss and damage during World War I reached unusually high totals; and at the end of the war, the loss and damage totaled almost $120 million. This was of concern to both carriers and shippers, and more positive preventive measures were instituted, with effective results. During World War II, loss and damage claims rose steadily; and in 1948, the railroads' loss and damage claim bill was $132 million. This had been lowered to $122 million in 1962, or more than $320 thousand a day. Since a greater volume of traffic subjects shippers to more potential hazards, however, a better comparison than the total dollar figures is the ratio of loss and damage claims to freight revenue. Despite the larger dollar total in 1948 as compared with 1920, the 1948 ratio of loss and damage claims to freight revenue was 1.60 per cent, as compared to 2.74 per cent in 1920. By 1962, this ratio had been reduced to 1.44 per cent.

Carrier claims personnel feel that the yardstick to be used in determining the efficiency of their claim department is to find out what percentage of claims is paid within 30 days after receipt. If the carrier pays 75 per cent of all claims within 30 days after presentation, it is considered to be doing a good job. In 1960, the railroads disposed of 76 per cent of all claims within 30 days after receipt, while 9 per cent of the claims required more than 90 days for adjustment. Included in the latter group are claims for grain losses and damage to fruits and vegetables, many of which are settled at the end of the season's movement at the convenience of claimants and the railroads, whereas others require additional time to determine the facts about liability of the carrier.

Motor

Motor carriers have been active in claim-prevention work, particularly through the National Freight Claim Council of the American Trucking Associations, Inc. The Freight Claim Rule Book contains a loss and damage claim-prevention and recommended practices section which lists fifteen points which should be observed. Another section outlines how

---

[11] Information supplied by the Association of American Railroads.

shippers can co-operate to prevent claims. Included are such subjects as packaging, marking, preparation of bills of lading, and other matters.

The figures for 119 Class I motor carriers for 1962 show a claim ratio of 1.08 per cent. Of these claims, 74 per cent were settled in 30 days, 16 per cent in 30–90 days, and 8 per cent beyond 90 days. The leading causes for claims in a representative year were shortages, 24 per cent; visible damage, 37 per cent; concealed damage, 21 per cent; wreck or fire, 5 per cent; heat, cold, or water damage, 5 per cent; theft and pilferage, 4 per cent; and delay, 1 per cent.[12]

INSURANCE

The traffic manager may have the responsibility for arranging for insurance, when necessary, on shipments in transit. This is true particularly of air and water-borne traffic. Air shipments move under a released value per pound, and the bill-of-lading conditions used to cover water shipments have many exceptions under which the carrier is not liable for loss or damage to the goods. It may be necessary, therefore, to arrange for marine insurance on movements which involve export, import, coastwise, intercoastal, and inland water transportation. It may be necessary occasionally to insure shipments of unusually high value; and it has become customary for the traffic manager to secure insurance on the shipment of household effects of employees who are moved at company expense, such shipments being shipped on a released valuation in accordance with the household goods carriers' bill of lading. Although the household goods carriers' tariffs provide for three released valuations, the most commonly used is the one in which, under the bill of lading, their responsibility is limited to 30 cents per pound per article. The employee declares the value of his household goods effects, and insurance is arranged to cover the difference between the carrier's liability and the full value.

Some business firms make a practice of taking out insurance on any items moved on a released valuation, as well as insuring all parcel post shipments.

DISCUSSION QUESTIONS AND PROBLEMS

1. What caused the establishment by the railroads of a code of principles and practices governing the investigation and disposition of freight claims?
2. Why is loss and damage claim prevention a joint responsibility of shipper and carrier?
3. Summarize the nonrailroad responsibilities which may contribute to loss or damage.
4. Carefully explain how loss or damage to goods caused by delay is determined when the shipment has moved by rail.

---

[12] National Freight Claim Council, American Trucking Associations, Inc.

5. There is no need to carry insurance on goods moved by common carriers operating in the United States. Do you agree or disagree? Why?

6. Is there any difference between common-law liability of common carriers and the liability under the Bill of Lading or related acts? Why?

7. Explain why there are certain exceptions to the liability of a carrier.

8. What are the different types of loss or damage? How can you differentiate between them?

9. What are the requirements for the filing of loss and damage claims? With whom are they filed?

10. Reference is often made to overcharge and reparation claims. How would you distinguish between them? Which one is most frequently presented to rail carriers?

11. Discuss some of the situations which often give rise to reparation claims against railroads.

12. What are some of the causes of typical overcharge claims? How would the traffic manager go about finding these causes?

13. List the documents which must accompany the various types of claims.

14. What is the purpose of the indemnity bond? Stipulation form?

15. Should the Commission have jurisdiction and authority to order motor carriers to pay reparation? Why, or why not?

16. What are undercharge claims? List some typical causes. Why are they not as common as overcharge claims?

17. List and compare the rail and motor carrier regulations governing the inspection of freight.

18. Establish a loss- and damage-prevention program for such a section of a traffic department.

19. In what way can the claim activity of the traffic manager be used for control purposes by him?

20. Compare motor and rail loss and damage claim ratios. Would a traffic manager's maintenance of the claim ratio record on his shipments be of value?

Chapter

16

REGULATION AND REGULATORY PROCEDURE

ALL modes of for-hire transportation which operate on an interstate basis are governed to some extent by federal regulation. The degree of regulation is not necessarily the same for different types of carriers or for different operations within a mode, some types of operations being subject only to safety regulation, whereas others are subject to economic as well as safety regulation. The laws governing the regulation of transportation are contained in several acts administered by different federal regulatory bodies or agencies. The latter report directly to Congress and are independent agencies.

An estimate by the Bureau of Transport Economics and Statistics of the Interstate Commerce Commission, in 1961, of the percentage of freight transportation subject to federal economic regulation transported by each mode of transport showed railroads to be 100 per cent; motor carriers of property, 33.4 per cent; water carriers, including inland, Great Lakes, and deep sea coastwise, 14.9 per cent; oil pipe lines, 86.1 per cent; and air carriers, 100 per cent.

The federal government plays an important role in the provision of airways, airports, waterways, and highways. About 98 per cent of total federal expenditures for transportation since 1946 have been expended for basic facilities and their maintenance. The Undersecretary of Commerce for Transportation in the Department of Commerce has responsibility for the formulation of over-all transportation policies and programs within the executive branch of the government.

FEDERAL REGULATION OF DOMESTIC SURFACE CARRIERS

A knowledge of the state and federal statutory acts governing transportation is necessary in order that the traffic manager may carry out successfully his management responsibilities on behalf of the company he represents. These are two broad categories of regulation. The extent to which each field must be comprehended is dependent in part on the transportation activities of the individual business organization. These two phases of regulation are (1) economic regulation, which is often termed "regulation of business practices," such as rates charged; and (2) safety regulation, which deals with such matters as maximum hours of work and rules regarding safety. The traffic manager has an interest in both of these phases of regulation. Where his company engages in rendering its own or part of its own transportation service, it must abide by the same safety regulation prescribed for those carriers engaged in the transportation business as their primary activity.

An important part of the traffic manager's activities is concerned with appearances before regulatory bodies in economic proceedings. Every ethical effort should be made to avoid the necessity for recourse to regulatory proceedings; but there are many instances when the best interests of his company require the traffic manager to make presentations before regulatory bodies, so that the procedure to be followed should be mastered. A thorough familiarity with rules of practice will insure efficient performance of this phase of a traffic manager's duties. The traffic manager also should have a knowledge of the Interstate Commerce Act, which regulates domestic surface carriers, including railroads, pipe lines (except water and gas lines), the Pullman Company, express companies, motor carriers, water carriers, private-car lines, and freight forwarders; the Federal Aviation Act, which has regulatory control over both United States domestic and international air carriers; and the Merchant Marine Act and related maritime statutes, which regulate the United States flagships operating in foreign commerce; as well as the various amendments to these acts, in order to have an understanding of the purposes of these regulatory acts. Each of the acts will be discussed briefly, a description will be given of the regulatory agency administering the respective act, and the procedure before the administrative bodies will be outlined.

Development of the Interstate Commerce Act

The Act to Regulate Commerce was approved on February 4, 1887, and thereafter has been amended many times. (Part I has been amended more than 140 times. The Constitution, which is 100 years older, has been amended 22 times.) It became the Interstate Commerce Act by a provision in the Transportation Act of 1920, approved on February 28, 1920. Originally, the jurisdiction of the Commission was confined to common carriers engaged in interstate transportation wholly by railroad, or partly by railroad and partly by water. Later, this authority was extended to include common carriers by pipe line, transporting in interstate commerce oil or other commodity, except water and gas; and it included carriers by water, under the Panama Canal Act. As the act was further amended, it was amplified and enlarged by the Motor Carrier Act of 1935, now cited as Part II of the Interstate Commerce Act.

The provisions of Part II apply to the transportation of passengers or property by motor carriers engaged in interstate or foreign commerce, as well as to the procurement and provision of facilities for such transportation. Regulation of these motor carriers is vested in the Commission. The statute distinguishes between common, contract, and private carriers; and the degree of regulation varies among these kinds of carriers. Special provision is made also for the regulation of brokers engaged in motor transportation. Provision is made in the act for the regulation of rates, carrier financial control, accounts, and other phases of the motor carrier business in a manner similar to that used for regulating rail carriers in the same matters.

The Transportation Act of 1940 made numerous amendments to Parts I and II and added Part III, which relates to domestic water carriers. In general form and content, Part III closely resembles Part II. The three parts of the Interstate Commerce Act as a whole are cited as such, but the declaration of National Transportation Policy is outside the particular parts. Part IV, concerning freight forwarders, was added by the act of May 16, 1942. Under Part IV, the Commission is given broad regulatory authority over freight forwarders engaged in interstate or foreign commerce. Part V, added in 1958, provided for government guarantee of loans made to railroads but expired June 30, 1963.

By amendment to the Interstate Commerce Act in 1940, it was declared to be the national transportation policy of the Congress to provide for fair and impartial regulation of all modes of transportation subject to the act's provisions, so administered as to recognize and preserve the inherent advantages of each, and to promote safe, adequate, economical, and efficient service; to encourage the establishment and maintenance of reasonable charges for transportation services without unjust discriminations, undue preference or advantages, or unfair or destructive competitive practices; further, that all the provisions of the act shall be administered and enforced with a view to carrying out this declaration of policy.

The Transportation Act of 1958 added a new Part V to the act and amended other parts of the act, including the rule of rate making; redefined private motor carriage; provided a procedure for discontinuing certain intrastate rail operations; and froze the agricultural exemption by truck.

The Interstate Commerce Act is a remedial statute, and its provisions are to be construed liberally.[1] By its terms, it affords remedies through Commission action for carriers, shippers, and others who have complaints and other matters to present that have arisen out of interstate transportation, which problems the Commission is the only body vested with authority to decide.

The Commission also has certain duties under various acts supplemen-

---

[1] *Crescent Express Lines* v. *U.S.*, 320 U.S. 401, 409 (1943).

tary to the Interstate Commerce Act, such as the Clayton Act, Elkins Act, Standard Time Act (as amended), Parcel Post Act (as amended), Medals of Honor Act, Railway Mail Service Pay acts (as amended), Railway Labor Act, Railroad Retirement Act, and Railroad Unemployment Insurance Act.

Composition of Interstate Commerce Commission

There are 11 members comprising the Interstate Commerce Commission. Each commissioner is appointed by the President, with the consent and approval of the Senate, for a period of 7 years. Not more than 6 members of the Commission may be appointed from any one political party, and the chairmanship and vice chairmanship shall be rotated each year among the members. The staff of the Commission is divided into 3 major offices and 10 bureaus. Seven of the bureaus report to a vice chairman, as shown in the organization chart of the Commission in Figure 16–1.

The Interstate Commerce Commission, in 1963, had some degree of economic and/or safety regulatory control over all forms of surface transportation, comprising some 1,000 rail carriers, 159,000 motor carriers, 83 pipe-line companies, about 300 water carriers, and approximately 100 freight forwarders, the Pullman service, and express service, as well as certain transportation brokers. The regulatory tasks of the Commission were being performed by 2,400 employees, of which 800 were stationed in field offices in 90 cities.

Divisions of the Commission

There are three divisions of the Commission, which are known as Divisions 1, 2, and 3. Three commissioners are assigned to each division, and the chairman does not serve with any division.

Division 1 is the Operating Rights Division and deals primarily with the issuance of certificates, permits, and licenses for motor carriers, brokers, water carriers, and freight forwarders. Division 2 is the Rates, Tariffs, and Valuation Division, and handles freight rates and charges, and valuation of rail and pipe-line carriers' property. Division 3 is the Finance, Safety, and Service Division. It has jurisdiction over the issuance of carrier securities, consolidations, mergers, purchases, and acquisitions of control of carriers, and also takes care of service and safety matters. The divisions handle matters of general transportation interest.

Employee Boards

A number of three-man boards have been created to handle many matters referred to the Commission. Matters assigned to these boards are those that do not involve taking testimony at a public hearing or submission of evidence by opposing parties. The decisions of the boards may be appealed to the appropriate division of the Commission, whose decision is

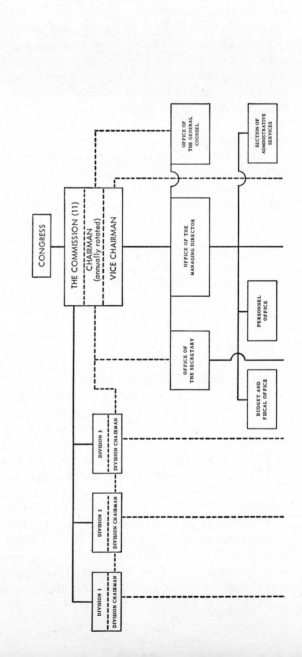

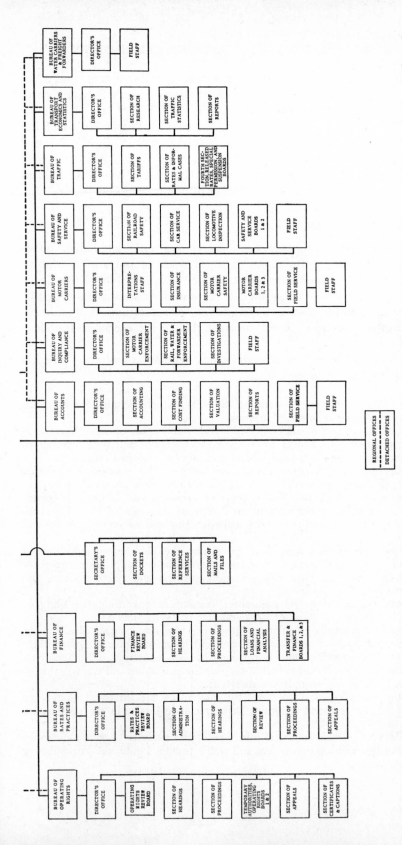

FIG. 16-1. An organization chart of the Interstate Commerce Commission. The three bureaus to the left are "procedural" and process cases for action by the divisions; the seven to the right are "regulatory" and administer the Commission's rules and regulations.

then administratively final. There are 19 boards at the present time, 15 of which were created in 1961. These boards are: Fourth Section Board; Suspension Board; Temporary Authorities Board; Transfer Board; Finance Boards Nos. 1, 2, and 3; Safety and Service Boards Nos. 1 and 2; Motor Carrier Boards Nos. 1, 2, and 3; Special Permission Board; Released Rates Board; Finance Review Board; Operating Rights Review Board; and Rates and Practices Review Board. The boards handle more than 30,000 matters formerly requiring action by the commissioners.

Functions of the Commission

The Interstate Commerce Commission has quasi-legislative, quasi-judicial, and executive functions. The extension of operating authority and the establishment of rates are examples of its quasi-legislative functions. Quasi-judicial functions include revocation or suspension of certificates, permits, and licenses and the granting of reparations. Enforcement of statutes and the rules issued pursuant thereto are executive functions of the Commission.

The broad areas of economic and safety regulation under the jurisdiction of the Commission include:

1. Duty to grant carriers operating authority, which includes, for railroads, authority to construct or abandon lines.

2. Duty to prescribe rules governing the publication of rates, fares, and charges, together with power to conduct investigations and hold hearings to determine the justness and reasonableness of new or changed rates.

3. Duty to authorize consolidations and mergers, the issuance of securities, and—in the case of railroads—approval of reorganizations in bankruptcy.

4. Duty to provide uniform systems of accounts and insure compliance therewith, set up depreciation rates to determine the costs of rail transportation, and maintain inventories of original costs and land values of railroads and pipe lines.

5. Duty to prescribe regulations governing the publication and filing of rates and charges, and insure compliance therewith; and adjudicate complaint proceedings involving tariff interpretation, justness and reasonableness, and discrimination.

6. Duty to prescribe and administer regulations governing the filing of liability insurance by motor carriers and freight forwarders.

7. Duty to prescribe regulations governing the use, control, distribution, and interchange of locomotives and cars, and insure compliance therewith.

8. Duty to prescribe rules governing the safe operation of locomotives, trains, and interstate motor vehicles; also for the packaging and transporting of explosives, and insure compliance therewith.

9. Duty to investigate violations by carriers of the Interstate Commerce Act and related acts, and assist the Department of Justice in the prosecution thereof.

10. Duty to provide statistical information and analyses of carrier finances, physical characteristics, operations, and traffic to afford guidance in regulatory problems.

Procedure before the Commission

Traffic managers may find it necessary to participate in proceedings before the Interstate Commerce Commission. Therefore, they must be familiar with the Interstate Commerce Act, with the actions of the Commission as contained in its orders and reports, and with relevant court actions. They must also have knowledge of the Rules of Practice which the Commission has adopted. This is available at nominal cost from the U.S. Government Printing Office.

The Commission maintains a register in which is entered the names of all persons who may practice before it. These people are called practitioners and comprise two classes: Class A is composed of attorneys at law who are admitted to practice before the highest court of any state or territory or the District of Columbia; and Class B is composed of those persons, not attorneys at law, who can satisfy the Commission that they possess the necessary legal, technical, and educational qualifications to enable them to render valuable service before the Commission. Since 1954, a total of 4 years of college is required, or a minimum of 2 years of college plus technical education, training, or experience which is regarded by the Commission as the equivalent of 2 additional years of college education. Class B admissions to practice are made only upon the successful passing of a written examination, which is given by the Commission twice each year. Many of the persons who pass the examination are traffic managers. During a 12-month period ended June 30, 1961, 16 per cent of those admitted to practice were nonlawyers; and since the Commission bar was established in 1929, 29,039 have been admitted, of which 67.9 per cent were attorneys and 32.1 per cent nonlawyers.[2]

The Administrative Procedure Act, which was enacted in 1946, established a general procedure for all governmental administrative bodies. However, it did permit the continued use of the rules of procedure of those bodies whose rules were in conformance with the new act or where, by modification, they would meet the requirements. Some changes were made in the Commission's Rules of Practice, and it is the document which should be consulted for procedure before the Commission.

A traffic manager can utilize two methods in handling complaints before the Commission—the "informal" and the "formal."

The informal complaint merely consists of a letter indicating the complaint, which might be against a carrier, in which case the latter is notified of the complaint. The entire matter may be handled through correspondence, without appearances before the regulatory body. In those instances where an informal complaint is made seeking damages, such as might be the case if reparations are sought, it must be filed within the statutory

---

[2] Interstate Commerce Commission, 76th *Annual Report* (Washington, D.C.: U.S. Government Printing Office, 1962), p. 123.

period. If the carrier is willing to pay the damages, a special docket proceeding can be instituted, inasmuch as reparations cannot be made without the authority of the commission.

The formal complaint must be carefully drawn in a prescribed manner, and those filed by the traffic managers are often brought under Sections 1, 2, 3, 4, 5, 6, and 15 of the act, alleging violation of one or more of these sections by carriers which either actually transport the goods or are par-

---

BEFORE THE INTERSTATE COMMERCE COMMISSION

COMPLAINT

_____

v.

_____

[*Insert without abbreviation the names of complainant and defendant (including each of the receivers, operating trustees, or other legal representatives of defendant), and whether a corporation, firm, or partnership, specifying the individual names of the parties composing the partnership; and the post-office address of any motor-carrier defendant.*]

The Complaint of the above-named complainant respectfully shows:

I. That [*complainant should here state nature and place of business, also whether a corporation, firm, or partnership, and if a firm or partnership, the individual names of the parties composing the same.*]

II. That the defendant above named is [*here state whether: (a) A carrier by railroad, express, motor vehicle (common or contract), or water (common or contract), a freight forwarder, or otherwise; (b) the transportation is of property or passengers, or both; and (c) the transportation involves a freight forwarder or more than one type of carrier, specifying particulars*] between points in the State of _____ and points in the State of _____ _____ [*a complaint under part II should specifically name the States in and through which the transportation which gives rise to the complaint is performed*] and as such defendant is subject to the provisions of the Interstate Commerce Act.

III. That [*state in this and subsequent paragraphs to be numbered IV, V, etc., the matter or matters intended to be complained of, naming every rate, fare, charge, classification, regulation, or practice the lawfulness of which is challenged, and also, if practicable, the points between which the rates, etc., complained of are applied. Where it is impracticable to designate each point, describe clearly the rate territory or rate group involved. Whenever practicable, tariff or schedule reference should be given.*]

[*Where unlawful discrimination, preference, or prejudice is alleged the particular elements specified in the act as constituting such violation (see sections 2, 3, 4, 13, 216, 217, 218, 305, and 406) and the*

FIG. 16–2.   Interstate Commerce Commission form used in presenting formal complaint.

*facts upon which complainant relies to establish the violation should
be stated clearly. Where any provision of the act other than those
just mentioned, or any requirement established pursuant to the act,
is alleged to be violated, the pertinent statutory provision, or established requirement, together with the facts which are alleged to
constitute the violation, should be stated. If two or more subsections
of the act or requirements established pursuant thereto are alleged to
be violated, the facts claimed to constitute violation of one subsection,
or requirement, should be stated separately from those claimed to
constitute a violation of another subsection, or requirement, wherever that can be done by reference or otherwise without undue
repetition.]*

X. That by reason of the facts stated in the foregoing paragraphs
complainant has been subjected to the payment of rates [fares or
charges, etc.] for transportation which were when exacted and still
are (1) unjust and unreasonable in violation of section _____
of the Interstate Commerce Act, and (2) unjustly discriminatory in
violation of section _____, and (3) unduly preferential or
prejudicial in violation of section _____, and (4) in violation of the long-and-short-haul [or aggregate-of-intermediate-rates]
provision of section 4 thereof. [*Use one or more of the allegations
numbered (1), (2), (3), and (4), or other appropriate allegation according to the nature of the complaint.*] That [if recovery of damages is sought] complainant has been injured thereby to his damage
in the sum of $ _____ .

Wherefore complainant prays that defendant be required to answer
the charges herein; that after due hearing and investigation an
order be made commanding said defendant [and each of them] to
cease and desist from the aforesaid violations of said act, and establish and put in force and apply in future to the transportation of
_____ between the origin and destination
points named in paragraph _____ hereof, in lieu of the rates
[fares, or charges, etc.], named in said paragraph, such other rates
[fares, or charges, etc.], as the Commission may deem reasonable and
just [and also, if recovery of damages is sought, pay to complainant
by way of reparation for the unlawful charges hereinbefore alleged

FIG. 16–2—*Continued*

ties to the freight rates, rules, and regulations under which the goods are
transported. The approved ICC form for the formal complaint is shown
in Figure 16–2.

Upon receipt of a formal complaint, the Commission ordinarily will
set it for oral hearing. However, the Rules of Practice provides for the
use of shortened procedure or modified procedure. Under shortened procedure, if the parties involved agree, the matter is handled by corre-

the sum of $_____, or such other sum as, in view of the evidence to be adduced herein, the Commission shall determine that complainant is entitled to as an award of damages under the provisions of said act for violation thereof], and that such other and further order or orders be made as the Commission may consider proper in the premises.

Dated at _____, 19___.

_____
(Complainant's signature *)

_____
(Office and post-office address)

_____
(Signature of practitioner)

_____
(Post-office address)

VERIFICATION *

*State of*_____
}*ss:*
*County of*_____

_____, being duly sworn, deposes and says: That he is the complainant [or, one of the complainants; or, is the (insert title of the affiant if complainant is a corporation) of the _____ Company, complainant] in the above-entitled proceeding; that he has read the foregoing complaint, and knows the contents thereof; that the same are true as stated, except as to matters and things if any, stated on information and belief, and that as to those matters and things, he believes them to be true.

_____

Subscribed in my presence, and sworn to before me, by the affiant above named, this_____day of_____, 19____.

[USE AN

L. S.

IMPRESSION SEAL]

_____
(Title of officer)

Commission expires:_____

FIG. 16–2—*Continued*

spondence. This procedure has been used where there is no disagreement as to the facts of a controversy but rather it is largely a question of law or tariff interpretation. If the use of the shortened procedure does not resolve the matter prior to the issuance of a report by the Commission, an oral hearing may be held.

The modified procedure may be used upon request of any of the parties involved; or the Commission may, on its own initiative, decide that a case could be handled by this method, in which case it notifies the parties by an order which specifies the time for filing statements of facts and argument, and counsels the parties on each side to consolidate their case. No alternative is offered the parties in such an order; it is a case of the modified procedure or a default. However, it is possible for a litigant to file a formal petition with the Commission explaining in detail why this method is not feasible. Few such petitions have been filed.

BEFORE THE INTERSTATE COMMERCE COMMISSION

ANSWER

----
        v.   } DOCKET No._____

The above-named defendant, for answer to the complaint in this proceeding, respectively states:

I. [*Here set forth appropriate and responsive admissions, denials, and averments, specifically answering the complaint paragraph by paragraph.*]

Wherefore defendant prays that_____

Dated_____, 19_____.

_____
(Name of defendant)

By _____

_____
(Title of officer)

_____
(Office and post-office address)

_____
(Signature of practitioner)

_____
(Post-office address)

FIG. 16–3.   Form used to answer complaint before Interstate Commerce Commission.

One of the rules provides that the defendant, in the statement of facts and argument, and complainant, in its reply, may request cross-examination of certain witnesses on specified subject matter; and an oral hearing will be held to that extent only.

Those proceedings known as investigation and suspension or I.&S. proceedings usually result from the filing by one or more carriers of some freight rate, rule, or regulation which, before its effective date, is alleged by some shipper or receiver of freight to be detrimental and unlawful. By petition to the Commission, there may be suspension by the Commission for investigation and determination as to the lawfulness of the schedule. Any party having an interest may participate without formal intervention in such proceeding. I.&S. proceedings may be handled under shortened or modified procedure.

Ordinarily an I.&S. case differs from a complaint case in three ways: the rate is not in effect while its lawfulness is being determined; in order to expedite the disposition of I.&S. cases within the statutory seven-month suspension period the preparation and service of recommended reports and orders is usually omitted; and the burden of proof, with certain excep-

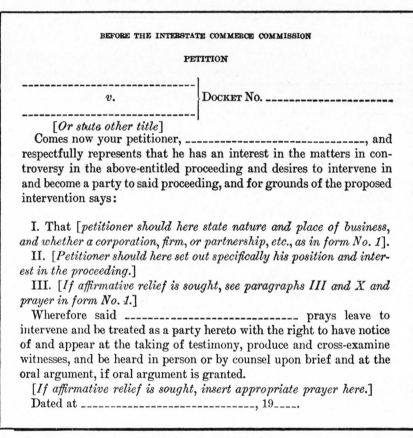

FIG. 16–4.   Petition for intervention form in complaint before the Interstate Commerce Commission.

tions, is on the carrier filing the rate to establish its lawfulness rather than on the complainant as in a complaint case. The exceptions referred to are the initial filing of a tariff rather than a change in an existing rate, or the investigation of an existing rate on Commission orders.

A formal complaint is given a docket number, and the defendant carriers are served with the complaint. They are given a limited number of days in which to answer. The form which is used to answer a complaint before the Commission is shown in Figure 16–3. If an answer to the complaint is not received, the issue is considered joined, and the defendant will still be given a hearing.

It often happens that a proceeding to which a traffic manager is originally not a party deals with some transportation matters in which his company has an interest. In such a case, he may petition for leave to intervene. The form for such petition is shown in Figure 16–4.

In the formal cases, the time for the hearing of a particular docket is set; and it is held before an examiner, who calls the meeting to order. Appearances are made by the complainant, defendants, and interveners, in that order. Some testimony is "canned," i.e., it is prepared in advance, and the witness merely reads it; whereas in other instances, testimony is given orally, without being set down in writing. The procedural order of appearances at hearing and oral argument is as follows: complainant, defendant, and complainant's rebuttal; respondent, protestant, and respondent's rebuttal; and applicant, protestant, and applicant's rebuttal.

At the end of a hearing, the examiner will announce the specific date by which all briefs must be received. The briefs are summaries of the case by the party who files it, containing an abstract of evidence, argument, requested findings, and conclusion.

Later, the examiner issues a proposed report of his findings. If no exceptions are filed within a specified period or the order is not stayed by the Commission, the recommended order becomes the order of the Commission. If the proposed order is stayed, a hearing may be held before a division of the Commission; and after that, recourse may be had to the entire Commission, which will issue an order or a report. The orders or reports of the Commission can be and are appealed to the courts. There are wide variations in the length of proceedings, depending upon the complexity of the case. Some cases are handled in a matter of days, whereas others take months. The routine steps, by days, in the progress of rate proceedings, from filing to decision, are shown in Table 16–1 on the next page.

Certain types of cases, principally those applying to operating rights and involving not more than three states, can be referred to *joint boards* by the Commission. The members of the joint boards are usually members of state regulatory commissions, with one member from each state within which the motor carrier operations are conducted or proposed. The procedure before a joint board is similar to that which applies to the Commission.

In complaint actions before the Commission, one should be as specific as possible as to violations substantiated by facts. Further, if a complaint is entered, one should be prepared to carry through on it. Such actions require careful preparation, organization, and presentation. The best-informed witnesses and concise testimony, based upon firsthand knowledge of the facts, are very important. Pretrial analysis of testimony of witnesses on the same side can eliminate overlapping.

TABLE 16–1

Steps from Filing to Decision	Investigations and Complaints (Oral Hearing) (Days)	Investigation and Suspension Proceedings, Rail and Motor (Oral Hearing) (Days)	Modified Procedure (Days)	
			Investigations and Complaints	Investigation and Suspension
Hearing set 30 or more days in advance, or modified procedure directed	40	40	15	15
Parties file briefs............	30	30	...	...
Filing of parties' statements on modified procedure.....	...	...	60	60
Preparation of proposed reports (including tariff check) and service thereof........	40	No proposed reports	30	No proposed reports
Filing of exceptions to proposed reports, and replies...	60	...	50	...
Oral argument, if requested, and if granted............	30	30	30	30
Preparation of final draft of decisions	15	30	15	30
Review and circulation of final drafts of decisions.....	17	17	17	17
Decisions by divisions and Commission, and service thereof	30	30	20	20
Totals, days	262	177	237	172

SOURCE: Statement of Interstate Commerce Commission to House Committee on Government Operations, May 3, 1957.

An important case before the Commission is indicative of the development of a record and the exhibits and statements introduced. In this case,[3] there were 15,768 pages of record, and 765 exhibits presented in 140 days of hearing.

FEDERAL REGULATION OF AIR TRANSPORTATION

Development of the Federal Aviation Act

Prior to the passage of the Civil Aeronautics Act in 1938, the Department of Commerce had administered the provisions of the Air Commerce Act of 1926, under which only matters directly affecting safety were regulated. The Post Office Department, under its authority to contract for the carrying of air mail, exercised limited economic regulation over commercial air carriers; and the Interstate Commerce Commission exer-

[3] I. & S. No. 7656, *Grain in Multiple-Car Shipments, River Crossings to the South* (1962).

cised a measure of economic control over commercial air carriers through its power to revise rates to be received by air-mail contractors for the transportation of mail.

The Civil Aeronautics Act, enacted in 1938, centralized in a single agency the various pre-existing regulatory functions of the federal government relating to civil aeronautics. It created a five-man authority to exercise semijudicial and legislative functions regarding economic and safety regulations.

At that time, a three-man Air Safety Board was established to investigate accidents, and an administrator was appointed to develop and operate air navigation facilities, as well as other promotional activities. The members of the Authority and Board, as well as the administrator, were appointed by the President, with the advice and consent of the Senate. This entire unit was an independent agency called the "Civil Aeronautics Authority."

A reorganization in 1940 abolished the Air Safety Board. The five-man Civil Aeronautics Authority was given the title "Civil Aeronautics Board" and reported directly to Congress. The administrator of the Civil Aeronautics Authority became the administrator of the Civil Aeronautics Administration, which was placed within the Department of Commerce.

The Federal Aviation Act of 1958 (Public Law 85–726) supplanted the Civil Aeronautics Act, created the Federal Aviation Agency, and continued the Civil Aeronautics Board. The Federal Aviation Act, like its predecessor, the Civil Aeronautics Act, contains promotional as well as regulatory provisions.

Federal Aviation Agency

The Federal Aviation Agency combined the aviation functions previously performed under the President; those of the Civil Aeronautics Administration, the Airways Modernization Board, and the Secretary of Commerce; and the safety regulations of the Civil Aeronautics Board.

The administrator of the Federal Aviation Agency is charged with the management of the national air space, including responsibility for establishing and enforcing air traffic rules, the development and operation of air navigation facilities, the determination of airworthiness of aircraft, and certification of airmen, as well as numerous other responsibilities. An organization chart of the Agency is shown in Figure 16–5. It currently has 44,000 employees.

Composition of the Civil Aeronautics Board

The President annually designates one of the 5 Board members as chairman and another as vice chairman. The Board members are appointed for 6-year terms, which terms are staggered as to expiration date. The Federal Aviation Act limits the number of members from any one political party to a maximum of 3.

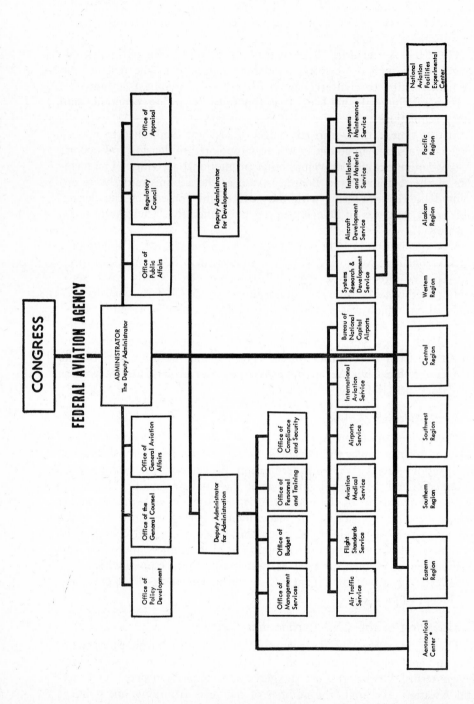

CONGRESS

FEDERAL AVIATION AGENCY

• Programs conducted at the Aeronautical Center are under the direction of the respective Services and Office.

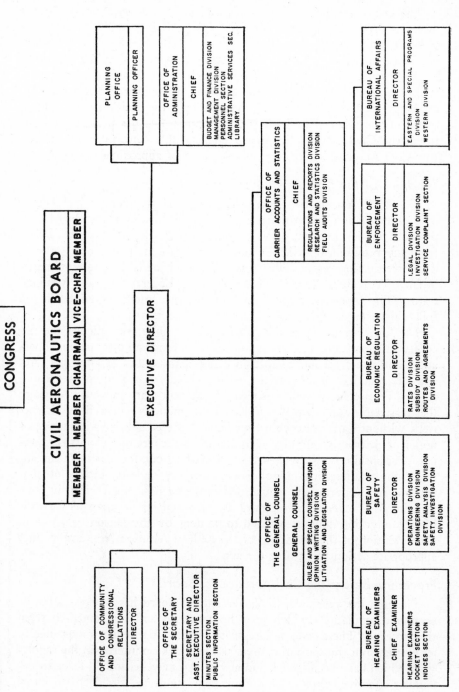

FIG. 16–6. Organization chart of the Civil Aeronautics Board.

The chairman, in addition to his duties as a member of the Board, serves as presiding officer at meetings of the Board and determines the order in which day-to-day matters will receive the attention of the Board. He is also spokesman for the Board before committees of the Congress. In the absence of the chairman, these duties are performed by the vice chairman. All of the opinions and decisions of the Board are voted on by the Board members, and the majority opinion is the decision of the Board.

An organization chart is shown in Figure 16–6. As presently constituted, the Civil Aeronautics Board consists of 5 bureaus and 6 offices. The Civil Aeronautics Board employs a staff of approximately 750.

Functions of the Civil Aeronautics Board

The Civil Aeronautics Board has economic regulatory jurisdiction over domestic and international air carriers. In addition, the Board may promote the development of air transportation, as well as exempt carriers from any provision of federal economic regulation. The Board has accident investigation responsibility and can participate as an interested party in air safety rule-making proceedings of the Federal Aviation Administrator. The economic regulatory functions are briefly described in the following paragraph.

The Board grants or denies certificates of public convenience and necessity to American-flag carriers for both domestic and international operation, and issues permits to foreign carriers; prescribes or approves rates and rate practices of air carriers, and determines mail rate compensation; fosters the safe and expeditious transportation of mail, and seeks to insure that reasonable and adequate service to the public is rendered by air carriers, without unjust discriminations, undue preferences or advantages, or unfair or destructive competitive practices; approves or disapproves business relationships between air carriers, including contracts, agreements, interlocking relationships, consolidations, mergers, and acquisitions of control, and issues appropriate regulations for the purpose of carrying out these functions. The Board investigates, upon complaint or upon its own initiative, anything done or omitted to be done by any person or group in contravention of the provisions of the Federal Aviation Act; and it takes appropriate action to enforce the act.

Procedure before the Civil Aeronautics Board

Through the years, the Civil Aeronautics Board has issued a series of economic regulations which have been revised and supplemented from time to time. These economic regulations are of particular importance to air carriers, but transportation users also have a keen interest in the regulations which have been issued, and any which may be issued. Prior to becoming effective, proposed economic regulations are circulated to interested parties for comments. Even after they have become effective, petitions may be made for changes. In order to be well informed on civil

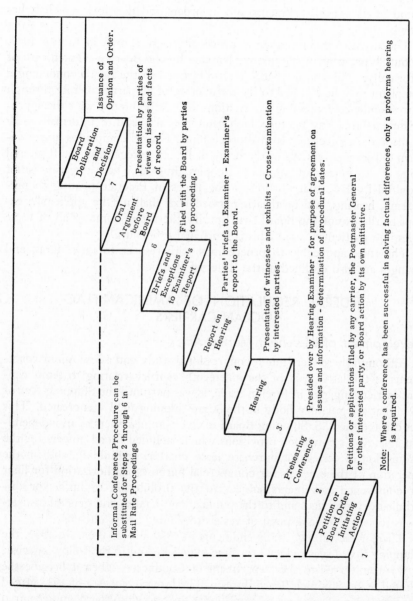

FIG. 16-7. The usual steps in economic proceedings before the Civil Aeronautics Board.

air matters, one should be familiar with the Federal Aviation Act, the composition of the Civil Aeronautics Board, the economic regulations, the rules of practice in economic proceedings, and the Board's policies as found in its policy statements and in orders and decisions which it has issued.

The usual steps in economic proceedings are shown in Figure 16–7. About 80 per cent of the matters handled by the Board are taken care of informally. This means that a letter addressed to the Board containing a complaint may be handled to the satisfaction of all parties merely through correspondence containing explanations, or by conference with the appropriate persons. Any matter which cannot be disposed of informally may be made the subject of a formal proceeding. Formal complaints must conform to the requirements of the Rules of Practices regarding the form and filing of documents and number of copies. In cases where a hearing is not required by law, that portion of the Rules of Practice relating to prehearing, hearing, and posthearing procedures shall not be applicable, except to the extent the Board shall specify the use of some or all of these rules in a particular case. This is shortened procedure.

The rules applicable to proceedings with respect to rates, fares, and changes are also outlined in the Rules of Practice.

FEDERAL REGULATION OF AMERICAN-FLAG OCEAN CARRIERS

Development of Merchant Marine Act

Although there were much congressional study and a few minor enactments in the latter part of the nineteenth century relating to American-flag carriers engaged in foreign trade, it was not until the Shipping Act of 1916 that a regulatory body in the ocean-shipping field was created. This act created the U.S. Shipping Board of five commissioners as an independent agency. It contained provisions which included broad powers for the acquisition of vessels for purchase, lease, charter, or building, and for the operation of these vessels for commercial purposes; authorization for liner or conference agreements subject to the prohibition of unfair or discriminatory practices and to the publication of rates; and general instructions for the sale or disposal of vessels to United States citizens.

There were subsequent amendments in 1920 and in 1928. In 1932, the Shipping Board was reduced to three members; and in the following year, it was transferred to the Department of Commerce, when it became the United States Shipping Board Bureau. The Intercoastal Act of 1933 placed the regulation of intercoastal rates under the Shipping Board, and required common and contract carriers to file and make public schedules of rates and fares. In 1940, the regulation of these carriers became the responsibility of the Interstate Commerce Commission, although, in certain particulars, the regulation of interstate transportation provided for in 1940

MARITIME ADMINISTRATION

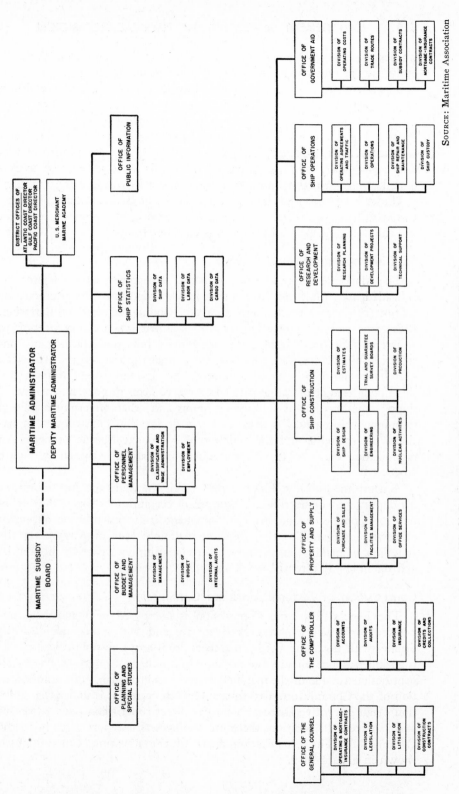

Source: Maritime Association

FIG. 16-8. An organization chart of the Maritime Administration.

was less comprehensive than that to which water carriers had been previously subject under the Intercoastal Shipping Act of 1933.

The Merchant Marine Act of 1936 established a Maritime Commission of five members as an independent agency which assumed the duties, functions, and obligations which earlier had been performed by the Shipping Board. The Merchant Marine Act of 1936 was both promotional and regulatory. In 1950, under Reorganization Plan 21, the Maritime Commission was abolished; and its functions and duties were transferred to two organizations—a Federal Maritime Board and a Maritime Administration.

Under Reorganization Plan No. 7 in 1961, the Federal Maritime Board was abolished. In its place, a Federal Maritime Commission was created, and the Maritime Administration was continued.

Maritime Administration

The Maritime Administration is in the Department of Commerce. It is headed by a Maritime Administrator who reports to the Secretary of Commerce through the Undersecretary of Commerce for Transportation. It is responsible for fostering the development and maintenance of an American Merchant Marine. Its functions include the awarding of construction-differential and operating-differential subsidies to the American Merchant Marine, the construction, repair, and operation of merchant ships, maintenance of national defense, reserve fleets of government-owned ships, administration of subsidy programs and other government aids to shipping, maintenance of reserve shipyards for ship construction in national emergencies, and the training of Merchant Marine officers. An organization chart of the Maritime Administration is shown in Figure 16–8.

A Maritime Subsidy Board, composed of the Maritime Administrator, his deputy and comptroller, act under direct authority from the Secretary of Commerce and exercise judgment independently of authority otherwise delegated to the Maritime Administrator in performing the functions of making, amending, and terminating construction differential and operating differential subsidies.

Composition of Federal Maritime Commission

The Federal Maritime Commission is composed of 5 members, appointed for 4 years by the President by and with the consent of the Senate, with not more than 3 members from any one political party. It is an independent agency which reports directly to Congress. The President designates one of the members to serve as chairman. The administration of the Commission's day-to-day regulatory duties is under the direction of an Executive Director who has direct supervision over 5 bureaus and 2 offices. In addition, there are 4 offices that report directly to the Commission. The organization chart of the Maritime Commission is shown in Figure 16–9.

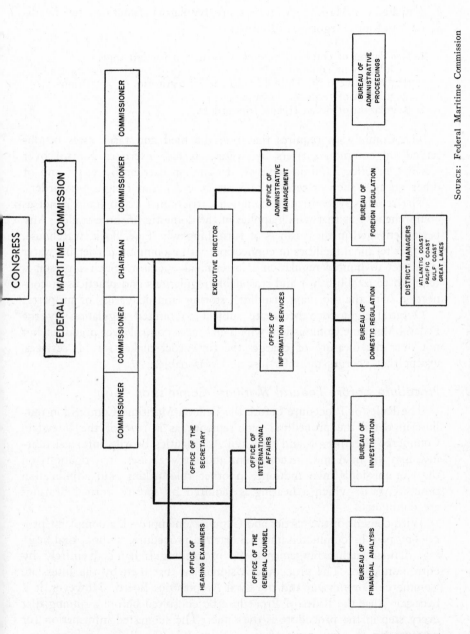

SOURCE: Federal Maritime Commission

FIG. 16-9. An organization chart of the Federal Maritime Commission.

Functions of the Federal Maritime Commission

The Federal Maritime Commission's regulatory functions can be divided into four categories, as follows:

1. Regulation of common carriers by water in foreign trade.
2. Regulation of common carriers by water in domestic offshore trades—that is, between the United States and its territories or possessions.
3. Regulation of terminal operators.
4. Regulation of ocean freight forwarders.

The Commission requires that rates be filed and tariff rates be observed by common carriers by water. It also exercises control over services, practices, and agreements of common carriers by water and of other persons, such as terminal operators and ocean freight forwarders.

The regulatory control of common carriers in foreign trade is not as comprehensive as that which applies in the domestic offshore trades. Any person engaged in the business of furnishing wharfage, dock, warehouse, or other terminal facilities in connection with a common carrier by water is subject to limited regulation as a terminal operator. Such a person is required to establish just and reasonable regulations and practices in connection with the receiving, handling, storing, and delivering of property.

Ocean freight forwarders are subject to limited regulation by the Federal Maritime Commission, which embraces control over practices, but not over the measure of charges the forwarder makes for his services, except that charges must be just and reasonable.

Procedure before Federal Maritime Commission

The Rules of Procedure before the Federal Maritime Commission outlines in detail the procedural requirements, as is true of the Interstate Commerce Commission and the Civil Aeronautics Board. Informal hearings may be held and, in complaint and answer cases, investigations on the Commission's own motion. In other rule-making and adjudication proceedings in which a hearing is required by statute, formal hearings are conducted.

With consent of the parties and Commission approval, a complaint proceeding may be conducted under shortened procedure, without oral hearing. Under such arrangements, the proceeding is handled entirely by correspondence. The procedure is similar to that used by the Interstate Commerce Commission and the Civil Aeronautics Board. However, it is necessary that the Rules of Procedure be consulted before assuming that every step in the procedure is the same. The suggested information for presentation in regulatory cases is outlined in the Rules of Procedure, which would be helpful in such proceedings.

An outline of the formal procedure in the complaint and answer cases before the Federal Maritime Commission is given below:

1. Pleadings.
2. Prehearing conference and hearing before an examiner.
3. Examiner's recommended decision and exceptions thereto.
4. Oral argument before the Commission.
5. Report and order of the Commission.
6. Petition for reconsideration.
7. Appeal to the courts.

RE-EXAMINATION OF REGULATION

Regulation constitutes an institutional or man-made restraint which was first imposed on rail operations about seventy-five years ago. As newer modes of transport developed, much the same type of regulation was applied to the newcomers despite quite variant economic characteristics of the modes and carriers within the modes. In the latter case, large segments in motor and water, however, were exempted from regulation.

The ease with which private carriage can be, and is being, undertaken has radically changed the need for reliance upon regulated for-hire carriers, and this has led to a degree of competition unthought of two or three decades ago. Coupled with this have been technological changes and federal promotional activities that have substantially altered the capabilities of carriers and thereby intensified competition. The changed competitive situation should allow us to relax regulation and permit greater reliance upon the forces of the market place to establish rates and services.

Most affected by increased competition have been railroads which have sought modifications in regulation to enable them to compete more effectively. Generally, motor, water, and air carriers have favored, as a minimum, the maintenance of the regulatory status quo, although expansion of the scope of regulation to embrace carrier segments now exempt from regulation would be more desirable in their views.

Originally, regulation was enacted for the protection of shippers and travelers; but since the vast changes in transportation have occurred which offer the shipping and traveling public many alternative methods to use, a great deal of regulation now appears to be maintained for the protection of segments of the carrier industry, thus relegating the shipping and traveling interests to a secondary position.

The weaknesses of our regulatory pattern have been evident for a number of years, and, since World War II, studies of federal transportation policy have been made by Congress, government agencies and departments, and organizations outside the government. A report in 1955 made by a Presidential Advisory Committee on transport policy and organization under the chairmanship of the Secretary of Commerce recommended placing greater reliance upon competitive forces in rate-making, revising the national transportation policy, and strengthening common carrier transportation by the adoption of specific proposals.

This resulted in some changes being enacted in the Transportation Act of 1958. The Department of Commerce issued a report, in 1960, containing many recommendations, some of which were meant to liberalize certain aspects of regulation.[4] A draft report on "National Transportation Policy," prepared by a special study group for the Senate Committee on Commerce was issued in 1961. Among the many recommendations were those advocating a department of transportation, a single transport commission, a new statement of transport policy, the imposition of adequate user charges on government-provided facilities, and modernization of rate-making policies.[5] Little action, other than the holding of hearings by Congress, was taken on the latter two reports.

In April, 1962, the first Presidential Message on Transportation was sent to the Congress.[6] It referred to the chaotic patchwork of inconsistent and often obsolete legislation which did not reflect the changes in transportation technology or in the structure of competition. Less federal regulation and subsidy were stipulated as prerequisites for a healthy intercity transportation network. The Message further stated that a more co-ordinated federal policy was needed with greater reliance on the forces of competition. Among the recommendations were the elimination of minimum rate regulation of bulk commodities and agricultural and fishery products; the sanctioning of experimental rates by regulatory agencies; the application of more equitable user charges; the formation of an intergovernmental group to formulate policies on mergers; the encouragement of through routes and joint rates; rate simplification by the Secretary of Defense and Administrator of General Services; and a continuous and co-ordinated program of research. Legislative proposals to implement the many recommendations were presented to Congress.

The most controversial provision was the elimination of minimum rate regulation for rail transportation of bulk commodities and agricultural and fishery products. Railroads and other regulated carriers have to compete with exempt water transportation and exempt motor carriers for this traffic. If such deregulation occurred, it is estimated that 76 per cent of rail tonnage representing 50 per cent of their revenues, 56 per cent of motor carrier tonnage producing 21 per cent of their revenues, and 85 per cent of water tonnage producing 50 per cent of their revenues would move without minimum rate control.

The Message suggested that Congress should make certain that in the absence of minimum rate regulation the existing laws against monopoly and predatory trade practices would be applicable. There appear to be a

---

[4] Department of Commerce, *Federal Transportation Policy and Program* (Washington, D.C.: U.S. Government Printing Office, 1960).

[5] Senate Committee on Commerce, *National Transportation Policy*, 87th Congress, 1st session (Washington, D.C.: U.S. Government Printing Office, 1961).

[6] Message from the President of the United States, "The Transportation System of Our Nation," 87th Congress, 2d session (Washington, D.C.: U.S. Government Printing Office, 1962).

number of remedies under the Sherman and Clayton acts. The Attorney General could: (1) prosecute such practices as criminal violations with attendant stringent penalties; or (2) institute a suit in equity to prevent and enjoin monopolistic rate practices or collusive rate agreements. In addition, an aggrieved competitor of a carrier allegedly engaged in unlawful practices could institute a suit for an injunction against the unlawful practices or a person injured by violation of the antitrust laws could institute an action for damages to his person, in which case the private party could obtain treble damages if successful in proving the alleged violation.

One of the criticisms of regulation is the lack of consistency in regulatory policies which may be caused, in part, by the Commission's view that each case is decided on the facts in that case. The Commission also has often implied that certain sections of the national transportation policy have been, or will be, violated without making a specific finding to that effect. The latter allusion is used as a substitute for substantive law.

One method that could be employed to inject a greater measure of flexibility in carrier pricing would be to permit competitive rates to be established without the usual 30-day notice. If these rates could be established without any notice whatsoever, regulated carriers would be able to institute rates immediately which, in their judgment, were necessary in order to meet competition.

Another proposal that would introduce a greater degree of flexibility to meet competitive conditions would be to stipulate that rates could not be suspended until they had been in effect for 60 days. As it now stands, a carrier can have its proposed rate suspended for a period of seven months. The rigidities caused by this may preclude its adoption of a rate structure to meet competitive conditions. Certainly, it would be reasonable to permit rates to become effective for a period, such as 60 or 90 days, and if the dire consequences forecast as a result of the rate change come to pass, then the regulatory body could suspend the rate. Under existing conditions, there are altogether too many instances of rate suspension occasioned by competitive carrier protests.

Of all the areas in which there has been general dissatisfaction for a long period of time, none surpasses the small shipments field. Carriers have complained of inadequate revenues and have instituted various changes in an attempt to make this segment of traffic compensatory. Shippers have repeatedly charged that these actions by the carriers place an unreasonable burden upon this traffic and, in addition, have consistently pointed to what they feel is the poor service associated with small shipment movements. With such irreconcilable views of shippers and carriers under existing conditions, it is suggested that the time has come for positive steps to ameliorate these conditions. Why should we not eliminate all regulation of small shipments? Of necessity an arbitrary weight would have to be designated as to what constituted a small shipment. It is suggested than 500 pounds or less could serve this purpose. Certainly, under competitive conditions, some carriers will actively seek such traffic if this is a profitable business. The fact that packages within certain size and weight limitations can be moved by parcel post will be some measure of protection against inadequacy of service.

EMERGENCY FEDERAL TRANSPORTATION AGENCY

During emergency periods, such as World Wars I and II and the Korean armed conflict, new agencies were created which affected transportation service and regulation. Transportation planning now includes the possibility of a nuclear attack.

By Executive Order the Secretary of Commerce is assigned the responsibility of preparing national emergency plans and developing preparedness programs designed to develop a state of transportation readiness with respect to all degrees of national emergency including attack upon the United States. The Office of Emergency Transportation was established to carry out these emergency transportation preparedness functions. There are two major planning factors involved in its work. These are (1) effective operation of carrier physical systems; and (2) centralized control of the use of transportation. The Office of Emergency Transportation may be thought of as concerning itself with balancing the supply-demand transportation equation under emergency conditions.

This office is part of the staff of the Undersecretary of Commerce for Transportation and under the direct guidance of the Deputy Undersecretary for Policy, who serves also as the Director of the Office of Emergency Transportation. (See Figure 16–10.) The Office of Emergency Transportation is organized to perform the task of furnishing policy guidance and direction to peacetime planning and is the nucleus wartime emergency transportation organization.

OET is organized along functional lines rather than according to modes of transportation. It relies on the transportation agencies for matters relating to the operation and utilization of each of the transportation systems. In emergency, the regulatory agencies, such as the Interstate Commerce Commission, would exercise the day-to-day control over common and contract carriers of all modes. These agencies are responsible for implementation of plans, priorities, and other controls. Each of them has developed a framework of orders which will guide the individual carriers in their emergency transportation operations.

The assignment of emergency preparedness responsibilities to various transportation agencies and to the Secretary of Commerce reflects the national policy that maximum use should be made of the regular departments and agencies in carrying out emergency preparedness programs. This approach is designed to achieve maximum effectiveness and efficiency through building into the on-going programs of the agencies an

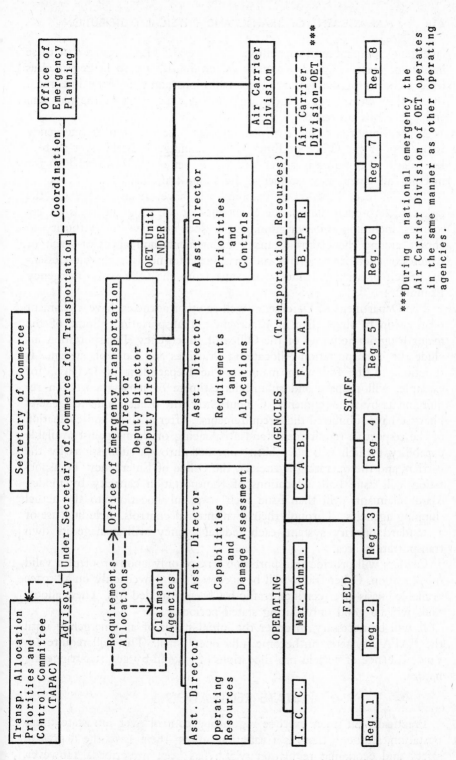

FIG. 16–10. An organization chart of the Office of Emergency Transportation.

***During a national emergency the Air Carrier Division of OET operates in the same manner as other operating agencies.

emergency preparedness capability. The President has stressed that these important emergency preparedness responsibilities are to be regarded as basic elements of the agencies' broad missions and should be integrated thoroughly with other agency programs at every step of the planning and operations processes.

A very important aspect of planning for transportation in emergency is the role of the Office of Emergency Planning. It is the over-all top-level national resource manager and the keeper of the National Plan for meeting all emergency problems, including transportation.

The Office of Emergency Planning will have, in an emergency, the task of determining the relative essentiality of the program needs for resources, including transportation. OET does not have the authority to choose among the claims of many departments and agencies—each of which considers its programs and transportation needs as the most essential. Such priority guidance will come from the Office of Emergency Planning.

The Department of Defense, as well as other agencies, have a claimant relationship to the Office of Emergency Transportation. Some of the major program activities of the Office of Emergency Transportation include the Transportation Allocations, Priorities and Controls system. It functions in the following manner: The Department of Defense, for example, will prepare and submit its estimate of its transportation requirements by time segments. Concurrently, the other claimant agencies likewise have submitted their requirements. After analysis and evaluation of the respective requirements and a balancing of them against available capability (which will have been compiled through submissions by the carriers and the operating agencies), the Office of Emergency Transportation will issue bulk allocations of transportation capacity by modes. Major claimants will then issue their own suballocations to the actual shipping agencies. Through their own internal controls, including use of a standard priority system, each federal agency will manage its own transportation area.

Carriers will provide transportation service only upon proof of a valid suballocation. Other traffic will be accepted and moved only on a "space available" basis after certified traffic has been provided for. These allocations will be good only during stated periods.

It will be necessary to cover the initial stages of an emergency until the TAPAC system can become fully operational. This will require advance issuance of certain pre-allocations of a stand-by and self-triggering nature.

STATE REGULATION

Practically all states exercise regulatory control over intrastate transportation, although there is a variation among them as to the degree of safety and economic regulation which has been prescribed. However, some states began regulating transportation prior to the first federal legislation dealing with transportation in 1887.

Representative functions of state regulatory bodies pertaining to transportation are collection of public utility taxes; formal and informal hearings of complaints of users of the service or carriers; formal and informal hearings of carrier applications; receipt and filing of carrier tariffs; receipt and recording of public liability insurance policies; acting as statutory agents for out-of-state carriers; investigation and adjudication of local commuter fares; and serving notice of charges developing from various violations of state laws pertaining to taxes, safety, and operating authority.

Many state transportation regulatory statutes differ from the federal statutes, so that where intrastate transportation is involved, a traffic manager should know the requirements and procedure of the applicable state statutes. About half of the states permit nonlawyer practitioners to appear before their regulatory bodies.

CASE

During the past two decades, an increasing amount of private and exempt transportation has developed. There are many factors responsible for this, including the rate structure of common carriers, the lack of, or low, user charges, and promotional and regulatory policies of the federal government. In 1939, regulated common carriers handled about 75 per cent of all intercity freight ton-miles but, by 1959, their share had declined to 67.5 per cent. This has been a slow but rather steady decline. Based on past linear relationships between freight ton-miles and the economic indicators of GNP, population and industrial production, a projection to 1970 shows the estimated common carrier share will be only slightly more than 63 per cent.

As a result of the increase in nonregulated transport, serious consideration has been given by the federal government over a period of years to changes in transport promotional and regulatory policies. This has met with quite varied reactions from carrier and shipper groups. Historically, regulation of transportation has increased and, as new modes have developed, some measure of regulation has been applied to them. In the case of motor carriers, common carrier operating authority has been granted to general commodity carriers and to specialized commodity carriers, such as household goods carriers, tank truck operators, automobile transporters, and others. The latter although common carriers, are permitted under their operating authority to limit their service to the transportation of a single or very limited number of commodities. This is a deviation from the historical concept of common carriage as the acceptance of any and all types of commodities. For many years, the carriers' solution to common carrier problems has been to advocate expansion of regulation to the nonregulated and to encourage vigorous enforcement of the newly regulated. Basically, this is still the position of many carrier groups. The railroads, however, are now seeking equality in regulation so they will be able to compete on an equal basis in so far as regulation is concerned with nonregulated transportation, i.e., have freedom to establish competitive rates on certain traffic.

The inertia of many shippers has, in the past, given the impression of satisfaction with the status quo, yet, at the same time, they are instituting an increasing amount of private carriage. The latter can be accomplished relatively easily with little or no capital, using leased equipment; or, if equipment is purchased, a comparatively small expenditure need be made, with the expectations of savings and service improvement. In order to provide back hauls for private carriage where the company itself is not able to provide its own products for hauls in both directions, these companies may transport exempt commodities, such as agricultural and fishery products, on the return haul. In this capacity, they are serving as a for-hire carrier of exempt commodities and are competing with exempt carriers, as well as regulated for-hire carriers, some of which transport exempt commodities as well as commodities under regulation.

The arguments that have been used favoring common carriage are that it serves both large and small shippers without discrimination in rates or service; and without such service, shippers—small shippers in particular—would be at a disadvantage.

1. Do you feel that common carriers are essential?
2. Should any restrictions be placed upon private carriage?

DISCUSSION QUESTIONS AND PROBLEMS

1. List the agencies of transportation which are regulated under the provisions of each of the transportation regulatory acts.
2. Give a brief historical background of the Interstate Commerce Act, including amendments.
3. What are the aims of the National Transportation Policy? Would you amend it in any way? Has this will of Congress been followed by the Interstate Commerce Commission?
4. Describe the make-up of the Interstate Commerce Commission, including the number of commissioners, length of term, chairmanship, and other pertinent matters.
5. In what manner is the work of the Commission divided? After a matter has been assigned to a division, may the Commission recall it and bring it before the entire Commission or assign it to another division?
6. What particular assignments are reserved for consideration and disposition by the Commission?
7. What is your opinion regarding the increased responsibilities of the Commission and the budget under which it operates?
8. Give the names of each of the three divisions of the Commission according to the work assigned to each, and summarize the functions of each division.
9. What document should be consulted for the correct procedure to be followed in appearances before the Commission? Where may it be secured?
10. Name and explain the methods which may be utilized in handling complaints before the Commission. Under what circumstances is each used?
11. In addition to being a regulatory act, the Federal Aviation Act has another function. What is this function? How important is it in the development of air transportation?
12. Compare the composition of the Civil Aeronautics Board to that of the Interstate Commerce Commission, including the administration of each body.
13. List and briefly describe the chief functions of the Civil Aeronautics Board.

14. Considering the functions the Civil Aeronautics Board performs, and with the information supplied regarding the duties of the various offices and bureaus, draw a new organization chart for the Civil Aeronautics Board, which may have a different number of offices or bureaus or different names that might appear logical to you.

15. Describe the functions of the Federal Maritime Commission, indicating those performed independently of the Secretary of Commerce and those performed in line with the general policies of the Secretary of Commerce.

16. Outline the formal procedure in complaint and answer cases before the Federal Maritime Commission.

17. Describe some of the federal agencies created during emergency periods which affect transportation service and regulation. As they are now constituted, do you feel they are adequate to meet any transportation emergency?

18. What criteria would you use, as a traffic manager, in determining whether to support a carrier seeking new operating rights before a regulatory body?

Chapter

17

MANAGEMENT OF PRIVATE INTERCITY TRANSPORTATION

THE traffic manager, as a part of his responsibility, is constantly seeking improvements in service and cost. This often leads to analysis of the practicability of private carriage instead of for-hire carriage for part or all of his company's transportation needs. In the postwar period, there has been a relatively rapid rate of growth of private motor and water transportation.

Domestic water transportation by private carrier is not subject to federal economic regulation, although safety requirements are prescribed by federal authority. Interstate private carriage by motor vehicle also is not subject to federal economic regulation. It is subject, however, to safety regulation by the Interstate Commerce Commission, and to size and weight limitations of the state or states through which the operations are conducted.

In determining what constitutes private carriage by motor vehicle, the Commission has made use of the "primary business" test. When the Commission has found an operator to be primarily engaged in some business other than transportation, and transportation was performed as a bona fide incident to manufacturing, merchandising, or some other noncarrier commercial enterprise, and in furtherance of the primary business, such transportation has been found to be private carriage.[1] If the facts show that the primary business of an operation, on the other hand, is the supplying of transportation for compensation, then the status of for-hire carrier is established, even though the operator may be the owner of the goods at the time they are transported and may be transporting them for the purpose of sale. A private carrier is not precluded from realizing an incidental profit in its motor carrier operations.[2]

---

[1] *Woitishek Common Carrier Application*, 42 MCC 193 (1943).

[2] *Lenoir Chair Co. Contract Carrier Application*, 51 MCC (1949). Also included in this case was *Schenley Distillers Corp. Contract Carrier*. The primary business test was upheld by the Supreme Court in the *Brooks Transportation Co., Inc.* v. *United*

MOTOR

Advantages

There are numerous reasons why business organizations turn to private carriage. Some of these are:

1. Improved service.
2. Lower cost between points which have loads moving in both directions.
3. Prompt delivery of rush orders.
4. Greater control of the condition of the merchandise, since it is not mixed with goods of other shippers.
5. Better control over scheduling of loading and unloading at the docks, with less congestion.
6. Less expensive packaging.
7. Assurance of on-time deliveries.
8. Transportation can become a self-supporting operation, since it is possible to charge for the service an amount equal to the rate of common or contract carriage.
9. Flexibility through freedom to operate wherever desired.
10. Advertising through the use of the company's own trucks which are, in effect, rolling billboards.
11. Lower inventory made possible through reduced transit time.

Feasibility of Conversion to Private Carriage

The consideration of private carriage may be occasioned by the feeling that rates are unreasonable and attempted adjustments have been unsuccessful, or that service provided by for-hire carriers is not adequate. Before converting to private carriage, the traffic or physical distribution department should make a very careful analysis of the proposed operation. The commodity or commodities and the area of the proposed operation must be selected. The estimated cost of a company truck operation should be computed on a monthly basis and divided between fixed expenses and variable expenses. Under the fixed expense category will be such items as depreciation for tractors and trailers, if equipment is owned; expense of leasing, if equipment is leased; licenses; and insurance. The Commission requires minimum amounts of insurance for the protection of the public, to be carried in the form of public liability, bodily injury, and property damage. Arrangements must be made to insure that there is compliance with this requirement of the Commission and that amounts beyond the minimum are adequate to protect the private carrier in the event of accident. If a mechanical refrigeration unit is required, its operating cost should also be included.

Variable costs include gasoline, oil, tires, and maintenance; drivers' salaries and expenses; a percentage for payroll overhead, social security, and the like; a charge for supervision; and toll charges, if any.

States, 340 U.S. 925 (1951). The Congress, in 1958, wrote the primary business test into the definition of private motor transportation, contained in Part II of the Interstate Commerce Act.

	PROPOSED TRUCK TRANSPORTATION PROJECT	DATE SUBMITTED
TITLE		PROJECT NO.

ESTIMATED ANNUAL SAVINGS $	SAVINGS PER CWT. $	CAPITAL EXPENDITURE $

DIAGRAM OF OPERATION

PRODUCTS HAULED	FROM	BRANCHES SERVED		CUSTOMERS SERVED

EQUIPMENT REQUIRED

EQUIPMENT TO BE BASED AT	LOADS PER WEEK	AVERAGE WEIGHT PER LOAD	LBS.
ESTIMATED TOTAL ANNUAL TONNAGE TO BE CARRIED			LBS.
REGIONS	DISTRICTS	PLANTS	

FIG. 17–1. Summary sheet for proposed truck transportation project.

The basic information can then be summarized and entered on a form such as that shown in Figure 17–1.

In addition, a schedule should be prepared, showing the routes and the service that can be rendered. If a schedule can be worked out so that there are return loads, the financial feasibility of conversion to private carriage will be greatly increased. It is not always necessary, however, that there be full loads in both directions. For example, there may be a 400-mile route in which deliveries are made at three points, with the load being completely discharged at the third delivery point. It may then "deadhead" to a further point, perhaps 50 to 100 miles distant, where a full load is secured for the company, to be returned to the point of origin. Triangular routes are also established, in which loads are carried on two sides of the triangle and the truck deadheaded back by the most direct route. Even a one-way haul may be economically feasible on high-rated commodities because of the cost if hauled by a for-hire carrier.

There may also be less-truckload quantities that are to be delivered to consecutive points and make up a truckload but which, if transported by a for-hire carrier, would take the higher less-truckload rates. The company, by operating its own vehicles, can perform a one-way haul actually cheaper than the less-truckload rates.

Where only a one-way haul is possible, some private carriers have found that they can secure return loads of agricultural commodities which are exempt from regulation. The revenue received from such traffic is sufficient to cover out-of-pocket costs and enables them to institute private carriage even where there is only a one-way haul.

Some indication of the cost of operating a truck is given in Table 17–1.

TABLE 17–1
PER-MILE COST OF OPERATING A
TRACTOR-SEMITRAILER

	Cents per Mile
Wages:	
Drivers' wages	11.638
Administrative salaries	1.002
Social security, compensation, group insurance, etc.	2.190
Fuel and oil	4.211
Tires	0.703
Maintenance and repairs:	
Labor	1.945
Material	3.629
Insurance	0.210
Licenses and taxes	0.621
Petty cash (including tolls)	1.146
Miscellaneous	0.139
Depreciation	6.666
Total, per mile	34.100

SOURCE: *Dun's Review and Modern Industry*, June, 1958, p. 21.

These figures are based on a Diesel tractor and a standard 35-foot aluminum dual-axle semitrailer costing $20,000. Depreciation is based on 300,-000 miles. The operating cost per mile is based on a one-way movement of 450 to 600 miles. For distances of less than 450 miles, the costs would be higher than the 34 cents per ton-mile shown in the table.

Private carriage has certain cost advantages over for-hire carriage. It does not have terminal expenses; it can use the most direct routes and does not have to cope with a rate structure as do for-hire carriers. Documentation requirements also are minimal, and the private carrier does not have to show a profit. Furthermore, a very large portion of drivers of private trucks are not unionized, and registration and miscellaneous fees in many states provide a tax advantage for private carriers.

A study of private carriage indicated that adequate cost records were not maintained by many companies with private fleets.[3] Clearly, it should be the responsibility of management to know what the costs are. This study recommends that the minimum basic cost records should include daily records of all current expenditures and operating statistics; monthly summaries of cost and operating statistics for each vehicle; and yearly summaries of all items including cost per-mile computations for each expense.[4]

Service aspects are of primary importance in considering conversion to private carriage. One of the areas in which service has been improved has been in reduction of transit time. This permits company salesmen to guarantee delivery since it is in company equipment and delivery schedules can be carefully controlled. Customer relations can also be improved through more responsiveness to emergency needs of customers where perhaps the customer is running out of materials for a production line, or a sale would have to be canceled because of the failure of goods to arrive as planned. With private carriage, it is possible to dispatch a truck with the necessary material which will allow operations to continue without interruption. Another factor of increasing importance to business is the desire to reduce inventories. The company fleet provides flexibility in transportation that is geared to production and delivery schedules. The reduction of the amount of time in transit when private carriage is used is an effective means of inventory control.

Traffic managers usually call in representatives of for-hire carriers when private carriage is being considered. The service and cost relationships between private and for-hire carriage, as shown by the analyses, are described. The for-hire carrier is then given the opportunity to see what it can work out on one or both of these aspects. If the carrier can make changes which more nearly meet the requirements of the company, there may not be conversion to private carriage. If it cannot, and the analyses show that there is a distinct advantage in private carriage, it is likely to be instituted.

Conversion to private carriage does not necessarily mean that the company turns completely to the use of its own trucks. It may be that certain segments of its traffic in particular areas will be most favorably suited

---

[3] Charles R. Haning, *Private Trucking Costs and Records,* Texas Transportation Institute, College Station, Texas (1958).

[4] *Ibid.,* p. 6.

for this type of operation. Furthermore, a company may use both private and for-hire carriage in the same area, with the result that the private operation will be favored in terms of traffic, quantities, schedules, time of loading, etc.

Private carriage is probably more attractive to the traffic manager of a large organization. There is sufficient traffic, and the traffic manager knows that he can assign the responsibility for the operation of private carriage to a subordinate. Some of the problems which are added, such as labor negotiations, can be handled by the labor relations experts of the company. In small industrial or commercial organizations, on the other hand, private carriage may mean a great deal of additional responsibility to the traffic manager, without any additional help. The limited capacity of trucks, however, enables even small firms to convert to private carriage.

Equipment Purchase or Lease

An important determination that must be made in conversion to private carriage is whether the equipment should be purchased or leased. If the traffic department or section has the responsibility for procuring the equipment, it should prepare specifications of required equipment and submit these to a number of leasing companies, as well as to tractor and trailer manufacturers, for cost quotations. When other departments have the responsibility for procurement of such equipment, the specifications may be prepared in co-operation with the department concerned, which may be the purchasing department or operating department. The lowest lease rate quoted, usually on a per-mile basis, is compared with the estimated cost of owning the equipment. If the differential is slight, leased equipment probably would be used. Some companies have a policy which states that leased equipment, on a long-term basis, is the only type which shall be secured.

One of the factors often considered in truck leasing is whether or not the company could make a greater profit by using the capital required for a company-owned truck fleet in some other phase of the business. For example, a truck fleet might represent an investment of $200,000 for a company which had a capital turnover rate of 10 times a year. In terms of capital utilization, the truck fleet for this company represents $2 million. If the company can get a 1 per cent cash discount on inventory purchases, leasing should be credited with $20,000 in an analysis of its value to this business.

There are several national or regional associations of truck-leasing companies which have member organizations in many cities. Currently, about 2 per cent of the nation's trucks are in leased fleets. Types of leasing arrangements are varied. One is referred to as the "full-service" type. Under this arrangement, the private carrier, or lessee, leases the truck under a long-term arrangement from the truck-leasing company, or lessor. The lessor provides the maintenance of the truck, fuel, repairs, tires, lubrication, garaging, and insurance—in fact, everything but the driver. The lessee provides a driver for the vehicle. When a leasing arrangement is made which involves a custom-tailored vehicle for the lessee, the leasing arrangement is for a period of five to six years, with a proviso that at the end of the first year, the contract may be canceled, but the vehicle must be purchased at its depreciated value. Long-term leases of ordinary equipment are usually for three years.

Another type of leasing on a long-term basis provides that the lessor furnish only the vehicle. The lessee provides the driver as well as maintenance, fuel, garaging, and insurance. Although these are two common types of long-term contracts, such leases can be drawn on a basis tailored to and agreeable to the parties concerned. This kind of leasing arrangement is available from truck manufacturers as well as leasing companies and is sometimes termed "finance leasing." In this type of lease, the title does not pass to the lessee.

A third type is a short-term lease, which may cover any length of time desired, such as a day, a week, or a month. Such a truck-rental arrangement usually provides full service except for the driver, who is furnished by the lessee.

Truck manufacturers offer a variety of arrangements for the purchase of their equipment, including leasing. The equipment generally is financed by the manufacturer. If the purchaser desires, he may secure a contract which will guarantee all maintenance of the vehicle. The purchaser supplies the driver and periodically makes the vehicle available for maintenance work. As little or as much maintenance as desired may be purchased and thereby, this phase, or part of this phase, may be handled for the purchaser by the truck manufacturer.

The Commission has had before it on numerous occasions the question of whether or not, under leasing arrangements, the transportation is for hire or the circumstances are such as to constitute private carriage of the shipper. The Commission has stated that the distinction between the two types of carriage rests on a determination as to who has the right to control, direct, and dominate the performance of the service. In instances in which the operations consist merely of the furnishing of equipment to shippers, who in turn furnish the drivers, operations are considered by the Commission to be private carriage.[5]

The Commission has recently ruled that, for the operations of a shipper using motor vehicles under a leasing arrangement to be those of a private carrier, there must be a clear, unmistakable showing that the shipper exercises actual control and responsibility over the operation to the same degree as he would if he were the owner of the vehicle.[6]

[5] U-Drive-It Co. of Pennsylvania, Inc., Common Carrier Application, 23 MCC 799 (1940).

[6] R.N.G. Commercial Auto Renters, Inc., Contract Carrier Application, 73 MCC 665 (1957).

An operation by two companies having certain officers in common, in which one company or its division offers motor vehicles without drivers for lease, while the other company furnishes drivers for such vehicles, has been found by the Commission to constitute for-hire carriage and to require authority from the Commission to operate.[7] There are some motor common carriers which own or control separate leasing or rental corporations, which lease or rent vehicles to private carriers or shippers. The Bureau of Motor Carriers of the Interstate Commerce Commission has ruled that private carriers may lease vehicles from such a company if the separate leasing or rental corporation conducts a bona fide business of leasing or renting vehicles to the general public, irrespective of whether the transportation services of the carrier are used. However, a regulated motor common carrier may not use a leasing or rental company which it owns or controls as a device by which concessions or rebates may be granted to shippers, or allow the business to be conducted in such a way as to result in discrimination or other practices unlawful under the Interstate Commerce Act.[8]

Equipment Selection and Maintenance

The *selection of the equipment* to do the job is a very important responsibility. Truck equipment is available in such a wide range that the particular requirements of the job to be performed can be readily matched with equipment from a number of manufacturers. The desirable approach is to determine the general type of equipment required, whether straight trucks or tractor-trailer combinations; and the type of motive power—gasoline, Diesel, or other; as well as the body type—refrigerated or insulated, tank truck, flatbed, etc. There are many different sizes of truck units and trailers, and the particular size which suits the amount to be shipped can be chosen. The maximum capacity of trailers is about 2,500 cubic feet, and the loading capacity is limited by the states in which they are operated.

Consideration should be given to each of the component parts that make up a truck: engine, transmission, axles, brakes, springs, and tires. The selection of the proper engine must make allowance for the following conditions: type of operation (city or line haul); maximum loads and type of loads (fixed or variable); desired maximum and cruising speeds; maximum grades to be encountered and the extent of these grades; type and condition of roads; and other conditions, such as weather, which would influence power requirements.

If a company buys its own trucks, it will be necessary to provide *maintenance service* for them. This may be done on a contractual basis with an outside organization, but the more common practice is to have this per-

---

[7] *Driver Service, Inc., Trac-Tra Rentals, Division of Wisconsin A. & L. Co., Inc., and Wisconsin A. & L. Co., Inc., Investigation of Operations,* 77 MCC 243 (1958).

[8] Administrative Ruling No. 103, dated July 24, 1957.

formed within the company organization. If maintenance is handled on a contractual basis, the traffic department may be called upon by the purchasing department to suggest organizations which perform such a service and be prepared to give assistance in an evaluation of the quotations submitted for this work.

If the company performs its own maintenance, it is necessary to maintain records of the work performed. A preventive maintenance program should be established, with more thorough periodic examinations based on time or mileage. Each driver should have a check list of items to be used in his daily operation of the vehicle. He should also turn in at the end of his run, when necessary, a vehicle repair order, listing the items requiring adjustment or repair.

A study of fleet operations of a large group of companies revealed that there were a number of shortcomings in fleet operations. These were: lack of exacting vehicle selection standards; lack of planned replacement programs; failure to analyze useful records systematically; lack of adequate maintenance policies; lack of clear performance standards; and poorly executed dispatch practices.[9]

Driver Selection, Training and Supervision

One of the most important tasks in operating as a private carrier is the selection of drivers. This requires the establishment of minimum standards in terms of experience, age, and health requirements, and instructions and procedures governing driver specifications. A general application form, which is usually standard in the company, is used, but should be augmented by a section specially prepared for driver applicants.

A telephone or personal check with individuals or organizations that have been listed as references should follow, and there may be personal interviews by the personnel department as well as the traffic department. Aptitude tests may also be given to driver applicants. A written test covering particular types of larger equipment and their operation may be desirable as part of the selection process in addition to a road test. A chauffeur's license and a statement that the applicant has operated certain types of equipment should not be considered adequate, but a road test should be given under qualified supervision. A portion of such a test is shown in Figure 17–2.

Companies may require a physical examination; and when interstate operations are involved, the Interstate Commerce Commission requires such an examination. At the present time, this examination must be taken every three years, and the certificate indicating that the examination has been made must be maintained by the private motor carrier.

In order to secure the greatest degree of efficiency from driver opera-

---

[9] G.M.C. Truck and Coach Division of General Motors Corp., *Seven Common Profit Leaks in Truck Transportation*, 1962.

					YES	NO
A. STARTING (Assume Gas, Oil, Water, Tires, Lights, I.C.C. Equipment, etc. have been checked)	1	Observes conditions surrounding parked vehicle before entering cab				
	2	Adjust seat				
	3	Assumes erect and alert driving position				
	4	Checks rear view mirror				
	5	Disengages clutch when starting motor				
	6	Warms up motor				
	7	Races motor				
	8	Checks instrument panel (Amperes, gas, oil pressure, etc.)				
	9	Releases emergency brake				
	10	Checks knowledge of gear shift sequence				
	11	Checks air pressure and brakes for working efficiency				
	12	Observes on-coming traffic before starting up or before entering street from parking lot				
	13	Starts smoothly				
B. STOPPING	1	Stops before necessary	A	At traffic signals or signs		
			B	Intersections		
			C	At crosswalks		
	2	Overruns crosswalks or white traffic lines				
	3	Stops without skidding tires				
	4	Avoids jerky stops				
	5	Rolls to a smooth stop				
	6	Allows truck to roll back while stopped				
C. CLUTCHING	1	Engages clutch smoothly				
	2	Double-clutchs properly				
	3	Rides the clutch				
	4	Releases clutch while stopped				
	5	Stops and starts without killing the engine				
D. SHIFTING GEARS	1	Starts evenly in proper gear				
	2	Runs long enough in each gear to ease labor on motor				
	3	Proper selection of gear for speed and traffic conditions				
	4	Clashes gears				
	5	Fails to drop gears when necessary				
	6	In gear while waiting for traffic light to change				
	7	Changes gear while crossing railroad tracks				
E. TURNS (Left & Right)	1	Strikes curb				
	2	From improper lane				
	3	At improper speeds (too fast or too slow)				
	4	Does he shy left on right turns				
	5	Selects proper gear before turning				
F. SIGNALLING	1	When leaving curb				
	2	When stopping				
	3	For turns				
	4	Proper signal for	A	Right turn		
			B	Left turn		
			C	Stop		

FIG. 17–2. A portion of a road test to be given to driver applicants.

tions, there should be a continuing training program. This may take several forms. A supervisor may ride with each driver periodically; and/or weekly or monthly meetings may be held, at which various subjects—such as operation of equipment, familiarity with Commission safety requirements, and others—may be discussed.

Inasmuch as trucks operate outside the plant and often over substantial distances, there must be adequate management control of such operations. Routes may be prescribed and, if necessary, a set schedule established. Check-in points along the way may be designated, so that the traffic department will know the whereabouts of the truck.

An aid in the supervision of drivers is the use of *mechanical operations recorders*, such as the Tachograph. A mechanism of this type is installed in the cab of the truck and records on a circular chart a great deal of information concerning the time that the engine was started, how long the truck was in motion, and the different speeds at which it traveled. Since the device is sealed, the chart can be removed at the end of the trip by a supervisor only; it can thus be ascertained whether there were violations of company rules or traffic laws. To be effective, the charts must be analyzed and remedial action taken, when necessary.

Another method of supervising drivers is the use of *road patrols*. The supervisor of drivers may occasionally undertake a road patrol, but a more general practice is to employ the services of one of the numerous companies which specialize in furnishing road patrol service. Insurance companies also furnish this service for insured private carriers. Regardless of how the road patrol is undertaken, the information in the reports can be helpful in the promotion of safety and a greater degree of control.

In order to assure enforcement officers and others that the operations are those of a private carrier, a letter may be addressed "To Whom It May Concern" and carried in each vehicle, advising that the equipment is operated for the industrial firm as a private carrier and that nothing is being transported for compensation.

Scheduling

To accomplish maximum utilization of equipment, it is necessary that trips be carefully scheduled and controlled. This requires close co-ordination with the sales department, since it will be receiving the orders for products to be shipped to customers, and with the purchasing department, in order that supplies purchased by the company F.O.B. the suppliers' plants can be picked up by the vehicles in conjunction with other trips.

There must be a central point at which this information can be assembled, and it is from this information that the trips can be scheduled. In many companies, shipments are on a repetitive basis, which makes scheduling largely a routine matter. In other instances, however, the weekly schedules of trips vary greatly.

One company has a planning department which schedules production with sales, sending a copy of the shipping schedule for each period to the general traffic manager. The traffic manager arranges to have the required number of vehicles ready at each plant when they are needed. The company's products move from the plants without any delay, and damage in transit is minimized by the tight control exercised by the traffic manager. A copy of each plant purchase order is sent to each local plant traffic manager, who selects the orders for materials and supplies that are to be shipped F.O.B. the suppliers' plants. Upon receipt of this information, the headquarters traffic department screens the data and notifies the supplier when the material will be picked up by the buyer's truck. This information is given to the truck supervisor or to the dispatcher, so that every time a driver leaves a plant with a load of products for a customer, he has instructions to make certain stops on the back haul; in this manner, a balanced operation is secured. If there is need for changing shipments to allow for emergency shipments, this would have to be worked into the schedule perhaps by holding another shipment for the next trip.

A driver's trip sheet or manifest should be prepared for each trip. It should provide complete instructions for the driver assigned to the trip. and list the shipments and destination point or points. The shipping documents used vary, some companies using a regular bill of lading and others a so-called "delivery ticket" which lists the items consigned to them.

Safety

Safety of operation is a paramount factor in private carriage. Interstate operations of this nature are subject to the safety regulations prescribed by the Interstate Commerce Commission, while intrastate operations are subject to safety regulations applicable in most states. Further, the highways are shared with the general public, and the advertising value of company identification on a private truck can be nullified by the actions of the company's drivers.

The Commission prescribes safety regulations concerning the qualifications of drivers, driving of motor vehicles, parts and accessories necessary for safe operation, reporting of accidents, hours of service of drivers, inspection and maintenance, and explosives and dangerous articles. The Commission requires that a *driver's log* be maintained by each driver when in service, which will show the time off duty, time driving, time on duty but not driving, and time in sleeper berth.

A safety program should be established which receives the full support of top management. It should include the careful selection of driver personnel and periodic meetings with drivers for training and accident-prevention purposes. Special meetings may be necessary for such matters as the introduction of new types of trucking equipment.

Some type of handbook or driver's manual, which is small enough to be carried in the driver's pocket, should be compiled to supply guidance and helpful information for the driver on a number of matters. The handbook may be divided into sections which include such items as safe driving and equipment-handling practices, what to do if an accident occurs, the handling and protection of products being transported, a digest of the Interstate Commerce Commission's motor carrier safety regulations which have application in interstate commerce, and a prescription of speed limits and penalties for violations.

There should be an inspection of the vehicle before it is operated. This should be done by means of a safety check sheet. It should be determined if all the required equipment is on the vehicle, such as fire extinguishers, spare bulbs, fuses, etc.; and a check should be made of the tires, windshield wipers, air-brake hoses and connections, and other items contained on the check sheet. A tractor-semitrailer combination can have as many as 3,228 things wrong, and the Interstate Commerce Commission check covers many of them. A safety check is essential because a vehicle can have an "out-of-service" sticker pasted on it by the Commission after examination, and it may not move until faulty parts are replaced or repaired.

A safety award program of cash or merchandise provides an incentive for more careful operation by the drivers. In order that such a program be successful, it is necessary that the awards be sufficiently large.

WATER

Some of the larger companies have established a private fleet of marine equipment, which may be purchased or leased. There is general purpose equipment as well as specialized equipment. The traffic department can assist in preparing equipment specifications based in part on the goods to be transported.

Fewer companies engage in private water transportation operations than is the case with private motor transportation. One of the principal reasons for this fact is that plants must be located adjacent to water facilities. There must also be substantially greater quantities to be transported than in private motor transportation. The commodities which are carried in private water transportation are generally bulk commodities. Because of the high cost of large, efficient power units, it may be that in the future private carriers might supply the barges and for-hire carriers the power unit.

The same general type of analysis must be made in determining the feasibility of private water transportation as is true with private motor transportation. Furthermore, it is essential that effective controls be established covering operations, personnel, and maintenance.

CASE

The Brown Manufacturing Corporation is a medium size company, headquartered in southern Virginia, producing various commercial and industrial chemical products. Caught in a recent profit squeeze, the company has become very conscious of the need for controlling costs, and each department throughout the firm has been urged to make some contribution toward cost reduction.

Mr. Phillips, the firm's industrial traffic manager, has been contemplating for some months the idea of the company's purchase of several trucks so as to meet certain of its transportation needs. He has read in trade journals of instances where other companies have engaged in "private transportation" and have saved substantial amounts of money. While he is not concerned solely with costs, Phillips recognizes that evidence of a possible cost reduction will be an inducement in securing the approval of the management committee of his plan.

Equally important to the Traffic Department is the improved service which Mr. Phillips feels certain would be gained with a portion of transportation under his direct control. The organization uses all forms of common carriers (i.e., rail, water, and motor) but has become increasingly disturbed at the deterioration in the quality of service offered by the motor carriers serving the firm and also by the upward trend of freight rates and charges. The company has experienced production holdups several times while waiting for a motor carrier to arrive, and the department has found that when a large claim against the carrier arises, lengthy conversations by telephone are necessary and frequently a meeting must be arranged with the carrier's claim representative. Of even greater importance is the fact that when a claim, either for damage or for overcharge, occurs after the company has paid the freight charges, it must wait a long period of time, often several months, before it receives reimbursement. Mr. Phillips has never kept an accurate account of monies due, but knows that at any given time it is usually substantial.

He recognizes that, if the company were to provide its own service, production schedules could be more closely co-ordinated since he would be responsible for scheduling the movement of the vehicles. Further, since company employees would be performing the handling and transportation of the freight, loss and damage would decline noticeably. In light of anticipated savings and improved service, Mr. Phillips has decided that it would be beneficial for the company to engage, to a limited degree, in its own private carriage. Operations at first would be conducted on a relatively small scale to determine their feasibility.

The Traffic Manager estimated that the firm last year transported some 7,000 tons of outbound traffic by motor carrier. Of this tonnage, it is estimated that about 4,000 tons a year, or 80 tons a week, moved in large lots or "volume" with a relatively high degree of regularity. It is this volume traffic which Phillips expects to move in the company's own trucks. He reasons that the 80 tons weekly could be moved by three trucks, one of them a 25-ton capacity tractor-trailer combination and the other two single-unit vans, gasoline-powered of 12-ton capacity. This traffic moves for the most part in the Boston, New York, eastern Pennsylvania, and eastern Ohio area where company warehouses and distribution centers are maintained.

Since Phillips knew approval of management would probably depend on cost reduction, he presented Table I as a comparison of the costs of transporting one hundred pounds of this volume freight by common motor carrier and the costs when using the company's own vehicles.

The cost of transporting one hundred pounds by common carrier is estimated on the basis of past expenditures at $1.10. The cost under the proposed method is $.90. Mr. Phillips is pleased because his cost figures, percentagewise, compare favorably to an "industry average" made up of other firms conducting private trucking operations.

The company would perform its own maintenance using facilities and

TABLE I

ESTIMATED COSTS OF COMMON AND PRIVATE TRANSPORTATION

Common Carrier Costs per Hundredweight

80 tons per week $\times$ 52 weeks $=$ 4,160 tons per year
4,160 $\times$ 2,000 $=$ 8,320,000 pounds per year
8,320,000/100 $=$ 83,200 hundred of pounds
Estimated 1962 expenditure for this transportation $=$ $91,520.00
$91,520.00/83,200 $= 1.10 per cwt. (hundredweight)

Private Costs per Hundredweight

4 Drivers (salaries, overtime, meal allowance)	$34,600.00	(45)%
Fuel, oil, lubricants, etc.	11,300.00	(15)
Maintenance and repairs	8,985.00	(12)
Depreciation ($40,000 over 5 years)	8,000.00	(11)
Insurance, licenses, taxes	6,000.00	(8)
Tires	2,250.00	(3)
Miscellaneous (fines, uniforms, special taxes, etc.)	3,745.00	(5)
Total	$74,880.00	99%

$74,880.00/83,200 $= 0.90 per cwt.

mechanics presently occupied in servicing the fleet of 15 official company automobiles and local delivery equipment. It was thought that the use of four drivers would enable the firm to conform to I.C.C. regulations governing the maximum hours of service which any one driver may work. Any driver not engaged in driving could be put to work around the traffic department in odd jobs according to Mr. Phillips' plan.

The expenditure on equipment would be approximately $40,000, and since the savings under the proposed plan were substantial, Phillips felt certain that management would approve.

Mr. Thompson, a member of the management committee, has some knowledge of transportation, and is reluctant to abandon or decrease the company's use of common carriage. He pointed out that the decreased use of common carriers would probably lead to a further deterioration of service on other types of freight. He was skeptical of the cost savings and was not certain that Phillips had included all pertinent factors. He stated that, with some pressure, the carriers could be made to improve their service and that the company was in the chemical business and not that of transportation.

Mr. Williams, another member of management, is decidedly in favor of the proposal. He argues that the expenditure is minimal in view of the potential savings. He also points out that if the experiment proves a failure, the firm can eliminate or dispose of its newly acquired fleet with little loss. He is also of the opinion that with more efficient service between the company and its distribution outlets, customer sales will be improved.

1. What factors, if any, has Phillips overlooked in compiling his cost estimates?

2. Is the argument of Mr. Thompson regarding a lessening of service by common carriers a valid one?

3. Are the savings sufficient to merit management's approval of the plan in its present form?

DISCUSSION QUESTIONS AND PROBLEMS

1. "Traffic managers have an obligation to use for-hire carriers if they are available rather than turning to private carriage." Do you agree? Why, or why not?

2. Discuss five reasons which cause business organizations to convert to private motor carriage.

3. As a traffic manager, how would you determine the feasibility of private carriage for your company?

4. Prepare an outline of the facts necessary to determine whether it would be better to own or to lease trucks.

5. Prepare an organization chart for the private truck section or division which operates thirty intercity trucks. Explain how and where it would fit into the traffic department.

6. Differentiate between the different types of leasing, and explain which one you would choose if you planned to lease truck equipment.

7. "Only large companies can engage in private carriage." Briefly comment on this statement.

8. What regulatory problems are involved in determining whether leasing arrangements are for-hire or private transportation?

9. Enumerate the factors influencing the choice of motor-truck equipment to be used in private operations.

10. Prepare a short paper stating how you would select and supervise drivers in a private carrier operation.

11. In analyzing private truck costs, what elements would you consider to be controllable by the traffic department?

12. Would you recommend a "token" private carrier operation by the traffic department to serve as a yardstick of the for-hire cost of transporting your shipments? Why, or why not?

Chapter

18

EXPORTING AND IMPORTING

THE intricacies of foreign trade are of such a nature that additional technical knowledge is necessary for the handling of these shipments beyond the continental limits of the United States. How extensive the responsibilities of the traffic manager are in export and import operations will depend in part upon the organizational make-up which has been created to handle foreign trade.

Basically, two methods are used in exporting. One of these is to sell *direct*, in which case the multiplicity of details and the responsibility and risk are upon the company. *Indirect* exporting is the other method, in which the American firm employs skilled export specialists. Company policy will dictate the choice between the two methods.

TERMS OF SALE

In foreign trade, a quotation signifies not only price but all the fundamental conditions of sale. It specifies what the prospective seller is willing to do and what he expects of the party to whom the quotation is made, in case it is accepted. In addition to actual price, it takes into account such matters as the place of delivery, the form and method of payment, the insurance coverage, methods of transportation, and all necessary items concerning quantity and kind of merchandise, as well as the time of delivery or shipment. An export or import quotation, except when qualified, is an offer, the final acceptance of which by the purchaser constitutes an export or import sales contract.

In computing price, the seller needs to consider many items of cost which differ greatly according to the circumstances of each transaction. Many of them will be determined by the extent to which the seller assumes the payment of transportation costs, the method of insurance coverage and service, and other fees or expenses involved in the shipping operation.

There are a number of forms used in making foreign trade quotations which designate the different stages in the transit of merchandise over which the shipper specifies he will assume transportation expense and be responsible for the goods. These generally are expressed through the use of abbreviations, the meanings of which are well defined within a particular trade or country. For example, the seller may make a quotation which obligates him to pay transportation expenses only until the goods are placed on board the vessel at the port of export—say, New York. The term then would be designated as F.O.B. (free on board) vessel, New York. Where the seller makes a quotation which includes the cost of the goods, marine insurance, and all transportation expenses to a named port of destination—say, Buenos Aires—the terms would be C.I.F. (cost, insurance, freight) Buenos Aires.

Through common usage, such terms have become more or less standardized as representing mutual understanding concerning costs, risks, and obligations of both seller and buyer. A number of these terms are given in the following list and are taken from the *Revised American Foreign Trade Definitions—1941.*[1] It is most important that United States buyers and sellers engaging in exporting and importing agree that their contracts are subject to the *Revised American Foreign Trade Definitions—1941,* for there are many foreign trade definitions which have been issued by various organizations.

1. Ex (point of origin), as EX FACTORY, EX MILL, EX MINE, etc.
2. F.O.B. (Free on Board)
   a) F.O.B. (named inland carrier at named inland point of departure).
   b) F.O.B. (named inland carrier at named inland point of departure) FREIGHT PREPAID TO (name point of exportation).
   c) F.O.B. (named inland carrier at named inland point of departure) FREIGHT ALLOWED TO (named point).
   d) F.O.B. (named inland carrier at named point of exportation).
   e) F.O.B. VESSEL (named port of shipment).
   f) F.O.B. (named inland point of country of importation).
3. F.A.S. (Free Along Side), as F.A.S. VESSEL (named port of shipment).
4. C.&F. (Cost and Freight), as C.&F. (named point of destination).
5. C.I.F. (Cost, Insurance, Freight), as C.I.F. (named point of destination).
6. Ex Dock, as EX DOCK (named port of importation).

EXPORTING

Direct Export Selling

Most of the manufacturers in the United States who are now exporting products originally started their business to produce for the domestic market. Over a period of time, many factors may have influenced their

---

[1] The *Revised American Foreign Trade Definitions—1941* is issued in pamphlet form and has been widely distributed by the National Council of American Importers, National Foreign Trade Council, Inc., U.S. Chamber of Commerce, and other organizations. It is reproduced in foreign-trade textbooks and other publications. Since the buyer's and seller's obligations are outlined under each quotation, the list should be consulted by those engaging in foreign trade.

move to send a portion of their output into foreign markets. If an early venture into foreign markets was successful, a manufacturer may have decided to seek a permanent foreign market. This has often led to the appointment of an export manager. Frequently, a company appoints its traffic manager as the head of the export department, inasmuch as many manufacturers feel that the more complex aspects of exporting are those involving shipping movements and the detailed documentation pertaining to clearance of shipments.[2]

Types of Direct Exporting

There are two different types of company-operated, direct exporting departments: (1) the built-in and (2) the separate. In the built-in export department, there is a department called the "export department." Under this arrangement, the only addition in personnel frequently is that of an export manager, for the personnel engaged in domestic responsibilities are interchanged with the export department. In effect, the traffic personnel handling domestic traffic will have the details of the export traffic to handle also. In a similar manner, financial arrangements and credit terms are handled by company officials along with their domestic operations. This type of export department is widely found where the volume of goods which the company sells in foreign trade is relatively small.

The second type of direct exporting is the separate export department. In this type of departmental organization, there is a separate department which performs all export functions except the actual production of the goods. Such departments will operate according to company policy. The export manager in this type of department has full responsibility for his staff, which will include a traffic manager, who may have under him a marine insurance specialist, a commercial invoice specialist, and a consular invoice specialist. The breakdown of the traffic personnel in this type of setup is related to the volume of shipments handled, as well as the geographical area in which distribution is made.

The separate export department in some of our larger business organizations may be established as a separate international company, which is a subsidiary of the parent organization. Such subsidiaries may even establish their own manufacturing and selling facilities in other countries, as has been done by some larger corporations. The general traffic manager may have a number of departments which are his responsibility, such as the packing and shipping department, marine insurance department, and foreign documentation department.

Traffic Responsibilities

In addition to documentation and packing responsibilities, the traffic manager in direct exporting usually has the responsibilities of advising

[2] Philip MacDonald, *Practical Exporting* (New York: Ronald Press, 1949), pp. 3–4.

on and managing details of routing to seaboard; selection of ports; export freight rates; bills of lading; seaboard handling; overseas shipping, including freight rates and ocean bills of lading; marine insurance; and use of foreign trade zones and free ports where available and appropriate.

The first consideration in making the ocean shipment is the selection of inland routes and their cost to seaboard by the various modes of transportation. The correct routing of freight by an inland carrier is important from the point of both economy and time. In choosing the carrier, the port facilities available will be a factor, as well as possible port congestion. The amount of switching or warehousing necessary also must be considered. Usually, merchandise must arrive at a port within certain time limitations to make specific sailing dates. Therefore, the choice of carrier is important.

Unless the export order specifies a particular port, the selection of the port from which the ocean shipment will be made depends to a great extent upon the ocean freight rates to the port of destination, the frequency of sailings, and transfer and storage facilities.

Other factors to be checked are whether or not there is absorption by railroads of switching, terminal, and lighterage charges and the extent of free time privileges for wharfage or storage.

For many years, port differentials existed which reflected competitive relationships between ports on the east coast. For example, differential rail rates to Philadelphia, Baltimore, and Norfolk were 2 or 3 cents per hundred pounds below those of Boston and New York on certain traffic. After extensive litigation, the Supreme Court in 1963 upheld a district court which had previously ruled that rail rates must be equalized on import and export traffic from and to North Atlantic ports and southern tier ports (such as Baltimore and Norfolk). There are differential rates to other ports, however, that have been unaffected by this order.

Packaging and Packing for Export

Redesigns in the product being exported frequently necessitate changes in the design of the export container. There are a number of rules which, if followed, will contribute a great deal toward a better export package. There are the following:

1. Domestic-type corrugated cartons should not be used for export. Solid fiberboard containers should be used instead.
2. All cases, cartons, and crates should be steel-strapped or wired with staples.
3. Whenever possible, new wooden cases should be used, properly lined and filled completely, but not overloaded.
4. The use of separators or special wrapping is recommended for interior packing.
5. Secondhand boxes or green lumber should not be used in new cases.

Adequate packing methods and an understanding of the transportation phases are a necessity in maintaining foreign markets. Goods prepared for shipment abroad must be adequately packed in order to give reasonable assurance of their safe arrival at ultimate destination. Generally, the packing considered to be sufficient for domestic shipping is not strong enough to withstand the rigors of export shipping. There are normally more handlings in export shipping than in domestic transportation, and the handlings are under conditions not as favorable as they are domestically.

When an order is received from abroad, consideration should be given to every handling which the shipment will receive from factory to destination. The following factors of handling should be given serious consideration:

1. Assembling and packing of commodity in the manufacturing plant.
2. Loading, stacking, and discharging rail cars and/or trucks.
3. Handling in transit, in warehouses, and on piers.
4. Loading and discharging of ocean vessels.
5. Warehouse facilities or open-storage conditions at port of discharge.
6. Transportation in country of ultimate destination by rail, truck, barge, etc.
7. Customs handling at destination.
8. Climatic conditions, including humidity and changes in temperature, such as from extreme heat to cold.

Another factor to be considered in export packing is that the distance involved is so great that, if the percentage of breakage is high, the purchaser of the goods may be unable to replace them because of the length of time it would take a reorder to reach him. This may result in financial hardship to the purchaser. He wanted the merchandise, paid duty on it, then had to arrange for an insurance survey, and eventually collected the insured value of the goods, which may not even reimburse him for his out-of-pocket loss.

The customer's instructions are very important in packing. A request to the shipper that no package should exceed a certain weight or dimension is probably a reflection of transportation conditions or facilities existing in the country of destination. In other instances, the customer's request to place only one kind of goods in each container should be followed. Some countries do not permit the importation of different kinds of goods in the same container, and a fine will be imposed by customs authorities unless there is compliance with this requirement.

The climatic conditions in the country of destination may be of such a nature that protection must be afforded freight by means of waterproof packing or other special protection. The selection of protective packing must be considered in terms of weight as well. The basis on which articles are dutiable varies in different countries throughout the world; but in some of them, it is based on the gross weight of the shipment—which, of course, would include the contents plus the packing and container. The traffic manager may recommend packing which will be just as protective but will not weigh as much; and thereby, he will save money for the customer. Because of the wide variations in the foreign tariff systems, it is necessary to have information available on the specific commodities shipped because the tariffs may have a more stringent application solely because of the manner in which the goods are packed.

Loss through pilferage of goods moving in foreign trade had reached alarming proportions by the end of World War II. Pilferage usually occurs on products of high value, but the problem is by no means confined to this group of goods. Almost any packaged article seems to be a target for pilferage. The method of packing can do much to minimize this type of loss. Metal and wire strapping have proved to be effective deterrents.

Packing for foreign shipments must be given careful attention and is a subject on which much has been written. Constant admonitions are made to follow the best packing procedures; yet, the percentage of loss and damage to goods due to inadequate packing remains too high. Since steamship companies engaging in foreign trade do not have the extent of liability that our domestic rail and motor carriers have, insurance is used by the shipper to protect against many contingencies.

There are many sources of information concerning all phases of packing in foreign trade, both governmental and nongovernmental. Many of the latter are packaging or testing laboratories or trade associations whose members manufacture particular types of containers. With data and advice available from these sources, it should be possible to pack adequately for foreign trade with proper consideration for cost factors.

Use of Containers

There is a growing use of containers for moving goods in foreign trade. The advantages of expeditious handling and the minimization of losses will undoubtedly accelerate their use. Unfortunately, the rates that apply on containers are port-to-port rates, and a single-factor rate for the land-water-land transportation has not been established. In the movement of containerized freight, as in the movement of other freight, a door-to-door type of rate is needed to simplify the rate aspects of international transportation. In addition, customs rules should be modified to permit the validation of export declarations at interior points rather than at the port where the cargo has to be removed from the container and checked.

With the development of the Common Market in Europe, American manufacturers are having to control costs more closely both in production and physical distribution. Greater utilization of containers is one method which could improve this situation. The development of containerization in the marine field has moved at a snail's pace because of lack of enthusiasm by labor, carrier management, and steamship operators. In 1962, the steamship conferences had not approved a single factor freight rate covering both marine and inland transportation services. Coupled with the need for a single factor rate should be simplified documentation.

A part of the labor difficulties has been overcome by the establishment of a system of royalty payments. In New York, this payment amounts to 35 cents a ton for loading a container aboard a conventional ship and is graduated upward to $1.00 for ships where more than 40 per cent of their capacity is fitted for containers. In international transportation, the container offers the common denominator system.

Causes of Preventable Losses

The responsibility for adequate packing is that of the shipper of the goods, for the steamship lines cannot require or enforce proper packing as rigorously as they would like. The United States Carriage of Goods by Sea Act of 1936 states in Section 4 (2): "Neither the carrier nor the ship shall be responsible for loss or damage arising or resulting from insufficiency of packing." The losses which occur as a result of breakage, pilferage, and theft exceed the losses caused by major maritime casualties, which include fires, sinkings, and collision of vessels. Thus, the largest of these losses is a preventable loss.

Some of the causes of preventable losses are described in the following paragraphs:

Leakage is caused by poor outer containers which do not protect the contents, lack of interior cushioning, inadequate handling marks, overpacking, insufficient ullage, and improper sealing of inner container.

Pilferage generally can be attributed to the use of frail, secondhand cartons or cases, or other inadequate containers; use of green lumber for outside containers; failure to protect removable parts; use of open crates; and lack of banding and other pilferage-prevention devices.

Corrosion results from failure to use preservatives and improper lining of the container.

Slackage can be attributed, in many cases, directly to the overloading of the container (particularly bags) and the use of the wrong type of container for overseas shipments; it may also be due to the use of reused bags, paper bags, and poor sewing.

Water damage, in many cases, results from exposure in open storage and failure to use waterproof liners.

Hook damage caused by freight handlers is, in many cases, caused by the lack of proper cautionary marks (such as "Do Not Use Hooks"). Heavy bags and bales should be provided with ears for handlers to grip.

Breakage can be attributed to lack of interior bracing and reinforcements, failure to disassemble breakable parts, and use of frail or otherwise improper packaging.

Nondelivery can often be attributed to poor and illegible markings, which may result in short delivery or delivery at the wrong port.

Marking

The proper marking of packages is necessary to effect delivery. The marks and numerals placed on the packages must conform to those placed in the commercial invoice, the consular invoice, the bill of lading, and any other shipping documents. Instead of writing out the full name and address of the consignee, symbols of either the exporter or the importer may be used. The symbol may be initials of the consignee in large letters enclosed in a square, circle, diamond, or triangle. Above the symbol should be the country of origin, and below the symbol should be the name of the port of destination. Below the port mark is the number of the individual package, if it is necessary or desirable to number packages. Below the number of the package are the gross weight, the legal weight, the cubic measurements of the package, if this information is helpful to the importer or is required by customs regulations.

The use of symbols instead of writing out the full name and address of the consignee makes identification easier. A provision of the ocean bill of lading states that all packages covered by a symbol must be stored together on a pier, so that the importer does not have to do any sorting. The use of symbols also may facilitate the handling of goods, since the packages may be handled by people who cannot read English. The most commonly accepted method of marking is stenciling. Cautionary phrases, such as "Handle with Care" or "This Side Up," may not be very effective. However, a heavy arrow pointing to the top of the case stands a better chance of being understood. In some instances, stickers which show palm trees are used instead of arrows to indicate "This End Up" on a package.

Documentation

Documentation is a very important part of the export shipment. The proper execution of the documents to conform to the pre-arranged terms of sale, as well as to meet the regulations pertaining to clearance at United States ports and entry in foreign countries, must be handled by individuals who are well trained in this field. Some of the documents are the same for every shipment, but there are specific forms which vary from country to country, and it is necessary that care is taken to insure that the personnel handling the phases of documentation are posted on the current regulations of individual countries. A good source of this information is the *Exporters' Encyclopedia*.

An outline of some of the documents required on ocean shipments is given below:

Export declaration	Delivery instructions
Ocean bill of lading	Insurance certificate
Packing list	Shipping instructions
Pro forma commercial invoice	Letter of transmittal
Final commercial invoice	Delivery permit
Dock receipt	

In addition to, or in place of, some of the above documents on some shipments, it may be necessary to have an export license, import license, intent for drawback, lighterage orders, letter of credit, consular invoice, and certificate of origin.

In the usual routing from an inland point by rail of freight which is moving in export, the shipment will originate on a domestic bill of lading marked for export. The domestic bill of lading used may be an order bill, in which case the party to be notified is shown, as well as the destination and other necessary data. A *uniform through export bill of lading* can be used. If it is not available at the point of origin, it will be issued by the commercial agent of the railroad at the nearest point of shipment in exchange for the railroad domestic bill of lading. Under the uniform through export bill of lading, the rail movement from a location in the interior of the United States, plus the movement by water, is covered by a single document. Since World War II, uniform through export bills of lading have been largely confined to shipments from interior points through Pacific Coast ports and shipments to the Far East. The use of these bills of lading through North Atlantic and Gulf ports was eliminated during the war, and their use has been discouraged since that time by the carriers.

The through export bill of lading contains three separate sets of terms and conditions: namely, Part I, covering transportation of goods from the inland point to the port of export; Part II, covering transportation by water from the port of export to the foreign port; and Part III, covering reshipment by water, where necessary, from the foreign port shown in the bill of lading to the ultimate port of discharge. The use of this bill of lading is restricted to cargo charged on a weight basis for the ocean portion of the shipment. However, the restrictions which exist in the use of this bill of lading are offset by several advantages, one of the most important of which is that the inland exporter, upon turning over his shipment to the railroad, knows that it will be routed to its ultimate destination without any further action on his part.

One of the procedures in the exportation of goods is arranging with the steamship company for cargo space in advance of the shipment. This is referred to as "booking." The traffic department may have a *booking request* form, to be prepared by the particular department which has an export shipment. Such a form is shown in Figure 18–1. The traffic department, acting upon this booking request form, can make arrangements for space on a steamship loading at a particular port at about the specified date. The *Journal of Commerce* and the *Shipping Digest* are good sources of information as to steamship operations. There must be sufficient time between receipt of the booking request and the sailing date of the steamship to prepare the documents, perhaps a minimum of 4 or 5 days. It is possible to make tentative bookings; but where large cargoes are involved, it is customary to book the space and enter into a formal contract of affreightment. The steamship company assigns booking numbers to the vessel's space, so that an exporter can use the booking number on all papers that he has in connection with the delivery of the cargo to the pier.

REQUEST FOR SPACE

ORDER NOS.

ORIGIN -	DATE	PLANT READY DATE - NOW
IMPORT LICENSE EXPIRES	LETTER OF CREDIT EXPIRES	EXPORT LICENSE EXPIRES
NO. AND KIND PKGS.	COMMODITY GROSS WEIGHT	CUBE LABEL ON PKGS.

CONSIGNEE

PORT	OR	DEPARTMENT -

FOR TRAFFIC DEPARTMENT RECORDS

BOOKED	S/S	SAILING DUE AT PORT OF	ON
S/S LINE	FLAG	PIER	
BOOKING NO.	DECLARATION NO.	PERMIT NO.	
DATE TO BE SHIPPED	DATE TO BE DELIVERED		
REMARKS:	CONSULATE DEADLINE		
	DEC. MAILED		
	FILE MAILED		

FIG. 18–1.   An example of a booking request form used in exporting.

Delivery permits or *steamship permits* are secured on each shipment. This document contains instructions to the receiving clerk at the specified pier for receiving, within the time limit specified, the freight described in the delivery permit. Traffic departments, where possible, obtain delivery permit numbers by telephone from the ocean carrier. Where the delivery permit number cannot be obtained in this manner, arrangements have to be made to have a messenger pick up the permit at the steamship office by presentation of an authenticated export declaration. The traffic department, having secured the booking, can place the following information on the booking request form: steamer name; sailing date; steamship line; flag of registry; pier number and location; steamship delivery permit number, if available at time of booking; delivery date to pier; and long- or short-form ocean bill of lading. With this information on the plant's booking request form, it can be returned to the plant, after which it is merely a matter of releasing the shipment.

The United States government, on all shipments to foreign countries, requires an *export declaration*, which shows the name and address of the shipper, name of the carrier, destination of the goods, marks and numbers, name and address of the consignee, number and kinds of packages, description of commodities, classification number, quantity, value at time and place of shipment, and origin. The export declaration is filed with the Customhouse at the port of export and is usually prepared by the traffic department. An export declaration must be examined to ascertain that the goods are described in sufficient detail to permit their classification in accordance with the commodity descriptions required by the Department of Commerce.

The export declaration presented to the Collector of Customs at the port of export for approval will, if approved, bear a serial number and validation stamp inserted by the Collector's office. As indicated earlier, this can be used in securing a delivery permit from the steamship company. Figure 18–2 is a shipper's export declaration. If the volume of business justifies it, a firm may have its name imprinted in the appropriate spaces, thereby saving time in the preparation of the export declaration.

At the time the export declaration is prepared, a check is made to see whether the commodity requires a U.S. Department of Commerce *export license*. If the commodity is on the "positive" list of controlled commodities, it is a commodity or product for which an export license is needed. Application for such a license is made to the Office of International Trade of the Department of Commerce. General licenses, as well as several other different types, are issued. Some foreign governments require the importer to secure from the exchange control board of his respective country an *import permit*. The permit describes the shipment in detail and is sent to the exporter for presentation to the consul with the necessary export documents.

The *dock receipt* is issued by a steamship agent upon delivery at the dock of the goods moving in export. This indicates that the goods have been received by the steamship company. These receipts are usually nonnegotiable. The inland carrier which has delivered the goods at the dock is usually given the dock receipt, and it turns the receipt over to the exporter.

The traffic department always checks the dock receipt to determine whether a short delivery has been made or if shipments arrived in damaged condition. It may be necessary to replace goods or make arrangements for recoopering. Some of the factors which will govern the action necessary on short or damaged shipments are the shipping date instructions, the letter-of-credit expiration date, the nature of the goods—hazardous or nonhazardous—and consular deadlines.

A dock receipt usually gives the name of the consignor, the name of the vessel, the port of discharge, the marks and numbers on packages, number of packages, description of the goods as it will appear on the bill of lading, gross weight of the shipment, and cubic measurements.

The *ocean bill of lading* is prepared by the traffic department. The number of copies required will depend on the requirements of the country

Form 7525-V (Rev. Nov. 1945)
EXPORT CONTROL
FOREIGN COMMERCE
STATISTICAL REGULATIONS
(See Instructions on Reverse Side)

U. S. DEPARTMENT OF COMMERCE
BUREAU OF THE CENSUS—OFFICE OF INTERNATIONAL TRADE

SHIPPER'S EXPORT DECLARATION

OF SHIPMENTS TO FOREIGN COUNTRIES OR NONCONTIGUOUS TERRITORIES OF THE UNITED STATES

READ CAREFULLY THE INSTRUCTIONS ON BACK TO AVOID DELAY AT SHIPPING POINT
Clearance will not be granted until shipper's declaration has been filed with the Collector of Customs. This declaration shall not be used to effect any exportation after the expiration date of the export license referred to herein, except as specifically authorized by export regulations.
DECLARATIONS SHOULD BE TYPEWRITTEN OR PREPARED IN INK; INDELIBLE PENCIL IS NOT PERMISSIBLE.

FORM APPROVED.
BUDGET BUREAU NO. 41-R597.2

CONFIDENTIAL (See Instruction 2(k) on reverse side.)
Do Not Use This Area

Do Not Use This Area | District | Port | Country (For customs use only)

FILE NO. (This Space for Use of Customs)

1. EXPORTING CARRIER (if vessel, give name, flag and pier number) | 2. FROM (U. S. Port of Export)

3. EXPORTER (Principal or seller—licensee) | ADDRESS (Number, street, place, State)

4. AGENT OF EXPORTER (Forwarding agent) | ADDRESS (Number, street, place, State)

5. PURCHASER OR ULTIMATE CONSIGNEE | ADDRESS (Place, country)

6. INTERMEDIATE CONSIGNEE | ADDRESS (Place, country)

7. FOREIGN PORT OF UNLOADING (For vessel and air shipments only) | 8 PLACE AND COUNTRY OF ULTIMATE DESTINATION (Not place of transshipment)

(9) MARKS AND NOS.	(10) NUMBER AND KIND OF PACKAGES, DESCRIPTION OF COMMODITIES, EXPORT LICENSE NUMBER, ISSUANCE DATE, EXPIRATION DATE (or GENERAL LICENSE SYMBOL) (Describe commodities in sufficient detail to permit classification according to Schedule B. Do not use general terms. Insert required license information on line below description of each item)	(11) SHIPPING WEIGHT * (Gross weight in pounds) Not required for truck, rail, and mail exportations	(12) SPECIFY "D" OR "F"	(13) SCHEDULE B COMMODITY No	(14) NET QUANTITY IN SCHEDULE B UNITS (State unit)	(15) VALUE AT TIME AND PLACE OF EXPORT (Selling price or cost if not sold, including in land freight, insurance and other charges to place of export) (Nearest whole dollar, omit cents)

16. WAYBILL OR MANIFEST NO. (of Exporting Carrier) | 17. DATE OF EXPORTATION (if Vessel, Date of Clearance)

18. THE UNDERSIGNED HEREBY AUTHORIZES .... TO ACT AS FORWARDING AGENT FOR EXPORT CONTROL AND CUSTOMS PURPOSES. (Name and address—Number, street, place, State)
(DULY AUTHORIZED
EXPORTER .... BY OFFICER OR EMPLOYEE) ....

▶ 19. I DECLARE THAT ALL STATEMENTS MADE AND ALL INFORMATION CONTAINED IN THIS EXPORT DECLARATION ARE TRUE AND CORRECT.

20. Subscribed and sworn to before me on ...., 19...... | SIGNATURE ....
(Duly authorized officer or employee of exporter or named forwarding agent)

FOR ....
(Name of corporation or firm and capacity of signer, e. g., secretary, export manager, etc.)

(TITLE OR DESIGNATION) Notary Public, etc., or those authorized to administer oaths under Sec 486, Tariff Act of 1930. | ADDRESS ....

▶ Declaration should be made by duly authorized officer or employee of exporter or of forwarding agent named by exporter
* If shipping weight is not available for each Schedule B item listed in column (13) included in one or more packages, insert the approximate gross weight for each Schedule B item. The total of these estimated weights should equal the actual weight of the entire package or packages.
² Designate foreign merchandise (reexports) with an "F" and exports of domestic merchandise produced in the United States or changed in condition in the United States with a "D"
NO AUTHENTICATED DECLARATION RELATING TO ANY COMMODITY REQUIRING AN EXPORT LICENSE MAY BE ALTERED, CHANGED OR AMENDED WITHOUT PRIOR WRITTEN AUTHORIZATION FROM THE COLLECTOR OF CUSTOMS OR FROM SUCH OTHER PERSON AS MAY BE EMPOWERED BY EXPORT REGULATIONS TO GIVE SUCH WRITTEN AUTHORIZATION. (See also Instruction 2 (e).)
16—66603-2

Do Not Write in This Area

FIG. 18–2. A copy of a shipper's export declaration.

of destination. Sometimes, as many as fifty copies have to be prepared. The ocean bill of lading contains a description of the goods, the port marks, the weights and measurements of the packages, and the numbers on the shipping packages. Like the domestic bill of lading, the ocean bill of lading may be either a straight bill or an order bill of lading. The straight bill of lading is a nonnegotiable document, and it is possible for the customer to take delivery without presenting the bill of lading, except where necessary for identification. The title to goods which move on order ocean bills of lading remains with the shipper until he transfers it to the bearer of the bill of lading by endorsing it on the back in blank, or to a special party by endorsing it specifically to that party. A copy of an ocean bill of lading is shown in Figure 18–3.

AMERICAN PRESIDENT LINES, Ltd.
Home Office—311 California St., San Francisco, California
(SPACES IMMEDIATELY BELOW FOR SHIPPERS MEMORANDA—NOT PART OF BILL OF LADING)

FORWARDING AGENT—REFERENCES | EXPORT DEC. No.

DELIVERING CARRIER TO STEAMER: | CAR NUMBER—REFERENCE

BILL OF LADING

SHIP | FLAG | PIER | PORT OF LOADING

PORT OF DISCHARGE FROM SHIP

SHIPPER ....

CONSIGNEE .... AT .... Port of Destination

NOTIFY ....
(Order Bill of Lading must show name and address of party to be notified.)

PARTICULARS FURNISHED BY SHIPPER OF GOODS

MARKS AND NUMBERS	NO. of PKGS.	DESCRIPTION OF PACKAGES AND GOODS	CUBIC FEET	GROSS WEIGHT IN POUNDS

....LBS. @.... PER 2000 LBS. $....
....LBS. @.... PER 2240 LBS. $....
....CU. FT. @.... PER 40 CU. FT. $....
....CU. FT. @.... PER 40 CU. FT $....
.... $....
.... $....
.... $....

FREIGHT PREPAID TOTAL $....

Dated At New York, N.Y. ....

PRINTED IN U.S.A. FORM F.T.-87-N.Y.-1-1-52

(CONDITIONS CONTINUED FROM REVERSE SIDE HEREOF)

IN WITNESS WHEREOF, THE CARRIER BY ITS AGENT HAS SIGNED .... BILLS OF LADING, ALL OF THE SAME TENOR AND DATE, ONE OF WHICH BEING ACCOMPLISHED, THE OTHERS TO STAND VOID.

AMERICAN PRESIDENT LINES, Ltd.

This is a SHIPPED on BOARD Bill of Lading When Validated

BY ....

B/L No. ....

FIG. 18–3. A copy of an ocean bill of lading.

There are both a long-form and a short-form bill of lading, as has been developed in domestic transportation. The short-form bill of lading is now in general use; many of these merely refer on the reverse side of the bill of lading to the terms and conditions, which are not reproduced.

If, at the time a dock receipt is issued, a steamship agent makes a notation on the dock receipt regarding insufficiency of packing, a notation such as this is transferred to the bill of lading. An ocean bill of lading which contains such notations is known as a "foul" bill of lading, and some banks will not receive it as an acceptable shipping document against a letter of credit. A dock receipt without the notation results in the issuance of a clean bill of lading. Some exporters will issue guarantees to steamship companies in order that the notations on the dock receipt are not transferred to the bill of lading; therefore, they can receive a clean bill of lading.

Steamship companies issue on-board and received-for-shipment bills of lading. The former are isssued only after the merchandise has been loaded on the vessel, and it is a widely used bill of lading. The received-for-shipment bill of lading, which is extensively used in United States export trade, is one in which the steamship agent issues a bill of lading acknowledging receipt of the goods and names the vessel on which the goods are to be shipped; but it does not state that the goods have been loaded. In effect, the commodities are delivered several days prior to sailing; and the loading is frequently done some time after delivery, so that a received-for-shipment bill of lading is issued before the goods are placed physically aboard the vessel. Generally, the on-board bills of lading are required in those transactions involving payment by letter of credit.

The majority of ocean bills of lading are prepaid bills of lading. However, some shipments are covered by a collect ocean bill of lading, provided the steamship line is willing to accept the goods under this arrangement.

Steamship companies have established minimum bill-of-lading fees. These establish a minimum charge, ranging from $5.00 to $15.00, for small-quantity shipments.

Special requirements are noted on the face of the bill of lading, such as "Below Deck Storage" and similar notations.

The REA Express provides for single, through charges and a single, negotiable, through export bill of lading on surface shipping to foreign countries. The service is available on traffic consigned to or shipped from countries where REA Express has foreign agents. The usual ocean bill of lading is then unnecessary; and banks will accept the express company's through export bill of lading in lieu of a letter of credit, when that is required.

At the time the cargo is loaded by the ocean carrier, a *manifest* is prepared, containing the shipper's name, consignee, number of packages, marks, weight, and measurement. There are so-called "charges manifests" which, in addition to the foregoing, contain the freight rate, other charges, and total charges.

The *commercial invoice* is a statement of the transaction between the seller and his customer. The pro forma commercial invoice and the final commercial invoice are usually prepared by the manufacturing plant or the sales department. Final invoices differ from pro forma invoices, in that they contain draft and invoice numbers. These invoices are of importance to the traffic department, inasmuch as the value of the shipment is reflected therein; and the traffic department will determine the amount of insurance necessary to cover the shipment. Some foreign countries require commercial invoices for goods which may be subject to custom duties based on value.

The *packing list*, which is also prepared by the plant or sales department, is forwarded to traffic to accompany the shipping order.

The *draft* is a means by which the exporter obtains payment from the importer. There are different types of drafts. The most widely used are documentary sight drafts, which are payable at destination and to which all original documents must be attached. The other type in widespread use is the draft drawn under a letter of credit. Drafts on letters of credit are payable when presented to a named United States bank. Commercial documentary credits may be either revocable or irrevocable. The procedure for completing the draft varies. Sometimes, it is entirely completed by the sales department. In other instances, the date and amount of draft are left blank, to be completed by the traffic department when all shipping expenses have been tabulated.

Ordinarily, the exporter arranges for insuring the export shipment from his plant to the warehouse of the consignee. Some foreign buyers carry blanket insurance policies and will insure their cargoes upon being notified by cable of the departure of the shipment. The traffic department usually secures *insurance certificates* or policies. The certificate of insurance is a document which certifies that the merchandise named in the certificate is insured under a marine insurance policy which contains the complete terms and conditions of the insurance contract. The certificate describes the quantity and nature of the goods shipped, their identifying numbers, value, identification of the vessel carrying the goods, and the terms of the insurance provided for in the insurance policy. Certificates of insurance in lieu of marine insurance policies are widely used.

Consular invoices are required by many foreign governments for shipments imported from other countries. Such an invoice is generally necessary for the clearance of merchandise through customs at the country of destination. It contains a description of the merchandise, its quantity, and its value, as well as other relevant information; and it is written in the language of the country to which the goods are destined. It must be presented and sworn to by the shipper or his representative at the proper foreign consulate in the American port of shipment.

In some cases, consular requirements include the certification of commercial invoices and bills of lading in addition to the consular invoice. Consular invoice blanks may be purchased in advance, in which case the traffic division of the export department maintains an inventory record of the dispersion of these forms.

The requirements of foreign governments regarding consular invoices vary widely. Most Latin-American countries require such invoices. The

Exporters' Encyclopedia is a good source of information concerning this matter.

The *certificate of origin* is required by some countries in lieu of or to supplement the consular invoice. For example, Brazil requires both a certificate of origin and a consular invoice. In some countries, the United States enjoys favorable custom rates due to treaty arrangements, and certificates of origin are necessary in order to benefit by the favorable treaty rates. This form is merely a certification by a disinterested agency that the goods shipped are a product of the United States.

Manufacturers often import raw materials which are dutiable and on which the duty is paid at the time they are brought into the United States. Later, the manufacturer exports finished goods which contain the imported raw materials on which duties have been paid. The manufacturer can obtain a refund on the duty paid on the raw materials under such circumstances, and this is referred to as an *intent for drawback*. This is filed with the Customhouse, Drawback Division, which gives it a number and retains four copies.

In handling foreign shipments, it is necessary that prescribed procedures and positive responsibility be established for the documents which are necessary. In the assignment of such procedures, it often will be found that one department or division is responsible for working up more documents than other departments. The majority of export documents, in practically all instances, can be prepared by the traffic department, but the significance of complete documents makes it mandatory that the fullest co-operation exists between the traffic department and other departments concerned with export shipments. The following assignment of responsibilities is an example of the manner in which export documents can be prepared:

Sales Department	*Traffic Department*
Packing list	Export declaration
Commercial invoice	Dock receipt
Shipping instructions	Bill of lading
	Certificate of origin
	Insurance certificate
	Payment of freight
	Distribution of documents
	Completion of commercial and consular invoices

One of the very important factors in foreign trade is to have all the necessary documents on hand at destination on or before the arrival of the shipment. The documents may go on the same ship which carries the cargo, on a faster ship, or by air mail. It has become very common to use a dual method to insure that the necessary documents are at the destination when needed by sending the originals by air mail and copies by regular steamer mail.

Indirect Exporting

Some relatively small producers may feel that there is no justification for an export organization as a part of the company. Even larger firms sometimes find it more feasible to rely on middlemen to handle their export activities. Under such circumstances, the traffic manager may not be completely relieved of traffic responsibilities regarding these shipments. Whatever responsibilities there are in connection with this work, such as deciding the type of indirect method best suited to the company's needs, the traffic manager should be prepared to assume them.

Types of Indirect Exporting

American exporters who, for one reason or another, may desire to use external organizations to handle their foreign trade for them can secure a resident foreign outlet, such as a sales agent or a distributor; or they may choose one of a number of different types of American export middlemen. The latter include:

1. Export merchant.
2. Combination export manager.
3. Export agent.
4. Export commission house.
5. Export trade associations.
6. Large-company facilities.
7. Buyers for export.

The *export merchant*, which is often referred to as an "export house," purchases goods from a manufacturer. Export merchants buy and sell for their own account. Such purchases may be F.O.B. factory. However, the traffic manager will usually find that, even under such terms of sale, the shipment must be packed, crated, and labeled for the export market, with the export merchant supplying the necessary instructions.

A *combination export manager* is one who handles the entire export functions for a number of manufacturers of allied but noncompetitive lines. Among other functions, he arranges all documentary details in filling, financing, and shipping orders. Often, his correspondence is on the letterhead of the firm he represents; and he is, in effect, the firm's export manager. Most of this type of organization will be found in port areas.

An *export agent* is an individual or firm usually handling noncompetitive but related articles for a number of manufacturers on a commission basis. Manufacturers may place their entire line with one export agent, or they may divide different items among several export agents.

The *export commission house* serves as a buying agent for foreign customers. However, it does not buy for its own account but, rather, places orders with manufacturers for the account of their foreign customers. This type of organization renders much the same kind of services for the manufacturer as does the export merchant.

A group of business organizations organized to co-operate in export trade on an industry basis is referred to as an *export trade association,* or Webb-Pomerene corporation. Such associations, which have been formed under the Export Trade or Webb-Pomerene Act, perform the export services for the members of the association, subject to the provisions of the act.

Some of the larger companies which engage in direct exporting may offer to distribute noncompeting products of other manufacturers. Under such arrangements, the *large-company facilities* are used to perform the export functions for other companies which make use of their services.

Foreign government purchasing commissions, United States branches of large foreign import firms, or the purchasing agents of large foreign industries, such as railroads and mines, are termed *buyers for export.* They purchase, in the United States, goods for which they handle the details of exporting.

The indirect methods of exporting which have been described can be grouped into three types:

1. The buyer and seller for his own account.
2. The buyer for the foreign customer.
3. The seller on behalf of the American supplier.

IMPORTING

The methods used in importing may be classified in the same manner, direct and indirect, as they are in exporting.

Direct Importing

The procedure in the importation of goods is the reverse of that in exportation, although the documents are not identical. The terms of sale in importing will have an influence on the arrangements which the traffic department has to make. If purchases are made F.A.S. vessel, the importer will have to provide freight space. However, the majority of imports are purchased on terms providing that the foreign exporters arrange the details involving documents and freight space. Under these circumstances, importers have the task of clearing goods through customs. This movement can be facilitated if the importer understands all aspects of importing which would, thereby, enable him to suggest to his suppliers in foreign countries how to prepare documents and select the routes which will be to his advantage. Importers may or may not handle routing to inland points. Goods may be purchased *ex dock,* in which case the buyer, or his traffic manager, takes delivery of the goods on the dock at the named port of importation within the free time allowed and arranges for its movement to the inland plant.

Customs Entries

There are many different types of customs entries with which the traffic manager has to be familiar in handling import shipments. A number of these are described in the following paragraphs:

1. The *consumption entry* is divided into two classes: the free consumption entry and the dutiable consumption entry. The free consumption entry is applicable to merchandise entered as not being subject to duty, for which a consumption permit is granted. The dutiable consumption entry covers merchandise on which the importer desires to pay the duties and secure the release of the merchandise from customs.

2. A *warehouse entry* is one in which the duties are not required to be paid at the time of entry. A warehouse entry bond must be given by the importer, and the merchandise must be deposited in a bonded warehouse. Each withdrawal from a bonded warehouse requires a particular form of entry, such as *warehouse withdrawal for consumption entry, warehouse withdrawal for exportation for transportation and exportation entry*, and *warehouse withdrawal for transportation entry*.

3. If merchandise arriving under a warehouse withdrawal for transportation entry is to be placed again in a bonded warehouse, a *rewarehouse entry* is made. This entry is the same as the warehouse entry, and the warehouse period is computed from the time of arrival of the goods in the United States.

4. The *combined rewarehouse entry and withdrawal for consumption entry* is used to secure delivery from customs of the merchandise upon arrival at the destination of the transportation entry and requires payment of the duties. The place of unloading is considered a constructive warehouse in this case, and no actual rewarehousing occurs.

5. Merchandise arriving in the United States and destined for a foreign country may be transported in bond through the United States for exportation under the *transportation and exportation entry*.

6. Imported merchandise to be used in the manufacturing of articles, such articles being exported without duty being charged on the imported merchandise, is entered under the *bonded manufacturing warehouse entry*.

7. One of the commonly used methods of merchandise entry is that of *immediate transportation without appraisement entry*. This is the type of entry in which the imported merchandise is not required to be cleared from customs at the port of arrival but, rather, the goods are forwarded in bond and will be appraised and the duty assessed at another point.

8. The type of entry used for merchandise exported from the port of arrival in the United States is an *exportation entry*.

9. At the discretion of the Collector of Customs, merchandise not exceeding $100 in value may be entered on an *informal entry* at places where there are customs officers competent to examine and appraise the articles and assess duties. This also may be used for household effects not imported in pursuance of a purchase or agreement for purchase, and not intended for sale, regardless of value, when arriving from a contiguous foreign territory.

10. The *mail entry* is used for merchandise imported through the mails when the value of the importation does not exceed $100. Formal entry is required when the value is more than $100.

11. The *baggage declaration and entry* is used for clearing through customs the baggage of persons arriving in the United States.

12. *Entry of returned American products* from abroad entitles such products to free entry under proper affidavit.

13. The *drawback entry* is used when there are claims for drawback duties on merchandise exported from the United States with benefit of drawback.

14. The *six-month bond entry* is used for certain classes of merchandise which may be brought into the United States for special purposes under bond for a limited period without payment of duty. Unless exported (or in certain cases, destroyed) within the allotted time, liquidated damages are collected under the temporary importation bond. There may be cash deposits authorized in lieu of the bond.

15. The *permanent exhibition entry* is for importation of works of art and certain other kinds of articles which, under specific conditions, may be brought into the United States without duty for exhibition.

Customs entry must be made within the normal time allowed after arrival, which is two days after the vessel enters at the Customhouse. If the time is not extended and the entry is not made in the time allowed, the merchandise can be transferred from the dock to general-order storage at the owner's risk and expense. Customs entries can be made, even though no documents have been received from the shipper at the time the shipment arrives, by posting bond for later presentation of the consular invoice; and in lieu of the missing bill of lading, a carrier's certification can be secured from the steamship company. The ocean carrier issuing such a carrier's certificate would require a guarantee from the shipper, which would hold it harmless from damages, through another party presenting the original documents in claiming the shipment.

Liquidation of the entry is the closing of the file by customs officials on a particular entry. An entry is considered to be liquidated if customs has determined that all required documents have been submitted and are in proper order; that weights, values, classification of merchandise, and the like are in proper order; and that correct duty has been paid. If an importer is not satisfied with the liquidation of an entry, he may file a protest with the Customs Bureau, which will make a review. If this is not satisfactory, it can be carried to the Customs Court for review and decision. Where there is doubt in the importer's mind as to the correct dutiable value of his shipment, he can submit to the customs appraiser, prior to filing a customs entry, all information available concerning the commodity. If it is later found that the entered value is not the correct dutiable value, no penalty for undervaluation will be assessed, for the importer will have been considered to have acted in good faith in seeking an appraisal.

Indirect Importing

Many manufacturers and retailers depend upon middlemen in importing goods. These middlemen include (1) the import merchant, (2) the indent house, (3) the import commission house, (4) the resident agent, (5) the wholesaler or jobber, and (6) the broker or factor.

The *import merchant* buys goods in foreign countries and imports them for his own account. He then sells to buyers in this country at his own established price. He assumes the risks in getting the goods from origin to the United States, and he may even provide storage facilities. There are two general types of import merchants: (1) the import merchant who imports goods of all types from all over the world and (2) the import merchant who specializes in certain commodities or groups of commodities. The trend among import merchants is toward specialization. This specialization is often carried to the point where an importer will handle only a certain grade or type of commodity, such as one coffee importer handling only Brazilian beans, while another may handle only Colombian beans.

Indent houses are importers which buy only on orders received from domestic firms. The term "indent" means an order or specification which is sent abroad for price quotations. Indent houses ordinarily quote cost, insurance, and freight prices; and they derive their profit from their specialized buying skill, their ability to obtain lower transportation costs, and their experience in handling exchange at a profit.

Import commission houses sell goods which have been shipped on consignment and receive their commission from the foreign producer. Sometimes, the import commission house buys small quantities of goods for a commission which is paid by the purchaser. An import commission house may also conduct one phase of its business as an import merchant.

Some foreign manufacturers have *resident agents* in the United States who sell for the account of their principals on a commission basis. The resident agents are usually assigned to a specific territory and, very often, represent a number of foreign manufacturers who offer related but noncompetitive products. The resident agent may receive goods in his principal's name and store them in anticipation of their sale and delivery. He usually handles the customs and shipping details to the United States.

Some domestic *wholesalers* or *jobbers* will handle a limited number of imports. They usually import nonperishable items not subject to style changes or wide price fluctuations. Such wholesalers are referred to as "importing wholesalers" or "jobbers"; and they usually will buy through import merchants, brokers, and resident agents. In a few cases, they may have their own importing department.

The import *broker* or *factor* brings together the buyer and seller, and negotiates the contract of sale. The broker or factor buys goods for the account of a client but never takes title to the goods. After the sale is completed, the domestic buyer imports the commodities purchased in his own name and makes payment directly to the foreign seller. The import broker or factor receives his fee from the party which arranged for his services. He does not service shipments or assist in the movement of goods.

Foreign Channels of Supply

An American firm which imports goods can also use firms located abroad to purchase foreign goods for its importation. These include exclusive buying agents, foreign manufacturers' agents, foreign export merchants, foreign brokers or factors, foreign commissionaires, and American traveling buyers.

Customhouse Brokers

It has become very common to make use of a customhouse broker who will handle the routine work involved in making customs entries. Such brokers are licensed to operate in compliance with the laws of customs procedure. The customhouse broker is usually given power of attorney by the importer, which gives him authority to sign the necessary forms for customs clearance of the goods, including the bill of lading. The service of the customhouse broker is performed for a nominal fee and will vary according to the type of service performed and the amount of work involved.

Forwarding from Port

Order bills of lading are widely used in importing goods, so that the bill of lading, properly endorsed, should be filed with the steamship agent immediately upon the arrival and discharge of the cargo. Since there is no extension of credit on import shipments, if the freight is collect—which is customary—it must be paid at that time. If the customs entry has been made and the bill of lading properly filed, the importer should arrange for inspection of the goods on the pier. This will facilitate the handling of claims, particularly with steamship companies, since they do not acknowledge any liability after the goods are out of their hands. Insurance companies, however, will consider claims filed after the goods have been removed from the pier.

The routing of imported goods to inland points is handled in a manner similar to the routing of shipments for export. Bills of lading are prepared, with the import certification certificate applied to each bill of lading. This will include the steamer name, where the shipment originated, and declaration that it moved direct from the steamer or pier to the inland carrier. In the case of small shipments, the bills of lading may be sent to the customhouse broker, who will see that the inland carrier will get them, along with his delivery order, when the customs release has been secured. On carloads or truckloads, the bills of lading and delivery order may be sent directly to the inland carrier.

Because of the existence of port differentials, explained earlier, the inland movement from the port on imported goods is less from certain ports than from others, which factor must be considered at the time that the over-all cost of the imported goods is computed.

OCEAN FREIGHT RATES

Space Weight Rates

Ocean freight rates are quoted on a weight or measurement basis, ship's option. Under this arrangement, the rate named will be applied either per ton of 2,240 pounds (in some trades, 2,000 pounds) or per measurement ton of 40 cubic feet, whichever will result in the higher revenue for the vessel. The manner in which rates quoted on this basis apply is as follows: [3] Assuming that the general cargo rate is $20.00 per ton, weight or measurement, ship's option, if the goods to be shipped weighed exactly 56 pounds per cubic foot, they would stow in 40 cubic feet (a measurement ton) to the ton of 2,240 pounds. Under these circumstances, the question of whether the rate to be applied should be on a weight or a measurement basis does not exist, since the rate is the same whichever application is made.

On the other hand, if a shipment of goods weighed 50 pounds per cubic foot, a different situation would prevail. At 50 pounds per cubic foot, it would occupy 44.8 cubic feet per ton (2,240 divided by 50, the weight of one cubic foot), [4] and one long ton of such goods would occupy more than a measurement ton of space, which is 40 cubic feet. The steamship company, quoting on the basis of $20.00 per 40 cubic feet, will charge $22.40 for 44.8 cubic feet. If the goods had been accepted on a weight basis, the steamship company would have received only $20.00 for the one long ton.

In ocean shipping, traffic managers need to examine the effects of the ship's option on each shipment. A United States firm which planned the construction of a 30-inch oil pipe line in a foreign country asked its traffic department to analyze the various traffic aspects of the operation. The traffic department studied several alternatives. Its recommendation was that half the pipe procured should be 30-inch and the remainder 31-inch, which could be accomplished at very little additional cost and without affecting pipe-line operation. The 30-inch pipe was then inserted into the 31-inch pipe for shipment. Bags of cement needed in connection with the construction were placed inside the 30-inch pipe. The result was a $7-million saving in shipping costs.

Another method of quoting is to name two rates, such as 45/80, which means that the cargo will pay 45 cents per cubic foot, or 80 cents per 100 pounds, whichever provides the greater revenue. Rates computed on this basis are designed to provide approximately equal revenue from goods which stow at 40 cubic feet per ton. As an illustration, 40 cubic feet of cargo or a measurement ton would pay 40 times 45 cents, or $18.00. On the basis of weight, the cargo would pay 22.4 times 80 cents, or $17.92.

Units other than these are used, such as rates for lumber, which may be quoted per 1,000 feet, board measure, or 1,000 superficial feet; poles and piling, per linear foot; and lubricating oil, per barrel. Articles of especially high value are sometimes charged ad valorem rates. The weight or measurement ship's option may be the basic method used by a steam-

---

[3] Board of State Harbor Commissioners of California, *Ocean Shipping Handbook,* 1950.

[4] *Ibid.*

ship company; and in the case of valuables, the additional option of charging on the ad valorem basis is established.

Conference Rates

Ocean freight rates have not made use of freight classifications to the extent that is true in domestic transportation, although there are classifications of freight in this field. Specific rates and ratings are published by each steamship conference. This often results in the same commodity having different rates and ratings in different trades. Furthermore, there can be a substantial difference between the outbound rate and the inbound rate on the same commodity. For example, in 1963, from the Pacific Coast to Japan the outbound rate on rubber tires and innertubes was $110.75 while the inbound rate was $24.75, or less than one-fourth as much. On 26 selected commodities with substantial export potential, the outbound rates were 70 per cent higher than the corresponding inbound rates. Outbound rates on the same commodities from U.S. Atlantic ports to Germany were about 21 per cent higher than inbound rates.

Ocean common carriers are required to file rate increases 30 days before their effective date, except on bulk cargoes, and they must distribute freight tariffs to shippers.

Steamship conferences constitute a method of collective rate making which has existed for many years, a number of them having been formed over a hundred years ago. Conference members are required to charge the same freight rates and other charges, and the conference issues the freight contract to be used by its members in their operations. The conference further agrees upon contract and noncontract rates.

The steamship conference contract with shippers will differ from conference to conference, but one of the provisions that has tended to become uniform is that the shipper will agree to ship all of his goods from a given group of ports, such as North Atlantic, to another group of ports, such as Baltic ports. The shipper is obligated to use only conference vessels, and conference carriers offer a concession in rates to encourage a regular flow of traffic. The steamship conference, under these circumstances, will charge such a shipper rates lower than those for the shipper who does not enter into such an exclusive patronage agreement. In the past, this spread has been as much as 20 per cent.

In 1948, a number of conference members advised shippers that the carriers proposed to reinstate the exclusive patronage contract and the dual-rate system, which had been in use prior to World War II. Nonconference carriers challenged this rate system, and there have been regulatory and court actions concerning the differential between the rates for contractors and noncontractors.

A nonconference shipping company carried its attack of the dual-rate system, as practiced by a particular conference, through the lower courts, where its charges were upheld. The case was then ruled upon by the

Supreme Court, which held that, in the particular circumstances which existed in the case of the complaining nonconference carrier, the dual-rate system was employed as a "predatory device" and instituted for the purpose of curtailing the competition provided by this carrier. As such, it was illegal under Section 14(3) of the Shipping Act of 1916. The Supreme Court did not rule upon any other phase of the dual-rate system and stated that it did not need to consider the various treatments of dual rates by the Federal Maritime Board under different circumstances.[5]

As a result of the Supreme Court decision, Public Law 85–626 was enacted in August, 1958, permitting the dual-rate system to be used until mid-1960. Public Law 87–346, passed in 1961, allowed a continuation of the dual-rate system and established a maximum difference between contract and noncontract ocean steamship rates of 15 per cent.

In numerous cases, the Federal Maritime Commission has expressed its belief in the concept of the dual-rate system. It has disapproved dual rates, however, in instances in which it felt that the rate differential was too wide, or where other factors were unjustly discriminatory. In 1963, there were 113 steamship conferences operating on the foreign trade routes of the United States, of which 63 used the dual-rate system.

It should be emphasized that where the shipper has a contract with a conference, he is under obligation to use only conference ships when the terms of sale require him to provide freight space. If a sale is made F.A.S. vessel, the buyer is under obligation to provide the freight space, in which case any vessel of his choice may be used.

Some indication of the general export cargo in long tons carried by liner services on the North Atlantic route from United States North Atlantic ports to ports in Belgium, Holland, and Germany, excluding

TABLE 18–1

GENERAL CARGO LINER CARRYINGS AND SAILINGS ON
NORTH ATLANTIC ROUTE

Year	1,000 Tons	Conference	Nonconference	Total Sailings	Conference Sailings	Nonconference Sailings
1948	1,485	76%	24%	621	89%	11%
1949	......	66	34	642	84	16
1950	1,812	57	43	613	80	20
1951	2,590	74	26	559	83	17
1952	990*	66†	34†	688‡	79‡	21‡
1953	2,044	64.5	35.5	675	72	28

* January–June, 1952, only.
† Percentage figures based on 9 months' statistics for conference lines and 11 months for nonconference lines.
‡ Estimated for full year, based on statistics mentioned in footnote *.
SOURCE: Docket No. 725, Federal Maritime Board, February 29, 1956.

[5] *Federal Maritime Board v. Isbrandtsen Company, Inc., et el.; Japan-Atlantic and Gulf Freight Conference v. U.S. of America, Federal Maritime Board, et al.; Nos. 73 and 74, May 19, 1958.

German-Baltic ports, and the number of eastbound sailings for the years 1948–52, are shown in Table 18–1. The division of sailings and tonnage between conference members and nonconference members is shown.

Additional Charges

In ocean shipping, there are basic freight charges, to which additional fees and surcharges may be added, such as tolls and port and handling charges. There are heavy-lift charges for weights beyond those considered maximum normal weights. For example, a package weighing over 6,000 pounds may be subject to graduated heavy-lift charges for anything above 6,000 pounds. A long-length rate may be imposed also because the length exceeds a specified maximum. Sometimes, these charges are referred to as "penalty charges."

Some steamship lines accept small packages on a parcel receipt basis to which the minimum bill-of-lading charges are not applicable. These are called "parcel rates."

In checking ocean freight rates, the tariff should be used, if available, and determination should be made whether a specific rate is published on the commodity. If there is no specific rate published, a check should be made to see whether the rate is published for a category in which the commodity could be included. If neither of these steps produces an applicable rate, the rate for the commodity would be under the grouping "General Cargo, N.O.S." (Not Otherwise Specified).

Where there is no tariff available, the conference or the lines which are members of the conference must be consulted to obtain the applicable rate. If there are no specific rates applying, and the shipper has volume movements of commodities, the traffic department should seek an adjustment in rates if the data assembled indicate justification for the initiation of such a proposal. Steamship conferences have their own forms on which formal applications for rate adjustments must be submitted.

At some ports, there is a top wharfage charge, assessed by pier operators for the use of piers. This is in addition to the regular freight charges and is assessed against the shipper. In some instances, this charge is applicable only when the shipment is delivered to the pier by motor carrier, since the piers at some ports are owned by railroads. At certain ports, the charge is asssessed against the water carrier when the inland shipment is by other than rail. A side wharfage charge assessed against all freight discharged to barge or lighter over sides of vessels docked at piers is also charged at some ports.

OCEAN FREIGHT FORWARDERS

The Federal Maritime Commission has defined a freight forwarder as any person engaged in the business of dispatching shipments on behalf of other persons, for a consideration, by ocean-going vessels in commerce from the United States and its territories or possessions to foreign countries, or between the United States and its territories or possessions, or between such territories and possessions; and of handling the formalities incident to such shipments. This definition includes independent freight forwarders, common carriers, manufacturers, exporters, export traders, manufacturers' agents, resident buyers, commission merchants, and other persons when they engage, for and on behalf of any person other than themselves, in return for a consideration, money or otherwise, in the aforementioned activity.

The technical details connected with the handling of a shipment of goods for export have given rise to the use, by many sellers, of foreign freight forwarders. Some companies even go so far as to have all of the traffic aspects of their exporting handled by freight forwarders. A competent and reliable freight forwarder should be prepared to look after numerous phases of shipping problems for the exporter, including all functions connected with transferring, documenting, and dispatching. He should be well informed on ocean freight rates in the ports through which the exporter's merchandise moves and be able to advise on all ocean-shipping matters. His activities keep him in constant touch with the many conditions of entry in foreign countries; thus, he is prepared to execute all necessary foreign consular and other documents.

Ocean freight forwarders perform a number of the following services: examine instructions and documents received from shippers; order cargo to port; prepare export declarations; book cargo space; prepare and process delivery order and dock receipt; prepare instructions to truckman or lighterman, and arrange for or furnish such facilities; prepare and process ocean bill of lading; prepare consular documents, and arrange for their certification, in the language of the country to which the goods are shipped; arrange for or furnish warehouse storage, when necessary; arrange for insurance, when so instructed; clear shipment in accordance with United States government regulations; prepare advice notices of shipments, sending copies to bank, shipper, or consignee, as required; send completed documents to shipper, bank, or consignee, as directed; and advance necessary funds in connection with the foregoing.

They also provide supervision in the co-ordination of services rendered to the shipment from origin to vessel; render special service on unusual shipments or when difficulties in transit arise; and give expert advice to exporters as regards letters of credit, licenses, inspection, and similar matters.

Forwarders may handle a shipment merely through the port of export. On the other hand, by means of their correspondents abroad, they may take care of the shipment to almost any foreign destination.

To a limited extent, the ocean freight forwarder acts as a consolidator and will forward small shipments on one ocean bill of lading, thus avoiding payment of a minimum bill-of-lading. The charges for forwarder service vary, depending upon the range and scope of the services performed.

Some of the services rendered to steamship carriers by freight forwarders include handling and facilitiating the delivery of cargo to steamship piers at the right time; working with carriers to overcome difficulties because of late arrivals and sailings; adjusting bookings when a carrier has overbooked his vessel capacity; preparing and, to some extent, processing the bill of lading; and often, passing information on to ocean carriers as to possible prospects.

Ocean freight forwarders are registered with the Federal Maritime Commission and receive a registration number. Among other requirements, registrants must show their registration numbers on their forwarding documents; itemize their charges to shippers, except under specified circumstances; and furnish to the Commission special contracts, specimen copies of invoices covering charges to shippers and services rendered, and such other information as the Commission may prescribe. About 1,000 ocean freight forwarders have registered with the Commission.

FOREIGN-TRADE ZONES

Of particular importance in foreign trade is the existence of foreign-trade zones in New York, New Orleans, San Francisco, Seattle, and Toledo. A subzone consisting of cold storage has also been established at New Orleans. A foreign-trade zone is a segregated, fenced-off, policed area within a port where foreign merchandise may be landed, stored, re-packed, sorted, mixed, or otherwise manipulated, manufactured, and exhibited, with a minimum of customs control and without customs bond. Foreign merchandise held in a zone may be re-exported without customs formalities; but if such merchandise is brought into customs territory from the zone, it is subject to all customs laws and regulations. (See Figure 18–4.)

The provisions for the establishment of foreign-trade zones were created by the passage of the Celler Act in 1934, which offered flexibility in import customs regulations. The act permits the Foreign Trade Zones Board in the Department of Commerce to grant charters to corporations to operate such zones. Zones must be operated as a public utility.

Some importers are inclined to regard foreign-trade zones simply as enlarged bonded warehouses. Technically, this is incorrect, as merchandise in a foreign-trade zone holds an entirely different status from merchandise in a bonded warehouse. As no customs entry is made on merchandise held in a zone, it is not subject to the various restrictions imposed on imported merchandise by customs regulations. As long as foreign merchandise remains in a foreign-trade zone, it retains the same status as if it were still in a foreign country.

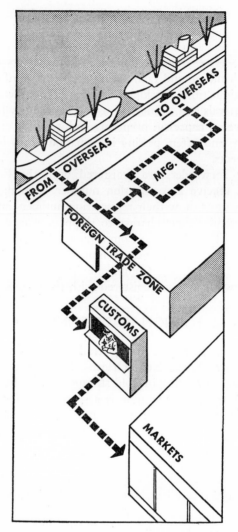

FIG. 18–4. Method of operation of Foreign Trade Zone.

Examples of some advantages to be derived from foreign-trade zones are:

1. The foreign exporter bears none of the expense for bonds or customs inspection when imports are stored or manipulated in foreign-trade zones—this applies whether the merchandise is dutiable or nondutiable.

2. Imports may remain in storage with no time limit until entry into customs territory is desired.

3. Ships, lighters, railroads, motor trucks, or parcel post make direct delivery to or from zones, insuring speedy, efficient, and frequent carrier service.

4. Foreign exporters or their agents, by utilizing foreign-trade zones for storing and holding merchandise, are in a position to obtain dollar bank loans

in the United States on negotiable warehouse receipts, thereby releasing their capital for other transactions.

5. Commodities under "quota" restrictions may be received in any quantity in excess of quota and held without customs liquidation awaiting the next quota period.

6. Alcoholic beverages forwarded to the zone in bulk by foreign exporters may be bottled, labeled, reduced in proof, and packaged prior to customs entry without being subject to state or federal licensing agencies. When such merchandise is later brought into United States customs territory it must, of course, comply with all requirements affecting imports.

7. The convenience available to the purchaser to examine foreign merchandise in the United States foreign-trade zone to ascertain its condition may save costly transportation expense to interior points on damaged or defective merchandise which must be later returned. Examination prior to customs entry precludes the possibility of payment of duties on damaged or unsalable merchandise.

8. Goods improperly marked may be remarked without penalty.

9. Private firms may erect their own structures within the zone to perform manipulating operations adapted to their needs.

MARINE INSURANCE

Marine insurance is secured to cover the risk of losses while the goods are being transported by water. It is used primarily for protection of the goods while the vessel is at sea; but the insurance has been substantially extended and can be applied, if desired, to more than just the water portion of the movement. Some marine insurance companies have provided insurance coverage also for international shipments by air.

Three primary interests insurable are (1) hulls or vessels, (2) cargoes, and (3) freight.

Hull policies are written on vessels and cover losses from the perils of the seas and fire. The perils of the seas covered are unexpected accidents or casualties of the sea, such as heavy weather, stranding, sinking, collision, and striking the ground, ice, and rocks, or other obstructions. The coverage of fire is the same as fire coverage provided in a fire contract, except that numerous exclusions included in the standard fire policy are absent in the marine contract.

The cargo policies are written to cover cargoes of vessels against similar perils but include coverage against loss of or damage to the insured cargo. Policies can cover a number of risks other than the perils of the seas, but they do not cover every loss or damage which might be sustained during the course of a voyage. Only those losses fortuitous and beyond the control of the assured may be covered, and not damages inevitable or usual because of the nature of the goods, the packages, or the voyage in question.

Freight policies are written on freight transportation charges; this use of the term "freight" is as used by the British. In the case of collect freight, the freight is not earned or due until there has been actual delivery of the goods at destination. The carrier, therefore, may effect insurance on collect freight, whereas prepaid freight is usually in the cargo insurance.

The primary activity of the traffic manager is with cargo insurance. However, in those instances where his company owns and operates vessels or tugs or barges, the traffic manager must become equally familiar with the details of hull insurance. The various types of insurance can be secured from insurance underwriters or through the intermediary of an insurance broker. The matter of whether insurance should be placed with an underwriter or through an insurance broker is a matter of choice which a company can make. Smaller organizations tend to make use of insurance brokers, although larger companies use them as well, so there is no established criterion to govern this selection. Hereafter, reference will be made in this discussion to the underwriter only.

Most marine insurance policies are issued as open policies. Under such policies, the importer or exporter is insured against loss or damage on all of his shipments within specific geographical areas. All the shipments are insured under this type of policy, even though the exporter or importer who placed the open policy does not know that the goods have been shipped. The assured, in an open policy, is to report all shipments to the insurance company immediately upon securing knowledge of such shipments, and the contract is of indefinite duration.

Rights and Liabilities of Ocean Carriers

The rights and liabilities of ocean carriers are defined in the Harter Act and the Carriage of Goods by Sea Act. The owners of ships must equip, man, and provision the ships and make them seaworthy. They are liable for loss and damage due to their negligence and failure to load or stow properly or care for the goods. They are not liable for losses due to perils of the sea, acts of God or the public enemy, inherent defects of the cargo, or negligence on the part of the shipper or owner of the merchandise. Although ocean carriers have certain liabilities, insurance underwriters have extended policies, in some instances, waiving their rights in connection with some of the legal liabilities of the carriers and insuring the exporter or importer against loss or damage which is the result of conditions for which the carrier is liable under the statutes.

The owner of the cargo makes contracts with the carrier and the underwriter. There may not be a contract between the carrier and the underwriter regarding the cargo; but because of the agreements which the carrier and the underwriter have with the owner of the cargo, they may have a mutuality of interest or a conflict of interest in the event of loss. In this connection, subrogation clauses are frequently included by underwriters. It is customary to use three of these clauses. The first clause voids the policy in the event of assignment of it to any party without the specific consent of the underwriters. The second prohibits the assured from giving any third party a release from a claim against that party which, if it was paid by the third party, would relieve the underwriters from the necessity of paying. The third provision is an agreement by the underwriters to loan the assured the amount of any claim until it has been finally determined whether the carrier or some other party is liable.

Types of Losses

There are several different types of losses. These are described as follows:

Total Loss.   A total loss may be divided into actual and constructive losses. The actual total loss is a case in which there is complete destruction of a shipper's cargo, such as might occur with the sinking of a vessel. A constructive total loss might be the result of an accident which caused an individual shipper's cargo to be badly damaged to the extent that the cost of salvage would exceed the possible proceeds from a sale. The shipper and the underwriters, therefore, will agree to abandon the cargo. In both of these cases of total loss, the underwriters pay the full insured valuation.

Particular-Average Loss.   Another type of loss is that known as "particular-average loss." This term means a particular damage to or loss of a shipment. The term "average" is widely used in marine insurance and means loss or damage which may be caused by marine perils. In a particular-average loss, the loss is borne entirely by the owner of the goods, and the owners of the remaining cargo do not contribute. There are many variations in the application of particular-average insurance.

Free of Particular Average.   Because of the susceptibility of some commodities to damage, marine insurance companies may insure only against total loss or against partial loss due only to certain circumstances. Where this situation exists and the underwriters do not give a broad coverage for partial loss or damage, the insurance is termed "free of particular average." The F.P.A. clauses used by American and English underwriters are quite different. Under F.P.A. American conditions, the underwriters do not require that the damage be caused by the named accidents but merely that such accidents must occur before their liability occurs. Generally, the English clause is more favorable to the shippers.

If cargo is insured F.P.A. under 3 per cent, and the whole or any part of the shipment is damaged by one of the insured perils to the extent of 3 per cent or more of the sound value of the entire shipment, the underwriter agrees to pay the same percentage of the amount for which the damaged property is depreciated by the damage. However, if the loss is less than 3 per cent of the value of the entire shipment, the insurance company is not liable under this clause.

General-Average Loss.   Another type of loss is termed "general-average loss." General average is a sacrifice in the interests of all concerned in an adventure to which the interests benefited must contribute according to the saved values. General-average loss can be a total loss or a particular-average loss. Such a loss occurs because in the face of danger from marine risks, it may be necessary to jettison some cargo, which is done voluntarily, in order to safeguard the vessel and balance the cargo. The loss of this particular cargo represents a sacrifice of a specific interest in order to save the entire venture. Thus, a levy will be made on those components of the venture saved so as to reimburse that portion of the venture sacrificed. The most common causes of general average are fire, sinking, or stranding.

A general-average adjuster is used by the vessel owner in order to make the adjustment. To insure the collection of the ratable share from the various interests, security, which is termed "general-average deposit," is required before any goods are released by the vessel owner. When the individual share is determined, it is deducted from this deposit; and the excess, if any, is returned to the principal involved. These charges are covered by marine policies; and upon request, the underwriter will make the general-average deposit.

Kinds of Insurance Coverage

The value at which a shipment should be insured for export may be determined by taking the invoice value plus freight, consular, and other charges and insurance premiums (the C.I.F. value), and adding 10 per cent or any other percentage to cover contingent expenses that might arise. These expenses occur due to general average, survey fees, bank charges, or duties assessed by the country to which the shipment is exported. The exact percentage is decided upon by the traffic department, or on instructions from the customer or terms of the letter of credit.

The following computation shows the value to be insured, using the above formula. This method can be used on shipments sold F.A.S.; and when the shipment is on C.I.F. basis, it is only necessary to add the desired percentage to the C.I.F. value.

A = C. & F. value plus desired insurance advance
B = the rate of premiums plus the same desired insurance advance

Assume A = $1,000 plus desired advance of 10 per cent, or $1,100
Assume B = All-inclusive insurance rate—i.e., war risk, marine, etc.— of 20 per cent plus desired increase of 10 per cent, or 22 per cent (which includes insurance cost)

Then $\dfrac{\$1,100 \times 100}{100 - 22} = \$1,410,25$, value at which shipment should be insured

One of the important matters in securing marine insurance is the determination of what portion of the movement is to be covered by the marine insurance.

Warehouse to Warehouse. If a warehouse-to-warehouse clause is added to the policy, the shipment is covered while in transit between the initial point of shipment to the final point of destination. However, this clause does not extend protection of goods during unusual delays, unless special permission is received from the underwriter. This usually involves payment of an additional premium.

Under Deck. It is assumed that all goods are shipped under deck. If the shipper has deck cargo, he is obligated to notify the underwriters, and the policy can be so amended. An additional premium is paid for this protection.

Deviation. If a vessel deviates from a direct voyage between two ports, the underwriter will provide coverage of the goods for an additional premium.

War Risk and Other Insurance. There are many additional risks that can be insured against, such as theft and pilferage, leakage and breakage, sweat damage, and even an all-risk insurance, as well as others. These are usually added to the basic policy. One of the added risks which has been used in recent years is war risk insurance. This is written as a separate policy for which an extra charge is made. The demand for war risk insurance continues because since the end of World War II, more than four hundred vessels have been lost or damaged by striking derelict mines.

Surveying of Losses

Underwriters maintain surveying organizations which make reports to the insurance company on the value of losses. On cargo, these losses are determined by surveyors who compute the percentage of loss by comparing the arrived damaged value of cargo with the arrived sound value. The percentage is applied to the amount of insurance to determine the amount to be collected from insurance.

If the insurance carried on a valued form equals the arrived sound value of the goods, the cargo owner can recover in full; while if the amount of insurance is less than the arrived sound value, he will become a coinsurer for the deficiency.

The assured, in filing a claim, must show that the loss is one within the scope of the contract and should include the following documents:

1. The master's protest,[6] which states that certain perils were encountered during the voyage.
2. Invoice.
3. Bill of lading.
4. Certificate of insurance.
5. The surveyor's report of damage.

Many aspects of marine insurance are beyond the scope of this book, such as clauses which will limit, modify, or expand, as is desired, marine insurance coverage. The subject of marine insurance is a study in itself.

INTERNATIONAL AIR SHIPMENTS

A growing volume of shipments move by air in foreign trade, but it is a fraction of that which moves by ocean carrier. The traffic manager can use scheduled air carriers, nonscheduled air carriers, international air freight forwarders, international air parcel post, or a shipping agent, such as American Express.

The domestic scheduled air carriers offer world-wide service and the benefit of joint rates to many countries. The shipper can prepare a "Shipper's Letter of Instruction" or the "International Air Waybill." One air waybill covers the shipment from origin to destination. Customs procedure and other nontransportation documents are usually the same whether the shipment to a foreign country is by surface or air carrier.

The tariffs of scheduled international air carriers are individual publications, and there is some variation in the provisions. The transportation charges consist of a weight or measurement charge and sometimes a valu-

---

[6] A protest is a formal document which contains an attested declaration made by the master of a vessel upon his arrival in port after a disaster, showing that any damage or loss sustained was not the fault of the vessel or his officers or crew.

ation charge or value surcharge. The weight or measurement charge is assessed at a certain rate per pound or fraction of the gross weight of the shipment, or at a measurement rate per unit of 250 cubic inches or fraction as the equivalent of one pound, whichever is greater. The greatest rectangular dimensions of each package, or group of packages tied together, are used in determining the cubic measurement of a shipment. Two or more packages forwarded by one shipper to one consignee under one air waybill are usually charged for at either the total gross weight of all packages or at the total weight of all packages determined by measurement, whichever is greater.

The valuation charge and value surcharge are charges assessed on the Shipper's Declared Value for Carriage, the amount of which, as shown in the air waybill, is the limit of the carrier's liability in the event of loss or damage to the shipment, and the chargeable weight or volume. As a general rule, shippers declare, as a value for carriage, the customs or actual value plus all shipping charges.

A value for carriage must be declared on each shipment. Shipments on which the declared value is in excess of $7.48 per pound are subject to valuation charges. Valuation charges start as low as 15 cents per $100.00. Shipments on which the actual value is $88.91 per pound or more are subject to value surcharge rates. However, certain commodities, including gold bullion and platinum, take specific commodity rates on which no extra valuation charges are assessed.

The inherent advantage of speed in international air transportation is a factor of importance in the shipment of certain commodities. The traffic manager, in performing his traffic responsibilities in foreign trade, will utilize those transportation services which meet the requirements of particular shipments.

CASE

The Rainbow Machinery Company of Beloit, Wisconsin, has been engaged for many years in the production of paper-making machinery. The company was located in this small Wisconsin community because the local banker was receptive to financing the business enterprise and because extensive forest reserves in the area had resulted in the formation of a number of paper manufacturing companies. For a number of years, Rainbow confined its production to a relatively small distribution area. Its machinery, however, was well made and, as the company grew, it began receiving inquiries from paper manufacturers around the country. Its product was competitive, and Rainbow found it could operate successfully in any of the market areas in the United States. Occasionally in the late 1940's and early 1950's, it received orders for its equipment from abroad, and in 1959 the company decided to develop an export market. Since the Rainbow Company had filled a number of orders from European countries, it was decided to seek to capitalize on the good will developed by the successful operation of the equipment over a number of years.

Rainbow was confronted with many problems. It needed to determine the proper markets to penetrate, the intermediaries to use to market its product, and the proper organizational structure in its own company to handle this undertaking. After considerable study, an export manager was appointed and given complete authority over all phases of the export activities of the company.

In the past, the overseas shipments had been of such a sporadic nature that very little attention had been given to any of the management aspects of their movement. With the prospect of the active development of specific markets, it was important to have analyses made of marketing and transportation costs in order to insure that Rainbow would be competitive. As a result of a market analysis, Stockholm, Sweden was selected as an initial market because of the large number of paper interests located in the area. A study of comparative rates from Beloit to Stockholm was also undertaken as a part of a distribution analysis.

Rainbow had a rail siding on the Chicago, Northwestern Railway and used principally rail transportation in its domestic shipments, particularly because of the size of the machinery. In its earlier foreign sales, shipment of machinery had been made by rail to the east coast and then by ship to Europe. In 1959, however, the improved St. Lawrence Seaway was opened with its deeper draft permitting larger ships to use the Seaway. The opening of the Seaway intensified the activities of steamship companies serving the port of Milwaukee, and the nearness of Beloit to Milwaukee made this an alternative to be considered in transportation to foreign markets.

Barge transportation was also available from Dubuque, Iowa, a short distance from Beloit, down the Mississippi River to New Orleans, and then by ship to Europe.

A representative shipment to Stockholm of 416,475 pounds of paper-making machinery was used in an analysis of comparative transportation costs. The shipment was 185.9263 gross tons, 13,330 cubic feet, and 333.25 measurement tons. The freight charge from Beloit to Milwaukee on the shipment at 36 cents a hundred pounds totaled $1,499.31. The ocean freight charges from Milwaukee to Stockholm via the Seaway, based on 13,330 cubic feet at $1.20 per cubic foot, amounted to $15,996. Seaway toll charges were based on $.90 per net ton for 208.24 net tons, or $187.42. The total freight charges, Beloit to Stockholm via the Seaway for the shipment, were $17,632.

Analysis of the freight charges applicable from Beloit to New York via rail was $1.67 per 100 pounds, amounting to $6,955.13. The ocean freight charges on 13,330 cubic feet was $1.20 per cubic foot and amounted to $15,996.00. The total freight charges via New York were $22,951.13. The steamship heavy-lift charges were the same at each port, marine insurance rates were comparable, and transit times were comparable.

1. Since there is a substantial saving, would you recommend that the delivered price of the machinery should be reduced by the amount of the saving?

2. Or should the transportation savings be used to cover some of the expenses of establishing the foreign market?

3. In what manner might the route via New York be made more competitive? Outline your plan.

4. Should other alternatives have been explored?

DISCUSSION QUESTIONS AND PROBLEMS

1. Describe the two methods that may be used by a company in its exporting.

2. What fundamental conditions of sale are covered when a quotation is made in foreign trade?

3. Select and explain three of the terms likely to be used in expressing terms of sale in foreign trade.

4. What are the differences between built-in and separate direct exporting departments?

5. List some of the responsibilities of the traffic manager in a direct exporting department.

6. Explain the significance of port differentials in line-haul rail rates as a factor in attracting cargo to a port.

7. There are a number of packaging rules which, if followed, will insure a better export package. What are these rules? What factors in handling should be considered in packaging for foreign shipment?

8. Preventable losses account for the greater portion of loss and damage in export shipments. Describe some of the causes of preventable losses.

9. Give a brief description of the following documents: shipper's export declaration, export license, import permit, dock receipt, commercial invoice, and consular invoice.

10. What are the different types of ocean bills of lading? Is the preparation of the ocean bill of lading different from that of a domestic bill of lading?

11. Can through bills of lading be issued which will cover the rail movement from a U.S. interior point, thence via steamship to a foreign destination? Why is this practice not universal?

12. Assume that your firm engages in direct exporting, and you have been asked to recommend the procedure and assign the responsibility for the various export documents. Prepare your recommendation, with necessary justifications.

13. Compile a list of those publications which would be helpful in determining the steamship companies rendering service to various foreign ports.

14. Briefly describe the following: export merchant, combination export manager, export agent, export commission house, and export trade associations.

15. Name and briefly describe eight types of customs entries. Would the nature of the goods being imported influence the type of entry?

16. Carefully explain what is meant by liquidation of entry.

17. Briefly describe five of the middlemen which may be used in indirect importing. What is the function of the customhouse broker?

18. In quoting ocean freight rates, the term "weight or measurement basis, ship's option" is used. Explain, by illustrations, just what is meant by this term.

19. What difference, if any, is there between a foreign freight forwarder and a domestic freight forwarder?

20. Briefly explain what foreign-trade zones are and some of the advantages they offer.

21. Why is extensive use made of cargo insurance by shippers and consignees for shipments moving via steamship to foreign ports?

22. What are the different types of cargo insurance coverage? Describe the types of marine losses.

23. Describe the types of international air carrier freight charges. Does the documentation procedure differ for international air shipments as compared to ocean shipments?

Chapter

19

PERSONAL EFFECTS AND
PASSENGER TRANSPORTATION

With the decentralization of industry and its general growth, there have been widespread shifts in company personnel. An increasing number of companies have established a policy of paying the moving expenses occasioned by new plant openings or shifting of personnel. The amount spent by individual companies for moving household goods of employees is from $250,000 to $400,000 annually, and the practice of moving at company expense is growing. The armed services also spend substantial amounts to move their personnel. The Department of Defense spends more for the transportation of household goods than for the transportation of any other commodity group, such as ammunition and explosives. In fiscal 1962, about $100 million was received by motor carriers of household goods from the Department of Defense for moves within the United States alone.

The responsibility for arranging the movement of employees' household effects is often delegated to the traffic manager. A 1962 survey by the magazine, *Distribution Age*, showed that 1,850 traffic managers, or 92 per cent of those answering the questionnaire, were responsible for the movement of household goods for the personnel of their companies.

Careful attention to the manner in which these shipments are handled is warranted. A traffic manager may successfully move large quantities of freight in a most efficient manner and yet find himself judged by the way in which the household goods of company officials and employees are moved. A pleasant attitude toward the traffic department can be fostered within the company through effective management of household goods movement. Such good will is worth any extra effort needed to assume competent handling of this responsibility.

There are several methods available for the movement of household goods. Although the vast majority of household goods is moved by motor transportation, rail carriers, freight forwarders, and air carriers also participate in this traffic. One of the competitive disadvantages in the past of freight forwarder, rail carrier movement of household goods has been the necessity of crating the items, which cost has increased greatly in the last few years. At origin and destination, it is also necessary for local cartage service to pick up and deliver the household goods from and to the dwellings, which is a cost factor in the line-haul rate and means extra handling of the goods. The development of compartmentized freight cars in which pads are used, thus eliminating the necessity of crating, is a recent development which may strengthen the competitive position of freight forwarders and railroads in the movement of household goods, particularly for the longer distances.

The density of household goods is such that the limited carrying capacity of aircraft has been a restricting factor in the development of the movement of household goods by air carriers. With new, larger aircraft, however, greater use is being made of air transportation.

Since motor carriers move the majority of household goods, the discussion will deal with motor carrier service.

The commodity description of household goods, as prescribed by the Interstate Commerce Commission for motor carriers, consists of three parts:

1. Personal effects and property used or to be used in a dwelling when a part of the equipment or supply of such dwelling.
2. Furniture, fixtures, equipment, and the property of stores, offices, museums, institutions, hospitals, or other establishments.
3. Articles, including objects of art, displays, and exhibits, which—because of their unusual nature or value—require specialized handling and equipment usually employed in moving household goods.[1]

It is possible, through the use of motor carriers, to move to a new location with a minimum of handling of household possessions, since they may be loaded into the moving van from one residence and carried to the destination residence. There is no packing required for the majority of household goods. Only such items as dishes, lamp shades, paintings, and other fragile articles require any packing. This is in contrast to some of the other methods of shipping household goods, in which everything, including the furniture, must be crated.

Recently freight forwarders using rail transportation have made use of pads and not required any more packing than has been customary in motor carriage, although this service by freight forwarders is applicable only to relatively long distances. They have made a relatively small penetration of the market, however.

Nationwide household goods carriers are represented in all the major cities by local agencies which, in the majority of cases, are engaged in

---

[1] *Practices of Motor Common Carriers of Household Goods,* 17 MCC 467 (1939).

the local moving and storage business. In some of the larger cities, some of the nationwide movers maintain branches to serve the public. Some carriers with limited operating territory have combined their service, through co-operative arrangements, in order to handle shipments over a larger part of the country through interline or interchange arrangements.

Other carriers have appointed only local companies having warehouse facilities as their agents, whereas some motor carriers have appointed primarily booking agents. The latter agency is one which makes the arrangements for the movement of the household goods as an agent on behalf of its principal but does not necessarily own storage facilities; it may merely "book" the shipment. The local agent is a key figure in household goods movement, since he handles the selling, packing, and storage (if he has such facilities), prepares shipping papers, arranges for the extra labor used to load and unload, and handles the investigation and settlement of claims.

The Interstate Commerce Commission's rules and regulations governing transportation of household goods by motor vehicle were first issued in 1939, and there have been subsequent modifications and additions so that at the present time, there are a number of rules having specific application to the operation.[2] Traffic managers should be familiar with these rules, since they cover such subjects as weights, rates, insurance, liability, and other matters.

Order for Service or Estimate Sheet

The traffic department is usually notified by the personnel department, or department concerned, of a transfer of company personnel. This notification is used as the basis for preparation of a traffic form which is given to the household goods mover. Such a form is shown in Figure 19–1. The mover will then go to the home of the employee being transferred and will make an appraisal of what the move entails. One of the rules which govern household goods motor carriers authorizes them to furnish to shippers or prospective shippers an estimate form which may contain statements of the weights of average pieces of furniture and other household articles of various types, for use by the shipper in making his own estimate of the total weight of his goods. Any instructions necessary to enable the shipper to use the estimate form shall be printed in the form. If cubic foot measurements are used in arriving at the weight, the form will state that a weight factor of seven pounds per cubic foot shall be used. When the company is paying the cost of transfer, the carrier's order for service is usually sent to the traffic department, and the carrier will be notified to effect the move.

---

[2] *Practices of Motor Common Carriers of Household Goods,* 17 MCC 467 (1939); 47 MCC 119 (1947); 48 MCC 59 (1948); 51 MCC 247 (1950); 53 MCC 177 (1951); 71 MCC 113 (1957).

Place_____

To: _____
    Moving Van Company

    _____
        Place

    _____
        City

Please make arrangements to cover the following transfer of household goods, account
Billbarrose Corporation

1. Name of party to be transferred.
2. Date of desired transfer from origin.
3. From:
    a. City
    b. State
    c. Street address
    d. Telephone number
4. To:
    a. City
    b. State
    c. Street address
    d. Telephone number
5. Number of rooms in which furniture now placed.
6. Description of unusual articles:

                                No.   Size

    Piano
    Refrigerator
    Other

    _____
    _____
    _____

7. Insurance required.
8. China, glassware, books, pictures, etc., are to be packed by_____
    _____.

9. Jewelry and valuables have been removed from bureaus, etc.

                                    Yours very truly,

                                    Signed_____

                                    Title_____

FIG. 19–1. Traffic department form for notifying mover.

Rates and Charges

There are a number of tariff-publishing agents of household goods
rates and charges for goods moving interstate via motor carriers. The
largest membership of household goods movers is in the Household Goods
Carriers' Bureau, Inc. The second largest group is that of the Movers' and
Warehousemen's Association of America, Inc. Although it is not unusual
in the motor carrier field to find independent action taken in rate matters
—with the result that an individual carrier may have a rate slightly less

than the rate published by the tariff bureau on behalf of its members—in the household goods field, there were two general levels of rates for many years. The rates of the members of the Household Goods Carriers' Bureau were referred to as the "high level," and the rates of the carrier members of the Movers' and Warehousemen's Association of America, Inc., were referred to as the "low level" of rates. Shortly after federal regulation of motor carriers was enacted, the difference between these two groups of carriers was as great as from 20 to 30 per cent, depending upon weight and distance. In more recent years, this difference was narrowed to about 4 per cent for line-haul rates. In 1963, the Household Goods Carriers' Bureau proposed the elimination of the rate differential by a reduction of their rates to the same level as their competitors, and this became effective.

Each of these agencies publishes a mileage guide which shows the mileages between all the points. These publications are more widely used than just for computation of distances for the moving of household goods, and there are other types of motor carriers which participate in the mileage guides. The second tariff is the scope tariff, which contains the list of members of each of the respective tariff-publishing agencies, and each carrier's scope of operations. The third tariff, the rate tariff, names local, joint, export, and import rates on household goods between points within the United States, and also between points in the United States and points in Canada and Mexico. This tariff also contains the general rules and regulations and a uniform household goods bill of lading and freight bill.

In contrast to interstate moving, local moving is usually performed on an hourly or a per-job basis. For example, in New York, a charge of $4.00 an hour for the van and $4.00 an hour for each man is charged. In local moving, rates may be established for small lots on a piece basis.

Released Value Rates

There is some difference between the bill of lading used by rail and motor carriers in the movement of general commodities and the bill of lading used by household goods motor carriers. The latter bill of lading gives a released value of "not exceeding ...... cents per pound per article." Where released rates are used by rail and motor general commodity carriers, the shipper releases goods to "not exceeding ...... cents per pound." This is a matter of some importance in so far as loss and damage are concerned.

It is important to recognize, in the movement of household goods by motor carrier, that the liability which the household goods motor carrier has is limited. This limitation of liability is the result of a released rate order by the Interstate Commerce Commission, which limits the liability of household goods movers to 30 cents per pound per article.[3] However,

---

[3] *Released Rates Order*, MC–No. 2A, January 29, 1948.

the shipper may release his household goods shipment at higher valuations; and the rate, of course, is higher. Where the shipment is released to a value exceeding 30 cents per pound per article but not exceeding 75 cents per pound per article, the rate is 110 per cent of the base rate—that is, the rate that applies on a shipment moving at a released value not exceeding 30 cents per pound per article. The rate which applies on a shipment released at a value exceeding 75 cents per pound per article but not exceeding $1.50 per pound per article is 120 per cent of the base rate. The great majority of shipments, however, are made at the rate which applies on a shipment moving at a released value of not exceeding 30 cents per pound per article.

Frequently, the shipper will purchase insurance to protect the full value of the articles against loss or damage. A living room lamp, for example, that weighs 5 pounds might be a complete loss; and carrier's liability at 30 cents per pound would be only $1.50, a wholly inadequate sum in terms of replacement. This insurance can be secured by the shipper from an insurance company, or it can be secured through the household goods carrier.

If arrangements are made for insurance, it should cover the full actual value of the shipment. If this is not done, the insurance company may invoke its coinsurer clause, which will result in the shipper sharing a proportion of the loss or damage. Insurance can be secured in multiples of $500 or $1,000.

An increasing number of household goods carriers are using a valuation basis. Under *Released Rates Order* MC–No. 362, a carrier which uses this method in its tariff can offer to the shipper greater carrier liability, for which the shipper pays 50 cents for each $100 of the declared value of the entire shipment. The shipper declares the value of the shipment in a lump sum, and the charge is currently at the rate of $5.00 for $1,000 of declared value. The carrier receives this valuation charge which, in effect, is like carrying insurance.

A new released rates order, proposed by an examiner of the Commission in 1962, would increase the carrier's liability to 60 cents per pound per article, or set a cash value of up to $500 on any article in the shipment, whichever is greater. An estimated 98 per cent of loss and damage claims are for less than $500. In addition, it was recommended that carriers be required to notify shippers by telephone or telegraph of the amount of charges when they exceed pre-shipment estimates by 10 per cent or $25; that carriers notify shippers of any delay beyond the date of delivery designated by the shipper; that a deadline of 120 days be established for carriers to act on claims, and the shipment-weight sheet used by carriers be revised.

Accessorial Services

Household goods tariffs provide for numerous accessorial or additional services. These services are at additional charges to the line-haul transportation rate and include such items as packing and furnishing wardrobes and mattress cartons. It is possible for the shipper to have his entire personal effects and household goods packed for him and, when he arrives at his destination, to have all of the furniture and other household goods placed as he desires, provided he is willing to pay for this service.

One rule of the household goods tariffs provides for storage in transit. This is usually defined as the holding of a shipment in the warehouse of the carrier or its agent for storage, pending further transportation, and it is effected only at specific request of the shipper, subject to certain specifications. Shipments which move under this rule may be stored only once, and for a period not to exceed sixty days from the date of unloading into the warehouse. Additional charges are applicable for this service; and if a shipper does not indicate final delivery instructions within the storage-in-transit period, the shipment is placed in permanent storage. When this is done, the warehouseman becomes an agent for the shipper; and the property is subject to the rules, regulations, and charges of the warehouseman.

General Rules and Regulations

The minimum charge contained in most of the household goods tariffs for interstate movements provides for 500 pounds. Tariff provisions exist for the exclusive use of a vehicle, in which case the transportation charges are based upon seven pounds per cubic foot of the total vehicle space furnished. A shipper can secure so-called "expedited" service, which is defined to mean tendering delivery of shipment of less than 5,000 pounds on or before a specified date. Where this is requested, and subject to the availability of equipment, the shipper may obtain this expedited service by paying for the shipment on the basis of 5,000 pounds.

Most shipments are made without a guarantee of shipping and delivery dates. The usual procedure is for the carrier to indicate a specific range of days, with the customer being informed that the carrier will pick up the goods on any one of the days. Another factor not understood by most shippers is the latitude granted by the statement: "No carrier is bound to transport property otherwise than with reasonable dispatch." The interpretation of this by carriers is very flexible. On an average shipment from New York to California, one mover may construe this to be approximately 10 days, whereas another may interpret it to mean 3 weeks.

On individual shipments, the carrier will not deliver or relinquish possession of any property transported by it until all tariff rates and charges involved in the shipment have been paid in cash, money order, or certified check. Where other arrangements have been made between the carrier and the consignee or the consignor, in cases where the company pays the cost of moving for its employees, in accordance with the rules and regulations of the Interstate Commerce Commission, arrangements can be made by the traffic department to have the bills submitted periodically. These so-called "commercial accounts" are solicited by household goods carriers. One of the large household goods carriers has established branch offices in many of the larger cities in order to secure the commercial accounts, for it feels that an agent is not as active in seeking this business.

Claims

Claims filed for loss and damage, overcharges, and reparations, are not subject to Interstate Commerce Commission jurisdiction, but a shipper has recourse to the courts if he does not feel that a proper adjustment has been made, or if no adjustment has been made. The filing of claims for loss, damage, or overcharge should be made in writing and should be accompanied by the original bill of lading and the original paid freight bill for transportation, if they have not already been furnished to the carrier. The carrier may require a certified or sworn statement of the claim. Where there is concealed loss or damage, the carrier should be notified immediately, so that it can inspect the concealed damage or loss in the original package. The carrier's liability is largely determined by who has done the packing—the shipper or the carrier.

Upon notification by the employee that loss or damage has been incurred to household goods moved at company expense, the traffic department notifies the household goods carrier. The claims are usually prepared on behalf of the employee and filed for the amount of carrier liability as indicated in the tariff; also, a claim is filed against the insurance company for the remainder of the actual loss or damage, where additional insurance covered the shipment. The traffic manager handling company accounts on household goods moves is more familiar with the handling of loss and damage claims than individuals who may move but infrequently and know nothing of the procedure involved in the handling of claims. He can be very helpful in assisting in the proper adjustment of claims of company employees. The actual loss or intrinsic value of the goods to their owner constitutes the measure of damages; and although there can be misunderstanding on the interpretation of this, the carriers recognize their responsibilities and make every effort to be fair and reasonable in their adjustment.

The released or declared valuation liability is settled on the basis of the carrier's bill of lading, and trip transit insurance claims are settled according to the terms of the trip transit insurance policy. The majority of bill-of-lading forms used by household goods carriers provide, under the contract terms and conditions, that claims must be filed in writing within nine months after delivery of the property or, in the event of failure to make delivery, within nine months after reasonable time for delivery has elapsed. The bill-of-lading terms further provide that suits must be instituted against the carrier within two years and one day from the day when notice in writing was given by the carrier to the shipper that the claim or any part thereof has been disallowed.

Movement of Office Equipment

The office and laboratory moves which companies make are handled along the lines outlined for household goods. However, if it is a large move, it may be necessary to inspect personally the articles to be moved with the company doing the moving. Packing and crating requirements should be reviewed. It is sometimes necessary to plan the move to occur over the week-end period or at night, in order to avoid any interruption of regular business.

PASSENGER TRANSPORTATION

Almost all of the larger industrial concerns with traffic departments have established a passenger division or section, although the transportation responsibilities of the traffic manager in this regard vary widely from company to company. The primary purpose of this section or division is to secure reservations for company employees traveling on company business. However, many traffic departments perform the service of securing these reservations for company employees even when they are not traveling on company business.

Another important function of this division is the responsibility for company-owned or company-leased equipment used for passenger transportation. In some organizations, this means the supervision of corporate aircraft used for executive purposes, as well as the leasing of automobiles for salesmen's use. Charter arrangements may need to be made from time to time for such affairs as group tours of company plants, and the traffic manager may be responsible for these arrangements.

The purchase of scheduled transportation for individual travel by rail, air, bus, or water is a relatively simple matter as compared to freight traffic management, but it is one which should not be slighted. Rightly or wrongly, traffic managers are sometimes judged by company executives on their ability to secure reservations and the type of accommodations secured. As many traffic managers know, requests for specific reservations with specific accommodations frequently are made on short notice and at a critical time, when reservations are difficult to secure, such as a holiday season. Another aspect of this problem is the fact that such a travel request often includes the necessity of securing accommodations for the executive's family as well.

Three of the primary sources of information concerning scheduled passenger transportation which are indispensable in the passenger transportation division are the *Official Guide of the Railways and Steam Navigation Lines,* the *Official Airline Guide,* and *Russell's Official National Motor Coach Guide.* The *Official Guide of the Railways and Steam Navigation Lines* contains the list of railroads and railroad passenger schedules, as well as air-line schedules. It includes an index of points reached by water routes, an index of points served by air passenger transportation lines, and an index of railroad stations. Trans-Atlantic passenger sailings are also listed. *Russell's Official National Motor Coach Guide* contains bus-line schedules and a list of bus depots. Also included are maps of many of the bus lines. The *Official Airline Guide* contains both domestic and inter-national scheduled air carrier schedules, as well as information about air freight, air express, air mail, and air parcel post. Points served and maps of the air lines are included.

None of these *Guides* is a tariff on file with the Interstate Commerce Commission or the Civil Aeronautics Board. Their usefulness lies in the fact that they are issued monthly and are therefore current, and that they contain practically all of the timetables of rail, air, bus, and water passenger services. Depending on the transportation service needed, it is possible to plan an entire itinerary by consulting one or more of these publications. The information contained in these publications is supplemented by the individual schedules of the different lines. Some passenger traffic departments make it a practice to distribute a timetable when the tickets are delivered to the passenger traveling on company business.

There has been a decline, particularly in the postwar period, in railroad passenger schedules. By 1962, passenger trains operated over less than half of the railroad trackage in the United States. This compares with 4 per cent of the trackage without passenger train operation 35 years earlier, and 10 per cent 25 years earlier. On the other hand, air carrier routes and services have been expanded considerably. They accounted for approximately 43 per cent of domestic intercity passenger-miles rendered by common carriers in 1962, as compared to 6.5 per cent in 1946.

The average revenue per passenger-mile for rail coach was 2.89 cents, rail sleeping car 3.97 cents, buses 2.71 cents, first-class air 6.08 cents, and air coach 5.01 cents in 1962. Passenger carrier fares are based on a per-mile basis. However, in comparing them on such a basis, it should be noted that air-line distances average about 17 per cent less than rail distances.

The volume of scheduled passenger transportation purchased by traffic departments is rather surprising to persons unfamiliar with this phase of traffic management. Some traffic departments spend more than $1 million a year on scheduled passenger transportation alone. In addition, the passenger section may be responsible for securing hotel reservations. To accomplish effective management control, it is necessary to have a passenger division of the industrial traffic department. This division should have sufficient personnel—on a full-time basis when this is warranted by travel volume—in order to serve the company adequately. Personnel who devote full time to passenger activities are better able to establish contacts with carrier agents, including the commercial account personnel of the carriers, and can maintain files indicating the transportation characteristics and desires of each executive. The primary emphasis in the management of this phase of traffic management is upon the benefits derived from the correct selection of the mode of transportation to meet the requirements of the particular journey.

When a substantial volume of passenger transportation is purchased from for-hire carriers, it is customary for the carriers to bill the traffic department. Transactions are usually in cash when the volume is small, and a petty cash fund may be maintained for this purpose. Sometimes, large organizations also use this arrangement for payment through a larger petty cash fund.

Travel Agents

An estimated 3,700 travel agents in the United States perform a variety of services in connection with passenger travel. Their primary activity is securing passenger accommodations and arranging tours of various types. The itinerary is planned, and the desired accommodations are secured for individual customers. Travel agents sell the tickets and are given a commission by the carrier. The price of the ticket is the same amount as that which the carrier charges. However, because of their volume of business, travel agents may have better accommodations available than the individual passenger could get from the carrier itself.

Travel agents do not represent all forms of passenger transportation in individual ticketing, since railroads do not give them any commission for selling individual tickets. Commissions presently being paid travel agents by steamship carriers are 7 per cent; domestic air carriers, 5 per cent; international air carriers, 7 per cent; and charter bus carriers, 10 per cent. The commission on cruises is higher, being 10 per cent for steamship, domestic and international air, and railroad tours. The carriers that grant commissions to travel agents look upon them as a sales force.

An increasing number of traffic departments have arranged to have all passenger reservations handled by a travel agency with no cost involved except for the expense of the direct telephone lines between the traffic department and the travel agency.

Rail Reservations

The passenger usually leaves to the passenger traffic section the choice of carrier which can furnish the best accommodations if comparable service exists. The passenger section also ascertains whether the passenger desires return or continuing space. With this basic information, the passenger section places the request with the carrier. This is generally done with the carrier's reservation bureau. However, a carrier may have assigned a particular person to handle the account of the industrial traffic department, in which case that person is contacted. This special service may be established by a carrier if it feels that the industrial traffic department is entitled to it because of the large volume of freight and passenger transportation given to the carrier. The passenger traffic section may request that the carrier assign someone to handle its account during a heavy travel season when there would otherwise be long delays in contacting the carrier representative.

The carrier representative, upon receipt of request for accommodations, checks his reservation diagram to see what space on the train is available. Diagrams vary slightly among carriers, but there is a separate diagram for each car on the train for each date. Some carriers arrange their diagrams according to date and keep the diagrams for each car in a separate package. If the carrier representative can grant the request for space, the passenger's name or corporation name will be inserted in the correct block on the diagram. If the requested space is not available, the usual procedure of the passenger traffic section is to accept the next best space and ask the carrier representative to have its name placed on the waiting list for a better accommodation.

When a carrier representative receives a request for accommodations at a point where the space is not controlled, he must contact the bureau which holds the diagrams; therefore, there is some delay. If there is need for return or continuing space, it is usually handled with the carrier representative who has arranged the original space or with the carrier's wire desk. Where space must be wired for, the passenger traffic section will hold its file in abeyance until these accommodations are confirmed. When the request is made on such short notice that the carrier cannot get the return or continuing space before departure, then the person wiring for the space marks it "en route." Under these circumstances, the traveler picks up his reservation for return or continuing space at his original destination.

Where Pullman accommodations are requested and the accommodations have been secured, the passenger traffic section inserts the Pullman space obtained, the railroad's time limit for buying the ticket, the train by name or number, the departure time, and the station from which it departs. The continuing or return space accommodations are completed in a similar manner. The location of the most convenient ticket office and the total itemized cost may be shown. The originating carrier usually issues the complete ticket, and it is either mailed or delivered to the passenger traffic department. Upon receipt of the ticket, it is checked against the file to insure that it is correct, after which it is forwarded to the passenger, with payment made by the appropriate company department.

If there is not sufficient time for this procedure to be followed, or if the carrier is hesitant about delivering or mailing the tickets, the original request containing the requested accommodations can be given to the person who has made the request. It is then his responsibility to arrange for buying the tickets.

Occasionally, it is necessary for a group movement to be handled by the passenger traffic section. The number of persons traveling in a group is the determining factor as to how arrangements should be handled concerning reservations. Rail carriers usually require that at least 30 coach tickets be purchased if exclusive use of the car is desired. If the group is traveling by Pullman and wishes to use the car exclusively, it must be engaged for a minimum of 3 days with a minimum rate applicable per day, so such charges should be compared with the cost of reservations handled individually. There are many additional ramifications to group movement that the passenger traffic section must check.

The passenger traffic section handles all claims for unused space or incorrect charges and will have a company form which will include the necessary information for filing the claim.

Private Air and Charter

The traffic manager may have the responsibility for the operation of aircraft maintained for company use. This may involve the hiring of pilots and co-pilots, the maintenance of all of the records in connection with the flights and equipment, and the scheduling of the aircraft in order to secure greater utilization of equipment. Where it is necessary to charter a plane to transport employees to a particular place for any purpose, such as participating in the opening of a plant, the passenger division will make the necessary charter arrangements. Although charter rates are on file with the Civil Aeronautics Board, the rates will vary with the size and type of aircraft. The per-mile rate varies on two-engine aircraft and four-engine aircraft; and the seating configuration, of course, varies, depending upon the equipment. It may be necessary, as well, to make arrangements for the serving of an in-flight meal, since charter rates usually do not include this service. The Civil Aeronautics Board limits the amount of charter service which can be rendered by scheduled air carriers in any calendar quarter to not more than $2\frac{1}{2}$ per cent of the revenue plane-miles flown during the preceding twelve months, excluding charter and special flights.

Air-Line Reservations

The procedure in securing air-line reservations is much the same as in securing rail accommodations. There are two basic types of scheduled air transportation services: first class and coach. The coach service is at a lower cost per mile and is usually one of two types: (1) travel by plane with a high-seat density and (2) travel at off-peak hours. The same high-seat density is found in certain first-class accommodations, however. There are also other types of service although, by 1963, coach revenue passenger-miles were 66 per cent of total trunk line passenger-miles.

In securing air accommodations, some people show a preference for jet or four-engine planes, as well as nonstop flights, so that these factors are given consideration. Air-line reservations may be handled by the regular air carrier's reservations department, or they may be handled by a special service group which handles reservations for a limited number of accounts. Whether a particular passenger traffic section deals with the latter group depends in part upon its volume of air transportation. If the desired air accommodations are not secured, a reservation is made for the next best flight and the name of the company placed on the waiting list for the flight originally requested. Air carriers have virtually pre-empted the long-haul field for distances beyond 500 miles and are gaining a monopolistic position in this area.

The air lines do not usually deliver tickets. Under these circumstances, the person who originally requested the reservation may be required to buy the ticket. The passenger traffic section handles all claims for unused space or incorrect charges involving air carriers.

Bus Transportation

A limited number of tickets are purchased for travel by bus; therefore, the passenger traffic section does not usually have a special form for handling such requests but uses the air or rail form, with necessary changes inserted. There are numerous points, however, which are not reached by air or rail service for which scheduled bus service is used. In other instances, the departure or arrival points of buses are conveniently located, which makes it desirable to use this form of transportation. Most intercity bus service is what might be termed "standard service," although in recent years, there has been the establishment of so-called "limited" scheduling, in which buses do not stop at the usual intermediate points but only at a very limited number of points. Seat reservations are sometimes made, but this is dependent upon the particular schedule.

The chartering of buses for moving company employees a limited distance to participate in a company activity or for group tours of company plants may be handled by the traffic department. As in the case of aircraft, the charge varies, depending upon the equipment. The selection of buses to be used in charter work affords greater latitude to the traffic manager than is true in the chartering of aircraft, for there is greater availability of equipment in this field. Charter rates are on file with the Interstate Commerce Commission but will vary, depending upon the type of equipment.

Automobiles—Company-Owned, Leased, or Rent-a-Car

Although the policy of furnishing automobiles to salesmen or allowing them a per-mile allowance for the use of employee-owned cars has been followed for many years, leasing of automobiles by companies for use by their salesmen has developed in more recent years. In the past, the sales department usually handled the arrangements; but with the development of leasing, there is a growing trend toward the absorption of this function by the traffic department. The reason for this is to effect management control over these transportation arrangements through the delegation of this responsibility to the department which is technically qualified and responsible for transportation matters.

The establishment of company policy and procedures for company-operated automobiles is necessary. Purchased or leased vehicles should be required to conform to company specifications; and the authority to purchase, lease, transfer, or replace any vehicles must be obtained from a designated section. It may be that employees will be given the option of purchasing company-owned cars assigned for use on company business and operating these cars under contract. When company cars are assigned, employees may be permitted to use them for personal use on a limited basis at a weekly charge or mileage charge, as provided by company policy.

Whether a company owns or leases automobiles, records should be maintained for management purposes. A typical form is shown in Figure 19–2. A preventive maintenance program may be established and equip-

OPERATING COST REPORT
PASSENGER CARS ON FIXED MONTHLY PLUS MILEAGE ALLOWANCE PLAN

DIVISION_____   DISTRICT OR DEPARTMENT_____   MONTH OF_____ 19____

MAKE OF CAR	YEAR	MODEL	TYPE	NO. OF CYLS	REGISTERED IN STATE OF	GARAGED AT

MILEAGE ACCOUNT		FIXED CHARGES	
SPEEDOMETER READING - END OF MONTH			
SPEEDOMETER READING - BEGINNING OF MONTH		REGISTRATION FEE (1/12 of Annual Amt.)... $	
TOTAL MILES TRAVELED FOR MONTH			
TOTAL BUSINESS MILES FOR MONTH		● TAXES (1/12 of Annual Amount)	
VARIABLE COSTS			
GASOLINE - NO. OF GALS. USED DURING MONTH	$	INSPECTION FEES (1/12 of Annual Amt.)	
MOTOR OIL - NO. OF QTS USED DURING MONTH			
LUBE, WASHING AND POLISH		TOTAL FIXED CHARGES $	
TIRES AND TUBES			
▲ REPAIRS		SIGNATURE OF OPERATOR _____	
		▲ Include batteries, tire chains, anti-freeze, accessories, etc. (Sales taxes on gasoline, oil, etc. to be included in cost of items.)	
		Do not include garage rental, parking fees, tolls, radio repairs, finance charges, drivers license.	
TOTAL VARIABLE COSTS .... $		● Include personal property taxes, use taxes, State rate taxes.	

FIG. 19–2. An example of an operating expense report of company automobiles.

ment checked on a planned and scheduled basis. Provisions may be made to staff a repair shop or shops in order to perform maintenance on company-operated cars. These records can be used at the next negotiation for leasing arrangements and will be helpful in determining the feasibility of continuing the leasing arrangement.

It is estimated that there were 500,000 rented or leased cars in 1963, of which 90 per cent were leased. Generally, cars available on an hourly, daily, or weekly basis are said to be rented, in contrast to those on a term lease, which is considered to be 30 days and usually longer. The nature of the lease depends upon the contract between the lessee and lessor. A basic lease may cover a one-year period with cancellation provisions which may be instituted upon proper notice by either party. When 5 or more cars are leased from one company, it is termed "fleet" leasing.

There are a number of firms that specialize in rent-a-car service. They endeavor to get their customers on the road fast and at a reasonable price. Under some circumstances, the cost of using rent-a-car service is less than taxi fees, the rental charge varying among the firms and depending also upon the type of equipment rented. The least costly cars to rent are the small foreign or compact cars which are available at some locations, and the most costly are the larger cars. Currently, to rent a Chevrolet, Ford, or Plymouth in a large city, the representative rates are $1.00 per hour plus 10 cents per mile; $10 per day plus 10 cents per mile; and $40 per week plus 10 cents per mile. Gas, oil, and $100-deductible insurance are included. For a nominal additional charge, the car is fully insured against all loss. The customer leaves with a full tank of gas. If he buys more while using the car, the cost is deducted from his bill, but he must bring in receipts for all purchases made.

Motorcar rental firms issue credit cards. Either individuals or a business is billed, and cards of other companies are honored. If the customer does not have a credit card, he can usually get a car by showing suitable identification and his driver's license, and by posting a deposit ranging upward from $15.

Some companies permit the rental of a car in one city and its return in another city where they have an office, without making a return charge. This service is sometimes restricted to specific models of cars and may be permitted only when the rental is a minimum amount, such as $25.

DISCUSSION QUESTIONS AND PROBLEMS

1. Explain the significance to the traffic department of the effective handling of movement of household goods of company personnel.
2. Distinguish between radial and nonradial operating authority as held by motor carriers of household goods.
3. What are the two main organizations of household goods movers by motor carrier, based on rates? Describe the difference in their rate levels. Why was there such a difference?
4. Discuss the liability of motor carriers of household goods, including released value rates. What arrangements can be made to secure insurance on household goods? What would you suggest as the best arrangement?
5. What are some of the accessorial services offered by motor carriers of household goods? As a traffic manager, what accessorial services would you authorize to be used at company expense? Give your reasons.

6. What are commercial accounts? Are these terms available to individual shippers of household goods?

7. Assume that, as a traffic manager, you are helping a company employee to file a claim or claims for damage to an item during its transportation at company expense by a motor carrier of household goods, the entire shipment having been covered by additional insurance obtained from an insurance company. What steps would you advise the employee to take?

8. Describe briefly the services which may be performed by the passenger section of a company traffic department.

9. What are three primary sources of information concerning scheduled passenger transportation which are available to the passenger traffic section, and what does each contain?

10. Suggest a plan which, in your opinion, would assure the traffic manager of the necessary passenger reservations at all times.

11. Why is the handling of passenger reservations of such importance to the traffic department, even though, in terms of transportation expenditures, it is of secondary importance?

Chapter

20

INVENTORY MANAGEMENT

ABOUT 30 per cent of the total assets of industry is in the total inventories, the dollar figures for business and the federal government amount-

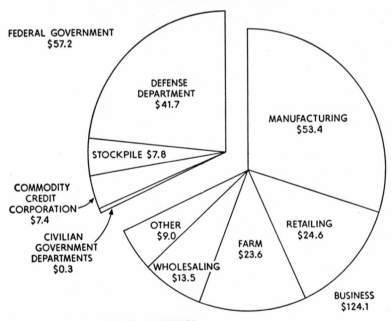

BUSINESS AND FEDERAL GOVERNMENT INVENTORIES
TOTALED $181 BILLION IN MID–1961

FEDERAL GOVERNMENT
$57.2

DEFENSE
DEPARTMENT
$41.7

MANUFACTURING
$53.4

STOCKPILE $7.8

COMMODITY
CREDIT
CORPORATION
$7.4

CIVILIAN
GOVERNMENT
DEPARTMENTS
$0.3

OTHER
$9.0

FARM
$23.6

RETAILING
$24.6

WHOLESALING
$13.5

BUSINESS
$124.1

DATA: OFFICE OF STATISTICAL STANDARDS

FIG. 20–1. Business and federal government inventories for 1961.

ing in 1961 to $181 billion (Figure 20–1). Of the business total of $124 billion, manufacturing accounted for $53.4 billion, the trade category— wholesaling and retailing—$38.1 billion, farm inventories $23.6 billion, and other business $9 billion. The federal government's inventories totaled $57.2 billion, of which the Department of Defense was $41.7 billion.[1]

General recognition of the magnitude of monetary commitments in inventories is resulting in an emphasis on inventory management. In addition, distinct efforts are being made to correlate the business functions which have, or can have, an effect upon the size of inventories, such as production, purchasing, transportation, warehousing, packaging, and handling.

Frequently, it has been stated that the real concern of businessmen regarding inventories arose following World War I when sharp price declines created significant losses for holders of large inventories. This led to the development of so-called "hand-to-mouth" buying which, in effect, was merely an effort to maintain inventories at lower levels than had previously been the case. The rise in mass-production industries, particularly of automobiles, focused additional attention upon the amount of capital tied up in inventory and the need to control its size.

Managing Inventory

Inventory management is of great importance because too much inventory results in high carrying costs and potential obsolescence which affect profits. On the other hand, too little inventory can cause high restocking and production costs and the risk of loss of sales which also have adverse effects upon profits. The critical problem is to secure the proper balance in inventory in order to enhance the general economic position of the company. There is a normal tendency to permit inventory to expand beyond its economic limits. One of the reasons for this is that there is no danger of running short. The sales department is happy with such an arrangement and so is production. This, however, ignores the cost aspects of inventory and the management aspects. Excessive stocking does not make itself felt immediately but a slight change in either general economic conditions or economic conditions within an industry can have immediate and sometimes disastrous effects. It has been authoritatively stated that "inventories are the graveyard of American business."[2]

The problem of inventory management is found in all stages of the business process from acquisition of material to production, through middlemen, and the retailer. Even the consumer has often placed before him the giant economy size, presumably at a lower cost per ounce, yet it will take considerable amount of storage space on the kitchen shelf and require a bigger investment. Some housewives actually equate the price reduction with the added inventory and investment they will have to carry.

Retailers in their inventory management are confronted with basically the same problem of quantity discounts, yet how much inventory can

[1] Chase Manhattan Bank, "Business in Brief," September–October, 1962.
[2] Benjamin Melnitsky, *Management of Industrial Inventory* (New York: Conover-Mast Publications, Inc., 1951), p. 5.

they afford to carry and should they carry, and what turnover of stock will occur? With improvements in transportation, the tendency on the part of retailers has been to replenish their stocks often and carry minimal inventories. As a matter of fact, one chain has sought to purchase in quantities to receive the quantity discounts but has timed deliveries so that the only inventory they have is on the shelves in front of the customers. There is no inventory in the stockroom.

As the pressures for holding inventory to minimal levels by retailers have been applied, this function has been, in part, pushed back upon job-bers, wholesalers, and other middlemen. Businessmen experiencing reces-sions have become very sensitive to the level of inventories, and the un-certainties that accompany too large inventories. The tendency is to get someone else to carry as much inventory as possible and yet obtain quan-tity discounts. These general pressures have accentuated the need for improved inventory management.

There are three elements that determine the size of inventories: the value of the units; their volume; and the time required in their processing and distribution. The value is the cost at which a unit is carried in inven-try. The volume of units in the inventory is ordinarily related to the rate of sales. The element of time is extremely important in inventory man-agement for this can influence the length of time required to assemble, process, and distribute, and therefore the total volume of units in the "supply pipe line." Since goods in the pipe line can be measured in mone-tary terms, the time element in all aspects of this process becomes of very substantial importance.

The desirability of a balance is obvious, and yet accomplishing it is dif-ficult unless adequate management controls are applied. The controls formulated must be consistent with the managerial philosophy of a com-pany. Some companies are very records conscious whereas others wish to maintain only minimal records with which to aid in management. Many companies rely upon periodic reports, personal consultations, and some even have inventory audits to insure adherence to the program. Generally, inventory reports are detailed for use in day-to-day management of in-ventories as well as being used in accounting records. The summary reports are also used for top management control purposes. Plant reports may be put into a consolidated report that will provide at a glance what the status of inventory is for the company as a whole or for individual products or plants.

Inventory management involves a great deal of planning and co-ordi-nating effort. It has to be responsive to changing economic environment and to changes in company product lines or programs.

Interdependence Aspects

Inventory management requires a broader perspective than has tradi-tionally been the case if its objectives are to be accomplished. The relationship of inventory management with sales and production is well-recognized, but there is still a great deal of managerial emphasis that needs to be placed in this area. If inventory is viewed as a pipe line in which raw materials enter, may be stored for a period of time prior to processing, and after processing may be moved to a warehouse or directly to customers, then it can be seen that inventory at any stage in the pipe line must be as carefully managed as that which is in the plant preparatory to processing.

The capital value of inventory causes management to seek methods of keeping the inventory level within reasonable bounds. Improved purchasing and more accurate sales forecasting are of great value in helping to accomplish this. Inasmuch as inventories are generally accumulated in anticipation of sales, good sales forecasting is mandatory in developing a sound method of inventory control. Sales department forecasts are often supplemented by independent sales forecasts that serve as another source.

Effective traffic management in the movement of products and warehousing that is used in conjunction with traffic management are additional areas where efficient management can result in measurable improvement. In spite of appreciable differences in transit time and comparable rate structures, many shippers continue in established shipping patterns. The average freight train speed between terminals at the present time is slightly less than 20 miles per hour, whereas motor carriers attempt to average 35 miles an hour between terminals—a difference of 75 per cent. Store-door to store-door time must be taken into account, as well as pickup and delivery aspects; but, on the average, motor carriers also have the advantage here. Transportation, in some instances, can be substituted for warehousing space, particularly in the shipment of finished goods. This is especially true in rail transportation where circuitous routing can be practiced. Shipments which by a direct route may take six days can be routed at no greater charge and may take twelve to eighteen days to reach destination. Where there are repetitive orders of products of not too high a unit value, routing can increase the volume of goods which are, in effect, in storage although being transported, and thereby lessen the demands on warehousing space.

As dramatic as the transit time change brought by motor carriers, an even greater change has occurred in the development of air transportation although the rates are about three times as high. The terminal-to-terminal speed of larger air carriers will average 250 to over 550 miles an hour for jet transports. These impressive changes in speed can have a very great effect upon reduction of inventory in the pipe line. Obviously, the value of the units in the pipe line will be an influencing factor in a decision to use a more expensive means of transportation. An item which has a value of $50 a pound would on a value basis alone be more susceptible to air movement than an item that had a value of 10 cents a pound. In both motor and air transportation, size limitations are not of the importance they were in earlier years since the development of larger equipment, particularly in air transportation where technological changes have been very great.

Transportation, then, can be used as a partial substitution for storage facilities under the right conditions, and conversely, it is possible to use transportation to reduce the total volume of goods in the pipe line by accelerating their movement.

A great deal of management effort has been expended in the development of a program in the Air Force relating to accelerated transportation and inventory management, with resulting reduction in total volume of inventories.

The Air Force, in its modernization of its logistics system, has established programs designed to develop a more responsive logistics structure that will, at the same time, support the weapons systems more effectively. With approximately 1,300,000 items in its inventory, the Air Force felt it was almost impossible to maintain uniform management of that number of items through the logistics cycle, and, therefore, it turned to management on a selective basis. Early studies indicated that a large portion of money was spent for a limited number of high-cost items. These became known as Hi-Valu items, and the term "Hi-Valu" is used to identify the program and the items designated for special management. All documents are stamped "Hi-Valu" to indicate that special attention, special handling, and special procedures are necessary. Three categories have been established: Category 1, limited to Hi-Valu items only; Category 2, items with unit cost of $10.00 or more and not designated as Hi-Valu; and Category 3, items having a unit cost of less than $10.00. By the establishment of selective management of Hi-Valu, it was expected that low-level, high-velocity inventories could be maintained.

Emphasis was originally placed on aircraft engines because they number over 100,000 and cost an average of $70,000 a unit, with some ranging as high as $300,000. The total value of inventory for this item is $7 billion. Hi-Valu control has been applied to about 64 per cent of the funds spent for aircraft spares support for newer weapons but a little over 1 per cent (about 14,000) of total items in Air Force inventory. The plan as applied to aircraft engines has resulted in the use of more costly and faster means of transportation, such as air transport. The higher cost of transport is considerably less than the cost of carrying a larger inventory.

The Air Force has estimated that the value of a day's pipe line—that is, spare parts, such as engines, etc., which are in transit, in storage, and in procurement—is $6.8 million. By speeding up the movement of Hi-Valu items, the transportation pipe line has been reduced from 30 to 8 days in the United States and from 96 to 16 days overseas which, allowing for the relative percentages of domestic and overseas shipments, has resulted in an average reduction in the transportation pipe line of 33.6 days worldwide. This is a monetary reduction of $228.5 million in spares.

Manufacturers' and Retailers' Inventories

The inventory problems of the manufacturer and the retailer are somewhat different. Generally, manufacturers use substantial quantities of basic raw materials with standard specifications. Obsolescence is not usually a problem since the diversion of materials from one end product to another minimizes the effect of shifts of consumer demand from one product class to another. In general, raw material inventory on a cost-per-unit basis is also considerably less than a finished goods inventory. A portion of manufacturers' inventories consists of goods in process of fabrication, and the volume of such stocks depends to a large extent upon the rate of production. Other factors that influence the manufacturers' inventory include the trend of sales, new orders, the volume of unfilled orders, price pressures, the level of inventories, the ratio of stocks to sales, interest rates on business loans, and the rate of capacity utilization in manufacturing. When a manufacturer produces goods "to order," the backlog of unfilled orders gives him a high degree of accuracy in the inventory of raw materials necessary. Even where goods are not produced "to order," many manufacturers rely upon the build-up or the depletion in the backlog of unfilled orders in determining inventory needs.

The inventory holdings of a manufacturing firm consist of a mixture of raw materials, goods in process, and finished goods. According to the Department of Commerce, purchased materials account on the average for approximately 30 per cent of producers' stocks; goods in process for another 30 per cent; and finished goods for the remaining 40 per cent. The optimum amount of finished goods held by a firm is the minimum with which orders can be efficiently filled.

The retailer's inventory consists of specific items of given size, style, color, and model. These items cannot be changed and may be made unsalable or obsolete due to shifts in consumer demand. The unit cost is considerably more than the raw materials inventory, and consumption is directly influenced by the adequacy of supply at a myriad of points.

The book value of the retailers' and wholesalers' inventories or so-called "trade inventories," totaled $38 billion at the end of 1960, with approximately two-thirds held by retail stores and chain store warehouses. This inventory category is affected by several factors which appear to cause the level of stocks to decline in the long run. Included among these is the introduction of new processes that speed up production and increase capacity. Coupled with the improvement in transportation, this permits lower stocks to be carried at the wholesale and retail level for a given volume of sales. Standardization of lines, with the resulting reduction in the number of products carried, and improvements in inventory control that will provide a more efficient movement of goods from the time of purchase to the time of sale are additional factors that will influence the level of stocks.

Cost of Possession

The cost of carrying inventory is called the "cost of possession." It often has been stated that inventory costs are as high as 25 per cent of the value of the inventory. The primary cost factors are obsolescence which is estimated at 10 per cent, interest on capital invested in inventory 6 per cent, and physical deterioration or its prevention 5 per cent.[3] The relative importance of these costs will vary among different industries and for specific inventory items. Ownership of perishable items in an inventory, for example, is more costly than that of a durable, staple item. The use of 6 per cent interest on capital invested might be considered too high if related to earnings on money invested. On the other hand, if that amount of money was reinvested in the business, this figure could easily be too low.

Lead Time

A factor of importance in inventory management is the amount of lead time required, for this has a direct influence on the level of inventory that must be carried. Lead time is the elapsed period between the time when it is determined that material is needed and when it is actually manufactured and delivered. The wide variation in lead time is due in part to the product and the proximity of suppliers. General business conditions also have an effect, lead time being somewhat longer during prosperous periods when the supplier is furnishing more products to a larger number of customers whereas the converse is true when business conditions are depressed.

Conditions of Certainty and Uncertainty

Under conditions of certainty, that is, when the demand for a product is certain, inventory control can establish minimum inventories. The assumption is that the demand for the product will continue to be certain and constant, and the lead time is known. The order to replenish the supply can be routinized since under the assumed demand the exact number of units that will be needed is known. The result is that good customer service can be assured with a minimum of inventory. In most cases, however, inventory management must be adapted to conditions of uncertainty since business demand is irregular or seasonal. Under these conditions, control of inventory is much more difficult.

Inventory Standards

One of the problems in inventory management has been the establishment of inventory standards against which performance can be meas-

---

[3] L. P. Alford and John R. Bangs, *Production Handbook* (New York: Ronald Press Co., 1955), pp. 396–97.

ured. Where these are in use, they usually have been established for raw materials, finished goods, work in process, and total inventories. Common standards include the minimum-maximum stock level, often termed the "mini-max"; the rate of return or the ratio of inventories to annual sales; the number of days' supply; and the return on investment.

In the mini-max method, a minimum and a maximum limit, which serve as general guides, are set for each inventory item. The "standard ordering point" is the minimum level of stock established to insure that orders are placed before the minimum is reached. With the use of computers, this can be an almost automatic function. The maximum stock level is a limit placed on the stock levels usually as a result of executive action. In using the mini-max standard for finished stock, an analysis of past sales, customer order practices, obsolescence potential, the time required to manufacture an item, promptness of delivery, storage factors, and sales forecasting are all considered. In dealing with work in process stock levels, companies attempt to secure the lowest possible unit production cost. Of necessity, these stock levels are generally the result of a compromise between the needs for finished stock and the desire to maintain an economical manufacturing program. An increasing number of firms are trying to arrange production schedules based on the expected sales of each item for the full year, as well as any seasonal pattern that must be accommodated. Obviously, the type of item being produced and its relative sales activity will have substantial effect upon the inventory levels of work in process. If the item is a standard part of the line and the relative volume of sales is high, the tendency is for companies to have more liberal work in process inventories since there is less risk of surpluses that could not be worked off through normal sales. On the other hand, where an item has a peak selling season, companies will provide an average production program that will build up inventories in advance but will allow a return to the minimum inventory at the end of the peak season. Stock levels for raw materials are established so as to meet the needs of manufacturing. In order to maintain a reasonable investment in raw material stocks, however, such elements as the adequacy of storage space, the reliability of transportation, and the volume of items must be considered.

The establishment of minimum-maximum stock levels does not constitute a substitute for good management nor does it assure effective inventory management. On the other hand, this inventory standard can provide very useful guidelines and be of considerable assistance in the attainment of inventory control.

Another inventory standard is the rate of return or the ratio of inventories to annual sales. The usual method is to review records and estimate the average inventory that will be required to support the existing rate of sales. Then rates of inventory turnover will be set for raw materials, work in process, and finished goods. The rate of turnover is secured by dividing estimated annual sales by total value of inventories.

Sales figures are used in a number of ways. In some companies, net sales are used whereas in others the cost of sales is used. Some employ annual rate of current monthly sales, and others project the sales year to date to an annual rate. Rate of turnover is also used in some instances because it is felt to be a good measure of the efficient use of inventory investments, and a rate of return approach is a good way of reporting to management. One of the dangers that must be guarded against is the acceptance of historical rates of inventory turnover as being adequate standards for present operations.

Another standard used is that of the number of days' supply. The usual approach in establishing such a standard is to develop a maximum and minimum level for each item or group of items, taking into consideration such factors as economic production runs, lead times for receipt of materials, reliability of suppliers, and customer service requirements. Supplementing this is a study of the historical performance of each item in the inventory at various levels of sales and manufacturing. The total value of average stock levels of individual inventory items of raw materials divided by average daily demand on that inventory to maintain given rates of sales results in the number of days' supply of raw materials required under varying sales conditions. The same procedure is used for work in process and finished goods inventories. The establishment of the number of days' supply standard enables management to compare its current performance with the standard. If, for example, the standard number of days' supply of finished goods is determined to be 45 days and existing finished goods inventory is equal to 60 times the cost of average daily sales, overstocking is obvious.

Not as frequently used is the method of employing return on investment. This has been applied by some companies to the rate on total investment required to produce a given amount of sales. In this method, a company might allocate a specified amount of working capital to a plant based on a forecast of sales. It is then up to the manager to secure an adequate return through effective management of all of the components under his jurisdiction, one of which is inventories. Return on investment probably causes the responsible executive to examine more carefully the size of his inventories since, as an item of cost, it has a bearing on return on investment.

Economic Order Quantity

Where a company produces to a customer's order or, in those instances, where the product is manufactured on a schedule for a certain number of each finished article within a given time, the quantity of materials to be ordered can be easily quantified. On standardized items produced in varying quantities over a period of time, the control of quantity is not as easy although the types of materials are standardized. Regardless of the types of products, the quantities of materials carried in inventory should be held at levels which permit the maximum amount of business with the minimum amount of capital invested per unit of product.

A number of standards are used in addition to the maximum-minimum in a control program. One of these is the reordering point which represents the addition of the minimum or cushion stock plus the quantity necessary for use during the period between placing an order and its delivery. When the stock falls to this point, a new order is placed. If the stock falls below the minimum, it falls to what is termed the "danger point" and emergency action must be instituted to replenish the stock.

Influencing the level of inventory is the economic order quantity (EOQ). This is the size of order at which the combined cost of procuring and carrying inventory is at a minimum. This can be determined as follows: those costs that increase as inventories increase, such as interest, obsolescence, risk, depreciation, and storage; and the set of decreasing costs which includes items such as quantity discounts, decreased procurement costs, and freight differentials. Procurement costs may be reduced for any item by placing fewer and larger orders. On the other hand, the result is an increase in inventory, with higher carrying costs. The EOQ will be the quantity that represents a balance of these cost factors.[4] Procurement costs vary directly with the number of orders and inversely with the amount of investment. Carrying costs vary directly with inventory investment and inversely with the number of orders. A decrease in one cost causes an increase in the other.

A number of different formulas have been devised since the cost components can be quantified. Although many companies do not use such a formula, those that do feel that it is a technique which enables them to exercise better inventory management.

A simple EOQ formula is:

$$Q = C\sqrt{Y}$$
Q = Amount to order (in dollars)
C = Cost factor
Y = Yearly demand in dollars

In this formula, the amount to order in dollars is the square root of annual demand times the cost factor. There are numerous variations to this basic formula. One that is commonly used where the unit price is the same regardless of quantity orders and where usage is reasonably steady is:[5]

[4] Thomson N. Whitin, *The Theory of Inventory Management* (2d ed.; Princeton, N.J.: Princeton University Press, 1957), p. 32.

[5] Dean S. Ammer, *Materials Management* (Homewood, Ill.: Richard D. Irwin, Inc., 1962), p. 176.

$$EOQ = \sqrt{\frac{2 \times (\text{Annual Usage in Units}) \times (\text{Order Cost in \$/Order})}{(\text{Unit Cost of Material in \$/Unit}) \times (\text{Carrying Cost in \%/Year})}}$$

Where a quantity discount is allowed, the formula would have to be refined to include this factor. Obviously, the refinements must be put into the formula. Some companies will prepare an EOQ table. These calculations require hours of work and are costly to make. Each item requires a different study. It is considerably easier to make the calculations involved if a company has a computer.

The development of the formulas has simplified the process of determining the EOQ and is helpful in the management of inventory levels. The use of mathematical and statistical techniques, however, has not supplanted the need for good judgment in inventory management. Such factors as market trends and planned program changes must be weighed and their effects are matters of judgment which cannot be ignored.

Order Processing

Cost of procuring and processing the order is often referred to as "cost of acquisition." Order processing consists of those operations necessary to enable a customer's order to be acted upon. Generally, it is not identified as a separate function but rather cuts across departmental lines of functional areas such as sales and production. The degree to which order processing has been subjected to analysis by a company may depend upon such factors as the size of the firm, its product mix, and its competitive position. The problem in order processing is not so much to identify and measure its cost as it is to analyze how the process can be accelerated from the time of customer placement to customer receipt of the order, and thereby facilitate product flow.

The advantage of the systems approach is the careful examination which each component receives. It may be found that an unnecessary amount of time is spent in processing the order and that it can be improved through better management. In one instance, a manufacturer found that only 6 per cent of the total time between the customer's order and his receipt of the shipment applied to the transportation of the product and the rest was consumed in processing the order. The application of improved communications, such as teletype or data processing, can appreciably speed up order processing. Tied in closely with order processing is the warehousing operation. Computers can be used to prepare an invoice and, at the same time, automatically update the inventory record. If inventory stock falls below a specified point, the computer will issue a production order from the plant. Since orders come in daily, the computer has permitted this information to be translated more quickly into inventory control, and production can also be more responsive to this information.

CASE

The Department of Defense recently established a Uniform Military Standard Requisitioning and Issue Procedures (MILSTRIP). Its purpose is to secure an over-all improvement in the time cycle of requisitioning and delivery of material. In order to accomplish this, twenty priority designators are used—one of which is assigned to each requisition. The priority designators are assigned according to the relative importance of the general mission of the military unit requisitioning the particular item and the relative urgency of need of the particular item in respect to the unit's ability to fulfill the assigned mission.

Response times are established by prescribing a maximum elapsed time from requisitioning to receipt of material. To accomplish this, a priority system is used in which the highest priority is attached to those items most urgently required.

This system integrates the requisitioning and transportation of material so that the entire time cycle is established under the various priority designators. This allows for tighter control of inventories and improved response to material requisitioning. The program is one in which supplies are matched more rapidly with detailed military needs, the effect of which is to reduce the general level of inventories. It is expected that even a slight decrease in pipeline stocks and locally held emergency inventories may bring large savings in procurement under existing conditions in which expensive weapon systems have high rates of technical obsolescence. The MILSTRIP procedure uses high speed computers which accelerate processing.

The following table gives the response times that have been established:

PRIORITY DESIGNATOR	MAXIMUM ELAPSED TIMES FROM REQUISITIONING TO RECEIPT OF MATERIAL (TIMES IN PARENTHESES ALLOTTED FOR DOMESTIC TRANSPORT LEG)	
	Domestic U.S.	Overseas
1 through 3	120 hours (72 hours)	168 hours (24 hours)
4 through 8	8 days (4 days)	15 days (2 days)
9 through 15	20 days (8 days)	45 days* (5 days)
16 through 20	30 days (14 days)	60 days* (9 days)

* Providing timely surface transportation is available.
SOURCE: DOD Instruction 4410.6 (ASD [I&L]), dated 24 April 1961. The times in parentheses are typical times allowed by military services for the transport segment.

On the basis of the Air Force experience in using priority assignments, it has been estimated that the number of shipments in priorities 1–3 may be 5 to 10 per cent of the total.

1. Could this program be adapted to a multiplant, industrial corporation which manufactures consumer goods?

2. Would the existence of private carriage make any difference in such an analysis?

QUESTIONS AND PROBLEMS

1. You are asked by the Executive Vice President for an analytical report on a proposal to create the position of inventory manager. How would you proceed? Prepare a one-page outline of the items that you think should

be covered. Assume your corporation manufactures hardware supplies and has nationwide distribution through wholesalers.

2. What factors influence the size of inventories? What suggestions do you have for control of them?

3. In what situations would you be likely to find "trade-off" potentials in inventory management?

4. Critically comment on "cost of possession." Should such an item as imputed interest be included? Why or why not?

5. Consult a number of books on inventory and explain an inventory model. What is the purpose in using such models?

6. Carefully discuss the different types of inventory standards. Is it possible to determine which one would be best to adopt?

7. In what way is EOQ important to inventory management?

8. How would you formulate a method for quantifying inventory which would improve management's ability to manage inventory more effectively?

9. How is order processing important to the management of inventories?

10. Consult several books on inventory and explain the different types of inventory systems.

Chapter

21

MATERIAL HANDLING
AND PACKAGING

$\mathbf{M}$ATERIAL handling is associated in the minds of many people with fork trucks and pallets. Actually, material handling encompasses much more than that. It is methods improvement and has been defined as the preparation, placing, and positioning of materials to facilitate their movement or storage.[1] The fork truck is but one piece of equipment of more than three hundred different handling devices on the market today. Material handling was developed in connection with productive processes, but the principles have been applied to improve handling techniques in many phases of industrial activities not involved in production.[2]

The responsibility for this function varies widely from plant to plant. It may be delegated to the production department or other departments. In other instances, it may be the responsibility of the traffic or physical distribution department; or it may be divided between the production department, which may have responsibility for material handling on the production line, and the traffic or physical distribution department, which has responsibility up to and from the production line.

Material handling is a part of the movement system and its efficiency has an important bearing on cost and flow of goods. The movement cost in the areas of warehousing, plant shipping and receiving, and yard storage can be disproportionately high in the absence of the application of sound management practices. Modern material-handling methods can also increase the capacity of existing warehouses and substantially reduce the unit cost of handling products. Additionally, the material-handling

---

[1] John R. Immer, *Materials Handling* (New York: McGraw-Hill Book Co., Inc., 1953), p. 4.

[2] Two of the professional societies active in the material-handling field are the American Material Handling Society and the Society of Industrial Packaging and Material Handling Engineers.

system should, to the maximum extent possible, be made compatible with the transportation movement system in order to facilitate the flow of products from plant to customer.

Several examples are given of the benefits which can be derived through the proper application of material handling in order to demonstrate the practical aspects of this field. A manufacturing plant purchased cast-iron bearing housings from a nearby foundry. The castings were irregular in shape and weighed from 5 to 150 pounds, with each shipment containing a number of different types and sizes. They were delivered by truck and unloaded to a pile in the receiving area, without consideration for type and size. Later, they were sorted and stacked in storage. The possibility of palletizing them in storage, since they could be nested, led to the discovery that the foundry which produced them used pallets but took the castings off when loading them on the truck. Arrangements were then made with the foundry to leave the castings on the pallets. The savings in handling and sorting by the manufacturing plant, as a result of this action, amounted to about two man-hours per ton, and the foundry also was saved a rehandling.[3]

Another instance where improved material handling had a substantial effect upon efficiency and cost is that of a plant which purchased carbon electrodes, each 24 inches long and 2 inches in diameter. These were always stacked and bulkheaded in a boxcar. It took 80 man-hours to unload and store the individual pieces contained in a boxcar. All the way through processing, this individual handling had to be performed. After a thorough study of this problem, arrangements were made to purchase the electrodes on a disposable pallet. This made it possible to unload and store, in palletized units, in $1\frac{1}{2}$ hours, with a fork truck and a driver, the same amount that had formerly taken 80 man-hours. In addition, the palletized unit cut down on delivery and handling all the way through to processing. Other advantages this company cited were that the unit load lent itself to better inventory control and eliminated demurrage on boxcars in which the palletized units had been shipped.[4]

Although there was considerable activity and interest in material handling prior to World War II, the real impetus in this area occurred during the war, when there were labor shortages and the emphasis was upon a heavy volume of production. The military services made widespread use of material-handling equipment, so that by the end of World War II, the benefits of the proper use of material-handling equipment had been widely demonstrated in a relatively short period of time.

---

[3] Neil Drake, "Better Shipping and Receiving," *Modern Materials Handling*, May, 1953, p. 111.

[4] Travis E. Parish, "Purchasing and Traffic," *Modern Materials Handling*, May, 1953, p. 168.

OBJECTIVES OF MATERIAL HANDLING

The broad objectives of material handling have been outlined by the American Material Handling Society as follows:

1. Reduction of handling costs.
   a) Reduction of labor costs.
   b) Reduction of material costs.
   c) Reduction of overhead costs.
2. Increase of capacity.
   a) Increase of production.
   b) Increase of storage capacity.
   c) Improved layout.
3. Improvement in working conditions.
   a) Increase in safety.
   b) Reduced fatigue.
   c) Improved personnel comforts.
4. Improvement in distribution.
   a) Improvement in routing facilities.
   b) Strategic location of storage facilities.
   c) Improvement in user service.
   d) Increase in availability of product.

An examination of these objectives indicates that some of them have primary application to production aspects. However, certain of these objectives of material handling are identical to the general interests of the traffic manager.

There are various estimates as to what improved material handling can accomplish. One such estimate is that, through the application of improved material handling, productivity can be raised by 15 per cent without any replacement of existing buildings or equipment.[5] A further estimate has been made that American industry could reduce the cost of plant movement and storage of materials by $2 billion through the use of modern material-handling methods and the proper equipment.[6]

The efficiency of material handling is measured by the number of units —such as tons, pieces, or other units of measurement—handled per man-hour. In computing the performance of the equipment plus the labor involved, tons per man-hour are used. This is secured by taking the total weight of the material handled in tons during a given period of time and dividing it by the actual number of man-hours used. However, this ratio is useful only in comparisons of operations handling similar materials. For example, bulky materials which have little weight might require the same number of man-hours to move as an equal cubic quantity of material

[5] Organization for European Economic Cooperation, *Materials Handling Equipment and Methods in the U.S.A.* (Paris, France, 1953), p. 14.
[6] Address by Allen K. Strong, National Material Handling Exposition, 1951.

weighing several times as much. Therefore, they should not be compared on the basis of tons per man-hour. The relative efficiency of two material-handling crews can be determined by having each crew do exactly the same work, use the same equipment, and travel the same route in the same elapse of time.

One of the classifications of material handling is in terms of the materials handled, as follows:

1. Unit materials handled, which include boxed, cartoned, and packaged goods.
2. Bulk materials handled, which include loose bulk materials, such as coal, grain, liquids, and similar materials.
3. Parts handled, including such items as castings, subassemblies, bar stock, sheet metal, and similar items.

Each of these three broad types may represent important phases where methods improvement can be effected. Probably the most widely recognized one of these is that of unit material handling. In this particular area, there have been very great advances in recent years. Part of this may be attributed to the fact that the higher wages paid to unskilled labor have accentuated the desirability of reducing costs in this field. Improved material-handling methods are one way in which this can be done.

EQUIPMENT SELECTION AT SHIPPING AND RECEIVING DOCKS

Various factors must be considered before the selection of material-handling equipment is made for use on shipping and receiving docks. These are:

1. Type and amount of materials handled, whether in bulk or in packages.
2. Available receiving or loading dock floor space, including amount of clearance and headroom, and floor loading factors.
3. Distance goods must travel from docks to departments where used.
4. Whether unit loads are used, such as palletizing, and the methods of packaging.
5. The material-handling equipment used throughout the rest of the plant.[7]
6. The types of carriers used—motor, rail, water, and air.

One of the most widely used material-handling methods is the utilization of pallets and fork lift trucks. Some of the advantages of palletization to the traffic manager are:

---

[7] An interesting account of the origin and historical development of many of the major types of handling equipment in use at the present time is found on pages 183–244 of the May, 1953, issue of *Modern Materials Handling*. Included in this account are belt conveyors, overhead cranes, hoists, industrial trucks, power shovels and yard cranes, roller conveyors, freight elevators, straddle carriers, monorails, hand lift trucks, and trolley conveyors.

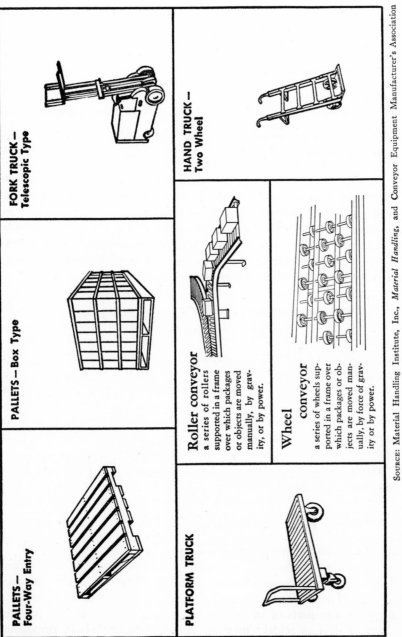

PALLETS— Four-Way Entry

PALLETS—Box Type

FORK TRUCK— Telescopic Type

PLATFORM TRUCK

Roller conveyor a series of rollers supported in a frame over which packages or objects are moved manually, by gravity, or by power.

Wheel conveyor a series of wheels supported in a frame over which packages or objects are moved manually, by force of gravity or by power.

HAND TRUCK— Two Wheel

SOURCE: Material Handling Institute, Inc., *Material Handling*, and Conveyor Equipment Manufacturer's Association

FIG. 21–1. Typical handling equipment.

1. Loading and unloading are efficient and convenient.
2. Palletization lends itself to tight loading in carrier vehicles because the nature of palletization dictates the need for the bonded block method, a recognized method of stacking.
3. Palletization eliminates, to a great degree, inaccuracies in counting and inventory controls.
4. It is not necessary to mark each package.
5. Palletizing adds a false flooring to which steel strapping can be anchored.
6. Palletization can reduce claims.
7. Palletization makes easier efficient warehousing, uniform placement of stock, neat aisles, and clean floors, and allows for proper lighting, as well as utilization of full ceiling height.

There are many different types of material-handling equipment with which the traffic manager should be familiar, some typical examples of which are shown in Figure 21–1. It is possible, from the data given in manufacturers' catalogs, to calculate the actual performance of a piece of material-handling equipment. Verification of this can be secured by timing in operation. Manual handling of the same task can be timed and an estimate made of the savings in manpower which would be possible through the use of the particular piece of equipment under consideration.

An important part of shipping is to have the correct package design. This usually means selecting a light, strong package which provides adequate cushion. The trend is toward substituting paper, fiber, and wirebound containers for wood and metal. Another method is the use of unit loads. Pallets reinforced with steel strapping have been used successfully to give strength and reduce the weight of the packaging needed for individual packages. Unit loads without pallets can be formed by using steel strapping. Often, articles of odd sizes and shapes can be strapped into a unit. Some carriers have special equipment which has reduced the amount of dunnage necessary, such as a compartmentized boxcar with adjustable steel frame and wire-mesh bulkheads.

A shipment in bulk instead of in containers can effect substantial time and cost savings where articles lend themselves to that type of shipment. Flour which can be shipped in hopper cars designated for pneumatic loading can effect substantial savings.

LOADING AND UNLOADING TO PREVENT DAMAGE

One of the methods of preventing damage in loading and unloading is that of combining packages into a unit. This lends itself to mechanical handling, as well as reducing the number of handlings which the packages would have. The unit loads are stronger and are damage-resistant, whereas the component parts of the unit loads are very susceptible to damage. Unit-loading devices widely used are standard pallets, skids, disposable pallets, steel strappings, glued loads, and pallet packs. *Unitizing* is a more inclusive word than *palletizing*, and its proponents feel there will be a great future development in this field.

The use of special shipping containers for bulk or packaged material is a method of securing maximum protection of material. The placement of bulk commodities in various containers or hoppers prevents spillage and contamination while loading and unloading. The use of pneumatic systems, mentioned earlier, for loading and unloading bulk commodities can also prevent damage.

There are various less-carload-lot merchandise containers, as well as shipload cargo containers. These containers may be fitted with various handling devices, such as casters, hooks, and sling eyes, which facilitate their movement.

Loading and unloading can be facilitated if it is possible to extend the handling system beyond the edge of the dock into the carrier's equipment. Another method is to use adjustable docks or dock boards, so that the handling vehicles can move easily into the carrier's equipment. Overhead systems that extend into the carrier's equipment, such as hairpin hooks, retractable arms, and monorail extensions, can accelerate loading and unloading.

The unit loading of packages can be speeded by the use of mechanical handling devices, such as industrial trucks, tow conveyors, tractor-trailer trains, and other means. Even with loose bulk commodities, there are many methods of loading such bulk by machinery to accelerate this operation. Some of these methods are cranes, shovels, scoops, magnets, fork trucks with scoops, car unloaders, and car dumpers, as well as others.

The prevention of damage en route is accomplished in much the same manner as in loading and unloading. Combining smaller packages into a larger unit adds strength to the unit and protects it. Good packaging methods must be used, involving proper sealing of the package, adequate cushioning, and interior packing to protect packages against moisture, shock, and pilferage. It is necessary, as well, that the goods be stowed properly in the carrier's equipment. Correct stacking methods for such things as bags, barrels, and rolls must be used. The use by carriers of especially designed equipment, such as damage-free loaders, compartmentizers, and similar devices which hold loads securely in place without undue pressures or weights, has accomplished much in the way of damage prevention.

Canvas shipping hampers similar to the hampers used in laundries have been successfully employed by some traffic managers in moving small packages. The hampers have a spring-steel frame to which is stitched heavy-duty canvas, leather-reinforced at points of wear. Wood runners enable the hamper to be pulled along the floor. Such a hamper measures $27\frac{1}{2}$ inches by 26 inches by 36 inches, and its capacity is the equivalent of 12 bushels. Many small packages can be placed in it, and its hinged top can be sealed with a boxcar-type seal. The hampers can be stacked, and other goods can be placed on top of them.

As is so often the case with unitized or mechanized handling equipment, one of the problems has been that of adjusting rates on the returned empty pallets, skids, hampers, and the like. In the case of hampers, adjustment was secured by apprising the carriers of the advantages of the use of the hampers to the carriers, particularly in reduced loss and damage. The carriers agreed to a lower empty return rate, which was approved by the regulatory body.

Another problem in the use of hampers was the increased shipping cost due to the weight of the hamper and to the increased freight rates on items within the hampers which by themselves would carry rates lower than the hampers. With agreement of both the carriers and the regulatory body, a sixty-day test of hamper use was conducted. Data gathered during the test period indicated that the carriers could charge lower than published rates for loaded hampers and still obtain the same revenue as when articles were shipped loose. As a result of the test, a lower rate on loaded hampers was granted. Loaded outbound hampers in the particular movement studied during the test period move at 72 per cent of Class 100, and empty hampers at 35 per cent of Class 100.

CONTAINERIZATION

A cargo container is a type of shipping container of weatherproof construction which can be stored outdoors and transported in open cars or trucks. Containers of this kind are used for handling bulk commodities as well as merchandise and are especially adaptable for interchange between open-truck, rail, and water transportation. They are of rugged construction for crane handling.

Cargo containers were originally designed primarily for transportation in gondola rail cars equipped with intermediate bulkheads dividing the cars into compartments. Six cargo containers, each with a maximum dimension of 112 inches by 96 inches by 8½ feet, and each with a capacity of 485 cubic feet, can be placed on the ordinary gondola car, as shown in Figure 21–2. Such a container may be insulated and refrigerated. It may

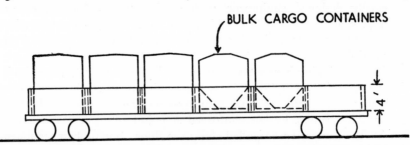

FIG. 21–2. Cargo containers in gondola container cars—capacity 6 large or medium or 12 small cargo containers.

be flat-bottomed, mounted either on skid runners or on four legs (Figure 21–3).

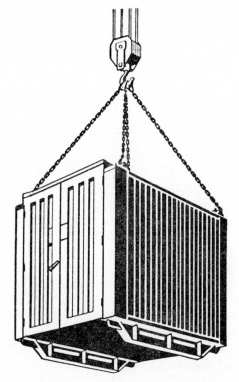

FIG. 21-3. Cargo container with skid runners.

Shippers have frequently pressured carriers to provide container service because of its many advantages. Containers require less protective packing and take less time and labor to load and unload. In addition, better rates are often available for container shipments, loss and damage may be reduced, and contamination from outside sources is minimized.

Cargo containers transported on special open-container cars usually are considered by the railroads to be demountable, sectionalized bodies that take the place of boxcar or covered hopper car bodies and therefore are exempt from freight charges, both loaded and empty.

Smaller containers are available—some of 65 cubic feet capacity, with 5,000 pounds loading capacity, which will fit 28 such units on a flatcar or 10 on the average truck trailer bed. There has also been a trend toward larger containers, particularly involving a combination motor, rail, or water haul. Even larger containers up to 40 feet in length, called "van containers," are used; these are, in effect, trailer bodies. The van container generally has to be of more rugged construction than a corresponding highway trailer body, since it must be able to stand the handling in railroad classification yards. In 1962, container production by truck-trailer manufacturers was about 10 per cent of the total trailers produced.

Extensive use has been made of containers by the military services, particularly since 1950. These containers—the largest of which weigh 1,400 pounds and are 8 feet, 6 inches long, 6 feet, 3 inches wide, and 6 feet, 10½ inches high—are capable of carrying 9,000 pounds. Although the containers were originally designed for the transporting of household goods to overseas points, it was found that about 26 per cent of military dry cargo could be containerized; and increasing use has been made of the containers for troop support supplies to overseas destinations.

The Transportation Corps of the Army, which was instrumental in the development of the containers, has approximately 70,000 containers in use.

There are many different types of pallet containers for intrafactory use and interplant transfer. These include pallet boxes, baskets, racks, bins or hoppers, and carton containers. They may have open tops, top covers, or side or end doors, and may be collapsible or expandable. Pallet containers can be used in either boxcars or trailers.

There is also what is termed a "jumbo" pallet container which can be rolled broadside into a van on its own casters with either side guides or channels attached to the floor of the van to guide the casters. Some jumbo pallet containers are used as a unit which will just clear the door of a trailer and in varying lengths, sometimes the full length of the van body. A container of this type is sometimes referred to as a "truck liner." The van can be loaded in a matter of seconds by rolling the entire unit into the trailer, and a rapid turn-around of the truck equipment can be accomplished.

Bulk shipping containers are used for handling crushed, powdered, or fluid materials. They are ordinarily sealed or weathertight and can be transported in boxcar or gondola container cars, in covered or open vans, or in barges or ships. They generally are arranged for either lift-truck or crane handling and can be tiered.

The different types of bulk cargo containers include a drop bottom, a controlled discharge gate, a sealed rubber container, and an air-activated container, the latter being one in which compressed air is attached to the container and the pulverized contents blown into a nearby elevated tank or silo. Rubber containers are collapsible and are handled by crane by means of a lifting eye. The flexibility possible with different-sized containers is a factor of considerable importance. Some containers have retractable legs that will support the container and allow the truck chassis to be driven away. Such units can be left on legs at terminals or at shipper platforms. Furthermore, several containers can be put on a 40-foot trailer and transported over long distances.

Standards for van and cargo container sizes have been established by the American Standards Association in 10, 20, 30, and 40 foot lengths with height and width dimensions of 8 x 8 feet. It is felt that smaller cargo and pallet containers will be made compatible with the van containers. By 1963, eleven nations affirmed proposed international standards for the 10 and 20 foot van containers. When adopted, these standards will facilitate transport co-ordination in international shipping.

Three elements are necessary in standardization of containers. These are: a systematic group of sizes that can be loaded in any combination with one another; standardization of all fixtures on the units; and systems capable of handling every container. It would appear that there would be advantages in standardization on a limited number of types of different containers in each of the broad categories given. This would make for a greater degree of interchangeability.

Rubber containers which can be inflated by filling them with liquid have been developed, particularly for use in connection with truck transportation. These are being transported by tank truck operators and, within certain limitations, by general commodity haulers. Up to 15,000 gallons can be transported in the sealed tanks.

The transportation of explosives and other dangerous articles is subject to specific safety rules with which the traffic manager must be familiar. If he is unable to procure authorized containers for dangerous articles or is confronted with a serious shipping problem which can be overcome without sacrificing safety, a special permit can be secured from the Commission covering such a shipment.

INDUSTRIAL PACKAGING

It is currently estimated that packaging is about an $18 billion industry. Approximately half of this amount is the manufactured value of packages and components shipped to packagers, and the remainder is the value added in the plant by labor, overhead, handling, testing, and designing. A survey of 98 food and grocery firms revealed packaging costs to be equal to 10 per cent of total sales.[8] The cost of packaging in the military services is estimated to be about 9 per cent of the military budget.

There are two types of packaging, but their functions are overlapping. Generally, industrial packaging deals with the preparation and protection of merchandise for shipment and storage; and consumer packaging is designed to affect sales acceptance. In some instances, the cost of consumer packaging exceeds the cost of the contents, as in the cosmetics industry. Obviously, consumer packaging may also be designed to provide a measure of protection to the merchandise while it is being shipped or stored, although it is usually necessary for industrial packaging to be used as exterior packaging. This sometimes has led to a simplified differentiation that industrial packaging is exterior packaging and consumer packaging is interior. Industrial packaging amounts to about 30 per cent of total packaging costs.

---

[8] A. C. Neilson, Jr., "Packaging Is a Dominant Factor for Today's Consumer," *Marketing Research Reports on Packaging* (New York: American Management Association, 1957), p. 3.

The responsibility for packaging involves problems of design, formation, filling, closing, and preparation for shipments. A few large companies have a separate packaging division but ordinarily packaging is under one of the existing departments, such as manufacturing, sales, or traffic. Consumer packaging is generally oriented to sales and advertising whereas industrial packaging is more closely allied with traffic and physical distribution. Some of the reasons for this are:

1. Weight of the package is a part of gross weight of the shipment and goes at the same rate as the shipment.
2. Material not correctly packed can result in a higher rate or penalty charge being applied.
3. Claims can be declined on the basis of improper packaging.
4. In the establishment of freight rates, the load factor and susceptibility to damage are considered, and these factors are affected by packaging.
5. Freight which is likely to damage other freight because of improper packing or packaging may be refused by the carrier.
6. Dangerous articles must be packed in accordance with state and federal requirements.

A packaging engineer with a working knowledge of the operations and facilities of the traffic department can accomplish substantial improvements in packaging. In one company, the container which had been used to ship aircraft components to the vendor for machining was fabricated of wood; but when another packaging material was substituted, the freight savings paid for the container. The production department in this company had authorized shipments in multiples of 6 weighing a total of 3,600 pounds, at which weight the freight charges were based on the 5,000-pound rate. After the initial shipment in the new container had been made, the production department was informed that 10 pieces could be shipped at no increase in freight costs, with the result that freight per piece was reduced by 40 per cent.

Packaging materials are divided into two groups—hard and soft. Hard materials include wood, plastics, fiber, masonite, glass, and metals. Soft materials include paper, cellophane, laminated products, and fabrics.

In an effort to reduce the transported weights in the future, it is expected that plastics will be increasingly used. At the present time, plastics are used as unit packs, as closures, and as outer containers. One of the military services which spends $70 million annually to ship packaged materials carefully analyzed this cost and found that about 20 per cent of the total was occasioned by the weight of packaging material.

Some of the factors that affect the design of a package and apply to all types of containers—fiberboard or wooden boxes—are given in the check list below. In designing a container, one should consider:

1. Shape of the object to be packaged (round, square, oblong, etc.).
2. Size (over-all dimensions).
3. Weight.

4. Shockproof requirements.
5. Stacking requirements, which include the effects of stacking, as well as humidity.
6. Shipping method (the number of cartons which will make up a unit).
7. Whether the package is for a single trip or for a return trip as well.
8. Storage life.
9. Handling techniques—a package for a unit load can be lighter and cheaper than one handled individually.
10. Quantities of items to be packaged in one container.
11. Type of box opening required—in general, an opening across the least dimension of a package will take less packaging material and will be cheaper.
12. Whether it has to be shipped in closed pack or open pack.
13. Whether the package has to be opened for inspection.
14. The type of packing method, whether packaged on an assembly line or in a separate area.
15. The type of closure to be used (wire stitching, glue, tape, and the like).[9]

The traffic manager of one corporation has given some tips on packaging machine parts. His procedure is to analyze the problem before packaging any of their products. This analysis will seek to answer these questions:

1. Is the product to be shipped to a customer for further fabrication in his plant?
2. Can the customer order large-enough quantities to warrant the palletization of his materials?
3. Can the customer handle palletized shipments?
4. Is the product to be stored and shipped in small lots?
5. What is the best method of packing, from the transportation standpoint, in order to comply with regulations?

After these questions have been answered, specifications can be issued to direct the packaging of the product.

The results of palletization in the example cited by this traffic manager are savings on material handled and packaging material. The example used was that of 60 motors which, if packed in individual cartons, required 665 square feet of fiberboard and would occupy 36 cubic feet of space. If the 60 motors were palletized, the palletized unit would require 194 square feet of fiberboard and would occupy only 27 cubic feet. The difference is a saving of almost 70 per cent of the amount of fiberboard needed and 25 per cent of the cubic space occupied. The cost of individual cartons for the 60 motors would be $12.80, whereas the cost for material for a palletized shipment would be $4.99, or a savings in material of 60 per cent of the individual package. The savings in packing were reflected also in lower transportation costs.

The arrangements for the use of palletized shipments to customers of

---

[9] "Factors That Affect Package Design," *Modern Materials Handling*, February, 1953, pp. 77–81.

this company's hydraulic brake line encompass 98 per cent of their hydraulic brake shipments.

CASE

The Citizens Chemical Company is a relatively small chemical operation conducted in the city of Galveston, Texas. The operation is devoted entirely to the reduction of chemical compounds into other chemical solutions. This process involves the purchase of acetylene from various producers of industrial chemicals and the manufacture of the chemical compounds of amyl acetate and acetic acid. The firm is the owner of a patent which is a greatly improved process over the traditional methods used by other chemical firms. So revolutionary is this method that it allows the Citizens Chemical Company to operate at a much lower volume than would be possible using other methods and still receive a profitable return on the operation.

The firm has been primarily a supplier of smaller purchasers of acetic acid and amyl acetate. For the most part, the sales of the acetic acid are to firms involved in leather tanning, laundry souring, the manufacture of solvents, the business of printing, and the dyeing of silk. Sales of this chemical have remained fairly constant over a period of years, showing a gradual and steady growth trend with no seasonal pattern. Amyl acetate is sold widely for use in preservation of fruits in warehouses. This process involves the vaporization of the amyl acetate in the warehouse and then sealing of the warehouse for desired storage periods. In contrast to the acetic acid, the amyl acetate shows marked seasonal fluctuations which correspond to the picking and storage of fruits, especially apples. There has also been a steady growth in the trend-cycle of the sales of the amyl acetate. The latter account for approximately 38 per cent of the dollar-sales while the acetic acid accounts for the remainder.

TABLE I

	Dollar Volume of Acetic Acid	Dollar Volume of Amyl Acetate
1958	$2,228,000	$1,384,000
1959	2,709,600	1,706,400
1960	2,950,100	1,866,700
1961	3,122,500	2,081,600
1962	3,515,000	2,242,400

The distribution channel of the two chemicals is comprised of the central office, plant, and warehouse at Galveston, Texas, and seven branch warehouses located one each in Atlanta, Georgia; Scranton, Pennsylvania; Rochester, New York; Dayton, Ohio; Kansas City, Missouri; Portland, Oregon; and Bakersfield, California. Warehousing of acetic acid is quite simple as there is a constant turnover of stock, and no great accumulation. However, the amyl acetate as a by-product of the acetic acid accumulates over the year and creates a warehousing problem. The warehouses average a percentage of occupancy as low as 55 per cent in the month of December and as high as 95 per cent during the month of September.

All processing and bottling of these fluids is done at the Galveston plant. The only container used is the 13-gallon wood-encased glass carboy. From Galveston, they are shipped in carload lots to the respective warehouses.

TABLE II
MONTHLY SALES PERCENTAGES FOR 1962

	Acetic Acid	Amyl Acetate
January	8.2%	1.1%
February	9.0	.7
March	8.7	.4
April	8.0	.5
May	8.3	1.7
June	8.3	2.0
July	7.9	11.9
August	8.5	22.7
September	8.6	28.7
October	8.4	15.1
November	7.9	10.2
December	8.2	5.0
	100.0%	100.0%

Seldom is it necessary to ship less than carload lots. However, the warehouses serve as break-bulk points, and shipments are made from warehouses to customers in their designated sales region. The average order size for 1962 was 133 gallons of acetic acid and 105 gallons of amyl acetate. About 92 per cent

TABLE III
FREQUENCY OF SIZE OF SHIPMENTS IN GALLONS IN 1962

Gallons	Acetic Acid	Amyl Acetate
0–13	79*	31*
13–55	195	94
56–110	268	178
111–210	115	117
210 up	300	92

* Unfilled due to absence of appropriate container.

of the volume of shipments from the warehouses to the customers in 1962 were made by rail. The remainder was delivered to a vehicle of the customer at the warehouse.

The present container used by Citizens Chemical Company is the glass carboy, which is wood encased. The initial cost of each carboy is $15, and the average length of usage is three years, seven months. When a customer purchases a chemical in a carboy, he must place $10 as deposit for the carboy, which amount is refunded when he returns the carboy to the warehouse. At present, Citizens Chemical Company owns 95,000 carboys, of which 7,000 are maintained as safety stock. The average age of the presently owned carboy is one year, ten months. It is estimated that each carboy makes approximately 4.2 trips per year through the plant. The prices presently effective per gallon for acetic acid and amyl acetate are $18.40 and $23.50 respectively, F.O.B. Galveston. Although the glass carboys presently being used by the Citizens Chemical Company are satisfactory from the firm's standpoint and very little complaint has been received from the customers, the possibility of changes in the packaging of chemicals has arisen.

Amyl acetate is of such a nature that it must be stored and shipped in glass or stainless steel containers. On the other hand, acetic acid is a chemical which is able to be stored and shipped in glass, stainless steel, or several of the new plastics which have recently been introduced on the market.

One of the directors of the company introduced the possibility of a change in the packaging material at a board meeting. He suggested the use of a polyethylene container for acetic acid and quoted from a 1963 issue of one of the trade journals in support of its excellent properties. The possibility of storing and transporting acetic acid and amyl acetate in stainless steel containers, as does the Fisher Chemical Corporation, was also suggested by the director. Before rashly changing containers for either chemical, however, the board of directors wished to have the problem thoroughly researched.

The ensuing study of packaging developed the following facts: Differences in packaging costs are quite significant. As previously stated, the glass, wood-encased 13-gallon carboys cost $15 each to purchase. The polyethylene container, steel encased, comes in various sizes and prices, as follows:

TABLE IV

POLYETHYLENE CONTAINER COSTS AND WEIGHTS

Size	Cost	Weight
5 gallons	$ 5	8 lbs.
15 gallons	12	23 lbs.
30 gallons	18	40 lbs.
55 gallons	24	65 lbs.

The stainless steel carboys also vary in price according to volume:

TABLE V

STAINLESS STEEL CONTAINER COSTS AND WEIGHTS

Size	Cost	Weight
5 gallons	$ 18	14 lbs.
15 gallons	40	28 lbs.
30 gallons	75	45 lbs.
55 gallons	135	85 lbs.

The wood-encased glass carboys also come in a variety of sizes and their relative prices are presented below:

TABLE VI

WOOD-ENCASED GLASS CARBOY COSTS BY WEIGHTS

Size	Cost	Weight
5 gallons	$ 6	12 lbs.
13 gallons	15	34 lbs.
30 gallons	26	62 lbs.

The present equipment at the Galveston plant is of the size and nature to handle the filling of the 13 gallon glass carboy. With adjustments in the filling time and the nozzle positions the same equipment could also be used to fill 15 gallon containers of either polyethylene or stainless steel. To fill 5 gallon containers of polyethylene, glass, or stainless steel would require the purchase of a bottling machine at a price of $13,492.77. There is a heavy-duty bottling machine available which would be able to fill either the 30 or 55 gallon containers. The cost for this piece of equipment would be $18,236.61.

Under the present system of using wood-encased glass carboys, the chemicals receive a first-class freight rate on the railroads due to the special handling necessary for their protection. If the stainless steel or steel-encased polyethylene line containers were used, the rail rate would be third class and would result in a freight savings of approximately 40 per cent.

While the average length of usage of the glass carboy is three years, seven months, the stainless steel and polyethylene containers are of considerably longer life. The stainless steel containers have a projected average life usage of about nine years. The polyethylene-lined containers are estimated to have an average life usage of 4.4 years. Also, it has been determined that the customer deposit for the polyethylene container should be 75 per cent of the cost of the original container. Due to the many uses for the stainless steel containers, it is felt that the deposit by the customers on the stainless steel containers would have to be 100 per cent of the original purchase cost.

At five of the eight warehouse locations, there is adequate space available both on the roof and adjacent property to maintain outdoor storage of some of the chemicals. The storage of the glass carboys with their wood cases in the weather was estimated to shorten the usage life of these carboys by 50 per cent, but it is felt there would be no change in the life of the stainless steel containers as a result of outdoor storage. The life of the steel-encased polyethylene container would probably be 20 per cent less if it were to be stored in the elements.

At the present, there is no foreseeable obsolescence to any of the three containers under discussion nor does sales promotion of the chemicals revolve on the type of packaging being utilized but rather on the cost and quality of the product and the services available. Packaging of the chemicals shapes consumer demands only in so far as any of these factors are enhanced by the packaging materials.

1. Should poly or stainless steel be used in shipping acetic acid?

DISCUSSION QUESTIONS AND PROBLEMS

1. What is material handling? How does it relate to traffic management?
2. List the objectives of material handling. What are some of the possible effects of improved material handling?
3. One of the aspects of material handling of interest to the traffic or physical distribution manager is the selection of equipment at shipping and receiving docks. Name the factors which must be considered in the selection of such equipment.
4. Palletization offers many advantages to the traffic manager. Describe these advantages.
5. What are some of the methods which can be used to prevent damage in loading and unloading? To prevent damage en route?
6. Describe the use of shipping hampers to move numerous small shipments. What were some of the problems encountered in their use, and how were these solved?
7. List the factors to be considered in designing a package container.
8. Describe the traffic or physical distribution manager's role in material

handling. Should he have complete responsibility for material handling? Why, or why not?

9. Identify the principal problems of material handling relating to traffic management, and give suggested solutions to these problems.

10. Assume that the production department has been given complete responsibility for material handling. How would you, as the company's traffic manager, proceed to utilize material-handling techniques?

11. Name the different types of containers. Do you feel that standardization of a "family" of containers should be required?

12. What role do you feel containers will have in the future movement of commodities? Carefully consider whether you would expect opposition to container use from any group.

13. Formulate the organizational position and role of industrial packaging in a large corporation producing consumer goods.

Chapter

22

WAREHOUSING

THE systems approach considers all components of physical distribution, of which warehousing is one. The cost of carrying inventories, the cost of warehousing, transit times, and the density of market areas are all factors analyzed in company warehousing. The increasing use of simulation to determine the optimum number and location of warehouses, as a part of a physical distribution analysis, enables a company to examine various alternative methods. Since the necessary data can be quantified and models developed through the use of the computer, the best balance based on available data can be secured.

There is a wide difference in the cost of warehousing different products. Therefore, the application of an average storage cost can be misleading. In the analyses made, a product-by-product warehousing cost analysis has usually been found advisable.

Warehousing is also closely associated with the transportation responsibilities of the traffic manager. He needs to have a basic knowledge of warehousing so that he may be able to advise management on the distribution aspects of warehousing.

Warehousing is usually considered to be the storage of goods prior to their use, although other aspects of warehousing are important in the distribution of goods. It is necessary in order to effect an equalization of seasonal production for more uniform consumption during the year, as well as to equalize uniform production for a more or less seasonal consumption, such as toys for the Christmas season. Storage, then, can achieve a better balance between supply and demand.

In the economic sense, warehousing can create time utility. This means that the value or usefulness of a good can be increased through storage. Transportation and storage are two of the functions which involve physical transfer of goods from producer to consumer.[1] Many manufacturers

---

[1] C. F. Phillips and D. J. Duncan, *Marketing Principles and Methods* (rev. ed.; Homewood, Ill.; Richard D. Irwin, Inc., 1952), p. 20.

spend much in the way of advertising and sales effort in order to place their product before the customer. However, it is necessary that the manufacturer's product be physically available to satisfy the demand for it which has been created. Warehousing can be of help in accomplishing this.

TYPES OF WAREHOUSING

There are two basic types of warehousing: *private* and *public*. The private warehouse is one which is operated by an individual company for the storage of its commodities or merchandise and involves the use of company-owned or company-leased warehouse facilities. A public warehouse can be defined as a place where a person is lawfully engaged in the business of storing goods for profit. The public warehouseman holds himself out to accept goods for storage, depending upon the type of facilities he possesses. Since storage is such an integral part of distributing goods, the public warehouse has become extensively used by buyers and sellers of goods.

The choice for individual companies between the two types of warehouses is a matter of evaluation to determine which will best satisfy individual requirements. In some of the different types of public warehouses, the availability of space is much greater than in others, which factor may influence the charges for such warehousing. Another factor a company considers in deciding whether to construct its own warehouse facilities is the tying-up of so much of its capital, which might be more usefully employed in some other phase of its operations. Since World War II, this factor has not been as important as it was previously, since it is sometimes possible for a business firm to arrange with financial organizations for the latter to buy the warehouse after it has been constructed by the business firm and lease it back to the company. Some companies feel that, for control purposes, all of their warehouses should be owned and operated by them.

In this respect, some products may be of such technical nature that they require such services as fitting, assembling, and finishing; or the volume of orders of certain lines of merchandise may be sufficiently high to justify a manufacturer in his maintenance of his own personnel in branch warehousing. However, many public warehouses will lease space to accommodate such situations, and the total cost to the manufacturer is usually less. As a rule, insurance rates are lower in public warehouses, the traffic facilities are geared to handling a volume of traffic, and the seasonal need for more space can be easily accommodated. A survey on the use of public warehouses by shipper companies made by the periodical, *Traffic World*, in 1957, gave some interesting information on the use of public warehouses. Of 2,391 shipper companies which indicated they used public warehouses, the average number used by each of these companies was 14.

The average number of states in which each of these companies used public warehouses was 9.

A large firm which processes food, as well as other products, at eight points in the United States, geographically serving large areas, still uses more than sixty public warehouses for distribution. There is also the experience of a manufacturer who was faced with continually rising costs in the operation of branch warehouses and changed to public warehousing. In the operation of one branch warehouse, this manufacturer had been paying $250 per month for rent, $8.00 for electricity, $20 for janitor service, and $10 for telephone service. This represented a total of $288 per month to operate the branch house. The public warehouses provided the same amount of space on a railroad siding at $86 per month, including heat, light, and janitor service. The manufacturer got the same amount of space and had less cartage cost, since the public warehouse was on a railroad siding, at a saving of $202 per month. Further, the insurance rate in the public warehouse was less than 30 cents per 100 pounds, whereas it had been $2.00 per 100 pounds in the branch house.

Many large food chains, on the other hand, have private warehouses that are strategically located close to the center of distribution areas to reduce the secondary transportation cost to a minimum. Over 4,000 items may be stored under controls that limit the amount of storage time on numerous items to a single day. The merchandise is stored according to the frequency of turnover with the most-used products conveniently located on main aisles. The trend has been toward single-story warehouses of the general merchandise type that may be spread over several acres.

A number of fully automated private warehouses are expected to be in operation by 1964. They will utilize a computer system that will direct operations involving storage and retrieval of palleted products and their automatic transfer to shipping docks. Cartons will be lifted onto pallets by suction cranes and moved by conveyor. The pallets will be assigned to a tier, stored, and retrieved by computer-directed stacker cranes.

It has often been pointed out that the public merchandise warehouse will perform all of the functions of a branch house except selling. Some of the additional services which they offer are repacking goods; listing a manufacturer's name in a telephone directory using the warehouse's telephone number, with the warehouse handling all calls for the manufacturer; sample and display rooms; stenciling; weighing; marking for redistribution; bottling; and cooperage, fumigation, and appliance delivery and installation.

The manufacturer who uses the public warehouse will ship a carload or truckload by sending, in advance of the shipment, a manifest which lists the contents of the shipment. The warehouseman checks the shipment upon arrival with the manifest. If there is any shortage or damage to the shipment, the warehouseman will furnish the manufacturer with the necessary claim papers. The contents of the shipment are placed in the warehouse with each marked brand or variety stored separately and in a space area as required by the nature of the product. Warehouse receipts are issued to the manufacturer, and a warehouse record is made for the goods stored.

Upon the sale of a commodity or product, the manufacturer or his sales representative issues an order which instructs the warehouseman to deliver to a jobber or a retailer a specified quantity. The order may be given to a jobber who will pick up the goods at the warehouse, or the warehouseman may make delivery to the store door. The manufacturer is notified of deliveries which are made and therefore can keep adequate stock moving to the warehouse.

If the manufacturer wants to do so, he can furnish the warehouseman with a list of the company's local and out-of-town customers. The warehouseman can then accept orders directly from the customers in quantities which are specified by the manufacturer for each of them. When the warehouseman fills these orders, he checks the quantities ordered with the amount authorized on the manufacturer's accredited list and then reports to the manufacturer all orders that have been filled, so that the latter may bill them.

Public warehouses are able to blend the fluctuating requirements of many manufacturers into a reasonably constant volume which permits maximum utilization of facilities. The manner in which this is accomplished is shown in Figure 22–1. Company A, in the illustration, would

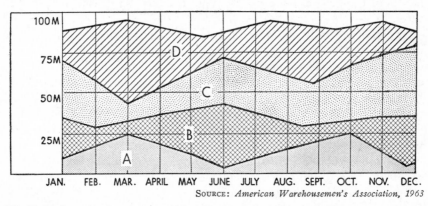

SOURCE: *American Warehousemen's Association, 1963*

FIG. 22–1. Example of manner in which public warehouses blend fluctuating requirements into reasonably constant volume.

need 25,000 square feet of storage space for March and October peaks; and during June, it would use less than 5,000 square feet. In June, Company B needs 37,500 square feet; in December, Company C uses 40,500 square feet; and in March, Company D uses 50,000 square feet. The public merchandise warehouseman can meet the needs of these demands with a plant of 100,000 square feet, whereas individually operated private warehouses of each company would require a total of 153,000 square feet to meet separate company peak requirements.[2]

Stock Location

The factors that ordinarily influence the layout of warehouse and stock location are similarity, popularity, size, and physical characteristics of the stored items. In the operation of the warehouse, the popularity or frequency of movement factor becomes most important. The fast moving items are located closest to the shipping area, slower moving items farther away, and the slowest moving items in the areas most remote from the shipping area.

In the past, observation has provided the principal means of determining the frequency of movement of items in a warehouse. When data-processing equipment is used for inventory control, however, information can be easily tabulated at regular intervals showing the frequency products in storage are called for. Comparative figures on the call frequency of fast-moving items can be developed that will show whether an item continues to be in as great demand from one audit period to the next. Since the frequency at which goods are moved changes, rewarehousing should be undertaken when data indicate that a change in location is justified.

The average time required to move stock from different locations to the shipping area can be checked. This enables a company to determine what the average cost is to move a unit such as a pallet load; and it can also show what the material-handling cost is to move from different zones. These cost data are most useful in connection with evaluation of the stock location.

Types of Public Warehouses

Because of the varied needs of commodities at different stages from production to ultimate consumption, a number of different types of warehouse facilities are needed. A classification of public warehouses has been made, based upon the type of operations performed.[3] These are: (1) general merchandise warehouses, (2) refrigerated warehouses, (3) special commodity warehouses, (4) bonded warehouses, (5) household goods and furniture warehouses, and (6) field warehouses. Some public warehouses offer a combination service in terms of types of operations, such as general merchandise warehouse facilities as well as refrigerated or bonded facilities, which may be operated as separate departments.

---

[2] American Warehousemen's Association, *The Modern Method of Distribution*, Chicago, 1963.

[3] See John H. Frederick, *Using Public Warehouses* (Philadelphia: Chilton Co., Inc., 1957).

General merchandise warehouses are facilities used by manufacturers or other shippers for storing merchandise until such time as it is needed by retailers, distributors, or ultimate consumers, which may be industrial organizations or the general public. Material or goods of many varieties, which are packaged or are readily handled and which do not require refrigeration or controlled humidities, are stored in this type of warehouse. A number of additional functions may be performed in this kind of warehouse, as was discussed earlier. A survey of the public general merchandise warehouses, undertaken by the Defense Transport Administration, showed that as of October, 1951, 80 per cent of the space available in this kind of warehouse was occupied, as compared to 74 per cent ten years earlier.[4] Also, 86 per cent of the public general merchandise warehouses are located in or within a radius of 25 miles of cities of 50,000 population.[5] This kind of warehouse is usually located in the center of the wholesale district.

In some states, a public merchandise warehouse must be licensed by the state before it can legally do business; and in fifteen states, a bond is required. In these states, the warehouseman files a bond or a warehouseman's legal liability insurance policy with a state agency, court, or other official, which protects the depositor of the goods in the event that the warehouseman defaults in meeting his liability as a warehouseman under law.

Refrigerated warehouses are used for the storage of perishable items. The widespread development of frozen foods has resulted in an increase in refrigerated space, although the increase is not necessarily in direct ratio to the increased production of frozen foods. The space in a refrigerated warehouse is divided according to the needs of the storing public. Generally, it is divided into two categories: (1) that which is above 29 to 50 degrees Fahrenheit, referred to as "cooler" space; and (2) freezer space, in which the temperature is below 29 degrees Fahrenheit. The freezer space which is maintained from 0 to 29 degrees Fahrenheit is termed "normal freezer," and "sharp freezer" is 0 degrees Fahrenheit and below. These temperatures may vary somewhat in different warehouses. As an example, shell eggs are considered as a "cooler" commodity but will be held at 29 degrees Fahrenheit or lower.[6]

The occupancy of "freezer" storage space in public refrigerated warehouses averaged 77 per cent in 1962; and in the same year, the average occupancy of "cooler" space in these public refrigerated warehouses was 63 per cent.[7] It is estimated that, in 1931, about 80 per cent of the total refrigerated warehouse space was "cooler" temperature and 20 per cent

    [4] Defense Transport Administration, *The Storage Picture* (Washington, D.C.: U.S. Government Printing Office, September, 1952), pp. 3, 4.
    [5] *Ibid.*
    [6] Defense Transport Administration, *Refrigerated Storage: A Look Ahead* (Washington, D.C.: U.S. Government Printing Office, May, 1953), p. 6.
    [7] Department of Agriculture, *Cold Storage Report*, Monthly.

"freezer," whereas today it is 20 per cent "cooler" and 80 per cent "freezer."[8]

The refrigerated warehouse is an excellent example of how seasonal production can be stored and released for year-round consumption. The frozen food aspect of refrigerated warehouses serves the consumer in allowing him to purchase, at any time during the year, in frozen status, foods which, in their fresh state, would be available to him only seasonally. For the producer or distributor, the opportunity is provided of storing foods when they are plentiful and placing them on the market at intervals instead of at one time, thus depressing the price.

Special commodity warehouses are widely used for storing agricultural commodities. Tobacco, cotton, grain, bulk liquids, peanuts, fertilizers, naval stores, and lumber are examples of products stored in this type of warehouse.

Bonded warehouses are ones which store commodities or merchandise for which they bond themselves to the U.S. Treasury to secure payment of certain import duties or internal revenue taxes, which must be paid before the goods are released. In addition to the storage function, the bonded warehouse makes possible the importation of goods and their storage in a bonded warehouse without payment of the import duty until such time as arrangements have been made for their sale and release from the bonded warehouse, at which time the import duty must be paid.

There are two types of bonded warehouses—United States Customs bonded warehouses and United States Internal Revenue bonded warehouses. The bond of either of these types of bonded warehouses assures the federal government that the goods will not be released from the warehouse until all the duties and taxes have been paid. In itself, the bond is not protection for the depositor of the goods.

Household goods warehouses are used for storing household furnishings, furniture, and personal effects of individuals. Three types of storage are provided in these warehouses: (1) open storage, where the goods are stored on the basis of a stated amount per cubic foot per month on the open floor of the warehouse; (2) container storage, in which a large container or box is used to pack the goods; and (3) private room or vault storage, in which a vault or private room of sufficient size to hold all of the storer's goods is used.

Some of the incidental services by such warehouses include packing and crating; repairing and cleaning furniture, rugs, and draperies; fur storage; and trucking and transfer service.

A *field warehouse* is one which stores, on the property of the owner, certain products under the custody of a bona fide public warehouse employee. The purpose of the so-called "field warehouse" is to broaden the credit of the storer of the goods. Inasmuch as, technically the goods are

---

[8] National Association of Refrigerated Warehouses.

under a public warehouseman, negotiable or nonnegotiable warehouse receipts can be issued to cover the products stored on the owner's premises. The owner possessing these receipts can use them in securing credit. Field warehousing arrangements are not generally of a permanent nature; for as soon as there is no longer a credit need, the arrangement will be discontinued. There may be as many as 9,000 or 10,000 field warehouses in the United States.[9]

Field warehousing services are usually available in connection with general merchandise warehouse companies. However, there are some companies which specialize in this particular type of warehousing. In effect, it is the conversion of private storage into a public warehouse primarily to accomplish credit; and therefore, most of the normal facilities provided by a public warehouseman are not necessary. Field warehouses are operated on premises usually leased by them from the owners of goods in their custody.

In field warehousing, the material subject to such warehousing is kept locked or guarded in some way. It is also posted to show that the property is in custody of the warehouse company. Field warehousing has been used for such diverse items as garden seeds, watch springs, steel, fuel oil, and canned goods. One of the factors in field warehousing that the traffic manager should point out is that such warehousing saves the expense of hauling to a public warehouse, as well as storage charges.

Where the demand for a product is seasonal but the product can be maintained the year around, field warehousing can help get production started before the seasonal orders are received. The benefits of a year-round staff and the fact that financing can be arranged enable the producer to take advantage of quantity discounts, as well as getting carload and truckload freight rates into his producing point due to the large-quantity purchases. Too, the manufacturer might desire to build up an inventory of raw materials, in order to plan production schedules in a more efficient manner. One distributor was offered a franchise which would double his yearly sales volume. However, it meant that he had to carry twice the inventory that had been the case formerly. By establishing a field warehouse, he could carry the required stock.[10]

THE UNIFORM WAREHOUSE RECEIPTS ACT

The Uniform Warehouse Receipts Act, enacted in all states, establishes the responsibilities of the public warehouseman as the custodian of the property of the public. Under the provisions of this act, uniformity of rules concerning the issuance of public warehouse receipts has been ac-

---

[9] "Field Warehousing Gets Popular," *Business Week*, August 9, 1952, p. 82.
[10] "A Warehouse in Your Own Plant," *Business Week*, December 11, 1948, p. 33.

complished, and the responsibilities for the storage and delivery of goods in the custody of the public warehouseman have been stipulated.

The Uniform Warehouse Receipts Act requires that the operator of a warehouse must be a bona fide warehouseman, which is defined as a person lawfully engaged in the business of storing goods for profit. He is a bailee for hire. The act further stipulates that a valid warehouse receipt can be issued only by a bona fide warehouseman.

Negotiable and Nonnegotiable Warehouse Receipts

There are two types of warehouse receipts defined in the Uniform Warehouse Receipts Act. A warehouse receipt in which it is stated that the commodities referred to thereon will be delivered to the depositor or to any other specified person or company is a nonnegotiable warehouse receipt. A warehouse receipt on which it is stated that the commodities will be delivered to the "bearer" or to the order of any specified person or company is a negotiable warehouse receipt.

There are standard forms of negotiable and nonnegotiable warehouse receipts. These forms were developed by the American Warehousemen's Association and the American Bankers Association. The Uniform Warehouse Receipts Act specified that each warehouse receipt must show: [11]

1. The location of the warehouse where the commodities are stored.
2. The date of issue of the warehouse receipt.
3. The consecutive number of the warehouse receipt.
4. A statement whether the commodities received will be delivered to the bearer, to a specified person, or to his order.
5. The rate of storage, which can be included by reference to the warehousing agreements between the depositor and the warehouseman.
6. The description of the commodities or of the packages containing them.
7. The signature of the warehouseman, which may be made by his authorized agent.
8. If the warehouse receipt is issued for commodities of which the warehouseman is owner, either solely or jointly or in common with others, the fact of such ownership.
9. A statement of the amount of advances made and of liabilities incurred for which the warehouseman claims a lien. If the precise amount of such advances or of such liabilities incurred is, at the time of the issuance of the warehouse receipt, unknown to the warehouseman or to his agent who issues it, a statement of the fact that advances have been made or liabilities incurred and the purpose thereof is sufficient and may be included on the warehouse receipt by reference to a warehousing agreement between the depositor of the commodities covered by such warehouse receipt and the warehouseman.

Figures 22–2 and 22–3 are samples of nonnegotiable and negotiable ware-

---

[11] American Warehousemen's Association, *Warehouse Receipts as Collateral*, 1945.

	NON-NEGOTIABLE WAREHOUSE RECEIPT			ORIGINAL
				CONSECUTIVE RECEIPT
	AMERICAN WAREHOUSE COMPANY			
	2121 AMERICAN AVENUE			
	AMERICA			·No. 3 4 6 2

THIS IS TO CERTIFY THAT WE HAVE RECEIVED FROM:	DATE	STORED IN WAREHOUSE	LOCATED AT
EX P. R. R. 562343	July 15, 1958	B	2125 American Ave.

FOR ACCOUNT OF

Evergreen Canning Company
Evergreen, U.S.A.

DEPOSITOR

LOT	SAID TO BE OR CONTAIN	WEIGHT	STORAGE RATE	DAMAGE AND EXCEPTIONS
5852	1000 cs. Early June Peas in tin - 24/#2-1/2's	58,000	.05 cs.	

The goods listed hereon were received in apparent good order, except as noted hereon (contents, condition and quality unknown) subject to all the terms and conditions contained herein and on the reverse hereof. such property to be delivered to the depositor upon the payment of all storage, handling and other charges.

Advances have been made and liability incurred on such goods as follows:

None

AMERICAN WAREHOUSE COMPANY claims a lien for all lawful charges for storage and preservation of the goods, also for all lawful claims for money advanced, interest, insurance, transportation, labor, weighing, coopering, and other charges and expenses, in relation to such goods.

The property covered by this receipt has NOT been insured by this Company for the benefit of the depositor against fire or any other casualty

AMERICAN WAREHOUSE COMPANY

By   A. JU.

No Delivery Will Be Made On This Receipt Except On Written Order

FIG. 22–2. An example of nonnegotiable warehouse receipt.

house receipts. If any of the preceding factors are omitted from a negotiable warehouse receipt, the warehouseman is liable for the omission. Figure 22–4 shows the standard terms and conditions on back of warehouse negotiable and nonnegotiable receipts.

A nonnegotiable warehouse receipt can be assigned to a second holder, and this is regularly done in the normal course of business, although the form of assignment may differ. The second holder of the nonnegotiable warehouse receipt, the assignee, should inform the warehouseman of the assignment of the nonnegotiable warehouse receipt to him. The person or company in whose favor the nonnegotiable warehouse receipt is assigned does not get any greater rights than the transferor had when the endorsement was made.

The negotiable warehouse receipt is similar to the other negotiable instruments, in that through endorsement, it can pass from one person to another. If it is issued to the order of "bearer," it may be passed, of course, without endorsement.

The merchandise covered by nonnegotiable warehouse receipts may be released upon written instructions to the warehouseman authorizing such release. Such releases are usually made out in ink or indelible pencil, or typewritten, in order to minimize forgery or alteration. Some warehousemen will accept oral release instructions in urgent situations, al-

			AMERICAN WAREHOUSE COMPANY					Consecutive No. 3 4 6 2				

AMERICAN WAREHOUSE COMPANY
2121 AMERICAN AVENUE
AMERICA

Consecutive No. 3 4 6 2

Date of Issue July 15, 1958

THIS IS TO CERTIFY that we have received in Storage Warehouse __B__ situated at 2125 American Ave.

for the account of __Evergreen Canning Company, Evergreen, U.S.A.__

in apparent good order, except as noted hereon (contents, condition and quality unknown) the following described property, subject to all the terms and conditions contained herein and on the reverse hereof, such property to be delivered to x̶̶ order, upon payment of all storage, handling and other charges and the surrender of this Warehouse Receipt properly endorsed.

LOT NO.	QUANTITY	SAID TO BE OR CONTAIN	EX CAR NO. INITIAL	STORAGE PER MONTH		HANDLING IN AND OUT	
				RATE	PER	RATE	PER
5852	1000 cs.	Early June Peas in tins 24/#2-1/2's Evergreen Brand	P.R.R. 562343	.05	cs.	.14	cs.

NEGOTIABLE

This Receipt is Valid Only When Signed by an Officer of the Company.

Advances have been made and liability incurred on such goods, as follows
None

American Warehouse Company claims a lien for all lawful charges for storage and preservation of the goods, also for all lawful claims for money advanced, interest, insurance, transportation, labor, weighing, coopering and other charges and expenses in relation to such goods.

The property covered by this receipt has NOT been insured by this company for the benefit of the depositor against fire or any other casualty.

AMERICAN WAREHOUSE COMPANY
By Richard Roe   Secretary

FIG. 22–3. An example of a negotiable warehouse receipt.

though the warehousemen prefer that there be a written order for warehouse release. In order that delivery instructions be effective, negotiable warehouse receipts must be surrendered if the total amount of merchandise covered thereby is being released, or they must be surrendered for endorsement of the amount for delivery if only a portion of the merchandise is taken out of the warehouse.

The Uniform Warehouse Receipts Act provides that, except where goods have been lawfully sold to satisfy a warehouseman's lien and charges, where a warehouseman delivers goods for which he had issued a negotiable warehouse receipt and he fails to take up and cancel the receipt, or where he delivers part of the goods and fails to take up and mark plainly upon the negotiable receipt a statement of the goods or packages before delivered, he is liable to anyone who purchases such receipt for value in good faith if he should fail to deliver the goods to such purchaser. For example, a warehouseman may issue a negotiable warehouse receipt for 500 bags of sugar. Upon the request of the storer, the warehouseman may deliver 250 bags but fail to endorse the delivery upon the receipt. The storer, without notice of this fact, sells or negotiates the receipt to a purchaser who has no knowledge of the facts, in which case the purchaser may claim the full amount of the negotiable receipt, 500 bags. The fact that the 250 bags were delivered by the warehouseman in good faith to the original holder is meaningless in so far as the rights of the purchaser are concerned. On the other hand, the assignee of a nonnegotiable warehouse receipt would have no such rights against the warehouseman in a like situation.

Where warehouse receipts are used for credit or financing, the banks or financial institutions usually prefer nonnegotiable warehouse receipts.[12]

TENDER FOR STORAGE—Sec. 1. (a) All goods for storage shall be delivered at the warehouse properly marked and packed for handling. The storer shall furnish at or prior to such delivery, a manifest showing marks, brands or sizes to be kept and accounted for separately and the class of storage desired; otherwise the goods may be stored in bulk or assorted lots, in freezer, cooler or general storage at the discretion of the warehouseman and will be charged for accordingly.

(b) The word "lot" as used herein means the unit or units of goods for which a separate account is to be kept by the warehouseman. Delivery of all or any units of a lot shall be made without subsequent sorting except by special arrangement and subject to a charge.

(c) The warehouseman undertakes to store and deliver goods only in the packages in which they are originally received.

STORAGE PERIOD—Sec. 2. (a) All goods are stored on a month to month basis, unless otherwise provided. A storage month shall extend from a date in one calendar month to, but not including, the same date of the next and all succeeding calendar months, but if there be no corresponding date in the next succeeding calendar month it shall extend to and include the last day of that month. When the last day of a final storage month falls on Sunday or a legal holiday, the storage month shall be deemed to expire on the next succeeding business day.

(b) Except where other procedure is provided by the warehouse receipts act, the warehouseman may, upon written notice to the storer of record and to any other person known by the warehouseman to claim an interest in the goods, require the removal of any goods by the end of the next succeeding storage month. Such notice shall be given by delivery in person or by registered letter addressed to the last known place of business or abode of the person to be notified.

INSURANCE, STORAGE RATES, EXPIRATION AND TRANSFERS — Sec. 3. (a) All charges for storage are on a month to month basis unless otherwise provided. Charges for any particular lot shall begin at the receipt of the first unit of that particular lot in store and shall continue and include the storage month during which the last unit of the particular lot is delivered. Charges shall be made on the basis of the maximum number of units in any particular lot in store during a storage month. All charges for storage are due on the first day of a storage month and all other charges are due when incurred.

(b) Instructions to transfer goods on the books of the warehouseman are not effective until delivered to and accepted by him, and all charges up to the time transfer is made are chargeable to the storer of record. If a transfer involves rehandling the goods, it will be subject to a charge.

(c) The warehouseman reserves the right to move, at his own expense of transfer, and upon notice sent by registered mail to the storer of record and to the last known holder of the negotiable warehouse receipt, any goods in storage from any room of the warehouse in which they may be stored to any other of his rooms or warehouses; but if such storer or holder takes delivery of his goods in lieu of transfer, no storage charges shall be made for the current storage month.

(d) When rates are quoted by weight they will, unless otherwise specified, be computed on gross weight and 2,000 pounds shall constitute a ton.

(e) Goods are not insured nor do storage rates include insurance unless so specified in writing. (Adopted with the understanding that in any state requiring insurance by statute the words "or required by statute" would be considered a part of the standard terms and conditions.)

HANDLING—Sec. 4. (a) Handling charges cover the ordinary labor and duties incidental to receiving goods at warehouse door, stowing and delivering to warehouse door, but do not include unloading or loading of cars, vehicles or vessels, unless so specified. Handling charges will be billed with the storage for the first month.

(b) Goods, at the request of a storer, received or delivered during other than usual business hours will be subject to an additional charge.

CAR UNLOADING AND LOADING—Sec. 5. (a) Charges for unloading or loading of cars include use of switch track, labor required to or from warehouse door, and billing of car.

FIG. 22–4. Standard terms and conditions on back of warehouse receipt.

[12] Robert L. Gordon, "The Issuance and Use of Non-negotiable and Negotiable Warehouse Receipts," before the 26th Annual Meeting of the American Warehousemen's Association, 1947.

(b) Dunnage and fastenings supplied by the warehouseman and used in loading out cars are chargeable to the storer.

(c) Any additional costs incurred by the warehouseman in unloading cars containing damaged goods are chargeable to the storer.

(d) The warehouseman, unless he has failed to exercise due care and diligence, shall not be responsible for demurrage, nor for delays in unloading inbound cars, nor for delays in obtaining cars for outbound shipments.

DELIVERY REQUIREMENTS—Sec. 6. (a) No goods shall be delivered or transferred except upon receipt by the warehouseman of complete instructions properly signed by the storer.

(b) When a negotiable receipt has been issued no goods covered by that receipt shall be delivered, or transferred on the books of the warehouseman, unless the receipt, properly indorsed, is surrendered for cancellation, or for indorsement of partial delivery thereon.

(c) When goods are ordered out, a reasonable time shall be given the warehouseman to carry out instructions, and if he is unable, due to causes beyond his control, to effect delivery before expiring storage dates, the goods will be subject to charges for another storage month; except when the warehouseman has given notice in accordance with the provisions of Sec. 2b, or because of fire, acts of God, war, public enemies, seizure under legal process, strikes, or lockouts, riots and civil commotions, if he is unable, due to causes beyond his control to effect delivery before the expiring storage date, the goods shall be subject to storage charges only for that part of the month during which the goods remain in store.

BONDED STORES—Sec. 7. A charge in addition to regular rates will be made for merchandise in bond.

MINIMUM CHARGES—Sec. 8. A minimum charge will be assessed for storage, handling and other services.

EXTRA SERVICE—Sec. 9. (a) Extra services in the interest of the storer, such as special warehouse space, material, drayage, repairing, coopering, sampling, weighing, repiling, inspection, physical warehouse checking, compiling stock statements, collections, revenue stamps, reporting marked weights or numbers, handling railroad expense bills, etc., are chargeable to the storer.

(b) Stock statements submitted in duplicate by the storer will be checked with the books of the warehouseman without charge.

(c) Shipping includes marking, tagging, billing, procuring and forwarding bills of lading and is chargeable to the storer.

(d) Freight and other disbursements made on behalf of the storer are due and payable on demand and subject to interest from date billed by the warehouseman.

(e) Storers, including holders of negotiable receipts, may, subject to insurance regulations and reasonable limitations, have access to their goods in store when accompanied by a warehouse employee whose time is chargeable to the storer.

LIABILITY—Sec. 10. (a) The responsibility of a warehouseman, in the absence of written provisions, is the reasonable care and diligence required by law.

(b) Perishable goods, or goods which are susceptible to damage through temperature changes or other causes incident to general storage, are accepted in general storage only at owner's risk for such damages as might result from general storage conditions.

(c) When no declaration of values is declared on merchandise when entering storage the warehouseman's liability shall be based at 500 times the base storage rate, not to exceed $50.00 for any one item.

SCHEDULE OF CHARGES—Sec. 11. Whenever provision is made in these Standard Contract Terms and Conditions for a charge or charges by the warehouseman such charge or charges will conform to the warehouseman's tariff in effect at the time the charge accrues or the service is performed, except that no increase in charges within the direct control of the warehouseman will be made on goods that are in storage without a thirty-day notice mailed to the storer of record or the last known holder of a negotiable warehouse receipt.

FIG. 22-4—Continued.

LICENSING OF WAREHOUSES

The United States Warehouse Act was passed in 1916 and provides for the licensing of warehouses for the storage of certain agricultural products. The public warehouses which can be licensed under this act are regularly inspected by the United States Department of Agriculture. Such inspection was felt to be a means by which it would be easier to secure loans on those receipts issued by federally licensed warehouses. However, the mere licensing of a warehouse or the issuance of a warehouse receipt under the United States Warehouse Act, or a state warehouse act,[13] does not guarantee the validity of the licensed warehouse receipt. Only a bona fide warehouseman can issue a valid warehouse receipt. Since licenses under the United States Warehouse Act are issued only for the storage of basic agricultural products, generally in connection with bulk storage near the point of production, few public merchandise warehousemen have occasion to be bonded and licensed under that act.

WAREHOUSE SERVICES

"Spot Stocks"

Through public merchandise warehousing, there has been created the widespread adoption of the use of "spot stocks" by manufacturers. Spot stocks are the locating of stock supplies in numerous market areas, so that a customer's order can be filled immediately. Spot stocking is used particularly in connection with the sale of "convenience goods," which are referred to in marketing as consumers' goods, purchased in the most convenient store with a minimum of effort and include such items as groceries and drugstore products. Since, in this category of goods, it is very important to place the products in as many stores as possible, a manufacturer usually finds it advantageous to carry spot stocks in public merchandise warehouses in addition to his own warehouses. The manufacturer can ship a carload or truckload at the carload or truckload rate to the public warehouse and have the warehouseman fill the orders for small quantities from the many stores which stock his product.

There are a number of advantages of this type of stocking:

1. It is a means by which products can be stocked at all times.
2. The orders of the majority of the retail outlets would take only less-carload and less-truckload quantities if filled from limited branch houses of the manufacturer. The difference between the higher freight rates which apply on these smaller quantities and the lower carload or truckload rate usually more than covers the cost of warehousing.
3. With the trend toward "hand-to-mouth" buying, many retailers order only by the dozen or fraction of a dozen instead of by the gross, as was formerly the case; and a manufacturer who does not make arrangements for spot stocks may lose orders.
4. The manufacturer who supplies his retailers through spot stocks is able to make immediate deliveries to his customers and thereby be assured that his product is before the buying public. Sales and advertising efforts are wasted if consumers are not able to buy a product when they want it.

The Corn Products Sales Company was reported as carrying spot stocks in 44 of the 48 states, in 230 different public warehouses. These were in addition to its own warehouses.[14]

---

[13] Some states have a warehouse act similar to the United States Warehouse Act.
[14] Corporation Trust Co., *More Sales with Spot Stocks* (New York, 1947), p. 3.

Many items which are not convenience goods are also handled in spot stocks. One of the manufacturers of kitchen cookstoves has maintained spot stocks in warehouses for many years. The experience of this manufacturer has been that if he is not able to take care of the demand as it arises, he loses business.[15] A great factor in reducing sales resistance is the ability to beat a competitor by quicker delivery after the sale.

In a public merchandise warehouse, the manufacturer pays only for the space he uses, whether it is for 100 cases or 1,000 cases. In general, 100 small warehouse stocks in different localities will cost approximately the same for storage and handling as 12 large stocks.

Some manufacturers, in addition to carrying spot stocks to increase and maintain sales volume, look upon spot stocks as a partial hedge against an unexpected contingency, such as a fire at the factory or a work stoppage.

Handling of Pool-Car Shipments

Due to selling methods or the perishable nature of commodities, a manufacturer may not maintain stock at numerous distributing points. In this case, he may combine shipments of a number of his customers in an urban area into pool cars or pool trucks, thereby securing a carload or truckload rate considerably lower than the less-carload or less-truckload rate which would apply if the shipments went from the factory to each individual customer.

Many public warehousemen have delivery equipment for making local deliveries, so the manufacturers will consign the pool car or pool truck to a public warehouseman, who will distribute the contents. Where the manufacturer's customers pay the freight, the warehouseman collects the prorata carload or truckload charges from them. The public warehouseman, then, may handle pool-car or pool-truck shipments, just as do many local cartage companies.

Distribution-Center Public Warehousing and Storage in Transit

One of the recent developments in public warehousing has been the move toward distribution-center warehousing. This involves the setting-up of large transit warehouse stores of from 50 to 500 carloads of a manufacturer's complete line of products at key points. The distribution-center warehouse systems use from 1 to 15 warehouse locations throughout the United States. Some public warehouses have been designed to serve food manufacturers. They perform the service of consolidating less-carload or less-truckload orders, as they are received from manufacturers and their sales representatives, into solid carloads or truckloads going directly to one customer. This has reduced transportation cost and has brought about a faster turnover of stock. The consolidation service is available only to those manufacturers which carry an inventory in the warehouse and is

---

[15] *Ibid.*

governed by individual conditions established by each participating manufacturer. Some of the distribution-center warehouses reship outbound more carload and truckload freight than LTL and LCL freight.

Public warehouses may be the point at which the storage-in-transit privilege is granted. Although this privilege has been limited in its application for commercial shippers, it has been granted more extensively on certain military items.

Distribution-center public warehouses also sponsor a transit tariff which meets the special requirements of the food industry. The storage-in-transit privilege operates in the usual manner; but in addition, the warehouse acting as the food manufacturer's agent can combine less-carload quantities of his merchandise in pooled cars and still retain the transit privilege on the less-carload quantities. This transit privilege permits both transit and nontransit items to be pooled. Under this plan, the manufacturer can take advantage of the carload or truckload freight rate, not from the distribution-center warehouse location but from the original producing plant or plants. Furthermore, as shown in Figure 22–5, the through

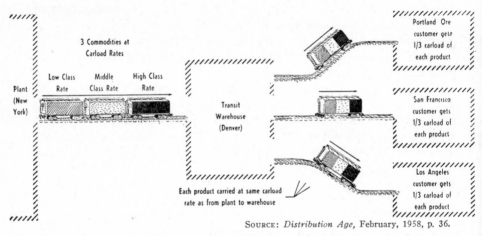

Source: *Distribution Age*, February, 1958, p. 36.

FIG. 22–5. Sample of storage in transit, with the public warehouse acting as the food manufacturer's agent.

freight rate applies on each commodity classification and not on a mixed-carload rating, which would be higher.[16]

RATES AND CHARGES

Warehouse charges are largely a matter between the warehouseman and the customer. Although all public warehousemen have schedules of charges, they may vary and are not usually open to the public. A rate

---

[16] "Transiting—Revolution in Warehousing," *Distribution Age*, February, 1958, p. 36.

STANDARD CONTRACT TERMS AND CONDITIONS.

GENERAL.

Section 2. STORAGE PERIOD.—(a) All goods are stored on a month-to-month basis, unless otherwise provided. A storage month shall extend from a date in one calendar month to, but not including, the same date of the next and all succeeding calendar months, but if there be no corresponding date in the next succeeding calendar month, it shall extend to and include the last day of that month. When the last day of a final storage month falls on Sunday or a legal holiday, the storage month shall be deemed to expire on the next succeeding business day.

(b) Except where other procedure is provided by the warehouse receipts act, the warehouseman may, upon written notice to the storer of record and to any other person known by the warehouseman to claim an interest in the goods, require the removal of any goods by the end of the next succeeding month. Such notice shall be given by delivery in person or by registered letter addressed to the last known place of business or abode of the person to be notified.

Section 9. EXTRA SERVICE.—(a) Extra services in the interest of the storer, such as special warehouse space, material, drayage, repairing, coopering, sampling, weighing, repiling, inspection, physical warehouse checking, compiling stock statements, collections, revenue stamps, reporting marked weights or numbers, handling railroad expense bills, etc., are chargeable to the storer.

(b) Stock statements submitted in duplicate by the storer will be checked with the books of the warehouseman without charge.

(c) Shipping includes marking, tagging, billing, procuring, and forwarding bills of lading, and is chargeable to the storer.

(d) Freight and other disbursements made on behalf of the storer are due and payable on demand and subject to interest from date billed by the warehouseman.

(e) Storers, including holders of negotiable receipts, may, subject to insurance regulations and reasonable limitations, have access to their goods in store when accompanied by a warehouse employee whose time is chargeable to the storer.

RULES COVERING CHARGES.

RULE 1.—STORAGE

A—Unless otherwise specified and agreed to in advance of receipt of goods, the rates of storage cover a period of one month or fraction thereof, dating from the arrival of the first lot or package, and apply from that date to, but not including the same date of the following month, but if there is no corresponding date in the final storage month, it shall extend to and include the last day of that month.

If the last day of final storage month falls on Saturday, Sunday or a legal holiday, the next succeeding work-day will be the expiration date.

B—Provided that when specified and agreed to in advance of receipt of goods, in which case Rule 2-A will not apply, Storage rates may be prorated on the following basis:

Actual number of days from the date received to the last day of the current calendar month or an agreed monthly date. Prorating will not be agreed to except in cases where accumulative stock is carried in these warehouses and then only for the purpose of simplicity of billing or accounting.

A full month storage charge to be made on the balance on hand on the last day of the current calendar month, or the agreed monthly date.

C—At option of the warehouse, the following method of billing storage charges may be arranged in advance of the receipt of the goods.

On goods arriving from the 1st to the 15th of the month, there shall be charged a full calendar month's storage. On goods arriving from the 16th to the last day of the month, there shall be made a charge of only one-half month's storage. Recurring storage charges shall be due on the balance of stock in the warehouse on the 1st day of the next calendar month, and the 1st day of each calendar month thereafter.

D—Minimum charges provided for in Rule No. 19 will apply on the first month, on all goods handled under Rule 1-C. The unit storage rate will apply on all such goods on hand on the first of each succeeding calendar month thereafter, if one charge is made for the total.

If required by the storer to retain identity of each lot of goods in the warehouse, or to show each lot, mark, etc., separately on the bill, the regular minimum charges shown in Rule 19 will apply.

RULE 29.—HIGHER CLASSIFICATION FOR DENSITY, ETC.

When, because of conditions other than density, a commodity is classified higher in Cols. 6 and 8 of the Commodity Section of this Tariff, than the density in Col. 5 indicates it should be classified, and it is offered in other densities, it is to be advanced the same number of classes in the tables referred to in Cols. 10 and 11.

RULE 30.—CLASSIFICATION.

A—Classifications in this tariff are based on a piling height of 8½ feet, or a floorload of 250 pounds per square foot.

B—If the commodity, because of the nature of the package, or for any other reason, cannot be piled to those limits, rates will be advanced according to the classification and pile heights in Table No. 3. See also Rule 26-D.

FIG. 22–6. Portions of a typical warehouse schedule.

quotation is usually furnished by the warehouseman in response to a rate inquiry. The American Warehousemen's Association has devised a standard rate quotation form which is widely used. Such a form has the advantages of avoiding later disputes as to rates and liability, and simplifies the settlement of claims; it is a contract, if accepted, between the parties, and is a complete definition of the services to be performed. In California, Minnesota, and Washington, warehousemen are subject to regulation by the Public Utilities Commissions of those states. Therefore, in these states, the warehouseman's tariffs containing rates and rules are on file, are open to the public, and have a legal status like the tariffs of rail and motor carriers.

Storage charges are usually on a per-package or per-hundredweight basis. Most warehousemen base their storage charges on the "standard

PACKAGE RATES.

COMMODITIES.	Kind of Package.	Note.	(3) C. W.	Storage Per Case.	Handling. (1) Per Case. 5 and less separations.	Handling. (2) Per Case. 6 to 10 separations.
Canned Goods................	Cases, Cartons.					
Fish: In Tin................. Meats: In Tin...............		{Storage Class B. {Handling Rule 8.				
Milk: Condensed: In Tin—						
24 Tall..................			28	1.2¢	3.8¢	4.3¢
48 Baby.................			24	1.0	3.2	3.7
48 Tall..................			52	2.0	7.0	8.1

Handling (1) covers 5 and less separations.
Handling (2) covers 6 to 10 separations.
Separations in excess of ten (10) will be charged for at 25 cents per separation.

SERVICES, Canned Goods—
 Labeling
 Stripping
 Overhauling
 Cleaning
 Transferring to new cartons.
 Gluing
 Branding
 Opening
 and other similar service— LABOR—See Rule 13 (Extra Services)
 MATERIAL—at cost plus 10%.

(3)
C.W. —Computing Weight.

The average or fixed weight for computing the rate shown. The weight which is always used regardless of the weight of the package. This is seldom the actual weight of a particular package.

FIG. 22–6—Continued.

stack"—a column 1 foot square at the base and 7¼ feet high, weighing 250 pounds—regardless of the ceiling heights or floor loads of the warehouse.

Some factors considered in determining storage charges are: the type of package; the weight and density of the item; value of the commodity and the services required; fragility, susceptibility to damage; volume of business; the need for protective services; difficulty of handling because of hazardous nature; and piling requirements which may cause the loss of space.

The most common charges are for storage and handling. Sometimes a third charge is used which is an accessorial charge. The latter includes the services beyond the normal storage and handling.

Rate quotations often contain reference to the liability of the warehouseman. Some forms state the liability shall in no case exceed 500 times the base storage rate, unless an excess value is declared by the storer at the time the goods are stored, in which case there will be a charge for two tenths of 1 per cent per month on the excess valuation in addition to the base storage rates. Some rate quotations contain no reference to liability. The schedules of warehousemen will contain a rule or section dealing with liability.

Some portions of a typical warehouse schedule are given in Figure 22–6.

CO-OPERATION BETWEEN TRAFFIC MANAGERS AND PUBLIC WAREHOUSEMEN

Co-operation between traffic managers and public warehousemen can be beneficial to both. An example of the close co-operation between the traffic manager and a public warehouseman which resulted in a reduction in rates by the warehouseman, thus reducing the manufacturer's distribution cost and improving the service, has recently been pointed out. A public warehouseman was furnished a list of every customer in the delivery area served by his trucks. The warehouseman numbered each of the customers in the rotation in which he desired to have such orders loaded at the factory in the rail car or truck which would carry the goods to him. As the plant received orders for the customers, they were consolidated into truckload or carload quantities, with all orders filled in numerical sequence according to the code numbers which the warehouseman had assigned and loaded accordingly into the vehicle. A night letter was then dispatched, indicating that a movement was en route which contained orders for Numbers 1, 10, 25, 60, 400, and so on. By referring to his code, the warehouseman could plan the routing of his local delivery trucks, since he knew that a truckload would be on hand at his receiving dock at a certain predetermined time. This made it possible for his delivery trucks to take the merchandise directly into those trucks without the need for unloading the various orders onto the receiving dock and then later reloading them into his delivery trucks.

CASE

The Apex Foods Company, located in western New York State, has manufactured canned goods in the grocery field for the past fifteen years. Although the firm first began operations on a small scale, they have now expanded and become a relatively large producer in this field. Originally Apex had two distinct markets for their products. Their major market had consisted of sales of unbranded canned goods to large grocery chains. The foods were canned at the factory, however, and then branded with the chains' desired labels and shipped by motor common carrier to the various retail outlets. This market for unbranded products originally constituted approximately 70 per cent of the company's dollar sales volume. Their other market consisted of sales of branded canned goods which were shipped to a number of smaller independent retailers.

Company sales were concentrated mainly in the northeast for some time. After several years the firm really began to grow and their branded goods began to earn a name for itself. When sales of Apex canned goods began to surpass unbranded sales volume, Apex ceased marketing unbranded canned goods entirely in 1954.

Other significant changes had also taken place. The firm's market area expanded, rapidly, creating significant distribution problems. Jack Nelson, the firm's industrial traffic manager, made several extensive studies in 1954 to examine the feasibility of establishing warehouses in several of their heavily concentrated market areas. He found that this would result in substantially lower total distribution costs to the company. Consequently, three warehouses were constructed and put into operation in 1955. These were located in Boston, New York City, and Pittsburgh.

Both public and private warehousing costs had been examined by Mr. Nelson, but he concluded that the cost of operating private warehouses would be cheaper in the long run than using public warehouse facilities. Public warehouse estimates were $1.20 per square foot, on an annual basis. (Nelson estimated that the company stored 50 pounds per square foot.)

In the following years transportation costs were greatly reduced, and the entire distribution system functioned much more efficiently. The salesmen immediately seized upon this warehousing idea as a tremendous aid to their sales appeal. If warehouses could be established and operated near their major market areas, they could effectively compete with the dealer serviced by larger nationwide manufacturers. Not only could the company's ability to meet specific service requirements be stressed, but also if retail customers could be assured of quicker delivery they could carry a larger variety of the company's products while keeping their inventories at the same level, and reordering their "popular sellers" more often. So the salesmen began pushing for the establishment of additional warehousing facilities each time they built up an existing area or opened a new sales territory.

Management was quite pleased with the relative success of their three pilot warehousing operations and were willing to go along with the salesmen when the sales in any given area appeared to warrant the establishment of warehouse facilities.

As a result of the company's new distribution policies, their warehousing system was not well planned nor controlled. There was no logical pattern to the development of their warehousing network. Warehouses were built and operated after the salesmen had put sufficient pressure upon management—without the aid of any cost analysis to establish the actual cost feasibility of their existence.

At a Board of Directors meeting in early 1960 the company's growth in size and sales volume was discussed at great length, but the question arose as to why profits had not risen proportionately. Top management was also concerned about the fact that such a large amount of capital was tied up in warehousing facilities. As a result of their discussion, a decision was made to discontinue the practice of establishing additional warehousing operations. For some time the distribution problem was again forgotten, and the company focused its attention upon new product development. But then as additional marketing areas were developed at greater distances from the Apex plant and existing sales areas, several salesmen began receiving numerous complaints that transit time was excessive, and dealer service requirements were not being met in many of the newer sales territories.

Consequently, a three-man committee, composed of the department heads of the Traffic, Sales, and Economic Research departments, was appointed to make a detailed analysis of the company's present distribution network.

An examination of the present distribution system yielded the following results:

EXHIBIT 1

Warehouse Location	Monthly Sales Volume (lbs.)
Boston	5,500,000
Albany	2,000,000
New York	4,000,000
Baltimore	3,500,000
Philadelphia	2,000,000
Pittsburgh	3,500,000
Cleveland	2,500,000
Cincinnati	3,000,000
Memphis	4,000,000
Proposed warehouse—Atlanta	5,500,000

The average inventory turnover has consistently run twelve times per year at all of the warehouses. Sales have been fairly regular throughout the year, so all of the warehouses were built to accommodate a one-month inventory plus a small reserve for any demand fluctuations which might occur. All of the existing warehouses were constructed to handle a 6,000,000 pound inventory, so each warehouse presently has a 120,000 square foot capacity.

Mr. Ferris, the firm's chief cost accountant, was called in by the committee to make a detailed cost estimate of the warehouse operations presently being conducted, plus an estimate of the proposed Atlanta warehouse. The results of Mr. Ferris' analysis are shown in Exhibit 2.

EXHIBIT 2

Interest and insurance on inventory	$ 1,000
Taxes	500
Manual labor	30,000
Administrative and clerical expense	20,000
Material-handling equipment depreciation	3,000
Building depreciation	8,000
Utilities	3,500
	$66,000

EXHIBIT 3

Location	Rate per Cwt		Local Cartage	Total Transportation Expense		Warehousing Express	
	L/TL	T/L		L/TL	T/L	Public	Private
Boston	86¢	52¢	$34,320	$567,600	$343,200	$132,000	$84,150
Albany	74	44	10,560	177,600	105,600	48,000	72,600
New York..........	74	44	21,120	355,200	211,200	96,000	79,200
Baltimore–Washington	76	46	19,320	319,200	193,200	84,000	77,550
Philadelphia	78	42	10,800	187,200	100,800	48,000	72,600
Pittsburgh	86	52	21,840	361,200	218,400	84,000	77,550
Cleveland	70	42	12,600	210,000	126,000	60,000	74,250
Cincinnati	74	44	15,840	266,400	158,400	72,000	75,900
Memphis	90	54	25,920	432,000	259,200	96,000	79,200
Atlanta (proposed) ...	90	54	35,640	59,400	356,400	132,000	84,150

This estimate, according to Mr. Ferris, was based on an average inventory of 2,000,000 pounds, but he further noted that 90 per cent of these costs were fixed while 10 per cent varied with the volume handled. All of the firm's warehouse operation costs were approximately the same regardless of their location, and it was felt by the committee that this cost estimate would also hold for any new warehouses which might be built and put into operation in the future.

Mr. Nelson made a detailed cost analysis of the transportation savings which resulted from the use of the present warehouses and for the proposed Atlanta warehouse shown in Exhibit 3.

However, it was decided by the committee that regardless of any changes which might be suggested in the distribution network, customer service requirements of forty-eight-hour delivery must be met.

1. Of those warehouses presently in operation, are each of these economically practical? Which, if any, should be eliminated?

2. Should the proposed warehouse in Atlanta be constructed?

3. How might the company's distribution network be revised for better efficiency of operation? Could dealer service requirements still be met?

4. Are there any other relevant factors?

DISCUSSION QUESTIONS AND PROBLEMS

1. Of what importance is warehousing to the traffic manager?

2. What are the two basic types of warehousing? List some of the factors which should be considered in choosing between the two.

3. In addition to the physical storing of goods, a public warehouse may perform many additional functions. List a number of these functions.

4. Assume that you are using all the services which it is possible for a public warehouse to offer in the distribution of a shipment. Describe the procedure followed by the warehouseman from the time he receives the shipment and checks it with the manifest previously supplied by you.

5. List the various types of public warehouses. Describe each type briefly. What particular advantages are there to field warehousing?

6. The Uniform Warehouse Receipts Act establishes the responsibilities of the public warehouseman as the custodian of the property of the public. What are some of the provisions of this act?

7. There are standard forms of negotiable and nonnegotiable warehouse receipts. List the items which must be contained in a standard warehouse receipt.

8. Examine Figures 22–2 and 22–3. What difference or differences do you find between a nonnegotiable and a negotiable warehouse receipt?

9. What is "spot stocking"? How is it used, and what are its advantages?

10. In what manner may pool-car shipments be used in conjunction with a public warehouseman?

11. Ascertain and explain any similarities or differences between carrier rates and charges and those of public warehouses.

Chapter

23

LOCATIONAL FACTORS

W<small>HEN</small> adequate transportation facilities were lacking, our markets were local, with each community being self-sufficient. With the growth of transportation, there developed an exchange of many commodities and a territorial division of labor until, today, modern transportation has made the United States a highly specialized free-trade area. Large-scale production, like the division of labor, depends upon the extent of the market, which is influenced in part by the efficiency of transportation. Although the market may expand through growth in the population of a given locality, the tendency has been toward its expansion in a territorial sense.

Industries have been classified as market-oriented, material-oriented, or attracted to intermediate locations.[1] An example of a market-oriented industry is the bakery, and the turpentine industry is an example of a raw-material-oriented industry. The intermediate location industries, sometimes referred to as "weight balancing" industries, are exemplified by the manufacturing of livestock feeds in which in-transit rates are important.

One expert has indicated that the location of a manufacturing industry depends primarily upon transfer costs, which are basically transportation costs. Such an industry will seek to locate at a point where its total transfer costs can be minimized, other things being equal. The advantage which analysis of transfer costs offers is that they are easily quantified.

One study of plant location came to the following conclusions:[2]

1. When firms sell to a given buying point, they seek the least-cost location in reference to this consumption center and ignore the locations of rivals in their plant sites.
2. When firms sell over a market area, their site-selections are influenced greatly by the location of rivals.
3. In selecting a plant site each firm seeks that place which offers the optimum sales output at a cost that cannot be matched elsewhere.

---

[1] Edgar M. Hoover, *The Location of Economic Activity* (New York: McGraw-Hill Book Co., Inc., 1948), chap. iii.

[2] Melvin L. Greenhut, *Plant Location in Theory and in Practice* (Chapel Hill, N.C.: University of North Carolina Press, 1956), pp. 268–69.

4. When firms sell over a market area the force of concentration is greater in the event of unequal costs at alternative locations than in the case of equal costs at all sites.

5. When firms sell over a market area, the tendency to disperse depends upon the height of freight cost, the elasticity of the demand function, the characteristics (slopes) of the marginal costs, the degree of competition in location, the degree of competition from substitutable products at the various locations, and the homogeneity or heterogeneity of the firms belonging to the industry.

According to this study, these five tendencies are sometimes distorted by imperfections in the market, such as delivery time, personal contacts, custom, and different types of discriminatory pricing.

Through the promotion of the division of labor and large-scale production, transportation is a factor in the determination of the extent to which industry is concentrated. Since the choice of an industrial site logically involves a balancing of costs, of which transportation rates are an element, transportation influences the location of industry. Changes in transportation rates may, therefore, cause the relocation of industry.

PRINCIPAL FACTORS

Some of the principal locational factors are markets, sources of raw materials, power, labor, and transportation. An examination of these typical locational factors will reveal that even they are to a considerable degree actually products of transportation. Thus, metropolitan cities, such as New York, Chicago, and Los Angeles—which themselves constitute large and important markets and, therefore, desirable sites for many industries—owe their existence largely to transportation.

One of the least understood of the various locational factors is the transportation factor. The importance of this factor will vary in the different types of economic activity which may be classified as agricultural, extractive, manufacturing, wholesaling, and retailing. An important transportation factor is the availability of the different modes of transportation—rail, motor, water, pipe lines, and air. Associated with this aspect is that of the number of carriers available. Some companies prescribe that new factories must be located on at least two railroads and be accessible to highways.

The element of competition has ramifications concerning the quality and quantity of service, such as frequency of schedules, reliability, and speed. The availability of different types of carriers also will be a rate factor of importance. There is keen competition among all modes of transportation for many shipments; and the location of plants adjacent to inland waterways, for example, may result in the railroad establishing water-compelled rates—that is, rates required to meet the lower water rates. Even potential water competition may result in such rates, for

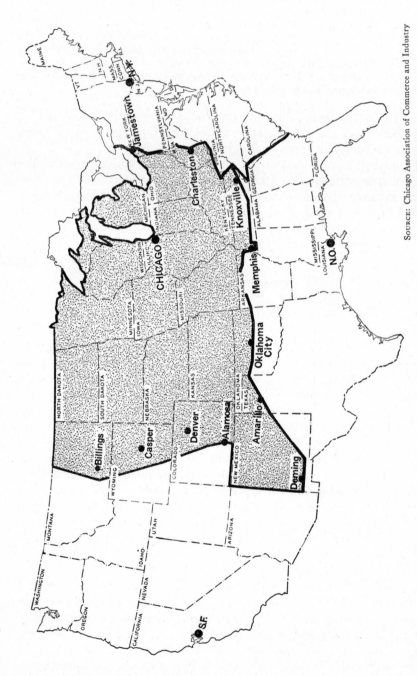

SOURCE: Chicago Association of Commerce and Industry

FIG. 23-1. Map showing area (shaded) served from Chicago within which Class 1 or 100 rates are lower than from New York, New Orleans, and San Francisco.

there have been instances where a new plant location adjacent to a waterway was without dock facilities, and yet rail rates were adjusted downward to compete with this potential water movement.

Such a case was that of a large company which located a new plant on the Mississippi River. There were railroad tracks between the river and the plant, and on the other side of the plant was a good highway. The property extended a short distance beyond the railroad track, so that it included frontage on the river. When the announcement about the new plant location was being prepared, an artist was called upon to prepare a drawing of the building and the area. He included, without instructions, a pier on the waterfront, so that barges on the river, trains, and trucks all appeared to be serving the plant. Immediately after the drawing appeared in the newspapers, the traffic department of this company was contacted by the railroads, which indicated that they planned to establish rates which would be competitive with barge rates. Prior to that time, there had been no indication that any of the raw material would be shipped other than by rail.

Among the most active organizations in promoting site location or site relocation have been railroads, chambers of commerce, and public utilities. An example of typical activities of a chamber of commerce relating to transportation is demonstrated in Figure 23-1, which has been prepared to show the area (shaded) served from Chicago within which Class 1 or 100 rates are lower than from New York, New Orleans, and San Francisco. The industrial development departments of railroads are also very active in aiding in industrial site selection. They not only have a considerable amount of land which can be used for this purpose adjacent to their rights of way but also will purchase property which has industrial location potential. The sale of land to an industrial plant does not necessarily conclude the railroad contribution. In one instance, the Western Pacific Railroad played an important role in getting the Ford Motor Company to locate a new assembly plant at Milpitas, California. The Western Pacific contributed $400,000 toward an enlargement of the county sewage system and spent $150,000 in constructing a drainage ditch to accommodate the new plant. It also constructed a 500-car railroad yard to serve the plant.

Some railroads sponsor industrial parks, and others co-operate in their development, there currently being about 1,200 such parks seeking occupants. Railroads that develop these parks secure the land at strategic points, divide it into factory or warehouse sites, provide streets and utilities, and sell or lease the improved sites. Other railroads own land and provide buildings that are either sold or leased to industries.

DECENTRALIZATION OF INDUSTRY

Among the factors responsible for the acceleration of decentralization of industry are shifts in population during the present century, the increasing emphasis on decentralization for defense purposes, cost of labor, the modification of the basing-point system subsequent to the Cement Institute Case in 1948, the tax policy of local communities, the increasing speed of transportation, and the percentage increases in the freight rates and charges that have been authorized by the Interstate Commerce Commission since June 30, 1946. Prior to 1940, nearly half of our industrial plants were in cities of 100,000 population. However, by 1955, only about 33 per cent were so located; and 30 per cent of the new plants which have been established since 1940 are in towns of 10,000 or less. This decentralization has been influenced by transportation.

DEPARTMENTAL ROLE IN PLANT LOCATION

A survey of industrial traffic managers showed that 1,025, or 81.7 per cent, were consulted before location of new plants. The general traffic manager of a large retail chain indicated that the traffic organization surveyed an area as to rail facilities, truck service, highway junctions, and rates, and also plotted on a map the location of the prospective warehouse site in relation to the stores served from it. Since all outbound deliveries to the retail outlets move in and on trucks, the location must be economically made.[3]

In contrast to the results of this survey is the following example. Some years ago, a plant location was being sought which required, among other factors, an adequate water supply. A site was chosen, and an option was taken on the property, which was adjacent to highways and railroads. Upon further investigation, it was found that the needed water supply would necessitate more drilling than had been first anticipated. This would add an estimated $1 million to the cost of this location, but it would provide the needed water supply. Another site was selected, however, because in the new site, this extra expenditure to provide water would not be necessary. Unfortunately, transportation factors were not considered, nor were transportation personnel consulted, and the transportation facilities in the new location cost $3 million more for access roads and rail trackage than the transportation facilities at the original site.

The experience of another company illustrates the significance of consideration of transportation aspects in choosing new sites. Land had been purchased for a new plant. Rates had been computed and recommendations made regarding the site, but there was a delay of several years in building plans. When the company decided to go ahead with its building on the purchased land, a notification was sent to each of the departments. During the interim years, the personnel of the traffic department had increased in quality and responsibility. When the notice of the proposed building was received by the traffic department, the traffic manager

---

[3] *Traffic World*, March 30, 1957, p. 136.

pointed out to top management that the main source of their raw material was located on water, and its primary users were located on water. The nature of the commodity, also, lent itself to water transportation; yet, the land which had been purchased was not adjacent to water transportation. The traffic department's recommendation was heeded and a new location found where water transportation could be used and savings effected.

EVALUATION OF FACTORS

A common method for evaluating the rate aspect of the transportation factor in plant location is to examine a number of potential sites—for example, six—in which the rates on raw materials inbound and the outbound rates on processed goods are computed for each of the possible locations. This will give an indication of the relative rate status of each

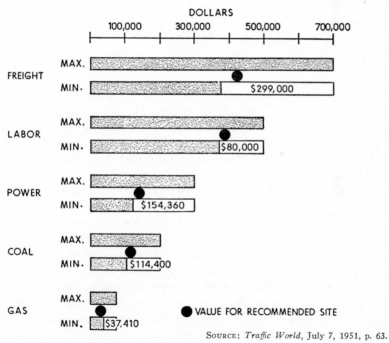

SOURCE: *Traffic World,* July 7, 1951, p. 63.

FIG. 23–2. Range of value of the five most important factors in specific plant location survey.

of the locations. The nature of some products, however, is such that the rate analysis should be on a weighted basis, in which an arbitrary weight of perhaps 60 per cent is given to finished products and 40 per cent to the rates on raw materials.

In addition to rates, there must be a check as to the adequacy of transportation facilities at a new plant location, for there are many considerations that must be analyzed regarding this aspect. Some of these are proximity to freight houses, necessity for rail trackage within the plants and roads within the plants, location of railroad yards and truck terminals, proximity of wharves or docks, proximity of highways and access streets, and adequacy of parking facilities and mass transportation for workers.

In a report of the location of a plant for a chemical company, 5 factors were given primary consideration. The cost of all of the 5 factors varied with different locations, the range from the lowest-cost location to the highest-cost location being $400,000. Figure 23–2 shows the range of value of the most important factors in a particular plant location, in which transportation cost was the most important single factor. A value was established for each of the factors for the recommended site.

In another type of industry where transportation is not the dominant factor but labor is, a weighted rating scale was used, totaling 100 points, and divided among five factors to which weights were assigned. These were:

Labor—58
Transportation—16
Community—12
Taxes—7
Specific site—7

Each of the items was further subdivided with percentages assigned according to relative emphasis. Labor, for example, was comprised of 50 per cent for wage rates, 15 per cent for benefits, such as pensions and insurance, and 35 per cent on availability of labor, union domination, and lack of labor unrest.

Due to transportation costs, the establishment of a transit privilege may cause manufacturing concerns which ordinarily would locate at the source of the raw material, or at the market, to locate instead at intermediate points, if the transit privilege is granted. Under the transit privilege, plants may be located at any intermediate point between the origin raw material and the finished product market. Thus, other locational factors may be accorded relatively more weight under such circumstances because the granting of the transit privilege makes possible a lower through rate. Transit privileges accord a greater degree of freedom in choosing a plant location.

The traffic manager for a manufacturer of breakfast cereals where milling and storage in transit privileges existed indicated that the location of a new plant depended upon the securing of the transit privilege at that particular point. A new location would be sought primarily to offer better service to customers, as well as to take advantage of raw material sources. In both cases, transportation was considered as the most important single element of the factors considered. The traffic manager's recommendation as to plant location for this company was the dominant factor in plant location.[4]

A factor frequently overlooked is the direction of the preponderance of the company's traffic flow and how it would fit into the over-all picture of existing traffic flow at the proposed location. Perhaps there is at present a directional movement of empty transportation equipment which might be utilized.

The traffic manager, in making his analysis as to various possible sites, also must consider what the freight rates to and from the proposed location should reasonably be, as contrasted with what they actually are at the time the survey is being made. The absence of traffic moving to and from the proposed location may result in "paper" rates, since there is no actual movement of traffic. Thus, the potential—that is, what the rates should reasonably be—must be properly evaluated in such a situation.

The compilation and analysis of transportation cost data, then, are very important in the determination of the location of the points from which goods may be most advantageously transported. The Office of the Chief of Transportation, Department of the Army, made a study of the distribution of coffee from four roasting plants to consuming installations in the United States. The transportation costs from the roasting plants to consuming installations were based, for the purposes of comparative transportation cost relationships, on all-rail, carload freight rates.

The facts developed in this study show the area which can be economically served on a cost-comparison basis from four points as shown on the map in Figure 23–3. It can be seen that two of the points have a limited distribution territory. The area which could be advantageously served if there was a change in the location of one of the points is much greater, as shown in the map in Figure 23–4. This would result in sizable transportation savings.

As is true with any organization—business or government—there are factors other than transportation that enter into the relocation of a site or the selection of a site. However, the important point is that benefits are derived by participation of transportation personnel in early determinations concerning site selections.

In the true economic sense, freight rates are a cost of production and enter into the prices of commodities. Of equal significance is the fact that once a price has been established, the ability of an individual producer to sell, as well as the price he will receive, will depend upon the freight rate he must pay. The availability of carriers, the adequacy of their equipment and facilities, and the level of rates and charges are dominant factors in economic development.

In spite of the most careful analysis made, the whim of a high-ranking

---

[4] "Selecting New Plant Sites," *Railway Age*, November 2, 1953, p. 56.

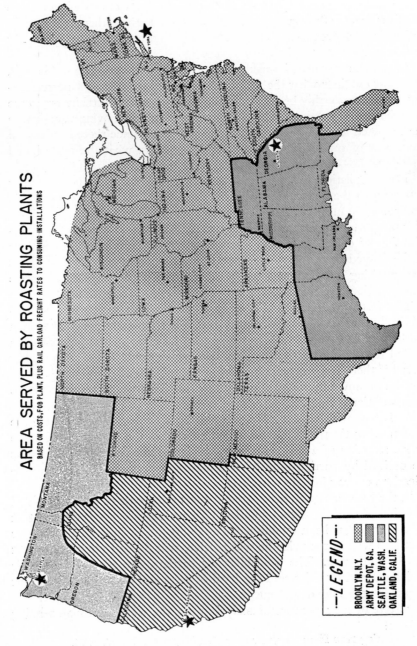

AREA SERVED BY ROASTING PLANTS

BASED ON COSTS, FOB PLANT, PLUS RAIL CARLOAD FREIGHT RATES TO CONSUMING INSTALLATIONS

--LEGEND--

BROOKLYN, N.Y.	
ARMY DEPOT, GA.	
SEATTLE, WASH.	
OAKLAND, CALIF.	

FIG. 23-3. Map showing area to be economically served on cost-comparison basis from four points.

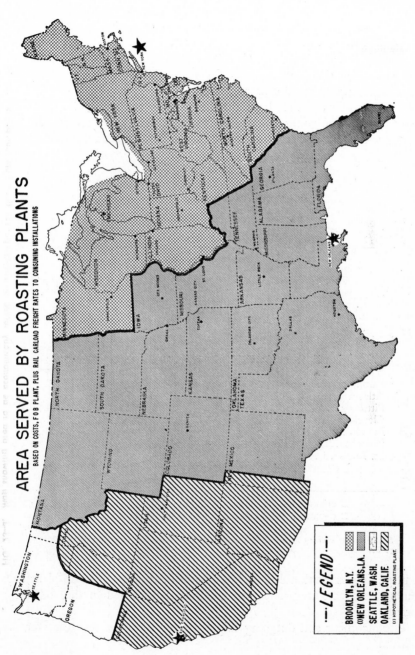

AREA SERVED BY ROASTING PLANTS

BASED ON COSTS, F O B PLANT, PLUS RAIL CARLOAD FREIGHT RATES TO CONSUMING INSTALLATIONS

-· LEGEND ·-

BROOKLYN, N.Y.
(1) NEW ORLEANS, LA.
SEATTLE, WASH.
OAKLAND, CALIF.

(1) HYPOTHETICAL ROASTING PLANT.

FIG. 23–4. Map showing area to be economically served if one of four points on previous map (Fig. 23–3) is relocated.

official of the company may result in the location of the plant in his boy-hood home town. The accolades and recognition he receives from his childhood friends overshadow all other considerations in his eyes.

ESTABLISHING THE CENTER OF DISTRIBUTION

A somewhat simple method of determining the "ideal" site for a new plant is the mathematical center of distribution technique. This least-cost distribution point is based on the firm's past traffic records of both incoming and outgoing shipments. Because freight rates on finished products are approximately double those on raw materials, the outgoing

TABLE 23–1
LOCATION OF WEIGHTED CENTER OF DISTRIBUTION:
RECORDED DATA AND CALCULATIONS

(1) Material Sources	(2) X Units	(3) Tonnage Weights	(4) (2) x (3)	(5) Y Units	(6) Tonnage Weights	(7) (5) x (6)
Pittsburgh .... (A)	65	5	325	52	5	260
Wheeling .... (B)	60	5	300	48	5	240
Cincinnati .... (C)	42	3	126	42	3	126
Cleveland .... (D)	58	3	174	61	3	183
Chicago .... (E)	24	2	48	61	2	122
Knoxville .... (F)	49	2	98	23	2	46
Markets						
Washington ...... (G)	80	12	960	42	12	504
New York .... (H)	95	6	570	59	6	354
Baltimore .... (I)	83	6	498	45	6	270
Atlanta .... (J)	43	4	172	5	4	20
Pittsburgh .... (A)	65	2	130	52	2	104
Cleveland .... (D)	58	2	116	61	2	122
Buffalo .... (K)	68	2	136	68	2	136
Chicago .... (E)	24	2	48	61	2	122
St. Louis .... (L)	9	1	9	39	1	39
		57	3,710		57	2,648

Σ column 4 $\div$ Σ column 3 $(3,710 \div 57) = 65.1$ (X)
Σ column 7 $\div$ Σ column 6 $(2,648 \div 57) = 46.5$ (Y)

SOURCE: James H. Thompson, *Methods of Plant Site Selection Available to Small Manufacturing Firms* (Morgantown, W.Va.: West Virginia University, 1961), p. 31.

tonnage figures are doubled. A hypothetical example of a small plant that wants to relocate its production facilities is described in the following paragraphs:[5]

The incoming and outgoing shipments for the previous year were as follows:

---

[5] James H. Thompson, *Methods of Plant Site Selection Available to Small Manufacturing Firms* (Morgantown, W.Va.: West Virginia University, 1961), p. 31.

INCOMING SHIPMENTS		OUTGOING SHIPMENTS	
Source	Tonnage	Destination	Tonnage
Pittsburgh	5,000	Washington	6,000
Wheeling	5,000	New York	3,000
Cincinnati	4,000	Baltimore	3,000
Cleveland	3,000	Atlanta	2,000
Chicago	2,000	Pittsburgh	1,000
Knoxville	2,000	Cleveland	1,000
		Buffalo	1,000
Total	21,000	Chicago	1,000
		St. Louis	500
		Total	18,500

A map of eastern United States was traced on graph paper, which identified all of the company's markets and material sources on the map

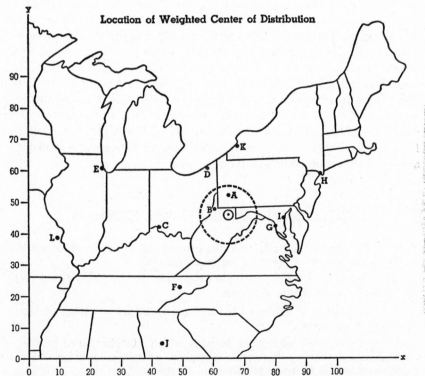

Location of Weighted Center of Distribution

SOURCE: James H. Thompson, *Methods of Plant Site Selection Available to Small Manufacturing Firms* (Morgantown, W.Va.: West Virginia University, 1961), p. 34.

FIG. 23–5. Location of weighted center of distribution.

by a letter or other symbol. A table was then prepared with columns for (1) source or destination, (2) number of X units, (3) tonnage weight, (4) X times tonnage weight, (5) number of Y units, (6) tonnage weight, and (7) Y times tonnage weight as shown in Table 23–1. Horizontal (X)

and vertical (Y) axes were constructed on the graph, as shown in Figure 23–5, in such a way as to include all sources and markets within the two axes. The material sources and markets were entered in Column 1, and the tonnage weights in Columns 3 and 6. The tonnage weight for each market was double the actual tonnage while actual tonnages were entered for material sources. This allowed for the assumed differential in freight rates.

X values were then calculated by counting the number of spaces from the vertical (Y) axis to the market or source, and entered in Column 4, Table 23–1. Y values were figured by counting the number of spaces from the horizontal (X) axis to the market or source and entered in Column 7, Table 23–1. Columns 3, 4, 6, and 7 were totaled. The Column 4 total was then divided by Column 3. The result was the weighted average value for X. Column 7 was divided by Column 6, and the result was the weighted average value for Y. The "ideal" distribution point was located on Figure 23–5 by starting at the point of origin (0) and counting off, along the horizontal axis, a number of spaces equal to the weighted average value of X; from this point, the number of spaces equal to the weighted average value of Y were counted off vertically upward. This point (encircled in Figure 23–1) was the "ideal" or least-cost distribution point from the transportation standpoint. Another circle around the point was then marked off as the area to be investigated. In this instance, the circle was about one hundred miles in radius, but it may be smaller or larger depending on what management believes is necessary in order to select a site meeting additional requirements.

DISCUSSION QUESTIONS AND PROBLEMS

1. How has transportation affected the growth and development of markets? What are the other principal locational factors?

2. The availability of different types of carriers will be a rate factor of importance. Explain this statement.

3. Decentralization of industry has been accelerated by a number of factors. Name these factors.

4. Using the example of the site location which was abandoned because of inadequate water supply, explain why there must be a balancing of factors in site selection to insure proper plant location.

5. What is a common method for evaluating the rate aspect of the transportation factor in plant location?

6. What are some of the factors concerning the adequacy of transportation facilities which should be checked when consideration is given to a possible site location?

7. Examine Figure 23–2. List the five factors considered there.

8. Why is it important that transportation aspects be considered *before* the plant site is selected?

9. Prepare a list of location factors important in the location of a new plant for a canner of food products; and indicate the weight, if any, which you would assign to each factor.

10. What impact have the newer modes of transportation had upon plant site location?

11. Consult the industrial location department of a railroad, and find out what efforts they have made, and how successful they have been, in the past year to attract industry to their line.

Appendix A

TARIFF CONSTRUCTION

Tariffs are schedules which contain rates and charges, as well as the special conditions or restrictions which govern the movement and handling of persons or property by commercial means. Where carriers must file rates, charges, and rules with a regulatory body, their form and manner of publication are prescribed by that body.

The interpretation of a tariff is considerably simplified if a knowledge of the method employed in its construction is acquired. The requirements which the Interstate Commerce Commission has prescribed governing the form and manner of publication of tariffs of carriers subject to the Commission's jurisdiction are set forth in a number of tariff circulars.

Section 6 of the Interstate Commerce Act authorized the Commission to establish and publish a uniform code of rules to govern the construction and filing of tariffs. Since 1891, the Bureau of Traffic of the Interstate Commerce Commission has issued twenty tariff circulars for railroads. Tariff Circular No. 20 and supplements thereto provide the rules to govern the construction and filing of freight rate tariffs, including classifications, schedules, and tariffs containing joint rail-motor, motor-water, and rail-motor-water rates. This tariff circular also governs freight rate tariffs for pipe lines. Tariff Circular No. 21 covers tariffs for water contract carriers, and No. 22 applies to water common carriers. Circular FF–2 covers freight forwarders; and currently, MF No. 3 contains the rules governing the construction and filing of tariffs and classifications of motor common carriers of property. The tariff rules which govern the construction, filing, and posting of schedules of contract motor carriers are currently contained in MF No. 4.

RAIL AND MOTOR COMMON CARRIERS

The extensive experience gained with the early tariff circulars that governed railroads was helpful in the preparation by the Commission of tariff circulars of carriers which later became subject to the Interstate Commerce Act. In the case of motor carriers, the Commission prepared a preliminary draft of a tariff circular, after which a series of conferences were held with representatives of motor carrier associations, large motor carriers, and shippers. The preliminary draft was revised as a result of the suggestions and criticisms made; and another draft was forwarded to the original participants in the conferences, as well as to others. The comments received were studied and submitted to the Interstate Commerce Commission, which, without a formal hearing, issued the circular. Subsequent circulars and supplements or modifications have been made without hearings.

Section 6 of the Interstate Commerce Act provides that the Commission is authorized to reject any schedule filed with it which is not in accordance with its regulations concerning the form and manner of publication filing and posting. Tariffs filed with the Interstate Commerce Commission are examined by Commission tariff examiners, who can recommend the acceptance or rejection of a tariff if it does not comply with the tariff circular rules.

Form of the Tariff

The tariff circular requirements start with the title page and prescribe the basic information which shall be shown there. In subsequent rules, the various parts or sections of the tariff are covered. Although tariffs and supplements are required by tariff circular rules to be in an 8×11-inch size, they may be in book, pamphlet, or loose-leaf form. The great bulk of tariffs are published in pamphlet form rather than loose-leaf form. Where loose-leaf tariffs are used, each page must be designated as "Original Page No. . . . ." In addition, each page must show the name of the carrier or agent, the page number, and the ICC number of the tariff. At the bottom of each loose-leaf tariff page must be shown the date of issue; the effective date; and the name, title, and street address of the issuing carrier or agent. The prescription of the size of paper to be used facilitates matters for the tariff user. It is well to point out that the Commission may permit deviation from the requirements contained in the tariff circular, an example of which are the mileage tariffs of the Movers' and Warehousemen's Association of America, Inc., and the Household Goods Carriers' Bureau, Inc., which make use of large Rand McNally maps which it would be impractical to reduce to 8×11-inch size. Therefore, these two publications are 12×16 inches.

All tariffs and supplements filed and posted are to be legible and are to be plainly printed, planographed, stereotyped, or prepared by other similar desirable process on paper of good quality. Such detail as the size of type contained in these publications is also prescribed. Not less than 8-point bold or fullface shall be used, except in the upper right-hand corner of every title page. The ICC number is to be shown in boldface type which, on printed tariffs, shall be not less than 12-point type. In the explanation of reference marks and column headings, 6-point boldface type may be used.

The following are sample sizes of type:

This line is set in 12-point type.

This line is set in 8-point type.

This line is set in 6-point type.

Another rule provides that a margin of not less than ⅝ of an inch without any printing on it is to be allowed at the binding edge of each tariff or supplement.

Title Page of the Tariff

The title page of a tariff and supplement determines the application of the tariff and, for that reason, is most important. In the upper right-hand corner of every title page is shown the ICC number. In the case of rail carriers, this is ICC No. 1, with the numbers running consecutively with each additional tariff published by a particular rail carrier or its tariff-publishing agent. Motor common carrier tariff ICC numbers are preceded by the letters "MF" followed by a dash, thus "MF–ICC No. 1," and consecutive numbers for each additional tariff. ICC numbers of freight forwarders are preceded by the letters "FF," in the same manner as motor carriers of freight. Under this number, the numbers of any tariffs canceled are to be shown. If the cancellations are too numerous to list on the title page, they can be shown immediately preceding the table of contents in the body of the tariff. The requirements for the title page of a rail tariff are outlined below:

Title Page	Rule of Tariff Circular No. 20 Covering
ICC No. and cancellation, State No. and cancellation.	3–b
Corporate name of carrier or name of agent..........	4–b
Nature of tariff:	
Local, joint, proportional, export, import..........	3–d
Class or commodity rates........................	3–d
Territorial application	3–e
Governing classification and exceptions thereto......	3–f
Issued date	3–g
Effective date	3–g
Name, title, and address of officer or agent issuing tariff	3–i

Figure A–1 is a title page of a rail tariff.

Where a tariff or supplement is filed in which all rates, rules, or regulations are made effective on less than thirty days' notice, if authorized by the Commission, a notation is made on the title page similar to the following:

Issued on 5 days' notice under authority of Special Permission of the Interstate Commerce Commission, No. M–98765, dated January 1, 1964.

NO CHANGE IN RATES, EXCEPT AS INDICATED BY REFERENCE MARK "♦".

Subject, except as otherwise provided herein, to Tariff of Increased Rates and Charges No. X-175-B, Agent R. G. Raasch's I. C. C. No. 764, Ill. C. C. No. 385, supplements thereto or successive issues thereof

Ill. C. C. No. 1116.
(Cancels Ill. C. C. No. WL-1027.)

For additional cancellations, see page 2.

I. C. C. No. 24111.
(Cancels I. C. C. No. WL-10822.)

The Baltimore and Ohio Railroad Company

TARIFF 460
Cancels
TARIFF No. H-2439-R.

JOINT AND PROPORTIONAL FREIGHT TARIFF

——APPLYING ON——

COMMODITIES

FROM STATIONS ON	TO POINTS IN
THE BALTIMORE AND OHIO RAILROAD COMPANY. (In Illinois.) (Named on page 7.)	ILLINOIS, KENTUCKY, SOUTH DAKOTA, INDIANA, MINNESOTA, WISCONSIN. IOWA, MISSOURI, (Named on pages 8 to 11.)

Governed, except as otherwise provided herein, by the Illinois and Western Classifications, ALSO by EXCEPTIONS to said Classifications (see Item 130, page 17).

NOTICE.

This tariff contains rates that are higher for shorter than longer distances over the same route.

Such departure from the terms of the Fortieth Section of the Illinois Commerce Law is permitted by authority of Illinois Commerce Commission order in Ex Parte 1139, of June 26, 1913, in conjunction with General Order No. 125, of July 7, 1931; also Illinois Commerce Commission Fortieth Section Order No. 29 of September 6, 1933.

Issued June 25, 1953.

STAMP HERE

DATE RECEIVED

Effective August 5, 1953.

By W. E. BRADLEY,
Chief of Tariff Bureau,
B. & O. Annex Building, Liberty & Lombard Streets,
Baltimore-1, Md.

File 249182-57.   A. S. C-1973, 2029, 2104.   (P. O. 98110)   1200

♦ Increase.

Made in U. S. A.

FIG. A–1.   A title page of a rail tariff.

If a tariff or supplement is issued in compliance with an order or decision of the Commission, regardless of whether it is effective on less than statutory notice under special authority granted in the order or decision in the particular case, or upon statutory notice, the title page of the tariff or supplement should bear a notation similar to the following:

> In compliance with the decision (or order) of the Interstate Commerce Commission in Docket No. 98765.

One very important item that will be found on the title page is the reference to governing publications, if any. This information must be placed on the title page, or the title page must refer to an item or page number of the tariff where a statement of the publications governing the tariff is to be found. An example of such a statement on the title page is as follows:

> For reference to governing publications, see Item 10, page 9; or as amended.

The name of the person or organization issuing the tariff should be shown near the bottom of the title page. The requirement differs according to whether it is published by an individual, an individual agent under powers of attorney, or an agent of a named tariff bureau. In Tariff Circular No. 20, there are powers of attorney starting with FX–1 through FX–9, all of which are different types of powers of attorney. In motor, Form MFXA–2 is used in appointing an individual to act as agent for a common carrier in the publication and filing of freight rate tariffs and supplements thereto, while Form MFXA–3 is used in appointing a corporation which is not a carrier to act as agent in publishing rates.

It sometimes happens that a tariff is issued to expire with a specified date, in which case a notation to this effect will be found near the bottom of the title page. The importance of detail in tariff construction can be secured from a sample expiration form. For example, a notice reading "Expires June 30, 1964, unless sooner canceled, changed, or extended" is not considered to be the most definitive statement, because the meaning of "expires" is not entirely clear, according to Commission interpretation. A more satisfactory notation, in the opinion of the Commission's tariff examiners, would be the use of "expires with," because that indicates the end of the day to which referred.

Main Body of Tariff

The main body of the tariff is to be compiled in the following order:

1. Table of contents.
2. List of participating carriers.
3. An index of commodities.
4. An index of points of origin and destination.
5. An explanation of symbols, reference marks, and abbreviations found in the tariff.
6. A list of exceptions.

7. Rules and regulations governing the tariff.
8. Rates applicable on the commodities covered in the tariff.
9. Routing.

Table of Contents

Tariffs must contain a table of contents with a complete statement, in alphabetical order, of the exact location of information under general headings, by subjects, specifying page or item numbers. However, when tariffs are so small that the title page or the interior arrangement clearly shows their contents, it is not required to have a table of contents. The legal names of participating carriers, the city of their principal office, and certificate numbers are shown alphabetically, as well as the form and number of power of attorney or concurrence of each. Where the carrier is an individual, or individuals, operating under a trade name, the trade name precedes the name of the owner or partners. However, this procedure may be reversed if the trade names are shown in alphabetical order and in a prominent manner, with the individual name or names indented. In motor carrier operations, there are many individual proprietorships and partnerships operating under trade names.

List of Participating Carriers

A motor carrier tariff which has not more than four participating carriers can show them on the title page rather than in the main body of the tariff. In the case of rail, not more than ten participating carriers can be shown on the title page. If a participating carrier is eliminated by means of issuance of a supplement, that supplement must also cancel rates for that carrier.

The extent of participation can be shown by the following symbols:

(x) For origin carrier.
(y) For intermediate carrier.
(z) For terminal carrier.

Index of Commodities

A tariff has to contain an alphabetical index of all articles on which commodity rates are named in that tariff. There must be reference, as well, to each item or page where a particular article is shown. If nouns are not sufficiently explanatory, articles are indexed under the names of descriptive adjectives. All of the articles relating to different kinds or species of the same commodity are grouped together. For example:

paper, building
paper, printing
paper, wrapping

If all the commodity rates to each destination in a general commodity tariff, or a combined class and commodity tariff, are arranged in alphabetical order by commodities, the index of commodities may be omitted.

Index of Points of Origin and Destination

Those tariffs which name specific point-to-point or station-to-station rates must provide an alphabetical index of all points in the case of motor carriers and an index of stations for rail carriers, from which rates apply, in a separate alphabetical index showing the states in which the points or stations are located; and when the tariff names rates of more than one carrier, the names of carriers serving each such point or station must be given. Where desirable, the rate tariff may refer to a separate publication, although not a rate tariff, for the names of carriers serving the points or stations in the rate tariff.

When all or practically all of the rates named in a tariff apply in both directions between the points or stations shown in the tariff, the points or stations of origin and destination may be shown in one index. If there are not more than 12 points or stations of origin or 12 points or stations of destination, they can be shown alphabetically on the title page of the tariff, in which case there need be no index of points or stations. If rates are shown in a tariff by rate bases or by named or numbered territorial groups, indexes of points or stations of origin and destination shall show the base or group to which each point or station is assigned. However, an exception exists to the foregoing where reference is made to a separate publication, as provided in Rule 14 for motor carriers and Rule 15 for rail carriers, for lists of points or stations in such groups. Such groups may be omitted from the indexes, provided that there is shown in the table of contents the item or page giving reference by MF–ICC number or ICC number to the separate publication, and also provided that there is shown at the beginning of the index points or stations, if the tariff contains such an index, MF–ICC or ICC reference to the separate publication.

If the rates in a tariff are arranged geographically, the alphabetical indexes of points or stations of origin and of destination should show index numbers corresponding to those assigned to the points or stations in the rate tables. Unless the rate tables themselves indicate that all points or stations shown in the tariff are arranged in geographical order for the carriers shown, there shall be included also a separate geographical list of points or stations; or reference must be made by MF–ICC or ICC number to a separate publication, filed in accordance with Rule 14 for motor and Rule 10 (i) or Rule 15 for rail, containing such a geographical list of points or stations with corresponding index or station numbers. There are additional requirements for motor carriers governing arrangement in items and arrangement in rate tables. A specific requirement governing tariffs of irregular route motor carriers is that they must clearly define the territory within which they operate; or their tariffs may refer to a separate publication, which is not a rate tariff, on file with the Commission, clearly defining the territory.

Symbols, Reference Marks, and Abbreviations

To facilitate the use of a tariff in which changes are made, widespread use has developed of reference marks, abbreviations, and symbols. The tariff circulars prescribe that certain symbols must be used for the purposes indicated. In the tabulation below, it will be noted that, for rail and motor, there is little difference:

- ⬇ to indicate reductions—or (R) for motor.
- ◆ to denote increases—or (A) for motor.
- ● to denote no change in rate.
- ✳ to denote prepay stations or points—not applicable to motor.
- ✚ to denote intrastate application only.
- ☐ to denote reissued matter.
- ▲ to denote changes in wording which result in neither increases nor reductions in charges—or (C) for motor.

It is a requirement that if the explanation of the reference mark, symbol, or abbreviation does not appear on the page on which it is used, the page on which the character is used shall indicate where the explanation is given.

If a change of the same character is made in all or nearly all rates in a tariff or supplement, that fact and the nature of such change can be indicated in distinctive type at the top of the title page of such issue or at the top of each page, as the case may be, in substantially the following manner: "All rates in this issue are increased," or "All rates in this issue are reductions."

List of Exceptions

If there is a list of exceptions to the classification or a classification exceptions tariff or tariffs governing the tariff, this must be shown. A rate tariff cannot refer to another rate tariff or classification ratings, exceptions to the classification, rules, or other governing provisions.

Rules and Regulations Governing Tariff

Rules or provisions which govern the tariff may be incorporated in the tariff. However, clarity is important in rules, for the controversial wording of a tariff rule revision cost carriers a loss of revenue of $1.5 million, as well as upsetting the marketing of lumber in the West, until there was a clarifying revision of the rule. If it is not practicable to include these rules and provisions in the rate tariff, they can be published in a special tariff, provided that specific reference is made in the rate tariff to the separate publication.

Tariffs containing rates for the transportation of explosives, inflam-

SECTION 1
APPLICATION OF RATE BASES

RATE BASES APPLICABLE (For rates, see pages 282 to 337)

BETWEEN (See Item 100) — AND (See Item 100)	Adrian, Mich.	Akron, Mich.	Akron, Ohio	Alba, Mich.	Albany, N.Y.	Alberta, Va.	Alexandria, Mo.	Allenstown, N.H.	Alliance, Ohio	Allingdale, W.Va.	Alma, Mich.	Alpena, Mich.	Altamont, Md.-Chaffee, W.Va.	Altavista, Va.	Altoona, Pa.	Amelia, Va.	Amherst, Va.
Adrian.............Mich.	40																
Akron..............Mich.	156	40															
Akron..............Ohio	56	278	40														
Alba...............Mich.	264	153	397	40													
Albany.............N.Y.	581	570	499	608	40												
Alberta.............Va.	698	818	504	939	539	40											
Alexandria..........Mo.	433	523	553	543	1012	932	①										
Allenstown.........N.H.	839p	768p	697p	896p	233p	701p	1208p	40p									
Alliance............Ohio	186	307	40	426	489	561	582	687p	40								
Allingdale.........W.Va.	213	563	302	682	649	492	778	845p	275	40							
Alma..............Mich.	136	163	269	142	608	811	487	806p	299	554	40						
Alpena............Mich.	242	131	375	132	677	919	615	875p	405	660	155	40					
Altamont, Md.-Chaffee, W.Va.	397	519	257	638	464	368	754	661p	261	183	511	616	40				
Altavista............Va.	598	718	517	837	556	101	881	718p	516	410	709	818	329	40			
Altoona.............Pa.	384	506	232	625	356	420	780	562p	200	310	497	603	125	380	40		
Amelia.............Va.	678	800	567	919	512	67	966	674p	534	471	791	896	341	98	393	40	
Amherst............Va.	608	730	529	849	518	122	896	680p	500	400	721	838	308	40	359	98	40
Annapolis (See Note 9) . Md.	616	723	465	851	263		995	516p	432	424	729	829	241	280	259	236	242
Ann Arbor.........Mich.	40	115	169	228	559	711	464	757p	198	454	101	207	410	609	397	691	631
Ansonia............Pa.	426	433	300	561	256	463	827	462p	286	433	170	539	258	478	133	436	442
Anthony...........W.Va.	481	603	389	722	603	249	769	788p	362	245	594	700	200	167	325	225	155
Arcade.............N.Y.	326	319	235	417	292	576	753	490p	225	446	356	425	332	598	208	549	555
Arlington............Vt.	679	608	537	736	51	590	1048	187p	526	699	646	715	515	607	402	563	569
Ashley.............Mich.	119	80	252	159	594	794	482	792p	282	539	40	172	490	692	480	774	704
Ashtabula..........Ohio	194	316	86	434	414	601	596	622p	75	353	307	483	301	540	221	574	540
Athens..............Ohio	232	354	152	473	639	469	556	837p	151	222	345	457	198	367	304	149	379
Atlantic City.........N.J.	687	741	535	869	279	376	1083	436p	503	532	778	847	348	393	303	349	355
Augusta............Me.	806	885	814	1013	339	795	1325	187p	804	939	923	992	755	812	679	768	774
Aurora..............Ill.	246	444	377	338	825	854	①	1023p	406	626	290	418	602	752	594	832	762
Avondale...........Pa.	593	670	441	798	265	284	989	427p	409	438	706	776	254	301	209	257	263
Bad Axe...........Mich.	173	64	298	193	549	841	563	747p	328	583	103	171	539	739	499	821	751
Baltimore...........Md.	580	687	429	815	332	227	959	464p	396	388	693	793	205	244	223	200	206
Bangor.............Me.	971	960	889	1088	419	870	1400	262p	879	1014	998	1067	830	887	754	843	849
Barry................Ill.	446	548	566	583	1023	964	①	1221p	594	756	512	640	737	863	772	948	878
Barstow.............Ill.	363	444	494	434	943	961	①	1141p	523	741	390	535	717	859	722	941	871
Batavia.............N.Y.	426	319	244	447	255	590	755	453p	234	482	356	425	371	605	244	563	569
Bath................N.Y.	400	393	315	521	238	512	832	444p	305	494	430	499	324	527	196	485	491
Battle Creek........Mich.	84	134	236	229	638	778	390	836p	265	521	110	226	477	676	461	758	688
Beckley............W.Va.	424	546	345	665	667	306	711	852p	344	259	517	643	292	205	417	288	218
Bedford.............Pa.	423	545	272	664	403	373	819	600p	239	263	536	612	78	333	47	346	312
Bellaire............Mich.	288	176	420	40	722	963	544	920p	450	705	166	143	661	861	649	943	873
Bellefontaine.......Ohio	124	251	143	370	608	591	435	806p	168	351	242	348	327	490	355	505	505
Bellefonte...........Pa.	431	503	279	631	313	432	827	519p	247	357	540	609	172	427	47	405	406
Bellows Falls.........Vt.	760	689	618	817	139	639	1129	94p	608	775	727	796	591	656	480	612	618
Bennington.........N.H.	783	712	641	840	218	648	1152	89p	631	791	750	819	607	655	506	621	627
Bens Run.........W.Va.	297	419	157	538	587	527	630	793p	130	181	410	516	187	440	231	500	443
Benton Harbor......Mich.	152	218	295	244	722	801	325	920p	329	557	163	311	533	699	522	781	711
Berlin..............N.H.	887	814	745	942	278	778	1256	174p	735	914	852	921	730	793	619	751	757
Berwick.............Pa.	525	561	374	689	230	396	926	440p	353	441	598	667	257	411	156	369	375
Bethel..............Me.	866	853	784	981	322	806	1295	193p	774	950	891	960	766	823	663	779	785
Bethel..............Vt.	824	753	682	881	203	705	1193	115p	672	839	791	860	655	720	544	676	682
Bethlehem..........Pa.	607	626	456	754	189	368	1004	386p	424	461	663	732	277	385	224	341	347
Big Blizzard Run....W.Va.	470	592	331	711	679	522	807	975p	304	138	583	689	212	440	340	500	430
Binghamton........N.Y.	489	482	399	610	143	495	918	349p	389	523	519	588	338	510	213	468	474
Birmingham.........N.J.	653	698	501	826	215	344	1049	374p	469	491	735	804	314	361	269	318	324
Blackstone..........Va.	675	797	593	916	538	64	963	700p	560	468	788	894	367	95	419	40	95
Blanchester.........Ohio	215	353	207	471	682	549	458	586p	280	217	344	450	316	448	378	533	463
Bloomington........Ill.	295	390	415	434	872	838	①	1070p	544	634	354	485	610	737	638	822	752
Bloomington.......Ind.	264	398	339	464	804	706	331	1002p	364	490	494	605	529	690	620		
Bluefield..........W.Va.	458	580	392	699	688	247	735	850p	391	306	571	677	362	146	474	240	170

For explanation of reference marks and notes, see pages 7 to 9.

FIG. A–2. An example of the alphabetically-by-name method, using headline, sideline points. The rate bases are used to secure the rate.

mable or corrosive materials, or other dangerous articles must also contain the rules and regulations issued by the Commission governing their transportation or must bear specific reference to the ICC number or MF–ICC number of the separate publication which contains such rules and regula-

TARIFF 44A.

Column "1" rates will not apply on Pyrites Ore Cinder.
Column "2" rates apply only on Pyrites Ore Cinder.

TABLE OF RATES
(Applies in cents per 2000 or 2240 pounds as indicated on pages 8 and 9)

RATE BASIS	Column 1	Column 2
210	361	315
250	429	...
277	475	...
319	548	...
332	569	...
341	585	...
361	619	514
381	653	...
388	667	...
402B	690	568
407	697	...
415	714	...
430	738	...
430B	738	605
440	755	...
446	766	...
455	781	...
458	787	642
462	792	...
471B	809	659
473	812	...
473B	812	662
485	833	...
488	838	...
499	857	...
499B	857	696
504A	866	716
506	868	705
510A	876	715
513B	881	715
515A	885	735
517	887	...
528	906	...
528B	906	735
539B	925	749
540	926	750
542B	930	...
546A	938	772
550	944	...
550A	944	768
550B	944	763
554	952	...
554B	952	769
557A	957	791
560	961	...
561	963	...
561A	963	782
561B	963	778
561C	963	792
572A	982	811

RATE BASIS	Column 1	Column 2
572B	981	792
582	998	...
583B	1001	807
590	1012	...
592A	1017	856
594A	1020	826
594B	1020	822
594C	1020	835
596B	1023	824
598A	1028	845
605A	1039	854
609A	1046	879
609B	1045	842
609C	1047	864
620	1064	...
620A	1064	861
627B	1076	865
631A	1083	907
631C	1084	901
634A	1089	912
638	1096	...
638A	1096	898
638B	1096	880
640	1098	882
640A	1099	900
642	642	...
647	1110	891
647A	1110	929
649A	1114	932
649C	1115	899
649D	1115	917
651A	1118	919
651B	1117	897
653A	1121	918
653C	1122	937
660A	1133	946
662A	1136	916
664A	1141	852
671A	1152	941
671B	1152	923
671C	1152	954
671D	1151	760
673A	1155	956
677	1162	931
679	1166	...
679B	1166	934
682A	1171	942
682C	1171	960
682D	1171	975
682E	1172	956

RATE BASIS	Column 1	Column 2
682F	1170	974
686A	1178	980
689A	1182	985
693A	1190	950
693C	1189	986
693D	1190	990
695	1192	...
695A	1193	973
697A	1198	996
699A	1045	842 plus 90 cents per 2000 pounds
700A	1202	986
702	702	...
703A	952	769 plus 266 cents per car
704A	1209	1005
704C	1207	1005
704D	1208	997
704E	1209	1004
706A	1212	1007
712	1221	977
715A	1228	1012
715C	1228	999
715D	1227	907
721	1238	...
721A	1238	989 plus switching charge of 1239 per car
721B	1238	989
722A	1240	1024
722C	1240	1035
724A	1244	1031
726A	1246	1033
728A	1249	1035
728C	1096	880 plus 90 cents per 2000 pounds
735A	1261	1041
737	1264	1010
737A	1265	1048
737C	1266	1049
737D	1264	1048
737E	1266	1048
738	738	...
739A	1269	1051
741A	1272	1040

RATE BASIS	Column 1	Column 2
741C	1117	897 plus 90 cents per 2000 pounds
743A	1020	822 plus 266 cents per car
745A	1023	824 plus 266 cents per car
748A	1284	1025 plus switching charge of 1239 per car
748B	1284	1025
752A	1045	842 plus 143 cents per 2000 pounds
754	1295	...
755A	1296	1067
756A	1298	1066
757A	1300	1074
757B	1298	1036
757C	1298	1036 plus switching charge of 1236 per car
759A	1302	1076
761A	1152	923 plus 90 cents per 2000 pounds
763A	1310	1078
766A	1316	1086
770A	1322	1091
770C	1322	1092
776A	1076	865 plus 266 cents per car
778	1335	1065
778A	1337	1102
781A	1341	1107
781B	1340	1068
781C	1096	880 plus 143 cents per 2000 pounds
781D	1340	1068 plus switching charge of 1239 per car
783A	1344	1095

FIG. A–3. Example of a sideline method of publishing rates.

tions. If the latter method is adopted, the tariff referred to shall contain nothing except the regulations promulgated by the Commission. There are two well-known publications of this kind that have been issued in the rail and motor fields: H. A. Campbell's Explosives and Dangerous Articles Tariff; and American Trucking Associations, Inc., Motor Carriers' Explosives and Dangerous Articles Tariff.

The practical effect of such publications is to simplify tariff publications. For example, there is a comparatively small rail tariff, comprising only 26 pages, which publishes rates from stations in Oregon and Wash-

		Tariff 431.		
Commodities, Carloads. (Unless otherwise specified.)	From Stations Designated by Station Number. (See pages 3 to 6.)	To	Miles. (See Note 1.)	Rates in Cents per 100 Pounds. (Except as noted.)
Ashes or **Cinders** (Coal). Minimum weight 90 per cent. of marked capacity of car, except when car is loaded to full cubical or visible capacity actual weight will apply. Shipments for which actual weight cannot be ascertained must be billed at 10 per cent. above the marked weight capacity of car, subject to minimum weight per car of 50,000 pounds, unless marked weight capacity of car is less, in which event the minimum carload weight will be the marked weight capacity of car, but in no case less than 40,000 pounds. When shipments so way-billed are received at destination at which there are track scales, receiving agents will have same weighed, and billing, corrected to the actual scale weight, subject to minimum weight per car announced above.	Station Numbers 12000 to 13775 ②13780 13785 to 15165 15185 to 15260 15300 to 15725	All Stations on The Baltimore and Ohio Railroad Company, in the States of ①Illinois, Indiana and Ohio, including ②Louisville, Ky., and St. Louis, Mo. (see Note 2 and Rule 25, page 10).	25 miles and under.... 40 miles and over 25.. 60 miles and over 40.. 75 miles and over 60.. 100 miles and over 75.. 125 miles and over 100.. 150 miles and over 125.. 175 miles and over 150.. 200 miles and over 175.. 225 miles and over 200.. 250 miles and over 225.. 275 miles and over 250.. 300 miles and over 275.. 325 miles and over 300.. 350 miles and over 325.. 375 miles and over 350.. 400 miles and over 375..	142 172 186 202 218 248 278 294 325 339 354 371 415 431 441 476 492 cents per 2000 pounds.
Blocks, Building, Cement or Concrete, not reinforced with metal. Minimum weight 50,000 pounds.	Station Numbers 12000 to 13775 ②13780 13785 to 15165 15185 to 15260 15300 to 15725	All stations on The Baltimore and Ohio Railroad Company, in the States of ①Illinois, Indiana and Ohio, including ②Louisville, Ky., and St. Louis, Mo. (see Note 2 and Rule 25, page 10).	10 miles and under.... 40 miles and over 10.. 60 miles and over 40.. 75 miles and over 60.. 100 miles and over 75.. 120 miles and over 100.. 140 miles and over 120.. 160 miles and over 140..	239 262 301 315 343 374 420 450 cents per 2000 pounds.

FIG. A–4.   Example of distance-scale method of publishing rates governed by a distance table tariff.

ington to stations in Idaho, Oregon, and Washington, and refers to Campbell's tariff for rules and regulations to apply in connection with the rates published therein. If the rules and regulations were not published in an agency tariff, such as Campbell's, it would be necessary to make specific publication in each of the various rate tariffs, which, in this particular instance, would increase the size of the small rail tariff by more than 300 pages.

Rates Applicable on Commodities Covered in Tariff

All rates must be clearly and explicitly stated in cents or in dollars and cents per 100 pounds, per ton of 2,000 pounds or net ton, per ton of 2,240 pounds or gross ton, per car, per truckload, or per other defined unit. Since reference is made to a definite unit, one will find rates per gallon, per barrel, and others. The tariff must show whether the named rates apply from, to, or between the named points or stations; and the rates are to be arranged in a simple and systematic manner. There are a

FREIGHT TARIFF No. 1-I

SECTION 2
COMMODITY RATES IN CENTS PER 100 POUNDS UNLESS OTHERWISE SPECIFICALLY PROVIDED
(See Rule 17)

Except as noted, L.T.L. Rates shown in Columns A, B and C will apply as follows:
COLUMN A: Applies on shipments weighing each less than 2,000 pounds.
COLUMN B: Applies on shipments weighing each 2,000 pounds or more but less than 6,000 pounds.
COLUMN C: Applies on shipments weighing each 6,000 pounds or more.

ITEM NO.	COMMODITY	FROM (Except as Noted)	TO (Except as Noted)	L.T.L. RATE (See Above) COLUMN A	B	C	T.L. RATE	T.L. Minimum Weight (In Pounds)
7780	CORK, Composition Stopper Disks, in boxes.	Wilmington.......Del. (File P-4860)	Pittsburgh.......Pa.	..	..	..	137	14,000
7800	CORK: Corkwood,in packages. Stoppers,in packages.	New York(Note 1)N.Y.: Zone 1............. Zone 2.............	Lancaster.........Pa. Lancaster.........Pa.	133 141	108 116	94 102	94 102	....
	APPLICABLE ONLY on shipments destined To Beaver Falls, Pa., or Pittsburgh, Pa. Minimum charge per single shipment 71 cents. (File R-39)							
7820	CORK: Granulated, in cloth or paper bags.	New York(Note 1)N.Y.: Zone 1............. Zone 2............. (File E-290)	Lancaster.........Pa. Lancaster.........Pa.	.. ..	.. ..	.. ..	112 117	12,000
7840	CORK: Sheets, with or without binder; Cork Waste; Cork, in shapes, N.O.I.; Insulating Brick; Infusorial Earth; Cement, Insulating;Linoleum Disks;Fibreboard; Shoe Bottom Fillers; in packages.	New York(Note 1)N.Y.: Zone 1............. Zone 2.............	Lancaster.... ...Pa. Lancaster.... ...Pa.	111 119	88 96	74 82	74 82	....
	APPLICABLE ONLY on shipments destined To Beaver Falls, Pa., or Pittsburgh, Pa. Minimum charge per single shipment 71 cents.							
7860	CORK or CORK PRODUCTS, in packages: Cork Bars, Rods, Sheets or Slabs,without binder, not coated. Cork Composition with cloth combined. Cork Composition. Cork Pipe Covering. Cork Chips, Shavings, Virgin Barks or Waste, in machine pressed bales having a weight density less than 20 pounds per cubic foot. Cork, ground.	Hillside..........N.J. Kearny............N.J. Newark............N.J. New York(Note 1)N.Y.: Zone 1........... Zone 2........... Wilmington.......Del. (File R-278)	Baltimore(Note 3)Md. Washington(Note 4)............D.C. Wilmington.....Del. Wilmington.....Del. Baltimore(Note 3)Md. Washington(Note 4)............D.C. New York(Note 1)N.Y.: Zone 1............ Zone 2............	.. ..	.. ..	.. ..	105 112 87 91 71 81 87 91	10,000
7880	COUGH DROPS OR TABLETS, Candy, in packages. GUM, Chewing, in packages. (Files P-6751-1a;L-923)	ⓧ New York(Note 1), N.Y.: Zone 1.......... Zone 2.......... ⓧ New York (Note 1), N.Y.: Zone 1.......... Zone 2..........	Philadelphia(Note 2)Pa. Philadelphia(Note 2)Pa. Trenton...........N.J. Trenton...........N.J.	86 93 75 82	79 86 70 77	66 73 58 65	46 48 40 42	23,000

FIG. A-5. An example of commodity alphabetical method of publishing rates.

number of different ways in which rates can be shown, and it should be noted that the tariff circulars do not prescribe a specific method. Some of the methods used are (1) alphabetically by name, using the headline, sideline method as shown in Figure A–2; (2) alphabetically by name, using the index number method (the index number is sometimes shown in a separate governing schedule such as the Open and Prepay Station List); (3) geographically by name, using the index number method; (4) rate basis method—headline and sideline method or only sideline method, as shown in Figure A–3 (p. 570); (5) distance-scale method, governed by a distance table tariff, as shown in Figure A–4; and (6) commodity alphabetical method, as shown in Figure A–5.

The tariff circulars contain definitions of different types of rates and the application of certain rates in considerable detail; but inasmuch as this material was covered in earlier chapters, no reference to it will be made at this point.

Routing

Tariff Circular No. 20 specifies that the routing over which rates apply must be stated in such a manner that the routes can be definitely ascertained. This can be done by providing that the rates in the tariff apply only via the routes specifically shown in the tariff; or by providing that the rates apply via all routes made by use of the lines of the carriers, parties to the tariff, except as otherwise specifically provided in the tariff. In the former case, a notation must be shown under the heading "Routing Instructions" as follows:

> The rates herein apply only via the routes specified on pages......
> (or in terms ......).

If the second plan—that of providing complete routing for shipment but not all of the rates in the tariff or incomplete routing for all of the rates— is used, the following must be included in the tariff under the heading "Routing Instructions":

> The rates herein apply via all routes made by use of the lines of any of the carriers parties to this tariff, except as otherwise specifically provided on pages ......, in individual rate items, or in connection with individual rates.

A separate publication called a "Routing Guide" may be used under certain circumstances. The form of the routing guide is prescribed, and it must contain three sections. There also exists an emergency routing clause which can be placed in the rate tariffs under the heading of "Routing Instructions."

Supplements to Tariffs

The price list of a company does not remain fixed; and in the transportation field, after a tariff has been issued, there are numerous changes that need to be made in the basic tariff, changes which cover not only rates but also items such as rules. New rates which have been formulated after the publication of the basic tariff need to be added. Tariff circulars provide rules which state that, when it is desired that changes be made to any rates, ratings, rules, or other provisions of a tariff, this is done by issuing an amendment which takes the form of a supplement to the tariff and is constructed generally in the same manner as the tariff which it supplements, although there are separate provisions which deal with the issuance of loose-leaf tariffs. Some of the types of supplements include cancellations, investigation and suspension and vacating, discontinuance of service, and special.

The tariff circulars prescribe the number of supplements permitted to a tariff. This is shown in Figure A–6, as well as the total number of pages

For Tariffs of:	Number of Supplements permitted
4 pages and less......................	No supplements
5 and not more than 16 pages.............	1 supplement
17 and not more than 80 pages............	2 supplements
81 and not more than 200 pages...........	3 supplements
More than 200 pages...................	4 supplements

FIG. A–6.   Number of supplements permitted to tariff.

which supplements to tariffs may contain, as shown in Figure A–7. As is true of many of the other provisions of tariff circulars, there may be deviations from the requirements of the rules which form the basis of the

For Tariffs of:	Volume of supplemental matter permitted
4 pages and less	None
5 and not more than 12 pages	4 pages
More than 12 pages	Supplemental matter aggregating not more than 33-1/3% of the number of pages in the tariff, except if the number of pages in the supplement which brings the volume of matter up to that authorized by the rule is not evenly divisible by 4, it may exceed the volume authorized to the extent necessary to bring the number of pages of such supplement to the next multiple of 4.
The smallest of 3 effective supplements to a tariff of more than 80 pages but not more than 200 pages shall contain not more than 8 pages, and the smallest of 4 effective supplements to a tariff of more than 200 pages shall contain not more than 16 pages.	

FIG. A–7.   Requirements regarding volume of tariff supplemental matter.

tables. In this connection, the Interstate Commerce Commission has, under special permission No. M–70560 of June 15, 1950, permitted motor common carriers and their agents to depart, where necessary, from the terms of the basic rules. The extent to which this departure is permitted is shown in Figure A–8, but the title pages of the supplements issued under

For Tariffs of:	Number of Supplements Permitted	Volume of Supplemental Matter Permitted
4 pages or less	None	None
5 and not more than 8 pages	1 supplement	4 pages
9 and not more than 16 pages	2 supplements	8 pages
17 and not more than 80 pages	2 supplements, and 2 additional supplements not exceeding 4 pages each.	Not to exceed 50% of number of pages in tariff.
81 and not more than 200 pages	3 supplements, and 2 additional supplements not exceeding 4 pages each.	Not to exceed 50% of number of pages in tariff.
More than 200 pages	4 supplements, and 2 additional supplements not exceeding 4 pages each.	Not to exceed 50% of number of pages in tariff.

FIG. A–8.   Exceptions allowed to requirements regarding tariff supplemental material.

this privilege have to bear a notation of the special privilege granted.

The majority of tariffs are published in pamphlet form, but a loose-leaf tariff is permissible, in which case such tariffs are not provided with separately published supplements but are amended by added or revised pages. The added or revised pages to the loose-leaf tariff are not construed to be supplements. Therefore, the limitations concerning the volume and the number of applicable supplements issued to the pamphlet form of tariff do not apply to loose-leaf tariffs. Although loose-leaf tariffs are basically subject to the same tariff instruction rules that apply to the pamphlet form of tariffs, there are a number of important distinctions. Loose-leaf tariffs are printed on only one side. Mention was earlier made of other characteristics of loose-leaf tariffs. Where a new page is added, say between pages 7 and 8, a letter suffix must be added; and the new page carries the same number as the preceding page—for example, "Original Page 7A."

In order to identify and check the pages filed in the loose-leaf tariff which are additions to or amendments of the tariff, a check-sheet method or correction-number-sheet method is used. In the check-sheet method, when the original tariff is filed, the page next to the title page, which is called the "check sheet," lists the original pages in the tariff. When the pages of the tariff are revised or new pages added, the check sheet is correspondingly amended and revised each time to include the added or revised pages. In the correction-number-sheet method, the added or revised pages show the correction number in the lower left-hand corner of each added or revised page, beginning with No. 1 and running consecutively. A permanent check sheet containing in numerical order a list of correction numbers beginning with No. 1 is filed with the original tariff, so that the corrected numbers can be properly checked off as received.

Sectional Tariffs

Among the important rules contained in tariff circulars is the rule regarding sectional tariffs. Often, a tariff is published containing different sections as a matter of convenience in arrangement. For example, a tariff may have two sections, one which names point-to-point or station-to-station rates and another which shows a mileage scale applicable in those instances where no point-to-point or station-to-station rates are named; or it might be a tariff which contains two or more sections based on geographical arrangement or different commodities. The second type of tariff published using the sectional form is one which is so published for the purpose of providing for the alternative application of the rates published in the tariff. The alternative use of rates can be provided[1] by publishing the rates in different sections of the same tariff. The first page of each section, which is the title page of that section, must contain the number of the section and the application of the rates published in that section. Each of these succeeding pages of rates has to bear the section number applicable to it. The title page of each section containing alternating rates must contain the following rule:

> If the charge accruing under section ...... or ...... of this tariff is lower than the charge accruing under this section on the same shipment over the same route, the charge accruing under section ...... or ......, whichever is lower, will apply.

A commodity tariff arranged in sections for alternative use must contain a nonalternating section, and each class and commodity tariff similarly arranged for alternative use must contain a commodity section which does not alternate with the other sections of the tariff. Where both class and commodity rates are published in separate sections of a tariff, the class rates must be published in a section preceding the commodity sections. Commodity rates which do not alternate with rates in other sections shall be published in the first commodity section. If an exclusive commodity tariff is issued, Section 1 of the tariff shall not have alternative application with other sections, and there must be a specific notation to this effect on the title page of Section 1. A sectionally alternating tariff permits a carrier to provide for so-called "catchall" rates between all points listed in the tariff by use of alternating sections when no specific point-to-point or

---

[1] Alternative application of rates is explained in Chapter 8.

station-to-station rates, the latter usually published on traffic moving regularly, are available in the tariff under its nonalternating Section 1.

There are a number of restrictions regarding the publication of alternative rates in different sections. One section of a tariff cannot alternate with more than three other sections. Another provision is that only one alternation of class rates against class rates may be provided, and not more than two alternating sections of commodity rates which may alternate with each other are permitted. There are other restrictions as well.

Provisions for Special Permission to Waive Statutory Period

The tariff circulars contain provisions which govern applications filed for special permission to make changes in rates or provisions on less than the statutory period of thirty days. They also provide for authority to waive and depart from the Commission's published rules, whether on short notice or on statutory notice. The granting of special permission is dependent upon the facts in each case. The tariff circulars outline the nature of the information desired by the Commission when applications are filed for special permission. For example, if permission is sought to establish provisions on less than statutory notice, the petitioner must indicate why the proposed provisions could not have been established on statutory notice.

Terminal and Special Service Tariffs

Each carrier or its agent must publish, post, and file tariffs which shall contain in explicit terms all of the rates and charges for, and rules governing, demurrage, switching, floating, lighterage, wharfage, and other terminal services; storage, transfer and drayage, weighing, diversion, reconsignment, icing, refrigeration, heat, elevation, feeding, grazing, and other transit services; and absorptions and allowances for rail carriers. For motor common carriers, the tariffs must show, in this connection, detention of vehicles, storage, weighing, diversion, reconsignment, icing, refrigeration, heat, C.O.D. services, transit services, absorptions, allowances, and other services. It is possible to secure modification of these general provisions, however.

In addition to the provision regarding the foregoing services, there is also the requirement for both rail and motor carriers that there must be included in their tariffs all other charges and rules which in any way increase or decrease the amount to be paid on any shipment, or which increase or decrease the value of the service to the shipper. The tariff circulars provide that these special services, and the charges therefor, in addition to those based on line-haul rates, shall be provided for in one of three ways:

1. By including in the tariff which contains the rate upon which charges

are based the specific authority for the service, the rules under which such extra service is to be performed, and the charge, if any, for the service.

2. By special reference in the tariff which contains the rate on which the charges are based to the ICC or MF–ICC number, as the case may be, of a separate publication which contains the provision for such service and the charge, if any, for the service.

3. By including in the tariff which contains the rates on which charges are based a clause providing that shipments made under the rates contained therein are entitled to the following services (those services which are permitted in connection with such rates are to be specifically named) and that shipments are subject to the charges for such service, if any, of participating carriers performing the services as shown in tariffs lawfully on file with the Interstate Commerce Commission.

Many carriers follow plan No. 3.

MOTOR CONTRACT CARRIERS

The tariff rules which govern the construction, filing, and posting of schedules of contract motor carriers are contained in Tariff Circular MF No. 4. The rules governing the publication of motor contract carrier schedules are not as comprehensive as is true of the rail and motor common carrier requirements. There are certain provisions which govern contract carrier schedule publication which are similar, although there are some basic differences. For example, a contract carrier cannot participate by concurrence in rates named in any schedule which is filed by another contract carrier, nor is the publication of the contract carrier schedule permitted by a tariff agency.

WATER

Tariff Circulars Nos. 21 and 22 govern water transportation, and are very similar to rail and motor tariff requirements.

AIR

Part 221, "Construction, Publication, Filing and Posting of Tariffs of Air Carriers and of Foreign Air Carriers," of the Civil Aeronautics Board's economic regulations, effective on July 1, 1954, governs the publication of tariffs of air carriers. These requirements are more comprehensive than those in the past and are comparable to the Interstate Commerce Commission requirements.

FREIGHT FORWARDERS

Tariff Circular FF–ICC No. 2 contains the rules which govern the publication of freight forwarder tariffs, and it is patterned after the rail tariff circular. There is no need for it to be as complete, nor is it as complete, as the Tariff Circular No. 20.

Appendix B

The American Society of Traffic and Transportation
Questions on Traffic and Transportation Management
for the Years 1959–63

1. Transportation costs and services play an important part in the manufacture and distribution of products in industry. However, the relationship of the industrial transportation department to other departments in the company is an area where improvement can be made. List the specific ways in which the industrial transportation department can be of help to the production, sales, and accounting departments.

2. Discuss fully the purpose of the Classification Committee as associated with both common rail and motor carriers.

3. What are the primary advantages of diversion and reconsignment from the viewpoint of:
   a) The shipper and the consignee?
   b) The carrier?
   c) The ultimate consumer?

4. a) Describe the procedure by which shippers may collect damages against interstate motor carriers for the payment of unlawful rates or charges of motor carriers.
   b) What provision is there in Part II of the Act for reparation in connection with interstate shipments?
   c) What provision is there in Part I of the Act for reparation in connection with interstate shipments?
   d) The award of reparations is the result of the use by a carrier of a "legal" rate which is "unlawful." Explain clearly the meaning of the terms "reparations," "legal," and "lawful" when used in actions of this kind.

5. Explain what "external economies of location" are and how these economies might be presented to management during an intra-corporation briefing on proposed new plant locations.

6. Air freight ordinarily is faster than other means of transport, but it usually is more expensive. Even so, when selecting a mode of transport, a business firm must consider the whole "transportation package" it really buys when it moves things from one place to another. Discuss how and under what conditions air freight might properly fit into the "transportation package" in physical distribution.

7. Your company has just started manufacturing a new product and the Distribution Department is suggesting a method of packaging that is not provided for in the NMFC No. A–6 or UFC No. 6. As traffic manager, you proceed to arrange with the Classification Committees for test shipments for the purpose of determining the merits or demerits of the new package.

Rule 185 of NMFC No. A–6 and Rule 49 of UFC No. 6 provide that test shipments will be accepted for this purpose without penalty under certain conditions. Name at least four of these conditions.

8. The Canadian railroads have made available to their shippers "agreed charges" since 1938. Such charges have grown in number quite rapidly since 1955. Answer (*a*) and (*b*) and either (*c*) or (*d*).

   a) Define agreed charges.
   b) Does the principle of agreed charges remove traffic from the competition of other forms of transport? Explain.
   c) In several instances in the United States, the Interstate Commerce Commission has refused to approve the agreed charge principle in rate making. Outline briefly your opinion about whether agreed charges should be made available to shippers in the United States.
   d) Outline briefly the advantages and disadvantages of agreed charges from the shipper's point of view.

9. The following is from *Traffic World's Questions and Answers Book*, Vol. 14, 1962:

   "A shipment, with visible damage, was delivered to us on September 28, 1959. Anticipating that the damage could be repaired for a nominal fee, we delayed the filing of a claim, or a letter of intent, until installation.

   "Installation was attempted eight months later and it was determined that doors could not be adequately repaired. Consequently, replacements were ordered.

   "On May 20, 1960, we wrote to the delivering carrier, informing him of our intent to file a claim as soon as the new doors and necessary documents were obtained.

   "An invoice for the replacement doors was received August 22, 1960, and a formal claim was filed that same day.

   "The delivering carrier has declined payment of the claim, on the basis that the statute of limitations was violated, and that a letter of intent is not valid protection against the violating of the nine-month clause in the bill of lading contract.

   "The delivering carrier also states that payment of this claim would constitute a rebate.

   "We would appreciate your opinion as to whether a letter of intent is sufficient to avoid violation of the statute of limitations, and if payment of this claim would constitute a rebate."

   Suppose the question had been directed to you. How would you answer it?

10. Define any *five* (5) of the following as they are commonly used in traffic management:
    a) Concentration Point.
    b) Mullen Test.
    c) Bond of Indemnity.
    d) Statutory Notice.
    e) Blanket Rate.
    f) Proportional Rate.
    g) Omnibus Clause.

11. You order an empty 50-foot DF car for an outbound shipment. Several days later the railroad brings the car into your plant on its daily switch, but it does not notify your track foreman that the car has been included in the switch. This car is physically in your plant for a week before your track foreman discovers it and calls it to your attention. The railroad bills

you for demurrage from the day the car arrives. Are you liable for this demurrage? Explain your answer.

12. Five common-law exemptions to the liability of common carriers are:
   a) Act of God.
   b) Act of the public enemy.
   c) Act of the shipper.
   d) The inherent nature of the goods.
   e) Authority of law.
   Explain or illustrate the application of each of these exemptions.

January, 1963, Questions

1. You are a traffic manager for XYZ Co., a multi-plant operation that produces a finished product used in the building trade. This product is produced at plants located at Newark, N.J., and St. Louis, Mo. Consideration is being given to building a third plant in the western section of the United States. The following factors are relevant to the cost consideration in this decision:
   a) Raw materials are shipped in equal quantities from XYZ plants located at Charleston, W. Va., and Memphis, Tenn.
   b) The finished product is sold F.O.B. destination.
   c) Market area for the finished product is closely related to population density.
   d) It takes three units of raw material to produce one unit of finished product.
   e) The transportation cost per unit of inbound material is approximately one-half that of the outbound finished product.
   f) Both the St. Louis and Newark plants presently are operating at optimum capacity; any increase in production would increase unit cost of production 10 per cent.
   g) It is estimated that the earliest a new plant could be placed in operation would be 1964. In addition, it has been estimated that the plant would not reach optimum production until 1968, and from 1964 to 1968 production cost would be 10 per cent higher than the present cost at St. Louis and Newark.
   Explain how you would evaluate the economics of establishing a third manufacturing facility.
   Explain how you would determine where the third manufacturing facility should be located.

2. The "pipeline concept" is integral to "physical distribution planning." Explain this concept in terms of: (*answer any five*)
   a) Customer service levels.
   b) The inventory cycle.
   c) The average inventory.
   d) Lead time.
   e) Probability theory.
   f) Inventory control.
   g) Stocks.

3. You have had several courses in economics and would like to use the knowledge gained to defend one of your proposals for a rate reduction. How might you conceivably use your knowledge of fixed costs? Variable costs? Average costs?

4. A fellow traffic manager is very enthusiastic about his private carriage operation and is encouraging you to start a similar operation. What factors

would you consider in deciding whether private carriage would be feasible for your plant?

5. President Kennedy has proposed that the Congress authorize the ICC to permit experimental rates. As traffic manager of a large company shipping and receiving scrap metals of all kinds, what kinds of experimental rates would you propose to rail, motor, and water carriers serving your plant? Why?

6. Your company manufactures and receives food products, some perishable, at Atlanta, Ga., and distributes them throughout the southeast. State and analyze the factors you would consider in constructing a routing guide for inbound and outbound shipments by rail, motor, express, and parcel post.

7. What must a rail carrier do if a shipper who prepares his own bill of lading:
   a) Specifies a particular route but does not specify the rate.
   b) Specifies a particular rate but does not specify the route.
   c) Specifies neither the route nor the rate.
   d) Specifies both route and rate, but the two are in conflict.
   What would a truck carrier be legally obligated to do under each of the above conditions?

8. In checking the freight rate on a particular movement, you find that the carrier's tariffs name the following: 98 cents per 100 pounds—based on the straight classification rating; 92 cents per 100 pounds—based on an exception to the classification; 95 cents per 100 pounds—based on a specific commodity rate.
   If the tariffs in question contained no provision for the alternation of class and commodity rates, which rate do you think would be the proper rate to apply? Give reasons for your answer.

9. The Apex Tire Co. purchased a truckload of automobile tires from a manufacturer in Akron, O. The terms of sale were F.O.B. Akron and shipment was forwarded via truck on an order/notify bill of lading.
   a) What would consignee have to do to obtain delivery of the shipment?
   b) Under the terms of sale, who would normally bear the cost of transportation?
   c) When would title pass on this purchase?

10. As traffic manager for a middle-sized company, you have been requested to obtain a classification for a new product manufactured by your firm.
   a) Explain in detail how this is accomplished.
   b) Explain the factors considered in establishing such classification and the arguments on which you would base your case for reasonable classification ratings for both rail and truck movement.

11. Briefly explain any five of the following:
   a) Released value rates; (b) rate bureau or association; (c) "spot stocks"; (d) consular invoices; (e) general-average loss; (f) the dollar system of measuring warehouse efficiency; (g) a "foreign trade zone"; (h) average agreement.

12. You are shipping a car to a consignee located in a large city served by many railroads. You are not sure which road your customer is located on, and because the road may not have reciprocal switching you want to route the shipment via the proper delivering carrier.
   a) If you cannot contact your customer, where might you find the above information?
   b) Suppose in error you shipped the car on a railroad that did not even

have an interchange agreement with the delivering carrier. What might be the nature of the additional charges to which you would be subjected?

JUNE, 1962, QUESTIONS

1. *a*) What are the functions of a bill of lading?
   b) Enumerate the various kinds (except short form).
   c) Explain the "no recourse" clause.
   d) Differentiate between bill of lading liability and that at common law.
2. The following are the rates per hundred pounds on a certain commodity by alternate modes of transportation between New York and Detroit:

	Rate/CWT	Time in Transit	Inventory Requirement to Serve Detroit Market
Air freight	$11.80	1 day	$1,000,000
Motor carrier .	7.50	3 days	3,000,000
Rail freight ...	6.75	6 days	6,000,000

If cost were the sole standard in determining the physical distribution system that you may choose, indicate what method of analysis you might use to determine the least cost method of physical distribution.

3. Water transportation, one of the earliest forms of access to distant markets, has been supplemented by rail, truck, air, and pipeline. In planning marketing strategy, what conditions would warrant utilization of each of these from the point of view of distribution costs considerations?

4. There are many motor carriers which engage in long haul operations. Comment on the future of these carriers with respect to:
   a) Their competitive position in the field of motor transportation.
   b) Internal operating problems.
   c) Competitive forces which might affect their competitive position in the future.
   If you so desire, (*a*) and (*c*) of this question may be combined.

5. The following is from the *Traffic World's* "Questions and Answers" column. Suppose the query had been directed to you. How would you have answered it?
   "We believe that the general practice in apprising a carrier that special damages will result for failure to make reasonable delivery is to place a notation to that effect in the bill of lading at the time of shipment.
   "On four occasions, different motor carriers have refused to sign for, or accept, a shipment with a notation of this kind in the bill of lading. As an example, on a shipment moving 100 miles for a special sale, the bill of lading is noted 'special damages will result if not delivered in 10 days.'
   "In your opinion, can the carriers legally refuse to accept the shipment?
   "What alternatives do we have if they can refuse to accept the shipment?"
   Explain your answers.

6. A number of the southern and western railroads permit "trans-loading" at specified points.
   a) Describe in detail the physical operation involved in this privilege and the manner in which freight charges are applied.
   b) What are the advantages of this privilege to the shipper?

7. As a result of the Supreme Court's decision in the T.I.M.E. case, considerable attention has been focused on the power or lack of power of the Interstate Commerce Commission to award reparation.

   a) Describe the growth of this power, and what it is today.

   b) In your opinion, what should be done to achieve uniformity under all four parts of the Interstate Commerce Act? (Bear in mind that your answer may be "Nothing should be done.")

8. The Vice President—Operations of a small firm producing a variety of large and small machine tools, generally to special order, has asked you as its Traffic Manager whether the company generally uses the carrier or mode of transportation with the lowest rates to transport its shipments. Prepare a memorandum in response to this inquiry.

9. Answer (a) and either (b) or (c).

   a) Briefly discuss the reasons for, the origins of, and the principal distinguishing characteristics of U.S. rail export-import rates.

   b) What is the principal pertinent difference between the Bill of Lading used in the U.S. land carriage and the one used in ocean carriage? Explain concisely.

10. a) What are the basic objectives of "good" materials handling? Briefly explain or illustrate each.

    b) How does unit loading and containerization fit into these objectives?

11. Briefly explain *any five* of the following:

    a) Rule of analogy.

    b) Aggregate of intermediates.

    c) Average agreement.

    d) Weight break.

    e) Penalty rule.

    f) Load factor.

    g) Mullen test.

12. Recently a railroad announced plans for an "integrated train." Explain what is meant by such a train.

    a) Tell what its function is to be and what brought it about.

    b) Suggest a rate system designed to meet this competition.

JANUARY, 1962, QUESTIONS

1. Answer (a) and (b) or (c):

   a) The particular form that a physical distribution system may take depends on the marketing problems faced by the firm. List four such problems, describing their characteristics in detail.

   b) Explain how the concept of "Physical Distribution Management" should be differentiated from the concept of "Traffic Management."

   c) State and explain at least three reasons for the recent emphasis upon physical distribution.

2. a) The XYZ Railroad runs from A to C through B. You have a shipment moving from A to B and upon checking the carrier's tariff you find that the only rate published from A to B is the class rate of 128 cents. There is, however, a commodity rate of 110 cents published from A through B to C. Under what circumstances might it be possible for you to apply the lower commodity rate on your shipment?

   b) A carload of bakery goods was shipped from New York City to Denver, Colo., routed NYC to Chicago and C B & Q beyond. Freight charges were assessed on the basis of a through rate of 250 cents which applied via all available routes. In auditing the bill you find that there is a rate of 120 cents published by the PRR from New York City to St. Louis, Mo., and a rate of 100 cents published by the Missouri Pacific from St. Louis to Denver. Are there any circumstances under which you, the shipper, might obtain the benefit of the lower combination rate on this shipment? Explain.

3. Answer (*a*), and two of (*b*), (*c*), and (*d*):
   a) Distinguish between the carrier's liability as a common carrier and as a warehouseman.
   b) When does liability as a common carrier end and that of a warehouseman begin?
   c) Within what period of time must claims for loss and damage be filed with railroads or motor carriers?
   d) Could a carrier by special rule in his tariff provide that claims must be filed within 12 months from date of delivery? Explain your answer.

4. Discuss the pick up and delivery of air freight by both airline-contacted motor carriers and regular drayage firms covering the following points:
   a) The applicable tariffs for assessment of charges.
   b) The geographic area within which the air carriers provide pickup and delivery service.
   c) The soundness of the method of using dimensional weight in connection with pickup and delivery.

5. As traffic manager of a company manufacturing and shipping small machinery, you have been requested to appear and testify in support of an application of a motor common carrier before the Interstate Commerce Commission for additional authority to serve your company. Prepare a memorandum to your management explaining why you should or should not appear and testify.

6. Special equipment is becoming increasingly important in rail transportation today. More shippers are asking for special equipment and more rail companies are providing this type of car.
   a) Analyze the advantages and disadvantages of this development from the shipper's viewpoint.
   b) Analyze the advantages and disadvantages of this development from the rail carrier's viewpoint.

7. From the viewpoint of an industrial traffic manager, name and concisely explain the possible factors which you might consider in determining the advantages and disadvantages of private truck carriage vs. for-hire carriage in moving your shipments.

8. A shipper placed a notation on a motor carrier's bill of lading requesting delivery at a specified hour and date. The carrier was unable to make delivery until a day later than requested, with the result that the consignee refused to take delivery, and ultimately the freight was returned to the shipper. The shipper refused to pay the return freight charges on the grounds that it was the carrier's fault that delivery was not made at the specified time. The carrier held that such charges could not be waived, that it was not bound to deliver with other than reasonable dispatch, and that a one day delay was not unreasonable.
   What right would the carrier and the shipper have?

9. "Agreed Rates" by rail carrier have been the subject of much controversy.
   a) Distinguish between these and other methods of charging and indicate the purpose of agreed rates.

b) What economic justification is there, if any, for agreed rates?

c) What legal precedent is there, if any, for agreed rates?

10. A carload shipment moved from Philadelphia, Pa., to Birmingham, Ala. The bill of lading specified routing via B & O—Southern Ry., and as no junction was indicated the B & O delivered the car to the Southern at Cincinnati, O. Charges were assessed on the basis of a rate of 120 cents per 100 lbs., which was the applicable rate via the route of the movement. There was in effect at the same time a rate of 105 cents per 100 lbs., which applied when routed B & O—Potomac Yard—Southern Ry.

a) As traffic manager for the shipper do you believe it would be possible for you to recover the difference between the rate charged and the lower rate of 105 cents and if so how?

b) Would your answer be the same if the shipment had moved by motor carrier? Explain why or why not.

11. Define or explain briefly any five: (*a*) A "foreign trade zone"; (*b*) particular average; (*c*) the proposed "constant charge" plan of the Eastern Central Motor Carriers Association; (*d*) "Project Horizon"; (*e*) the dollar system of measuring warehouse efficiency; (*f*) incentive rates; (*g*) ship's option.

12. Plant location procedure consists of an organized development of location factors within a working framework. Selection of a plant site is a compromise among various location factors and forces, the final decision resulting from the balancing of information found in two types of analyses.

a) Outline five items which might be found in the Plant Analysis which covers the specific costs and procedures of the plant itself.

b) Outline five items which you would expect to find in the Field Analysis relating to the region, the community, and the sites where the plant might be located.

June, 1961, Questions

1. As a transport consultant you are engaged to advise the board of directors of a medium-sized manufacturing firm on the advantages of a traffic and transportation division.

a) Define industrial traffic management to the board of directors. Also, discuss the newer concept of physical distribution management as a total function; and, elaborate on the advantages of a transportation program which is profit maximization orientated versus a cost reduction memorization program of operation.

b) Finally, outline for the board the important functions of the distribution executive in his role as administrator and coordinator with the production planning division, e.g., long-range and short-range forecasting; the pricing division; the purchasing division; organization planning division, e.g., establishing the boundaries of a traffic and transportation division organization structure and explaining the line and staff functions.

2. In May, 1961, the President of the Atlantic States Shippers Advisory Board wrote the Board members as follows:

"During our 114th Regular Meeting in Baltimore last month there was much discussion regarding Senate Bills S-1089 and S-1197, which bills, in brief, propose to further burden the railroads by changing the rate making provisions of the Transportation Act of 1958.

"At the end of this discussion, the undersigned was instructed by the Board to write the Chairmen of the Interstate and Foreign Commerce

Committees of the U.S. Senate and House of Representatives, informing them that the Board had gone on record as opposing these two bills.

"I would now like to urge all of our members to study the two bills in question and write your own Senators giving them the advantage of your views.

"I also urge that you do this promptly as hearings commence May 11th."

a) Is this a departure from the policy of the advisory boards, a policy of not being involved in rates? Explain.

b) What are the "rate making provisions of the Transportation Act of 1958" which the two bills propose to change?

c) As traffic manager of a large industrial concern, will you, or will you not, follow the suggestions in the letter? Explain.

3. *a*) Account for the rise of privately-owned trucking facilities.

   b) Should the federal government (1) encourage, or (2) discourage, this trend? Justify your answer.

   c) What steps should the government take to carry out the policy you chose in (*b*)?

4. As the Traffic Manager of a large metropolitan department store, set forth your views on the subject of the auditing and post auditing of transportation freight bills.

5. Senate Bill No. 1401 dated April 20, 1961 is a bill in the Legislature of the State of California. It is described as "An act to add Chapter 15.5 . . . to Division 3 of the Business and Professions Code, relating to the creation of a State Board of Certified Traffic Management, prescribing its organization, powers, and duties, and making an appropriation therefor." A significant portion of the proposed act is: "8854. The board shall prescribe regulations and prepare, approve, grade, or administer examinations for candidates for the certificate of certified traffic manager. The board may also prescribe rules of professional conduct for the practice of certified traffic manager."

   Also: "8857. No person shall engage in the practice of certified traffic management in this State unless such person is the holder of a valid certificate to practice certified traffic management issued by the board; provided, however, that all persons who, at the time this section goes into effect, are actively engaged in the practice of traffic management in California and have been so engaged for 10 years prior thereto shall be registered by the board as certified traffic managers without examination . . ."

   You are a member of the California State Chapter of the American Society of Traffic and Transportation. What position should you take on this proposal? Justify your stand.

6. The small shipment problem has caused great concern among all modes of transportation. Explain the causes of this problem, and recent steps or proposals which have been taken or offered to solve it.

7. A headline in the April 29, 1961 issue of the *Traffic World* read:

   "Merger With Other Eastern Traffic Groups Eyed by EITL to Avoid Duplicative Effort."

   In this case, EITL stood for The Eastern Industrial Traffic League.

   a) Develop the reasons why such a move might seem indicated to the EITL. With what other groups might it duplicate?

   b) Outline a plan which you as a traffic manager deem sound covering (and justifying your position in each case):

   1. Memberships in organizations which you think your company ought

to support, indicating whether support for attendance at meetings is included.

2. Subscriptions to services and periodicals which your company ought to support.

3. Activities or other items involving monetary cost which the personnel in the traffic department ought to carry themselves.

8. Identify or define briefly *any five:*
   a) Commercial zone.
   b) Gray area.
   c) Dual rates—present status.
   d) MTMA.
   e) Break bulk point.
   f) Ship's option.

9. As the Director of Traffic of a medium-sized multi-plant hardware manufacturer, you are a participant in a meeting of top management called to discuss methods of profitably increasing your company's sales. Each participant is asked to submit a program for his responsibility at the next meeting.
   a) How would you organize your program?
   b) What specific functional areas would you investigate? Why?

10. You are the Traffic Manager of a large single plant manufacturer of tires and rubber products. Shipments to date have been direct from factory to wholesale distributors. Your company has started thinking of using warehouses as distribution centers at two strategic locations. Prepare a memorandum to your President giving your opinions on points to be considered in locating the warehouses, type of warehouse to be employed, and placement of personnel and administration of the warehouses in your company's organization.

11. You are Traffic Manager of a company whose demurrage costs have been averaging $30,000 per year or approximately $2,500 per month. You have an average demurrage agreement and you handle 1000 inbound cars and 500 outbound cars per month. Your outbound demurrage costs are zero. Outline a program that you would propose to your management to reduce your demurrage costs.

12. Outline your recommendations for a department of local transportation for a large department store located in a city of one million population. The store serves a territory reaching out 25 miles and does $25 million gross business. Some of your recommendations may be in the alternative.

JANUARY, 1961, QUESTIONS

1. a) When material sent by a common carrier from a central manufacturing point to a company-owned regional warehouse is completely destroyed in transit, what is the amount of the carrier's liability?
   b) When the same material reaches the regional warehouse safely and is sent by common carrier from the warehouse to a customer and is completely destroyed, is the liability of the carrier the same as in part (a)?
   c) On what value is claim based when the item involved under circumstances similar to those outlined in part (b), is no longer manufactured?
   d) Under circumstances similar to those outlined in part (b), the damage to the material is partial rather than complete. Does the carrier's liability for the goods damaged require that the carrier pay more than the cost of repairs to the merchandise? Explain briefly.

2. You are the general traffic manager of a company similar in size to U.S. Steel. For executive use, you have a fleet of six aircraft.
    a) What sort of organization would you set up to operate this fleet?
    b) Your president asks you if the benefits from the use of the fleet justify its cost. What information would you give him?

3. Pan-American World Airways has announced the establishment of a number of modern air cargo terminals throughout the world and several domestic airlines have in process a large program of passenger aircraft conversion to freight aircraft. You are traffic manager of a large shoe manufacturer with an extensive line of shoes.
    a) What change in your company distribution system, if any, might follow the above developments?
    b) What recommendations would you make to the sales department concerning the possibilities of shipping shoes by air?

4. In an extensive program of diversifications of holdings, your company, which produces a line of industrial chemical products, secures controlling interest in: an active, hard-coal mine; a window air-conditioner manufacturer in the southwestern part of the United States; and a small visual aids film and projector manufacturing company. What general recommendations would you as traffic manager make as to organization of the traffic work of each of the new subsidiaries?

5. Motor trucking is often described as a small-scale business, particularly well adapted to short-haul carriage, yet we have a number of trucking company organizations of substantial size, and one carrier is said to have an average haul of 1,500 miles.

    Were (or are) the "small-scale, short-haul" descriptions inaccurate; has the industry changed; or is the development of the larger-company, longer-haul carrier uneconomic? Explain.

6. An economist recently described the railroad approach in the Paint Rate Case as amounting to the "design of a rate structure for the specific purpose of maximizing revenue contribution over incremental cost."
    a) What did he mean by this?
    b) Is the Paint Rate Case likely to be remembered for having established a landmark in the rate regulation? Explain.

7. Special transit services and privileges may be divided into two general groups: (1) Arrangements which imply the processing or manufacturing of a commodity and (2) arrangements for marketing or transportation.
    a) Give some examples of each type of special transit privilege.
    b) How are the freight charges collected on shipments stopped in transit?

8. A manufacturing company executive recently said that the personnel of the traffic department of his company lacked imagination—that a competitor had recently invaded the market in which his company had done a substantial amount of business and the competitor's price was lower than the price of his company's product. When the executive passed the problem to the various departments, including the traffic department, the solution of the latter was to ask the carrier for a freight rate reduction. The executive termed this an "inadequate and disappointing" response. Could you have done better? If so, explain.

9. *Traffic World's Questions and Answers Book,* Volume 8, on the question of loss and damage raised this question:

    "A shipper has been forwarding collect shipments of a released valuation commodity, but has neglected to note the released valuation on the bill of lading. The commodities take Class 100 ratings if released, but, if not released, the shipment is subject to the Class 200 rate in any-quantity, as per item 2180, Middle Atlantic Conference tariff No. 10-k. The carrier's rate department inadvertently rated the shipments as Class 100. The error was discovered by the carrier's claim department upon presentation of a claim by the consignee, who is claiming full value.

"We would appreciate your advising whether the carrier may now re-rate past shipments and bill the consignee for additional freight charges or, if that is not possible, can the carrier make payment of the claim on the basis of the released value rating."

How would you answer the question and why?

10. *a*) What should a traffic manager look for in selecting materials handling equipment for his firm?

b) List some cost factors that should be considered in purchasing materials handling equipment.

11. Discuss briefly:

a) Rules of the National Defense Transportation Association for the distribution of traffic of the Department of Defense among different types of carriers.

b) The position of any of the shippers' advisory boards in the recent Ex Parte No. 223 rate case (October, 1960).

c) The control exercised by the Civil Aeronautics Board in the issuance of airline company securities for the purchase of jet aircraft.

12. Comment briefly on three of the following: (*a*) The significance of plan III for the common motor carrier; (*b*) break-even analysis; (*c*) linear programming; (*d*) the bulk exemption; (*e*) a census of transportation.

JUNE, 1960, QUESTIONS

1. In recent years there has been much talk of "distribution management" and those who now carry the title of "traffic manager" are urged to be alert to this development.

a) What is included in this new concept; that is, what is "distribution management"?

b) What persons, by functional title, are in competition for the title of distribution manager?

c) What do you recommend to a traffic manager as a means of combating, or taking advantage of, this new trend?

2. *a*) Explain the difference in the time allowed for loading without additional charge for rail movements and for highway truck movements.

b) Upon what basis is the published charge for strike demurrage determined?

c) Outline in general the terms of an average agreement.

3. *a*) How does one railroad determine whether it should pay for freight cars owned by another railroad on the lines of the first railroad, and, if so, how much?

b) Explain the theory of per diem reclaim.

4. An obstacle to the development of air cargo has been the lack of an airplane which is suited to cargo transport.

a) What are the characteristics of a good cargo transport?

b) What is the responsibility of the following for the underwriting of the development of an efficient air cargo transport:

1. Trunkline air carriers.

2. Aircraft manufacturers.

3. The government.

5. *a*) Your company produces plaster and plaster products. It has determined that the increasing population, and increased building, in a western area including several states can support a new mill and products plant. You, the Traffic Manager, are asked to estimate the freight rates which could be established from a possible site near the raw materials source to the market area in the several western states. Explain fully how you would go about preparing the estimate.

   b) Afterwards the management of your company accepts your study and asks that you arrange to have the estimated rates published. Explain fully how you would go about accomplishing this.

6. The use of containers in the movement of commodities appears to be headed for an increase.

   a) What is the responsibility of a food products distributing company of substantial size, for underwriting and carrying on research into this problem?

   b) Suppose the food products company develops a very satisfactory container, and secures a patent on it. What is its responsibility:

      1. To its competitors, so far as permitting the use of the device is concerned?

      2. To the common carrier industry which might wish to supply the device to its shippers?

7. *Traffic World's Questions and Answers Book*, Volume 9, poses the following problems:

   "A load of passenger automobiles was moved by a motor carrier, who is a certified common carrier in interstate business, on a standard automobile transport tractor and trailer combination in an over-the-road haul. During the journey, part of which is through desert areas, the rig was caught in a sandstorm, which damaged the glass, the chrome, and the painted finish of the automobiles in the cargo. The autos were not covered, because tariff rules and regulations do not require the carrier to furnish such protection. No advance notice as to the storm was available to the truck driver. "Since sandstorms of the intensity to cause such damage are unpredictable, the damage resulting therefrom would not appear to be carrier liability under the act of God clause of the uniform bill of lading.' "

   Do you agree or disagree? Why?

8. Explain in detail the various methods and advantages of financing by the following:

   a) Shipper's Order Bill of Lading.

   b) Field Warehousing.

9. *Traffic World's Questions and Answers Book*, Volume 9, on the subject of Limitation of Action raised this question:

   "Is it true that in return for waiving the time period conditions of the statute of limitations on freight charges applicable to a government bill of lading, the United States Government has agreed that there will be no charge for interest, when discrepancies are revealed through audit and a request for overcharge is presented to the carrier?"

   How would you answer this question and why?

10. In March, 1960, the United States Department of Commerce published a report, *Federal Transportation Policy and Program*. In it were recommendations for new legislation, changes in the administration of present

regulation, and new programs for the government. The Senate Interstate and Foreign Commerce Committee asks you, as one of the nation's leading Vice Presidents—Traffic, to present your views on the report. What positions would you take in your testimony on a number of the recommendations of the report? Be specific.

11. The St. Lawrence Seaway, beginning in 1959, was opened for vessels of greater size than formerly.
    a) What industries should find it of greatest advantage to use the Seaway for the transportation of their products?
    b) To what industries will the Seaway make little difference?

12. What considerations would lead you as Vice President—Traffic to recommend to your company that it:
    a) Purchase a fleet of ten trucks for over-the-road hauling of its own commodities, both inbound, and outbound?
    b) Purchase a small plane for company use?

January, 1960, Questions

1. Identify or describe briefly any *five*.
   a) T.I.M.E. v. *United States of America* (or *Davidson Transfer & Storage Co.* v. *United States of America*).
   b) Three-way rule.
   c) Particular average loss.
   d) "Without Recourse" clause.
   e) The "Paint" case.
   f) A recent Post Office Department proposal.
   g) Burlington Mills Corp., *Transportation for Compensation*.

2. A spokesman for the Association of American Railroads recently stated that, "Piggy-back service is now offered by some 50 railroads and is one of the most promising developments in the industry's continuing program of improving methods and techniques to meet the needs of American shippers."
   Briefly discuss some of the present advantages and disadvantages of piggy-back service:
   a) To the railroads.
   b) To the shippers.
   c) To the motor carriers.
   d) To the freight forwarders.
   Include in your discussion how those mentioned in (b), (c), and (d) can utilize piggy-back service offered by the railroads.

3. "Contract" or "Agreed" rates have long been lawful in Canada and certain European countries. Many shippers and railroads in the United States believe that recent Interstate Commerce Act changes now permit this type of rate in the United States. (Answer any *three*.)
   a) Under what conditions could you as a Traffic Manager expect to negotiate this type of rate with the railroads?
   b) What would be some of the advantages to a shipper in having this type of rate available for his use? Disadvantages?
   c) What advantages could railroads expect if they agreed to publish this type of rate? Disadvantages?
   d) Do you believe that "Contract" or "Agreed" rates by rail would be harmful to the railroads' competitors? Explain.

4. Bills of lading are perhaps the most important single shipping document with which the Traffic Manager must be familiar. How would you, as a Traffic Manager, explain the following types of bills of lading and bill of lading terms to the person in your company's shipping department who is responsible for the issuance of bills of lading? (Answer any *five*.)

a) Straight bill of lading.
b) Order bill of lading.
c) Domestic bill of lading.
d) Export bill of lading.
e) Government bill of lading.
f) Uniform bill of lading.
g) Clean bill of lading.
h) Shipper's load and count.

5. Describe two ways a consignee may secure his shipment from a carrier when the original shipper's order bill of lading is apparently lost. As an industrial Traffic Manager, explain for each of the two ways the circumstances in which it would be wisest to use that method.

6. a) Explain "Diversion" or "Reconsignment," showing the situations that might arise and the factors to be looked for, and how the carriers have made provision for them.

b) To what extent are these practices available with different types of carriers?

7. The Senate Interstate and Foreign Commerce Committee has a research staff at work studying transportation problems. You are Traffic Manager for a large Chemical company moving substantial amounts of raw materials by different transportation agencies, and distributing a wide variety of finished products also by a number of carriers of different type. Your company also has a substantial expense for the movement of persons.

The top management of your company encourages you to take part in public affairs and you draw up a statement for the Senate committee to consider in deciding what problems are most worthy of study.

What four (or five or six) items would you include in your statement? Rank them in order of importance, and tell why you have chosen them.

8. What duty rests with a railroad with respect to its obligation to shippers when the following appears on bills of lading:

a) No route or rate is shown.
b) Route is shown and no rate.
c) Rate is shown and no route.
d) When both rate and route are shown but they conflict?

9. The following is from the *Traffic World's Questions and Answers Book*, Volume 4. Suppose the query had been directed to you. How would you have answered it?

"We should like very much to have the benefit of your opinion concerning what we believe to be a commercial zone situation.

"There is a military installation located near one of the towns which we are authorized to serve. This installation was established after our franchise rights were granted. The town near which this reservation is located has a population of about 8,000 and one of the gates leading to the reservation is within a distance of approximately one mile from the city limits of said town.

"Our question is, 'Would we be authorized under commercial zone rulings to include this reservation in the commercial zone of this town and would we be authorized to serve the entire installation once we have entered the gate referred to above?'

"We shall appreciate your opinion in this matter."

10. Common carriers publish class and commodity rates to cover the transportation services they are required by law to furnish. These rates fall into various forms and the designation of the particular form may also indicate the type of service offered, such as Local rates or Joint rates.

Name at least *five* other types of rates and briefly explain how they enter into the assessment of just and reasonable freight charges.

11. The following is from the *Traffic World's Questions and Answers Book*, Volume 4. Suppose the query had been directed to you. How would you have answered it?

"Is it unlawful to bill an interstate shipment via one motor carrier to an interchange point and issue a second bill of lading to another carrier from that interchange point to destination and in that manner protect a combination of rates lower than a through class rate from initial point of shipment?"

12. Though air cargo has been available over many airlines and between many points for years, its development has not lived up to what many expected. At present, however, many spokesmen anticipate a "break-through."

a) On what developments will a "break-through" depend?

b) Which would you advise an airline to do:
   1. Make a market survey to determine the air cargo potential for the line?
   2. "Sit tight" for the time being, taking whatever cargo is offered, but doing little to encourage it?

c) What steps, if any, do you think the federal government should take in encouraging air cargo development?

JUNE, 1959, QUESTIONS

1. Several different plans, designated Plan 1, Plan 2, etc., for operation of trailer-on-flat car business are in use or under proposals for use. Explain the fundamentals of each plan and how they differ.

2. *a*) Give your views as to the value of common carriers in the sound prosperous state.

   b) Do you think continuity of privately owned carriers in the United States is in danger? Why, or why not?

3. "Railroads Vow Rate Competition" was a headline in the *New York Times* on April 21, 1959, in a story on the opening of the St. Lawrence Seaway. In the same story a Pennsylvania Congressman was quoted to the effect that the Seaway tolls would not accomplish the mandate of Congress that the Seaway be self-liquidating.

   a) What changes in traffic flow may be expected as the result of the Seaway?

   b) What changes in service in rates will be introduced by the carriers already existing in the Seaway area?

4. As toll highways have been introduced, it has become the problem of the managing authorities to induce the drivers of different types of vehicles to use the toll facility. Different ones have experienced different degrees of success. As the manager of a truck line with a considerable number of vehicles, what considerations of toll charges, weight limitations, and operation costs, versus conditions of operation on alternate highways, would be

important to you in your decision to use, or not to use, the toll highway?

5. An I.C.C. Examiner recently reported the railroads "have good reason to believe that the principal underlying causes of their loss of passenger traffic has been the governmental promotion of air and highway transportation by financial outlay and other means." Do you agree? Why, or why not?

6. Business flying in the United States has grown to the point where it uses "about forty times more aircraft" and does "three and a half times more annual flying hours than the airlines." In the management of a commercial airline such measures as load factor, utilization factor, length of haul, and others, are used in determining the efficiency of the airline.

   a) Are these same measures, or similar ones, appropriate guides for determining the efficiency of the fleet of an industrial or commercial company? Explain your answer.

   b) If your answer to (a) is "no" or partially "no," what measures would you use?

7. From the *Traffic World's Questions and Answers Book, 1954:*

   "In your opinion, is it in order for an intercoastal steamship company to request a surety bond from shippers on cargo reconsigned when under a straight bill of lading?

   "The reconsignment does not effect a change in the port, simply a change in the consignee. The reconsignment rules under Interstate Commerce Commission Intercoastal tariffs provide for reconsignment. No mention is made in the intercoastal bill of lading as to any change in the reconsignment rules carried in the tariff."

   Suppose the question had been directed to you. How would you answer it? Justify your answer.

8. Controversy continues unabated over statutory or policy limitations upon one type of transport engaging in another form of transportation.

   a) What are the economic arguments for and against integration of this type, relative ease of private entry into all but rail transport considered?

   b) What reasons are there, if any, for treating air-surface integration differently from integration of surface carriers?

9. Identify or describe briefly any five:

   a) General average.

   b) Primary business test.

   c) *Illinois Central R.R. Co.* v. *Crail* (1930).

   d) Port equalization.

   e) Ship's option.

   f) Mullen test.

   g) Demurrage—motor carrier rules.

10. From the *Traffic World's Questions and Answers Book, 1954:*

    "We would like to have your opinion with reference to a claim we have filed with a carrier for concealed damage, which claim has been returned declined. The claim was declined for the reason that there had been no inspection by the carrier of the damaged merchandise.

    "The claim was filed with the carrier within thirty days after delivery of the shipment. The carrier was then advised that the merchandise was being held for inspection.

    "It is our rule to ask for inspection before filing a claim, but this claim slipped through before the carrier was asked to make an inspection."

    Suppose the question had been directed at you. How would you answer it? Justify your answer.

11. From the *Traffic World's Questions and Answers Book, 1954:*

"Item 21420 of Uniform Freight Classification No. 1, Agent W. S. Flint, I.C.C. No. A-1, provides ratings on Glassware, N.O.I.B.N. The item provides various ratings depending upon valuation.

"The classification description for the first rating reads 'Actual value not exceeding 25 cents per lb.' The description for the ratings of higher value all carry the phrase 'Actual value.' One of our shippers has asked whether under this classification the shipper may declare a value less than actual value or whether under the terms of the classification description, the actual invoice value must be declared."

Suppose the question had been directed to you. How would you answer it? Justify your answer.

12. Late in 1958 the New York Central announced that it was withdrawing from the express business on January 1, 1960. In March, 1959, the Pennsylvania proposed that the Railway Express Agency be "saved" by altering the rate divisions between eastern railroads and southern and western railroads. Other proposals were offered in the spring of 1959, under one of which a banking firm offered to buy the Agency and continue to operate it.

   a) Suppose the Railway Express Agency were discontinued. What would be the impact on our distribution system?

   b) Suppose you support the point of view that the Agency cannot be dispensed with. What steps would you take to keep it in operation?

January, 1959, Questions

1. State your concept of the responsibility of an industrial traffic department for provision and administration of *any four* of the following transportation activities:

   a) Owned or leased passenger automobiles and trucks.

   b) Owned or chartered airplanes.

   c) Owned, leased, or chartered barges or ships.

   d) Owned or leased railway cars.

   e) Passenger reservations via public carriers.

   f) Materials handling within plants.

   g) Packaging and loading of freight.

2. Railroads may be ready to request authority to establish *agreed rates* on certain traffic.

   a) Distinguish between these and other methods of charging *and* indicate the purpose of agreed rates.

   b) What economic justification is there, if any, for agreed rates? Legal precedent?

   c) Should other types of transport oppose the request? Explain.

3. Many motor carrier agency tariffs contain "rate stops" and "flagouts" on commodity rates, exception ratings, general increases, etc., for the account of individual carriers. Do you believe such exceptions to general application of rates are justified? Give reasons.

4. You are in need of information on items listed below. To what text or publication references would you go for the answers? (*Five of six*)

   a) The inside dimensions of a railway car, Southern 52148.

   b) The name and business address of the traffic manager of a large food products company.

   c) Whether a rail shipment may be made "freight charges collect" to a small station in Nevada.

d) Ocean cargo rates, New York to Cairo.

e) The population of the trading area of Dallas, Texas.

f) Possible motor freight routes, Chicago to Los Angeles.

5. Explain how you, as an industrial traffic manager, could use effectively the following types of warehousing:

a) Privately-owned warehousing.

b) Public warehousing.

c) Field warehousing.

6. Define or describe *five* of the following:

a) Rule 10.

b) Rule 34.

c) Tapering principle.

d) Reed-Bulwinkle Act.

e) Agreed weight.

f) Tolerance.

7. *a*) Is a carrier obligated to pay interest on freight overcharge claims brought to his attention by a shipper? If so, what is the currently applicable rate of interest?

b) Outline the procedure for collecting from the railroads claims for property damage.

8. What changes in regulation were incorporated in the Transportation Act of 1958 (or in other laws passed by the 85th Congress) which might be expected to bring substantial changes in the management of traffic, or the transportation facilities, of a large manufacturing industry?

9. From *Traffic World*, August 30, 1958:

"A shipment was picked up in Philadelphia, Pa., for delivery in Washington, D.C., freight charges collect. The consignee refused to pay the collect freight charges, claiming the terms of sale were delivered at Washington, D.C. Since this consignee was not on the credit accommodation list, the truck driver refused to deliver the shipment and returned same to his Philadelphia terminal.

"The shipment was returned to the shipper with the bill for freight charges to Washington, D.C., and also from Washington to Philadelphia, covering the return movement. The shipper is willing to pay the charges to Washington, but refuses to pay the return freight charges.

"We would appreciate your citing any reports of the Interstate Commerce Commission or decisions of the courts covering similar cases."

Suppose the question had been directed to you. How would you answer it?

10. Explain briefly the regulations governing the rendition of bills and the payment of freight charges on interstate shipments between shippers and (*a*) railroads, (*b*) motor common carriers.

11. You are General Traffic Manager for a large organization. Actual routing of traffic by types of carriers, or by competitors within types of carriers may be performed by you, or by a member of your staff, in the main office or at branch plants. You are concerned with the possibility that those who route your business may be influenced by other things than service and rates, for example, by "Christmas presents," which come from traffic solicitors.

Outline a directive of not more than a page in length, embodying the four, or five, or six (or any other number), points which you will send to those who route your traffic to guide them in determining how they shall do their job, and what part Christmas presents or other "gratuities" may play in their judgments. Make your "code" a realistic one.

12. Discuss the role of the consignor, the consignee, and the carrier:
   a) In expediting shipments.
   b) In tracing shipments.

Selected Bibliography

AITCHISON, C.B. *Fair Reward and Just Compensation, Common Carrier Service*. Washington, D.C.: Association of Interstate Commerce Commission Practitioners, 1954.

AMERICAN MANAGEMENT ASSOCIATION, INC. *Management of the Physical Distribution Function*. American Management Assn. Inc., 1515 Broadway, New York 36, N.Y., 1960.

AMERICAN TRANSPORTATION RESEARCH FORUM. *Papers—Third Annual Meeting*. Oxford, Ind.: Richard B. Cross Co., 1962.

AMERICAN TRUCKING ASSOCIATIONS, INC. *Highways, Trucks and New Industry—A Study of Changing Patterns in Plant Location*. Washington, D.C.: American Trucking Associations, Inc., 1963.

AMMER, D.S. *Materials Management*. Homewood, Ill.: Richard D. Irwin, Inc., 1962.

ASHBY, W.T., and OTHERS. *Motor Truck Red Book*. New York: Traffic Publishing Co., Inc., 1950.

ASSOCIATION OF INTERSTATE COMMERCE COMMISSION PRACTITIONERS. *Supreme Court Decisions Important to the Interstate Commerce Commission, and Abstracts of 39 Important Decisions since 1939*. Washington, D.C., 1954. A supplement issued in 1956 covers the period 1953–56.

AUERBACH, C.A., and NATHANSON, N.L. *Federal Regulation of Transportation*. St. Paul: West Publishing Co., 1953.

BAKER, G.P., and GERMANE, G.E. *Case Problems in Transportation Management*. New York: McGraw-Hill Book Co., Inc., 1957.

BARRIGER, J.W. *Super-Railroads*. New York: Simmons-Boardman Co., 1956.

BIGHAM, T.C., and ROBERTS, M.J. *Transportation*. 2d ed. New York: McGraw-Hill Book Co., Inc., 1952.

BLAINE, J.C.D. *Selected Cases and Case Studies in Transportation Regulation and Management*. Dubuque, Iowa: Wm. C. Brown & Co., 1963.

BROSS, S.R. *Ocean Shipping*. Cambridge, Md.: Cornell Maritime Press, 1956.

BRYAN, L.A. *Principles of Water Transportation*. New York: Ronald Press Co., 1939.

———. *Traffic Management in Industry*. New York: Dryden Press, 1953.

BUGAN, T.G. *When Does Title Pass*. 2d ed. Dubuque, Iowa: Wm. C. Brown & Co., 1951.

CAVES, R. *Air Transport and Its Regulators*. Cambridge, Mass.: Harvard University Press, 1962.

CHERINGTON, P.W. *Airline Price Policy*. Boston: Harvard University, 1958.

COLQUITT, J.C. *The Art and Development of Freight Classification*. Washington, D.C.: National Motor Freight Traffic Association, Inc., 1956.

COLTON, R.C., and WARD, E.S. *Practical Handbook of Industrial Traffic Management*. 3d ed. New York: Funk & Wagnalls Co., 1959.

COOLEY, HENRY B. *Transportation Management*. New York: Cornell Maritime Press, 1946.

COUGHLIN, E.W. *Freight Car Distribution and Car Handling in the United States*. Washington, D.C.: Association of American Railroads, 1956.

CUFLEY, C.F.H. *Ocean Freights and Chartering*. Cambridge, Md.: Cornell Maritime Press, 1962.

CUSHMAN, F.M. *Manual of Transportation Law.* Dallas, Tex.: Transportation Press, 1952.

——. *Transportation for Management.* New York: Prentice-Hall, Inc., 1953.

DAGGETT, STUART. *Principles of Inland Transportation.* 4th ed. New York: Harper & Bros., 1955.

DEARING, C.L., and OWEN, W.L. *National Transportation Policy.* Washington, D.C.: Brookings Institution, 1949.

FAGG, C.J.; WELLER, W.W.; and STRUNK, A.B. *The Freight Traffic Red Book.* New York: Traffic Publishing Co., Inc., 1955.

FAIR, M.L., and WILLIAMS, E.W., JR. *Economics of Transportation.* Rev. ed. New York: Harper & Bros., 1959.

FLOOD, KENNETH. *Traffic Management.* Dubuque, Iowa: Wm. C. Brown & Co., 1963.

FREDERICK, J.H. *Commercial Air Transportation.* 5th ed. Homewood, Ill.: Richard D. Irwin, Inc., 1961.

——. *Traffic Department Organization.* Philadelphia, Pa.: Chilton Co., 1956.

——. *Using Public Warehouses.* Philadelphia, Pa.: Chilton Co., 1957.

GERMANE, G.E.; GLASKOWSKY, N.A., Jr.; and HESKETT, J.L. *Highway Transportation Management.* New York: McGraw-Hill Book Co., Inc., 1963.

GREENHUT, MELVIN L. *Plant Location in Theory and Practice.* Chapel Hill, N.C.: The University of North Carolina Press, 1956.

GROSSMAN, W.L. *Ocean Freight Rates.* Cambridge, Md.: Cornell Maritime Press, 1956.

GWERTZMAN, M.J. *The Law of Transportation in Its Relation to Transportation Insurance.* Larchmont, N.Y.: Macade Press, 1950.

HARPER, DONALD V. *Basic Planning and the Transportation Function in Small Manufacturing Firms,* Small Business Management Research Reports. University of Minnesota, Minneapolis 14, Minn. 1961.

HAYNES, D. OLIPHANT. *Materials Handling Applications.* Philadelphia: Chilton Co., 1958.

HOBBAH, R.V. *Railroad Transit Privileges.* Chicago: University of Chicago Press, 1944.

HOOVER, E.M. *The Location of Economic Activity.* New York: McGraw-Hill Book Co., Inc., 1948.

HUDSON, W.J., and CONSTANTIN, J.A. *Motor Transportation.* New York: Ronald Press Co., 1958.

IMMER, J.R. *Materials Handling.* New York: McGraw-Hill Book Co., Inc., 1953.

INSTITUTE OF INTERNAL AUDITORS RESEARCH COMMITTEE. *Internal Audit & Control of a Traffic Department.* The Institute of Internal Auditors, 120 Wall St., New York 5, N.Y., 1958.

Interstate Commerce Act (revised to November 1, 1958). Washington, D.C.: Superintendent of Public Documents.

Interstate Commerce Acts Annotated, Vols. I–XVIII. Washington, D.C.: Superintedent of Public Documents, 1930, and subsequent years.

ISARD, WALTER. *Location and Space-Economy: A General Theory Relating to Industrial Location, Market Areas, Land Use, Trade, and Urban Structure.* New York: John Wiley & Sons, Inc., and the Technology Press, M.I.T., 1956.

JOHNSON, E.R. *Transportation Facilities, Services and Policies.* New York: D. Appleton-Century Co., 1947.

JOHNSON, E.R.; HUEBNER, G.G.; and WILSON, G.L. *Transportation: Economic Principles and Practices*. New York: D. Appleton-Century Co., 1940.

KAHN, F. *Principles of Motor Carrier Regulation*. Dubuque, Iowa: Wm. C. Brown & Co., 1958.

KNORST, WILLIAM J. *Interstate Commerce Law and Practice*, Vols. I, II, III, and IV. Chicago: College of Advanced Traffic, 1953 and 1958.

————. *Transportation and Traffic Management*, Vol. I (1947); Vols. II and III (1948); and Vol. IV (1949). Chicago: College of Advanced Traffic.

LANDON, C.E. *Transportation*. New York: William Sloane Associates, 1951.

LEDERER, E.H. *Port Terminal Operation*. New York: Cornell Maritime Press, 1945.

LEEMING, JOSEPH. *Modern Export Packing*. Washington, D.C.: U.S. Government Printing Office, 1940.

LEWIS, H.T., and CULLITON, J.W. *The Role of Air Freight in Physical Distribution*. Cambridge, Mass.: Harvard University Press, 1956.

LOCKLIN, D.P. *Economics of Transportation*. 5th ed. Homewood, Ill.: Richard D. Irwin, Inc., 1960.

LOSCH, AUGUST. *The Economics of Location*. New Haven, Conn.: Yale University Press, 1954.

LOWE, GUSTAV E. *Practice and Procedure before Rail Rate-Making Bodies*. Washington, D.C.: Traffic Service Corp., 1959.

LUNDY, R.F. *The Economics of Loyalty-Incentive Rates in the Railroad Industry of the United States*. Pullman, Wash.: Washington State University Press, 1963.

McDOWELL, C.E., and GIBBS, H.M. *Ocean Transportation*. New York: McGraw-Hill Book Co., Inc., 1954.

MELNITSKY, BENJAMIN. *Management of Industrial Inventory*, New York: Conover-Mast Publications, Inc., 1951.

Merchant Marine Act, 1936, and certain related acts (revised to 1957). Washington, D.C.: Superintendent of Public Documents.

METCALFE, J.V. *The Principles of Ocean Transportation*. New York: Simmons-Boardman Publishing Corp., 1959.

MEYER, J.R.; PECK, M.J.; STENASON, J.; and ZWICK, C. *The Economics of Competition in the Transportation Industries*. Cambridge, Mass.: Harvard University Press, 1959.

MILLER, C.A. *I.C.C. Law and Procedure*. Washington, D.C.: National Law Book Co., 1939.

MILLER, J.M. *Law of Freight Loss and Damage Claims*. 2d ed. Dubuque, Iowa: Wm. C. Brown & Co., 1961.

MILLER, R.E. *Domestic Airline Efficiency*. Cambridge, Mass.: The M.I.T. Press, 1963.

MORTON, N. *Digest of Selected Cases on Interstate Commerce Regulation* (Booklet). Washington, D.C.: Traffic Service Corp., 1963.

MORTON, N., and MOSSMAN, F.H. *Industrial Traffic Management*. New York: Ronald Press Co., 1954.

MOSSMAN, F.H., and MORTON, N. *Principles of Transportation*. New York: Ronald Press Co., 1957.

MURR, ALFRED. *Export-Import Forwarding and Traffic Management*. Cambridge, Md.: Cornell Maritime Press, 1957.

NATIONAL INDUSTRIAL CONFERENCE BOARD, INC. *Industrial Traffic Departments*. New York: 1950. (Booklet.)

————. *Inventory Management in Industry*. New York, 1958.

NATIONAL PETROLEUM COUNCIL. *Petroleum Transportation.* Washington, D.C., 1958. (Booklet.)

NELSON, J.C. *Railroad Transportation and Public Policy.* Washington, D.C.: Brookings Institution, 1959.

NICHOLSON, J.L. *Air Transportation Management.* New York: John Wiley & Sons, Inc., 1951.

NORTON, H.S. *Modern Transportation Economics.* Columbus, Ohio: Charles E. Merrill Books, Inc.

PEGRUM, D.F. *Transportation: Economics and Public Policy.* Homewood, Ill.: Richard D. Irwin, Inc., 1963.

RICHMOND, S.B. *Regulation and Competition in Air Transportation.* New York: Columbia University Press, 1961.

RODDA, WILLIAM H. *Inland Marine and Transportation Insurance.* New York: Prentice-Hall, Inc., 1949.

ROSENTHAL, M.S. *Techniques of International Trade.* New York: McGraw-Hill Book Co., Inc., 1950.

SENATE COMMITTEE ON COMMERCE. *National Transportation Policy.* Preliminary draft of a report prepared for the Committee. Washington, D.C.: U.S. Government Printing Office, 1961.

SHARFMAN, I.L. *Interstate Commerce Commission: A Study in Administrative Law and Procedure* (5 parts). New York: Commonwealth Fund, 1931–37.

SHINN, G.L. *Freight Rate Application.* New York: Simmons-Boardman Publishing Co., 1948.

———. *Reasonable Freight Rates.* Washington, D.C.: Traffic Service Corp., 1952.

———. *Routing and Misrouting of Freight.* New York: Simmons-Boardman Publishing Co., 1949.

SMYKAY, EDWARD W.; BOWERSOX, DONALD J.; and MOSSMAN, FRANK H. *Physical Distribution Management.* New York: The Macmillan Co., 1961.

SMYKAY, EDWARD W., and OTHERS. *Essays on Physical Distribution Management.* Transportation & Distribution Management, 815 Washington Bldg., Washington 5, D.C., 1961.

STARR, E.A. *The Practice of Traffic Management.* Dallas, Tex.: Transportation Press, 1952.

———. *The Tools of the Traffic Man.* 3d ed. Dallas, Tex.: Transportation Press, 1953.

———. *The Interpretation of Freight Tariffs.* Fort Worth, Tex.: Transportation Press, 1961.

STARR, M.K., and MILLER, D.W. *Inventory Control: Theory and Practice.* Englewood Cliffs, N.J.: Prentice-Hall, Inc., 1962.

STUFFLEBEAM, G.T. *The Traffic Dictionary.* 4th ed. New York: Simmons-Boardman Publishing Co., 1950.

TAFF, C.A. *Commercial Motor Transportation.* 3d ed. Homewood, Ill.: Richard D. Irwin, Inc., 1961.

———. *Operating Rights of Motor Carriers.* Dubuque, Iowa: Wm. C. Brown & Co., 1953.

TEDROW, J.H. *Regulation of Transportation.* 5th ed. Dubuque, Iowa: Wm. C. Brown & Co., 1955.

TRAFFIC SERVICE CORPORATION. *Traffic World's Questions and Answers Books,* Vols. I–XIV. Washington, D.C., 1950, and later years.

VAN METRE, T.W. *Industrial Traffic Management.* New York: McGraw-Hill Book Co., Inc., 1953.

WALDEN, C.F. *Fundamentals of Transportation.* New York: Traffic Publishing Co., Inc., 1950.

WAY, W. *Elements of Freight Traffic.* Washington, D.C.: Regular Common Carrier Conference, ATA, 1956.

WESTMEYER, R.E. *Economics of Transportation.* New York: Prentice-Hall, Inc., 1952.

WHITE, J.L. *Analysis of Railroad Operations.* New York: Simmons-Boardman Publishing Co., 1946.

WILLIAMS, E.W., JR. *The Regulation of Rail-Motor Rate Competition.* New York: Harper & Bros., 1957.

WILSON, G.L. *Elements of Transportation Economics.* New York: Simmons-Boardman Publishing Co., 1951.

———. *Freight Service and Rates.* Washington, D.C.: Traffic Service Corp., 1952.

———. *Freight Shipping Documents and Claims.* Washington, D.C.: Traffic Service Corp., 1952.

———. *Industrial Traffic Management.* Rev. ed. Washington, D.C.: Traffic Service Corp., 1949.

———. *Interstate Commerce and Traffic Law.* New York: Prentice-Hall, Inc., 1947.

———. *Railroad Freight Classification Rates and Tariffs.* Washington, D.C.: Traffic Service Corp., 1950.

———. *Railroad Freight Rate Structure.* Washington, D.C.: Traffic Service Corp., 1951.

———. *Traffic Management.* Englewood Cliffs, N.J.: Prentice-Hall, Inc., 1956.

———. *Transportation and Communications.* New York: Appleton-Century-Crofts, Inc., 1955.

WILSON, G.L., and BRYAN, L.A. *Air Transportation.* New York: Prentice-Hall, Inc., 1949.

WINTER, W.D. *Marine Insurance.* New York: McGraw-Hill Book Co., Inc., 1952.

WOLBERT, J.C. *American Pipe Lines.* Norman: University of Oklahoma Press, 1952.

YASEEN, LEONARD C. *Plant Location.* Roslyn, N.Y.: Business Reports, Inc., 1952.

TRADE AND PROFESSIONAL MAGAZINES

Some representative publications in transportation, physical distribution, and related fields are as follows:

Air Cargo, published monthly by American Aviation Publications, Washington, D.C.

American Aviation, published monthly by American Aviation Publications, Washington, D.C.

Aviation Week, published weekly by McGraw-Hill Publishing Co., 330 West 42nd Street, New York 18, N.Y.

Distribution Age, published monthly by Chilton Co., Inc., Chestnut and 56th Streets, Philadelphia 39, Pa.

Handling and Shipping, published monthly by Industrial Publishing Corporation, 812 Huron Road, Cleveland 15, Ohio.

I.C.C. Practitioners' Journal, published monthly except July and August by Association of I.C.C. Practitioners, 2218 I.C.C. Building, Washington 4, D.C.

Marine News, published monthly by New York Marine News Co., Inc., 26 Water Street, New York, N.Y.

Material Handling Engineering, published monthly by Industrial Publishing Corporation, 812 Huron Road, Cleveland 15, Ohio.

Modern Materials Handling, published monthly by Materials Handling Laboratories, Inc., 221 Columbus Ave., Boston, Massachusetts.

Modern Packaging, published by Modern Packaging Corporation, 575 Madison Ave., New York 22, N.Y.

National Defense Transportation Journal, published bimonthly by National Defense Transportation Association, 1001 Connecticut Avenue, Washington 4, D.C.

Oil and Gas Journal, published weekly by Petroleum Publishing Co., 211 South Cheyenne Street, Tulsa, Oklahoma.

Railway Age, published weekly, and *Railway Freight Traffic*, published monthly, by Simmons-Boardman Publishing Co., 30 Church Street, New York 7, N.Y.

Shipping Management—National Hi-Way Shipper, published monthly by Shipping Management, 425 Fourth Avenue, New York 16, N.Y.

Traffic Bulletin and Traffic World, published weekly, and *Traffic World Daily*, by the Traffic Service Corporation, 815 Washington Building, Washington 5, D.C.

Traffic Management, published monthly by Watson Publications, Inc., 201 N. Wells St., Chicago, Ill.

Transport Topics, published weekly by American Trucking Associations, Inc., 1424 16th Street, N.W., Washington 6, D.C.

Transportation and Distribution Management, published monthly by Traffic Service Corp., 815 Washington Bldg., Washington 5, D.C.

Transportation Journal, published quarterly by American Society of Traffic and Transportation, Inc., 22 W. Madison St., Chicago 2, Ill.

INDEX

A

Accessorial or ancillary rates, 177, 198
Accessorial services, 480–81
Across-the-board rate increase, 206
Act to Regulate Commerce, 389
Actual placement, 352
Actual value ratings, 200–201
Ad valorem rates, 208–9
Administrative Procedure Act, 395
Agency and individual carrier tariffs, 225–26
Agency tariffs, 226
Aggregate of intermediates, 195–96
Agreed charges, 189–90
Air-bus package express service, 85
Air cargo, 74–78
  international, 471–72
  rates, 210–13
Air express, 74, 77–78, 210, 471
Air rates; see Rates, air cargo
Air Safety Board, 403
Air tariffs, 210–13
Air taxi and helicopters, 75, 76
Airbill, 106–7
All-commodity rate; see Freight—All kinds
All-freight rates, 160
Allowances, 201
Alternative minimum weight rate, 188–89
American-flag vessels, 72
American Merchant Marine, 410
American Society of Traffic and Transportation, 24–26
  Questions, 1959–63, 579–98
Analogy, 140
Analytical methods, 50–58
Annual volume rate, 184
Any-quantity rates, 188, 209
Applied research, 52
Arbitraries, 186–87, 207
Arrival notice, 112–13
Associated Traffic Clubs of America, 26
Astray freight, 363
Auditing, 252–57
Average agreement, 353

B

Bare boat charter, 74
Bills of lading
  commercial
    air, 106–7
    express, 108
    freight forwarder, 108
    pipe line, 107
    rail and motor, 93–106
    water, 106–8
  government, 108–12
  rules governing, 158
Booking request, 446
Brokers, 89
Bunching, 354
Business logistics, 8–9
Buyers for export, 455

C

Car Demurrage Rules and Charges Tariff, 351
Car record, 349
Car service, 339–42
Cargo insurance, 467–68
Carloads, 163
Carmack Amendment, 94
Carrier classification
  motor, 65–66
  pipe lines, 79
  rail, 64
  water, 70
Carrier terminal services; see Terminal services
Central receiving department, 273
Central shipping department, 274
Certificate of origin, 453
Certificate of public convenience and necessity, 66
Certificated cargo carriers, 75–76
Charter rates, 208
Charter service
  air, 76–77
  water, 73–74
Chicago Switching District, 327
C.I.F. (cost, insurance, freight), 439
Circuity, 203
Civil Aeronautics Act, 403

Civil Aeronautics Board, 403–8
Claim prevention, 384–86
Claims; *see also* Household goods
  causes of, 358–62
  handling of, 18–19
  inspection of freight
    motor, 380–81
    rail, 379–80
  in loss or damage, 362–69
  measure of, 381
  overcharge and reparation, 369–77
  prevention of
    motor, 385–86
    rail, 384–85
  procedure, 358
  traffic manager's prevention of, 381–84
  undercharge, 377–78
Claims documents, 381–84
Class and commodity tariffs, 225
Class Rate Case, 128, 178–81
Class rate stops, 205
Class rate tariffs, 225
Class rates, 123, 178–82, 202–3, 207
Classes, 122, 135, 138
Classification
  air, 139
  committee procedure
    motor, 144–49
    rail, 140–44
  company, 149–50
  exceptions, 150–53
  freight forwarders, 140
  importance of, 19
  motor
    National Motor Freight Classification, 134–38
    New England Classification, 138–39
  rail
    Consolidated Freight Classification, 121–27
    development of, 118
    Uniform Freight Classification, 127–33
  REA express, 140
  rules, 155–75
  water, 139
Classification rules, 127, 155–74, 174–75
Clearances, 268
Coastwise transportation, 70
C.O.D. shipments, 172
COFC service, 84
Column rates, 182
Combination export manager, 454
Combination rates, 192–95
Combination service, 83–85
Commercial invoice, 451–52
Commingling, 80–81
Committees, use of in management, 31
Commodity rate tariffs, 225
Commodity rates, 171, 178, 182, 204, 207

Common carriers, 60, 66–67, 72, 81, 210–13
Common-law liability, 364
Company classifications; *see* Classification
Company-owned and leased equipment, 427–29; *see also* Equipment
Compensatory rates, 248, 250
Competition
  carrier, 248–49
  intermodal, 249
  private with for-hire, 413
Computers, 53–55, 114–15; *see also* Data processing
Concealed loss or damage, 366
Conditions of certainty and uncertainty, 498
Conference method of rate making, 232–33, 461–63
Consolidated Classification Committee, 140
Consolidated Freight Classification, 121–27, 155
Consolidation, 15, 273–84
Consolidator, 281
Constructive placement, 352
Consular invoices, 452
Containerization, 512–15
Containers, 84, 443–44; *see also* Containerization
Continuous movement, 326
Contract carriers, 60, 67–68, 72, 213
Coordinated Motor Freight Classification, 139
Cost of possession, 498
Crude-oil gathering lines, 79
Crude-oil trunk lines, 79–80
Cube rate, 196–97, 215–16
Customhouse brokers, 459
Customs entries, 456–57
Cutback rate, 188

D

Dangerous cargo rates, 209
Data processing, 7, 20, 53–55, 114–15, 272–73
Decentralized operations, 33–35
Deck cargo rates, 209
Defense Traffic Management Service, 116
Deferred air freight, 77, 211–12
Delivery permits, 447
Delivery receipt, 113
Delta Nu Alpha, 26
Demurrage, 20, 293, 347–56
Density, 135, 139
Department of Commerce, 408
Departmental organization
  centralized, 35–36
  committees in, 31

Departmental organization—*Cont.*
  decentralized, 33–35
  functional, 30
  line, 30
  line and staff, 30–31
  principles of, 28
  transition to physical distribution, 36–41
  types of traffic, 31–33
Detention, 20, 347–49, 356
Differential rate, 186, 207
Direct exporting, 439–40
Direct importing, 454
Discount rates; *see* Rates, incentive
Discrimination, 250
Distribution, 5–6
Distribution-center public warehousing, 537–38
Diversion, 18, 286–93
Dock receipt, 448
Docket No. 20660, *Class Rates, Transcontinental Rail, 1950*, 181–82
Docket No. 28300, *Class Rate Investigation, 1939*, 128, 178–81, 202
Docket No. 28310, *Class Rate Investigation, 1939*, 128, 202
Docket No. 30416, *Class Rates, Mountain-Pacific Territory*, 181–82
Documentation, 21–22, 93–117
Draft, 452
Driver training, 430–31
Driver's log, 433
Driver's manual, 433–34
Dual-rates, 461–62

E

Eastern Territory, 236, 238–39
Economic order quantity, 500–502
Elevation, 299–300
Embargoes and quarantines, 269
Employee boards, 391–94
"Envelope on the car" system, 277
Equipment
  air, 74
  company owned or leased, 17, 90, 427–29
  rail, 63
  utilization
    car service, 339–42
    demurrage and detention, 347–57
    private cars, 342–47
  water, 70, 71, 434
Estimated weights, 332
Examiner, 401
Exceptions, classification, 150–53, 178, 182–83, 203
Exempt transportation, 68
Expediting, 22, 304–5

Explosives and Dangerous Articles Tariff, 171
Export agent, 454
Export commission house, 454–55
Export declaration, 447–48
Export merchant, 454
Export license, 448
Export trade association, 455
Exporters' Encyclopedia, 445
Exporting
  direct
    documentation, 445–53
    marking, 444–45
    packaging and packing for, 441–43
    preventable losses in, 444
    traffic responsibilities in, 440–41
    types of, 439–40
    use of containers, 443–44
  handling of, 24
  indirect
    traffic manager's role in, 454
    types of, 454–55
  rates, 190–92
  terms of sale, 438–39

F

Federal Aviation Act, 402–3
Federal Aviation Agency, 403
Federal Bills of Lading Act, 94
Federal Maritime Commission, 410–13
Federal regulation
  air, 402–8
  American-flag ocean carriers, 408–12
  domestic surface carriers, 388–402
  re-examination of, 413–16
Ferry car; *see* Trap or ferry car
Fibre Box Association, 359
Finance, Safety, and Service Division, 391
"Fishy back," 84
Flagout, 205
Floating-in rates, 187–88
F.O.B. (free on board) vessel, 439
Foreign-trade zones, 465–67
Foreign water transportation, 72
Fourth Section departures or rates, 173, 193, 195
Fourth Section Order No. 9800, 194–95
Free of particular average, 469
Freight—All kinds, 183–84, 214
Freight bills
  auditing of, 23, 252–56
  processing, 22
  use of, 113–14
Freight Claim Division, A.A.R., 358
Freight classification territories, 120
Freight forwarders
  air, 87–88

Freight forwarders—*Cont.*
  ocean, 412, 463–65
  rates, 214
  surface, 86–87
Freight insurance, 467–68
Freight rate schedule, 220
Functional organization, 30

G

Gathering lines, 79
General-average loss, 469–70
General cargo, N.O.S., 463
General cargo rates, 208
General commodities tariffs, 227
Government bills of lading, 108–12
Great Lakes transportation, 71
Guaranteed rate, 189–90

H

Heater service, 297–98
Heavy-lift rates, 208
Horizontal rate increase, 206
Household goods
  motor
    accessorial services, 480–81
    claims, 482
    movement of office equipment, 483
    order for service, 477
    rates and charges, 478–79
    released value rates, 479–80
    rules and regulations, 480
  other carriers, 475–76
Household Goods Carriers' Bureau, Inc.,
  478
Hull insurance, 467

I

Icing, 297–98
Illinois Classification, 122
Import permit, 448
Importing
  customhouse brokers, 459
  customs entries, 456–57
  direct, 455
  foreign channels of supply, 458
  forwarding from port, 459
  handling of, 24
  indirect, 457–58
Incentive rates, 188–89, 215
Indemnity bond, 375
Indent houses, 458
Indirect exporting, 454
Industrial carrier, 72
Industrial railroads, 90

Inland water transportation, 71
Insurance, 386, 467–68
Insurance certificates, 452
Integrated trains, 62–63
Intent for drawback, 453
Intercity ton-miles, 60–61
Intercoastal water transportation, 71
International air carriers, 78
International air freight, 471–72
Interoffice letter, 218
Interstate Commerce Commission; *see
  also* Regulation
  Section 5a, 232–33
  supervision of rates, 245–50
  tariff interpretation, 229–30
Interterritorial class rates, 202–3, 232–37
Intraplant transportation, 90
Intraterritorial class rates, 202–3, 232–37
Intraterritorial motor rate territories, 240–
  41
Inventory
  carrying costs, 11
  management, 18
    conditions of certainty and uncer-
      tainty, 498
    cost of possession, 498
    economic order quantity, 500–502
    interdependence aspects of, 494–95
    lead time, 498
    manufacturers' and retailers' inven-
      tories, 497
    need for, 492–93
    order processing, 502
    standards, 498–500
Investigation and suspension proceedings,
  399

J

Job descriptions, 49
Joint agency tariffs, 226–27
Joint rates, 185
Joint tariffs, 225
Journal of Commerce, 446

K

Key-point operations, 66
Known loss or damage, 366

L

Lawfulness of rates, 177
LCL, 63–64, 163–64
  consolidation of, 273
  rates, 214
  ratings, 129
Leasing, 90, 427–29

Legal rates, 177
Liability
    air carrier, 369
    common carrier, 364
    ocean carrier, 468–69
    warehouseman, 364
Light and bulky articles, 135–37, 168
Lighterage and floatage, 333–34
Line and staff organization, 30–31
Line-haul rates, 177–98, 202
Line organization, 30
Linear programming, 57
Liner service, 72
Loading, 23–24
Loading and unloading, 332, 510–12
Local cartage, 69, 281
Local rates, 207
Local service carriers, 75
Local tariffs, 225
Locational factors
    decentralization of industry, 549–50
    establishing center of distribution, 556–58
    evaluation factors, 551–56
    principal, 547–49
    traffic department's role in, 17, 550–51
Loss or damage claims, 362–69
LTL, 66–67, 135

M

Management
    analytical methods, use of, 50–58
    budgeting, 50
    policies, 44–46
    reports, 50–51
    staffing, 49–50
Manifest, 433, 451
Manufacturer's inventories, 497
Marine insurance, 467–71
Maritime Administration, 410
Maritime Subsidy Board, 410
Marking, 157–58
Material handling
    equipment selection in, 508–10
    loading and unloading, 510–12
    objectives, 507–8
    traffic manager's role in, 16–17, 505–6
Materials management, 8
Mathematical model, 55
Mechanical operations recorders, 432
Merchant Marine Act of 1936, 410
Middle Atlantic Conference, 237
Middlewest Shipper–Motor Carrier Conference, 342
Mileage allowances, 342
Mileage blocks, 202, 203
Mileage guide, 479
Mileage tariffs, 225

MILSTAMP, 115
MILSTRIP, 115
Mine cards, 104
Mini-max stock level, 498
Minimum charge, 162
Minimum rate stops, 205
Minimum rates, 118, 208, 414
Minimum tender, 82
Minimum weight factor, 175
Misdescription, 335
Misroute claims, 372, 377
Mixed-carload provisions, 159–60
Modified Rule 10, 159–60
Money or traffic pools, 232
Motor-air service, 85
Motor Carrier Act of 1935, 389
Motor Carrier Directory, 267
Motor carrier rates, 177–206
Motor carriers, 65–69
Mountain-Pacific Territory, 202
Movers' and Warehousemen's Association of America, Inc., 478
Multiple car rate, 184

N

National Classification Board, 145–49
National Classification Committee, 149
National Defense Transportation Association, 26
National Diversion and Reconsignment Committee, 289
National Freight Claim Council, 358
National Freight Tariff Committee, 251
National Highway and Airways Carriers and Routes, 267
National Motor Freight Classification, 134–38
National Motor Freight Traffic Association, Inc., 149, 252
National Rate Basis Tariff No. 1, 180
National transportation policy, 390
National Transportation Policy Report, 414
Natural-gas pipe lines, 82
Nested, 164–65
New England Classification, 138–39
New York Lighterage and Terminal Tariff, 333
NOI, 135
NOIBN, 124

O

Ocean bill of lading, 448–50
Ocean freight rates, 459–63
Office of Emergency Planning, 418
Office of Emergency Transportation, 416
Official Airfreight Tariff, 107

Official Classification, 121
Official Classification Committee, 140, 232
Official Express Classification, 140, 214–15
Official Guide of the Railways, 263
Omnibus rule, 197
Open rates, 209
Operating authority, 66, 394
Operating Rights Division, 391
Operations research, 56
Optional cargo rates, 208
Order bill of lading, 94, 100, 291–92
Order for service, 477
Order notify bill of lading, 158
Ordinary operating convenience, 326
Organization; see Departmental organization
Over freight, 362
Overcharge claims, 369–77

P

Package cars, 64
Package service, 69
Packaging
  costs, 11
  for export, 441–43
  importance of, 20–21
  industrial, 515–18
Packing list, 452
Parcel post, 88–89, 216
Parcel rates, 209, 463
Particular-average loss, 469
Passenger miles, 60
Passenger transportation
  air
    private and charter, 486
    reservations, 487–88
  motor, 488–89
  rail reservations, 485
  traffic manager's role in, 483–84
  travel agents, 485
Peddler cars, 63
Penalties, 157
Perishable Protective Tariff, 298
Per-mile costs, tractor-semitrailer, 425
Personal effects; see Household goods
Physical distribution
  analytical methods, use of, 50–58
  concept, 5–10
  definition, 7–8
  functions of, 12–24
  management of, 11–12
  management principles, 45–46
  policy implementation, 46–47
  relationship with other departments, 47–48
  staffing, 49–50
  transition to, 36–41
Pickup and delivery, 212–13, 327–29

"Piggy-back"; see Trailer-on-flatcar
Pipe lines, 78–82, 213–14
Point-to-point rates, 182
Pool cars, 64, 281–83
Pool truck service, 282
Posting relief, 224
Practitioners, 395
Premium transportation, 273
Presidential Advisory Committee, 413
Presidential Message on Transportation, 414–15
Primary business test, 422
Principles and Practices for the Investigation and Disposition of Freight Claims, 359
Private carriage
  classification, 68
  motor
    advantages of, 423
    definition of, 422
    driver selection, training, and supervision, 430–32
    equipment purchase or lease, 427–29
    equipment selection and maintenance, 429–30
    feasibility of conversion to, 423–27
    safety in, 433–34
    scheduling, 432–33
  rail, 342–47
  water, 434
Private cars, 342–47
Private sidings, 323
"Pro" number, 303–4
Probability theory, 57–58
Product lines, 79, 80
Production, 5
Programming, 54
Propellor Club of the United States, 26
Proportional rate, 185–86
Protective services, 297–98
Protest, master's, 471
Public team tracks, 177
Pure research, 52, 53

R

Rail classification; see Classification
Rail rate territories, 233–35
Rail service, 62–65
Railway Equipment Register, 63
Rate bureaus and conferences, 232–39
Rate card system, 4
Rate cards, traffic department, 218–21
Rate factors; see Rates
Rate formulation, 223–50
Rate making procedure, 246–47
Rate scale, 178–80
Rate tariff; see Tariffs
Rate territories, 232, 234–37, 240–41

Rates
  accessorial or ancillary, 177, 198
  actual value ratings, 200–201
  aggregate of intermediates, 195–96
  agreed, 189–90
  air cargo
    common, 210–13
    contract, 213
  air express, 216
  allowances, 201
  alternative minima, 188–89
  any-quantity, 188
  arbitraries, 186–87
  class, 178–82
  combination, 192–95
  commodity, 178, 182
  cube, 196–97
  cutback rate, 188
  determination of, 14
  differential, 186
  exceptions to classification, 178, 182–83
  export and import rates, 190–92
  factors affecting, 205–6
  floating-in, 187–88
  freight—all kinds or all commodity, 182–83
  freight forwarder, 214
  how to look up a rate, 227–28
  I.C.C. supervision of, 245–50
  incentive, 188–89
  joint, 185
  line-haul, 177–78
  litigation involving, 15–16
  local rate, 185
  minimum, 188
  motor contract, 206
  negotiation of, 15
  omnibus rule, 197
  parcel post, 216
  pipe line, 213–14
  priority of, 228–29
  proportional, 185–86
  REA Express, 214–16
  released value ratings, 198–200
  reshipping, 196
  Section 22, 196
  standard, 188
  structures of, 201
  surcharge, 197–98
  through rate, 186
  traffic department forms for, 218–21
  trailer-on-flatcar, 187
  trainload or multiple car, 184
  volume, 184
  water; see also Ocean freight rates
    ad valorem, 208–9
    arbitraries, 207
    class, 207
    commodity, 207
    dangerous cargo, 209

Rates—Cont.
  water—Cont
    deck cargo, 209
    general cargo, 208
    heavy-lift, 208
    local, 207
    minimum, 208
    open, 209
    optional cargo, 208
    parcel, 209
    refrigerated cargo, 209
Rates, Tariffs, and Valuation Division, 391
Ratings, 122, 129–31, 138, 157, 178
REA Express, 74, 82–83, 140, 210, 451
  Air Express Division, 77–78, 216
Reconsignment, 18, 286–93
Records, 19–20
Reed-Bulwinkle Act, 233
Refined-oil pipe lines; see Product lines
Refrigerated cargo rates, 209
Refrigeration service, 297–98
Regulation
  Civil Aeronautics Board
    composition of, 403–6
    functions of, 406
    organization chart, 404
    procedure before, 406–8
  economic, 388
  emergency transportation agency, 416–18
  Federal Aviation Act, 389, 402–3
  Federal Aviation Agency, 403
  Federal Maritime Commission
    composition of, 410
    functions of, 412
    organization chart, 411
    procedure before, 412–13
  Interstate Commerce Act, 389–91
  Interstate Commerce Commission; see also Interstate Commerce Commission
    composition of, 391
    divisions, 391
    functions of, 394
    organization chart, 392–93
    procedure before, 395–402
  Maritime Administration, 410
  Merchant Marine Act, 389, 408–10
  re-examination of, 413–16
  safety, 388
  state, 418–19
Regulatory agencies; see Regulation
Released rates order, 198–99
Released value rates, 479–80
Released value ratings, 198–200
Reparation claims, 369–77
Research and development, 22–23, 50–53
Reshipping rate, 196
Retailers' inventories, 497

Revenue, ton-mile
  motor, 64
  rail, 62
Revised American Foreign Trade Definitions—1941, 439
Reweighing, 330
Rhochrematics, 8
Road patrols, 432
Road test, 431
Routing
  air, shipper's rights in, 268
  factors considered in, 259
  freight forwarders, shipper's rights in, 268
  motor, shipper's rights in, 266–67
  policy
    Defense Traffic Management Service, 271
    Department of Defense, 269–70
    industrial, 269–70
  rail
    determination of, 262–65
    open, 265–66
    shipper's rights in, 261–62
  reciprocity, 260–61
  use of premium transportation in, 273
  value of, 14
Routing guides, 262–63
Routing orders, 271–72
Rule 100 Statement, 372
Rules of Practice, I.C.C., 395–401

S

Sea-land and sea-train rates, 249–50
Secretary of Commerce, 413, 416
Section 4 rates; *see* Fourth section departures or rates
Section 5a, 233
Section 15a, 248–50
Section 22 rates, 196
Sherman Antitrust Act, 232–33
Shippers Advisory boards, 340
Shippers' associations, 278–81
Shipper's Letter of Instruction, 471
Shipper's proposal, 242
Shipper's right to route
  air, 268
  freight forwarders, 268
  motor, 266–67
  rail, 261–62
  water, 267
Shipping Digest, 446
Short notice filing, 246
Sidetrack agreements, 19
Simulation, 55
Small shipments, 273, 415–16
Southern Classification, 121
Southwestern Freight Bureau, 236

Space weight rates, 459–61
Special Committee on Uniform Tariff Rules and Regulations, 252
Special service tariffs, 225
Special services, carrier, 286–305
Specific commodities tariffs, 227–28
Split deliveries, 163
Spot stocks, 536–37
Staffing, 49–50
Standard rate, 188
Standing Rate Committee, 242–44
State regulation, 418–19
Statistics, 19–20
Steamship conferences, 461–62
Stop off in transit, 293–96
Storage, 300–301; *see also* Warehousing
Straight bill of lading, 94, 99, 292–93
Streamlined Rule 10, 159–60
Substituted freight service, 63
Supplemental air carriers, 75
Surcharge, 197–98
Switching, 322–27
System and services, transportation; *see* Transportation
Systems analysis, 56–57
Systems approach, 7, 38, 48

T

Tachograph, 432
Tariff Circular MF No. 3, 198
Tariff Circular No. 20, 194, 198
Tariff circulars, 224, 561–78
Tariff construction, 561–78
Tariffs
  air, 210–13
  freight forwarder, 214
  how to look up a rate, 227–28
  I.C.C. requirements regarding, 223–24
  interpretation of, 229–30
  maintenance of, 22
  pipe line, 213–14
  simplification, 250–52
  traffic manager's tariff file, 230–32
  types of, 224–27
  unofficial, 230
  use in routing, 262
Tender of shipment, 107–8
Terminal services
  Chicago Switching District, 327
  estimated weights, 332
  lighterage and floatage, 333–34
  loading and unloading, 332
  pickup and delivery, 327–29
  switching, 322–27
  transfer and drayage, 332–33
  weighing and reweighing, 329–30
  weight agreements, 331–32
Terms of sale, 115–16

Through export bills of lading, 101, **446**
Through rate, 186
Time charters, 72
Title to goods, 115–16
TL; *see* Truckload
Todd-Knott award, 191
Ton-miles, 60
Total cost approach; *see* Systems approach
Total loss, 469
Tracing, 22, 301–4
Trade-offs, 18, 37
Traffic Bulletin, 142, 144
Traffic department; *see also* Traffic management
  analytical methods, use of, 50–58
  centralized, 35–36
  combination, 36
  decentralized, 33–35
  manual, 46–47
  organization chart, 35, 39
  policies, 44–47
  types of, 31–33
Traffic management
  analytical methods, use of, 50–58
  budgeting, 50
  claims procedure and prevention, 381–84
  definition of, 3
  development of, 1–4
  functions of, 12–24
  professional status of, 24–26
  rate forms, 218–21
  staffing, 49–50
  tariff file, 230–32
Traffic manager, 1–3; *see also* Traffic management
Traffic manual, 46–47
Traffic organizations, noncompany, 3–4, 256–57
Traffic policies, 45–47
Traffic World, 3
Trailer-on-flatcar, 83–84, 187, 249–50
Trailership, 84
Training courses, 49
Trainload rates, 184
Trainship, 85
Tramp service, 72–73
Transfer and drayage, 332–33
Transit privileges
  importance of, 23
  motor, 318–20
  rail
    application rules, 309
    explanation of, 306–9
    policing rules, 311–12
    rules governing, 309–11
    types of, 312–16

Transit privileges–*Cont.*
  rail–*Cont.*
    unit and split billing, 316–18
    traffic manager's role in, 320–21
Transport Topics, 144
Transportability, 21
Transportation
  costs, 10–11
  brokers, 89
  freight forwarders, 86–88
  motor-air service, 85
  parcel post, 88–89
  system and services
    air, 74–78
    common carriers, 60
    contract carriers, 60
    extent of, 59–60
    motor, 65–69
    pipe line, 78–82
    rail, 62–65
    water, 69–74
    trailer-on-flatcar, 83–84
    trailership, 84
    trainship, 85
Transportation Act
  of 1920, 389
  of 1940, 390
  of 1958, 68, 248–49, 390
Transportation Allocations, Priorities and Controls, 418
Transportation management, 32
Trap or ferry car, 296–97
Truck-air freight service, 85
Truck leasing, 427–29
Truckload, 66, 135
Trunk line carriers, 75

U

Umbrella rates; *see* Section 15a
Undercharge claims, 377–78
Undersecretary of Commerce for Transportation, 388
Uniform bill of lading; *see* Bills of lading
Uniform class rate scale, 178–80
Uniform Freight Classification, 127–33, 155
Uniform livestock contract, 101
Unit loading, 510
United States Official Postal Guide, 216
U.S. Shipping Board, 408

V

Ventilating, 297–98
Vertical increase, 206
Volume rates, 184–85
Voyage charter, 73–74

W

Warehousing, 523–45
    co-operation between traffic manager and warehouseman, 541–42
    handling of pool-car shipments, 537
    licensing, 535–36
    negotiable and nonnegotiable warehouse receipts, 531–36
    rates and charges, 538–40
    services, 536–38
    stock location, 527
    traffic management aspects of, 16
    types of, 524–27
    types of public, 527–30
    Uniform Warehouse Receipts Act, 530–36

Watching services, 231
Water rates; see Rates
Water transportation, 69–74
Waybill, 112
Webb-Pomerene Act, 455
Weighing and inspection bureaus, 331, 334–37
Weighing and reweighing, 329–30
Weight agreements, 21, 331–32
Western Classification, 121
Western Traffic Association Territory, 236
Western Weighing and Inspection Bureau, 334–37

This book was set on the Linotype in 10 point Janson, leaded 2 points, and 9 point Janson, leaded 1 point. Chapter numbers are in 24 point Futura Medium and 36 point Lydian; chapter titles are in 24 point Futura Medium. The size of the type page is 27 by 47 picas. Paper is 50# Tone-O-Paque.